The Supreme Court of Florida and Its Predecessor Courts, 1821–1917

The Supreme Court of Florida and Its Predecessor Courts, 1821–1917

Walter W. Manley II, editor and co-author

E. Canter Brown Jr., contributing editor and co-author

Eric W. Rise, co-author

Prepared for the Florida Supreme Court Historical Society

Contributing writers:
H. Glenn Boggs
Randall O. Reder
Gary M. Ketchum

University Press of Florida
Gainesville Tallahassee Tampa Boca Raton
Pensacola Orlando Miami Jacksonville

01 02 00 99 98 97 6 5 4 3 2 1

Library of Congress Cataloging-in-Publication Data

Manley, Walter W.
The Supreme Court of Florida and its predecessor courts, 1821–1917 / Walter W. Manley III, editor and co-author; E. Canter Brown Jr., contributing editor and co-author; Eric W. Rise, co-author; contributing writers, H. Glenn Boggs, Randall O. Reder, Gary M. Ketchum.
p. cm.
"Prepared for the Florida Supreme Court Historical Society."
Includes bibliographical references and index.
ISBN 0-8130-1540-5 (alk. paper)
1. Florida. Supreme Court—History. 2. Justice, Administration of—Florida—History. I. Brown, E. Canter. II. Rise, Eric W. III. Title.
KFF512.M36 1998
347.759'035—dc21 97-40291

The University Press of Florida is the scholarly publishing agency for the State University System of Florida, comprised of Florida A & M University, Florida Atlantic University, Florida International University, Florida State University, University of Central Florida, University of Florida, University of North Florida, University of South Florida, and University of West Florida.

University Press of Florida
15 Northwest 15th Street
Gainesville, FL 32611
http://nersp.nerdc.ufl.edu/~upf

Contents

List of Illustrations

Foreword

Until the publication of this superb work, there was no book that told the compelling story of the supreme court of Florida and the tribunal that preceded it, the territorial court of appeals. Several years of meticulous research and skillful writing have resulted in a well-documented and readable volume that provides one of the links long missing in the story of Florida. The book describes the state's judicial history and the eminent and often colorful members of the supreme court who forged Florida case law. The contributions of many of these justices to the development of our state have never been adequately recognized in previously published works.

The well-organized text divides the ninety-six-year period between 1821 and 1917 into five parts. Each one presents the significant historical events and circumstances and the life stories of the judges or justices within the particular time frame. The reader is then well prepared for the cases that follow—and for the decisions flavored by their authors and the circumstances.

This history would have been of immense value to me as a lawyer, attorney general, and supreme court justice. It historically depicts in flesh and blood images the litigators and jurists who participated in formulating the rules of law that govern in Florida today. The book vividly brings home these rules of law for the reader, who can apply them to myriad human controversies. For example, I would have understood how and when to use any of the extraordinary writs, those chameleons of law, if I had read the evolutionary and personalized story of these writs.

I highly recommend this book to all members of the bench and bar. When you have a personalized history of who made the law and the circumstances under which they made it, you remember and understand the law much better and use it more appropriately in your work. However, this book is not only for lawyers, judges, and law libraries. It has value for all who enjoy Florida history.

An important missing chapter has now been published that adds even more color and character to Florida's past.

RICHARD W. ERVIN
Attorney General of Florida, 1949–64; Justice of the Supreme Court of Florida, 1964–75; Chief Justice, 1969–71.

When acquired by the United States, almost fifty years after the Declaration of Independence, the territory of Florida was sparsely settled without the organized government, courts, schools, infrastructure, or learned professionals found in adjoining states.

This extremely interesting book begins in that setting with the efforts of General Andrew Jackson, as territorial governor, to establish a fledgling government and bring a semblance of Anglo-American order and jurisprudence to an underpopulated land most recently governed by Spain.

With skill the authors carefully track the formation of a judicial system beginning with the county courts established by General Jackson, the territorial court of appeals created by act of Congress in 1824, and transport the reader through the several organizations of the supreme court of Florida to that tribunal as it existed in 1916.

This major and outstanding work also reveals much about the economic and social life of the inhabitants, their struggles with disease and epidemic, and the Indian Wars. Moreover, it provides through fascinating biographical sections a profound insight into the lives of each of those men, mostly eminent, who held high judicial office, all of whom in the early years were immigrants from existing states. Further, the synopses of many early decisions of the Florida supreme court will enhance the reader's enjoyment of this volume.

For most of the period covered by this book, justices of the supreme court of Florida and judges of its predecessor courts were appointed. Therefore, the book discusses significant actions of the presidents, governors, and legislators and the patronage they exercised, as well as the influence of political parties until the supreme court reached a modicum of independence by popular election of its members.

The reconstruction of past events is difficult even for those who lived through them. It is even more trying to capture in printed word the atmosphere of the time or the character and spirit motivating the makers of history. Yet the authors accomplish these tasks in admirable fashion.

Writing this work has been a major undertaking requiring exhaustive research, accurate assimilation of and reflection on records, and then reduction of all to a most informative history of the supreme court of Florida.

This book, which establishes a lofty standard for state high court histories, is an important reminder of our past, which should convince all that our progress in search of the most effective judicial system is a continuous process.

Stephen C. O'Connell
Justice of the Supreme Court of Florida, 1955–67; Chief Justice, 1967; President of the University of Florida, 1967–73.

This unprecedented work offers a thoughtful, meticulously researched examination of the Florida judicial system's evolution during five highly distinct eras of the state's remarkable history. It is not only a scholarly reflection on Florida's court system. The authors have masterfully crafted a concise, penetrating analysis of pivotal national events—most notably the Civil War and Reconstruction—that played vital roles in shaping the ever-expanding Florida judiciary.

Each of the five sections clearly illustrates how individual and regional influences profoundly affected the judiciary's maturation process. The reader is given insight into opinions and specific rulings on crucial issues that concerned the growing state, such as the blight of slavery, taxation, women's rights, and educational reform. The journey eventually takes us from a court of limited influence to a highly influential panel of justices whose decisions played an integral part in shaping the state's destiny.

In this long-awaited historical look at the less-examined branch of government, the authors have written an absorbing, powerful explication of how the court has grown into the distinguished institution that it is today—a group of dedicated justices that perform indispensable roles in the preservation and continuing enhancement of Florida's legal structure and the rights and liberties of the people.

Kenneth W. Starr
Justice, U.S. Court of Appeals, District of Columbia Circuit, 1983–89; Solicitor General of the United States, 1989–93. Judge Starr is currently serving as Whitewater Independent Counsel.

Preface

This book describes and analyzes the development of appellate courts in Florida from the territorial period to the beginning of the First World War, covering the era in which state constitutional law was preeminent. Through the use of detailed biographical sketches of each judge or justice, the book also emphasizes the importance of individual personalities in shaping the law in Florida. For many of the judges and justices, these sketches are the most extensive biographical accounts that have yet been written. Considerable research in a variety of primary sources has brought to light significant material, some of which was heretofore obscure. At the same time, the work underscores the close relationship between the supreme court of Florida's jurisprudence and prevailing social, economic, and political conditions. By examining the court's opinions on issues such as slavery, internal improvements, and business regulation, this history demonstrates the ways in which the work of the court shaped, and was in turn fashioned by, the competing economic and social interests that transformed Florida. Similarly, the supreme court's frequent efforts to define the scope of the powers of each branch of government, coupled with the numerous adaptations of the character of the court, whether through constitutional revision, judicial elections, or the patronage powers of executive appointment, reveal the manner in which the quest for political domination influenced the court's work.

This book is the first in-depth exploration of the history of the Florida territorial courts, the supreme court of Florida, and the judges of both, and the work fills two significant voids in the historical and legal literature. First, despite the rich historiography on Florida's past, the state's legal history, and particularly the history of its judiciary, has been sorely neglected. The leading general histories of the state contain scant reference to the work of Florida's highest court, and even the specialized monographs and journal articles focus on the political and social history of the state. Yet as this book demonstrates, the supreme court of Florida and its territorial predecessors have often been at the center of leading political, social, and economic controversies. In addition, virtually every jurist on the appellate courts held other prominent positions in business or government. The biographical sections of the work establish that the political and jurisprudential philosophies of these men often overlapped in significant ways.

Second, this history provides an important contribution to the renewed interest in state courts spawned by the recent transformation in the importance of state constitutional law. For most of the twentieth century, several circumstances—including the nationalization of the economy after the New Deal, the centralization of governmental authority in response to world war and cold war, and the application of the Bill of Rights to the states through the Fourteenth Amendment—combined to establish the federal courts as the primary arbiters of governmental authority and personal liberty. Today, public institutions play an increasingly significant role in American society. In fact, they have become the loci of power, authority, and responsibility. There is renewed interest among lawyers, judges, historians, political scientists, and scholars of jurisprudence in the function and history of the highest state appellate courts because of the state constitutional law revolution that has occurred in the past two decades. The emergence of a "new federalism" and an increased emphasis by civil libertarians on state constitutions as independent sources of civil rights and civil liberties have spurred lawyers, historians, and political scientists to pay considerable attention to the processes of state constitution making and the adjudication of constitutional cases at the state level.

Surprisingly, this renewed interest in state constitutionalism has not produced significant scholarship in the history of state appellate tribunals, despite the fact that during the nineteenth century state courts were the primary venues for the creation and interpretation of constitutional law. *The Supreme Court of Florida and Its Predecessor Courts, 1821–1917* addresses that void by presenting the most comprehensive historical analysis of a state supreme court during this golden age of state constitutional law. Thus, at a time when state courts will assume greater responsibilities, this book will reveal to scholars and policymakers the challenges faced by an earlier court in shouldering the burden of arbitrating constitutional struggles over power and liberty.

This volume is divided into five discrete sections: Florida Territory, 1821–1845; Antebellum Statehood, 1845–1860; Civil War and Reconstruction, 1861–1877; Redemption and the Bourbons, 1878–1896; and Before the Great War, 1897–1917. Within each of the sections, the narrative offers an overview of Florida's social, political, and economic history; a discussion of the legal and structural evolution of the court; biographical sketches of jurists that enhance an examination in some depth of personal contributions to and influence upon the court and its antecedent tribunals; and key court decisions that permit insight into not only the evolution of Florida jurisprudence but also the manner in which the court addressed new issues arising with the passage of time and the state's growth and experience. Thorough portraits of life in Florida in each of the book's five sections from 1821 to 1917 comprise a mise-en-scène in order to provide a rich perspective of the court's and its antecedent tribunals' activities.

As part of the book's preparation, the authors incorporated the latest contributions to Florida historiography yet retained a balanced approach that facilitated critical examination of the court and its members while avoiding political favoritism or ideological bias. The work incorporates, for example, factual discussions of the court's partisan role in Florida's political redemption after the Civil War and of its efforts to ensure access of African Americans and African-American attorneys to the court system. The discussions include relevant interpretation but allow readers themselves to decide the soundness of decisions and the measure of the men who made them.

In line with this balanced approach, this history presents in even-handed fashion the facts of the court's development; the backgrounds, accomplishments, and, sometimes, weaknesses of its members; the circumstances under which the court labored and which impacted its rulings; and the general outlines of the process by which Florida jurisprudence evolved between 1821 and 1917. The narrative demonstrates that Floridians may be proud of the court's history for honesty and sincerity, while it points out the dangers inherent in politicization of such tribunals.

The Supreme Court of Florida and Its Predecessor Courts, 1821–1917 represents the first significant examination of the court and its antecedent tribunals in such a comprehensive fashion and offers a model by which the supreme judicial courts of other states may be viewed. The book provides a context for a contemporary understanding of Florida jurisprudence, and, as such, it will find a practical use within the judiciary and the bar while providing interesting, provocative, and informative reading for scholars, students, and the general public.

A number of organizations and individuals played an important role in this book project, either by laying its foundation or by rendering assistance in an extraordinary research effort or in a thoughtful review of the text. The Florida Supreme Court Historical Society, led by chairman Robert M. Ervin; past presidents Talbot D'Alemberte, Mark Hulsey, and M. Lewis Hall, Jr.; current president James E. Cobb; and current vice-president Russell Troutman, determined that there should be a written history of the supreme court of Florida and wholeheartedly supported this project—an effort of well over six years. Moreover, Talbot D'Alemberte, William Reece Smith, Jr., Chesterfield Smith, the Honorable Parker Lee McDonald, the Honorable Ben F. Overton, Mark Hulsey, and Douglas D. Friedrich, provost of the University of West Florida, ably served on the original advisory committee established in 1990 to determine the proper course of the book project. Without the aforementioned individuals' enormous encouragement, support, assistance, and extremely high standards of excellence, which were consistent with those of the authors, this book would have remained unwritten.

I am grateful for the constructive involvement of two foundations. In 1991, the Florida Bar Foundation, with Interest on Trust Accounts Program funding, provided substantial financial support to this project. Moreover, in 1996, welcome financial assistance was received from the McGregor Smith Foundation.

In particular, Nancy Dobson, executive director of the Florida Supreme Court Historical Society, was always a source of learned editorial suggestions and other wise counsel, based not only upon her immense knowledge of the subject but also on her sincere personality. She has my gratitude for her assistance in compiling photographs displayed in this book. Robert M. Ervin diplomatically relayed our progress to the many interested supporters and was a stalwart advocate of our effort. Like all who supported this effort, these two individuals' devotion to the supreme court of Florida as an institution was apparent and instructive.

The late circuit judge and regents professor Harold B. Crosby initially led the project and was assisted by historian Thomas Gilliam; Professor Crosby deserves recognition for establishing the project's credibility and a favorable environment for its successful completion. Alana Cain, now an assistant professor of history at Morehead State University, spent two years providing indefatigable and scholarly research assistance. Through their provision of research, Cynthia Waddell, Lelani Plendl, Donald Gardner, Anne Marsh, Michael Andrew, James Mathis, and Laura Waltke significantly enhanced my factual and bibliographic knowledge.

I owe special thanks to the staffs of several libraries and archives: Dean DeBolt, University of West Florida librarian for special collections; the distinguished scholar James Servies, former director of libraries at the University of West Florida, who provided excellent critiques of the early sections, which were important in shaping the final draft; David J. Coles, reference section supervisor of the Florida Department of State, Bureau of Archives and Records Management, who assiduously verified the references in the text; reference archivists Nadine Doty-Tessel and James Helms; supervisor Joan Perry Morris and photo archivist Jody Norman of the Florida Photographic Collection at the Florida State Archives; State Library of Florida director Barratt Wilkens and librarian specialists Mary Ann Cleveland, Elaine M. Dickinson, Karen Southwell, and Cynthia Wise; Suzanne Olson of the Key West Historical Society, who transmitted research from the archives of that organization; and supreme court librarian Joan D. Cannon and her assistant Jo Dowling.

The interest and support of the members of the supreme court of Florida, especially former chief justice Stephen Grimes, together with their staff are gratefully acknowledged. Supreme court clerk Sid J. White and chief deputy clerk Debbie Causseaux made special efforts to locate and allow access to obscure records.

Randall O. Reder contributed to this book and his interesting and meticulous research in the 1980s regarding the supreme court of Florida provided an important foundation for our substantial research effort. I especially appreciate the support and encouragement of Canter Brown, Eric Rise, and Michael Rosen during the thousands of hours I invested in the project. Thanks are due to Glenn Boggs, Gary Ketchum, Eyal Barnea, and Anthony Sinke for their assistance.

Through his wise experience, Ken Scott, director of the University Press of Florida, recognized the substantial merit of this book and supported its publication. He and his staff, especially Meredith Morris-Babb, editor in chief, and Michael Senecal, project editor, provided welcome and productive advice that improved the book.

No book could feature more prominent, learned, high-minded foreword writers: former chief justice Richard W. Ervin, former chief justice Stephen C. O'Connell, and former judge of the United States Court of Appeals for the District of Columbia circuit and Solicitor General Kenneth W. Starr. Their thoughtful and generous praise of this text validates our immense effort.

Finally, I express my love and thanks to my children, Marjorie and Benjamin, for their patience and support.

Walter W. Manley II
Project director, editor, and co-author

Part One

Florida Territory, 1821–1845

Chapter 1

Andrew Jackson and the Beginnings of the Florida Judiciary

The supreme court of Florida received its constitutional authorization with statehood in 1845, but its origins are traceable to events that occurred decades before.[1] Those events involved personalities of national importance, including a future president of the United States, and concerned issues with which the court was required to deal for generations after its creation. The surrounding circumstances helped to mold the fabric of Florida jurisprudence and influenced the course of Florida history to the present day.

Florida's path from Spanish colony to United States territory had been a tortuous one. An isolated and sparsely populated outpost of an increasingly troubled imperial domain, the colony by 1814 had seen its previously immense borders shrunken approximately to those of the present state. Administratively, it was divided into two parts. East Florida, with its capital at St. Augustine, comprised the area east of the Suwannee River. Its colonial settlers lived for the most part south of the St. Marys River and east of the St. Johns. The peninsula otherwise was uninhabited or else the domain of Indians and blacks. West Florida encompassed the land between the Suwannee and the Perdido rivers. Pensacola served as the center of its government and small colonial population. West Florida also was home to some Indians and blacks.[2]

The weakness of Spanish authority in Florida jeopardized the prospects of continued imperial control. By the 1810s many individuals residing to the north had begun to view the colony as ripe for plucking, and on several occasions during the decade the United States military had intervened in Florida affairs. Most significantly for the future, forces led by Andrew Jackson twice invaded the colony. During the second instance in 1818, Jackson had stirred an international incident when he occupied Spanish positions at Pensacola and St. Marks, battled Indians and blacks, and executed two Englishmen accused of inciting the natives.[3]

Jackson's second invasion, known to history as the First Seminole War, forced imperial officials to reassess Spain's interests in Florida. Faced with the likelihood of United States seizure of the colony at some not-too-distant time, they approved negotiations aimed at transfer of possession. Spanish minister Luis de Onis and Secretary of State John Quincy Adams commenced discussions in October 1818, a process that resulted on February 22 of the following year in the Adams-Onis Treaty. Ratification was delayed for two years, during which controversies ensued over land titles, Indian resettlement, and other issues. Tensions mounted between the two powers with war seemingly on the horizon. Finally on October 24, 1820, Spanish King Ferdinand VII broke the stalemate and approved the treaty. The United States Senate followed on February 19, 1821, with its own final action followed by the president's confirmation on February 22, 1821.[4]

Well before the diplomatic maneuverings reached their conclusion, the Congress and President James Monroe began to consider territorial organization, administration, and governance. An 1819 law, while offering few specifics, had granted authority to the president "to take possession of and occupy the territories of East and West Florida and the appendages and appurtenances thereof." The statute vested the military, civil, and judicial powers exercised by Spanish officers "in such person and persons" designated by the president.[5]

Treaty ratification delays rendered the 1819 law obsolete, but the Spanish king's eventual consent caused Monroe to look for a suitable governor pending renewed congressional action. By January 1821 Monroe's sights had focused on Major General Andrew Jackson. Should Jackson accept, the appointment would rid the president of several troublesome problems. Beyond the question of who would govern the new territory, it would resolve Monroe's dilemma about what to do with the powerful general. Although Jackson enjoyed national popularity, his volatility and unpredictability were legend, and his 1818 Florida invasion had lit a firestorm of criticism.[6]

Monroe, who strove to avoid unpleasant and difficult situations, agonized over what to do with Jackson. He first considered sending the old war hero out of the country as ambassador to Russia, but he had abandoned that course when Thomas Jefferson warned, as one historian put it, that "we should have a quarrel with Russia in a month."[7] The president's sense of urgency about the matter heightened when Congress mandated reductions in the armed forces, which resulted in the elimination of one of the nation's two major generals' positions. Friends of Major General Jacob Brown carried more clout within the Monroe administration, so the axe would strike elsewhere than on Brown. In the circumstances Monroe, in January 1821, offered Florida's governorship to Jack-

John Quincy Adams (1767–1848), U.S. secretary of state, 1817–1825. The diplomatic skills of Secretary of State Adams played a major role in the annexation of Florida. His success in obtaining the ratification of the Adams-Onis Treaty in 1821 followed two years of delays in negotiations with Spain. Aside from the geopolitical significance of the acquisition of Florida, the annexation stabilized the troubled territory and was welcomed by residents along the Georgia border as well as by foreign and domestic shipping interests.

son. "The climate will suit you," he wrote, "and it will give me pleasure to place you in that trust."[8]

Jackson's satisfaction at receiving Monroe's letter did not match the president's pleasure in sending it. Born March 15, 1767, to a widowed mother, Jackson's career had taken him from the border region of upcountry North and South Carolina to what became the state of Tennessee. Despite the handicap of a poor education, Florida's future governor and supreme judicial officer had prospered in his adopted state, serving it as prosecutor, member of the United States House of Representatives, United States senator, and state supreme court justice. As his career prospered, Jackson increasingly had invested in land and black slaves. His principal plantation, the Hermitage, stood on a site near Nashville.

His legal and political careers had offered Jackson economic security and social standing, but his fame arose from military exploits. A major general of Tennessee militia, he had led opposition to Red Stick Creeks during the Creek campaign of 1813–14. His defeat of the hostiles at Horseshoe Bend, Alabama, on March 27, 1814, had earned Jackson a commission as United States Army major general. He then turned his attention to problems arising from the War of 1812, particularly British designs along the Gulf of Mexico coast. His January 8, 1815, victory over British troops and their Indian allies at New Orleans, although it came after the successful conclusion of peace negotiations, propelled Jackson to the status of national hero.[9]

Subsequent to the Battle of New Orleans, Jackson's fortunes had waxed and waned. His continuing popularity fueled talk of a presidential bid, but the notoriety of his 1818 Florida invasion, coupled with other of his actions, provided ammunition to his enemies. The congressionally mandated cuts in the army infuriated him, and chronic health problems—including the legacy of a duel years in the past—drained his energy. Already indisposed to further impairment of his "fortune and constitution" in "the service of my country," he despaired of a return to Florida. He worried that voters might suspect poor motives, that his 1818 "Seminole Campaign was but a struggle for the present appointment."[10] More personally, his wife Rachel's feelings about Florida mattered greatly to him, what he described as "the repugnance of Mrs. J. to go to that country."[11]

Beyond Jackson's personal concerns, other voices soon compelled him to deny his inclinations and accept the gubernatorial appointment. The factors of which they spoke articulated themes that, after 1828, marked Jackson's presidency and also influenced the nature and evolution of Florida's judiciary. Appeals to the bonds of friendship and personal loyalty formed their basis. Many Jackson associates, such as his protégé and future Florida governor Richard Keith Call, already had invested in Florida property. Others intended to capitalize on Florida opportunities through speculation in lands and black slaves or else through the recapture of black runaways. Patronage through governmental appointments in the new territory also offered the possibility of lucrative employment, insider status, and rewarding contacts. Finally, old scores could be settled. A thousand or more Red Stick Creeks with some black allies had escaped Jackson's wrath during the Creek campaign and the War of 1812 engagements that followed. Jackson and his friends ached to render them powerless, something Governor Jackson might easily accomplish. To the entreaties Jackson submitted. From the Hermitage on February 11, he informed Monroe, "I have determined to accept [the government of Florida], provided it will answer your views, that I may resign as soon as the Government is organized and in full operation."[12]

The general's reluctant acceptance of the Florida position proved, for him, the cardinal point of his gubernatorial tenure. To fulfill his own desires and to satisfy the needs of his associates, Jackson required broad-based, if not plenary, authority. The need especially was great in the areas of land titles, patronage, and taxation. Monroe's enthusiasm about the appointment may have misled Jackson into false hopes, but, if so, they were quickly dispelled. The unwelcome news began to arrive at Nashville in March after enactment of a new law for executing the Florida treaty. In it the Congress served notice that the gov-

Andrew Jackson (1762–1845), governor, territory of Florida, July 17–November 13, 1821. Governor Jackson was disappointed and frustrated with the congressional act of March 3, 1821, for it assigned the power of appointment in the territory of Florida to President James Monroe and thereby limited his own authority to select those individuals with whom he would work. His practical solution was to promulgate eight comprehensive ordinances between July 18 and September 6, 1821. These first printed expositions of Anglo-American jurisprudence in Florida related to order, citizenship, preservation of health, fees, harbor regulations, and the creation of two counties. Complete texts of Governor Jackson's eight ordinances are included in the Acts of the Legislative Council of the Territory of Florida, 1822.

ernor's powers would be circumscribed in critical areas of authority. At month's end a frustrated Jackson informed a confidant, "I sincerely regret that I did not adhere to my first determination not to accept the government of [the] Floridas."[13]

Several provisions of the "Act for carrying into execution the Treaty between the United States and Spain," approved March 3, 1821, disappointed Jackson. The act's broad grants of authority rested in the president's hands instead of being directly delegated to the governor. Its terms permitted Monroe's appointees "all the military, civil, and judicial powers exercised by the officers of the existing government." Given Spanish practice and land title guarantees contained in the Adams-Onis Treaty, those words effectively forestalled gubernatorial power to grant or decide land titles. The law touched on the question of patronage by reserving to the president's judgment how many officers should be appointed, by whom they were to be appointed, and which of the specified powers each could claim. The act similarly withheld taxation authority from the governor by extending to the territory United States laws "relating to revenue and its collection."[14]

Once such powers were invested in Monroe's hands, he guarded them carefully. The commissions he executed for Jackson ventured little beyond the language of the congressional act. Jackson, as "Governor of the whole Territories," could accept transfer of East and West Florida and utilize "the powers and authorities heretofore exercised by the Governor and Captain General and Intendante of Cuba, and by the Governors of East and West Florida within the said provinces respectively."[15] Finally, the president granted Jackson "Special and extraordinary powers" that in vague terms permitted the governor "to administer the government . . . in the best manner in your power."[16]

The language of his commissions and of the Florida law left in Jackson's mind troubling questions about the extent of his authority, questions that he attempted to clarify. In particular he inquired, on April 2, about his powers in regard to "removing" Red Stick Creeks, runaway slaves, and free blacks who had concentrated in the southern peninsula. The response was an unwelcome one. For the administration, Secretary of War John C. Calhoun denied the desired power to the governor by directing him to take no immediate measures. Jackson's reaction to the rebuff is not known, but within days Indian leaders associated with him set out for southern Florida with a raiding party. By midsummer they had destroyed black settlements on the Manatee River, devastated Indian villages along their route, and returned to the United States with their black captives.[17]

This series of occurrences and circumstances affected Jackson's state of mind, perceptions, and goals and set the stage for his actions as governor. They encouraged a zealous protectiveness regarding his powers and office as well as a predisposition toward arbitrary and even autocratic action. On a different level they forced him into careful planning so that he could utilize his limited authority to its fullest extent. That this latter effort culminated in some success is evidenced by the manner in which Jackson coupled his concerns about patronage with the need for law enforcement and the administration of justice.

Although the governor-to-be did not arrive in Florida before June 1821 and did not accept the transfer from West Florida's governor José Callava at Pensacola until July 17, his thoughts since April had centered upon the promulgation of a basic legal structure for the territory.[18] The efforts assumed added importance in May when President Monroe signed a series of commissions for territorial officers, including ones for former Kentucky congressman William Pope DuVal and former United States senator Eligius Fromentin of Louisiana as judge of the United States, respectively, for East and West Florida. The appointments, made contrary to the governor's wishes, sharply contrasted the president's patronage powers with Jackson's patronage desires.[19]

Seeking alternatives and expertise in the formulation of an effective program, Jackson consulted a number of individuals. His physician James C. Bronaugh, among others, figured in the planning, as did aide Richard Keith Call. While en route from Nashville to New Orleans in April, Jackson encountered lawyer, author, and former editor Henry Marie Brackenridge, who spoke Spanish and was well acquainted with Spanish colonial policies. Since Brackenridge was eager to assist with the new Florida administration, Jackson enlisted him to coordinate administrative policies and to effectuate their results. In mid-May Edward Livingston contributed by forwarding to Jackson from New Orleans "some [S]panish books, which will be of use to [Brackenridge] in the organization of your Courts."[20] Livingston included a 1769 publication of Louisiana's Spanish governor Alexander O'Reilly, which established that colony's law through a series of gubernatorial ordinances.[21]

Design of a basic legal and administrative structure for the territory was hampered by a number of factors. Among them were the limitations of the 1821 congressional act, President Monroe's patronage policies and reluctance to grant Jackson the powers he desired, the territory's large size and minuscule population, and Florida's heritage of Spanish culture and traditions as contrasted with those of the United States. The Adams-Onis Treaty contained several provisions that complicated the task. Article 5 provided that "[t]he inhabitants of the ceded territories shall be secured in the free exercise of their religion without any restriction"; article 6 mandated that territorial inhabitants be "admitted to the enjoyment of all the privileges, rights, and immunities, of the citizens of the United States"; article 8 protected property rights granted or confirmed prior to January 24, 1818; article 9 established a procedure for settling claims against Spain; and article 15 assured Spain privileges at the ports of Pensacola and St. Augustine.[22]

These obstacles notwithstanding, Jackson and his aides were prepared to act by the time of the transfer of possession. On July 17 at Pensacola he first proclaimed that, until the Congress organized a territorial government, "all laws and municipal regulations which were in existence at the cessation of the late government, remain in full force."[23] By retaining the colony's two municipal governments, he preserved offices to which he might appoint men loyal to him and thereby enhance his power and extend his control over territorial affairs. Soon he designated Brackenridge as alcalde (or mayor) of Pensacola, while Edmund Law succeeded to the same office at St. Augustine. Until Monroe's appointees arrived in the territory, Jackson authorized others of his associates to administer those governmental responsibilities on a temporary basis.[24]

The governor's next step partially contradicted his first. While Jackson had promised to continue "all laws," he capitalized upon O'Reilly's Louisiana experience by issuing in July and August a number of ordinances to alter the form and nature of the government, thus effectively establishing the first system of United States law in the territory.[25] He provided new requirements for municipal governments and directed that alcaldes "exercise the powers of Judges of probate, Registers of Wills, Notaries Public, of Justices of the Peace, and such other powers appertaining to their said offices, as have not been otherwise distributed." He mandated observance of the Christian sabbath, established public health procedures, and regulated harbors. One ordinance addressed his continuing anger over the status of refugee Red Stick Creeks and blacks who, arguably, could claim United States citizenship under the terms of the Adams-Onis Treaty. To forestall the possibility he established registration requirements for those who desired their treaty rights to be protected, knowing that the Creeks and blacks would not appear.

Beyond these measures Jackson addressed the need for territorial administrative and judicial machinery. On July 21 he divided Florida into two counties with the Suwannee River as their mutual boundary. Escambia County corresponded with the old West Florida and St. Johns County with East Florida. To provide county government, he created in each a court composed of five justices of the peace. Any three of the justices could comprise a quorum. In addition to its administrative responsibilities, the court's judicial jurisdiction extended to "all civil cases originating in said county, where the matter in controversy shall exceed twenty dollars; and to all criminal cases; saving to these parties the right of appeal to the Governor, in all cases above the sum of five hundred dollars; and that there shall be no execution for a capital offence until the warrant of the Governor be first had and obtained."[26] The language asserted Jackson's personal authority as the territory's supreme judicial officer.

Respecting court procedures, the governor again contradicted his original proclamation. In civil cases he first permitted continued use of "existing laws, or the laws of Spain," although he excepted rules regarding examination of witnesses. Then on July 26 he offered revised rules for procedure that mixed "the usages in Spanish tribunals" with the needs of American businessmen and speculators used to other traditions. Moreover, Jackson again specified provisions for gubernatorial oversight of appeals.

Already on July 21 Jackson had issued rules for criminal procedure. To extend protections afforded by state and national constitutions, in section 3 of No.4 An Ordinance, he ordered that such cases be conducted "according to the course of the common law: that is, no person shall be held to answer for a capital or otherwise infamous crime, unless on a presentment or indictment of a Grand Jury; and in all criminal cases, the accused shall enjoy the right to a speedy, and public trial, by an impartial Jury of the county wherein the crime shall have been committed; and to be informed of the nature and cause of the accusation, to be confronted with the witnesses against him, and to have compulsory process for obtaining witnesses in his favor and to have the assistance of counsel for his defence."

The reforms extended further as Jackson attempted to overcome congressional and presidential limitations on his authority. In section 9 of No.4 An Ordinance, he empowered judges of the county courts, for example, "to impose such taxes upon the inhabitants of their counties respectively, as in their discretion may be necessary to meet and defray the expenses which may be incurred in carrying this ordinance into effect." Jackson also addressed the question of revenues by permitting counties to collect license taxes and specifying that his appointees could require the payment of specified fees for judicial and other services rendered. Given that his courts claimed jurisdiction that Monroe's appointees might claim as their own, the governor acted through section 14 of No.4 An Ordinance, as well, to seize prosecutorial authority. "In all criminal cases," he proclaimed, "the process and indictment shall be in the name of the United States, and there shall be appointed a prosecuting Attorney for each of said counties, who shall receive in each case, a reasonable compensation, to be taxed by the court."

Jackson's 1821 ordinances established a strong basis for territorial government under gubernatorial control and permitted Jackson to place his protégés securely in positions of real power, affording them a lasting foothold in Florida. That Jackson could reach so far to establish his own authority resulted in great part from the delayed arrival of Monroe's other appointees. Resentment of Jackson's presumption, though, was not long in surfacing.

The governor's principal early rival for authority, and the man who tested his resolve most directly, was Eligius Fromentin of Louisiana. Boasting a background in the baroque politics of his state, the French-born former Roman Catholic clergyman greeted political conflict lustily. Only two years out of office as United States senator, Fromentin eagerly anticipated taking up the position to which Monroe appointed him on May 18, 1821—that of "Judge of the United States for West Florida and for that part of East Florida which is westward of the cape, to reside at Pensacola."[27]

Earlier in his career Fromentin had defended Jackson's military conduct, but the potential for conflict between the two men appeared evident from the outset of their Florida acquaintance. The month prior to his judicial appointment, the Louisianian had engineered an encounter with Jackson in New Orleans, claiming without success the right under an old presidential commission to "receive the Floridas" for the United States.[28] Following Fromentin's late July arrival at Pensacola, the breach between them widened as each maneuvered for political advantage. By August 4 the governor was imploring the president to counter the judge's standing. "I should not like to continue in the administration of the Government with such an associate," he proclaimed. "And I can assure you this confidence does not exist either in the Spanish or American population here, in the case of Judge Fromentin." Jackson added, "[H]e is a polite, Gentlemanly man, but from the character given of him both here and in New Orleans, both as to his capacity as a judge and his moral character, I cannot confide in him."[29]

As Jackson's letter made its way to Washington, the smoldering resentments burst into full flame. The eruption grew out of a pending legal case involving the estate of former Spanish West Florida official Dr. Nicolas Maria Vidal. Because of certain debts owed to the powerful trading concern of John Forbes and Company, the estate had not been settled at the time of the transfer of Florida to the United States. Upon the exchange of flags, Vidal's mulatto daughter employed as her counsel Brackenridge and Call to obtain from the former Spanish government's archives documents vital to the case. When local authorities refused them access, they appealed to the governor.

By the time of the appeal, the Florida governor's fuse had grown quite short. Among others things, disputes with former West Florida governor Callava had proved to be a source of continuing frustration. In the circumstances, when approached about the apparent injustice in the Vidal matter, Jackson ordered Brackenridge, several other officials, and a military detachment to Callava's residence to demand the papers. After a series of incidents, the Spaniard was escorted under armed guard into Jackson's presence. The men argued heatedly through interpreter Brackenridge before the governor ordered Callava jailed and the records seized.

These events raised important legal questions, including whether Jackson had authority under principles of diplomatic immunity to arrest Callava. Into the legal breach stepped Fromentin. During his brief stay at Pensacola, the judge already had befriended Callava as well as the suit's principal defendant, John Innerarity, Jr. When Innerarity learned of the detention, and in order to secure Callava's release, he applied to Fromentin orally for a writ of habeas corpus, used in Anglo-American jurisprudence as a protection against illegal imprisonment. Innerarity offered no written petition or supporting affidavits, but Fromentin complied nonetheless and required that Callava be brought before his court.

The governor's reaction to Fromentin's order resulted predictably. "Old Hickory" exploded in rage and demanded that the jurist be brought before him. Jackson lectured Fromentin as to the governor's supreme judicial authority and insisted that the judge's jurisdiction extended only to those national laws specifically enumerated in the 1821 congressional act providing for the Florida transfer—that is to say, to laws on revenue and the importation of slaves. Fromentin temporarily backed down, subject to Jackson's threat of jail if the judge ever again interfered with the governor's authority. In the case of *The Heirs of Vidal* v. *John Innerarity*, the governor eventually ruled in favor of the plaintiff heirs.[30]

The Callava affair, as some named it, occurred at isolated Pensacola, but its repercussions were national in scope. Newspapers trumpeted reports, and politicians of all persuasions used the matter for their own purposes. The incident embarrassed Jackson, a circumstance that Call blamed on the "weakness and folly" of Brackenridge.[31] The controversy persisted for months and, quickly enough, landed in President Monroe's hands. Fromentin naturally defended his stance, labeling Jackson a "grand inquisitor" and imploring of Secretary of State John Quincy Adams, "because my enemy, like the swine, which delight in nothing as much as filth, has thought it convenient to seek a refuge in the quagmire of billingsgate abuse, shall I let go the hold I have of him?"[32] Yet in the end Adams and Monroe had little political choice but to support the still-popular Jackson. Attorney General William A. Wirt might assert that "for the Governor of a Territory, to summon a judge of the U.S. to his tribunal to answer for the discharge of a conscientious duty, will not be tolerated by the people of this country," but Monroe, through Adams, acquiesced in Jackson's interpretation of the governor's judicial authority.[33] Final words on the matter, though, would not be spoken until the next session of the Congress.

Once the furor receded, Jackson and his friends emerged triumphant within the context of territorial power sharing. His authority stood virtually unchallengeable. Fromentin avoided direct confrontation and soon left for New Orleans. Others of Monroe's appointees present in Florida carried out their duties quietly. East Florida's judge, William Pope DuVal, did not arrive in the territory until November, so he took no part in the controversies. Nonetheless, by the time of DuVal's arrival, the wheel of change had revolved, and the future of Florida's government and judiciary suddenly had become uncertain. New power cards were about to be distributed, with the president again sitting in the dealer's chair.[34]

The change once more was initiated by Jackson. He had not desired to come to Florida, and he had not enjoyed his stay. Seemingly, the Callava affair proved to be the last straw. "Having Organised the Government of the Floridas, and it being now in full operation," he wrote Monroe on October 5, "I have determined to take a little respite from the laborious duties with which I have been surrounded."[35] He and Rachel left the territory two days later and reached Nashville on November 5. On the fourteenth he dispatched a letter of resignation. "I can only observe for the present that I am truly wearied of public life," he remarked to the president, "I want [to] rest." He closed, "[A]ll things progress in harmony in Pensacola . . . and . . . the Citizens appear hap[p]y under the Government as Organized."[36]

Andrew Jackson bequeathed a great legacy to Florida, its law, and its judicial system. He provided the organizational basis from which its government grew. He ordained the first laws, instituted reforms, and demanded respect for them. He lent the authority of his person, power, and reputation to the majesty of the supreme judicial bench. Most important, he foresaw a Florida more closely akin to the United States than to Spain. He sought guidance from English and United States legal traditions and looked to the common law for wisdom. As one Florida historian observed, "Within three months' time Jackson turned Florida toward the American way of life." He concluded, "Florida still had a long route to travel, but her start was a good one."[37]

Eligius Fromentin, United States Judge for West Florida, 1821–1822

Born in France during the reign of Louis XV, Eligius Fromentin received his education at a Jesuit college after which he was ordained a priest. He undertook a ministry at Étampes during the days of unrest prior to the French Revolution. Abbé at Étampes and likely a member of the Society of Jesus, he escaped the Terror in 1795. Fromentin settled and conducted religious services at Azelum, a colony of émigrés founded in 1794 on the Susquehanna River in Bradford County, Pennsylvania. Subsequently he moved to Maryland, where he taught French, acquired fluency in English, and studied law. His marriage to the daughter of an influential Maryland family improved his social and financial prospects significantly.

Fromentin later relocated to Louisiana and settled at New Orleans. He practiced as an attorney during 1805–7, gaining experience in the intricacies of French and Spanish law and legal traditions. For four years thereafter he worked as clerk to the Orleans territory house of representatives. Fromentin also cultivated a friendship with William C. C. Claiborne, the territorial governor. In 1812 the former priest was chosen as secretary of the territory's statehood constitutional convention. That body selected him as an agent to convey its proposed charter to President James Madison, along with a memorial to the Congress requesting annexation of West Florida to Louisiana. Claiborne described him at the time as a person who "deserves and possesses a great share of public confidence" and as "a man of education and strict moral rectitude."[38]

The honor accorded Fromentin by the convention presaged further recognition. Also in 1812 he gained election as secretary to the Louisiana senate. One year later the legislature named him United States senator, in which office he remained until March 1819. Changing political fortunes denied Fromentin reelection in 1819, and the impact of the loss proved dramatic. He left his wife for a mistress and, with the restoration of the Bourbon regime in France, returned to his native country. The French Catholic church, wary of his personal problems, denied him any important ecclesiastical position.

Disappointed by the results of his return to France, Fromentin sailed for New Orleans, reconciled with his wife, reestablished a law practice, and regained political favor. In 1821 he presided as a judge of the criminal court in New Orleans and was accorded increased recognition in the legal community for his essay *Respecting Land Titles in Orleans and Dominique*. Given his fiery emotions and strong sentiments, the judge naturally made enemies. Rumors swirled about his indiscretions and adventures, and, reportedly, "men of high standing" were "astonished" that the president might consider him for preferment.[39] In politics, as was true of many other men during the "era of good feelings," Fromentin considered himself a Democratic-Republican.

Fromentin's Florida connections had begun in 1819, when he had received a commission to accept the Floridas from Spain pursuant to the Adams-Onis Treaty and to assure the proper transfer of Spanish archives. Passage of time had rendered the commission obsolete, but Fromentin had pursued the matter with governor-designee Andrew Jackson at New Orleans in April 1821. That meeting had displeased Jackson and exposed the potential for conflict between the two men. One month later, Fromentin's political connections yielded him a temporary appointment by President James Monroe as judge of the United States for West Florida.[40] Opponents insisted that his wife Elizabeth's family influenced Monroe's action, an accusation Fromentin countered by asserting that the appointment fittingly acknowledged his special knowledge of Spanish law, customs, and language.[41]

As detailed previously in this chapter, Fromentin's brief stay in Florida resulted disastrously in his quarrel with Jackson. Because of the governor's insistence upon retaining most court jurisdiction within his own hands and those of his appointees, together with Monroe's acquiescence to the claim, Fromentin found himself with little work to do. Probably he took some comfort in personal sentiments supporting his integrity expressed by Secretary of State John Quincy Adams and the president. "In the different view which you have taken of the Subject," Adams informed the judge, "[President Monroe] is persuaded that your motives and intentions were entirely pure, though he deeply regrets the collision of authority and misunderstanding."[42] In his next message to the Congress, Monroe repeated his belief in the purity of Fromentin's "motives and intentions," offering in the process indirect criticism of the governor.[43]

Whatever comfort he received from Adams and Monroe, Fromentin was left an unhappy man. Jackson's friends—including Escambia County justices of the peace, the bar, and the Pensacola city council—demanded the judge's replacement by Henry Marie Brackenridge. In mid-December 1821 one official observed, "That Sapient Judge [Fromentin] but rarely crawls out of his shell."[44] By month's end local report noted that "Judge Fromentine intends leaving this place, having been appointed President of the College at New Orleans."[45] In January 1822 he and family left Pensacola for New Orleans. Fromentin resumed his legal practice. On October 6, 1822, he and Elizabeth died there, victims of yellow fever. Though formerly a priest, he was buried without benefit of clergy.[46]

William Pope DuVal, United States Judge for East Florida, 1821–1822

William Pope DuVal, though he served only briefly as Judge Eligius Fromentin's East Florida counterpart during 1821–22, emerged as one of Florida territory's preeminent men. DuVal was born in 1784, at Mount Comfort, near Richmond, Virginia. His parents, William and Ann Pope DuVal, belonged to aristocratic families. His father William had distinguished himself as a military officer during the American Revolution and was associated in friendship or the practice of law with numerous prominent men, including Patrick Henry, Thomas Jefferson, and George Wythe.[47]

While Virginia society offered comfort and refinements, William Pope DuVal early yearned to make a life on his own. At age fourteen, with his father's blessing, he accompanied an older brother to the Kentucky frontier. Four years later he commenced reading law in the Bardstown office of Judge Henry P. Broadnax.

William Pope DuVal (1784–1854). DuVal was appointed by President Monroe to serve as the first federal judge of East Florida in 1821 and by Monroe and successive presidents as territorial governor from 1822 to 1834. Later responsibilities included service as a delegate at the 1838–39 constitutional convention, a member of the territorial senate, and senate president in 1840.

He achieved admission to the bar in 1804, and in the same year married his life's great love, Nancy Hynes. Her death in Florida thirty-seven years later would devastate him. "The fairy spell is broken," he wrote friend Richard Keith Call, "and the rich sunshine of the heart is changed to cold and starless night."[48]

Death was long in the future for the DuVals in 1804, and for years they and their family, which eventually included seven children, fared well. William involved himself at Bardstown in law, society, and politics. During the War of 1812, he served for a time as captain of the Kentucky mounted rangers, and in the year that conflict began he also was elected to the United States House of Representatives. DuVal held his congressional seat during 1813–15, then returned to Kentucky where he practiced law and acted as Hardin County attorney.

By 1821 family financial pressures had prompted DuVal to search for employment more lucrative than the practice of law in Kentucky. He appealed to an old Washington friend, John C. Calhoun, then secretary of war. "If a judge is to [be] appointed with a compitent Salary for this new country [of Florida]," DuVal wrote, "I will accept it or any other appointment." He added, "I would indeed prefer a situation nearer, Kentucky—but I know of none."[49] Calhoun subsequently recommended DuVal to Secretary of State John Quincy Adams as "a very worthy man [who] is very competent to fill the place of a judge or District attorney."[50] The secretary's intercession succeeded, and on May 18, 1821, President James Monroe commissioned DuVal as "Judge of the United

States for East Florida, with the exception of that part which lies Westward of the Cape."[51]

The DuVal judicial appointment commenced a Florida career that was to last, with certain intervals, virtually to the 1850s. As was the case with other of Monroe's appointments, it had not pleased Governor Andrew Jackson, who complained to the president about his failure to appoint "[anyone] of my personal acquaintance, and in whom I had confidence."[52] Still, DuVal proved a loyal Jacksonian for almost two decades and learned to work closely and fruitfully with many Jackson associates whom the governor left in Florida upon his departure.

Jackson's departure, in fact, resulted in DuVal's rapid elevation in Florida society and politics. He arrived at St. Augustine only in November 1821, after Jackson had left Pensacola the previous month. As also was the case with Fromentin in West Florida, DuVal's judicial duties were few. Consequently, he spent his early days touring East Florida, especially the St. Johns River area. Before the year was out DuVal had convened a grand jury, rejected a proposed clerkship appointment by Jackson's local representative William G. D. Worthington, recommended the appointment of fellow Kentuckian and future United States attorney for East Florida Greenbury A. Gaither, and inquired as to "whether the President has fixed on the allowance intended for the U.S. judge of E. Florida."[53]

Most of DuVal's days as a judge were spent in another pursuit. Jackson's resignation as governor set off a scramble for appointment to the vacancy, and DuVal quickly placed himself in the running. His early popularity with Floridians was attested to when leading residents of St. Augustine urged his appointment to the "Chief Magistracy of this territory." They proclaimed, "No choice would be so gratifying or acceptable to the people of East Florida."[54] The judge hurried to Washington to plead his cause directly, and his efforts paid dividends. On April 17, 1822, Monroe commissioned him as governor of a unified "Territory of Florida," under the provisions of a congressional act passed two weeks earlier. His first term was for three years and carried an annual salary of $2,500.[55]

In Florida's rough-and-tumble frontier political atmosphere, DuVal's tenure as governor was a troubled, though long, one. President John Quincy Adams twice reappointed him for terms of three years, and President Andrew Jackson continued the practice in 1832. Some of DuVal's actions and policies are discussed elsewhere in part 1. It is worthy of mention, nonetheless, that as governor he helped initiate representative government and a more workable system of courts and law enforcement in the territory, was involved in locating the capital at Tallahassee, worked diligently on behalf of positive relations with

Florida's Indian population, and extended his efforts in favor of numerous other good causes including education.

Troubles still attended DuVal continually. By 1828 he would confide to a friend, "I have never my dear Andrew [Hynes] felt at home in this country, and if I die here, my spirit will quit this country in twenty-four hours for old Kentuck."[56] Three years later Nancy returned to Bardstown to permit their children access to an adequate education. Particularly beset by criticism arising from his opposition to the creation of banks, an increasingly besieged DuVal remained in the territory only for about two years thereafter. A critic noted in March 1834 that, since DuVal's reappointment by Jackson two years earlier, "he has made the office a sinecure—[h]e was for seven or eight months before December last actually living in Kentucky—His Secretary acting as Governor."[57] By the spring DuVal's tenure of office had come to a close. Jackson designated his protégé John Eaton as the successor, and DuVal recommenced the practice of law in Kentucky.[58]

Florida's allure has remained alive in the hearts of many individuals who first experienced its delights and then moved away; DuVal was no exception. He and Nancy returned to the territory by 1836, and he revived his political career. The former governor narrowly failed to be elected president of the statehood constitutional convention during 1838–39, served in the territorial senate during 1839–41, was senate president in 1840, held office as United States civil law agent in Florida during 1841–42, and acted as United States boundary commissioner in 1845. Three years later, as a Democrat, he lost a congressional election in the Whig landslide that saw Zachary Taylor elected as president. He then moved to Texas, where he again plied his trade as a lawyer, this time in Austin and Galveston. He died at Washington, District of Columbia, March 18, 1854, and was interred in the Congressional Cemetery.[59]

Aside from the outfall of his political disputes, William Pope DuVal was well regarded in Florida and other parts of the country. His ebullient personality and his remarkable storytelling abilities endeared him to the nation's common folk. His exploits passed into legend with the fictionalization of his life and adventures by Washington Irving and James K. Paulding. Of him one early Floridian reminisced: "The Governor did not accumulate property out of the salary of his long public service. He was too openhanded and openhoused for that. He died poor in this world's goods, but rich in the estimation of his country and the affection of his personal friends."[60]

Chapter 2

Superior Courts and a Territorial Court of Appeals

Andrew Jackson's tenure as Florida's provisional governor generated long-lasting legacies. He turned the former Spanish province toward a different orientation, that of a United States territory, and he left behind him numerous of his friends and protégés who would themselves significantly affect the course taken by Florida's development. Still, Judge William Pope DuVal's arrival in November 1821 may symbolize more appropriately Florida's early territorial years than did Jackson's brief presence. DuVal served the territory for well over a decade as Jackson's successor, and during his time in office dramatic changes occurred that left an indelible mark upon the future state, its legal system, and its judiciary.

The changes that were to mark DuVal's years as governor began prior to his April 1822 appointment by President James Monroe. The 1821 law under which Jackson had chafed had not been intended as a permanent legal foundation for the territory, and Jackson's judicial quarrel with Judge Eligius Fromentin had demonstrated to the Congress the need to act with dispatch in designing a more permanent framework. During February and March 1822, both the House of Representatives and the Senate debated the proper course of action, spurred by petitions from the territory pleading "the necessity of acting on the bill without delay."[1] The resulting law, "An Act for the establishment of a Territorial Government in Florida," was approved by the president on March 30.[2]

The new territorial act entailed profound changes in Florida's governmental structure. It created a balance of powers by establishing three separate branches of government and specifying the jurisdiction of each. The governor, appointed by the president, held executive power. He commanded the militia, acted ex officio as superintendent of Indian affairs, could grant pardons and reprieves, and was empowered to "appoint and commission all officers, civil and of the militia, whose appointments are not herein otherwise provided for."

The legislative power, previously exercised solely by the governor, now rested with a legislative council composed of the governor and thirteen of the "most fit and discreet persons of the Territory." Members of the council were to be appointed annually by the president. The body received powers over "all the rightful subjects of legislation," but the Congress imposed important restrictions. The council could not, for instance, exercise control over land and land claims; the Congress would dispose of those matters by creating special land commissions in subsequent statutes. Most significantly, the Congress retained veto power over territorial laws, authority it proved more than willing to exercise. As an early resident recalled, "Congress was active and profuse in annulling acts of the Governor and Council, and curbing the lavish expenditures for clerk hire, and other incidentals." Congressional vetoes at times also affected millage rates, divorce, public printing, and revenue.[3]

The statute addressed reorganization of the territory's judiciary as well. In place of the confused overlap created by Jackson and Monroe, it established two superior courts and authorized "such inferior courts and justices of the peace as the Legislative Council of the Territory may, from time to time, establish." One superior court, for West Florida, was to be held at Pensacola, while that for East Florida would sit at St. Augustine. Judges, together with marshals and district attorneys, received their four-year appointments from the president, subject to Senate approval.

Anxious to avoid imbroglios such as those that had beset the Jackson administration, Congress carefully delineated superior court jurisdiction. Basically, the courts were intended as the system's "workhorse" trial courts, and their judges received authority so substantial as to alarm many Floridians. "Within its limits, herein described," the law read, "each court shall have jurisdiction in all criminal cases, and exclusive jurisdiction in all capital cases, and original jurisdiction in all civil cases of the value of one hundred dollars, arising under, and cognizable by, the law of the Territory now in force therein, or which may, at any time, be enacted by the Legislative Council." Specified national laws were made applicable to the territory, and the superior courts granted jurisdiction. Each "free male white" person could act as a grand or petit juror so long as he was a housekeeper who had resided in the territory for one year or more. Appeals ran to the United States Supreme Court "in the same cases, and under the same regulations, as from the circuit courts of the United States."[4]

Having granted power within the state, the territorial law also enumerated certain rights that the new government could not infringe. Harking back to Jackson's refusal to acknowledge Fromentin's authority to issue against the governor a writ of habeas corpus, the act guaranteed "the benefit of" that order. It also provided that "to the end that the inhabitants may be protected in their liberty, property, and the exercise of their religion, no law shall ever be valid which shall impair, or in any way restrain, the freedom of religious opinion, professions, or worship." It continued: "They shall be bailable, in all cases, except for capital offences, where the proof is evident or the presumption great. All fines shall be moderate and proportioned to the offence; and excessive bail shall not be required, nor cruel and unusual punishments inflicted." The provision concluded, "No *ex post facto* law, or law impairing the obligation of contracts, shall ever be passed; nor shall private property be taken for public uses, without just compensation."

The 1822 congressional act constructed a foundation for Florida government, but its effectiveness depended greatly upon actions of the legislative council and other factors. That territorial governance would encounter huge obstacles became apparent from the first days of the law's effectiveness. Just getting from place to place, for example, posed enormous problems. Few dependable roads connected those settlements worthy of the name, while most of the four-hundred-mile-wide area separating St. Augustine and Pensacola remained virtually uninhabited, save for scattered villages of Indians and their black vassals. Water afforded one means of transportation, but in those pre-steamboat days water travel carried substantial risks and involved great uncertainties.[5]

These problems evidenced themselves at the legislative council's first session. The body required more than a month after its first meeting to obtain a quorum. It officially convened at Pensacola on July 22, 1822, but only after several St. Augustine delegates survived a hazardous fifty-nine-day sea voyage. One East Florida colleague failed to arrive and was believed to have been lost en route. Thereafter the council strove to maintain a quorum until an outbreak of yellow fever forced its members to seek refuge at a nearby farm. Council president James C. Bronaugh and clerk Joseph Coppinger Connor died of the malady.[6]

While circumstances made legislative activity difficult, the 1822 council session accomplished a good deal. It elected a territorial delegate to the Congress, organized the militia, called for army surveys of the interior, and established two new counties: Duval in East Florida and Jackson in West Florida. It continued Governor Jackson's county courts as administrative bodies and created circuit courts as "a temporary expedient" to balance the "novel and dangerous" power Congress had vested in superior court judges. Each county was authorized eight justices of the peace.[7]

The legislators also provided a body of territorial law, although the achievement relied heavily upon borrowing. "Foreseeing . . . the difficulty under which the Territory would labor for the want of a suitable code of laws," Henry Marie Brackenridge remembered, "I had procured a volume of the digested Legislative acts of Missouri, which had been similarly situated, having been also a province of Spain." Brackenridge continued, "The volume . . . was the result of fifteen years experience in that State, and yet contained for the greater part, little more than the adaption of the joint labours of Jefferson, Wythe and Madison, and of some of the Pennsylvania Legislators, to the circumstances of the country."[8]

With Missouri law as their guide, council members enacted a series of measures governing various aspects of civil and criminal matters, including probate, commercial transactions, civil proceedings, conveyances, guardianship, apprenticeship, slavery, and alimony.[9] Additionally, the common law and statutory laws of England in force down to July 4, 1776, were adopted by the governor and legislative council in 1822. Brackenridge described the step as "among the few [council actions] which can be called original."[10] Subsequent councils raised his ire, though, by daring to formulate new codes. His anger at the complications and uncertainties of statutory change still ring true today for many who work with the law. "Our Territory, has ever since experienced the pernicious effect of this example," he proclaimed in 1831. "The whole body of the law criminal as well as civil, not even excepting the fundamental act which adopted the common and statute law of England, has since been repeatedly repealed, and re-enacted, and partial alterations have been made, by which they have been rendered vague and uncertain, instead of permanent and generally known."[11]

As the council endeavored to furnish the territory with a basic law, the superior courts slowly organized. President Monroe had moved quickly to fill the judicial vacancies after approval of the territorial act, his criteria again resting upon his political needs and the patronage desires of those whom he chose to please. For East Florida, on April 30, 1823, he commissioned Yale-educated former army officer Joseph Lee Smith of Connecticut. Smith, father of future Confederate general Edmund Kirby Smith, had been recommended by his home state senator James Lanman as well as by Andrew Jackson's rival Jacob Brown, commanding general of the United States Army.[12] The West Florida nomination took more time. Monroe first offered the position to former North Carolina governor John Branch (future governor of Florida, 1844–45), but he declined. Jackson associates at Pensacola pressed the candidacy of Henry Marie Brackenridge. Governor DuVal on behalf of the council also urged action in favor of their fellow council member. "[N]o man can be found who is better qualified," he wrote Secretary of State John Quincy Adams, "and who would be so acceptable to the people here [as Brackenridge]." DuVal's letter proved unnecessary, as Monroe had decided in favor of the Jackson man before it was sent. He issued Brackenridge a commission on June 5.[13]

Both judicial commissions had been issued by early June, but legal technicalities delayed court business. The situation was not so deficient in West Florida, where in late July Brackenridge announced that he would begin to organize the court immediately in anticipation of its October term. Unfortunately, East Florida's experience was otherwise. Smith arrived at St. Augustine to discover that the governor's residence at the territory's western extremity forestalled the judge from taking office. "[I]t would not be in my power to hold a Court in October, or to do any official act," he informed Secretary of State Adams on October 31, "because Governor Duval, from whom alone, by the Act of Congress, I could receive the Oath of Office, was at Pensacola."[14] Only when DuVal reached St. Augustine for the 1823 legislative council session did Smith take his oath. On May 5, 1823, District Attorney Alexander Hamilton finally could report to the president, "The Superior Court has this day commenced its first session, under the direction of Judge Smith, to the very great satisfaction of the community, and it is with pleasure I inform you that the Judge is considered a valuable acquisition to the Territory."[15]

Judge Smith's problems mirrored others the territory experienced in establishing its judicial system. The Congress overturned territorial laws relating to the county courts, and the circuit courts had come under scrutiny as well. Another important concern involved appeals. The 1822 territorial act had permitted appeals to the United States Supreme Court in cases under federal law, but no right of appeals had been specified in territorial cases.[16]

In light of this situation, judicial reform once more commanded attention during the 1823 session of the legislative council. When that body met at St. Augustine in May, Richard Keith Call, among others, offered solutions and pursued their adoption. As a result, the council abolished circuit courts and transferred most of their powers to reorganized county courts. The same year Call was elected Florida's delegate to the Congress. After that body convened in December 1823, he pressed for supplementary federal legislation.[17]

Call's congressional work achieved success in 1824. The act of May 26 of that year first authorized the addition of a third superior court judge for a district encompassing "that part of the Territory, situated between the Apalachicola and Suwannee rivers." The statute then created a "Territorial court of appeals" composed of the three superior court judges, any two of whom could comprise a quorum. The appeals court was directed to convene "at the seat of government of said Territory" on the first Monday of January in each year. The panel held complete appellate jurisdiction over the superior courts, subject to the right of Congress to provide differently in distinct areas of law, such as land claims. Its jurisdiction extended, as well, to inferior territorial court decisions. Writs of error and appeal from the court of appeals were permitted to the United States Supreme Court, subject to a $1,000 minimum threshold for territorial civil cases.[18]

The new law recognized increasing complexities present in Florida's society by 1824 and anticipated future needs of its legal system. The third superior court, for instance, acknowledged settlement and investments in the area that became known as Middle Florida. That region's dynamic growth and its impact upon Florida is discussed at greater length in chapter 3, but already the council had authorized the location there of the territorial capital. Still, the act was no cure-all. The design of the appeals process was far from ideal. For instance, the court's objectivity could be questioned, since the same judge would examine cases at the appellate level that he previously had decided at the trial level. Moreover, no statutory provision augmented the salaries of the judges when they sat in distant Middle Florida as appellate jurists. Since payment of these costs had to come from the judge's established compensation, service as an appeals judge from any district other than Middle Florida required an extraordinary sense of duty, a large measure of ambition, or both.

The new law's weaknesses notwithstanding, President Monroe acted quickly to implement the statute. On May 27, 1824, one day after its approval, he appointed a friend of Delegate Call, East Florida resident and former Kentucky jurist William W. Blair, to the Middle Florida judgeship. Blair had long sought Florida positions in order to take advantage of the territory's climate for the benefit of his health. Unfortunately, Florida's curative powers proved insufficient, and Judge Blair died at St. Augustine on July 27, 1824, before assuming his duties. Within one month Monroe had turned to former Michigan federal judge Augustus Brevoort Woodward as his replacement.[19]

The early days of the superior courts and of the territorial court of appeals were a time of trial, error, adaptation, and uncertainty. A brief examination of the lives and careers of the first four jurists who sat upon them—Joseph Lee Smith, Henry Marie Brackenridge, William W. Blair, and Augustus Brevoort Woodward—permits an insightful glimpse of that pioneering era, the circumstances under which courts operated, and the jurisprudential legacy that emerged.

Joseph Lee Smith, Eastern District Superior Court Judge, 1822–1832

East Florida's first superior court judge, Joseph Lee Smith, was the son of Elnathan and Chloe Lee Smith. Born May 28, 1779, at New Britain, Connecticut, he possessed a brilliant mind coupled with an often troubled disposition. He graduated with honors from Yale University and studied law under Tapping Reeve at the prestigious Litchfield Law Academy. He joined the Connecticut bar in 1804 and, thereafter, practiced law at Hartford until 1812. By 1807 he felt sufficiently secure in his professional standing to begin a family. He and his bride, Frances "Fanny" Marion Kirby, eventually parented four children.[20]

Smith's years as a lawyer did not pass quietly. He held his personal and political opinions deeply, and he was outspoken about them, a trait that marked the entirety of his life. One event vividly portrays these characteristics. In 1807 at the renowned Litchfield Festival, Jeffersonian Republican Smith condemned federal politicians who had imprisoned editor Selleck Osborn on libel charges. Smith's reward was swift in coming. The Federalists soon had him arrested. The charge accused him of uttering "false, malicious, scandalous, and defamatory words."[21]

As was true of others of his generation, Smith's legal career was interrupted by the War of 1812. Both his and his wife's families boasted proud military traditions, and his son Edmund Kirby Smith would become the last Confederate general to surrender his troops during the Civil War. Given tradition and his political opinions, Smith likely hesitated little before offering his services to the country. As a major of the Twenty-fifth United States Infantry regiment, he proved a natural leader and accomplished officer. One acquaintance described him at the time as "six feet in height, strong & well proportioned, and his natural bearing prepossessing and commanding," as well as "the best and finest looking man in the [army]."[22] On one occasion he narrowly escaped death when fever struck his men. On another, at Stoney Creek, New York, on June 6, 1813, he displayed profound qualities of leadership and a fine sense of tactics in ordering a strategic maneuver that saved his troops from a surprise British attack. Afterward, he led the men in withstanding three charges at close ranks. Noted one observer, "[N]o troops, however well-disciplined, could long stand before such a shower as was poured upon them by the gallant 25th."[23]

Smith's actions during the War of 1812 provided him with access to an army career. While the conflict still raged, he recruited enlistments at Hartford, a dangerous assignment given the antiwar, pro-British sentiments of many Connecticut Federalists. Afterward he remained in the service until the army reductions of 1821, when he retired as a colonel. In this second career, as in his first, he earned friendships and enmities. Jacob Brown, the army's commanding general, later recommended his subordinate for a Florida judgeship and for territorial governor. On the other hand, William Pope DuVal, who bested Smith in the contest for the gubernatorial appointment, labeled his rival as "a man dismissed with disgrace from our army, as too vile to hold any command."[24]

Fortunately for Smith, in 1822 his friends outnumbered his enemies within President James Monroe's administration. Accordingly, he was able to secure a four-year appointment on April 30 as "Judge in and over that part of the Territory of Florida known as East Florida."[25] His difficulties in taking office and organizing his court prior to May 1823 have been discussed earlier in this chapter. They were complicated by the jurist's unhappy reaction to his new home. St. Augustine, he remarked, was "out of the world." He added, "Everything here is extremely dull."[26]

Health also became a factor in Smith's judicial tenure. Before arriving in Florida he had suffered through frequent health difficulties, brought on in part by excessive drinking. The territory's hot, humid climate exacerbated the concerns. Shortly after his arrival he was stricken by yellow fever or, as it was known, "yellow jack." He survived but in a weakened condition. Stress of judicial travel probably weakened him further. He encountered danger from such threats as snakes and alligators. On one judicial journey he rested the night with a rural family. Not long after his departure the following morning, the family was attacked, apparently by Indians, and most of its members murdered. Smith once remarked to a friend that, if he had possessed an independent fortune, he would never have resided in Florida for one season. In his opinion, the climate was too hot and the land scarcely "good enough for Indians & rattlesnakes."[27]

The judge's temperament, combined with unhappiness, stress, and health problems, launched him into numerous quarrels and controversies during the remainder of his life. Future Florida supreme court chief justice Thomas Douglas, who served under Smith as United States district attorney, remembered the judge as a "gigantic man, both mentally and physically; and, but for his rebounded prejudices and ungovernable passions and dissolute habits, would have been qualified to fill any, even the most exalted station in government." He then added, "He had the advantage of an excellent education; was a sound lawyer; read much; had fine conversational powers; a highly discriminating mind, and could equally adorn the bench or the drawingroom . . . [b]ut he was intemperate in his habits and of most uncontrollable temper."[28]

Sometimes the controversies involved physical violence. St. Augustine's Levoritt Coe reported on August 12, 1824, "my missfortune on Saturday last to have my person unwarrantably attacked, and unmercifully beaten by his Honor, Judge, Joseph L Smith."[29] According to Coe, he had been present while Smith was playing billiards. Suddenly the judge "took a large Stick that was near and beat me." The victim recalled a Smith boast that "he is above the Law or at least that it cannot reach him."[30]

The incident illustrates, as well, that some of Smith's quarrels concerned fellow officials and carried political overtones. When District Attorney Edgar Macon investigated the fight with Coe, Smith reportedly retaliated. Seemingly bad blood already existed between Macon and Smith because the judge had not recommended the prosecutor for his position. Smith, Coe insisted, now threatened Macon with "imprisonment for suffering witnesses to be sworn to give evidence to the Grand Jury."[31]

The Smith-Macon feud continued long after the judge's threat. Six months later Macon complained to a political friend, Florida's congressional delegate Richard Keith Call, that Smith improperly was charging fees for judicial services. Call carried the matter to the House Judiciary Committee, which declined to investigate due to "the distance of the parties . . . from the seat of Government" but also indicated that it was "not able to perceive how any law of the Territory can authorize the Judge to receive any compensation in the shape of fees, for his official services."[32] The judge countered by asserting his innocence and demanding an official inquiry.[33]

Events then moved quickly. St. Augustine lawyer John Rodman, a friend of Smith's, complained against Macon for contempt of the judge. Smith submitted to himself a personal affidavit in support of the complaint, had Macon brought before him, convicted the prosecutor of contempt, and ordered his dismissal from the bar. The judge also appointed a new district attorney. "Judge Smiths personal feelings towards me," Macon protested to Secretary of State Henry Clay, "preclude me from anything like a fair and impartial hearing." No hearing could be held before Smith, he believed, "without subjecting me to the indignation and anger of the court."[34]

The matter finally was settled in Smith's favor, thanks to an intervening election. Delegate Call delivered to the House of Representatives a passionate attack on the judge, but a House committee tabled his resolution. Call's successor, Joseph M. White, reversed his predecessor's stand and advocated Smith's cause. His arguments won over President John Quincy Adams, who, on May 22, 1826, commissioned Thomas Douglas to replace Macon. The political ramifications required the president to take yet another step before the controversy could be put to rest. Smith had recommended lawyer Benjamin A. Putnam for the post. Since Adams had opted for Douglas, he needed to assuage Smith's feelings somehow. The opportunity did not arise until early the next year when

Adams appointed the judge's friend William A. McRea as United States attorney for Florida's Middle District.[35]

A second political struggle affected Smith's career far more than the dispute with Macon. By the early 1830s political power in Florida increasingly revolved around a loose alliance of Andrew Jackson protégés, land speculators, Middle Florida planters, and their allies. Formed by Call and known as the "Tallahassee Nucleus," the group used patronage, particularly in the federal land office, to influence the legislative council and to assist its backers in banking, land speculation, and other development schemes.[36] Groups opposed to Nucleus power centered upon congressional delegate White and Judge Smith. Smith especially irritated Nucleus members by judicial rulings in favor of East Florida's small landowners and less-well-to-do settlers in Spanish land-grant cases arising out of the Adams-Onis Treaty of 1819.[37]

As will be seen in later chapters, land issues loomed large in Florida territorial politics, law, and litigation, and they ultimately proved Smith's undoing as a judge. He had been recommissioned to a second four-year term by President Adams in 1828, but by 1832 his appointment neared its expiration. In that year Andrew Jackson, mentor of Call and other Nucleus members, occupied the presidency. Still sensitive to the needs of his political friends and protégés, he heeded their complaints about the East Florida judge. Smith pled his case through testimonials "from every County in East Florida, of the just and faithful manner, in which I have uniformly discharged my official duties," but the efforts failed.[38] The bitter disappointment abated very slowly. "I have been denounced," Smith declared three years later, "for making a decision in favor of the poor pre-emption settlers in Florida, which conflicted with the schemes of the speculators, and the pride and vanity of government officers, favorites and proteges of Andrew Jackson."[39]

Few Floridians protested Jackson's failure to reappoint Smith. Although small landholders applauded his liberal interpretation of limits on preemption parcels, his unstable, often volcanic temperament alienated potential supporters. Allegations of abuse of judicial power, drunkenness, and profanity dogged him. In spite of it all, Smith had an important impact. His jurisprudential legacy was beneficial, for his decisions aided in unraveling the complexity of real property law, a prerequisite for subsequent Florida development. Politically, his alliance with White against Nucleus power presaged evolution of the territory's Democratic party. Finally, Smith's exercise of his judicial duties maintained independence from the dictates of the powerful, thereby lending credibility to a judicial system still aborning.[40]

After the expiration of his judicial tenure, Smith remained in Florida, practicing law at St. Augustine. In 1833 he successfully ran for a seat on the legislative council, regaining some of his lost prestige. He served, as well, a term as St. Augustine's mayor. The former judge and war hero died at home on May 22, 1846, apparently while formulating plans to return to the North to live with relatives. Noted a biographer, "[H]e was found in his room one morning in a fit of apoplexy or paralysis of which he died in the course of 48 hours." The account continued, "He had his senses perfectly, and fervently and devotedly prayed that God would pardon and accept him through the merits of the Savior."[41]

Henry Marie Brackenridge, Western District Superior Court Judge, 1822–1832

Henry Marie Brackenridge, West Florida's counterpart to Joseph Lee Smith as first superior court judge, came to Florida prominence with the 1821 arrival of Andrew Jackson. At the time Brackenridge already was an individual of national renown, with skills and talents that were to be of considerable use to Floridians and their government. After his mentor's departure, he continued to exert himself in territorial judicial and political affairs with immediate and long-lasting results. Beyond those accomplishments, Brackenridge represented to nineteenth-century Floridians the epitome of urbanity and sophistication. Truly, he was a gifted man.

Born May 11, 1786, at frontier Pittsburgh, Pennsylvania, Brackenridge experienced a difficult childhood. His mother died before he attained two years of age, and his father, Hugh Henry Brackenridge, proved a distant and demanding parent, one with great expectations. Hugh traveled in the highest circles of American political life. A friend and schoolmate of James Madison at what became Princeton University, he served as a chaplain in George Washington's colonial army during the American Revolution. His legal career began after he read law in Maryland under Salmon Chase.[42]

Hugh's accomplishments contributed to young Henry's unhappiness. Preoccupied with politics, literature, and the law, he afforded his son little time. The elder Brackenridge effectively disregarded the child until he appeared to display an "improvable intellect."[43] He dispatched Henry at age seven to the distant village of St. Genevieve, near St. Louis in French Louisiana, to learn the French language. There the child blossomed under his instructors and the tender attention of a Mrs. Beauvais, in whose care he had been placed. He became a Roman Catholic, excelled at his studies, and learned a good deal about morality and personal responsibility. Brackenridge later wrote movingly of the Beauvais family's influence, acknowledging his debt to them. From them, he asserted, he learned "reverence [for his] parents, [to] respect . . . the aged, to be polite to my equals, and to speak the truth to every one." He added, "I was taught to restrain my temper, to practice self-denial, to be compassionate to man and beast, . . . and to be thankful to God for every blessing."[44]

After several years at St. Genevieve, Brackenridge was returned to his father's custody. The stern parent introduced the boy to a three-year regimen of classical studies, together with readings in history, German, and French. Young Henry's desire for approval and caring attention, such as he had grown used to from Mrs. Beauvais, was met only by Jane Marie, who had tended the child after his mother's death. Prophetically, Marie on occasion placed in the boy's arms her infant daughter Caroline, whom Henry later would marry.

Brackenridge's education continued after studying under his father. He attended Pittsburgh Academy, where he developed a concern for the institution of slavery that was to influence his actions as a Florida judge. On one occasion his interest moved from intellectual to physical action when he assisted a fugitive bondsman's escape by smuggling bread and meat to him. Subsequently, Henry worked for a time away from Pittsburgh, then returned to read law with his Pittsburgh Academy professor James Mountain. He achieved admission to the bar in 1806.[45]

Acceptance into the legal community marked another beginning, not an end, of Henry's preparatory work. His perfectionist father prescribed readings in numerous treatises on general and international law as well as standard texts on technical aspects of jurisprudence. Notwithstanding a twelve-hour-per-day, year-long commitment, he found time to improve his proficiency in German. Finally released from his father's supervision, Brackenridge launched upon a time of professional wandering. He lived for two years at Baltimore but found himself displeased with the city and its bar. From there he moved to Somerset, Pennsylvania, where he dreamed of Louisiana and the Beauvais family. In April 1810 he relocated again to St. Genevieve, by then in the Missouri District within the extreme northwestern frontier of the United States. Briefly he practiced law at St. Genevieve and edited the St. Louis *Louisiana Gazette.* He also found time to explore the huge territory with Manuel Lisa, who earlier had participated in the Lewis and Clark expedition. Brackenridge's account of the trip, *Views of Louisiana; Together with a Journal of a Voyage up the Missouri River in 1811,* was published in 1814.[46]

The young lawyer's travels soon took him to New Orleans, where he settled in December 1811. He obtained appointment to a job unwanted by others, that of deputy attorney general for Orleans Territory. He traveled a 1,000-mile circuit before helping to design Louisiana's judicial system. His contributions received their reward when he accepted the position of district judge at Baton Rouge. There, he developed further legal expertise while continuing a correspondence with Thomas Jefferson about his visits to the frontier.[47]

Brackenridge remained in Louisiana during the War of 1812. The conflict afforded him opportunity to praise Andrew Jackson in verse as victor of the Battle of New Orleans. The result was the poem "Ode on Jackson's Victory." Later he scripted his *History of the Late War.* The book found wide popularity after its 1816 publication, moving through ten editions. Its success came at a crucial time for the author, as it helped him stave off the penalties of bankruptcy.[48]

The affairs of Spain's rebellious South American colonies soon turned Brackenridge's attention away from poetry and history. By 1817 he had become, as one historian put it, "[the] foremost advocate and chief propagandist [for the rebels], recognized as such in the United States and in Europe."[49] His pamphlet *South America: A Letter on the Present State of that Country, to James Monroe, President of the United States* reached many Americans. By stressing the hemispheric solidarity of North and South America, the writing, it has been asserted, "foreshadowed not only the Monroe Doctrine but the Monroe Doctrine in its Pan-American interpretation [by Franklin Delano Roosevelt] of 1940."[50] President James Monroe designated him secretary to a study commission on the subject, and in that capacity he traveled the continent. From the journey's experiences, he penned *Voyage to South America, Performed by Order of the American Government in Years 1817 and 1818, in the Frigate Congress.*[51]

Brackenridge's South American interests had developed after his return to Baltimore subsequent to the War of 1812. In Maryland he served a term in its house of delegates but found himself again frustrated in pursuing a legal career in the state. Once more he set his sights on Missouri, arriving at St. Louis in late 1820. There he received news of Andrew Jackson's designation as governor of the new Florida Territory. Intrigued at the possibilities for employment and reward there, he boarded a steamboat for New Orleans with President Monroe's assurance that he would be favorably considered for an early appointment in the provisional government. On the way he encountered Jackson and his party; the two men recognized the good they could do for each other, and Brackenridge became the governor's advisor. Effectively, he soon acted as Jackson's right-hand man.[52]

The eager lawyer immersed himself in Florida affairs. He researched Spanish law codes, translated for Jackson, wrote speeches and state papers, and helped craft the provisional governor's Florida ordinances. Jackson, in turn, quickly placed Brackenridge in a position of power, that of alcalde of Pensacola. In that capacity he exercised the functions of "mayor, chief of police, sheriff, superintendent and inspector of prisons, and notary public."[53] Somehow the alcalde also found time to establish the territory's first private law partnership. As the *Pensacola Gazette* of September 1, 1821, explained, "H. M. Brackenridge & R. K. Call, Attornies at Law, [h]ave associated themselves in their profession and may be addressed on any business connected therewith, at Pensacola, W. Florida."[54]

The previously peripatetic lawyer loved his new home and determined to stay after his mentor's departure in October 1821.[55] Jackson offered his assistance. "[A]s far as my influence will extend," he informed Brackenridge, "it will afford me much pleasure in using it in your behalf." Jackson needed only to know whether his friend desired "a seat in the Judiciary, or any other office within the Floridas."[56]

Jackson fulfilled his commitment to Brackenridge, but for the time being it availed the Pensacola alcalde little. President Monroe was addressing his own patronage needs rather than the provisional governor's. Other friends joined the effort. Judge Eligius Fromentin's departure from the territory seemed certain, and the Pensacola bar, town council, and Escambia County court petitioned for Brackenridge as a replacement, lauding his "known character and standing" while stressing his "knowledge of the Civil and maritime laws, and of the French and Spanish languages."[57] Positive results were not forthcoming, though, until June 5, 1822, when Monroe designated Brackenridge a judge of the superior court for West Florida, a position created two months before by the Congress. Even then, the president acted only after former North Carolina governor John Branch declined the honor.[58]

Praise greeted the president's announcement in West Florida. "The appointment of Judge Brackenridge," reported the Pensacola *Floridian*, "has given universal satisfaction here, . . . [and] it is [the] very best appointment which could have been made."[59] The judge, as ever eager to pursue his responsibilities, rapidly organized his court and entered upon his judicial duties. His tenure would not be marked by the same degree of scandal that beset Judge Joseph Lee Smith in East Florida, but it contained moments interesting, significant, and controversial.

During a decade on the bench, Brackenridge considered a broad range of cases. Some dealt with exotic subjects, such as the 1822 piracy charges against the schooner *Carmen* and her crew. The incident had begun when the *Carmen*'s men confronted a United States naval cutter off Cuba. Once in custody, crew members admitted that the ship contained arms and that their cruising orders

Judge Henry Marie Brackenridge (1786–1871). As federal judge of the superior court in West Florida from 1822 to 1832 and one of the first members of the territorial court of appeals, Brackenridge used his education, experience in the Louisiana Territory, and knowledge of foreign languages to assist Jackson in organizing a government. A dedicated and conscientious public servant, his major concern was Florida's lack of a suitable code of laws in the early territorial years.

could not be produced. At first, Brackenridge evidenced little sympathy. "These circumstances formed to my mind the strongest presumption of guilt," he declared while finding the grounds "sufficient to justify their arrest and commitment for trial."[60] The judge's mind remained open despite the presumption of guilt. He allowed the captain and first officers free bail and ensured that the remaining prisoners received respectable treatment while confined. A jury ultimately found the men not guilty after hearing witnesses testify that the ship was owned by a Havana merchant and often sailed armed. Brackenridge concurred in the verdict. "[I] did not believe the evidence sufficient to return a conviction," he recorded, even though the facts were "sufficient to justify the arrest and capture."[61]

The case of the *Carmen* and her crew illustrates Brackenridge's personal search for equity and justice. The theme carries through his known decisions, as he sometimes used technicalities as loopholes to justify doing what he believed was right and other times called for strict enforcement of just such technicalities. He pursued an activist approach to justice in a time when the law and the judicial system were in their formative stages.

Examples of Brackenridge's search for justice are apparent. In 1825, for instance, the slave Ambrosio was convicted of grand larceny for stealing $35. Territorial law defined the crime of larceny but provided no penalty for stealing money. Arguably Brackenridge should have relied upon common law, which mandated death in such cases. In the dilemma the judge released the slave rather than adhering strictly to the law.[62]

Another example is afforded by the case of *William M. Loftin* v. *William S. Mooring.* Both men claimed the office and duties of Jackson County sheriff, with good foundations for their claims. Brackenridge considered the choice between the men a crucial one. The case, he explained, was of "great importance to the Country inasmuch as the interests of parties may be seriously affected by the acts of an illegal officer." It involved, he concluded, "a much higher interest than a mere question of right between two individuals." Apparently, he believed Loftin to be better qualified, for he ruled in Loftin's favor based upon a technical reading of the relevant statute.[63]

The frontier territory's violent criminal behavior and its social consequences alarmed Brackenridge, and the judge stood foursquare in favor of law and order in such cases. In 1827 he presided over the trial of Benjamin Donica, indicted for murder of Saunders Donoho. The jury found Donica guilty but recommended clemency. As required, Brackenridge forwarded the trial records to Governor William Pope DuVal for review, but he nonetheless condemned Donica to death. "[I]t is not [my] intention . . . ," he told the defendant, "to harrow up your feelings [but rather to] characterize your crime." He did so to "exhibit [the] conviction as an awful warning to others." Ultimately, Donica was hanged.[64]

The judge developed a reputation for being fair and impartial. The purpose of the court system, he believed, was to ensure that the "weak must be protected; the lawless and violent must be restrained." He would add, "On this the peace of society, as well as the security of the individual depends." Key to the system was the role of grand and petit jurors. "In all communities of civilized men," he observed to a grand jury, "this is one of the most important duties of government."[65]

Brackenridge's 1831 charge to the Jackson County grand jury remains one of the very few preserved from the territorial period. "Although all human institutions are imperfect," he declared, "I am yet satisfied that nothing better was ever contrived to accomplish this great object than the introduction of Grand Juries." Such panels served to protect the weak from the powerful. "Where in a word, they have no Grand Jury—a body, which with us may be justly styled, the terror of the guilty, and the shield of the innocent," he explained, "another must interpose before final conviction or acquittal. In the countries to which I have alluded, crimes may be committed with impunity by the great and powerful; the poor and humble, dare not complain, because they can seldom hope to prevail, and might be made to feel the consequences of their temerity."

Legal uncertainties caused by repeated statutory changes, Brackenridge informed the jurors, undermined law and order and made their task more difficult. He had encouraged the adoption in 1822 of English common law, but subsequent councils had ignored his warnings with new laws and codes. "The definitions of the Common Law," he remarked, "are the preductions of ages of experience, and every term, is so explicitly understood, as to leave but few questions to be settled. In a new code, many questions must arise; a circumstance, which militates against that certainty so necessary in criminal jurisprudence." Still, the jurors should fall back upon the common law to make sense of the new laws and to ensure proper law enforcement. "The greater part of the definitions contained in the code we have enacted, have been, it is true, almost literally borrowed, or copied from that Law," he continued, "and I incline to the opinion, that it would have been more advisable, for the present, to have referred the whole to that source." Brackenridge concluded, "By pursuing this plan, some of the puzzling, and perplexing abstractions, to be seen in our code, and some of its dangerous novelties might have been avoided."[66]

Every judge of the territorial era, given the powers of his office and the freedom for personal assertion that they allowed, made enemies, and Brackenridge was no exception. Peter G. Williamson was infuriated when the judge convicted him of inhuman treatment of his slave Katy, for fastening a chain "to her neck . . . with her arms tied fast behind her" and ordering the slave pulled through the streets.[67] John and James Innerarity, heirs to the vast Forbes land grant, similarly were angered when Brackenridge rejected their claim to approximately 1 million acres.[68]

Not all of Brackenridge's opponents were private citizens before his court. William F. Steele, district attorney for West Florida, infuriated the judge when he presented twenty-three bills of indictment to a grand jury but secured only a single conviction. Brackenridge thereafter sought Steele's removal from office. "It is impossible for me to give an account of his strange and unaccountable deportment," the judge complained to Secretary of State John Quincy Adams. "[I]t became my duty," he added, "to reprimand him at almost every moment."[69] Steele retaliated by accusing Brackenridge, though indirectly, of attempting to destroy him. The affair made the local papers and became a public cause célèbre.[70]

The Brackenridge-Steele feud came to a head during the May 1824 court term. Letters presumably written by Steele appeared in newspapers throughout the United States charging Brackenridge with five counts of impropriety. Pensacola editor William Hasell Hunt attempted to discount the letters by offering his own account of the proceedings. "The attorney," he wrote, "[stated] that the Judge of this Court is [his] personal enemy." Further, only "after he had been repeatedly ordered to sit down [was] an order of imprisonment for three hours" leveled at Steele by Brackenridge.[71] Steele's ruination was imminent. His open defiance of the powerful judge would not be tolerated, and, in September 1824, he left the territory, eventually to be replaced by Albert J. Clagget of Maryland.[72]

Beginning in 1827 Brackenridge brought trouble on himself by absences from the territory, causing District Attorney Benjamin Drake Wright to express concerns about delays in the administration of justice. The cause involved the judge's personal life. Still a bachelor, in late 1826 he had journeyed north to Philadelphia, where he wooed Caroline Marie, daughter of his former governess. Without her, he insisted, his life was "joyless and unhappy."[73] They married on March 22, 1827, and then hurried to Pensacola for the superior court's May term. Caroline's delicate health suffered in Florida's summer heat and humidity, and Brackenridge was compelled to send her back to Philadelphia. To be with her, he unsuccessfully sought appointment as Henry Wheaton's successor as reporter for the United States Supreme Court. Given his disappointment, he retained his Florida judgeship, while spending his recess periods with his wife and growing family.[74]

Brackenridge's tenure lasted for five years after his marriage, but, in 1832, the man who had initiated Brackenridge's Florida career ended it. The judge had been reappointed in 1824 by President Monroe and in 1828 by President Adams. At a White House "family dinner" in 1831, President Jackson reportedly promised to retain his old friend as well. By the next year, though, the fickleness of politics undermined that commitment, and Jackson instead had turned to Virginia's James C. Bryce, whose nomination was rejected by the Senate on a tied vote. The president then named North Carolina's John A. Cameron, and Brackenridge's service ended on May 26, 1832.[75]

Sacrificed by Jackson to his patronage machine, Brackenridge thereafter despised the man and castigated him unmercifully during the 1832 election and afterward. He appealed to the public with his pamphlet *Judge Brackenridge's Letters*, a powerful indictment of Jackson's integrity. The former judge became a Whig and in 1840 was elected a member of the United States House of Representatives from Pennsylvania. In 1841 Whig president William Henry Harrison appointed him to the Mexican Claims Commission, on which he served ably and honorably. He then returned to Pennsylvania, practiced law, and sat for one term in the state legislature.[76]

Henry Marie Brackenridge died near his Pittsburgh birthplace—at the home of his deceased son's wife, Phillipine—on January 18, 1871. At the time of his death, apparently he was the oldest native-born Pittsburgher.[77] Floridians, and especially jurists, owed him a great deal. He maintained the independence of the judiciary, while he labored zealously for the improvement of the law, the court system, and the territory. He had sought justice on the bench, and in the process had been found to be a wise and incorruptible man.

William W. Blair, Middle District Superior Court Judge, 1824

In 1824 President James Monroe commissioned William W. Blair as Florida's first superior court judge for the Middle District. While Blair's subsequent death prevented him from discharging the duties of his new position, his appointment deserves recognition. It suggested, as had been the case with Henry Marie Brackenridge, that resident Floridians increasingly received consideration for important federal patronage positions within the territory. Blair's appointment also underscored the continuing influence in Florida affairs exercised in national circles by Andrew Jackson's Florida-based protégés.

Like Richard Keith Call and William Pope DuVal before him, Blair moved to Florida from Kentucky. Born about 1795, the young lawyer had served his home state as a district attorney and state court judge. His health troubled him, though, and he soon sought relief through a move to a milder climate. In 1821 he unsuccessfully applied for a position as United States attorney in Florida and, through State Department influence, received consideration for a territorial judgeship. His supporters included many of Kentucky's leading political figures. The contacts ultimately brought results three years later with his appointment to the land commission for the East Florida District.[78]

The question of land titles and the implications of land policies stood as major issues in the territorial period. As mentioned earlier and discussed further in chapter 3, the Congress enacted a series of laws concerning claims to real property based upon British and Spanish grants, legislation required by provisions of the Adams-Onis Treaty. United States attorney for East Florida, Alexander Hamilton, Jr., reported in 1822 on problems with existing legislation, particularly as it related to East Florida. The Congress responded in 1823 by establishing an East Florida land commission to be composed of three individuals. President James Monroe then designated Hamilton to serve on the new panel with Blair and David Floyd (a presiding judge of an Indiana circuit).[79]

The early days of the East Florida land commission were marked by conflict among its members, a situation made worse by Blair's poor health. Soon Hamilton refused to cooperate with his fellow commissioners because he disagreed with their procedural methods. He criticized Blair and Floyd for what he characterized as their repeated refusal "to adopt any arrangement of the business of the Commission"; their failure to employ "written evidence" in determining important questions of land ownership; their unwillingness "to examine and secure the original records"; their reluctance "to report the proceedings of the commission to Congress"; and their appointment of Blair's brother-in-law and future Florida supreme court justice Joseph B. Lancaster as assistant secretary to the commission. Hamilton charged Blair, as well, with misrepresentation to the secretary of the treasury and to a member of the local bar.[80]

The land commission controversy may have spurred Monroe's interest in finding a new position for Blair, a case pressed by Blair's friends Richard Keith Call, Sam Houston, and Henry Clay. The president issued him a four-year commission on May 27, 1824, to the newly created superior court judgeship for Middle Florida. The appointment came too late. Earlier in the month an East Floridian had noted of Blair and land commission affairs: "At present we have but two Commissioners [Hamilton had resigned] & one of them (Judge Blair, a truly good & worthy character) is so very ill that he can scarcely attend to the duties of the board, nor is he expected to be much longer for this world!! [H]is loss would be great to this Country."[81] The forecast of Blair's early death came to pass. He died at St. Augustine of consumption on July 27. Observed a local editor at the time, "Judge Blair had resided among us exactly one year, and during this period he had exhibited such traits of amiability, as to command the affections of all who knew him." He added, "He was a Christian, and his life corresponded with the Christian character."[82]

Augustus Brevoort Woodward, Middle District Superior Court Judge, 1824–1827

Augustus Brevoort Woodward, William W. Blair's successor as judge of the Middle District superior court, was a brilliant but eccentric visionary whose varied talents produced innovations in government, education, science, and jurisprudence. He was born at New York City in 1774, the second son of John and Ann Woodward. His father's forebears were middle-class Englishmen, while his mother's were influential and prosperous Dutch burghers. Woodward was raised in the Reformed Dutch Church and with family members who were considered to number among the leading residents of Manhattan. At age fifteen he entered Columbia College, from which he graduated with an A.B. degree in 1793. As a student, Woodward mastered Greek, Latin, and French. He "appeared eager, on all occasions," it was said, "to display his knowledge."[83]

As had been true for Henry Marie Brackenridge, Woodward's early professional life involved a series of moves and contacts with persons of influence. Following graduation from college, he lived for two years in Philadelphia, where he worked as a Treasury Department clerk. Then he taught school and read law in Rockbridge County, Virginia, where he was befriended by Thomas Jefferson. A family bequest afterward permitted him to relocate to Georgetown in the District of Columbia. There, dressed in "a long, loose-fitting blue coat with enormous brass buttons, a scarlet cravat, and buff waistcoat . . . [with] pantaloons . . . hung in folds to his feet, meeting a pair of boots which were always well greased," the young lawyer was admitted to the bar. He practiced law at Alexandria as well as in nearby Maryland.[84]

Woodward's personal appearance failed to suggest his future professional success. Some believed him ungainly and even grotesque. A prototype of Washington Irving's Ichabod Crane, he stood six feet, three inches tall. Additionally, he appeared lean, stooped, sallow-complexioned, long-faced, and big-nosed. Coupled with his physical attributes, the lawyer exuded an extreme self-confidence, which more than a few acquaintances interpreted as pomposity or "audacious impudence." On the other hand, his intelligence was respected by many. A friendly jurist described him, for instance, as "one of those strange compounds of intellectual power and wisdom in great emergencies."[85]

The District of Columbia's political environment and small bar—it boasted only eleven members in 1802—offered Woodward a comfortable launching pad for his career. A man of strongly held opinions, he early indulged in the art of political pamphleteering. Writing under the pseudonym "Epaminondus" during 1801–3, he advocated municipal government and home rule for the district and broad extensions of the franchise. His essays received wide distribution and earned him a serious readership among Federalists and Democratic-Republicans. One principal admirer was Jefferson.

Woodward's success at the bar equaled his achievements as a pundit. He represented clients in a number of significant matters. With the execution of murderer James McGurk, Woodward became the first lawyer to lose a capital case in the District of Columbia, but his ability as an attorney was not faulted for the outcome. More happily, he obtained for a different client a substantial settlement from the Congress for unreimbursed funds advanced in support of the Rebel cause during the American Revolution. In many instances his writing skills played an important role, permitting him to prepare, publish, and circulate briefs in aid of the causes he undertook. They also allowed him to claim credit for his successes, as when he discussed the congressional reimbursement case in his A *Representation of the Case of Oliver Pollack,* published in 1803.[86]

Professional success earned Woodward substantial fees, but financial obligations arising from real estate investments left the lawyer chronically short of cash. His friend Jefferson, by then president, offered relief by appointing him, in 1805, to be a judge in Michigan. Woodward gratefully accepted the favor, moved to Detroit, and began a career of public service in that territory which lasted until 1824. While there, he acted instrumentally in the founding of the University of Michigan, assisted in planning the city of Detroit (one of its main streets bears his name), and helped to develop and name the city of Ypsilanti. He also authored *The Laws of Michigan* ("The Woodward Code"), *Considerations on the Executive Government of the United States of America*, and *The System of Universal Science*. The judge found time, as well, to serve during the War of 1812 as a colonel of Michigan militia.[87]

Woodward's judicial appointment required that he preside over Michigan's supreme court as well as execute the duties of a superior court judge. He carried out the responsibilities with distinction. Several of the most important cases with which he dealt involved slavery. By then the judge ardently opposed the institution, as did many of his fellow Detroit residents. The Northwest Ordinance of 1787 had prohibited bondage in Michigan, but those who already held slaves were allowed to possess them. Consequently litigation regarding bondsmen often came before the territorial courts.

One such slavery case involved a petition for a writ of habeas corpus applied for on behalf of the Denison family, slaves owned by a widowed British citizen. Woodward's opinion in the case illustrates that, while he would not hesitate to express his personal views, he felt compelled to enforce the law regardless of those opinions. "The slave trade is unquestionably the greatest of enormities which have been perpetrated by the human race," he declared, and the existence of slavery in the United States "is universally and justly considered their greatest and deepest reproach." Nonetheless, he dismissed the petition after ruling that possession of slaves in the territory was not illegal and that the Denisons were the property of their owner.[88]

The judge's concern with slavery and the question of the Denisons' freedom did not end with the Denison decision. About one month later two slaves fled to the United States from Canada. They were seized and brought before Woodward's court. In this instance the judge found a lawful way to grant their liberty by ruling that no treaty required their return to Canadian slavery. "Under the law of nations," he decreed, "property of a subject or citizens of one country found within the territories of another country ought to be restored, but there is no obligation under such law to restore persons." Without a reciprocal agreement between Great Britain and the United States, the Canadians could not regain their bondsmen. With the decision, the Denisons also claimed their freedom. They slipped across the international border and asked for sanctuary. When they returned years later to Detroit, they were allowed to live unmolested.[89]

His conduct as a judge gained Woodward respect and sometimes admiration, but other aspects of his Michigan service prompted controversy and caused him torment. Under the peculiar provisions of federal law for the territory, the governor, secretary, and three superior court judges (including Woodward) comprised the government. As a legislative board, they crafted the law, enforced it, and managed territorial affairs. In acting his part, Woodward unfortunately revealed a personal weakness, what was described as "his impatience—both with people and events." An account continued, "[He] was more the architect than the mason[.] . . . The slow pace of territorial advancement discouraged him; he had a tendency to sulk when his vision was not immediately shared by others." Particularly the judge's republicanism clashed with traditions and concepts held closely by Michigan's many French inhabitants. As a result, after the territory was granted home rule Woodward on three occasions was defeated in elections for territorial congressional delegate.[90]

The judge's problems extended to a feud with Governor William Hull and served as context for his relocation to Florida. The personal animosity between the governor and the judge resulted in a complaint about Woodward's judicial conduct at a time when Woodward was attempting to secure appointment as Hull's successor. The charge asserted that the judge had attended court while intoxicated. Woodward countered by insisting that he had been under a physician's care and that, to permit court attendance, he had taken "medicine and brandy to help him leave his sick bed." President James Monroe hesitated to take action in favor of Woodward's Michigan appointment, but at the behest of the judge's friends he compromised by designating the jurist as Middle Florida superior court judge to replace the deceased William W. Blair. The commission was signed August 26, 1824, and Woodward subsequently was reappointed by President John Quincy Adams for a four-year term on March 25, 1825.[91]

Woodward thus arrived in Florida in 1824 with a distinguished record of service and accomplishment, though not without questions concerning his behavior. In his new home he found what amounted to a retirement haven. The Middle Florida judicial district remained sparsely populated. Its urban center at Tallahassee, where Woodward would make his home, constituted little more than a frontier outpost with a newly constructed log-cabin capitol building. The presence of few residents translated into few legal cases before the superior court. One local man recalled that the jurist "did not seem to find much to do at his first [court] sitting."[92] A historian added, "Judge Woodward's duties in Tallahassee do not seem to have been onerous nor very complicated."[93]

A man of Woodward's background and temperament could not take easily to enforced idleness. Rather than whiling away his hours, he sought activity. Beneficially, he took an interest in the newly authorized, but unorganized, territorial court of appeals. He laid the groundwork for its first session and took pride on January 3, 1825, in informing Secretary of State John Quincy Adams that "The Court of Appeals of the Territory of Florida was, this day, fully organized, according to law."[94] Observers of the Florida judiciary note that date as a milestone in the state supreme court's history, as it marks the effective beginning of the territory's first formal judicial system and the first Florida appellate tribunal with jurisdiction throughout the territory.

The judge made some influential Florida friends during the early days of his territorial service. Especially he grew close to Governor William Pope DuVal, a fact that rebounded in the governor's favor. Woodward, for example, credited DuVal to Secretary Adams for his able administration of territorial affairs. "I found that the public measures here had been modelled," he remarked, "according to my conception, with such sound judgment, and with such resolution and foresight, as to render unnecessary a farther prosecution of that intention."[95] On a more practical level, Woodward ruled in the governor's favor concerning a claim to preemptive rights in lands near Tallahassee that the Congress had granted to the Marquis de Lafayette.

The subject of preemptive rights and land claims took up a good deal of the time Woodward spent on judicial duties, and his decisions sometimes made him enemies. As mentioned earlier, questions of land ownership and land policy loomed high among the territory's fiery issues. Occasionally superior court judges were required to adjudicate claims under the federal preemption act, which permitted settlers on Florida's public land prior to January 1, 1825, to enjoy certain favorable purchase rights in preference to others. As demonstrated in the DuVal litigation, Woodward tended to rule in favor of small preemptive claims rather than large holdings. Opposing such a policy were speculators, planters, and men affiliated with the federal Office of Register and Receiver (of lands).

Two individuals connected with the Office of Register and Receiver, Richard Keith Call and George W. Ward, particularly were angered by Woodward's rulings in preemption cases. They charged that he "never examined the evidence" in some cases and argued the "inattention and incapability of Judge Woodward at that period to discharge his official duties." Citing federal policies, they "truly called absurd" a Woodward decision in favor of one claim as small as eighty acres. The United States land commissioner buttressed their position while noting, "Judge Woodward has given a decision not in conformity to the letter of the law."[96]

The Middle Florida judge also heard a major case involving banking and legislative power, two concerns of ever-increasing importance in territorial politics. The litigation concerned a bill that chartered banks in Pensacola and St. Augustine. DuVal, who opposed creation of such institutions, vetoed the measure. The legislative council then overrode the veto by a vote of six to three, which constituted a two-thirds majority of those present and voting. Territorial Secretary George Walton refused to record the act, contending that federal law mandated a veto-override requirement of at least two-thirds of the entire membership of the council (thirteen members sat in the body). A legislator subsequently brought the matter before Woodward seeking a writ of mandamus to compel Walton to record the law. The judge again opted to side with the governor's desires, agreeing with Walton's interpretation and denying the writ.[97]

During 1826 and 1827 two matters distracted Woodward from his relatively few judicial responsibilities. His health was suffering, and he found it necessary to tidy up some personal affairs in Michigan. Judge Henry M. Brackenridge aided Woodward during his journey out of state by holding court for him. Back in Florida in 1827, the Middle Florida judge's health declined further. He died at Tallahassee on June 12, 1827, still a bachelor. Though he had lived in the territory only for a short time, he had earned the respect of the community by his contributions. He had organized the Middle Florida superior court and the territorial court of appeals. He had given heart, as well, to ordinary citizens by his decisions in favor of their rights in land cases. In the circumstances Woodward's accomplishments had been significant and of lasting consequence.[98]

Chapter 3

A Maturing Judicial System

By the time Florida's court of appeals held its first session on January 3, 1825, the territory had begun to experience dynamics of change that were to exert extraordinary influences upon its future and especially that of its judicial system. Four short years previously, the new American possession had consisted primarily of two small towns, St. Augustine and Pensacola, and rural settlements clustered in their vicinities. The huge panhandle region that lay between them, as well as the peninsula west and south of the St. Johns River, for the most part remained unpopulated save for occasional groupings of Indians and their black vassals. Florida's cultural and social accent was Spanish, with pronounced flavorings of a myriad of other ethnic and national influences.

From the first days of American occupation in 1821, the territory under Governor Andrew Jackson and his successor, William Pope DuVal, commenced a process of reorientation toward the culture, mores, and practices of the United States, including those related to jurisprudence. The changes involved in that process differed, though, according to the portion of the territory concerned. East Florida (east of the Suwannee River) and West Florida (west of the Apalachicola River) retained significant Spanish influences. Accordingly, their social and race relations patterns afforded somewhat more flexibility than did those of adjacent areas of the Old South. Moreover, their economies continued to be dominated by grazing, herding, subsistence farming, and naval industries.[1]

The experience of Middle Florida, that portion of the territory lying between the Apalachicola and the Suwannee rivers, differed markedly from that of East and West Florida. The land and climate of much of this middle region was well suited for cotton culture, and soon land speculators and immigrants laid the seeds of an affluent plantation economy similar to the plantation regions of the Old South. Many of the settlers belonged to leading, even aristocratic, southern planter families and brought with them to frontier Florida the social graces, culture, and connections of their old southern homes. The region's economic foundation increasingly rested upon the work of black slaves.[2]

A number of additional factors encouraged development of Middle Florida, and immigration into the region quickly rebounded on territorial politics, government, and judicial organization. The legislative council in 1823 located the territorial capital there, and commissioners William H. Simmons and John Lee Williams decided upon a site in Gadsden (subsequently Leon) County near an Indian village named Tallahassee. A log cabin was erected on the site in 1824, Governor DuVal took up residence, and a small community began to coalesce. The same year congressional delegate Richard Keith Call, who would become one of the town's most important citizens, achieved passage of a federal law that created a superior court district for the region and provided for the seat at Tallahassee of the new territorial court of appeals.[3]

The development and growth of Middle Florida and other portions of the territory depended upon a satisfactory resolution of the problems of resident Indians and their black subjects, and DuVal gave the matter his early attention. At Moultrie Creek near St. Augustine in September 1823, certain chiefs agreed on behalf of the natives to remove themselves principally to a large reservation in the peninsula's interior south of present-day Alachua County. Negotiators rewarded a few leaders with parcels of land along the Apalachicola River. This Treaty of Moultrie Creek failed to resolve in any final sense the questions involved, and, by 1835, Indian and race war would ravage the territory. Still, the treaty opened for exploitation the rich Middle Florida lands so desired by incoming planters.[4]

Once Middle Florida settlement became feasible, the federal government offered additional encouragement by establishing at Tallahassee a federal land office and by conducting sales of federally owned lands. Wildcat speculation quickly became the order of the day, prompting one historian to characterize the period by its "mania for buying land."[5] In 1828 alone the office realized $189,182 from the sale of 140,587 acres. The land purchase mania, in turn, spurred renewed immigration. By 1830 Middle Florida contained 45 percent of the territory's 34,730 residents. Leon held the largest county population with 6,494 black and white inhabitants. Ten years later Middle Florida boasted approximately 42 percent of Florida's 27,943 whites but a large majority of the territory's 25,717 slaves. Leon continued as the most populous county with 10,715 residents, about two-thirds of whom were slaves.[6]

Population growth translated itself into political power. The Congress in 1826 changed the method of selection of members of the legislative council from presidential appointment to popular election. The law mandated creation of thirteen electoral districts equally apportioned by population. Three years later a county-oriented scheme was substituted for the population-based districts, but with each change the power of Middle Florida legislators grew, their influence further enhanced by the fact that the council met in Tallahassee. As the decade of the 1830s dawned, this Middle Florida power found a loose organizational structure in "the Nucleus." It centered around Andrew Jackson protégés such as Richard Keith Call, who controlled the Tallahassee land office.[7]

Thus, by the late 1820s and early 1830s, Florida had split, geographically, socially, economically, and politically. East and West Florida had lost political power to Middle Florida, while control of that power within the territory had passed into the hands of Nucleus members. Some counterbalance was provided from 1825 to 1829 through judicial and other territorial appointments of President John Quincy Adams, who relied for patronage advice upon congressional delegate Joseph M. White, a Nucleus foe. Although actual events did not always transpire as anticipated, many observers expected President Andrew Jackson thereafter to support his old Florida friends and their interests and aspirations. Often those interests and aspirations involved claims to land.[8]

Within the context of these changes and events, Florida's judicial system itself began to evolve and mature. Its superior court judges accepted responsibility for assuring public safety, stimulating economic expansion, and establishing workable judicial—and sometimes legal—procedures for territorial governance. Consequently, as population increased, interests clashed, and affairs of state and politics grew ever more complicated, the jurists involved themselves more deeply in a greater number of significant matters.

One area in which territorial judges endeavored to bring order amidst chaos concerned salvage and wrecking. The combination of an extensive coastline, treacherous waters, and unpredictable weather made Florida a natural focus for shipping disasters. The situation particularly was severe in the Florida keys. "Wreckers," as salvage operators were known, helped to minimize losses but often were seen as a part of the problem. Constantly circulating rumors, not completely without foundation, suggested that some wreckers lured unsuspecting vessels into danger for their own pecuniary gain.[9]

Legislators turned their attention to the wrecking business early in the territorial period, but real solutions were slow to appear. In 1823 the territorial council enacted a salvage law. Under it, the municipal court nearest the port of claim assumed jurisdiction over a salvage dispute resulting from a shipwreck, but a notary or justice of the peace could gather a jury of five persons to decide how to dispose of salvaged cargo. Under this system wreckers could expect to receive from 50 to 95 percent of the goods saved.[10]

In practice, the 1823 salvage law created as many problems as it cured, as illustrated by the example of the cargo vessel *Point a Petre,* which wrecked in the keys in 1825. According to a contemporary account, "[t]he presiding magistrate was the judge who condemned—the auctioneer who sold—and the purchaser at the sale of some of the property." The cargo's insurers, angered at the award of 365 bales of cotton to a salvager, sued to overturn the decision. The suit, *American Insurance Company* v. *356 Bales of Cotton,* challenged the council's authority to establish jurisdiction in such matters, and it became the first case appealed to the United States Supreme Court from the territory. In 1828 that court denied relief while upholding the council's power as of 1823.[11]

Well before the *Point a Petre* decision, many Floridians had become convinced that the scales of justice had been biased to the wreckers' advantage. Responding to the complaints, the Congress in 1826 vested exclusive admiralty jurisdiction for the territory in the superior court at St. Augustine. Judge Joseph Lee Smith of that court, in an 1827 case involving a court-sanctioned award to wreckers of 95 percent of a salvaged cargo, found the territorial law invalid. The legislative council thereupon requested the Congress to establish an admiralty court at Key West, the principal settlement in the keys. Washington agreed, and a new federal law approved May 23, 1828, created a fourth superior court, to be seated at Key West, for the new Southern District. Its area included all of the peninsula south of Indian River and Charlotte Harbor. The Congress granted the court customary admiralty jurisdiction but, in a novel action, also permitted it to license and regulate parties engaged in the salvage business. Rules specified that all salvaged property within the district be placed in the court's custody, stored, and auctioned upon final disposition of the case. Proceeds of sales would be distributed according to the court's orders. The approach proved workable, and the licensing authority was continued into the statehood period.[12]

Florida's frontier society in the 1820s and 1830s stimulated law enforcement and judicial concerns far greater than those arising from the wrecking business. Criminal activity was commonplace, with offenses ranging from "gambling and fornication to murder on the high seas."[13] Cases touching crimes such as larceny were plentiful, and sentences included fines, restitution, and public floggings. Homicide figured prominently, as well, on superior court dockets. Despite the magnitude of the crime, authorities imposed capital punishment infrequently. Instead, courts often prescribed fines and whippings, reflecting the temperament of frontier pioneers and the abysmal financial status of the superior courts. During one period of extremely constrained funding, for example, Judge Henry Marie Brackenridge freed prisoners "in preference to allowing them to starve [since] no provision [was] made to their support."[14]

Admiralty, salvage, criminal, and everyday civil matters occupied court attention during the territorial period, but litigation involving land held a special and important place on court dockets. As suggested earlier, land speculation and development served as one of the principal foundations of territorial growth and economic enterprise. Intertwined with the legal issues were political complications, diplomatic intransigence, bureaucratic ineptitude, personal interrelationships, and returns for favors owed.

At first, controversies regarding holdover land claims from colonial days were considered not by the superior courts or by the legislative council. Rather, in line with provisions of the Adams-Onis Treaty of 1819, the Congress had created special commissions to hear claims. The process involved was cumbersome and often excruciatingly slow. Richard W. Meade's case, while extreme, illustrates the point. Meade, a Philadelphian, possessed a Spanish judicial certificate for almost $400,000 worth of Florida land. As often occurred, his attorneys and commission staffers found themselves unable to obtain from Spanish archives the original documents necessary to verify the certificate's legitimacy. The land commission disallowed the claim on a technicality. The matter dragged through an appeals process until the United States Court of Claims in 1866 declared that only Congress could resolve the matter. That body took forty additional years to act, reimbursing Meade's heirs in 1905 the amount of $1,166.14.[15]

Land commission actions, beyond other concerns, sometimes conflicted with the desires of powerful Floridians intent upon an efficient decision-making process better designed to promote their interests. Consistent with their wishes, congressional delegate Richard Keith Call in 1825 obtained passage of a federal law that placed jurisdiction over claims of less than 1,000 acres into the hands of the register and receiver of the federal land office, where Call's friends were entrenched. During the same year the delegate arranged for his own appointment as land office receiver.[16]

Call's successor, Delegate Joseph M. White, took the matter one step further. An opponent of Call, a former land commissioner, and a political ally of East Florida's judge Joseph Lee Smith, White arranged for an amendment to the federal law by which claims involving more than 3,500 acres would be considered in the superior courts, and not by Call's land office or by the commissions. The amendment specified grounds for decisions in such cases and permitted "the testimony of intelligent witnesses" to overcome the unavailability of documentation. District attorneys would represent the government in responding to claims, and cases determined against the legal position of the government would automatically be appealed to the United States Supreme Court "within four months after the decision." Disappointed private claimants were permitted the same appeal. The law authorized salary supplements for district attorneys and superior court judges, while it also empowered the president to appoint assistant counsels to aid the district attorneys.[17]

White's legislative coup gathered enormous power within the grasp of superior court judges and unleashed a relative deluge of litigation. According to District Attorney Thomas Douglas, "130 claims were filed in East Florida embracing upwards of four million acres of land," many of which "turned out to be almost worthless."[18] Nonetheless, a number of credible claims involving millions of acres of land were presented for determination by the superior court judge for the district in which the land was located. Effectively this procedure allowed flexibility for local considerations within each district to play a role in the decision-making process.

The particulars of three of the most important land-grant cases—each heard in a different district—illuminate the issues involved, the complexities of decision making, and the powerful interests at play within the territory and its court system. The first arose in the superior court for East Florida and concerned a grant to Don Fernando de la Maza Arredondo and his sons of almost 300,000 acres located, for the greater part, in today's Alachua County. The second and third cases involved grants of a total of 2,700,000 acres in West and Middle Florida to the merchant concern John Forbes and Company.

Simply finding counsel to litigate claims such as those of Arredondo and Forbes required complex maneuvering, given the small size of Florida's bar. President Adams's principal advisor in such matters was Attorney General William Wirt of Maryland. In 1827 Wirt had established a plantation near Tallahassee and in the same year had arranged for his son-in-law and business partner Thomas Randall to be appointed Middle Florida's superior court judge to replace Augustus Brevoort Woodward. When Congress awarded superior courts jurisdiction in cases involving large land grants the following year, Wirt pressed the president to employ the most capable legal counsel to defend the claims; after all, planters such as Wirt and Randall could purchase prime lands less expensively from the government than from private owners. As was their custom, Adams and Wirt turned to Delegate Joseph M. White to oversee such territorial matters, but Arredondo and Forbes claimants already had retainted Florida's congressional delegate, along with John Berrien and Daniel Webster, to represent them. Eventually the federal authorities employed White to research Spanish laws and to appear for the United States in certain other land-grant cases.[19]

Because of White's conflict of interest, the attorney general did not appoint counsel for the United States in the Arredondo and Forbes cases until after Andrew Jackson's inauguration as president. The complications then intensified when Jackson designated Berrien as his attorney general, but the appointment resulted only after an agreement was reached by which Berrien gained authority to continue representing the grant claimants. The president then hired Wirt as government counsel along with Jackson's protégé Richard Keith Call, the receiver at the Tallahassee land office. At the time Call's compensation as receiver depended upon the volume of land transactions through his office, which obviously would be reduced if the Forbes grant were upheld. Call intended, as well, to develop a town, St. Marks, within the grant's limits.[20]

As the litigation proceeded, counsel for all sides encountered the longstanding problem of unavailability of documentation from Spanish sources. Call and others traveled to Cuba with little success. Thereafter, United States diplomats applied pressure upon Spanish officialdom, although only with partial satisfaction.

The Arredondo case was the first of the grants to be tried. The venue lay in the East Florida superior court at St. Augustine, and the presiding judge was Joseph Lee Smith, Call's political and personal antagonist. Call and District Attorney Thomas Douglas argued that the Spanish grant had been processed illegally and that, even if the grant were legal, conditions contained within it regarding the settlement of homesteaders on the property had not been met. Smith did not hesitate to rule against Call's assertions, interpreting the grant as requiring only that Arredondo begin arranging for two hundred families to settle. The government's counsel quickly appealed to the United States Supreme Court, which upheld Smith's ruling in 1832.[21]

Call's clients found greater satisfaction in the Forbes cases, but the results were mixed. The litigation actually concerned two grants separated by the Apalachicola River, which also served as the boundary between the West and Middle Florida superior court districts. The portion of the claimed property that lay in the West Florida district encompassed 1.5 million acres between the Apalachicola and Choctawhatchee rivers. The grant document clearly had been altered to avoid the sanction of that portion of the Adams-Onis Treaty that declared grants made after January 24, 1818, null and void. Call established the forgery, Judge Henry Marie Brackenridge ruled in the government's favor, and the claimants declined an appeal.[22]

The Middle Florida Forbes grant litigation was more complicated. The cession had been based upon an Indian grant ratified by Spanish authorities with questionable authority. Call naturally argued that title could not be transferred by chiefs who held no title or ratified by officials lacking the power to act. Thomas Randall agreed, but the judge stressed his own observation that watermarks on the grant documents suggested that the paper had been manufactured after the dates inscribed upon them. The claimants appealed to the U.S. Supreme Court. In 1835 the high court disregarded Randall's emphasis on forgery, focusing instead upon treaty obligations as the deciding issue. The court not only found for the claimants but awarded them an additional 7,000-acre island not previously disputed.[23]

The Arredondo and Forbes cases represent the importance of land cases to the superior courts and also the personal and institutional factors that affected the processes of adjudication. They were not, of course, the only land cases litigated or appealed. Call argued fifteen cases, all told, before the Supreme Court, losing fourteen of them. Even after the discontinuance of land-claim salary supplements for superior court judges in 1834, petitions continued to appear. As late as 1840, one judge's docket still disclosed thirty cases involving almost 1 million acres.[24]

Florida's judges by the early 1830s took for granted their jurisdiction over a plethora of concerns, including matters involving great fortunes. No doubt they enjoyed the opportunity to dispense their version of justice, while sometimes buttressing their social and economic interests or else avenging what they considered to be political wrongs. Coincidentally, though, they often seethed over their own circumstances. By way of example, the territorial court of appeals law, which placed each superior court judge on the appellate bench, required all but one of the jurists to undertake difficult and sometimes hazardous annual journeys to the frontier capital at Tallahassee. Judge Smith's narrow escape from death, already noted, affords one illustration of the problems. In the circumstances judges occasionally declined to accommodate the law, further impeding the already slow advance of justice. In 1828, for instance, the court of appeals failed to convene, as Richard Keith Call reported, due to the "absence of the Judges [Brackenridge and Smith]."[25]

The increasing workload also sparked complaints. In 1833 Congress appropriated insufficient funds to pay land-case salary supplements to all the judges. As Delegate White explained to the treasury secretary, "[P]rovision is made for the extra compensation of only *two* Judges, when there are *four* & land cases depending before each." The secretary aggravated the situation by advising that, since the treasury could not determine "which of the two out of the four Judges of said Territory, the provision was intended, no further payment under that appropriation, will be made to either of them."[26] The judges protested, of course, with three of them joining to demand the extra pay, plus the sums in arrears, for their increased workload. Unfortunately, the pleas fell upon deaf ears.[27]

During the period of the late 1820s through the mid–1830s, the judiciary enjoyed a time of relative stability and continuity despite the problems faced by its members. President Adams appointed Thomas Randall in 1827 to replace the deceased Judge Woodward, and the following year he also designated Florida resident James Webb as first judge of the Southern District. These individuals, together with judges Brackenridge and Smith, served together until 1832, when the commissions of the latter two men expired.[28]

President Jackson resolved for a number of reasons to modify Florida's judicial composition during the presidential election year of 1832. Among other factors, Brackenridge had moved away from his political association with Richard Keith Call and, instead, had allied himself with Nucleus opponent Joseph M. White. Smith long had opposed Call and his associates. In the situation the president appointed North Carolinian John A. Cameron to the West Florida judgeship. For East Florida he named Robert Raymond Reid, Jr., of Georgia as Smith's replacement. The appointments permitted Jackson to favor Call's political friends. Jackson's actions also acknowledged election-year politics by allowing him to placate factions in North Carolina and Georgia that were displeased by his stand on South Carolina and nullification.[29]

After Jackson's 1832 appointments, stability on the superior courts and, consequently, the court of appeals again became the rule. Webb and Cameron remained in office until 1838, Reid until 1839, and Randall until 1840. Their personal experiences disclose in greater depth the nature of the era's judicial system and the circumstances within which it matured.[30]

Thomas Randall, Middle District Superior Court Judge, 1827–1840

The combination of ability, experience, and high-level connections possessed by the individuals selected during the territorial period as Florida's superior court judges is exemplified by the life and career of Thomas Randall. He came into the world at Annapolis, Maryland, in 1792, the son of John and Deborah Randall. His father conducted a respectable mercantile establishment there and was deeply ensconced in the society and politics of his city and state. His brothers similarly enjoyed success. John joined his father in the family business, Richard taught as a professor of medicine and later served as governor of Liberia, and lawyer Alexander held office as a Whig congressman during the 1840s and also served as president of an Annapolis bank.[31]

Thomas's early life revolved around schooling and military service. He attended the Annapolis Latin Grammar School and later graduated from St. John's College in 1810. Afterward he studied law under the elder chancellor Thomas Johnson. During the War of 1812, Randall entered the army as a lieutenant. He was seriously wounded in a frontier engagement and captured by British forces. For the remainder of the conflict he was detained as a prisoner at Quebec.

After the war's end Randall's career took several turns. Until 1820 he remained in the army, where he advanced to the rank of captain. After the military was downsized at the decade's end, he pursued his calling as a lawyer in Washington, D.C. There he established numerous personal and professional friendships. A surviving description suggests how he came by them so easily. "[He was] a man of remarkable determination and coolness, of fine address and grace of manner, and of great versatility of talent," the account noted. "To extensive and varied reading and a tenacious memory he added great powers as a conversationalist, and was a most agreeable companion." The characterization concluded, "His attainments as a polished and forcible writer were very marked."[32]

Rewards soon were forthcoming for Randall. In 1823 President James Monroe designated him a special minister of the United States to travel to Puerto Rico and the West Indies regarding piracy in the area. The following year he visited Cuba seeking to gain custody for the United States of Florida land records and archives. The trip, coupled with encouragement from family friend and United States Attorney General William Wirt, spurred Randall's interest in Florida. Wirt, in fact, was attempting at Richard Keith Call's urging to organize an extended family-and-friends scheme for investments in the territory. His plans included himself and Randall as well as the Gamble, Cabell, and Parkhill families.[33]

By early 1827 Randall had decided to relocate to Florida, but he could not yet have known the opportunity that would appear for him. Already under consideration for appointment as territorial secretary, he paid a courtesy call on his friend John Quincy Adams before departing Washington. "Colonel Randall came to take leave of me," Adams recorded. "He is going to Florida—first, upon a speculation to purchase land at one of the public sales to be made there in May; and, secondly, to settle there."[34] Then, on June 12, Middle Florida superior court judge Augustus Brevoort Woodward died at Tallahassee. Immediately, associates made contacts on Randall's behalf. "[O]f Mr. Randalls honorable character there can be no doubt," Maryland chancellor Theodorick Bland informed the president, "and from all I have known or learned of his professional skill I am confident he would be perfectly adequate to the correct discharge of the duties of that station."[35] On July 6, as soon as Adams received an "authentic account" of Woodward's death, he complied with the requests and commissioned his friend a judge. On December 27 he reappointed Randall for a full four-year term.[36]

The new judge arrived at Tallahassee as the business of the superior court and of the court of appeals was increasing dramatically. His role in land cases, especially the Middle Florida grant to John Forbes and Company, already has been noted. Criminal matters occupied much of his attention as well. According to one early resident, the judge held office through "most of the rioting, rough, duelling times of that lawless period." In the circumstances he "dispatched an immense amount of business, largely of a criminal nature," as trials for "gaming, assault and battery and duelling were profuse."[37] Numerous other criminal matters concerned him, including the "illegal importation into the United States of certain Negroes." As late as 1838, multiple indictments for that crime were entered and processed in his court.[38]

On the question of judicial ethics, Randall may have possessed more sensitivity than some of his judicial peers. In the 1830s investments in financial institutions, some of them quite speculative and unsound, attracted leading territorial figures. The jurist declined to join them, he reasoned, because he would then have to recuse himself from hearing cases in which he had an economic interest. "If I had been disposed & able to take stock in Banks my situation as a Judge would have restrained me," he explained to William Wirt. "My Court being the only one open to Banks to sue & be sued in, it would not in my opinion have been right for me to hold an interest in such institutions & thereby deprive them of a most . . . appropriate Court except at great inconvenience."[39]

At first the judge did not face life in territorial Florida alone. Shortly after his appointment, he returned to Maryland to marry Wirt's daughter Laura Henrietta on August 21. The gently reared woman did not easily embrace her rough frontier home. "There is such a destitution of everything like comfort," she told her parents. "They know nothing of cleanliness . . . coffee is served in a tea pot and the cooking is miserable[,] . . . burnt up[,] and . . . dirty."[40] Her chagrin was apparent to others. Of Laura, Henry Marie Brackenridge confided to his wife on October 2, 1827, "She is melancholy, & in low spirits as you were. She is . . . remote from the elegant and fashionable circle in which she had been accustomed to move."[41]

Laura's sentiments about Florida changed in 1828, with happy consequences for the Randalls. A terrifying accident threatened them as the couple traveled to Tallahassee in January to attend a ball. "I cannot tell you how much this accident has endeared us to each other," she related to her mother. "It is no exaggeration to say that now I can scarcely live out of his sight—I cannot bear him to go even to town on business." Laura finished by declaring, "Yes, my dear mother, I must be 'happy with such a husband!'"[42] By early 1834 she was said to be "highly gifted, accomplished, and amiable . . . [with] a very large circle of acquaintances and friends."[43] About the same time, an onlooker recalled of her husband: "[He was] a small, thin man, quick in all his movements. His head was covered with very light and soft brown hair, complexion very fair, face, chin and nose sharp and well defined, eyes light colored, restless, and a general expression which defied description. He was a man of culture, wit, affability, and an able lawyer."[44]

The couple settled in Jefferson County, twenty-seven miles from Tallahassee, on 1,000 acres given them by William Wirt as a wedding present. Their home, Belmont, developed as one of territorial Florida's premier slave-worked plantations, and Randall also contributed to the management of his father-in-law's nearby establishment, Wirtland. At Belmont the Randalls created the gentle life of hospitality that Laura had left behind. That desire for gracious living influenced their opinions of others. Laura expressed abhorrence of the habits of Governor William Pope DuVal's family, whom she described as "the rough, inhospitable, *don't care* Duvalls." Their budding friendships with Richard Keith Call, to the contrary, were enhanced. Randall soon was identified with Call's political associates and aspirations rather than the governor's.[45]

The paradise the Randalls made of their home was disrupted when Laura died on December 17, 1833, shortly after childbirth. Several months after her death, Thomas carried their four daughters to live with relatives in Maryland. Call's daughter Ellen remembered a girlhood visit to Belmont years after Laura's passing. "A grass covered mound in the rear of the garden," she wrote, "told the sad story of [Laura's] life; a bride she came, but this is all that is left, for [her] four orphaned girls find care in a distant home." She continued, "The Judge is thus a widower, and when not holding his court, he here finds rest and relaxation in the culture of his garden and fields."[46]

Randall enjoyed a long tenure on the bench, but his days as a judge were drawing to a close as the decade of the 1830s ended. He had been reappointed for additional four-year terms in 1831 and 1836, but in 1840 Martin Van Buren chose not to continue the judge's service. The president was sensitive to the fact that Randall, a Whig, along with Call had begun criticizing administration military and economic policies. Moreover, a number of Tallahassee lawyers, including many Democrats, had bristled at what they considered Randall's quick temper and authoritative demeanor. Andrew Jackson suggested to his former vice president that he appoint instead Nashville lawyer Alfred Balch, an early Van Buren supporter. Van Buren acceded to the request.[47]

After leaving the bench Randall farmed in Jefferson County and practiced law at Tallahassee with his nephew, Thomas Hagner. As a planter, he suffered from poor weather and the economic outfall of the Panic of 1837. Within a matter of weeks after the onset of that national depression, he was compelled to apologize to his former mother-in-law for not "remitting you the money I owe you."[48] Within a year his plantation had been attacked by Indian raiders, and several of his slaves were taken away. In 1839 his crops were said to be "in a bad way," and a relative would note of his affairs, "tis a sad business."[49] His professional endeavors suffered a similar fate. He became chairman of the ill-fated Union Bank in 1844, only to watch its fortunes sink ever lower.[50]

Randall's character, so evident during his judicial tenure, continued to shine even in adversity. Although his financial position required in the early 1840s that he sell his pew at Tallahassee's St. Johns Episcopal Church to his nephew Hagner, he willingly had assisted the young man to establish himself in the community upon his arrival from Virginia a few years before. As his daughters grew older, he also brought them home to Florida. With them near, he worked at his law practice and strove to rejuvenate his financial standing. To an extent Randall succeeded. In 1850 his land holdings totaled only $4,000, while ten years later his estate had increased in value to $15,000.[51]

The former judge never lost interest in civic activities or politics. During the Second Seminole War of 1835–42, Randall had served as adjutant general to Governor Call, providing valuable assistance. Later he engaged his talents on behalf of public education, believing that "all popular governments depend on the virtue and intelligence of the people, and that virtue and intelligence can be expected only as the result of a correct and efficient system of education."[52] Politically, Randall continued a Whig until that party dissolved in the 1850s. In 1848 he supported Zachary Taylor for president and saw Florida entered in Taylor's electoral column. Two years afterward he participated prominently at local debates regarding the Wilmot Proviso, the Nashville Convention, and the Compromise of 1850. He involved himself, as well, in projects for local improvements, such as construction of a plank road in the Tallahassee area. As late as 1868 Randall attended the national Democratic convention as a Florida delegate.[53]

As Randall entered the autumn of his life, he undertook several changes in his personal life. For one thing, he remarried at Tallahassee on December 29, 1864, to Hannah S. Craig, a widow. Sometime later he and Mrs. Randall moved back to his old home at Annapolis. He passed away near there during the summer of 1876.[54] Though he neither died nor was buried in Florida, Randall left in the state rich memories of civic contribution, ethical behavior, and judicial responsibility. It was an honorable legacy.

James Webb, Southern District Superior Court Judge, 1828–1838

By creating a Southern District superior court in 1828, the Congress signaled an intention to foster the development of admiralty law, a goal greatly furthered by the two men who occupied the judicial seat during the territorial period. The first judge, James Webb, was born in Essex County, Virginia, on March 31, 1792, the son of Francis and Frances Webb. The family resettled in Georgia in 1810, but James soon returned to Virginia to read law under John P. Lee of Tappahannock. He continued his studies thereafter in Milledgeville, Georgia, where he gained admission to the bar in 1816. For seven years he practiced his profession at the community of Linton. Webb married on June 24, 1813, and he and wife Rachel Elizabeth subsequently had three sons and one daughter. In 1823 the family sought its greater fortune in Florida territory, establishing a home in Jackson County. Webb founded there the town of Webbville, near Marianna.[55]

Though still a young man in the 1820s, Webb played significant roles in area affairs, and his extraordinary abilities earned him the favorable attention of many leading men. His success as a militia officer brought him promotion by 1828, thanks to Governor William Pope DuVal, to the rank of colonel. During the period he also was considered for, though he did not receive, appointments as territorial secretary and West Florida district attorney. His supporters included officials of stature such as Georgia senator Thomas W. Cobb.[56]

When the Congress authorized creation of a superior court at Key West in 1828, Webb thus enjoyed a good reputation and enviable political connections. In the situation, congressional delegate Joseph M. White favored his appointment to the judgeship, although it required him to break a "political promise" previously given to future Florida supreme court justice Thomas Douglas. President John Quincy Adams signed Webb's commission on May 26, for a four-year term. By August the secretary of the Navy was instructing the commander of the West India Squadron to "afford a conveyance to the Judge, Marshal, and District Attorney with their records and papers, to Key West."[57]

Although Key West appealed to Webb, at first he left his family in Middle Florida, a circumstance that nearly cost him his job before he had fairly commenced his tenure. "For the last two weeks, I have been a resident of this Island, & am highly gratified at the prospect it presents of health, comfort & convenience—no place has ever been more unfairly represented," he wrote in October 1828. He continued, "The town is handsomely situated, & contains at present, about six hundred souls, & will no doubt increase rapidly in size and commercial importance."[58] Still, he left the island to be with his family as soon as his court, which first convened November 3, was adjourned. That fact angered President Andrew Jackson, who instructed Secretary of State Martin Van Buren to correct the situation. "When a vessel is wrecked, and the Marshal takes possession of the goods there is no person to adjudicate the case," the president declared, "from which great injury accrues to the owners, & the wreckers." Jackson added, "You will write to Judge Webb . . . and bring to his view the necessity of his removing to Key West, and taking up his constant residence there, or he will have to resign his office as Judge."[59]

Webb heeded the president's directive. He transferred his family to the remote island, and the worldly atmosphere of the port town eventually worked its effect upon them. Upon one occasion early in their stay, straitlaced and somewhat elitist Judge Henry Marie Brackenridge had noted that Mrs. Webb was "quite a plain and unaffected woman, & pious withall" and that "I fear Mr. Webb is a little touched with it."[60] Soon he discovered otherwise. Webb's daughter, he declared disapprovingly, though "only half grown" was "unfortunately permitted to put on all the airs of a woman, & what is worse, of a fashionable woman, extravagant dresses, flirtation, fiddle-de-dees, & all such nonsense." He described, as well, "[the] most strange transformation [which] has taken place in Mrs. W from being a plain, natural, & unaffected religious woman, . . . all at once to have waded to the chin in the follies of the fashionable life, so as to be a subject of general remark." Webb's home, Brackenridge added, "is a complete thoroughfare at all hours, for the humblest & least to be esteemed officers of the Navy."[61]

Even though Webb's judicial tenure began with threats from an annoyed president, his actions while presiding over the Key West superior court overcame the reservations and objections held against him. Jackson, who felt little compulsion about continuing President Adams's men in office, in 1832 and 1836 reappointed Webb for four-year terms after receiving numerous commendations from local residents. Typically, Key West founder John W. Simonton observed in 1832, "Judge Webb is extremely popular through out his district, not only as a Judge but as a gentleman." Simonton continued, "[I]f his reappointment depended upon the voice of the people with whom he has resided nearly four years, two votes would not be recorded against him."[62] Local physician and *Key West Gazette* editor Benjamin B. Strobel concurred. "[T]he Hon. Judge . . . has always acted, in his official capacity, in a manner highly honorable to himself," he wrote, "with strict impartiality to those upon whose interests he has to decide."[63]

The principal business of Webb's court, about which he exercised such impartiality, was admiralty law and the licensing of salvors. The implications of the court's powers and its anticipated workload were suggested in a November 1829 issue of the Key West *Register*, in which the editor reported, without enthusiasm, the arrival from Middle Florida of a vessel with "an assorted cargo and seven lawyers."[64] Beyond the exercise of normal admiralty jurisdiction, Webb carried out numerous regulatory responsibilities. He was obligated, for example, to ascertain that each salvage master had a well-equipped and seaworthy ship, that the ship's owner was a reputable person, and that a fair and equitable distribution of salvage was made. Asked once about the principles that guided his regulatory management, the judge replied, "If they commit any offense against honor or justice, instantly I take from them their licenses."[65]

Due to what one resident called "a great want of moral feeling in the community," reputedly the salvage business at Key West was riddled with venality.[66] Specifically, the workings of boards of arbitration composed of local men advanced opportunities for fraud and bribery to interfere with the attainment of justice. That Webb could overcome such obstacles so relatively effectively resulted partly from his willingness to defend what was good about the salvage industry and to reward its practitioners when they performed in a particularly laudable manner. An example of the latter practice arose from the case of the schooner *Waverly*, which ran aground at Florida Key in 1831. The salvors, Webb determined, had acted in circumstances of "extreme peril and labor." As a result, where one-third or less of the cargo's or vessel's net value might usually be awarded as compensation, the judge authorized an award of one-half the salvaged goods' value.[67]

As to the judge's defense of wreckers' reputations, his own words speak most eloquently. "I am gratified with the opportunity of expressing on this, as I have done on other occasions, my entire conviction that the course pursued by the individuals now engaged in this occupation on the coast of Florida is as exemplary in regard to the rights of others as that of any other class of this or other communities," he once declared from the bench. "They are the instruments of saving an immense amount of property, which without their exertions would be wholly lost," he continued, "and so far as their conduct on rendering these services has come to the knowledge of this court (and it is often the subject of minute and critical examination) it has, but with few exceptions, been found correct, meritorious and praiseworthy."[68]

Moreover, Webb encouraged professionalization of salvors by refusing to compensate extraneous participants in rescue operations. During the same year as the adjudication of the *Waverly* case, for instance, he refused to grant a lighthouse operator a large award for assisting in cargo recovery because other keepers could well be induced to operate their light for purposes other than ships' preservation if the "temptation" of large fees existed. By doing so Webb set a precedent obeyed by his successors, and he moved the evolution of admiralty law another step upon its path of development.[69]

The problems and responsibilities of a territorial-era superior court judge often extended beyond the bounds of mere jurisprudence, and Webb's career offers multiple examples. He often was asked, for instance, to recommend persons for federal appointments. Congressional delegate White once drew him toward the realm of politics by seeking the judge's opinion on the creation of Dade County out of Key West's Monroe County and on establishing a superior court to the northeast at the Indian Key settlement. Webb's response suggests not just his willingness to involve himself in such matters but also some of the concerns with which he regularly dealt. "I can perceive no injuries except such as may grow out of the impossibility of obtaining Jurors for the trial of important cases in the Courts of either County," he informed White somewhat disingenuously. "Previous to the division, there were not more than One hundred persons residing within the limits of Monroe County . . . qualified to serve as jurors; [so that] difficulty was often experienced in procuring jurors." The judge then cited federal law, which freed prisoners if not tried by the third court term after their arrest, and sought the delegate's assistance in increasing juror compensation for "travel & attendance," noting that "people labor under some inconvenience in getting to the Courts." The impediments mentioned by Webb served the purpose intended. White opposed creation of the new superior court, and the proposal was forestalled.[70]

After a decade of service, Judge Webb tired of the primitiveness of the territory, the constant threat of diseases such as yellow fever, and persistent trouble in the salvage business. In 1838 he resigned his seat on the bench and moved to the republic of Texas. There he held a succession of important offices, including secretary of treasury (1838), secretary of state (1838–39, 1849–51), attorney general (1839–41), minister to Mexico (1841), senator (1841–44), reporter of the Texas supreme court (1846–49), and judge of the fourteenth judicial district (1854–56). He also served in 1845 as a delegate to the Texas constitutional convention. The former Florida pioneer died on November 1, 1856, and was buried in Goliad, Texas.[71]

Robert Raymond Reid, Jr., Eastern District Superior Court Judge, 1832–1839

Through the territorial period, patronage needs often served presidents as sufficient justification for the designation of Florida's judicial officials, most of whom were individuals who had resided elsewhere or had been in the territory for only a short time. Still, the presidential appointments brought to Florida a pool of men who possessed talents, contacts, and experience desperately needed on that thinly settled frontier. The appointment of future governor Robert Raymond Reid, Jr., provides a good illustration.

Reid hailed originally from Beaufort District, Prince William Parish, South Carolina, where he was born on September 8, 1789, the son of a prerevolutionary Irish immigrant. His early schooling at Beaufort was disastrous because of hazing and other problems. "I was at last, after acquiring the character of a dull, lazy, and unprincipled child, taken home," he later recorded. "My vices forsook me, and my joys returned." His struggles commenced once more when he again was dispatched from home for his education. "About a year after," he wrote, "I was sent to Savannah, in Georgia, to the care of an aunt." He continued: "The boys [at school] imposed upon me; my cousins cheated and scorned me; my aunt and uncle neglected and starved me. After some time, I returned to my beloved home."[72]

Happily for Reid, his educational experiences improved, leading to the beginnings of successful professional and personal lives. He finished his basic schooling at Augusta, Georgia, from whence he entered college at Columbia, South Carolina, about 1809. Although ladies' company, poetry, and novels occupied a good deal of his time there, Reid graduated and commenced a law practice at Augusta.[73] Having almost attained the age of twenty-one, he married the first of his three wives on April 2, 1810. Anna Margaretta McLaws, the daughter of a lawyer under whom he had studied, subsequently bore Reid five children before her early death in 1825. Six years after their marriage, he was named a superior court judge. He worked in that capacity during 1816–19 and 1823–25, leaving the position from 1819 to 1823 to represent his district in the United States House of Representatives. He also served the city of Augusta as municipal judge and as mayor.[74]

Reid's personal life alternated after his first wife's death between bliss and tragedy. He remarried on May 8, 1829, to Elizabeth Napier Delphia Virginia Randolph, but she died in childbirth after only a few years. He again married on November 6, 1837, to Mary Martha Smith. Their happiness was undermined in 1839, though, by the death of his daughter Janet and the drowning at sea of his son James. The following year Mary's infant child died, although the couple was blessed thereafter with the birth of a son. More tragedy would greet them in the years just ahead.[75]

Despite his professional achievements, the death of his second wife led Reid into serious depression, which included habitual drinking and physical deterioration. He ached to leave the memories behind by relocating. Friends approached President Andrew Jackson in 1832 for assistance. As a presidential elector in 1828, Reid had voted for Jackson, and he enjoyed a longtime friendship with Jackson favorite Martin Van Buren. The president saw a chance during that electoral year to endear himself to Georgia voters, while ridding himself and his Florida associates of the troublesome East Florida judge Joseph Lee Smith. Accordingly, on May 23, 1832, he appointed Reid to a four-year term as Florida's Eastern District superior court judge.[76]

As was true of his judicial peers, much of the business of Reid's court concerned land claims. In 1833 he noted "nearly one hundred" such cases on his docket and insisted to the president that "the land claims within my jurisdiction are nearly twenty times as many as the existing number in the other three Districts put together."[77] He chafed at the workload and the refusal of the Treasury to pay him a salary supplement for his efforts. "I've not been well and am greatly embarrassed by the manner in which I am treated at Washington," he confided to his diary. "They refuse to pay me for arduous duties rendered to the country and actually are withholding every cent of my salary." He queried of himself, "Do they want to get rid of me?"[78]

Demands upon the judge's time naturally included many responsibilities other than land claims, civil litigation, and criminal cases. An important one, which gave him influence upon a broad range of nonjudicial matters, regarded supervision of the grand jury. As judge, he charged the panels with their duties, in the process guiding them as to the subjects with which they should concern themselves.

An 1834 presentment of the St. Johns and Mosquito counties jury, prepared for submission to the legislative council and to the Congress, offers a glimpse of the numerous and sometimes controversial topics considered. Its members chastised the federal government, for example, for failing to maintain Fort Marion (the Castillo de San Marcos) properly and for neglecting the extension of the town's sea wall, both items "heretofore . . . repeatedly urged." It requested that "every aid should be given" to a steamboat company so as to improve mail service. The jurors also expressed bewilderment that the Congress had not appropriated funds for inland navigation along Florida's Atlantic coast, a matter that, they felt, "presses with irresistible force on the minds of all capable of appreciating its advantages." Finally, they asked for a military expedition into the southern peninsula to combat an "evil requiring the attention of the Government." Given the presence there of Indians and their black allies, the "most valuable division of the Territory" had "become a source of injury to its best interests, by affording a refuge for runaway slaves, and for bands of Indians of bad character, who are beyond the reach of civil prosecution."[79]

To a man with Reid's educational and professional background, the duties of his judgeship—however important and diverse—brought little stimulation. He found at St. Augustine a congenial environment, but of a typical day he still could record: "To work preparatory for Court. On the Bench from 10 A.M. to 3 P.M. Arguments dull and Judge sleepy—can hardly keep my eyes open."[80] Nonetheless, he was far happier when in coastal East Florida than when his presence was required in the territorial capital. "How far preferable is St. Augustine to Tallahassee!" he mused in 1835. "The latter place is full of filth—*of all genders.* I never knew such dirty houses and indifferent people. Gov. [John] E[aton] is a rowdy—his wife, drunk or crazy, and several other ladies but so-so."[81]

Tallahassee afforded some comforts to Reid, but not many. To the good, his daughter Janet lived near there at her plantation Blackwood. He resented, though, the discomforts of territorial travel, which sometimes kept him on the road for a week getting to and from sessions of the court of appeals. When other judges did not arrive, his mood worsened. He summed up his sentiments following the conclusion of the 1833 appeals court term. "I have seen a noisy senseless crowd," he wrote, "a legislative council with little wisdom, a fashionable circle with little taste. . . . a Governor's daughter, pretty, rouged, and sour; a Governor, shallow, blasphemous, and coarse; a Secretary, (sometimes Governor) rough, factious and egotistical." Of his fellow judges Reid added: "Judge Randall, [c]hivalrous, intelligent, and opinionated; Judge Cameron, Scotch! Scotch! Scotch!"[82]

Reid's interest in his judgeship waned as the years of the 1830s passed. His 1837 marriage to Mary Martha Smith permitted some relief from what to him was the boredom of his duties, and by all accounts she made an excellent partner. Described as "blond with light hair, rosy cheeks and blue eyes and inclined to be stout but [with] a very stately carriage," she was at once intelligent, kind, and sympathetic.[83] Yet even Martha could not distract him for long from his love of politics, and in that field he would render his major contribution to the territory.

The background to Reid's involvement in Florida politics related to Indian and race war. After late 1835 the territory was locked in a brutal conflict, known to history as the Second Seminole War.[84] During its seven years' duration territorial politics heated, and the previously small regional cracks in society and politics widened into fissures. Many East and West Floridians desired to separate from Middle Florida, and Middle Florida's planter elite, in turn, decided to press for immediate statehood to forestall the possibility. In Whig-oriented East Florida Reid, along with David Levy Yulee and a few others, constituted the core of what would become the region's Democratic pro-statehood leadership. Among other important issues the creation and regulation of banks also came to the fore, with Whigs often supportive and Democrats generally opposed.[85] "There is a passion for bank making existing at present in the Territory," Reid had written in 1833. "Such schemes are fit only for the brains of speculators."[86]

The statehood and banking controversies reached an early peak when Governor Richard Keith Call arranged for the call of a constitutional convention. The body met at St. Joseph in Middle Florida on December 3, 1838. Though a sitting superior court judge, Reid had been elected as a delegate from St. Johns County, and he had decided to make a difference in favor of limitations on banks and of statehood for the entire territory. To do so, he contested the presidency of the convention with former Governor William Pope DuVal, whom Reid finally bested by one vote. Seemingly, the outcome resulted from an arrangement between East Florida men and antibank delegates from Middle Florida.[87]

The political stakes were high at the convention over which Reid presided, and the body's actions profoundly influenced Florida's future. Reid skillfully maneuvered adoption of provisions calling for immediate admission of the entire territory to the United States, prohibiting the issuance of state "faith" bonds in favor of private corporations, and restricting banks. Call biographer Herbert J. Doherty offered a glimpse of the judge's personality and sensibilities, which helps to explain how he could make such a crucial difference. "Reid was a remarkable man," he observed, "an urbane scholar, a gentleman, an intellectual who shrewdly evaluated his fellow men." Doherty added, "In his calm introspection, his tact, his discretion, his humanitarian impulses, his shrinking from physical exertion, he presents a picture of a man quite opposite in temperament from Call [and many other territorial leaders]."[88] Upon its conclusion convention members joined to praise the man who seemed so different from their governor, expressing gratitude for "the dignity, ability and impartiality with which he has presided over these deliberations."[89]

While Reid's convention labors succeeded, each of the convention's steps was dogged by controversy, and the outcome divided the territory. In a referendum on its work, East Florida decisively opposed the document. Six years then would pass before Florida's admission as a state under its provisions. As the territory's "old way" of doing things found itself a casualty to the struggle, so, too, did Reid's judicial career. His enemies labeled him a "political judge," a charge that intensified as he emerged as a Democratic leader. President Van Buren, his old friend, rescued him from the dilemma on December 2, 1839, by naming him to replace Call as territorial governor. "The removal of Judge REID from the bench was a desirable event," declared a politically hostile St.

Augustine newspaper editor, "for *no politician* should ever be allowed its occupancy."[90]

Reid's tenure as governor was brief, lasting less than one and a half years. Democrats hailed his appointment. "He is the ardent and uncompromising supporter of the St. Joseph Convention," waxed the Tallahassee *Floridian*, "is in favor of the admission of Florida as a State, and unequivocally opposed to the scheme of immediate dismemberment and division."[91] But the bitter statehood controversy and territorial political polarization grew more intense and, over it all, loomed the Second Seminole War, which dragged on year after year. The struggle exasperated the governor, and he found himself describing the hostiles as "fiends in human shape." In frustration he even endorsed the use of bloodhounds to track and capture them.[92] Both actions earned him criticism. The war's tremendous impact affected territorial society as it did the normally cerebral Reid. He found that he could not combat the resultant lawlessness. Rather than face its causes, he policed Tallahassee's streets with militiamen to keep the peace.[93]

The Democratic governor's service ended with the inauguration of Whig president William Henry Harrison in March 1841, when Call received a second appointment. Reid remained near Tallahassee at his daughter's plantation Blackwood. During the summer yellow fever struck Leon County. The plague caused the deaths of Reid's daughter Rosalie, his granddaughter Rebecca Black, and, on July 1, the former judge and governor. His years in Florida thereafter were recalled with respect, and the unified state served in part as his memorial.[94]

John Adams Cameron, Western District Superior Court Judge, 1832–1838

When President Andrew Jackson decided in 1832 to utilize appointments to Florida's judiciary to enhance his reelection campaign as well as to rid himself of politically troublesome judicial incumbents, he replaced East Florida Judge Joseph Lee Smith with Robert Raymond Reid, Jr. For the West Florida position, he turned to an old friend and popular North Carolinian, John Adams Cameron.

The new West Florida judge was born in Virginia during the year 1788. His education included college-level training at the University of North Carolina at Chapel Hill. As a young man, he served in the Virginia legislature and, later, in its North Carolina counterpart. During the War of 1812, he rose to the rank of major. More important for the future, he earned the friendship of Major

General Andrew Jackson. Cameron was married on November 19, 1818, to Catherine and then pursued careers as a lawyer and as a diplomat. In 1822 President James Monroe appointed him consul to Brazil. Jackson followed in 1831 by designating him consul to Vera Cruz, Mexico.[95]

When, in 1832, Jackson began pondering a possible replacement for Judge Henry Marie Brackenridge, Cameron was not his first choice. Rather, he nominated James G. Bryce, a Winchester, Virginia, lawyer. The president's desires were frustrated, though, when the Senate declined on a tie vote to confirm the nominee due to his lack of substantial legal and judicial experience. In the circumstances Jackson turned to his old friend Cameron. The appointment of the popular former legislator pleased North Carolinians and enjoyed an easy confirmation.[96]

Meager available documentation provides little information regarding Cameron's service on the West Florida superior court. A letter written by him in 1833 to the treasury secretary regarding the ongoing judicial compensation controversy does provide insight into his actions and perceptions. In it, he detailed his responsibilities and circumstances, as follows:

> The original salaries of the Judges in West, East and Middle Florida were each $1500 per An: they were required to hold a Court, twice a year, at Pensacola, St Augustine & Tallahassee, each; and the Legislative Council of the Territory were authorized to require them to hold one other Court only in their respective Districts. When the Southern District was established, the salary of the Judge was fixed at $2000.
>
> Subsequently, Congress authorized the Legislative Council to establish other Superior Courts [the Act of Mar. 3, 1827], which the Judges were called upon to hold. By another Act of Congress, certain Land Claims were referred to the Superior Courts for adjudication, and for this Service, the sum of $800 was added, annually, to the salary of each one of them. . . . [I]n the Western District, they [now] have established Courts to be held in *six* counties *twice* a year—in the Middle Circuit there are *seven* Superior Courts annually—in the Eastern there are also *seven*, while the Southern has but one yet. While all the Judges are required to hold a term of the Appeal Court, of from two to four weeks in duration, once a year. Hence the duties of the Judges of the West, Middle, and East Districts have been multiplied more than *four fold* since the salaries were fixed—while those of the *West* (or my District) have been still more increased. I hold 12 Superior Courts in the year—no other Judge holds more than 7.

Cameron continued:

> I am compelled to travel more than 2,000 miles in a year: no other Judge is compelled to travel more than 800. I have *two* important Admiralty Courts in my District (Pensacola and Appalachicola): no other Judge has more than *one*. I am compelled to be from home . . . three months at a time: no other Judge is compelled to be from home, half that time.[97]

The judge's complaints about the hardships of travel only partially revealed the difficulties he faced in the frontier Panhandle area. Another of Cameron's 1833 letters mentioned, for example: "There are six Counties in West Florida, and of Course, six places where U.S. Courts are held twice a year; and yet, save in the County of Jackson, there is not a single Court House in the District, nor is there One Jail." He added, "Except in the County of Jackson, I hold the Sessions of the Courts in private houses, which are rented, for that purpose, by the Marshall."[98] Years later his concerns remained unresolved, and he still would declare: "Pray cast your eyes on the Map of Florida and look at my District! I have to hold Courts in five Counties, twice a year, besides on[e] yearly term of the Court of Appeals: my traveling is more than 2,000 Miles in the year." He concluded, "I am from home, on my official duties, more than 6 months in the year: . . . my health and even life are often hazarded."[99]

Cameron's tribulations and contributions did not pass unnoticed. Leading men of the territory supported his demands for better compensation and conditions. The Jackson County bar, for instance, lauded his service and joined in asking for relief. "Impressed with a high sense of the merit of the present Judge of the Western District and . . . by his able, impartial and faithful administration of the Laws," its members memorialized, "[we] respectfully suggest, that [the judge's present salary] is inadequate to his worth, his services, and the arduous labors he has to perform." Among the signatories were prominent individuals including Richard C. Allen, Thomas Baltzell, Augustus Brevoort Woodward, Richard Keith Call, George S. Hawkins, and James D. Westcott.[100]

Even with the challenging conditions under which he worked, Cameron's judicial future looked bright when, on March 14, 1836, Jackson commissioned him for a second four-year term. Nonetheless, two years later he was dead, a victim of drowning on July 14–15, 1838, when the steamship *Pulaski* was lost at sea. His assertions about the hazards of travel had been proved chillingly accurate.[101]

Chapter 4

Momentum toward Statehood and a Supreme Court

Florida entered the 1830s poised to enjoy sustained growth and increasing prosperity. Particularly in the Middle Florida area between the Apalachicola and Suwannee rivers, planters from the southern states invested heavily in plantation lands. In the region, cotton culture came to dominate agriculture as a genteel society superimposed itself upon what had been a raw frontier. East and West Florida also anticipated a share in the rewards of the territory's association with the United States. Federally subsidized road construction projects, harbor improvements, and military expenditures brought needed capital into both regions, as the arrival of steamboats on waterways such as the St. Johns River betokened a very bright future.[1]

The rosy prospects of the decade's beginning turned into dismal conflict halfway through its course, and the tragedies proved multiple. Serving both as tragedy and as catalyst for further problems were Indian and race conflicts. From the territory's earliest days, authorities had pursued efforts to force Florida's Indian population and the blacks who resided in Indian lands to relocate to the remote southern interior. President Andrew Jackson's administration redirected Indian policy to require the removal of the natives to the West. Federal negotiators concluded treaties under highly questionable circumstances toward that end, and, meanwhile, tensions increased. By 1835 the situation had erupted into bloody fighting across the peninsula, a struggle that constituted the largest slave rebellion in United States history and the nation's longest war.[2]

The Second Seminole War's impact especially was profound in East Florida, much of which was depopulated for prolonged periods of time during 1835 to 1842. Settlers who remained often clustered for protection in isolated forts or else in the region's few towns. Sugar plantations and other slave-worked agricultural enterprises along the southern frontier were abandoned as a number of their bondsmen allied themselves with the hostiles. Military expenditures supported a few communities such as Jacksonville and Palatka, but overall the economic and military picture became bleak. Resentments felt by East Floridians soon were translated into political animosities. The legislative council appeared to concern itself more with protecting the Middle Florida plantation belt and, at the same time, penalized East Florida slaveholders whose bondsmen had joined the war. The ensuing divisions thereafter underlay territorial and state political alignments for decades.[3]

While territorial residents fought the Second Seminole War and its effects, an additional catastrophe occurred. During the conflict's second year the national economy declined into a depression subsequently known as the Panic of 1837. Its outfall was not immediately pronounced in Florida because the war already had caused such widespread economic damage, except that the territory's few banks (the Union Bank headquartered in Tallahassee was the most prominent) soon were destabilized. The institutions were vulnerable, having been founded upon schemes by which territorial bonds were sold to investors outside Florida, with the proceeds distributed in the form of loans to planters who also owned and controlled the banks through stock purchased on credit. In the years following the Panic, many banking institutions first faltered and then collapsed, prompting demands for rigid banking restrictions and creating a political division to overlay the existing regional alignment.[4]

In this climate many Middle Florida planters, led by Governor Richard Keith Call, convinced themselves that statehood offered the only viable solution to the problems confronting them. Their reasoning involved many considerations, and the thought of statehood was not a novel idea. Still, the mid-decade conflicts had evoked a sense of urgency or desperation. First, the Middle Florida men wanted a government able to control all of Florida in order to protect their investments and way of life. The stirrings of abolitionist sentiments in northern states had created a climate in which East and West Florida's relatively more flexible racial patterns, coupled with the presence there of armed free blacks within the Indian lands, seemed to threaten Middle Florida slavery. East Floridians on the other hand, angered at Middle Florida's failure to protect them during the Indian war and the attempts to penalize them for desertions of bondsmen to the hostiles, had begun to demand autonomy through territorial division. Second, many of Call's planter allies had been major shareholders of firms such as the Union Bank. In addition to political demands that their influence be reduced in, if not removed from, the halls of power, pressures for punitive measures of civil and criminal natures increasingly were exerted.[5]

Call formally initiated the statehood drive in January 1837 by appealing to the legislative council for its endorsement. As summarized by one historian, he told the legislators that statehood offered a government "more responsive to the needs and wishes of the people." His justification depended upon references to judicial problems. Call noted, for example, that no session of the court of appeals had been held for three years due to lack of a quorum. A state government could compel the attendance of the judges, Call insisted, while the legislative council under federal law held no such power. The remedy to such problems, as he asserted, was "a State Government, under which all public officers may be held mediately, or immediately, responsible to the people."[6]

The constitutional convention summons gained momentum slowly. The council endorsed an election for delegates, but voters paid more attention to the Indian war and economic problems. Many East and West Florida newspapers labeled the statehood effort premature. In May "the bleeding, suffering East" emphatically rejected statehood, as did a number of West Florida counties. Heavy voting in Middle Florida and in growing West Florida towns such as Apalachicola and nearby St. Joseph nonetheless carried the proposal territory-wide. As a scholar of the statehood movement concluded, "The majority of 63.4 percent probably indicated a more favorable attitude than really existed, for there was considerable apathy in the election, particularly in the East."[7]

The convention met at the Gulf-coast boom town of St. Joseph in December 1838 and January 1839. Its deliberations proceeded tumultuously. The complicated crosscurrents at play within its membership were illustrated early on in the struggle for the convention presidency. Ultimately antibank but pro-statehood, East Florida superior court judge Robert Raymond Reid, Jr., defeated Call-backed former judge and governor William Pope DuVal by a single vote. The tally presaged the body's final antibank, pro-statehood positions, but the resulting constitution failed to heal the territorial divisions and problems. Instead, that document exacerbated them by focusing power in a Middle Florida-dominated legislature and permitting statewide election only of the governor. The charter achieved voter ratification by a margin so slight that Reid refused for three years to release the final figures. Even in Middle Florida only 55 percent of those voting approved the constitution. East Floridians overwhelmingly rejected it, and many of their leaders dedicated themselves to fighting statehood and promoting division.[8]

The political conflict sparked by the St. Joseph Constitution lasted for six years and, in the process, midwifed the birth of local Democratic and Whig parties. Sectional and partisan clamor failed to abate completely even when, in 1845, the Congress eventually admitted the territory to the union under the document's aegis. The decisions of that convention, achieved so controversially and narrowly, then guided the state's government until the Civil War. Out of the turmoil came the creation of Florida's first supreme court.[9]

The St. Joseph Constitution's judicial provisions—including those calling for a supreme court—had stirred few passions, certainly not the kind demonstrated in the fight over banking regulations. A committee appointed by Reid crafted them in a two-part process. Headed by newly appointed superior court judge Richard C. Allen of St. Joseph, the panel's other initial members included Middle Florida residents James D. Westcott and George T. Ward of Leon County, Thomas Baltzell of Jackson, and Jefferson County's John Partridge. This committee reported three days after its December 7 appointment, but resentments about its composition prompted Chairman Allen to request additional appointments more representative of East and West Florida and of other shades of opinion on the banking issue. Accordingly, on the tenth, Reid added Benjamin D. Wright of Escambia; Monroe County's William Marvin, the district attorney of the Southern District; David Levy of St. Johns County; and former judge and governor DuVal of Calhoun. The reconstituted panel then resolved most outstanding issues. Its revised report was debated on December 21. Approval came four days later after a last-minute attempt by a Leon County delegate to forbid the state courts to enforce the validity of several large Spanish land grants and to prohibit state residents from serving on federal juries in such cases.[10]

The organization of state courts under the St. Joseph Constitution will be discussed more fully in chapter 5. Here it suffices to note that regional and partisan factors played a role in their design, with Middle Florida planters and other pro-statehood advocates combining to approve a system in which all judicial officers, including members of the supreme court and its clerk, would be elected by a legislature presumably more sympathetic to their legal, political, and personal needs than the electorate at large. The same elected individuals could be removed from office by the legislature for "reasonable cause."[11]

Beyond these political factors, drafters addressed certain lessons of the territorial era in a practical manner. Governor Call, for instance, had criticized weaknesses in the court of appeals, and the new document, in providing for a supreme court, took them into account. Particularly, language forbade justices to participate in any appellate decision in "any case which shall have been decided by him in the court below" and expressly were made subject to removal for "wilful neglect of duty." Further, the constitution underscored the principle of separation of powers, as it prohibited the imposition of nonjudicial duties on supreme court justices and circuit court judges. Moreover, boards of commissioners for the conduct of county affairs were authorized apart from county courts. Finally, the example of Governor Jackson's defiant rebuke of judicial power in 1821 resulted in the grant of important authority to the Florida

Supreme Court. "[T]he said Court," read one provision, "shall always have power, to issue writs of injunction, mandamus, quo-warranto, habeas corpus, and such other remedial and original writs, as may be necessary to give it a general superintendence and control of all other Courts."[12]

The product of the 1838–39 constitutional convention drew upon Florida's territorial experience and cannot be understood without reference to it. That experience did not end, though, with the convention's adjournment. Six years elapsed before Florida's admission as a state, and during the period the superior courts and territorial court of appeals worked through the turmoil, enduring continued challenges and evolving with the times.

One important change in the court system occurred in the months prior to the St. Joseph convention's meeting. For more than a decade, Florida legislators had urged the Congress to authorize a new superior court for Apalachicola, the territory's bustling cotton port. "The extensive and increasing cultivation of the lands in the upper Country near the Rivers Appalachicola, Flint and Chattahoochee in the States of Georgia and Alabama, and in this Territory," noted the 1832 council, "justifies the assertion that in a few years a town must grow up at the mouth of the former river, second in size and importance to none in the Southwestern Country except New Orleans."[13]

Costs proved the roadblock to authorization of an Apalachicola superior court. "The Judiciary expenses in Florida," wrote congressional delegate Joseph M. White in 1836, "exceed that of any [other territory], more than 30,000 dollars a year."[14] White suggested, to avoid the problem, that the town and Franklin County be transferred into the nearby Middle District, but the idea drew opposition from leaders in both West and Middle Florida, including Judge Thomas Randall and prominent Apalachicola-area residents such as lawyers George Sydney Hawkins and Richard C. Allen. Allen conveyed the sentiments in opposition to the plan to Washington early in 1838, in the process making and reinforcing personal connections that were to prove invaluable to him. In July the Congress relented and passed enabling legislation, creating a new Apalachicola District composed of Franklin, Washington, and Jackson counties. President Martin Van Buren thereupon designated Allen as its first judge.[15]

Just as the Congress shied away from increased expenditures for an additional superior court, it also refused to pay for some expenses otherwise deemed essential by local judges. An example arose in 1838 when the court of appeals struggled to resolve complicated issues without benefit of a proper law library. "[A]t the present Term of this Court," the judges proclaimed in an appeal to the congressional delegate, "several most important causes in Admiralty have been submitted to its decision." They continued, "For the full investigation of all these important questions, the want of an adequate number of Law books is most Sensibly felt." A committee of the House of Representatives recommended a $5,000 appropriation, but the measure suffered defeat.[16]

While difficulties of travel, population growth, scarce resources, and politics complicated the lives of the superior court judges, the men saw their case loads increase with the bad economic times following the Panic of 1837. "The failure of the territorial banks of Florida to function as their promoters expected and of many borrowers to meet their interest," one historian explained, "led to numerous foreclosure suits during the period just prior to statehood and these suits greatly increased legal work." He added: "An examination of the latter territorial newspapers will show whole half pages of legal notices, many of which related to mortgage foreclosures, attachments and bankruptcy proceedings. The latter were especially numerous during 1841 and 1842."[17]

Through these troubled times the courts adjusted, as well, to far-reaching changes in personnel. As had been true previously, the selections better reflected presidential patronage needs than those of properly managing jurisprudence in the territory. Van Buren complemented Allen's July 1838 appointment by naming North Carolinian Dillon Jordan, Jr., as the drowned John Cameron's replacement on the Western District superior court. The same year Southern District judge John Webb departed the territory for Texas, occasioning the president to elevate William Marvin in March 1839. When one year afterward the terms of judges Randall and Reid expired, Alfred Balch of Tennessee and New Yorker Isaac H. Bronson, respectively, received the Middle Florida and East Florida honors. Balch resigned because of sickness in August 1841, and Virginian Samuel J. Douglas replaced him. Allen died about the same time, and another Tennessean, Samuel Williams Carmack, was called. Biographical sketches of the new members of the Florida bench further illustrate the trying circumstances and conditions under which these judges labored in the territory's waning years.

Richard C. Allen, Apalachicola District Superior Court Judge, 1838–1841

Unique among the superior court judges appointed for Florida from 1838 until statehood in 1845, the Apalachicola District's first judge, Richard C. Allen, resided in the territory. He enjoyed, nonetheless, important connections from earlier days and other locales. Premier among those associations was one with Andrew Jackson.

Allen was born in Newberry District, South Carolina, sometime around 1795. The details of his early life and education are not available, save that at age seven he moved with his family to Tennessee. During the early 1810s he served as a volunteer in General Jackson's forces during the Creek civil war and the War of 1812. William Pope DuVal, at a crucial moment in Allen's career, would remind the general of the young man's contributions. "[H]e is known to you," the governor opined, "both as a civilian & soldier, for he served with you in your military campain through Florida and was with you at New Orleans."[18]

The future judge seemingly liked what he saw in Spanish Florida and removed to the territory in 1825. At Tallahassee he speculated in lands and, apparently, practiced law. He furthered his interests by engaging in surveying, a pursuit in which he benefited from Governor DuVal's patronage. In one such instance early in his stay, he was charged with selecting lands granted by the Congress in support of "a Seminary of Higher Learning." Allen explained. "In the winter of 1825–6," he recorded, "[Romeo] Lewis & myself proceeded to the Chippola Country, where we remained six weeks industriously employed in traversing the Country, a labour of the most arduous and unpleasant description." Allen's tribulations arose from the condition of the Panhandle region and from some personal encounters with others interested in the area. "The Country was extensive and . . . entirely unsettled," he continued. "[M]y only reward [was] . . . the ill will, & sometimes abuse, of persons, who wished to purchase lands, which I thought it my duty to select."[19]

Despite his protestations of ingratitude, rewards did come Allen's way. He eventually was compensated with two sections of land in payment for his surveys of the seminary grant. In 1829, again with DuVal's support, he received from President Jackson a lucrative designation as a federal law agent for Florida. Richard Keith Call accepted a similar position. Allen held the office, which required him to represent the United States in certain land claim cases, through most of Jackson's administration. As he did, his relationship with Call grew closer. He worked with the soon-to-be governor as a part of the powerful political faction, the Nucleus. He invested in many of the bank and internal improvement schemes then the rage among leading Middle Florida businessmen and planters. In doing so he served as director of the Central Bank of Florida and of the Union Bank.[20]

When the position of federal law agent was abolished in the spring of 1835, Allen enjoyed further preferment from the Jackson administration. He contracted with the Government Land Office to survey the Forbes purchase or, as it was stated at the time, "the large land claim decreed by the Supreme Court at their January term 1835."[21] His responsibilities carried him to the Apalachicola and St. Joseph area, where he soon relocated. By 1838 he headed the Lake Wimico and St. Joseph Canal and Railroad Company, which constructed Florida's first steam railroad to connect St. Joseph with the Apalachicola River.[22]

Allen's business and professional interests, as well as those of the St. Joseph and Calhoun County vicinity, compelled him in early 1838 to lobby at Washington for creation of a superior court district for the Apalachicola River area. His success and the opportunities it afforded for renewing his government contacts led to his appointment by President Martin Van Buren on July 7, 1838, as its first judge. His term was to be of four years' duration.[23]

After accepting his judicial appointment and following the practice of other territorial judges, Allen remained involved in politics. Local voters chose him to represent them in the 1838–39 constitutional convention, and he participated actively in its deliberations. He influenced most directly the work of the judiciary committee, of which he was chairman. That panel—composed primarily of Middle Florida planters, professionals, and businessmen—designed a conservative judicial article to safeguard their interests against the forces of territorial division and what they considered the threat of excesses of democracy. Allen fought for legislative selection of all judges and other court officers, given the likelihood that Middle Florida would control the assembly. His forces defeated by a 48–to–6 vote an amendment to require popular election.[24]

Allen's popularity, as evidenced by his 1838 election, followed him through his judicial tenure. His standing suffered not at all when he reached beyond his responsibilities on the bench to advocate federal support of local internal improvement projects. Yet the pleasure of community leaders at his appointment soon was terminated abruptly. Yellow fever decimated St. Joseph during the summer of 1841, and, on July 30, friends and associates found the judge among its victims. Sorrow greeted news of his death in most of the territory. "[T]hose who knew Judge ALLEN, far and near, but more particularly the people of this District and his immediate neighbors," observed the *St. Joseph Times*, "will accord to his memory more than our feeble pen can express." Its editor concluded, "He has passed away in the meridian of a useful life without one blot upon his name."[25]

Dillon Jordan, Jr., Western District Superior Court Judge, 1838–1845

As Richard C. Allen died in 1841 from natural disaster, so, too, had his Western District counterpart John Cameron perished three years earlier. The cause in Cameron's case, rather than plague, had been shipwreck. While some territorial offices lay vacant for a considerable time awaiting appointments, President Martin Van Buren acted quickly in filling the Western District bench. In so doing he turned to a man with a background remarkably similar to that of the deceased and designated him for much the same reasons as had prompted his predecessor's appointment.

Dillon Jordan, Jr., was born in Cumberland County, North Carolina, about 1800. He received his formal education at Mount St. Mary's College at Emmittsburg, Maryland. After graduation he returned to North Carolina, where he read law with Louis D. Henry, and he afterward pursued the legal profession at Fayetteville. According to an obituary, "He commenced his political career when quite a young man."[26] In 1836 he represented Cumberland County in the lower house of the North Carolina legislature. The following year Jordan capitalized on political contacts with the Van Buren administration and experience in litigating claims for Indian depredations to gain employment as an Indian agent. He already had married. He and Ann Elizabeth Jordan subsequently had eight children.[27]

When news of Judge Cameron's death reached Washington in the summer of 1838, Jordan presented the president with an excellent political choice. He and Cameron both were popular North Carolinians and former legislators, and Jordan's loyalty to the administration could be assumed based upon his prior actions. Even his Indian-related experience might be helpful, since the Second Seminole War then was ongoing. In the circumstances Van Buren acted quickly, commissioning Jordan as West Florida superior court judge on July 7. President John Tyler would reappoint him in 1842 to a second four-year term.[28]

While Jordan's judicial tenure lasted seven years, his responsibilities were not as great as those imposed upon other superior court judges. West Florida's population had increased slowly, and its fastest-growing areas—those near the Apalachicola River—had been split off into the new Apalachicola District. The largest town remained a quaint but remote community. Of Pensacola at the time, a New York newspaper observed, "[It] now contained 2100 inhabitants, of whom the majority are Spanish or French by descent." The report continued: "Although Pensacola has been in the possession of the Americans for nearly twenty-five years, it still retains many of its old customs, and the peculiarities so characteristic of the Spaniard." The newspaper added, "The business of this place is considerable, but it derives its principal, if not sole support, from the squadron belonging to the West-India Station, and of which there are generally three or four vessels lying in its beautiful bay."[29]

Jordan's duties might not have been onerous, but, as was also true for his judicial peers, he was called upon to perform a variety of functions and to participate in matters having far-ranging significance. Judges constantly were asked, for example, to influence appointments to territorial positions. A case in point involved Vinton Butler, who wanted to remain United States attorney for the Middle District. Jordan had been favorably impressed with Butler's legal abilities, but Van Buren had canceled his commission in 1840, less than two months after signing it. The action stemmed from "information recently received" by the president containing accusations against the appointee. Jordan interceded on Butler's behalf with Van Buren, but he discovered what other politically influential men had realized after coming to the territory. The principle of "out of sight, out of mind" applied to him as well as to others, and his influence in Washington had diminished as he traveled away from it to his new Florida home.[30]

The judge's responsibilities naturally included presiding over countless civil and criminal matters, and Pensacola's status as a bustling port afforded him perhaps his most important case. In 1844 Jonathan Walker, a Boston abolitionist, attempt to smuggle a group of slaves out of the town. At sea, he suffered heatstroke and his vessel was discovered by a salvager. Walker was returned to Pensacola and brought before Jordan's court. The ensuing trial—at which the judge sentenced the defendant to one hour in the pillory, a fine of $150, and the branding of his hand—caused a national furor that aided the emerging abolition movement. Walker published his own account in 1845, while John Greenleaf Whittier's version of events as portrayed in his *The Branded Hand* further appalled a number of Northerners. Through it all, Walker insisted that he had received fair treatment from everyone but Jordan. The judge, he declared, "manifested a considerable degree of prejudice against me."[31]

Jordan's judicial career ended shortly after statehood was granted in 1845. He had continued to hold a federal judicial position but resigned on November 11 after he failed to be elected by the legislature to a circuit judgeship. His standing at Pensacola had not been harmed. As a local newspaper later declared, "The able and dignified manner in which he fulfilled the duties of the Judiciary, stamped him as a jurist of considerable legal attainments."[32] Ann Elizabeth Jordan died at Pensacola on February 1, 1846, and her widower thereafter practiced law at the town. During 1845–49 Jordan edited *The Florida Democrat, and Mechanic's and Workingman's Advocate* and served by appointment of President James K. Polk as collector of customs for the port.[33]

In the remaining years of his life, Jordan's partisan leanings earned him renown in West Florida. "He was looked upon for many years as the leader of the Democratic party in this county," remembered a local man, "and was familiarly styled the 'old War Horse' of the Democracy." Jordan died, still at Pensacola, probably at age seventy-two, on January 26, 1872. Noted an obituary, "He had been an invalid for several months before his death, and we trust that in his relief from the sufferings of this world he has found a happy eternity."[34]

William Marvin, Southern District Superior Court Judge, 1839–1845

For more than a decade following his 1828 appointment, Judge James Webb of the Southern District significantly aided the rational development of admiralty and salvage law. His publications earned him national and international repute, and his practical approach to the problems of salvage and wrecking permitted him to begin regulating the profession while defending its more reputable practitioners. In 1838, though, Webb determined to seek his fortunes in the republic of Texas. He attempted to arrange the appointment of his successor, but he learned to his chagrin—as Western District Judge Dillon Jordan, Jr., soon would—that his connections and achievements afforded him little influence against the needs of presidential politics. Still, while William Marvin was not the man Webb preferred, he would carry on and expand upon the traditions pioneered by his predecessor.

The Southern District's future judge was born April 14, 1808, at Fairfield, Herkimer County, New York, the son of Selden and Charlotte Pratt Marvin. Soon after the event, the family moved to a farm near Dryden in Tompkins County. There, in a small log cabin, William grew, working on the farm and attending local schools. At age fifteen he assumed teaching responsibilities, but within three years wanderlust compelled him to undertake a tour of discovery. He "walked the greater part of the way" to Bladensburg, Maryland.[35] At that town and later at Frederick City, he taught school and read law. In 1830 he achieved admission as an "Attorney and Counsellor at Law in the Courts of Maryland."[36]

At age twenty-two, a proud Marvin returned to the family farm and his widowed and remarried father. "I had brought home with me good clothes, a license to practice law in Maryland and three hundred and fifty dollars in good bank bills," he remembered. "I was in good health and fine looking," he continued, "being about five feet eleven inches in height and weighing one hundred and fifty pounds. My hair was black. My beard was black and thick but kept closely shaven." The lawyer added, "I gave a part of the money to my father."[37] His enthusiasm at being home diminished somewhat when he found that New York would not recognize his law license. To overcome the problem he entered a three-year clerkship, during which his father, stepmother, and an older brother died of fever. William settled the estates and arranged homes for his seven orphaned siblings. In 1834 he successfully completed a rigorous examination and was admitted to the New York bar.[38]

The young man's Phelps, New York, law practice proved short-lived. In 1835 Marvin traveled on business to Florida, visiting Jacksonville, St. Augustine, and nearby locales. He made the acquaintance of many prominent individuals, among them Charles Downing. The future congressional delegate, aware of a vacancy in the office of district attorney for the Southern District, brought the personable Democrat to the attention of Florida's then delegate Joseph M. White. White, in turn, urged President Andrew Jackson to offer Marvin the vacant position. Jackson accommodated the delegate, and in the summer a commission was issued.[39]

Marvin's career as a federal appointee began ominously but afterward proceeded more smoothly. He received his district attorney's commission at Phelps, and, little appreciating Jackson's temper, advised that he would remain there for a time to arrange his affairs. A presidential order directing his immediate relocation to Key West changed his mind soon enough. Once at the island, he was charmed in spite of its "millions of mosquitoes." He later recalled, "I became an inhabitant of Key West in October . . . [and the] whole population was then not very far from four hundred souls."[40] Within the small community he quickly made friends. Judge Webb, for instance, he found to be "a good lawyer[,] an impartial judge, and a genial gentleman."[41] Other friends came to him through his boarding house, an establishment overseen by Ellen Mallory. The "kind-hearted" widow and the district attorney grew close when she nursed him to health after an attack of yellow fever. He took an especial interest in her "bright and intelligent" son Stephen, teaching him the law and serving as mentor to the future United States senator and Confederate navy secretary.[42]

In Key West's friendly climate Marvin enjoyed lucrative professional opportunities. His official duties amounted to "very little." Since no statute barred him from practicing law, he grasped for a "full share as a lawyer." He reminisced, "In the four years that I was at the bar, I had earned, over and above my expenses of living, about fourteen thousand dollars." The sober-minded attorney then used his good fortune to plan for the future. "This money I invested in Chautauqua County, New York, in bond and mortgage securities," he explained. "Thus invested it became the nucleus of other savings in after life."[43]

The attorney's friendships and good fortune led him into politics. Before long the local Democratic party, although loosely organized and more social than political, coalesced around him and Mallory. In 1836 Monroe County residents elected Marvin a member of the territorial council, and two years later he was chosen as the Southern District's man in the new territorial senate. The district attorney similarly represented Monroe County in the St. Joseph constitutional convention during December 1838 and January 1839. In that capacity he served on the judiciary committee and helped to design the state's court system.[44]

In the 1830s Florida's frontier status encouraged a rough-and-tumble, if not outright violent, political atmosphere, and Marvin's career nearly was cut short because of that fact. Duels were common, and, in his first legislative session at Tallahassee, the new council member only narrowly avoided one. The quarrel came in January 1837 and involved Franklin County's Fred Wood, who possessed the reputation of a fighting man. Marvin explained:

> [Wood] was interested in having a bill for the charter of a Bank for St. Joseph, passed by the Council. I opposed the passage of the bill and made a little speech in the Council against it. I had been fully indoctrinated in the Tom-Benton theory of a hard money currency and was accustomed to the use of such money at Key West. I had also read a good deal about the miserable "*red dog*" banks of Michigan and other western States. I was naturally, therefore, opposed to the Charter of any bank for Florida that should have power to issue a currency.[45]

The Monroe County representative's attack on banks infuriated the bill's sponsor, who took the matter personally. "After I had done speaking," Marvin recalled, "he said of me to several members sitting around, in rather an undertone, but still, loud enough for me to hear distinctly: 'He is a damned rascal! damn him, I'll cut his damned ears off.'" Without considering the consequences, Marvin retorted, "You are a damned liar; damn you!" Marvin's friend James D. Westcott quickly filled the future judge's pocket with a loaded pistol and warned him of an imminent attack by Wood. For the moment, though, peace prevailed.[46]

At the council session on the following day, the dispute picked up in intensity. Several members urged Wood to apologize to Marvin, but his effort did not extend so far. "Mr. Speaker," he declared, "I do not know whether or not I ought to apologize to the Council for any of my conduct, but if the gentlemen think that I ought to do so, why, I now make the apology. I apologize to the Council, but as to the member from Monroe, I do *not* apologize to him." At that point Marvin began to seek out seconds for the impending duel, first asking Leon County's George T. Ward, who referred him to Hector Braden. The cool-headed Braden then approached Wood, but only after Marvin directed that "you can carry no message from me except a written challenge to fight." Fortunately for Marvin, Braden assuaged Wood's wounded pride, and the sure-shot marksman from Franklin County extended Marvin an apology. In later years, Marvin realized his good fortune. "My life was probably saved by the good sense and sound discretion of Colonel Braden," he wrote. "I thank God in my old age for this safe deliverance."[47]

By 1838 Marvin was well established in Key West legal, social, and political circles. When Judge Webb decided to leave the community, though, he turned for a successor to attorney Charles Walker, a New Yorker who had resided on the island a mere sixteen months. The district attorney's friends rallied around him, notwithstanding the judge's wishes, and pressed his candidacy. President Martin Van Buren realized that in Democrat Marvin he had a loyal political ally with intimate connections within the territory. As such, on March 11, 1839, he commissioned Marvin as superior court judge for the Southern District. A full four-year term followed on April 21, 1840.[48]

On the Southern District bench, Marvin followed in Webb's footsteps. He had gathered experience with admiralty practice and salvage laws as an attorney in the previous four years. Early in his tenure he capitalized on that knowledge by compiling his *Rules of the Superior Court for the Southern Judicial District of Florida: In Admiralty*. In 1858 he added *The Law of Wreck and Salvage*, an internationally acclaimed treatise that systematized the jurisprudence of wrecking and salvage. It served as a catalyst for raising the wrecking industry from a type of subtle piracy to a legitimate business in which wreckers and underwriters could settle or litigate claims and disputes with reasonable expectation that justice would prevail.[49]

Marvin's publications built upon the early work done by Webb and so did his approach to wreckers. He demanded adherence to his court's policies, but he favored the salvors when he felt that circumstances warranted it. As he noted in one opinion, liberal compensation granted to wreckers in his district was justified because the Florida salvor relied on wrecking for his livelihood, outfitted his vessel at significant expense, and spent "months and years near the place of danger." As a consequence, concluded the judge, the "interests of commerce and humanity [required] that his steady and active devotion to his regular employment be encouraged and rewarded."[50]

Southern Florida's volatile wrecker population and Key West's highly competitive admiralty bar for the most part reached happy accommodations with Judge Marvin. His Democratic politics continued to be popular on the island, as well. When statehood was granted in 1845, the Democrat-controlled legislature accordingly elected him judge of the new southern circuit, but he declined the position in order to practice law and start a family. On October 15, 1846, he married Harriette N. Foote. Marvin described the Cooperstown, New York, native as possessing "medium size, fair skin, with grey eyes and dark hair . . . [with] a cheerful and gay disposition, and graceful and easy manners . . . well educated in the schools and in domestic life." Sadly, the bride's health declined at Key West, and she died on March 31, 1848, six months after the birth of daughter Hattie.[51]

The former superior judge's judicial career resumed in 1847, when President James K. Polk appointed him as a United States district judge. He held the Key West position for fifteen years before he resigned for health reasons during the Civil War. Unlike many federal officials in the state, he had refused to deliver his court into the hands of Confederate authorities, a position he was able to maintain since Union forces occupied the island throughout the conflict. His stance on secession had been equivocal. He opposed immediate action after President Abraham Lincoln's November 1860 election but urged fellow residents rather to "wait for the border States and secede with them."[52]

From 1863 to 1865 Marvin practiced law in New York City, but the Civil War's end prompted his return to Florida. President Andrew Johnson appointed the former slaveowner as provisional governor, and in the position he prepared the state for readmission to the Union. His policies during the period are discussed in chapter 11, but they were marked by the conservative stances he displayed throughout his Key West residence. Aided by his friend and private secretary Samuel J. Douglas, he supervised revisions of the state constitution and elections for legislative and other state offices. Rewarding his efforts, the new legislature—still controlled by Florida's prewar power structure—elected him United States senator in December 1865. His old friend Wisconsin senator James R. Doolittle presented his credentials, but the Senate refused to seat him.[53]

After the Senate rejection, Marvin made a permanent home in New York, although Florida concerns remained close to his heart. When the Congress in 1867 enacted military Reconstruction, he declined to participate in the proceedings of a new constitutional convention. "I considered at the time," he recorded, "the enfranchisement of the negro so soon after he had come out of a condition of slavery, as unnecessary for the protection of his liberty, offensive to his late masters and in many other points of view wholly injudicious." He added, "In this manner, I became disconnected from the politics of Florida."[54]

Although he occasionally spoke out through letters to newspapers, Marvin's life after 1867 was marked more by quiet and reflection. He married again on July 11, 1886, to Elizabeth Riddle Jewett, and the couple lived at her Skaneateles, New York, home. Mostly, he gardened and read, but he did find time to write a new book, *The Authorship of the Four Gospels.* He died at Skaneateles on July 9, 1902.[55]

Alfred Balch, Middle District Superior Court Judge, 1840–1841

In the case of William Marvin, a president's political expedient served, as it had throughout the territorial period, to justify a judicial appointment. That such a dynamic extended to replacement of a popular, but politically unsupportive, sitting judge is evident in the lives of Thomas Randall and his successor, Alfred Balch. Balch's career offers another insight, as well. It portrays the continuing influence in Florida affairs of its first American governor, Andrew Jackson.

Balch's biography discloses a privileged background and powerful connections similar to many of the territory's other judicial officers. He was born on September 17, 1785, at Georgetown, Maryland, to Stephen Bloomer and Elizabeth Balch. After attending local schools, he entered the College of New Jersey (later Princeton University), from which he graduated with an A.M. degree in 1805. Subsequently he practiced law at Nashville, Tennessee. Following marriage, he and his wife Mary had a son, Alfred Newman Balch.[56]

At Nashville, Balch shared in the area's prosperity. He developed a plantation, gaining as his neighbor Andrew Jackson. A friendship blossomed between the two men close enough to permit Balch to offer a gentle lecture to his temperamental fellow planter. "Those who borrow are encouraged in their extravagant modes of dressing and living which are greater than their means will justify," he informed Jackson on one occasion. "Many are building little palaces, furnishing them in very expensive style, and . . . [dress their] children as though they were the sons and daughters of Princes."[57]

The connection with Jackson led Balch to federal preferment. Likely with the president's encouragement, he backed the presidential candidacy of Jackson's vice president and political ally Martin Van Buren. Van Buren, in 1837, then designated the Democratic lawyer as an agent to the Creek Indians, at a time of unrest when Florida Creeks had joined with Seminoles and blacks in fighting the Second Seminole War. Jackson interceded for his friend again in 1840, when Middle Florida superior court judge Thomas Randall's term was due to expire. Neither Jackson nor Van Buren desired to reward the prominent Whig by reappointment, and with Jackson's urging Van Buren turned to Democrat Balch. A commission followed on March 14.[58]

The new jurist presided in his Florida court little more than one year, although that time did not pass without incident. Balch's trip to the territory proved arduous, given bad roads and flooding. His predecessor's Tallahassee-area friends greeted him in a less than cordial manner, with some—such as Richard Keith Call—articulating their resentments. The political climate worsened the situation. "[T]he condition of affairs in this territory is deplorable," he reported to Van Buren in April 1840. "The leading men are divided into bitter parties and violence is the order of the day." He continued, "Heretofore the banking influence has been predominant, but now the most determined resistance is made to it and in fact it is tottering to its foundation." Balch entertained concerns about the president's strength in that electoral year but mistook Middle Florida Whig planter courtesy for Democratic political support. "Hardly any body can be found here," he informed Van Buren, "who is not in favour at least by *profession* of your re-election."[59]

The letter's mention of violence reflected an immediate concern. Judge William Marvin, in 1837, narrowly had escaped a duel while serving as a legislator, but others were not so lucky. A series of bloody encounters culminated the same year in a duel between Augustus Alston and Leigh Read. One historian described the clash as "essentially between the heads of the two rival political parties in Tallahassee."[60] Read killed his opponent. Thereafter, Alston's brother Willis returned to Florida from Texas and, on a third attempt, murdered Democrat Read. Normally Balch would have heard the criminal case against Alston, but the judge's worsening health in April 1841 forced the substitution of Apalachicola Judge Richard C. Allen. Even then, justice was delayed, if not denied. Alston escaped from jail and returned to Texas. He was lynched there in 1842 after a related killing.[61]

Although health concerns plagued Balch's stay in Florida, he was determined to render creditable service within his understanding of his responsibilities. "I shall make it my object to pursue an honest course," he recorded. "An honest man has nothing to fear before those amongst whom his lot is cast."[62] In at least one instance he was willing to reject the federal government's legal stance in order to support what he considered the honest initiative of local officialdom. The case involved William Pope DuVal and expenditures he had authorized while territorial governor. DuVal denied owing reimbursement to the United States and claimed instead that substantial sums were owed him for personal funds spent for Indians' supplies and advances to the territorial treasury. Balch agreed that DuVal's intentions had been proper and awarded him in excess of $18,000, despite government protests.[63]

The rigors of judicial responsibilities in a violent and troubled era wore at Balch's constitution. By spring 1841 "excessive labor in the discharge of official duties as Judge of the U States of America for the District of Middle Florida" had rendered him vulnerable to fever. A physician advised the judge to seek medical care in New York City, after which treatment he rested at Newport, Rhode Island. The treatment failed to restore Balch's health, and, on August 5, he resigned his judicial office, noting to President John Tyler that "I should have resigned my office of Judge several weeks ago."[64] He returned to Nashville and, in 1842, recommenced his law practice. He died there on June 21, 1853.[65]

Isaac H. Bronson, Eastern District Superior Court Judge, 1840–1845

President Martin Van Buren's 1840 election-year decisions caused a number of reverberations in Florida beyond Alfred Balch's designation as Middle District judge. The previous year, for example, Van Buren had replaced Governor Richard Keith Call with Eastern District judge Robert Raymond Reid, Jr. The vacancy thus created permitted the president to satisfy an old friend in need of a job, solidify his own political base in New York, and oblige East Florida Democrats. In the appointment of Isaac H. Bronson, he met each of the goals, and Florida gained one of its outstanding nineteenth-century residents.

Bronson's family boasted deep and respectable roots in Connecticut. His mother Hepzibah's father was lawyer Joseph Hopkins, and his father Ethel served at Waterbury as justice of the peace and member of the state legislature. Two years after Isaac's October 16, 1802, birth, though, the family removed to Jefferson County, New York. There Ethel pursued banking and investments. By the time of his 1825 death, he headed the Jefferson County Bank.[66]

Isaac's education and early career seemingly proceeded at an even pace. He attended local schools and read law under Micah Sterling, later a United States congressman. He was admitted to the New York bar in 1822 and opened a practice at Watertown in Jefferson County. He also married, and he and his wife Sophronia thereafter had two daughters, Gertrude and Emma. Professional standing and an interest in politics led to his 1836 election as a Democrat to the United States House of Representatives. During his one term in the body, he chaired the committee on territories. In that capacity he unsuccessfully proposed the admission of Florida as a state and—at the behest of congressional delegate Charles Downing—more successfully sponsored a bill to create a bicameral legislature for the territory. Once enacted, the 1838 law established a house of representatives composed of twenty-nine members and an eleven-member senate.[67]

The Whig resurgence of 1838 doomed Bronson's congressional career, and that change in the political environment presaged problems for the ex-representative. While successful professionally, Bronson's personal fortune had remained small. According to an 1835 state census, he owned only one acre in Watertown, three cattle, two horses, and two hogs. After leaving Congress a possibility for secure employment was presented to him, but due to poor health and financial concerns he declined the position of New York state circuit judge in order to resume his legal practice. For two years Bronson worked at the law in partnership with Micah Sterling, who by then was his brother-in-law. His health worsened under the strain, and in 1840 Sterling approached the president on his partner's behalf. Van Buren, who had not yet filled Reid's Florida vacancy, saw the potential for advantage to himself and to Bronson. On March 14 he appointed the former congressman as Eastern District superior court judge. President John Tyler later recommissioned him to a second term in 1844.[68]

Bronson received a warmer welcome in Florida than did some of his counterparts. Dillon Jordan's appointment two years previously, for example, had been met with wariness. "A North Carolina gentleman named Judon has been imported for Judge of the Western District," noted a Tallahassee newspaper at the time. "He may be a good man for aught we know—but we go against new importations and shall take occasion hereafter to say our say on this point."[69]

Bronson, to the contrary, was well known through his congressional work on Florida's behalf and was viewed with relief by Whigs and anti-statehood Democrats angry at Judge Reid's politicking from the bench. "The Honorable I. H. Bronson . . . arrived in this city on Monday last," the St. Augustine *News* reported on June 5, 1840. "Judge B., though a stranger among us, comes preceded by a high reputation of moral integrity, talent and industry. The stream of justice will now flow, we can believe, in an even channel and that the humblest individual of society will be protected by vigorous enforcement of [the] law." The editor added, "[W]ith a total separation of all *political* and *Judicial* character, the friends of order may expect to find in Judge Bronson, all of those qualities 'which were wanting in Judge Reid.'"[70]

In East Florida the judge assumed many of the same responsibilities faced by his predecessors. His docket was crowded with disputes, among them holdover land-claim cases. The burden forced Bronson in 1843 to object to a plan calling for removal of the public archives, including Spanish records, to the territorial capital. "There is not a term of my Court at St. Augustine that some of these records are not required particularly in all land cases," he protested. "I have had frequent occasion also to consult them in reference to the claims for losses of 1812 & 13—they are constantly referred to by the people on the subject of land titles, perhaps as much as the Co[unty] records."[71]

Crowded dockets and the availability of records were two of Bronson's many concerns. Although East Florida's population had grown in the previous two decades, most county seats were located in remote and sparsely settled areas, forcing upon the judge difficult and hazardous journeys along poor roads. Accommodations often ranged from the unpleasant to the unbearable. At the time of his June 1840 arrival, the Second Seminole War was ongoing, a fact adding to the challenges and dangers that he faced. One month previously, the hostilities had reached close to St. Augustine when a Seminole war party attacked a theatrical troupe, killing three. The frustrated judge finally joined other residents to demand forced relocation "to effect a termination of the war by the removal of the Indians to their destined homes West of the Mississippi."[72] Four years later conditions had improved little. When the legislative council created Marion County that year, the military post at Fort King was designated as its temporary seat. To obtain quarters and a courtroom, Bronson appealed to General William Jenkins Worth for assistance. As a result, a two-story cupola-topped barracks became Marion's first courthouse.[73]

Through the rigors of the job and the times, Bronson distinguished himself. His efforts on behalf of the Episcopal church drew praise, and, as an increasingly influential and highly esteemed Mason, he was elected Most Excellent

Grand High Priest of Florida. When statehood arrived, the popularity and high regard resulted in his election by the legislature as judge of the Western Circuit. Like his Southern District counterpart William Marvin, he declined the honor, preferring to await a federal appointment. The position came in 1846, when he was named United States district judge for the state. One year later Congress divided Florida into northern and southern districts, with Bronson receiving the judgeship of the former and Marvin of the latter. Bronson continued in that position until his death.[74]

Although Judge Bronson's principal court was located at St. Augustine, memory of him is more closely connected with the city of Palatka. In 1849, when Putnam County was created, he prepared a charter for the town and petitioned for its designation as county seat. He also donated the land upon which the county courthouse was erected. On a ten-acre tract at Sunny Point, overlooking a bend of the St. Johns River, he planted an orange grove and, after 1852, built a home of hand-cut cypress. Within the building's walls he entertained friends from throughout Florida, including neighbors Reid, first-elected state governor William D. Moseley, and county namesake Benjamin Putnam. Bronson died there on August 13, 1855. "His demise was very sudden, but not unexpected, as he has been in a low state of health for several years," reported a Tallahassee editor. "He had won during his long service on the Bench, the entire respect and confidence of the people of our State for his learning, and their affection by his impartiality. His loss will be deeply regretted."[75]

Samuel Williams Carmack, Apalachicola District Superior Court Judge, 1841–1845

Through Martin Van Buren's appointment of Isaac H. Bronson as superior court judge for the Eastern District, the urgencies of presidential politics had held sway over Florida judiciary personnel decisions. In 1840, though, Whig candidate William Henry Harrison defeated his Democratic opponent, Van Buren. Harrison then died on April 4, 1841, of pneumonia. His successor, Vice President John Tyler of Virginia, determined to change presidential patronage practices. Instead of the spoils system, he adopted a policy designed to ensure the integrity of judicial offices. The July 30, 1841, death of Apalachicola District judge Richard C. Allen afforded him an early opportunity to effect his plans. In those circumstances, Samuel Williams Carmack of Tennessee became the territory's newest superior court judge.[76]

Carmack's family had helped to press westward the edge of European settlement on the southern frontier or, as one account put it, "[His parents] were descendents from the bold and adventurous Pioneers, or first settlers of the then wilderness of Middle Tennessee."[77] Samuel was born in Davidson County, Tennessee, on January 9, 1802. He received "such an Education as the Common Schools of the Country afforded," after which he read law in the Nashville offices of Judge John Overton, a close associate of Andrew Jackson. From Overton, he gained a particular perspective on the law. "It was here," one friend remembered, "that he contracted that love for the 'Ancient Fathers of the Law' which harmonized so well with the taste of his venerable preceptor, and which caused him to predict for the Student a career of honorable distinction." The friend continued, "He studied Law as a science—a system of sound ethics, not as an art by which he was to be enriched at the expence of his fellow man."[78]

Overton's prophecy for his student proved accurate. In 1824 Carmack opened a legal office at Fayetteville, where he specialized in circuit and county court practice. In addition to his legal skills, he contributed to his efforts a concern for even-handedness and an open, friendly disposition. "Disdaining the petty arts and devices of the Demagogue," it was said, "he flattered no man for his wealth, his station or his influence." Rather, he was "Kind and courteous" and "yet more particularly the friend of the poor and oppressed."[79] A Florida editor later noted, "He brought from Tennessee the reputation of an erudite and accomplished lawyer, and a most estimable man."[80]

From youth, Carmack suffered from a frail constitution, a condition that led him to Florida. In the winter of 1837 at Nashville, he was stricken with "a disease which so prostrated his system, enfeebled by previous ill health as to render a removal to the milder climate of Florida necessary."[81] He and his wife, Margaret Greer Carmack, accordingly relocated their family to Tallahassee the following year, and the lawyer resumed his practice in the territory. His subsequent acts enhanced the reputation for probity and decency that he brought with him, a fact which friends brought to President Tyler's attention after Judge Allen's death in the summer of 1841. In Carmack, Tyler believed he had found the type of man who should be a judge. He commissioned him to a four-year term on the Apalachicola District superior court on September 13.[82]

Carmack's contemporary, Middle Florida judge Alfred Balch, had commenced his duties the previous year to discover how seriously the territory's economic problems had added to his court's responsibilities. At Apalachicola, Carmack found the same situation, and the problems continued through his tenure on the bench. Bankruptcy proceedings necessarily formed a good bit of his workload, something he discussed with Secretary of State Daniel Webster in 1843. "Twenty persons have been discharged and Eighteen applications are still pending," Carmack wrote. "As congress has probably ere this repealed the bankrupt law it is perhaps unnecessary for me to reply to the balance of your communication. I will however remark that I know of no modification of the law which I think would be useful. Its effects, in this District, have been to restore to business and active employment a number of useful and enterprising men who, until their discharge, were in a state of hopeless indebtedness." The judge concluded, "I know of no evils which have resulted from the operation of the law."[83]

In bankruptcy and other matters brought before his court, Carmack earnestly endeavored to do right as he saw it. Many Floridians believed that he succeeded. One newspaperman declared that he was "just, benevolent, wise and good," while a fellow lawyer asserted:

> As a judge he was humane—but firm and inflexible—clear of apprehension, of quickness sufficient, though not hasty; perspicuous in his opinions and instructions. To which may be added a perfect command of himself, never manifesting impatience, or betraying spleen or ill nature to any who had business in his Courts. To borrow the language of another we may well say, that when the spotless Ermine of the Judicial robe fell on Samuel W. Carmack, it touched nothing not as spotless as itself.[84]

Statehood and the elimination of federal superior courts came to the territory four years after Carmack's appointment. Florida's first state legislature considered him, along with fellow judge Dillon Jordan, Jr., and Apalachicola District Attorney George Sydney Hawkins, for the new western circuit judgeship. The Democratic body, not surprisingly, turned to Hawkins over Whig Carmack, an ironic result for the defeated judge as he earlier had appointed Hawkins to office. The solons did not turn their back completely on the well-regarded jurist. After William Marvin declined the southern circuit bench, they selected Carmack after thirty ballots for the position. One Whig journal hailed the election as evidence "of a spirit of liberality for which we had not given full credit to our democratic legislature."[85]

Legislative honors did not suffice to resolve the health concerns that had brought Carmack to Florida. Because of continuing weakness and indisposition, he declined the circuit judgeship and returned to his law office at Tallahassee. Reportedly, he "[enjoyed] it with as much arder and assiduity as his waning health permitted."[86] Carmack died while visiting at his friend and physician Edward C. Bellamy's Jackson County plantation on December 18, 1849, and was buried at Marianna in the Episcopal church cemetery. "He has left a rich legacy to his widow and children," observed one obituary, "in a character which it is the fortune of few in this world to achieve and sustain."[87]

Samuel J. Douglas, Middle District Superior Court Judge, 1841–1845; Supreme Court Associate Justice, 1866–1868

President John Tyler's desire to emphasize integrity in the judicial selection process evidenced itself during 1841 in the designation of Samuel Williams Carmack as Apalachicola District judge. In Tyler's second Florida appointment, which came one month later, his commitment was less evident although still visible. In fairness, the president's first choice—William Henry Brockenbrough—declined the office. As had been the case with Carmack, Tyler reached with Brockenbrough for a territorial resident where his predecessors generally had opted for non-Floridians. Still, Brockenbrough represented the highly political side of the legal profession. He had arrived in the territory from the president's home state of Virginia in 1837, and the next year he had been elected to the legislative council from Mosquito (later Orange) County. A Democrat, Martin Van Buren had appointed him the same year as district attorney for the Apalachicola District. In 1840 Brackenridge backed Whig William Henry Harrison for the presidency, while successfully pursuing election as Democratic senator for West Florida. Members of both parties tended to view him with suspicion as an opportunist.[88]

Thus, Tyler's first choice to fill the Middle Florida vacancy caused by Alfred Balch's resignation, while it may have centered on a politically oriented opportunist, dealt with an individual knowledgeable in Florida law and affairs. The president's next attempt settled on family friend from Virginia, and a young one at that. Samuel J. Douglas was born on October 10, 1812, at Petersburg. His educational credentials were excellent, including graduation with distinguished honor from the University of Virginia. For a decade thereafter he practiced the law in Southampton County. An acquaintance described him as "of fine presence—handsome in face and superb in figure—head and features large, open and manly, sprightly of humor and wit, social, urbane, and a sound lawyer, he made an agreeable impression on every one." His political beliefs eventually brought him into the Democratic camp, but early on his sentiments paralleled Tyler's. As the acquaintance added, "He was a very popular man with the old Whig party."[89]

Naturally, among those upon whom Douglas made an agreeable impression was Tyler, and the connection launched the younger man's Florida career. William Marvin later recalled fondly a dinner the three men shared at the Tyler White House, in celebration of a Douglas visit to the national capital. The president admired the young lawyer, remarking, according to Douglas family lore, that Samuel "was not afraid of the devil himself."[90]

When Brockenbrough declined the offer of the Middle Florida judgeship, he may have prompted Tyler to direct his attention to their fellow Virginian. "As we have no one now fit for the station," he observed, "I hope none will be appointed from Florida."[91] The president accepted the advice and named Douglas on October 12, 1841, recommissioning him for a four-year term on February 15, 1842.[92] At age twenty-nine, Douglas became the youngest man to sit on the territorial court of appeals.

Douglas's four years on the superior court bench tested him severely. Economic distress strained the fabric of society. Disorder and violence intruded themselves into daily life, and the wheels of justice turned slowly when they turned at all. "From the delay in executing the Laws," Douglas reported three months after his November 1841 arrival at Tallahassee, "society had become disorganized, and the best Citizens were unable to withstand the threats of violence made by the offenders." In the situation Douglas reacted sternly and with determination. "I found that it would require, firmness, promptness & decision, and that it would be necessary to make examples of some of the more hardened offenders, before the Laws & its officers would be respected. I have pursued this course with unwavering firmness, and it affords me pleasure to be able to say to you [that] I have succeeded beyond my most sanguine expectations."[93]

The judge's initiative met with some success, although it came at a price. He received threats of physical violence, and other, more sophisticated, malefactors attempted to "coax" him. The problems came not simply from common criminals but often from prominent Middle Florida planters and businessmen whose bank and other investments had soured, leaving them unable to repay loans or to secure new sources of credit. The men opposed Douglas's holding court since, absent a court session, no judgments could be entered against them for debt. Allies—many of them plaintiffs' attorneys such as Brockenbrough, Leslie A. Thompson, Thomas Baltzell, and David S. Walker—supported the judge's approach, and he persevered. "I have been engaged in Court from Ten in the morning, until nine at night (and very often much later)," he declared in February 1842. "I have disposed of Two thousand cases, and as many yet remain to be disposed of." He added, "I shall not be disengaged from the duties of the bench before the first of June; and shall have disposed of Four thousand cases, common law, criminal & chancery, having had a continuous session of six months."[94]

One particular case, although it ended with mixed results, was used by Douglas and his allies, including *Florida Sentinel* editor Joshua Knowles, to help their anticrime campaign. In early January 1842 Irishman Thomas Horan stabbed James Ramsey to death in a drunken brawl at Tallahassee. Douglas had him quickly tried. With conviction in hand, Douglas then delivered a condemnatory speech to the defendant so intense that Horan broke down and, amidst tears, begged for his life. The judge thereupon sentenced him to execution by hanging, after which Knowles published the judge's speech and attendant details on the front page of his newspaper. Doubtlessly, word of the judge's serious intent got out, but Horan avoided death nonetheless. He escaped from the local jail and, despite suffering a wound, got away, never to be heard from again.[95]

The responsibilities of the superior court bench included service on the territorial court of appeals. Few of its opinions have survived, although one written by Douglas appeared in an 1843 issue of *The Army and Navy Chronicle*. In it the judge overturned a local court decision releasing army private Thomas Downs from active duty due to a claim that Downs was not a United States citizen at the time of his enlistment. Reflecting his get-tough attitude, the judge held "that the enlistment of an alien for a term of years in the land or naval service . . . is nothing more than a contract" and that such an agreement "is unquestionably binding."[96]

Douglas's judicial stance made him both friends and enemies, but the friends were not sufficiently numerous in the 1845 legislature to secure him a judgeship after statehood. Instead he turned to the practice of law at Tallahassee until President Zachary Taylor in 1849 designated him collector of customs at Key West. He resigned the position in 1853 and followed the legal profession on the island until the Civil War. In 1847, after the death of a first wife, he remarried to Elizabeth "Lizzie" Brown, daughter of the state's second governor Thomas Brown. Their Key West home became recognized as a scene of gaiety, charm, and hospitality, as well as a gathering spot for prominent visitors and community members.[97]

The Civil War's advent caused Douglas's expulsion from Key West by United States military authorities. He supported secession once his native state of Virginia withdrew from the Union, and he relocated there. During the conflict he served as a Confederate military judge, but, at its end, he returned to Florida. At Tallahassee in the summer of 1865, he encountered provisional governor William Marvin who, happy to see his old Key West friend, asked Douglas to serve as his private secretary.[98] "His hair was white as snow," Marvin remembered. "[He] had been through the war and had . . . lost all of his property."[99] As Marvin's aide, Douglas helped to prepare the state for readmission to the Union under presidential Reconstruction.

The postwar Reconstruction efforts of Marvin and Douglas ended quickly but not before Douglas achieved a distinction held by no other judge of Florida's territorial period. The state's newly revised charter provided for gubernatorial appointment of supreme court justices. When Justice Augustus E. Maxwell resigned from the court in 1866, Governor David S. Walker—himself a former justice—placed Douglas on the high court. During his two years of service, the court did not conduct a great deal of business due to the uncertainties of federal Reconstruction policy. Douglas contributed, despite the problems, by mediating disputes between local officials and occupation forces. Of him as a justice, a fellow lawyer declared, "[He] illustrated his judicial character by the ability and impartiality which distinguished his judgments and the opinions he pronounced."[100]

After congressional Reconstruction ushered in a new Florida supreme court in mid–1868, Douglas resumed a law practice. Five years later, on November 14, 1873, he succumbed to a stroke at his Tallahassee home. His friend Marvin summarized his life:

> As a Judge, Judge Douglas was capable, and honest; as a practicing lawyer, loyal to this clients, and in arguing his causes before a court or jury was often eloquent. As a patriot he loved the whole Union, especially his native state, as a husband he was faithful and affectionate, as a father, considerate and indulgent. He was moderately fond of society, easy and graceful in his bearing, fond of dancing and always courteous and agreeable. He enjoyed, too, a dinner with his friends, at his own house or their, but was moderate both in his eating and drinking. In his church relations he was an Episcopalian.[101]

His fellow state capital lawyers added, "The members of the bar record with satisfaction, in the solemnity of the occasion, that no stain of dishonor rests on his professional or private character, and point to his career as a fit example for the imitation of those who are to follow the honorable profession he adorned by his life and conduct."[102]

Part Two

Antebellum Statehood, 1845–1860

Chapter 5

Florida in the Antebellum Era

Florida's years of statehood before secession and Civil War witnessed remarkable changes, and they began with receipt of important news that, although it was not perceived as such at the time, hinted at a tumultuous future. On June 6, 1845, former provisional governor and president Andrew Jackson died at his Tennessee estate. The word arrived at Tallahassee eighteen days later. The first state legislature thereupon adjourned its second day's session out of respect to the man who had led Florida into United States's possession and whose influence during the preceding twenty-four years had been pronounced throughout its political, governmental, professional, and social circles. Although the man's loss was felt deeply by many, his legacies to Florida remained intact. He had attracted to it scores of men who themselves or through their acquaintances exercised economic and political power. Further, the Democratic party, whose birth he had overseen, had brought the territory into the Union. Fifteen years later the party would lead efforts for the destruction of the same bonds.[1]

Few Floridians in 1845 paid careful attention to portents of future violent struggles, such as the sensational trial of abolitionist Jonathan Walker held at Pensacola the previous year. Instead they looked to good times in the aftermath of Indian war, economic depression, and the resultant plagues of crime and violence. They ached for prosperity, for which they had paid so great a price, and they were not to be disappointed.[2]

Several factors combined to help Floridians on the road to better days. First, after more than six years of conflict, the Second Seminole War had ended in 1842 with a cautious peace. Most Indians and their black vassals had been shipped to the American West, and the three hundred or more who remained were restricted to lands deep in the peninsula east and south of the Peace River. In 1855 a sequel to the struggle erupted, but its 1858 conclusion saw additional natives, including Chief Billy Bowlegs, transported West, with only a few Indians still seeking refuge deep in the peninsula's southern swamps and prairies.[3]

While the fighting had devastated broad portions of the territory, especially in East Florida, the contest had provided, as well, infrastructure improvements necessary for subsequent development. Funded by congressional appropriations, army teams and contract crews had surveyed and constructed roads, bridges, and ports; improved inland waterways; and erected buildings at sites such as Fort Pierce soon to be used by civilian settlers. The location of supply depots, maintenance centers, and headquarters facilities had spurred growth of towns and villages, particularly Jacksonville, Key West, Pensacola, and Tampa. Congressional generosity, in the form of the Armed Occupation Acts of 1844 and 1845, extended grants of acreage to families willing to move onto the newly opened lands and to protect them from further depredations.[4]

As war crisis eased, so, too, did financial concerns. The national economic depression induced by the Panic of 1837 abated with northern industrial expansion, urbanization, agricultural innovations, westward immigration, and the growth of the southern cotton kingdom to meet international textile-industry demands. In more recently cultivated cotton lands such as Middle Florida's, prosperity arrived with tremendous impact. Commodity prices, which had trended downward until 1842, rebounded during a time of "phenomenal growth" during the late 1840s and 1850s. Towns that supported the cotton trade—Tallahassee and Apalachicola being leading ones—thrived with the presence of planters and their suppliers.[5]

In the situation, Florida found itself welcoming thousands of new settlers. The total population outside Indian lands in 1830 had amounted to less than 35,000, of whom slightly more than half were white. By the time of statehood fifteen years later, twice as many residents were counted, with the total almost evenly split between whites and blacks, about 10 percent of whom were of mixed blood. In the following five years the population increased by about one-quarter, to 87,445. Florida stood as the least populous of the states, but its rate of increase was substantial. In the next ten years the total rose another 61 percent. In 1860 the state had 77,747 white residents, 61,745 black slaves, and 932 free blacks.[6]

As suggested by the percentages of white and black Floridians, state residents comprised a diverse lot. Black slaves represented the largest single cultural and ethnic group and, by 1860, they totaled a majority of the population in Alachua, Gadsden, Jefferson, Leon, Madison, and Marion counties. Otherwise, a mixed array of humanity stirred the dust of the state's rutted roads and streets. By 1850, for example, 2,700 persons hailed from foreign countries. In great part they were West Indian or Minorcan, but English, French, Spanish,

Irish, and others joined the throng. Most newcomers emigrated from the southeastern states. Still, St. Augustine and Pensacola preserved more cosmopolitan societies rooted in colonial days.[7]

Despite substantial rates of population increase, the greater part of Florida's territory remained barely settled or uninhabited, with the Middle Florida plantation belt marking the great exception. There, by 1845, the culture of the Old South dominated the capital and the cotton counties of Jackson, Gadsden, Leon, Jefferson, and Madison. Within the next fifteen years, planters' needs for new lands extended the cotton belt and its culture into East Florida's Columbia, Alachua, and Marion counties. The largest segment of the cotton area's white population shared similar attitudes toward political and economic issues—and corresponding social values—with their counterparts in the states Florida later would join in secession. Middle Florida's cotton-induced prosperity led the state's regions. By 1860, 70 percent of its $16 million in farm holdings rested in the area. There, too, lived a large majority of the slaves, who created economic security for their masters but posed a continuing threat of uprising.[8]

Middle Florida's Old South world afforded pleasure and comfort to many, but its reality was complicated. "A splendid hospitality was dispensed," typically remembered one Gadsden countian. "Hunting parties were of frequent occurrence and those who never lived that life little know the delights of real living."[9] Nonetheless, few planters enjoyed the luxury of a fictional Tara or Twelve Oaks, and none matched the rice and sugar grandees of South Carolina and Louisiana who owned 1,000 or more laborers each. In Florida, by contrast, only two men owned two hundred or more slaves. In 1850, 217 residents listed themselves on the census as planters, as compared to 5,700 farmers. The dividing line was drawn between those who owned twenty bondsmen or more and those who owned fewer than twenty or none. The average slaveholding for a planter fluctuated slightly above twenty. Most slaveowners—6,000 in 1860—held a single individual or perhaps a family.[10]

The agricultural economy provided little impetus for growth of a middle class in the antebellum era, although factors in port towns and professionals such as lawyers, medical doctors, and ministers often enjoyed social standing. Carpenters, brickmakers, chemists, millwrights, teamsters, tanners, and similarly skilled workers found employment, but industrial development enjoyed little more than modest progress. Some hope in that regard glimmered, though, in the construction of the state's first railroads. By 1860 six lines were operational on at least a limited basis. One interstate connection permitted travel from Pensacola to Alabama, and the Florida Railroad linked the Atlantic Ocean at Fernandina with Cedar Key and the Gulf of Mexico. All told, 401 miles of track, supplemented by a few plank roads, offered hopes of future transportation advances.

The cotton trade, the timber and naval stores industries, related commercial shipping businesses, government programs and expenditures, immigrants' needs for supplies, and railroads in turn encouraged town development. From two settlements worthy of the name in 1821, the state contained nine communities with more than 1,000 inhabitants by 1860. Pensacola and Key West, with economies derived primarily from maritime industries, ranked first and second with fewer than 2,900 residents. Tallahassee with 1,932 stood third, followed by St. Augustine, Apalachicola, Milton, Fernandina, and Monticello. All told, about 13 percent of Florida's people lived within the towns.[11]

Outside the towns and off the plantations lived the majority of the state's white population. Clustered on and near the Indian frontiers and in the East and West Florida backwoods were the legendary crackers. In appearance and manner, they impressed few sophisticated critics. "Florida is the Paradise of an idle man," an Englishman noted in 1857. "This easy, lazy, good-for-nothing kind of life is very common among all the 'poor whites' of the seaboard Slave States, but it seems to have reached its climax in Florida."[12]

Belying the appearance of lassitude, the crackers fought for possession of the land and to protect their families, herded cattle, raised hogs, and subsistence-farmed with success. Their efforts contributed substantially to the more-than-tripled corn production in the state during 1845–60. That vegetable product, necessary for human and animal consumption, served along with pork as the mainstay of the southern diet. Beef, sweet and Irish potatoes, peas, pumpkins, squash, molasses, honey, and other items supplemented the basic foods, as did wild game and fish. "I have yet to visit a country capable of affording a greater variety of fruits, many of them of the most delicious quality," a visitor added. Rye, barley, wood, rice, tobacco, and dairy production increased, as well, during the 1850s.[13]

As the numbers of crackers, planters, townsmen, slaves, and other inhabitants mounted, Florida's population density rose. In 1850, an average of 1.48 persons lived within each square mile. Ten years later the figure stood at 2. How sparse Florida settlement remained can be gleaned from a comparison with Massachusetts's 1860 ratio of 157 people per square mile. Even within the state the density figures mislead, as huge areas in East and West Florida, especially in the peninsula below Alachua and Marion counties, possessed few, if any, settlers. Somewhat to the contrary, the counties of Leon, Gadsden, and Jefferson contained about 12 persons per square mile, and Duval, Madison,

Alachua, Jackson, and Escambia possessed from 6 to 11.9. From 9,000 free households in 1850, the state gained an additional 6,000 within the decade.[14]

In the still frontier-like conditions in much of Florida, inhabitants often lacked amenities commonly available in other states. The sparse population, for instance, was more than matched by the scarcity of qualified medical personnel. An early statewide patient-to-physician ratio of 644 to 1 improved only to 522 to 1 before the Civil War. Compounding the problem, the greater number of health care professionals resided in Leon County. More than a few residents lived from cradle to grave without the care of a doctor or of any of the four dentists or fourteen druggists present in the state in 1850. Home remedies and patent medicines with names like Compound Gentian Bitters were advertised in local newspapers as capable of curing everything from asthma to worms, with special attention to a variety of digestive ailments.[15] Some commercial products used opiates. More benign panaceas contained cod liver oil, "Congress water," citrate of magnesia, quinine, and sulphur.[16] Not surprisingly the death rate was high. Often the cause could not be discerned given the knowledge available, but digestive disorders, respiratory problems, diarrhea, dysentery, fevers, smallpox, syphilis, measles, and whooping cough figured prominently.[17]

Religion and churches offered comfort in a world where natural and violent death were common. In Middle Florida, planters, professionals, and related families often attended Episcopal services, while those lower on the social scale might belong to a Baptist congregation. Slaves sometimes joined white churches or else heard preaching from black or white ministers. Elsewhere in the state, gatherings tended to be less class-conscious. Many leaders, though, adhered to the Presbyterian faith, and, in areas such as the southwest peninsula's Peace River settlements, Methodism predominated. Most cracker farmers and herdsmen declined to affiliate officially with any church but attended revivals and camp meetings or listened to circuit preachers when they visited. Roman Catholics were few in number, although the religion's adherents were sufficient to justify seventeen churches by 1860. An even smaller number of Jewish residents was present, but that faith also had been represented in Florida since the territorial era.[18]

Educational opportunities proved almost as hard to come by as health care and, in some areas, churches. The state's ministers, lawyers, and other professionals usually received schooling outside Florida. No college or university existed prior to the Civil War, although beginnings were made by the establishment of seminaries at Ocala and Tallahassee, which later became the University of Florida and Florida State University, respectively. Despite regional pride, many families chose to send their sons (but rarely their daughters) to the North for formal education, though they reserved the right to rail that Yankees corrupted the young peoples' minds. An important exception related to legal education, where the University of Virginia excelled and attracted some of the South's brightest young men. Several future justices of the supreme court of Florida would be listed among them.[19]

Primary and secondary schooling fared not much better than higher education. Differing little from the experience of other southern states, Florida failed to mandate public education or to fund adequately the school system it did contemplate. The trend in the North embodied the concept of public schools to provide basic education for all white children. The federal government provided support with the proceeds from the sale of the sixteenth section in each township of public lands. In 1853 Florida acted by establishing local school boards and a tuition fund for indigent families, assessing a school tax, authorizing additional county taxes, and appointing David S. Walker as state superintendent. Unfortunately, these limited efforts never enjoyed broad public support, nor were they fully implemented. Poor whites felt themselves too proud to ask for charity, the middle classes formed their own schools, and the wealthy hired tutors. Superintendent Walker lamented without impact "the apathy which has prevailed in the public mind on the important subject."[20] By 1860 ninety-seven public schools served only 4,900 of the state's 20,600 eligible students. The public contribution to their operations totaled $20,000. Twice as many students attended the 138 private upper-division academies, which were funded by almost $80,000, $4,000 of which came from public funds.[21]

Public schooling lagged, but the literacy rate of Florida's free population was high. Only 5,400 such adults were unable to read in 1860 at a time when slaves were not permitted to learn even the rudiments. Those who could read might utilize one of the state's sixty-six libraries or peruse any of the religious and literary newspapers in wide circulation. They also could enjoy one of the twenty political weeklies. Larger towns such as Jacksonville, Pensacola, and Tallahassee had two newspapers, one each for the two dominant parties. They mixed news, editorial comments, and advertisements on four to six pages. During the legislative sessions, laws and proceedings might fill page 1; otherwise, poetry and fiction often appeared. No resident listed an occupation as author on the 1850 census, but a celebrated one soon appeared. After publication of Harriet Beecher Stowe's *Uncle Tom's Cabin* in 1852, Yankee transplant and new Floridian Catherine Lee Whiting Hentz contributed her *Planter's Northern Bride* in response, portraying the plantation system as beneficial to all, slave and master alike.[22]

Samuel J. Douglas

Charles Breckenridge Parkhill

George Pettus Raney

Augustus Emmet Maxwell

James Bryan Whitfield

Robert Spratt Cockrell

William Adams Hocker

Law graduates, University of Virginia. As there were few law schools in the United States in the nineteenth century, most lawyers and judges acquired their legal education by reading the law under the tutelage of lawyers. Eight of the justices covered in this volume attended law school. Milton Harvey Mabry was a student in the Law Department of Cumberland University in Lebanon, Tennessee, and the above seven jurists were students in the Law Department and graduated from the University of Virginia.

The lack of commitment to public education represented more than a legislative failure to keep pace with national trends. The state's economic health, in particular that of Middle Florida, progressed well during the antebellum period. Nonetheless, in the agricultural economy the cash necessary to fuel programs such as schools always proved difficult to find. Most planters and farmers operated upon annual extensions of credit from factors and town merchants. Following the banking collapse in the wake of the Panic of 1837, the prevailing political winds had forced severe restrictions upon the chartering of new financial institutions. It took a decade after statehood before a new state bank received a charter, and, at the end of the antebellum years, only twenty-six small banks and bank branches served a few Panhandle towns, Middle Florida, Jacksonville, Fernandina, and St. Augustine. Accordingly, credit remained hard to attain. Floridians, as always, found themselves cash poor and with meager resources to manage economic bad times such as those brought on by the Civil War.[23]

Undergirding the social and economic dynamics that were propelling Florida through the evolutions of the antebellum era were the strictures of the Constitution of 1838 and of statutory law enacted pursuant to it. The governmental and judicial aspects of that law are discussed in chapter 6. Here, note should be made that the law mandated clear distinctions based upon gender and race, discrimination that both reflected and affected contemporary practice. In each area changes occurred during the antebellum period, with white women achieving gains and blacks, free and slave, suffering setbacks.

The adoption of the common law during the territorial period had afforded women few legal protections; in fact, some previously granted statutory guarantees had been withdrawn. Even a wife's separate property and income were placed completely within her husband's control. The dangers of the property provisions became apparent within the context of the banking collapse of the late 1830s and early 1840s. Many women and their children faced impoverishment through no fault of their own but rather from their husbands' independent and ill-advised actions. Since planter families faced greater concerns than others, they and their Whig allies labored during the final session of the territorial council to address the situation before elections turned legislative power more completely over to less concerned Democrats. The attempt succeeded in early 1845 with the passage of the Married Woman's Property Act to keep a wife's property free from the demands of her husband's creditors. In doing so, the council furthered an aspect of women's rights pioneered only six years before in Mississippi. Additional advances for women, though, would be slow in coming.[24]

The law's treatment of blacks reflected a very complicated situation. Legislators drew a basic dividing line, for example, between free blacks and slaves. The former theoretically possessed substantive rights protected by law and enforceable by legal processes. The relatively easygoing ways of Spanish Florida quickly began to give way, however, as lawmakers placed more and more restrictions upon free blacks. They were not allowed to serve on juries, vote, carry firearms without permits, gamble with whites, or engage in numerous other acts and practices. Laws forbade free blacks from coming into the territory, and the Constitution of 1838 expressly required the legislature to prevent such immigration. They were subjected to high taxes. After 1842 they were obligated to have a white guardian. Finally, in 1859 a law required each free black man and woman to choose a master and become a slave. The era's trend evidenced deep-rooted white hostility to free blacks.[25]

The position of free blacks held further complications under the terms of the Adams-Onis Treaty, by which Florida was transferred from Spain. It specified that inhabitants at the time of transfer were to be granted the rights of citizens of the United States. Early territorial court decisions upheld the provisions to some extent, and many territorial laws thereafter noted a distinction based upon the time a black entered Florida. While discrimination remained a fact of everyday life, some free blacks prospered. A few even owned slaves. An example of the possibilities for prosperity can be found in the Proctor family of St. Johns and Leon counties. Antonio Proctor earned a respectable position in society through his own efforts and with assistance from Governor William Pope DuVal. Proctor's son George, the builder of several of Tallahassee's fine homes, voted, entered into contracts with whites, sued whites in court, testified against them, and purchased his wife's freedom from slavery, a condition of servitude to which she returned when he traveled to California during the gold rush. A third generation produced two state legislators during Reconstruction.[26]

With regard to slaves, the law classed their status as personal property and placed wide-ranging power in masters' hands. It restricted, as well, their movements and actions off farms and plantations and specified penalties that might involve branding, whipping, and, in extreme cases, death. Despite prohibitions on cruel and unusual treatment by owners, corporal punishment often and fatal punishment sometimes resulted. Statutes did require masters to "feed, clothe, and provide for" their slaves or face charges of criminal neglect, but standards by which to judge treatment were not specified.[27] While any court proceeding concerning a slave risked biased treatment at the hands of a white jury, procedures were the same as those observed in trials of free persons, except that slave testimony was subject to a series of restrictions.[28]

Legal attempts to regulate and control free blacks and slaves intensified through the 1840s and 1850s, but the laws did not always reflect day-to-day reality. Especially in East and West Florida, somewhat more easygoing traditions survived. At Tampa in 1857, for instance, future Union general and Freedmen's Bureau head Oliver O. Howard still could observe, "Slavery here is a very mild form." He added, "You wouldn't know the negroes were slaves unless you were told."[29] Notwithstanding such regional variance, the lot of all blacks was a hard and occasionally terrible one. Historians have noted, additionally, that institutions such as slavery impacted upon society as a whole, negatively affecting owners along with those who were owned.[30]

Within this dynamic and divided society after 1845 and before 1861, legislators and legal practitioners created, organized, and implemented Florida's first state court system and supreme court. The needs of and issues at play within the society necessarily became those addressed by the courts, and the tensions they revealed affected the judiciary's deliberations and decisions. How that judicial structure came to be and with what significance is the subject of the following chapter.

Chapter 6

Creation and Organization of the Supreme Court

When Florida achieved admission to the union of states in 1845, its political divisions equaled, if they did not exceed, its social and economic ones. During the territorial council's session in January and February, influential East Florida Whigs, including future supreme court justices Joseph Bradford Lancaster and Ossian Bingley Hart, had opposed pro-statehood Democrats to forestall the action. In the complicated political environment, regional alignments continued sometimes to outweigh party identification in importance. For example, East Floridians blocked election of Jefferson County's pro-statehood Democrat William D. Moseley as president of the senate but did so only by supporting Key West's pro-statehood Whig-leaning George W. Macrae.[1]

The state's first election, held on May 26, 1845, in an atmosphere celebratory over statehood, resulted in large majorities for the Democrats. To avoid the likely landslide in favor of their opponents, Whigs initially had offered Jefferson County planter William Bailey as a nonpartisan candidate for governor. Democrats refused to take the bait, though. Their man, Moseley, then bested Whig nominee Richard Keith Call by 700 votes out of 5,900 cast in a contest one historian described as "hot."[2] In the seventeen-member senate, the Whigs achieved victory in only six races. The house of representatives contained thirty Democrats out of a total of forty seats. Similarly, East Florida Democrat David Levy, who soon adopted use of an earlier family name to become David Levy Yulee, defeated East Florida Whig senator Benjamin A. Putnam for the single seat in the United States House of Representatives.[3]

The legislature first convened at Tallahassee on June 23, 1845, to begin the process of state organization. Two days later, newly inaugurated governor Moseley outlined his desires for legislation, noting among them the need for establishment of the judiciary. While doing so he sounded a then-controversial note on nation-state relations. "I believe . . . ," he told his listeners, "[in] a government formed and established through the agency and express authority and assent of the States, as independent sovereignties."[4] Thoughts of future disunion quickly melted into the background, however, as the lawmakers immersed themselves in the details of the tasks at hand. To permit them to proceed, both house and senate authorized committees to consider specified areas of concerns. Significantly, in the senate Democrat George Sydney Hawkins and Whig David S. Walker, both future supreme court justices, secured appointment to the judiciary committee.[5]

The flow of money constitutes the lifeblood of any government, and, as such, the legislators early addressed the questions of expenditures and revenues. The results illustrate the unusually important role of the judiciary in governmental organization and operations. The state budget decided upon for 1845–46 totaled $41,500. Of this amount, the judiciary consumed the largest portion, $18,500. Since the costs of collecting taxes ran to approximately $11,000, legislators found themselves needing $52,500 in revenues. To meet the challenge, they imposed a poll tax on white males as well as other taxes on slaves, free blacks, money, bank stock, stock-in-trade, carriages, town lots, wharves, sawmills, incomes of medical doctors and lawyers, and real property. Due to the rate structure, the fiscal system encouraged investment in plantations, slaves, and cattle rather than in urban development or manufacturing.[6]

The politically delicate task of elections for prominent federal and state offices numbered among the additional tasks faced by the legislators. Florida's two United States Senate seats commanded the earliest attention. At the time David Levy Yulee and James D. Westcott held unchallenged roles as the state's most prominent Democrats. On July 1 they capitalized on the legislature's friendly Democratic majorities and easily won election as Florida's first two United States senators. Yulee became the first Jew to sit in that body. A subsequent race for Yulee's seat in the House of Representatives thereafter hinted at problems for his party, as Whig Edward Carrington Cabell appeared to have beaten Democrat William Henry Brockenbrough. The Democrat challenged the results and later was seated by the federal body's Democratic majority.[7]

The partisan environment surrounding the Yulee and Westcott elections affected other races subject to legislative authority, as Democrats sought to dispense patronage to members of their own party or else, as in the case of some judicial elections, to those believed sympathetic to Democratic perspectives. On the question of judge selection, the legislators possessed great powers. The St. Joseph Constitution of 1838 mandated most judicial elections "by the concurrent vote, of a majority of both Houses of the General Assembly."[8] The charter also specified that, for at least five years after statehood, the judges of the western, middle, eastern, and southern circuits would comprise a supreme court, a scheme reminiscent of the territorial court of appeals. Accordingly, major political overtones loomed over the election of the circuit judges.[9]

At first the lure of judicial selection proved almost too tempting, with both legislative houses on July 16 resolving to proceed with elections even though procedural rules had not been adopted and an organic act for the judiciary had not received consideration. When Franklin County representative Robert J. Floyd pointed out the problem, a Joint Select Committee on Election of Justices was formed to address the former concern while the judiciary committees worked on the latter. The select committee considered adoption of two basic rules. First, the two houses would act simultaneously. Second, legislators would vote for judges in each of the four circuits on one ballot, a process that, presumably, would sharpen partisan lines. The second recommendation's implications troubled many members who might need to support region over party as to a particular choice. In the circumstances, the proposal failed on a tie vote. At Senator Benjamin D. Wright's suggestion, a substitute plan attained approval by which a separate vote would be taken on each judgeship.[10]

Meanwhile, legislation to organize the judiciary wound its way through legislative corridors. Because constitutional provisions delineated the basic outline of court organization and jurisdiction, the statute mostly added necessary detail. The Act to Organize the Circuit Courts of the State of Florida, signed by Governor Moseley on July 22, determined boundaries for each circuit, established terms of court, specified some procedures, and authorized judges to adjourn court due to "the prevalence of infectious or contagious disease." It provided that "all writs, process, and other business" would be returnable to the first term and that "no recognizance, suit, or other matter, shall be dismissed, discontinued, or fail, by reason of the alteration in the time of holding said courts."[11] Subsequent acts added more detail. One empowered circuit judges and the supreme court's presiding judge to authorize payment of reasonable sums for necessary expenses, such as stationery, wood, candles, room rents, per diem for bailiffs and servants, court interpreters, bedding and blankets for prisoners, and guards' pay. It also prohibited counties from charging the state rent for court use of facilities and precluded "the payment of any jury."[12] Many legislators adhered to preelection promises on the question of judicial compensation by ordering that circuit judges receive the constitutional minimum of $2,000 per year. Some called the salary "niggardly and penurious," but it amounted to $500 per year more than that which the governor enjoyed.[13]

Judicial elections commenced—with partisan considerations at the fore—on the day following Moseley's approval of the first judicial organization act. The general assembly's Democratic majority proceeded expeditiously to select judges for the western, southern, and eastern circuits. After three ballots Senator George Sydney Hawkins, nominally a Whig but with excellent Democratic connections, defeated judges Samuel Williams Carmack and Dillon Jordan,

Jr., for the western district bench. In the south, Judge William Marvin bested Carmack, Key West's one-time federal prosecutor Adam Gordon, and former territorial senator L. W. Smith. For the eastern circuit, Judge Isaac H. Bronson easily overcame opposition from Whig leader and territorial house speaker Joseph Bradford Lancaster. Mariano D. Papy, chief clerk of the house of representatives, also had an easy time of it, enjoying near unanimous support for supreme court clerk.[14]

Middle Florida's judgeship posed greater problems. The area constituted the state's wealthiest region as well as the heartland of Whig planter strength. Democrats desired a strong judge who would not bend to planter needs by hampering enforcement of debt collection or impeding civil actions and criminal prosecutions in the wake of the territorial banking scandals. They settled on Thomas Baltzell, an outspoken antibank Democrat leader and member of the house judiciary committee. Against a variety of opponents, Baltzell found majority support in the house after five ballots, but in the senate Whig leaders struggled to frustrate his candidacy. Not until the thirty-sixth ballot in that body did he receive the requisite number of votes.[15]

The judicial selection controversies did not end with the legislature's July 26 adjournment. Marvin and Bronson, both federal territorial judges who likely expected reappointment to federal judicial positions, declined the state judgeships. On September 27 the governor chose District Attorney Thomas Douglas to take Bronson's place until the legislature met later in the year. Douglas's performance pleased many East Floridians, as suggested by testimonials in newspapers such as St. Augustine's *Florida Herald and Southern Democrat.* On December 6 the legislature concurred and elected him to a full term.[16]

As had the previous Middle Florida contest, the Southern District judgeship election presented troubling problems. Marvin's notice of refusal did not arrive in time for Governor Moseley to name a temporary appointment, so the contest remained open. East Florida Whigs backed Jacksonville's Joseph Bradford Lancaster, and many Democratic senators advocated their colleague William Augustus Forward of St. Augustine. Leon County Whig Leslie Atchinson Thompson also attracted consideration. Deadlock ensued, with candidates falling by the wayside and others entering the lists. Territorial senate president George W. Macrae stood among the disappointed. Finally, on the thirty-first ballot territorial judge Samuel Williams Carmack emerged as the victor—a compromise candidate.[17]

The December 1845 elections, at first, seemed to resolve in a satisfactory manner the question of which men would form the supreme court. Douglas's popularity crossed party lines to some extent, and the choice of a moderate

Whig such as Carmack furthered the impression that the rancorous partisanship of the summer legislative session had eased. Even friends of the losers appeared complacent. "We understand that Mr. Forward would have received the appointment had he not been a member of the Senate," observed the *Florida Herald and Southern Democrat*. "And we think this was a sufficient objection."[18] A correspondent of the Whiggish *Pensacola Gazette* condemned the "shifting, log-rolling, electioneering, & c., & c." but praised the senate for choosing in Carmack "the best man of the whole (a whig) and stick[ing] to him, as being the only way of coming to a decision." The writer continued, "The Senate have done themselves much credit in electing, as all seem to admit, two able men by a unanimous vote to that high office without distinction of party."[19]

The cooperative spirit soon vanished. Carmack declined the position, and the contest was resumed. Macrae and Lancaster emerged as the frontrunners, but neither could obtain the necessary majorities. After the twenty-fifth ballot Lancaster withdrew. Whig senators David S. Walker and Benjamin D. Wright thereafter entered the fray. Walker and Macrae then vied as leaders for the honor. Residents complained in letters to newspapers of waste of time and taxpayer funds as the struggle extended itself. Finally, the legislators postponed the election when the forty-eighth ballot ended inconclusively.[20]

The Southern District judgeship issue continued to haunt the legislative halls and prompted calls for popular election of judges. In March 1846 Governor Moseley temporarily answered the question by appointing Macrae until the assembly again met. Beginning in November that body recommenced its political tug of war. Whigs had increased their representation in the legislature during elections held earlier in the month, so the contest reshaped itself not as Democrat against Whig but as Middle Florida Whig against East Florida Whig. The contestants, respectively, were Walker and Lancaster. Following the forty-first ballot, legislators agreed to suspend the vote indefinitely. Moseley reappointed Macrae until further action occurred.[21]

Pending resolution of the southern judgeship question, the supreme court of Florida attempted to convene its first session at the state capitol on Monday, January 5, 1846, with justices Baltzell and Douglas present and Hawkins absent, thereby constituting a lack of quorum. Not until the following day, when Hawkins arrived, would the high court have a quorum. The constitution had elucidated the court's jurisdiction in article 5, paragraph 2:

> The Supreme Court, except in cases otherwise directed in this Constitution, shall have appellate jurisdiction only, which shall be co-extensive with the State, under such restrictions and regulations, not repugnant to

> this Constitution, as may from time to time, be prescribed by law; provided, that the said Court shall always have power, to issue writs of injunction, mandamus, quo-warranto, habeas corpus, and such other remedial and original writs, as may be necessary to give it a general superintendence and control of all other Courts.[22]

Paragraph 18 specified that "No Justice of the Supreme Court, shall sit as judge, or take part in the appellate court on the trial or hearing of any case which shall have been decided by him in the court below." Paragraph 20 added, "No duty not Judicial, shall be imposed by law, upon the Justices of the Supreme Court, Chancellors, or the Judges of the Circuit Courts of this State."[23]

Pursuant to these grants of authority and limitations on legislative control, the high court addressed itself to twenty-seven cases pending on its docket. Motions were received, oral arguments entertained, and opinions delivered. The justices referred several matters to the federal courts; otherwise, jurisdictional and procedural concerns predominated. The court's first decision established its authority to hear cases transferred from the territorial court of appeals, ruling that the organizational act passed in 1845 determined the issue with "no room to question the jurisdiction."[24]

The supreme court's first session passed in relative harmony. All but one of the decisions received unanimous approval. Baltzell wrote four court opinions and one dissent, Hawkins wrote three court opinions, and Douglas wrote five court opinions and one concurring opinion. The court also administered proper oaths to permit attorneys to practice before it. Among them were future justices Charles H. DuPont and David S. Walker. On the last day of its first session, February 4, the court approved rules of procedure to be followed in future cases and announced the election of Thomas Douglas as chief justice.[25]

Still pending the addition of the fourth circuit judge to the supreme court, the general assembly in late 1846 modified somewhat the tribunal's judicial powers. It reinforced the court's power "to abolish, alter, or amend, or add to the rules adopted at the last session of said court."[26] On the other hand, the legislature voided two of the rules previously adopted. Rule 23 had provided that, when "costs shall be allowed" in the supreme court, it would be the "duty of the Clerk to insert the amount thereof in the body of the mandate, or other proper process sent to the Court below, and annex to the same the bill of the items in detail."[27] Rule 24 had established that a rehearing "must be applied for by petition in writing within fifteen days after the judgment or decree, setting forth the cause or causes for which Judgment or decree is supposed to be erroneous."[28]

Housing the court, 1846–1902. The first session of the supreme court of Florida convened in January 1846, in the courtroom on the south end and second level of the three-story frontier capitol. A description in the *Florida Daily Times*, Jacksonville, dated January 28, 1882, noted that the courtroom was a "roomy chamber, with long windows on three sides and . . . two plain, old-fashioned wood fireplaces, and the side walls lined with plain, cheap, but commodious book shelving. The shelves now contain about 3000 volumes of reports, besides about 2000 volumes of statutes; also a few old Spanish law books."

With Governor Moseley's 1847 temporary reappointment of George W. Macrae to the southern circuit bench, the supreme court during its 1847 term finally realized its constitutionally intended form. The justices all possessed economic means and social connections well above the state's average. They all were slaveholders or else supported the institution. All had been active in politics. They had risen rapidly through the ranks of power in Florida's frontier setting and had served it in various capacities during the territorial era. The details of their lives further suggest the nature of their backgrounds, capabilities, individual and collective experiences, and contributions.

George Sydney Hawkins, Supreme Court Justice, 1846–1851

Like many of the men who would lead Florida into secession, George Sydney Hawkins was a northerner. Born at Kingston, Ulster County, New York, in 1808, he attended the area's common schools. Thereafter, he graduated from Columbia University and practiced law in New York City before moving to Florida

Thomas Baltzell, middle circuit

Thomas Douglas, eastern circuit

George Sydney Hawkins, western circuit

The supreme court of Florida convenes. The Constitution of 1838 provided that "the powers of the Supreme Court shall be vested in and its duties performed by the Judges of the several Circuit Courts within the state." The first session was scheduled by law to convene Monday, January 5, 1846, but the delayed arrival of circuit judge George Sydney Hawkins prevented a quorum. The term began on Tuesday, January 6, and adjourned February 4. No circuit judge from the southern circuit was present in 1846 since each of those elected declined to serve. The circuit was represented by Judge George W. Macrae in 1847 and by Judge Joseph Bradford Lancaster from 1848 to 1850.

in 1828. Hawkins initially settled at Pensacola but soon relocated to Marianna. He opened a law office in 1831 and the following year served the territorial council as an enrolling and engrossing clerk. He achieved the distinction in 1833 of admission to the bar of the United State Supreme Court. Two years later, Hawkins accepted Governor John H. Eaton's appointment as aide-de-camp. During the Second Seminole War, he rose to the rank of captain of militia. Hawkins was wounded during the summer of 1837 in a skirmish at Aloqua. When a subordinate asked if he were hurt, the captain replied jokingly, yet prophetically, "enough to send me to Congress."[29]

Hawkins's legislative career already had begun two years previous to the wounding incident. In October 1835 he had secured election to represent Jackson County in the territorial council. He entered the new senate in 1839, nominally a Whig. He achieved its presidency one year later with strong Democratic backing. Hawkins served, as well, on the Committee to Report on the Division of the Territory, delivering its majority report for statehood of a united Florida.[30]

The senate president's focus soon turned toward federal preferment. The Whig party had captured the presidency, and Hawkins approached New York's powerful Nathaniel Tallmadge for assistance in securing appointment as a United States attorney. He assured the United States senator of his conservative political beliefs and the existence of a Whig majority in the territory. The Apalachicola district's United States attorney, William Henry Brockenbrough, added his recommendation, and President John Tyler thereupon commissioned Hawkins to succeed Brockenbrough beginning in July 1842.[31]

While he fulfilled his federal responsibilities, Hawkins's pro-statehood beliefs and political involvements persisted. During the first statehood election, for instance, he canvassed for Democrat congressional candidate David Levy Yulee. At the same election Franklin County voters sent him to the state senate. He briefly acted as a member of the judiciary committee before Senator Joel Parker nominated him for judge of the western circuit. Hawkins's third-ballot victory prompted his resignation from the legislature.[32]

The new judge's work on the bench brought him praise. When Hawkins presided over John Grant's Wakulla County murder trial, to cite one example, the *Newport Gazette* reported, "[T]he impression which he made on our citizens was very favorable."[33] A Tallahassee newspaper concurred, declaring that Hawkins had proved "equal to the task." Its comments continued, "[H]is decisions, as well as his courteous deportment, and his firmness in administering the law, have met the approbation of the community."[34]

Map of Florida by S. Augustus Mitchell, circa 1844. Superimposed dotted lines identify boundaries of the western, middle, eastern and southern judicial circuits of Florida as established by acts of the general assembly in July and December 1845. The absence of good trails, roads, and railroads made circuit riding in Florida difficult for many years. Western circuit judge John Adams Cameron complained in January 1836 to U.S. Secretary of State John Forsyth: "Pray, cast your eyes upon the map of Florida and look at my District! I have to hold Courts in five Counties, twice a year, besides on[e] yearly term of the Court of Appeals: my traveling is more than 2,000 Miles in the year . . . my health and even life are often hazarded."

The judge's engaging personality assisted his overcoming some of his political problems and remaining on the bench. A friend described him as "ever cheerful, bright and sparkling, urbane, chivalric—the very soul of honor."[35] Those qualities permitted him to assuage Whigs who looked askance at his close associations with Democrats. They permitted his reelection in 1848 and 1850 with Whig support. After the 1850 election, he served three years. During the period his most notable trial concerned the slave Henry Prior, who was convicted of murder. Hawkins left his judgeship when he accepted appointment as federal collector of the port of Apalachicola, effective March 16, 1853.[36]

Through his period of service on the bench, Hawkins enjoyed better fortune than did some other judges. He had profited during the early 1840s, along with fellow justice Thomas Baltzell, from a directorship of the Apalachicola Land Company. He also had purchased Union Bank stock but, unlike many others, had disposed of it before the bank's collapse. By mid-decade Hawkins owned seven slaves, a Marianna town lot, improvements worth $2,250, and an expensive carriage. His legal practice brought an annual income of $1,200. With the security thus afforded him, Hawkins married on August 2, 1848, to William Henry Brockenbrough's daughter Mary. From the union was born a son, Charles. Hawkins continued to prosper, and, by 1850, his slaveholding had increased to ten. Sadness did cloud the picture for Hawkins when, on Christmas Day 1859, Mary died. After a period of mourning, though, he married Mrs. Emily Henry.[37]

Hawkins's politics during the 1850s increasingly were identified with the Democratic party's radical secession element. With the Whig collapse following the 1852 state elections, he moved officially toward the Democrats. Two years later he represented Escambia, Franklin, and Walton counties at the party's state convention. By then, his pro-secession sentiments were well known. At the decade's beginning he had chaired, while a circuit judge and member of the supreme court, a Marianna meeting to select Western District delegates to the Nashville convention. In 1856 the Democrats nominated secessionist Madison S. Perry of Alachua County for governor, and Hawkins eagerly joined the ticket as a candidate for Congress.[38]

Hawkins's 1856 campaign ended successfully, launching a two-term career in the United States House of Representatives. He adroitly kept his name before the public with widespread dissemination of his congressional speeches. Particularly, he became identified as a supporter and defender of William Walker, a filibusterer who sought to annex Caribbean territory for the benefit of the slave states. When Abraham Lincoln's election as president brought the secession question to a head in November and December 1860, Hawkins objected on the House floor to all attempts at compromise. Once Florida scheduled a secession convention, he refused to serve on the congressional committee dealing with federal-state relations. On January 21, 1861, Hawkins left the Congress, the first member of the House to do so. Afterward, he acted along with United States senators Stephen Mallory and David Levy Yulee as Florida commissioners to negotiate transfer of federal property to state control.[39]

Following his withdrawal from Congress, Hawkins's career took on a less prominent and more sedate character. He served from 1862 to 1865 as a Confederate district court judge in Florida. In 1866 Governor David S. Walker appointed him as a delegate to President Andrew Johnson's national union convention of conservatives, but that body's call for sectional accommodation faded with victories by radical Republicans who demanded a harsher Reconstruction policy. In his last years Hawkins practiced law at Marianna, sometimes appearing before the supreme court. He died at his Marianna home on March 15, 1878, while preparing a recodification of Florida law pursuant to a request of the legislature. Observed his hometown newspaper, "All who knew him will remember him for his courage, kindness, his congeniality and learning." It added, "He held almost every office in the State in the gift of the people, and discharged the high trusts reposed in him with credit to himself and acceptably to the people."[40]

Thomas Baltzell, Supreme Court Justice, 1846–1851; Supreme Court Chief Justice, 1853–1859

Thomas Baltzell's strong personality and willingness to venture where others feared to tread made him one of the most colorful justices to serve on Florida's supreme court. Among other things, he dueled with one justice's father, ordered another justice arrested, and inspired barrages of press criticism for his political views. Somewhat of a gadfly, he nonetheless pursued public affairs with sincerity, energy, and perseverance. His contributions proved substantive and helped to mold the court and its traditions.

Baltzell was born in Frankfort, Kentucky, on July 1, 1804. At age twenty he obtained a lawyer's license, after reading with Solomon P. Sharp and Q. Q. Crittenden. Friendship with William Pope DuVal brought him to Jackson County, Florida, in 1825. He opened a legal practice, and, penniless, he followed court sessions with his belongings in a backpack. Within two years he had established a favorable reputation. He became a trustee of the Webbville Academy—Jackson County's first legislatively chartered school—which opened in 1827. Later he served as trustee for the St. Andrew Bay and Tallahassee academies and acted as first president of the board of trustees responsible for supervising Florida's seminary lands. He remained interested in education throughout his career.[41]

The young lawyer's life took major turns in 1832. First, he engaged in October in an "affair of honor" with future United States senator James D. Westcott, whose son and namesake would follow Baltzell on the supreme court. The confrontation's cause is not known, and, fortunately, it resulted in only slight injury to Westcott.[42] More happily for Baltzell, he was elected to represent Jackson County in the legislative council. There he served on the judiciary committee, where he revealed a more progressive mind than that possessed by some of his peers. Particularly, he dissented strongly from a report arguing that debtors be imprisoned until after a fair surrender of their effects. An interest in internal improvements expressed itself, as well. As a result, the council asked Congress to provide partial funding for a canal linking Chipola and St. Andrew Bay.[43]

Although Baltzell did not return to the legislative council in 1833, his political and public lives continued to evolve. In 1834 Governor DuVal appointed him a justice of the peace for Escambia County, and four years afterward he represented Jackson County in the constitutional convention held at St. Joseph. His resolute antibanking stand at that assembly enhanced his populist-like reputation. In the process he authored the antibank faction's appeal to Congress to repeal or modify bank charters guaranteed by the territorial government. He worked, as well, on the judicial department committee and assisted in the writing of the constitution's judicial article.[44]

Following the constitutional convention, Baltzell capitalized on his prominence as an antibank man to vie for the territory's congressional delegate seat against East Florida Whig Charles Downing. While stressing his banking stance, he opposed division and urged early statehood through the slogan "The constitution; Florida a State and entire."[45] In the bitter political environment, he endured harsh personal attacks. A correspondent of the *Apalachicola Gazette*, for example, linked him with a faction whose members intended "plainly to get themselves into office . . . [at the cost of] the prostration of all banking . . . and the utter disregard of all the sanctions of the plighted faith of the Country."[46] In the end, sectionalism defeated Baltzell. He ran very well in Middle Florida, but many East Florida Democrats backed their fellow East Floridian rather than their fellow Democrat.[47]

The 1838 congressional defeat only temporarily halted the momentum of Baltzell's career. For the present he maintained a law office with Walker Anderson at Tallahassee, advertising their availability for practice throughout the Middle Florida area and in the court of appeals. As antibanking arguments grew more popular, he took pains to raise his profile as a Democrat in order to overcome his reputation for independence. In return Governor Robert Raymond Reid, Jr., in 1840 placed him in charge of the fund created for the construction of a new capitol building. The following year the legislative council began to meet in a portion of the structure, but funds ran out for further building. Baltzell then diligently pursued federal grants in aid of the project, blazed a path through contention and litigation, and eventually recommenced construction. He achieved final completion in 1845.[48]

As commissioner of the capitol fund, Baltzell benefited from better relations in Tallahassee's important political, business, and financial circles. He strengthened the ties with service on the city's rebuilding committee following its great fire in 1843. His rewards were not slow in coming. His political nemesis, the banking industry, reached out to him in 1840 when the Union Bank elected him to a directorship and allowed him to purchase its stock with a $2,000 mortgage. Soon he sat, as well, on the board of the Apalachicola Land Company. His personal finances additionally were enhanced when, in 1844, he gained federal designation, along with Walker Anderson and James Cooper, as Treasury Department agents to complete the selection of seminary lands. The appointment illustrated well the strengthening of Baltzell's political standing as a Democrat. It came with the blessing of David Levy Yulee, the powerful territorial delegate who had led East Florida Democrats in voting against him in 1838.[49]

The early 1840s also saw the revival of Baltzell's career as an elected official. Middle Florida residents chose him as one of their senators in late 1842, and he participated in the final three sessions of the territorial council. While strongly partisan, Baltzell retained a degree of independence as shown by his support in early 1845 for the compromise candidacy of George W. Macrae as senate president. When the first state legislature convened later in the year, the former senator sat in the house of representatives and on its committees on judiciary, schools and colleges, internal improvements, and elections. As recounted earlier, Baltzell's service as legislator terminated in July with his selection as Middle District circuit judge.[50]

The new judge's bench experience brought him praise, but his tenure ended for the time being in political retribution. One incident especially brought Baltzell favorable attention. In October 1846 a man named Holloman and others were caught and charged with murder of a Quincy man. Agitated citizenry petitioned Baltzell to call a special court term lest there be a "popular outbreak, and the summary punishment of the offenders."[51] The judge complied, declaring court power to hold an extra term to try criminal cases. A leading

Democratic newspaper observed, "Judge Baltzell is rapidly gaining in the confidence of the bar . . . and is an able and impartial administrator of the law."[52] It later lauded him, as well, for "diminishing the trial docket to a size truly alarming to lawyers."[53]

Democrat supporters might applaud Baltzell, but by the late 1840s the legislators who held power over his continuation on the bench identified more closely with the Whig party. Their leaders had not forgotten his earlier partisanship or his popular appeal. Accordingly, they united to defeat him. The setbacks occurred in 1851, when a supreme court was created independent of the circuit courts. Gadsden County's representative William E. Kilcrease nominated Baltzell for the higher position, but opponents stalled his bid, effectively removing the jurist from the supreme court. On January 14, again they combined to forestall his reelection as circuit judge.[54]

Involuntarily retired from the bench, Baltzell returned to his family and the practice of law at Tallahassee. He had married Harriet King in 1834, and by 1850 six children had been born. Additionally, Harriet's mother lived with them. The former judge enjoyed affluence, but by the early 1850s he needed the steady income of a legal practice or public salary. In the previous decade's poor economy, his Union Bank and other investments had soured; his slaveholdings had dropped from twelve in 1846 to eight in 1851; and other property had declined in value. The first years of the 1850s seem to have begun reversing the trend.[55]

Electoral defeat and financial strain did not dissuade Baltzell from active interest in politics and civic affairs. He emerged again as a Democratic party leader and played public roles in support of many local and regional improvement projects, such as the projected Gulf and Atlantic Railroad. The visibility reinvigorated his popularity and set the stage for a judicial comeback in 1853 with the state's first popular elections for supreme court justices. Baltzell entered his name in the race for chief justice. Democrats rallied to his side, endorsing "His sterling patriotism and unyielding devotion to Florida and her best interest."[56] He was hailed as "the uncompromising friend of liberal and progressive principles . . . [who] never faltered when they were in danger."[57] Needing only a plurality of votes cast, Baltzell defeated Justice Leslie Atchinson Thompson and Chief Justice Benjamin D. Wright with 1,260 votes to their respective totals of 876 and 515.[58]

The state's first elected chief justice took his oath in January 1854 and remained in office through the duration of his five-year term. Many aspects of Baltzell's service and of court history during his tenure are discussed later in this work. One facet of his leadership especially merits mention, however. Having supported education and its institutions since soon after his arrival in Florida, Baltzell used his position to urge the creation of a school to educate the state's future lawyers in a proper manner. He announced his plans in 1856. The chief justice intended the law school to be located at Tallahassee, meeting for two terms in each year. Its faculty—including Baltzell and, possibly, other supreme court justices—would offer instruction in jurisprudence, constitutional history and law, common law, commercial and criminal law, and equity. Through lectures, examinations, recitations, and moot courts, he hoped to "communicate a knowledge of these respective departments of the great system of law—to instil their principles into the mind and initiate the student into the rules of practice."[59] The proposal prompted favorable attention from the press, but nothing came of it.[60]

The last eight years of Baltzell's life, a period that began while he still served on the supreme court, proved personally and professionally difficult. In October 1858 his son, Thomas, Jr., was drowned at Apalachicola Bay while attempting to save a child. Perhaps the father's grief played a part in ensuing court events. The tribunal's 1859 term was scheduled to begin on January 3. Only the chief justice attended. Justice Charles H. DuPont arrived the next day, but Justice Byrd Murphy Pearson failed to appear due to problems with his eyesight. Baltzell and DuPont differed as to whether they should hold court with two justices or else appoint a circuit judge to sit in Pearson's place. DuPont then departed for his Quincy home. An irate Baltzell ordered that DuPont be notified to return and that Pearson be arrested and brought to the capital. DuPont vehemently objected to the procedure. When Pearson voluntarily presented himself, the two jurists ruled that Baltzell lacked the authority to demand Pearson's arrest and directed that the record of the order be expunged. The dispute attracted intense publicity and likely contributed to Baltzell's defeat by DuPont in his reelection attempt.[61]

Departing the court in 1859, the former chief justice again embraced a legal practice. As the secession crisis built, Baltzell initially opposed the breakup of the Union, but, like many other Middle Florida Unionists, he accepted and supported Florida's withdrawal once it seemed inevitable. Leon County elected him in 1862 and 1863 as its delegate to the state house of representatives. After the war Baltzell represented the county at the 1865 constitutional convention, at which he unsuccessfully vied for its presidency. Soon after the convention adjourned, Baltzell succumbed to fatigue and illness. He died at his Tallahassee residence on January 14, 1866. Both houses of the legislature adjourned the following day in his honor.[62]

Baltzell's contributions to Florida government and jurisprudence appeared evident to his peers, who met soon after his death to commemorate his "eminence, pure moral worth and sustaining dignity of character." They noted his fidelity to justice and the law and the clarity, comprehensiveness, and vigor of his intelligence. The jurists and lawyers applauded his rulings from the bench as "enduring monuments of judicial patience, diligence, thoroughness of investigation, profound learning, striking views and lucid expositions of the laws and the Constitution."[63] A Tallahassee editor added, "Judge Baltzell was too well known in this State to require at our hands any extended comments on the loss the State has sustained by his death."[64]

Thomas Douglas, Supreme Court Chief Justice, 1846–1851; Supreme Court Justice, 1854–1855

While Thomas Baltzell offered the supreme court spontaneity and eccentricity, Thomas Douglas provided it with experience and a strict moral tone. The future justice was born at Wallingford, Connecticut, on April 27, 1790. He received a public school education, where he was exposed to "reading, writing, arithmetic, as far as the rule of three, and grammar."[65] A teacher aunt also tutored him, providing Douglas educational advantages that he acknowledged warmly. After concluding his formal education, Douglas remained for a time in Connecticut, but, after he reached age twenty-four, important changes altered his life's course. First, on September 26, 1814, the future justice married Hannah Sanford. The next year the couple moved to Madison, Indiana, to seek their fortune. Douglas opened a general store and established a button and tin factory. He soon acquainted himself with local leaders, counting as friends Indiana's first governor, United States senators, and congressional representative.[66]

The financial crisis following the Panic of 1819 undercut Douglas's hopes for prosperity, forcing him toward a legal career in order to satisfy a $30,000 debt. He read two hundred pages of law each day, along with two hundred pages of the Bible. Community leaders rewarded his diligence by asking him to run for office as an associate judge. The venture succeeded, and, once elected, Douglas gained the confidence of other prominent men. He particularly impressed Judge Davis Floyd, who permitted the novice jurist to handle some matters by himself.[67]

Douglas's judicial duties led him to bar membership within two years after the election. The achievement occurred after he attended a fledgling attorney's bar examination. When Floyd invited his judicial protégé to question the candidate, Douglas accepted. "Deeming the examination rather too superficial," he recalled, "I took the young man in hand, and questioned him near an hour." Douglas then told Floyd, "[I]f that was the way he made lawyers, I would take a [local] license."[68] The judge agreed to the request on condition that Douglas not leave the bench. Afterward, Douglas continued reading the law and eventually took the Indiana supreme court's examination. That court admitted him to its bar on November 12, 1822.[69]

During the period of Douglas's preparation for the Indiana bar, an event transpired that resulted in his relocation. President John Quincy Adams appointed Judge Floyd to be a commissioner of land claims in East Florida. Floyd, in turn, encouraged the young lawyer to visit the new territory. He accepted the suggestion and, while in Pensacola, decided to apply for the vacant position of district attorney for the Western District. The application was denied, but Douglas nonetheless determined to make a permanent home in Florida. He was admitted to practice before the Pensacola-area courts on May 28, 1824.[70]

Douglas's advancement in Florida Territory came at a rapid pace. Two years after his arrival, friends proposed him for appointment as district attorney of the Eastern District, a position that had become available when incumbent Edgar Macon was dismissed by Judge Joseph L. Smith for contempt of court. This time President Adams acquiesced and on May 22 commissioned Douglas to the office. After a harrowing sea voyage, Douglas reached St. Augustine to assume his new responsibilities. One year passed before he could return to Indiana to gather his family and bring them to the territory.[71]

Because of certain personality characteristics, Douglas found St. Augustine's easygoing atmosphere difficult to accept and sometimes hostile. The lawyer held his religious commitments and beliefs firmly, and he judged others by the standards of those beliefs. Especially, Douglas entertained a hatred of alcoholic beverage consumption at a time and in a place where drinking to excess formed a way of life for many. Even his friend and mentor Judge Smith suffered in his critical eye. Douglas believed Smith to be a "gigantic man, both mentally and physically [who was qualified to fill] any, even the most exalted station in the government," yet he could condemn the same man for his "unbounded prejudices and ungovernable passions and dissolute habits." As Douglas explained of the judge, "He was intemperate in his habits and of the most uncontrollable temper."[72]

At St. Augustine the district attorney discovered that danger lurked in the moral condemnation of others. During the first decade of his residence, assassins on three occasions attempted to rid the community of his presence. The first incident happened not long after his arrival, when someone shot into his bedroom after midnight on a Sunday morning. Ten years later two similar efforts also ended unsuccessfully. "What motive could have induced [the assassin] to attempt the life of a valuable citizen is known only to himself?" wrote the local press. "Mr. Douglas is not aware of having given offence to any one, either in a private or official capacity." Although the mayor offered a reward of $300 on one of the occasions, no suspects were apprehended.[73]

Douglas's relationship with Smith illustrates the ambivalent character of his intercourse with many of his legal community peers. As mentioned, Smith mentored Douglas, but the district attorney regarded the judge contemptuously for his drinking and other "dissolute" habits. Still, as a friend, Douglas could advocate to President Andrew Jackson Smith's reappointment as judge, knowing that Jackson possessed personal and political hostility to Smith. At the expense of such a friendship, however, once Douglas grasped what appeared to him a question of morality, he could not relinquish it. An example arose out of the dismissal of District Attorney Macon. With partisan considerations playing a role, Douglas, as well as future congressional delegate Charles Downing, investigated the reasons for Macon's departure from office. An irritated Smith had related records removed from the court clerk's office. Then-delegate Joseph M. White took State Department copies under similar circumstances. Because of the situation and in spite of the older man's kindnesses, as Douglas later wrote, he developed "an opinion unfavorable to Judge Smith."[74]

The district attorney's sense of morality occasionally failed him when it came to his own dealings. The principal instance involved Douglas's actions as a trustee of a banking house named the Southern Life Insurance and Trust Company. The firm, formed in 1835 to develop land in East Florida, sold territorial bonds to speculators outside of Florida, using the proceeds to fund loans for local investment. The concern began as a legitimate enterprise involving prominent East Floridians, but control was seized by out-of-state speculators, and the business's practices degenerated into fraud. Numerous original backers—such as future justice Joseph Bradford Lancaster—separated themselves from its affairs in a timely manner, but Douglas maintained his involvement. After the state dissolved the bank in 1843 due to mismanagement, Douglas declined to accept any responsibility and argued disingenuously that the Second Seminole War, not fraud, had caused its demise.[75]

Questions of personal honesty raised by the bank incident did not typify Douglas's life or reputation. "I consider him a gentleman of great purity of character—honest and upright—and a good lawyer," testified Judge Isaac H. Bronson in 1845.[76] Douglas's personal financial condition supports the judge's assertion. In the hard economic times of the 1840s, his assets declined markedly. At the decade's beginning Douglas possessed a slave family of five and later purchased 440 acres of agricultural land. By 1848 his taxable holdings included only a town lot in St. Augustine and another in Ocala.[77]

Douglas's reputation as a lawyer and public servant, as also suggested by Bronson, brought him regard within the territory's legal and political communities. He developed expertise in Spanish land-grant cases, cooperating closely with Delegate White and federal officials in properly resolving them. Attorney General William Wirt praised his efforts, and the work reportedly won Douglas reappointment by President Jackson despite the district attorney's opposition to the president's candidacy. Douglas recalled that his opponents once sought to remove him from office with Jackson's approval. "They reckoned . . . without their host," he boasted, "[for] they did not know the old hero, or my standing with him."[78]

Six presidential administrations benefited from Douglas's service as East Florida district attorney, but in 1845 his career entered a new phase. The state's legislature had elected Florida's first circuit (and ex officio supreme court) judges, but the victor in the eastern circuit race, Judge Bronson, declined to accept. Instead Bronson suggested to Governor William D. Moseley another possibility. "I have no doubt [that Douglas] would make a good judge," he wrote, "better than any other man that could be appointed from that District."[79] The governor took the advice and made a temporary appointment, after which Douglas resigned as district attorney on October 8. The legislature ratified the designation on December 6.[80]

East Florida's circuit judge served on the supreme court from 1846 to 1851. After the court received an identity separate from the circuit courts, Douglas continued as circuit judge. In 1853, though, he entered his name as a candidate for justice in the first popular elections for the supreme court. His friends trumpeted his candidacy by noting that "the public mind appears to be anxious to discard every thing like political or partizun feeling in the selection of the various candidates to fill the Judgeships of the Supreme Court" and that "the people have never failed to appreciate [Douglas's] merits."[81] He achieved election and returned to the high court in 1854.[82]

Death from pleurisy cut short Douglas's second period of supreme court service. The end came at Jacksonville on September 11, 1855, four months after he fell ill during a journey from Tallahassee to St. Augustine. Six years before, an editor had spoken highly of his "great ability, untiring industry, and dignified deportment" and expressed wishfully, "May the evening of his days be as bright and as blessed as his life has been irreproachable."[83] After receiving news of the justice's passing, another added, "He has led a life of astonishing activity and usefulness, and has died in a ripe old age, covered in honors, and bearing the regrets of his fellow citizens."[84]

George W. Macrae, Supreme Court Justice, 1847–1848

If mystery surrounds the life of any member of Florida's supreme court, that individual is George W. Macrae. Available sources fail to disclose the date and place of his birth, his family history, or the path by which he gained federal appointment in the territory. One 1846 account hinted at his age and origins outside Florida by stating that "Judge Macrae is a young and comparatively new man." It added, "He has mingled little in the political strifes of the Territory or State."[85]

Macrae first emerged into prominence in Florida affairs in 1842. On August 24 of that year, President John Tyler appointed him United States attorney for the Southern District. After fulfilling the responsibilities of that office for two years, Macrae won election to the territorial senate from South Florida. His party identification appeared unclear then as now. The St. Augustine *News* believed him to be a Whig, while its crosstown rival, the *Florida Herald and Southern Democrat*, insisted that he was "a Democrat of the first water."[86]

Macrae's unwillingness to engage in rough partisanship, as well as uncertainties about his party preference, proved the linchpin to his political success. When the council began its deliberations in January 1845, regional rivalries and bitter divisions over the statehood question prompted efforts by East Floridians, mostly Whigs, to block the election of Middle Florida's William D. Moseley as senate president. Instead, the body's members selected Macrae, whom they perceived as fair and moderate, to oversee the balloting. Three days of votes ended in impasse, when Thomas Baltzell moved the South Florida senator's election in Moseley's stead. Macrae's subsequent actions as president "gave general satisfaction."[87] One man referred to his manner as "highly dignified and consistent."[88]

Following the council's adjournment, Macrae intended to pursue his political career. He announced his candidacy for the state senate seat representing Hillsborough, Dade, and Monroe counties. The news found a positive reception statewide, with one friendly editor declaring, "We feel assured that the people of that District cannot make a better selection."[89] The plan died aborning, however, as Macrae withdrew from the race. His reasons may be gleaned from the fact that, when the general assembly met in July, Macrae was working as an aide to Governor Moseley. In that capacity he delivered to a joint legislative session the governor's first official message.[90]

Moseley's respect for Macrae paid dividends for the former district attorney and senator. Legislators deadlocked over election of a southern circuit judge. When in December 1845 Samuel Williams Carmack was chosen, he declined to serve. The governor then turned to Macrae, whom the legislature also had considered. "We understand that his appointment was solicited by citizens of South Florida of both political parties," noted one newspaper. It continued, "[As a relative newcomer to politics, he] may well be supposed neither to have excited prejudices in the minds of others, nor to have suffered his own mind to become embittered against any portion of those whose rights and interests he will now become to a certain extent the [custodian]."[91]

Macrae's nonpartisan appeal earned him appointment in 1846 but frustrated any real hope of his eventual election by the legislature. At a time when judges alternated circuits, he earned approval from both sides of the political divide. "If we are not misinformed," commented the Whiggish *Pensacola Gazette*, "Judge M. gave equal satisfaction in the Middle Circuit as in the Western."[92] Still, in December 1847 the Whigs, who exerted greater influence in the legislature after 1845, chose their leader and house speaker Joseph Bradford Lancaster to replace Macrae. Justice Macrae had served a single year on the supreme court.

Macrae's activities after stepping down from the court are as uncertain as are his origins. He returned to Key West at least briefly but either died or departed from the state within a short time. He can be remembered nonetheless for the character he helped to bestow upon the Florida judiciary. As one acquaintance remarked of him, "[He was] highly esteemed as an upright, honest man, and of good legal abilities: the greatest requisites for an acceptable Judge."[93]

Joseph Bradford Lancaster, Supreme Court Justice, 1848–1851

Joseph Bradford Lancaster served on the Florida supreme court from 1848 to 1850, the last elected circuit judge to sit on the court by right of law. Though his tenure on the tribunal occurred early in statehood, his background and credentials hearkened back to those of the federal judges appointed in territorial days. He was born in Kentucky to John and Catherine Miles Lancaster about 1790. In preparation for what proved to be a wide-ranging public career, he read law and achieved admission to the Kentucky bar, establishing offices at Bardstown and Lebanon. In 1815 he married Presbyterian minister's daughter Annie Blair, with whom he eventually shared a large family.[94]

Kentucky family and professional contacts brought Lancaster to Florida and introduced him into territorial influence. Fellow Bardstown resident, William Pope DuVal, captured Florida's governorship in 1822. Apparently DuVal encouraged his colleague to relocate with him, arranging for the young lawyer a position as assistant secretary to East Florida's board of land commissioners. A legal practice at St. Augustine led, in 1825, to his admission to the bar of the territorial court of appeals and his appointment to the legislative council. The same year Lancaster emerged into Florida's political fray by siding with Judge Joseph L. Smith in defense of charges that the judge had misused the powers of his office.[95]

The connections network that brought Lancaster to Florida extended well beyond DuVal. Lancaster was cousin to Middle Florida planter and politician George T. Ward, and, through Ward and his sister Virginia Ward Braden, he enjoyed an entrée into Middle Florida planter society. His Kentucky origins also afforded him access to leaders such as Richard Keith Call and David S. Walker. By the early 1830s many of these men had associated as the powerful Nucleus.[96]

Such connections brought to Lancaster more than social acceptance. In 1826 he received appointment as St. Johns County justice of the peace. The next year he became judge of the Alachua County court and later acted as the county's 1830 federal census enumerator. He took a larger step in 1831 by accepting presidential designation as first collector of the Port of St. Johns at Jacksonville. There his circle of friends grew, and Lancaster prospered. He associated in business and politics with men such as town founder Isaiah D. Hart and area political figures including Jacob Summerlin, Sr., and Benjamin A. Putnam. They shared investments in the Union Bank and the Southern Life Insurance and Trust Company and planned together projects such as a Pensacola-to-Jacksonville railroad. Politically they identified mostly with the Whig party, and they trumpeted opposition to statehood and support for territorial division.[97]

Lancaster's roots sank deep into Florida's soil during the 1820s and 1830s. As they did, his influence expanded. As early as 1832, friends attempted to secure his election as chief clerk of the territorial council but failed by one vote. They succeeded in 1833, and he won reelection for six years thereafter. DuVal appointed him inspector of lumber for Duval County in 1834. Aided by distinguished service as a militia officer during the Second Seminole War (he was badly wounded near Micanopy in the conflict's opening engagements), Lancaster's political future seemed limitless. He received consideration for the 1838 Whig congressional delegate nomination. In 1839 Duval County voters rewarded him with election to the territorial house, where he served in 1840, 1842, 1843, and 1844. The final two years he presided over the chamber. Lancaster was remembered as a prompt and decisive legislator of "unvaried courteousness" who displayed "a comprehensive and well-stored intellect" and "sound, discriminating judgment."[98]

Lancaster's abilities won him respect, but his professional and political careers brought difficulties as well. Politically, his effectiveness drew resentment, and his willingness to take decisive stands added more enemies. Middle Florida Democrats especially found him distasteful, as he led East Florida pro-division forces in what became bitter political warfare during the early 1840s. Some of his Middle Florida Whig allies, unsympathetic with anti-statehood policies, angrily reacted to his insistence that taxpayers were not liable for defaulted bank bonds backed by the territorial government. Bondholders, Lancaster argued, should legally pursue bank stockholders for satisfaction. The banks, he asserted, deserved contempt for oppressing the territory with the issuance of worthless currency.[99]

The East Florida lawmaker's animus toward banks may have stemmed from personal as well as political reasons. In the wake of the Second Seminole War, the Panic of 1837, and the collapse of Florida's banks, his financial position had deteriorated drastically. The same situation recurred in the 1850s, after which his daughter Laura explained: "My own dear Father twice lost every thing he owned on earth and twice struggled thro—once when his children were all small. My mother being and having been at that time for years at death's door—the Second time most of his children were grown or large enough to share in his distress."[100]

The combination of powerful enemies and financial troubles forestalled Lancaster's governmental career. In early 1845 a Whig caucus nominated him for Congress, but the circumstances forced him to withdraw. The same year and in 1846 he received consideration for election as circuit judge. In the Democrat-controlled legislature, he lost first to Benjamin D. Wright and then to George W. Macrae.[101]

Lancaster rebounded after 1846, when he served as Jacksonville's mayor. The next year a hotly contested election resulted in his elevation to the house of representatives, although the cost ran high as his political opponents accused the Whig's supporters of election fraud. The body's Whig majority thereafter named Lancaster as its speaker. Son William B. Lancaster benefited, too, being chosen as chief clerk. The speaker's election permitted legislators to engage in the type of political humor beloved in the 1840s as much as it is enjoyed today. First, lawmakers—tongue firmly in cheek—called for the house to adjourn to Jacksonville. Further, their resolution directed members to wear red roses on their left shoulders and renamed the chamber the "House of Lancaster," a not very subtle reference to the English War of the Roses.[102]

The speakership catapulted Lancaster in December 1847 to the judgeship of the southern circuit. His detractors had feared "that worst of all functionaries—a political judge," but his work on the bench earned praise. One opponent found him to be "as unswerving, impartial, prompt, discriminating and sagacious a Judge as he was conceded to have been as Speaker." The man insisted that many of Lancaster's critics had "acknowledge[d] their mistake—they concede him to be an important accession to the Judiciary."[103] A courtroom visitor added in 1850, "Judge Lancaster at present occupies the bench, a gentleman of liberal views, large intelligence, and courteous manners—one of your old school gentleman lawyers."[104]

The judge remained on the circuit bench until 1853, when he lost a three-man race while seeking reelection in Florida's first popular judicial elections. Meanwhile, problems plagued Lancaster. Without a state salary he needed money, a fact that forced him to transfer from Key West to the village of Tampa in order to pursue possibilities in railroad development. About the same time his Whig party collapsed, a casualty of the 1852 state elections. He moved into the American or Know Nothing party, but it possessed little strength in South Florida. He attempted to soften its image by rejecting its anti-Catholic and anti-immigrant biases, but his 1856 race as party nominee for the house of representatives fell short of victory. More happily, on February 16 that year his fellow Tampans had elected him the town's first mayor. He died there, shortly after the legislative defeat, on November 25, 1856.[105]

One of Lancaster's protégés, future justice and governor Ossian Bingley Hart, well summarized his mentor's life and career. "Blest with a high order of intellect, with a heart full of kindly feelings," Hart declaimed, "he was the comfort and pride of his family, the ornament of every social circle in which he mingled, and was eminently useful to the people of our State." Hart continued: "As a lawyer few were his equals in point of talent, and in fidelity to those whose interests were in his hands; and, as a Judge, none more anxious that justice should be done. To say that he had none of the frailties of human nature, would be to call him perfect, which no man is, but I think I can truthfully say that he had less of those frailties than most men."[106]

Chapter 7

An Independent Supreme Court

During the first decade after the Florida supreme court's organization, a series of changes in its statutory basis and in personnel profoundly affected the court and its perspectives. These alterations occurred against a background of international war, sectional crisis, and partisan rancor. They created external and internal tensions with which the justices were forced to deal as they endeavored to meet the challenges of interpreting law and dispensing justice over a broad territory still, in great part, subject to frontier conditions. The response of court members, while varying in motive and substance, proved equal to the task and laid the foundation for the tribunal's work over the next century and a half.

As mentioned in the previous chapter, the court initially organized in 1846 with only three members. When its term began in January 1847, Justice George W. Macrae joined Thomas Douglas, Thomas Baltzell, and George Sydney Hawkins to complete the panel. As he did, the Mexican War continued to rage, provoking, in turn, controversy between northern and southern states over extension of slavery into any territory annexed as a result of the conflict. Five months earlier Pennsylvania congressman David Wilmot had proposed that "neither slavery nor involuntary servitude shall ever exist in any part of said territory, except for crime, whereof the party shall first be duly convicted."[1] This Wilmot Proviso, though adopted by the House of Representatives, was blocked by southern senators. The issue it raised persisted, though, and by 1849 cries of secession were heard through the South. The famed Compromise of 1850 stilled the furor for a time, but rising antislavery sentiment kept alive the threat of disunion.[2]

In Florida, politicians naturally reacted to national events, but local partisan differences usually predominated. By 1847 the Whigs—who generally opposed secession—had taken control of the state legislature, reversing the 1845 pro-

Democrat landslide. The following year they captured the executive branch as well. Thomas Brown, a Leon County planter, bested Democrat William Bailey by about 500 votes out of 8,000 cast to become governor. Brown's ticketmate, Edward Carrington Cabell, also defeated former governor William Pope DuVal for election to the United States House of Representatives. Whig presidential candidate Zachary Taylor, a commander of United States troops during Second Seminole War operations, earned 1,300 more Florida votes than did Democrat Lewis Cass.[3]

These elections ran "hot and heavy." The Whig victories emboldened party advocates, who were embittered by their experiences. They determined to allocate important governmental positions only to their allies, a practice at variance with the somewhat accommodationist attitudes of Democrats evidenced by the judicial elections of men such as Samuel Williams Carmack and George Sydney Hawkins. Sectional differences continued to overlay and undercut partisan alliances, however, with confusion and chicanery sometimes the result.[4]

Within this evolving political context, the 1847 and 1848 supreme court terms proceeded smoothly. At the January 1847 session, for instance, the tribunal rendered twenty-six decisions with opinions. The large majority of cases dealt with contract disputes among private citizens, mostly concerning bills of exchange and promissory notes. Virtually all of the opinions reflected a unanimous court. Baltzell authored nine decisions, Macrae and Hawkins six apiece, and Douglas five. Additionally, Hawkins and Baltzell each dissented on one occasion. The jurists spent the greater part of the year working as circuit judges. Under the "alternating plan" then in existence, each judge alternated holding court in the other judges' circuits. As a result, not until the spring of 1847 did all of the judges hold court within their own circuit.[5]

After the court's adjournment in 1847, the state's emerging legal system benefited from a most noteworthy accomplishment. Future justice Leslie Atchinson Thompson completed the digest of Florida law in time for the state to order 1,500 copies in July, paying $2,100 for them. Each county clerk received a volume. The rest were sold at cost to legal practitioners and to the public.[6]

The new Whig-dominated legislature, which convened in November, desired to work its influence upon the legal system, as well. A broad range of subjects came to its attention. Questions as to the expiration of justice of the peace terms found practical resolution with a request that the governor make temporary reappointments of sitting judges until scheduled elections were held. More important, the assembly permitted and outlined procedures for criminal appeals. The law achieved passage after representatives Thomas Hagner and William Augustus Forward forged a workable compromise. Lawmakers decided, as well, to base solicitors' compensation primarily on a set salary rather than upon fees collected by the court. A few matters were set aside, at least temporarily. Justice Baltzell objected to having to make specific requisition for supplies, arguing the unconstitutionality of imposing nonjudicial duties upon supreme court justices. The legislators delayed consideration of his complaint but directed county commissioners and the comptroller to audit sheriffs and clerks in order to "save the Judges an irksome examination of petty accounts."[7]

The general assembly usually adopted simple, practical solutions to judicial problems, as suggested by the issue of terms for justices of the peace. Much credit goes to Hagner, a Leon County representative and the nephew and partner of Thomas Randall. Sensitivity to everyday problems complemented his practical turn of mind. By way of example, he opposed draconian divorce-law changes, which he contended worked undue hardships on couples during "an [already] unhappy period of time."[8] The same commonsense approach, when directed at procedures for government property sales, led him to recommend Saturday rather than Monday sales, as the former day was "usually devoted by the citizens to business in their county towns, and of consequence the better suited for a public sale day."[9] Striking a note that would be sounded again soon, Hagner also supported popular election of circuit judges, but in 1847 the bill failed of passage.[10]

The 1847 general assembly directly addressed the supreme court's composition, even though it did not subject its members to popular election. Democratic newspapers had aired rumors since the October election that the Whig leadership intended to oust Democratic judges before their terms had expired. Supposedly, David S. Walker would be named Middle District judge, with Thomas Randall and Samuel J. Douglas selected, respectively, for the East and West. The political coup failed, but Whig legislators succeeded in electing their house speaker as southern circuit judge. Among those considered were appointed incumbent George W. Macrae and Key West's Adam Gordon. The race actually amounted to a regional contest, as Middle Florida backed Thomas Randall while East Florida supported Joseph Bradford Lancaster, a Whig like Randall. During the first day of balloting, Randall's nephew Hagner recused himself from voting, which resulted in deadlock. Randall then withdrew, permitting Hagner to participate. The Leon County man offered his vote to Lancaster, who achieved the necessary majorities on the eleventh ballot. In the succeeding race for Lancaster's speakership, a later justice, Augustus Emmet Maxwell, narrowly lost to Santa Rosa County's John Chain.[11]

Lancaster's selection as a justice, because of his longtime association with activist Whig politics, spurred fears among some Floridians that the supreme court might be politicized. The concerns, for the most part, proved unfounded. During his first court term, held in 1848, Lancaster joined the majority in each of the twenty-eight opinions rendered. Only three decisions lacked unanimity, and Justice Baltzell authored the only two dissents. Justices Douglas and Baltzell wrote nine and ten opinions, respectively. Lancaster penned five and Hawkins four.

The election year of 1848, which resulted so happily for Whigs, fairly roiled with political maneuvering. Legislatively, the general assembly's greatest task involved the election of a United States senator to replace Democrat James D. Westcott. By December, four Whig candidates challenged each other for the honor, but, as so often was the case, regionalism complicated partisanship almost beyond understanding. In the end Pensacola-area Whig Jackson Morton, an experienced legislator and prosperous businessman, emerged victorious, although twenty-two of his thirty votes came from Democrats. Stories circulated thereafter that vote swapping for railroad charters, an issue that for the time had supplanted bank charters in importance, had provided the difference for Morton.[12]

The increasing attention paid to railroad and other internal improvement schemes and to partisan infighting over appointments amounted only to a part of the legislature's workload. Judicial issues numbered among assembly concerns, but 1848 found Whig leaders more likely to chastise judges, particularly Democratic ones, than to praise them. The proposal of most significance or, as Governor Moseley put it, "one of the most immediate pressing wants," involved creation of an independent supreme court.[13] Unfortunately, the idea received lukewarm consideration and a "do not pass" recommendation from the house judiciary committee. Instead, lawmakers indirectly rebuked Justice Baltzell for his complaint of the previous year about the unconstitutionality of requiring justices to requisition supplies. They ordered that to obtain "all stationery and candles necessary for the use of the Supreme Court, the Chief Justice thereof shall issue a requisition upon the officer having charge of the same."[14] The solons additionally struck at Baltzell by overruling his 1845 precedent of declaring an extra court term to avoid the possibility of lynching or mob violence. A new law prohibited all judges from holding any "extra or adjourned terms."[15]

Additional court-related measures commanded legislative time. Frustrated assembly members penalized jurists who did not adhere to the legally mandated schedule for opening court terms. They specified a sanction of "a deduction of one hundred dollars from his salary for each and every such default."[16] The legislators, illustrating Whiggish reservations about mass opinion, declined to approve popular election of circuit judges. When a constitutional amendment permitting such elections for probate judges obtained initial approval, they reduced the term of office from service during good behavior to a period of eight years. Moreover, legislators disputed whether they could elect new circuit and probate judges in advance of the expiration of established terms, since months would elapse after expiration but before a new legislature convened. The specifics of constitutional language on the matter compelled them to authorize the governor to appoint interim judges. Finally, on January 13, 1849, shortly before adjournment, they selected Robert Hayward, an old political associate of governor-elect Brown, as supreme court clerk.[17]

For two years after the conclusion of the 1848 legislative session, state and national political tensions heightened. Debates over the Wilmot Proviso and calls for southern secession exacerbated fears in both North and South, apprehensions never completely calmed by the Compromise of 1850. An outspoken, radical wing of the Florida Democratic party cried for disunion. Some moderate party members, unwilling to go so far, nonetheless agreed with the slogan "May peace be our motto till war is inevitable."[18] The majority of Floridians and most Whigs held unionist sentiments. "Every true Southern representative will not fail to give his vote and lift his voice in opposition to the schemes of northern incendiaries," declared one Whig organ, "but few will be found rash enough to propose disunion for a remedy. It is not remedy. It will kill, not cure, the patient."[19]

While a majority of Florida voters stood with the Union in 1849 and 1850, the passion of radical Democrats brought out a higher percentage of their supporters to the polls than did the less dramatic appeals of unionist Whigs. In the circumstances the 1850 elections left Florida with a government narrowly balanced between the two parties. Whig congressional delegate Cabell defeated his Democratic opponent, and Thomas Brown's four-year term ensured continued Whig occupancy of the governor's office. On the other hand, Democrat majorities of one in the state house and senate permitted that party to organize the legislature. These conditions set the legislative stage for deliberations central to Florida's future: election of a United States senator to assume office upon the expiration of David Levy Yulee's term, how to use millions of acres of federally donated state lands to encourage internal improvements such as railroads, and what action to take in light of repeated calls for an independent supreme court.[20]

In the meantime and amid the tumult, the supreme court had maintained its early cooperative spirit, a fact that helped to lend some stability and credibility to a bitterly divided state government. During 1849 the tribunal issued twenty-four opinions, twenty-one of which were unanimous. Chief Justice Douglas penned just under half of them, authoring eleven. Justice Hawkins added seven, and Justice Lancaster wrote four. Because Florida law prohibited court members from sitting in matters over which they had presided as circuit court judges and since most cases appealed were derived from the middle circuit, Justice Baltzell offered only two court opinions and one concurring opinion. The following year the situation remained virtually the same. Douglas and Lancaster composed the court's voice in most cases, while Baltzell did so less often than his three fellow justices.[21]

When the legislature met in November 1850 (voters had limited its sessions to every other year), fundamental issues of judicial organization held a prominent place on its agenda, but other subjects drew the most attention. In fact, the economic good times that a rapidly developing Florida had begun to enjoy by 1850 gave birth to demands for legislative initiative that nearly stole the political show from the usual regional and partisan rivalries. To encourage further growth, the Democrat-controlled general assembly created a privately owned State Bank of Florida, an action that would have been inconceivable a few years previously. The lawmakers established, as well, an internal improvement board to supervise state lands and to draft overall plans for a statewide system of internal improvements. The scheme assumed state grants in aid of the construction of railroads, canals, plank roads, and other projects.[22]

The excitement stirred by such advances captivated legislators and opinion leaders but in the end did not eclipse consideration of other pressing concerns. Governor Brown's annual message had focused on judicial reform. He had noted "defects" in the current system and highlighted the "inequality" among judicial districts. About two-thirds of the 105 cases considered by the supreme court during the first five years of its existence, he explained, had arisen in the middle circuit, forcing its judge to recuse himself from participation in most appeals. Brown insisted that such a state of affairs was "prejudiced [to residents of the middle circuit] by the exclusion of their judicial officer from the bench of this tribunal."[23]

The need for judicial change stemmed from even broader concerns, Brown argued. On a four-man supreme court, the specter of deadlock by tie vote loomed as a possibility. Further, the great distance of some portions of the state from Tallahassee and difficulties of travel contributed to minimize appeals from districts other than the middle circuit. Southern circuit residents, Brown declared, "are practically excluded from the Appellate Court by their distance from the seat of government." To overcome the problems, the Whig governor recommended retaining the existent system but with significant alterations. He mentioned the possibility of a statewide chancery court to handle equity matters, the judge of which would sit as a fifth member of the supreme court. He favored, though, redrawing circuit lines to add a fifth district.[24]

With the question of judicial reform squarely before them, legislators entertained a number of proposals along the spectrum from Brown's suggestions to authorization of an independent supreme court selected by popular vote. Failure of all the plans would not have surprised many, given that the chambers were so narrowly divided politically and regionally. The need for resolution triumphed, however, when a compromise authored by Escambia County representative Walker Anderson, a Democrat, achieved final approval on January 11, 1851. An independent supreme court, though not a popularly elected one, resulted.[25]

The new law dealt with many of the issues raised by Brown and in legislative debates. "[T]he Supreme Court of the State of Florida," it mandated, "shall be composed of one Chief Justice and two Associate Justices," who were to "hold their offices for eight years." Each member would receive "an annual salary of two thousand dollars, to be paid quarter-yearly." The statute attempted to overcome distance problems by having the court go to the state rather than requiring appeals to come to Tallahassee. The supreme court would hold one term per year in each of the four circuits, beginning in 1852. The law provided, moreover, that "no Justice of said Court, shall sit upon the determination of any case which he may have decided as Circuit Judge or in which he may have been engaged as counsel." Finally, in the event of disqualification of a justice to sit on an appeal, the legislation instructed the remaining court members to appoint a circuit judge who was "invested with full authority, in conjunction with the remaining Justices of the Supreme Court, to hear and determine the causes [of action]."[26]

The judicial reform act generally enjoyed a positive reception from the judiciary, the bar, and the public, but its implementation was far from complete. A few Floridians opposed higher taxes to pay for the new court. Others expressed fears that increased expenses would compel decreased salaries. "A poorly paid judiciary," explained the *Pensacola Gazette*, "is an evil to be dreaded above all others."[27] These slight concerns amounted to little, though, compared to those regarding which men would sit upon the courts.

The judicial elections drama subsequently unfolded in the general assembly amid tumult, regional interest, and similar characteristics of Florida legislative politics as usual. The rough equality of party strength and the required election of a United States senator added flavor and enhanced opportunities for deal making. In particular, Democratic legislators from Tampa, Key West, and Pensacola held political grudges against senatorial incumbent Yulee, who had advocated construction of a cross-peninsular railroad against their communities' interests. These Democrats seemingly avowed a willingness to elect Whig judges, if Whigs would unseat the senator in favor of Key West Democrat Stephen Mallory. One additional factor weighed in the judge-selection process. Before balloting began, Attorney General David P. Hogue, a Whig, submitted his opinion that, under the Florida constitution, a sitting circuit judge would be ineligible for a supreme court seat. Whether the legislature would abide by the opinion remained to be seen.[28]

Voting commenced during a joint legislative session on January 14, 1851, and the influence of a loose coalition composed of Whigs and Tampa, Key West, and Pensacola Democrats evidenced itself. Circuit judgeships received initial consideration. At first, Southern District judge Joseph Bradford Lancaster withheld his name from that circuit's contest while awaiting supreme court nomination. After seven ballots he relented, though, and accepted reelection as circuit judge. Chief Justice Thomas Douglas then defeated William Augustus Forward for the Eastern District, also apparently eliminating Douglas from the supreme court balloting. Whig nemesis Thomas Baltzell's lack of voting strength resulted in his loss of the Middle District judgeship race to Whig lawyer J. Wayles Baker. Justice Hawkins thereafter achieved easy victory as western circuit judge.[29]

Supreme court selection followed, beginning with the election of a chief justice. Middle Florida Democrat and future governor John Milton, codifier and Whig editor Leslie Atchinson Thompson, and Pensacola's Democratic representative Walker Anderson vied for the position. Anderson had drafted the law creating the court and had helped to forge the Whig-Democrat voting group. The coalition persisted, and Anderson won after five ballots. Apalachicola Whig Albert Gallatin Semmes, an 1838 constitutional convention delegate, followed without serious competition to receive designation as justice. A bruising fight thereupon erupted when ten individuals contested the remaining seat.[30]

Six failed attempts at election of a second justice were undertaken before the legislature turned to a different, though not unrelated, task. The core of lawmakers who formed the voting coalition required four ballots to oust Yulee from the United States Senate and to position Mallory in his place. That success behind them, they chose John P. K. Savage as supreme court clerk. For six days afterwards competition for the final supreme court seat occupied the legislative agenda. In spite of the attorney general's opinion, Lancaster demonstrated electoral strength but could not obtain a majority. He withdrew on the second day, leaving Democratic senators William Augustus Forward and Augustus Emmet Maxwell as the leading contenders. Finally, Forward also withdrew, and Thompson again entered the lists. On the forty-fifth ballot, the coalition secured election for Thompson.[31]

The circumstances of the judicial elections of 1851 cast a cloud upon the court that within two years would cause another fundamental readjustment in its makeup and the manner of its selection. In the interim, Anderson, Semmes, and Thompson possessed a charge to establish an independent court. These men, who played such important roles in the court's history, are profiled in the following pages.

Walker Anderson, Supreme Court Chief Justice, 1851–1853

Walker Anderson's career abounded in paradox. An aristocratic Virginian, he found his home in a rough Florida Panhandle port town. A well-trained lawyer, he preferred teaching and business. Elected to the 1838 constitutional convention from alienated West Florida as a man with Whig principles, he subsequently led pro-statehood and antibank forces, while assisting in the formation of the Democratic party. He could entertain ideas of secession and, at the same time, enjoy the benefits of federal office. In spite of the convolutions, he engendered trust and respect, qualities that proved vital to the supreme court's first years as an independent entity.

The future chief justice was born in Petersburg, Virginia, on July 18, 1801, to parents Daniel and Mary Reid Cameron Anderson. He matured in that town's comfortable environment, then studied law at Raleigh, North Carolina, with his uncle, Judge Duncan Cameron. At age twenty-one Anderson married Phoebe Hawks of New Bern, North Carolina, and subsequently practiced law, except during 1831–32 when he served as professor of history and English at the University of North Carolina. Through this period, apparently, he yearned for the challenges a new environment might offer.[32]

Anderson's opportunity arrived late in 1835 when he decided to relocate to Pensacola. According to his son, the family journeyed "from North Carolina to Florida in carriages, with wagons and negroes following." The Second Seminole War was underway, and they traveled in fear of massacre. After arrival at Pensacola, Anderson learned that the dangers lurked where he least expected them. He opened lumber and mercantile businesses, but local denizens quickly tested the newcomer. "[T]hrough the dishonesty of persons whom he trusted," Anderson's son remembered, "he lost his money and property, and was reduced to poverty."[33]

The financial calamity pushed Anderson into a law practice and, eventually, politics. An 1838 murder trial especially heightened local regard for him. The "dignity and urbanity of [his] demeanor" and his "superior talents and acquire-

Walker Anderson

Albert Gallatin Semmes

Leslie Atchinson Thompson

An independent supreme court. The legislative council created a supreme court independent of the circuit courts on January 11, 1851, and court convened for the first time on Thursday, January 30. Two changes were made: a new term in July and August 1851 was held, and the court commenced annual sittings in three additional cities—Jacksonville, Tampa, and Marianna. The council's 1851 election of members of the supreme court would be its last. In 1853 a bill was enacted providing for popular elections of high court jurists.

ments" produced a jury recommendation of mercy for his guilty client, although the judge sentenced the man to death.[34] As a lawyer, Anderson, recalled his son, "speedily rose to eminence."[35] His election as an Escambia County delegate to the 1838 St. Joseph constitutional convention numbered among the rewards.

The nature of the Escambia delegate's role in the constitutional convention doubtlessly surprised some of his supporters. At Pensacola, Anderson had associated with men such as his fellow delegate Jackson Morton who later were identified with the Whig party. Yet on the convention's eve he accepted the presidency of a caucus called the Jeffersonian Republican Democrats, from which the territory's Democratic party emerged. Although West Floridians had suffered less than other territorial residents from banking scandals, Anderson embraced tough antibank policies as a member of the banking committee. Further, he backed statehood and opposed division, positions finding little favor in the alienated Panhandle.[36]

Anderson's actions during the constitutional convention may have risen out of conviction, but he may also have been eyeing a statewide political career. In any event, he secured election to the house of representatives in 1840 and redoubled his efforts on behalf of Florida statehood. He became one of the Democrats most closely linked to the issue, provoking criticisms from some East Floridians for his "desperate FRAUD."[37] Even in Escambia County his position faced rejection at popular assemblies, but other issues soon rehabilitated his local standing.[38]

The practice of law once again opened doors for Anderson. Shortly after the constitutional convention, he had commenced a partnership with fellow Democrat Thomas Baltzell, which exposed him to Middle Florida's influential social and political circles. Also, in May 1841 his Virginia connections assisted him in attaining appointment by President John Tyler as United States attorney for West Florida. In that position he successfully prosecuted one of the territorial period's most controversial cases, that of the abolitionist Jonathan Walker, discussed earlier in this volume. Anderson's success carried personal and political rewards. His professionalism earned the respect even of the defendant, who thanked the prosecutor for "his kindness and humanity towards me both in his private and official capacity."[39] Conversely, Anderson's seeming defeat of abolitionism propelled him back into the legislative council, this time to the 1845 senate.[40]

The chance for greater office teased Anderson in 1845, but the reality eluded him. He chaired the territorial senate's judiciary committee early in the year, but his energy focused on another chairmanship, that of a panel to identify the proper course of action to obtain Florida's speedy admission to the Union. Congress moved more quickly than expected, however, and statehood received approval while the council was meeting. Anderson did not return to the senate in the first state elections, but his standing kept his name before legislators. As a "ripe scholar, [whose] acquirements are extensive and varied with polished manners and an amiable disposition," he vied within the Democratic caucus for selection as United States Senate nominee.[41] In the day's politics, sparsely populated West Florida usually took third place to the state's middle and eastern regions; the same held true with the balloting, as Anderson's vote total lagged behind those of East Florida's David Levy Yulee and Middle Florida's James D. Westcott.[42]

Other interests occupied Anderson following the senatorial defeat. His civic and social responsibilities at Pensacola were numerous and important. A lay leader in the Episcopal church, he worked on behalf of numerous good causes. He opposed violent practices such as dueling, having on one occasion rejected a challenge from the notorious Augustus Alston "proffered on some trivial pretext of insult to the Whig party."[43] He had played a key role in the founding of the Pensacola Academy and long had expressed a particular concern for the education of the poor. In 1847 he assumed responsibility as commissioner of public schools for West Florida. Earlier he, Baltzell, and Thomas Cooper had worked as agents for the selection of Florida's congressionally donated seminary lands. After statehood he joined with other local leaders to urge creation of an institution of higher learning at Pensacola as one of the eight projected state seminaries. His appointment as president of the board of trustees of West College Institute ensued in 1848.[44]

Other civic and business concerns occupied Anderson's attention, as well. The same year as his West College Institute appointment, President James Polk named him navy agent for the port of Pensacola. The position, which he occupied for two years, carried responsibility for the government's valued Santa Rosa peninsula live-oak plantation. Anderson also promoted transportation development. Alabama designated him a commissioner of the proposed Alabama and Florida Railroad, and in 1849 he began emphasizing the urgency of road completion to Pensacola's citizens. He accepted subscriptions of the line's stock through his law office and traveled as far as New York City to attract other investors. As a stop-gap measure, he advocated immediate construction of a plank road to link Pensacola with Montgomery.[45]

The calls on his time and energies notwithstanding, Anderson's love of politics kept him interested in Democratic party affairs. His name became connected with further senatorial speculation in 1848, but fellow townsman Jackson Morton went to Washington. More significantly, he involved himself in the growing national crisis over slavery. Years earlier he already had revealed a sense of cautious sectional chauvinism. "The ear must be deaf which does not hear the muttering of the storm on our northern horizon," he had informed a St. Augustine audience. "To meet it, let us be united, but let us ever act on the defensive."[46] Reflecting Anderson's continued sensitivity on the subject, Governor William D. Moseley in 1849 dispatched him, as one of the state's senior Democratic statesmen, to a Memphis, Tennessee, southern convention where secessionist rhetoric filled the halls. Anderson's own expressions carried a more moderate tone. Still, Escambia residents, in electing him to the state house of representatives in late 1850, probably agreed with a leading Democratic organ's description of the former Virginian as "a gentleman of distinguished ability, a thorough-going Southern man in his feelings."[47]

Anderson chaired the general assembly's joint committee on federal relations at a time when the effectiveness of the Compromise of 1850 in preserving the Union was yet to be realized. Governor Thomas Brown had requested authority to call a southern secession convention under some circumstances. Perhaps because Anderson and other Democrats saw the Whig governor's move as an attempt to enhance the popularity of his own party, they sidetracked the effort. To underscore the Democratic position, the chairman nonetheless issued in January 1851 a strongly worded report. It warned, "Concession by the South, for the sake of the Union, has now been made to the very verge of dishonor, and every Southern heart revolts at submission to further injustice."[48]

The joint committee's actions came just in time to release Anderson to concentrate on duties as chairman of the judiciary committee. As such, he urged creation of an independent supreme court. He favored selection of justices by popular election, a method he had come to prefer for United States senatorial contests, as well. In order to obtain final passage, Anderson compromised and authored a plan for legislative election of the new court. Three days after the bill received gubernatorial approval, Representative Anderson accepted election as the tribunal's chief justice. As his term did not begin until assembly adjournment, he continued to vote in the house, supporting Albert Gallatin Semmes and William Augustus Forward for election as justices. Eventually he relented in Forward's case to back the election of Justice Leslie Atchinson Thompson. His own selection had been praised. Noted the *Pensacola Gazette*, "His habits of thought and research, his mild and patient temper; his profound legal learning, and his spirit of impartiality combine to qualify him in an eminent degree for the high office to which he has been chosen."[49]

The chief justice's tenure on the supreme court lasted only for two years. In

1852 the general assembly called for popular election of the court. In May of the next year, not long before the first elections, Anderson resigned to return to his Pensacola law practice and to accept a directorship of the Alabama and Florida Railroad Company. He accepted, as well, reappointment as Pensacola's local naval agent. But his health declined. At the time of his death on January 18, 1857, he had been "long confined to the house by lingering and painful illness."[50] Of Anderson, a Pensacola editor commented, "A Christian gentleman, a lawyer of eminent ability, and ever foremost in the advocacy of measures of general weal, his memory demands no eulogy at the hands of the public journalist, for his name and character are familiar to all."[51]

Albert Gallatin Semmes, Supreme Court Justice, 1851–1853

Albert Gallatin Semmes shared with Walker Anderson his southern heritage, legal skills, pro-statehood sympathies, and service in Florida's 1838 constitutional convention. Otherwise, the two men diverged by political preference and by the degree of their public service within the territory and state. Despite the differences, Semmes's story, like Anderson's, follows closely the pattern of many of his Florida judicial predecessors.

Semmes was born to Andrew Green and Frances Herbert Semmes at Sand Hills near Augusta, Georgia, on August 18, 1810. The extended family encompassed numerous individuals of note, including future Confederate admiral Raphael Semmes and Louisiana's Confederate senator Thomas Semmes. Albert completed his degree at the University of Georgia, then gained admission to the state bar by reading law. On February 22, 1834, he married his cousin, Cuban-born Isabella V. Semmes. The marriage coincided with his appointment by Georgia's governor as solicitor general for the state's southern circuit. He served in that office until 1837, when the couple removed to Florida.[52]

Once at Apalachicola, the Semmeses established themselves in church, civic, and business affairs. Albert developed a reputation as a "moralist." He was a man with the "fear of God" before his eyes, who acted primarily based upon his conservative religious principles in determining what was just and who was "diligent in the pursuit of that knowledge which is most useful to society."[53] Semmes engaged in the practice of law as well as the profession of religion. For one year after January 1838 he worked in partnership with W. G. M. Davis; thereafter, he pursued the law as a sole practitioner. By the early 1850s he was earning the considerable annual income of $2,000.[54]

Politically, Semmes cooperated with pro-statehood, pro-banking enthusiasts who, after the 1838 constitutional convention, typified the Middle Florida Whigs. He made his position on the former issue clear at Apalachicola's Fourth of July celebration in 1838. His toast to the United States flag declared, "May another star be emblazoned upon its folds, and that star be Florida."[55] A public meeting soon nominated Semmes as a Franklin County delegate to the St. Joseph convention, a post to which he enjoyed unopposed election.[56]

The Franklin County delegate's service at the constitutional convention and in public office for more than a decade thereafter proved limited. He served on convention education and seat-of-government committees but took leave of absence on January 1, 1839, and did not return to the assembly. He also failed to sign its final charter. At Apalachicola he remained interested in local politics, where he lost a close election for mayor in 1840 by his deciding a technical point in favor of his opponent. Territory-wide he supported Middle Florida Whig political positions and candidates. He came to be recognized as a "talented lawyer" with "studious habits" and great "moral worth."[57] Those qualities, combined with his Whig political credentials, earned him legislative election over three other candidates as a supreme court justice in January 1851.[58]

Semmes's tenure on the Florida supreme court lasted only until 1853. The voters approved a constitutional amendment requiring popular election of justices, and his popularity proved insufficient in 1853. Subsequent to the defeat of his reelection bid, Semmes left the state for New Orleans, where his relative Thomas Semmes had moved in 1850. He practiced law in that city, although he refuged at Amite during the Crescent City's Union occupation. He volunteered for Confederate service as a marshal. After the conflict's end Semmes returned to New Orleans. Reportedly, he later died there on November 25, 1883, and his funeral was held at St. Joseph's Catholic Church.[59]

Leslie Atchinson Thompson, Supreme Court Justice, 1851–1853

While Floridians remember Leslie Atchinson Thompson primarily for his digest of laws, he served creditably on the supreme court and in numerous state and local positions of trust and responsibility. He was born in Charleston, South Carolina, on October 8, 1806. His family moved to Savannah, where he attended college and studied law with Judge Thomas U. P. Charlton. He achieved admission to the bar on June 25, 1826. The following year Thompson moved to Tallahassee. One account suggests that, after paying his traveling expenses and those incident to setting up a law office, only $20 remained to him. That amount he loaned to a needy friend. On April 5, 1829, his finances rejuvenated, Thompson married a fifteen-year-old Georgian, Jane M. Everett.[60]

At Tallahassee the Thompsons established themselves in the community's society. They held membership in St. John's Episcopal Church, where Leslie served as warden and vestryman. Among the Masons, he became a grand warden. The couple moved easily in the highest social circles. By 1829 he held the town treasurer's position. In 1830, 1832, and 1840 Thompson presided as intendant or mayor. For six months in 1829 the young lawyer edited the *Florida Advocate* and, in June 1831, the *Floridian*. Governor William Pope DuVal appointed him auditor in 1832 and judge of the Leon County court in 1833. Governor Richard Keith Call reappointed him to the two positions five years later. Education constituted a special concern for Thompson, who acted as a trustee of Leon Academy in 1839. When in May 1843 fire ravaged Tallahassee, he worked with Thomas Baltzell and others on the town relief committee.[61]

Thompson found success in his profession and in business as well as in society and local affairs. By 1838 he earned an enviable income of $8,000 per year in fees. A decade or so later, after the economic ravages of the 1840s, he retained fifteen slaves, 480 acres of first-rate land, town property, and other valuables. His law partners included prominent men such as Thomas Hagner and George T. Ward. In business, the lawyer associated closely with banking interests. For a time he occupied cashier and director positions at the Central Bank, serving as its liaison with the territorial government. He left the bank in 1836, but four years later he accepted a directorship of the Southern Life Insurance and Trust Company, long after favoritism and fraud appeared evident in its policies. A decade afterward he associated as an incorporator and superintendent with the projected State Bank of Florida, along with Charles H. DuPont and others.[62]

Beyond these economic concerns, the larger stage of territorial and state politics appealed to Thompson. He represented Leon County at the 1838 constitutional convention, where he chaired the committee on revenues and taxation. Like most other Middle Florida Whigs he backed statehood. Unlike them, however, and surprisingly in light of his business associations, Thompson adopted an antibank posture, contending that territorial banks had been chartered illegally and that their debts could be repudiated by the people. Perhaps in recompense, Democratic governor Robert Raymond Reid, Jr., designated the Whig lawyer as an aide-de-camp. Future Democratic governor William D. Moseley promoted him to adjutant general.[63]

As suggested by his relationships with Reid and Moseley, Thompson could work in his own interest on both sides of the political divide. At home he stressed Whiggish leanings. He unsuccessfully represented the party as candidate for the legislative council from Leon County in 1841 and carried out other party leadership roles through the 1840s. On the state level he established friendships in all camps. This facility, combined with a reputation for legal scholarship, resulted in appointment by Governor Moseley as the "fit and proper person to form and arrange a digest . . . of the Laws of this State" in accordance with an act approved by the general assembly in December 1845. The law also required a committee to examine and report on the completed work. Commissioners Thomas Randall, William Henry Brockenbrough, and J. Wayles Baker expressed their "entire approbation of its plan and execution." Fifteen hundred copies of Thompson's digest, as it was popularly known, were published in 1847. Another act approved, at the same 1845 session, authorized the governor "to appoint some suitable person, to collect and arrange . . . the Statutes of Great Britain, of force in this State." Moseley again appointed Thompson. Committee members David P. Hogue, Charles H. DuPont, and William Augustus Forward gave a favorable review, but the completed work of more than 750 handwritten pages never saw publication despite a legislative appropriation.[64]

Thompson's election to the supreme court came amid the legislative wheeling and dealing of January 1851. His friendships, his legal reputation, and his recent involvement as adjutant general in an Indian crisis factored into the choice. A leading Democratic newspaper praised him as "a profound jurist" who "stands in the front rank of the Bar in Florida."[65] A few days later the journal added, "[T]here are none more eminent in the legal profession." It concluded, "He will adorn the Bench, and be a bright and useful auxilliary to his associates."[66]

As with his two colleagues elected in 1851, Thompson served on the court only until 1853. He met defeat that year in an attempt to secure the chief justiceship at the state's first popular elections for the court. The death of his first wife led the next year to his marriage to Jane Strange de Graffenreid on April 27, 1854. Two months later the couple left Tallahassee for Galveston, Texas, after receiving from prominent bar members "their deep regret at the loss of a highly valued professional associate and Friend."[67] Thompson served in Texas with distinction as mayor of Galveston and as state legislator before he died there on January 23, 1874.[68]

Benjamin D. Wright, Supreme Court Chief Justice, 1853

Benjamin D. Wright temporarily assumed the chief justiceship of the supreme court of Florida in 1853 after the resignation of his fellow Pensacolan, Walker Anderson. Unlike his predecessor, though, Wright did not boast a southern heritage, nor was he a Democrat. Instead his influence had derived from membership in territorial Florida's most powerful political faction, although his career had been marked by independent ideas and a willingness to defy his party friends.

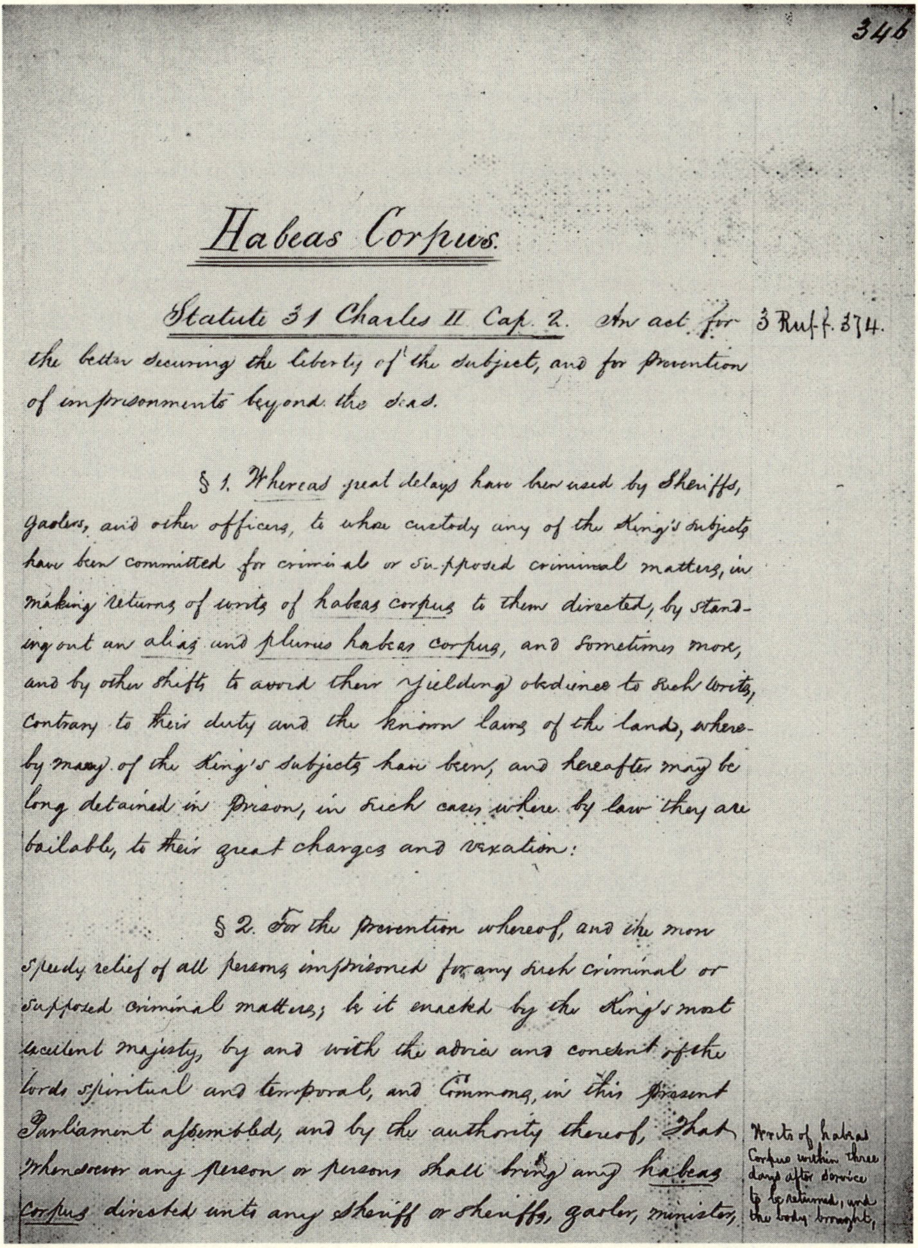
346

Habeas Corpus.

Statute 31 Charles II Cap. 2. An act for the better securing the liberty of the subject, and for prevention of imprisonments beyond the seas. 3 Ruff. 374.

§ 1. Whereas great delays have been used by sheriffs, gaolers, and other officers, to whose custody any of the King's subjects have been committed for criminal or supposed criminal matters, in making returns of writs of habeas corpus to them directed, by standing out an alias and pluries habeas corpus, and sometimes more, and by other shifts to avoid their yielding obedience to such writs, contrary to their duty and the known laws of the land, whereby many of the King's subjects have been, and hereafter may be long detained in prison, in such cases where by law they are bailable, to their great charges and vexation:

§ 2. For the prevention whereof, and the more speedy relief of all persons imprisoned for any such criminal or supposed criminal matters; be it enacted by the King's most excellent majesty, by and with the advice and consent of the lords spiritual and temporal, and Commons, in this present Parliament assembled, and by the authority thereof, That whensoever any person or persons shall bring any habeas corpus directed unto any sheriff or sheriffs, gaoler, minister, Writs of habeas Corpus within three days after service to be returned, and the body brought,

"Habeas Corpus," page 346 of a set of 751 handwritten pages prepared by Leslie Atchinson Thompson, Esq. The future justice was commissioned by Governor Moseley in 1845 to collect and arrange British statutes in force in Florida down to July 4, 1776. Although never published, Thompson's work is intact and preserved in the Florida Supreme Court Library.

The son of Irish immigrant William and Sarah Ann Osborne, Wright was born in Wilkes-Barre, Pennsylvania, on January 23, 1799. Few facts of his early life are available, except that he achieved admission to the Luzerne County bar on April 7, 1820. At age twenty-four he moved to Florida and settled at Pensacola. There he established a close and longlasting friendship with Richard Keith Call, Andrew Jackson's protégé and, at that time, ally of Governor William Pope DuVal. Wright joined Call's law partnership and received the governor's bounty, as well, with a commission as inspector of the militia's First Brigade. His friends' support brought him an April 1824 appointment to the territorial council, followed on May 27 with presidential designation as United States district attorney for Middle Florida. When a vacancy occurred late in 1825 in the same position for West Florida, Wright successfully petitioned President John Quincy Adams to transfer him. His new commission arrived in early February 1826.[69]

The district attorney's resettlement at Pensacola endured for the remainder of his lifetime, but, while it brought him good personal fortune, it also produced professional difficulties. To the good, on February 23, 1826, he married Josephine, the daughter of the well-regarded Colonel John De La Rua. On the other hand, the new prosecutor soon found himself battling Judge Henry Marie Brackenridge. The problems first surfaced in November 1827, when Wright accused the judge of neglecting his duties. Brackenridge answered by characterizing the charges as "unfounded and malicious."[70] Afterward the judge's embarrassment simmered for several years until the question of Wright's reappointment arose in 1829 and 1830. Then Brackenridge, through anonymous letters in the public press and the efforts of congressional delegate and Call opponent Joseph M. White, demanded the prosecutor's replacement.[71]

The judicial assault on Wright produced a flurry of excitement. The district attorney and his friends pled for administration support. Wright insisted that, if for no other reason, his work relating to valuable land claims offered justification for his reappointment. "[T]he interests of the government in this particular might suffer materially," he insisted, "if an individual unacquainted with these claims should now be appointed in my stead."[72] When President Andrew Jackson gave the job to another man, DuVal pointed a finger of blame, identifying Brackenridge as "the anonymous author of anonymous publications in the Florida newspapers."[73] Brackenridge responded unapologetically. "That [Wright] *deserved* to be removed for his conduct towards me, no man of correct feelings, who reads his own letter can doubt," he wrote. "He *admits* that he has been guilty of a deliberate falsehood, in relation to one of my official acts, but repels with indignation, the charge of being a *habitual* slanderer."[74]

Though he left his federal position in 1830, Wright's social, professional, and political standing suffered little. His association with Call had grown stronger over the years. By the early 1830s the power of Call's faction, the Nucleus, had reached its peak, and Wright stood within the front rank of what he called "our little caucus."[75] He returned to the legislative council, representing Escambia County during 1831–33 and 1837. His interests, as expressed through his committee assignments, concentrated most heavily on education, law, and the judiciary. Unlike his contemporary Thomas Baltzell, however, Wright's perceptions often tended to the more conservative positions. An example of this fact is offered by his support for imprisonment of debtors until a "fair surrender of [their] effects."[76]

Wright's leadership led to his election as a member of the 1838 constitutional convention. He later asserted that he and the other western delegates "went to St. Joseph prepared to act with the eastern delegation in opposition to the making of a constitution at that time," but understandings reached with antibank men from Middle Florida apparently changed the situation.[77] Though he later allied with Call in the Whig party, Wright's most vocal efforts were directed against speculative financial institutions. He worked, as well, on the judiciary committee to craft a state court system. Overall he supported statehood of a unified Florida, but for unknown reasons he resigned from the convention on January 5, 1839, before its work had been completed.[78]

The reasons for Wright's departure from the constitutional convention did not impede his return to territorial politics. Western District electors sent him to the new senate in 1839, and there he joined to oppose anti-statehood initiatives. At the session Wright's appointment as chairman of the banking committee reflected a continuing interest in that issue. For the remainder of the territorial period other responsibilities kept him from public office, but he joined in organizing and maintaining the Whig party. With statehood, however, he sat in the 1845 state senate, where he failed in attempts to elect Whigs as United States senators but forced selection of judges one circuit at a time rather than by partisan ticket. Before the session's final adjournment, he again resigned his office and returned to Pensacola, where other responsibilities awaited him.[79]

Politics had presented Wright during the 1830s and early 1840s with opportunity for contribution, but his true calling involved journalism. For five years beginning in 1834 he owned the *Pensacola Gazette*. Until July 11, 1846, the lawyer also served as editor. The *Gazette* earned the reputation of a Whig organ. Still, Wright brought to his editorial role a sense of objectivity, at least for the time and place. That fact sometimes raised the ire of his political allies, who occasionally warned that the newspaper's subscription list might suffer.

He refused to submit to demands that he produce a purely partisan sheet or else refrain from political commentary entirely. "My political opinions are what they have been," he declared, "but if I write, my thoughts must be free—free to denounce the entire Whig party, if I should have occasion for it—free to support loco-focoism [the Democratic platform] in all its features, if I should deem it right."[80] Eventually what he considered a conflict between his principles and his livelihood compelled him to withdraw from the paper.[81]

The integrity demonstrated by Wright brought him acclaim, and his resignation as *Gazette* editor simply opened for him other possibilities for involvement. One fellow journalist recorded that the Pensacolan not only enjoyed an enviable reputation throughout the state as a vigorous and pointed writer but "also in the still higher character of a most intelligent, urbane and accomplished gentleman." Especially the commentator noted the "vigor and comprehensiveness of [Wright's] mind."[82] The talents served him well as his careers in law, politics, and railroad development surged. He commenced in 1848 arguing appeals before the supreme court, while he also actively engaged in Whig organizational efforts. Along with Walker Anderson, he served by the general assembly's 1850 designation as a commissioner of the Alabama and Florida Railroad. When Anderson resigned as Pensacola's naval agent that year, Wright succeeded to the position.[83]

With business success Wright benefited from increasing prosperity, and his openness to Democratic ideas permitted greater honors as the body politic moved to a closer identification with that party. In 1830 he had held two slaves as his major assets. Twenty years later he possessed ten bondsmen and women, 980 acres of land, substantial investments in town lots, and other valuable property. He also had gained the respect of Democratic governor James E. Broome. When Walker Anderson left the supreme court in May 1853, the governor accordingly turned to Anderson's fellow Pensacolan, who had ties among Democrats and Whigs. Wright's stay on the court ended abruptly, though, when voters later in the year opted for Thomas Baltzell as the first popularly elected chief justice.[84]

The 1853 defeat returned Wright to Pensacola's business life and his law practice. Three years afterward he became president of the Alabama and Florida Railroad, and in 1859 he once more failed to win election as chief justice. During the Civil War, Wright followed the Confederate States, while his brother, Dr. Joseph Wright, served as surgeon general of the United States Army. Benjamin emerged again into the public eye with the coming of peace. He represented Escambia County in the 1865 constitutional convention, where he and Baltzell battled again. This time both lost a race for the assembly's presidency.

Wright received consideration for election to the United States Senate, also unsuccessfully, from the 1865 legislature, after which he attended President Andrew Johnson's August 1866 national union convention as Governor David S. Walker's designee. His reward came with appointment by Johnson as collector of customs for the port of Pensacola. Although family records suggest that his demise was on April 28, 1875, Wright died in Pensacola on April 28, 1874.[85]

Chapter 8

Popular Elections and Internal Divisions

In January 1851 legislators created Florida's first independent supreme court. During the following decade the tribunal and its members withstood, at various times, the tribulations of public indignation, conflicts of interest, difficulties of travel in a state still typified by the frontier, foreshortened terms, death, natural disasters, disease, Indian conflict, political divisions, personal animosities, and the onset of civil war. In spite of these challenges, the justices heard and decided upon scores of cases with direct and substantial impact upon the developing state, its businesses, and its people. That it could do so while offering Floridians a growing reputation for honest and thoughtful judicial action represents a singular achievement.

Justices Walker Anderson, Albert Gallatin Semmes, and Leslie Atchinson Thompson convened the first term of Florida's independent supreme court at Tallahassee on January 30, 1851. The event came only days after controversial legislative vote-swapping deals had ousted the state's most powerful politician, Democrat David Levy Yulee, from the United States Senate and fostered the three justices' placement on the supreme bench. Beyond public and political distaste for the legislative actions, the three jurists faced multiple concerns. Among them, state law held them responsible for organizing the high court, arranging for its sessions to be held in four widely separated locales, and ensuring that its members avoided participating in the adjudication of matters in which they previously had been involved.[1]

Problems presented themselves almost immediately. During 1851 state circuit judges were needed to decide most supreme court cases because the new justices had served as counsel for the matters under appeal. The following year, when the court scheduled its first meeting outside the capital, the justices failed to arrive at Marianna on time, and the session was delayed for five days. They then traveled the width of North Florida to Jacksonville, where one appeal awaited. Afterward, the difficult and sometimes dangerous journey to Tampa yielded but two cases. Back at Marianna in April 1853, only three matters commanded their attention.[2]

The judicial peregrinations exhausted court members, and, meanwhile, political events called their continued tenure into question. The 1852 national and state elections had worked a profound change upon the political scene. The Whig party suffered disastrous defeats. Democrat Franklin Pierce, a Mexican War hero, won the presidency. In Florida, Whig gubernatorial candidate George T. Ward lost his race to Leon County planter James D. Broome, a South Carolina-born Democrat who vociferously opposed the Compromise of 1850. Narrow Democratic majorities in the legislature expanded to margins of about two-thirds.[3]

The general assembly met on November 22, 1852, with Democrats intent upon using their majorities to enact the party's program, a portion of which demanded greater popular participation in government. Necessarily, some smaller matters required resolution before larger ones were addressed. In one such instance the two houses studied damage to the capitol from an October storm. Some supreme court books and records had been harmed, and the need for an officer to be "specially charged with the duty of preserving the Library properly assignable to the Supreme Court" appeared evident. Accordingly, the lawmakers directed the court's clerk to assume the charge and appropriated $200 for "taking care [of] and preserving" the library.[4]

Additional court-related questions received attention. The tribunal's 1851 decision in *In Re John Innerarity* v. *Curtis and Griswold, Trustees* had raised a question as to which governmental agency possessed jurisdiction over territorial court of appeals records. The legislature now decreed that the "files, rolls and books of record of the Court of Appeals . . . are hereby, placed in the custody and under the control of the Supreme Court." Further, it empowered the panel to take "such judicial cognizance and power over them, as the said Court may lawfully have and exercise over its own . . . records."[5] In a separate jurisdictional question, a new statute somewhat expanded court authority over appeals "from any interlocutory order, decision, judgment, or decree of the Circuit Courts . . . when sitting as Courts of Equity" or from orders and judgments of such courts related to new trials, amended pleadings, additional pleadings, or amended records of proceedings.[6]

These concerns melted into insignificance compared to the main supreme court question at hand, the popular election of justices. Through the United States the movement toward such a selection process had gained momentum, although many political leaders and voters, especially Whigs, had resisted the tide. As one Florida editor put it, "The judiciary should be as far as possible removed from the influence of partisan feeling."[7] By the early 1850s the experience of states such as New York and Pennsylvania had helped to shift the balance of opinion. Still, even many Democrats who preferred popular election opposed partisan contests.[8]

Selection of judges by the voters had been debated in Florida for decades by 1852. Franklin County delegate C. E. Bartlett had proposed the idea at the 1838 constitutional convention. Only five others supported him. The forty-eight opponents included Walker Anderson, Thomas Baltzell, Albert Gallatin Semmes, and Leslie Atchinson Thompson. After statehood Governor William D. Moseley, a Democrat, endorsed the concept, repeating his sentiments over the years. The general assembly in 1850, with its narrow Democratic majority, enacted legislation, but, under the state constitution, such a change required approval by successive legislatures. The lawmakers then aroused public sentiment in favor of the proposal by the manner in which they subsequently elected Anderson, Semmes, and Thompson.[9]

The Democratic victories in 1852 ensured adoption of the popular election legislation. During the interim Attorney General David P. Hogue, who had "not the slightest objection" to such elections, crafted appropriate language. He raised, though, concerns as to when the requirement could become effective. Specifically, he suggested that, although the general assembly could abolish positions, it could not rightfully divest a judge of his judgeship as long as the office continued. Hogue's warnings notwithstanding, lawmakers wholeheartedly embraced popular election for circuit and supreme court justices. Concerns about term interruptions were handled by noting vaguely in a committee report that the new law would not divest sitting judges. The bill passed the senate unanimously and received a single nay vote in the house. The provision called for elections beginning the first Monday in October 1853 and on the same day in each sixth year thereafter.[10]

The elections act would change completely the personnel on the supreme court, and anticipation of that transformation affected the tribunal. First, on May 19, 1853, Chief Justice Anderson resigned. Governor Broome temporarily appointed in his stead Escambia County's Benjamin D. Wright, a former Whig senator and yet another constitutional convention member who had opposed popular election of judges. When the court reconvened with the new justice in July, it encountered resistance to its authority, which hints that at least some individuals preferred that an elected court decide pending matters.[11]

The controversy arose during the hearing of *Griffin* v. *Orman*, when litigants demanded disqualification of Justice Thompson, who had served as trial counsel. Thompson then authored a court opinion stating that three judges must be present for the supreme court to reach a decision. He noted also that, when a justice was disqualified, the chief justice could appoint a circuit judge to act. Seemingly both Thompson and Justice Semmes anticipated their disqualification in other cases, and the court ordered southern and eastern circuit judges Joseph Bradford Lancaster and William Augustus Forward to sit on the court in their place. Both men declined to appear. From August 1 the court members waited. On September 6 the likelihood of Lancaster's continued absence appeared clear, and the court adjourned with about two-thirds of its docket remaining to be considered.[12]

As the court's conundrum deepened in July and August, candidates eager for election to the panel geared up campaigns. To avoid the appearance of partisan involvement, "friends" of hopefuls announced their candidacy. Perhaps one-time justice Thomas Baltzell's early July notice of intention to seek the chief justiceship came first. Chief Justice Wright and Justice Thompson declared for the office, as well. Justice Semmes entered the race to retain his position and was joined by Attorney General Hogue, former justice Thomas Douglas, Gadsden County territorial senator Charles H. DuPont, and Duval County lawyer Byrd Murphy Pearson. After the latter's withdrawal, Douglas remained as the sole candidate from East Florida.[13]

Public attention to the supreme court campaigns fluctuated from race to race, but overall the level of interest proved low. A yellow fever epidemic hampered candidate attempts to address the public. Newspapers exhorted a full turnout but contributed to general apathy by neglecting analysis of candidate merits and claims. Voters devoted most attention to the chief justice contest. Many Whigs backed Wright who, one party editor asserted, "will grace the official ermine with profound knowledge, the accumulation of great experience, guided by an intellect of the very first order."[14] They especially opposed Democrat Baltzell, whose appeal to the common man stoked fears. Since they could not voice such a complaint publicly, some editors insinuated that Baltzell's ties to railroads created conflicts of interest. At the polls the attacks meant little, as voters rejected all sitting members of the court and elected Baltzell as chief justice. Thomas Douglas and Charles H. DuPont similarly won seats as justices.[15]

The reconstituted supreme court gathered first at Tallahassee on January 2, 1854, and adjourned on February 7. Since the requirement of holding sessions at Marianna, Jacksonville, and Tampa remained the law, it reconvened in Jackson County in April to hear three cases. The remaining dozen or so matters on the docket received a hearing at Tallahassee during August 21 to September 23. Through the period and into 1855, as the court traveled around the state, it undertook determination of numerous matters of significance, as will be discussed in chapter 9. In 1855, particularly, the tribunal enjoyed one of its most productive and important years. Unfortunately, the period witnessed Justice Douglas's death from pleurisy. At a special election held December 1, Byrd Murphy Pearson led the voting to replace the deceased justice.[16]

Beginning in 1856 the court entered a troubled era that lasted through the decade, a circumstance that mirrored state and national experiences in the immediate pre-Civil War period. In the court's case, the happenings limited its ability to fulfill its duties and strained the cooperative atmosphere its members had preserved since 1845. The train of events began in January 1856 when "the detention at home by illness of the Hon. B. M. Pearson, the newly elected Associate Justice" delayed the court from considering "Several very interesting cases."[17] A few weeks earlier, incursions by whites into Indian lands had provoked open warfare in the peninsula. When the court prepared to travel to Tampa for a March 1857 session, it was forced to cancel the plans "in consequence of the interruption of the communication with that place."[18] In the next year the panel's docket witnessed substantial reduction due, report suggested, "to the failure to hold courts in many of the counties this Fall."[19]

The strains upon court members erupted into a different kind of warfare in 1859, as fiery Thomas Baltzell and strong-willed Charles H. DuPont locked horns in personal conflict. The feud stemmed from a difference of opinion about the court's authority to act with only two sitting justices, the recurring issue from 1853. Failing eyesight prevented Justice Pearson from attending at the court term's commencement. Baltzell and DuPont disagreed about summoning a circuit judge to serve. The former justice believed two justices had the authority to issue the order; the latter did not. They disagreed even as to whether the court could convene with only themselves present. Again, Baltzell thought yes, while DuPont insisted no.[20]

The dispute escalated when DuPont departed Tallahassee for his Gadsden County plantation. On January 18 Baltzell ordered Pearson's arrest and appearance in court. He also directed that DuPont "be notified to attend court . . . on Monday next the 24th" and recorded his actions in the court minutes in strongly worded language.[21] DuPont returned on the twenty-fifth, but he and the chief justice failed to resolve the matter. Angered by Baltzell's intransigence, DuPont entered in the minute book the substance of his sentiments regarding his fellow justice's actions. "I do most solemnly Protest," he wrote in part, "against the same as having been made without the authority of Law or the sanction of Precedent and as well calculated to bring the body into disrepute." Additionally, he objected to Baltzell's temerity in taking recourse to the official minutes.

"[N]o individual member . . . ," he insisted, "possesses the right to make or cause to be made therein any Entries purporting to be 'Orders' save such as declare an adjournment or become necessary to procure the Organization Contemplated by the . . . Act Establishing a Supreme Court."[22]

From that point the contretemps worsened. Baltzell blasted back at DuPont, mentioning several concerns. Particularly, he criticized the justice for making entries in the official minutes "without the knowledge or consent of the Chief Justice to whom is confided by law the records to see that proper entries are made subject to the examination of the Court."[23] DuPont waited patiently until February, when Pearson's health permitted him to join the court. An uneasy truce then reigned, while the interpersonal and legal problems remained unresolved.[24]

During February the judicial strife entered the public arena, which caused embarrassment and exacerbated the tensions. Newspapers published letters from Baltzell and DuPont urging their positions and offering explanations. The members cooperated sufficiently to travel to Jacksonville and, in March, to Tampa for the regular terms. Afterward they journeyed to Marianna before another flareup occurred on April 1. The match was struck when DuPont and Pearson disqualified the chief justice to sit on the hearing of a matter in which he earlier had been counsel of record. In turn they directed eastern circuit judge James McNair Baker to replace him. Baker refused, "citing the opinion of the Chief Justice, recently published . . . [in which he] denies to the Supreme Court the power to invite the aid of the Circuit Judges under such circumstances."[25]

With these events the intracourt dispute again surfaced. DuPont and Pearson ruled that the court could appoint a circuit judge to serve but, with an eye to their previously expressed positions, added a caveat. "[T]he members of the Court are upon the footing of the most perfect equality," the two jurists held. They then added, "The position of a Circuit Judge, when called to the Supreme Court bench, is the same as one of the Justices, and we therefore hold that we have no power to compel the attendance of his Honor Judge Baker." Baltzell retorted that his colleagues had missed the real issue. Attendance could be compelled because a circuit judge did not occupy the same position as a sitting justice. The majority opinion, he felt, necessitated or assumed a term-long appointment for the circuit judge, while the constitution permitted such designations for individual cases only. "[T]he authority to appoint is restricted to a case of disability in hearing and determining a cause or causes," he determined, "and the power of the Judge so appointed is confined to the hearing and determining the same."[26]

The drama's final acts were yet to be played. On April 15 the justices declared Baltzell's order for Pearson's arrest invalid and ordered it expunged from court records. "[T]o guard against the recurrence of similar errors in future," they determined, "it is made a standing order of this Court that no entries shall be made upon the minutes thereof in vacation and without the concurring authority and consent of a majority of the presiding Justices thereof, unless the same be for the adjournment or continuance of the legal terms of the same, or to effect the organization provided for by . . . the act . . . organizing the Supreme Court."[27] Newspapers carried word of the actions, with accompanying criticisms by Baltzell and rebuttals by DuPont. The controversy persisted with important court ramifications.[28]

Under the provisions of the supreme court organizational act, justices' terms lasted six years, with the next election scheduled for October 1859. For a time it appeared that the sitting justices, under one interpretation of constitutional language, might not be eligible for reelection. In 1858 compliant Democratic lawmakers resolved the problem, though, to permit the Democratic justices to run or, as it resulted, to run against each other. Pearson, whose health had declined precipitously, declined to enter the contest, but DuPont carried his ire at Baltzell into the race for chief justice. Former appointed chief justice Benjamin D. Wright ventured a candidacy, as well. For justice a variety of hopefuls announced.[29]

The supreme court elections were held as sectional divisions widened and fears of dismemberment of the Union intensified. The nation awaited some event to serve as catalyst, with John Brown's raid on the federal arsenal at Harper's Ferry, Virginia, only days away. Under these conditions many Floridians might have opted for southern radicals for the court, but that did not prove the case. DuPont, who held secessionist sentiments, defeated Baltzell with a plurality of votes, but the outcome reflected personality, public perceptions of their actions in the recent controversies, and the repayment of old political grudges more than it did other issues. A moderate former Whig and a moderate Democrat judge, David S. Walker and William Augustus Forward, respectively, won the justiceships to round out the new court.[30]

At various times in that era from 1851 until the Civil War, Walker Anderson, Albert Gallatin Semmes, Leslie Atchinson Thompson, Benjamin D. Wright, Thomas Baltzell, Charles H. DuPont, Thomas Douglas, Byrd Murphy Pearson, David S. Walker, and William Augustus Forward maneuvered through a myriad of problems to lay a foundation for Florida's independent supreme court and to lend it credibility in the wake of political crisis, personal differences, and other challenges. The individual natures of the men who took these steps offer important perspective on their actions and the events in which they were involved. Anderson, Semmes, Thompson, Baltzell, and Douglas previously have been profiled. A closer look at the lives of DuPont, Pearson, Walker, and Forward follows.

Charles H. DuPont, Supreme Court Justice, 1854–1859; Supreme Court Chief Justice, 1860–1868

Charles H. DuPont led Florida's supreme court through the trials and conflicts of the Civil War and presidential Reconstruction, but his service to the state already had been felt for three decades before he joined the tribunal in 1853 as a justice. Afterward his contributions continued, as he sought to offer farmers and planters options for renewed prosperity amidst the ruins of the South's former plantation cotton economy.

DuPont's early life was surrounded by comfortable circumstances. His relations, the DuPonts de Nemours, stemmed from French Huguenot roots, as did their more acclaimed Delaware cousins. Charles's branch had settled in South Carolina, where he was born in Beaufort District on January 27, 1805. The family enjoyed affluence, but Charles's father died during the son's childhood. His mother, when Charles was aged ten, sent him to Ohio for an education, by "working upon a farm and attending the common schools."[31] Later he returned to the South to complete formal studies and become a lawyer. DuPont graduated in 1826 from Georgia's Franklin College.[32]

The young man's Florida domicile began soon after his college graduation. In 1826 DuPont relocated to Gadsden County, where he established a law practice and engaged in plantation development. By 1830 he owned sixteen slaves, a figure that almost tripled within the decade. With planter prestige came social acceptance. DuPont took a leadership role in the local Methodist church and accepted membership on the board of trustees of the Quincy Male and Female Academy. He soon cultivated banking connections, as well. In 1833 Governor William Pope DuVal named him as an appraiser for the Union Bank. DuPont became a stockholder and director of the institution, eventually borrowing from it $32,500 secured by 1,614 acres of his land and forty-two slaves. Additionally, the Central Bank in 1834 claimed him as trustee.[33]

Governor DuVal's favor introduced DuPont to territorial politics. In 1834 the governor designated the lawyer as judge of the Gadsden County court and arranged for his appointment in that year and 1835 as member of the legislative council. DuPont worked closely on issues concerning the militia, internal improvements, and the judiciary. Middle District voters sent him to the territorial senate in 1838 as a statehood advocate. He remained there through 1841, during which time he associated himself first with Richard Keith Call's conservative faction, then with the Democratic party. In 1848 the Democrats acknowledged his efforts of their behalf by naming him a presidential elector.[34]

As DuPont's political career advanced, so, too, did his role in the state militia and as protector of his friends and neighbors. Beyond his service on the territorial council's militia committee, he participated in Gadsden County defensive efforts in anticipation of Second Seminole War violence. As an officer during the conflict, one historian remarked, "he made a creditable military record."[35] In December 1841 DuPont attained the rank of brigadier general, although five years later he suffered defeat in a contest for the major general's position at the hands of William Bailey.[36]

The 1846 defeat for promotion to ranking militia officer occurred at a time when DuPont was confronting other problems. The banking collapse and economic depression caused him losses, especially from default of loans he had endorsed for friends. One biographer suggested that "he was now penniless," but the true circumstances, while serious, were not so drastic. They did compel him, however, to concentrate on his plantation and on generating income through his law practice. In such circumstances DuPont became, for example, one of the first lawyers to argue before the new Florida supreme court. As with many of his contemporaries, he engaged in promoting railroad schemes and other internal improvement projects. The efforts succeeded in rehabilitating his fortune. By 1853 DuPont held eighty slaves and 2,266 acres of land, together with more than $6,000 in town property. He had become one of Florida's leading planters, and DuPont's wealth would grow greater yet.[37]

The challenge of financial concerns could not distract a man of DuPont's standing from the state and national political crises of 1849 and 1850. His thinking represented the ideas of the state's radical Democrats, who opposed accommodation with the national government over the question of extension of slavery. He attended the Nashville convention of 1850 and emerged from it as a secession advocate. He believed states retained under the federal constitution an "inalienable" right to secede. Any attempt by the federal government to deprive a state of the exercise of the right, he maintained, ought to be rebuked.[38]

DuPont's successes in the militia, at the bar, in agriculture, and among radical Democrats had not provided him by the early 1850s with a base of popularity sufficient to propel him to higher political office. The general assembly had rejected his candidacies for judgeships and for membership on the internal improvement board. His reputation as an attorney had garnered a gubernatorial appointment to join Attorney General David P. Hogue and William Augustus Forward to examine, for publication, Leslie Atchinson Thompson's work of collecting and arranging the statutes of Great Britain. DuPont searched for other opportunities as well. The state's first popular elections for the supreme court, held in 1853, provided one. At first he announced for chief justice. Reassessment of his electoral strengths moved him to contest a justiceship, though, and he emerged the victor. Six years later, in the wake of highly publicized disputes with Chief Justice Thomas Baltzell, DuPont achieved election to Baltzell's position.[39]

As chief justice, DuPont played a major role in supreme court activities, which are discussed for the period of the Civil War and Reconstruction in part 3 of this book. Once the conflict had ended, he received the prewar leadership's blessings for his work with reappointment to his office by Governor David S. Walker. In the immediate postwar era, he also participated with Anderson J. Peeler in drafting and urging legislative adoption of the "black codes." These laws attempted to secure a docile and dependable labor supply for planters by establishing restrictions and regulations governing the lives of freed blacks, virtually reinstituting slavery in all but name. The implementation of congressional Reconstruction in 1868 terminated the codes and DuPont's tenure of office.[40]

The Civil War's end found DuPont, like most southerners, a man of reduced circumstances. A great part of his wealth had been invested in slaves, who now were free. Apparently his plantation received damage, as well. Black Union soldiers had demonstrated their ire when the chief justice refused to reveal the whereabouts of his house slaves. Imminent repeal of the black codes convinced him that immigrant labor offered planters their only realistic hope for a dependable labor supply. Consequently, DuPont promoted a statewide association constructed around his concepts, and on December 1, 1867, the Agricultural and Immigration Association of Florida was born. Three years later DuPont attracted some Swedish immigrants to Gadsden County, although the experiment achieved little success.[41]

DuPont persisted in the face of adversity. He continued to urge the need for immigrant labor, and he also encouraged agricultural innovation and economic development. He stressed particularly tobacco's potential as a cash crop, a vision that resulted by 1900 in Gadsden County's production of the world's finest wrapper tobacco. One setback could not be overcome by perseverance. In his youth DuPont had married Georgia-born Mary Ann Hanson, who had become the mainstay of his life. Her death on July 10, 1877, left him disheartened, a condition from which he never recovered. He undertook a trip to the Middle West to recruit workers for Florida, but he fell ill at Minneapolis. He lived to reach the Quincy home of his son-in-law, William B. Malone. There DuPont died on October 14. "He was permitted, thanks to the good Lord, to reach home," a friend recorded, "and to breathe his last among relatives and friends."[42]

Other friends and colleagues gathered at the supreme court to bid DuPont farewell and to pay tribute to his memory. Governor Walker spoke on that occasion of the chief justice's "firmness, dignity, [and] gentleness," as well as "his noble bearing and courteous demeanor." Justice George Sydney Hawkins recalled that DuPont's "judicial integrity was never impugned." Edwin M. Randall, his successor as chief justice, concluded by noting "the cheerfulness which beamed from his kindly face on greeting an acquaintance [and] the courtly dignity and heartiness which graced his bearing and distinguished him as a gentleman of the olden time."[43]

Byrd Murphy Pearson, Supreme Court Justice, 1856–1859

Byrd Murphy Pearson served on Florida's supreme court for only four years, but during that time he witnessed the panel's transition from one of its most productive periods to one of its most trying times. His poor health indirectly provoked the first intracourt crisis. It subsequently contributed to his withdrawal from the tribunal's deliberations and brought about his early death.

Union District, South Carolina, was the site of Pearson's 1803 birth. His father's family claimed descent from a man who accompanied William Penn to the New World, and his mother's ancestors included Virginia's prominent Byrd family. Pearson pursued his education within his home state, graduating from South Carolina College. He then read law and practiced his profession, serving at one time as a state solicitor. He moved in 1838 to Fawnsdale, Alabama, where he established a plantation. Seven years later he again relocated with his wife, family, and twenty slaves to a plantation near Brooksville in Hernando County, Florida.[44]

Although Pearson came to reside in Florida's peninsula, his views of slavery, race relations, and states' rights resembled more closely those of his home state of South Carolina than they did the sentiments of many East Floridians. He defended the right of secession and attended the 1850 Nashville convention with his future supreme court colleague Charles H. DuPont. His fervor in defense of his beliefs persisted until his death.[45]

Peninsular Florida planters suffered during the 1850s from lack of reliable water or rail transportation, and Pearson proved no exception. Additionally, little legal business awaited the lawyers of the southern circuit at that time. In the situation Pearson resettled at Jacksonville in 1851, where he soon achieved admission to the state supreme court bar at its first regular term held in the town. He struck his new neighbors as "an able lawyer and a man of great urbanity and courtesy of manner." Added one historian, "His home was the seat of unbounded hospitality and the favorite resort of a large circle of friends."[46]

Pearson and his fellow radical Democrats began to think that his talents might be of use on the supreme court. In 1853 they considered his entry into the first popular elections for the court. In a state still pro-Unionist, the lawyer eventually declined to make the race. One report described that his decision came because "the expectations under which he consented to become a candidate have not been fully realized" and he did not desire "to become the instrument of still greater division in public sentiment in the choice of Judicial officers than already exists, or to resort to electioneering practices."[47] Whatever the "expectations" were, they did not keep Pearson from running to fill the vacancy caused by Justice Thomas Douglas's 1855 death. In December Pearson won the seat.[48]

Through Pearson's four-year tenure on the court, ill health plagued him. The condition forced the jurist in 1859 to decline seeking reelection. "We deeply regret that the Court is to [lose] Justice Pearson's services," commented a leading Democratic editor. "He has a fine legal mind, and, as a Judge, is singularly independent, impartial, and unprejudiced, while his consistent and unswerving States Rights sentiments make him politically precisely what every Southern State, in these times of threatened Federal aggression, should seek in filling the office of its supreme judiciary." The item concluded, "We hope that the State may yet enjoy the services, in some capacity, of one who would ever show himself so faithful to her honored institutions."[49] Despite the newspaperman's hopes, Pearson's services were not again made available to Floridians. His health worsened during his final sessions on the court. He returned to Jacksonville and died there on October 9, 1859.[50]

David S. Walker, Supreme Court Justice, 1860–1865

David S. Walker's influence upon nineteenth-century Florida affairs proved significant and enduring. His reputation stands most prominently upon his tenure as governor in the immediate aftermath of the Civil War. Still, Walker's contributions to the state judiciary, the development of a public school system, and antebellum politics and government deserve careful attention and recognition.

Walker was born near Russellville, Logan County, Kentucky, on May 2, 1815. At the time his father, also named David, already had enjoyed success as a state legislator and, for three months during the previous year, as an appointed United States senator. The elder Walker sat, as well, in the United States House of Representatives from 1817 until his death in 1820. Raised in affluent circumstances, David S. Walker attended private schools in Kentucky and Tennessee before studying law with his brother, George K. Walker. At age twenty-two, apparently at the urging of his cousin Richard Keith Call, Walker moved to Leon County, Florida. There, on May 22, 1842, he married Philoclea Alston. The couple then launched themselves into Middle Florida planter society, while David established a law practice with Call's nephew, Wilkinson Call.[51]

Just as Walker came to Florida under Richard Keith Call's influence, so also did he follow Call's lead into Whig political circles. He soon secured a leadership role in local party affairs, which resulted in his 1845 election from Leon County to the first state senate. As a Whig in the Democrat-controlled body, he found his initiatives stymied, although he received considerable support in an unsuccessful bid for election as circuit judge for the Southern District. He resigned from the senate in October 1845, due to his interpretation of a constitutional provision regarding the expiration of terms of office. He returned to his law partnership and, in January 1846, became one of the first attorneys admitted to practice before the state supreme court. Walker continued to be active in Whig politics and in civic affairs. When the Mexican War began, he helped organize Florida volunteers to fight in the conflict.[52]

Walker reentered elective office in 1848, when Leon County voters sent him to the state house of representatives. Whigs held majorities in both chambers, and the leadership designated him judiciary committee chairman. He attempted without success to create an independent supreme court and also fell short in an effort to elect Wilkinson Call as supreme court clerk. Walker worked on behalf of Whig causes and candidates, but he displayed an independent streak by joining Democrats in support of Jackson Morton for United States senator.[53]

The representative's pro-Morton vote may have represented an early effort to appeal to Democratic and middle-of-the-road voters in the state at large. Poor health had compelled Walker to consider employment less taxing than the practice of law, and he had set his sights on the position of registrar of public lands. Although considered the "best Whig" in the 1850 race, he softened his public image by straddling the fence on the sensitive issue of disunion amid the national crisis of 1849–50. He opposed secession, he declared, but he refused to endorse admission of California to the Union as a free state. The appeal worked, and Walker bested opponent Mariano D. Papy in the fall elections.[54]

For ten years after his 1850 election, Walker occupied the registrar's office with increasing public support. In a state where residents were eager to purchase newly opened lands, he streamlined procedures and facilitated transactions. He put property on the market quickly and advertised sales widely. By the summer of 1854, he had disposed of "126,101 78/100 acres" for "$219,073 42/100 and the average price is $1.74 per acre."[55] That year and in 1858 Walker won reelection without opposition, the final time when he was out of state.[56]

The registrar's position permitted Walker to engage in a seemingly unrelated cause that, nonetheless, he held dear to his heart. The office carried with it responsibilities for superintending state-supported schools. Since public schools virtually were nonexistent, Walker assumed the role of advocate for free and public education. He established one school at Tallahassee, and his work assured passage in 1853 of a law providing at least the future promise of public educational opportunities in Florida.[57]

Walker's popularity and visibility during the 1850s launched multiple attempts to secure other statewide offices. The Whig party for the most part dissolved after the 1852 elections. Like many of his fellows, Walker then moved into the American or Know Nothing party, a movement that based its appeal upon nativism and anti-Catholicism. As that party's 1856 gubernatorial nominee, Walker lost to Democrat Madison S. Perry by fewer than 400 votes out of 10,500 cast. His subsequent ventures ended more pleasantly for him. Tallahasseeans elected him to their town council during 1858–59, and, as fears of disunion hovered over the nation late in 1859, his moderate perspectives and reputation as an honest and effective public servant secured him a seat on the supreme court. Of the honor a Tallahassee editor later noted, "[H]e was elected . . . by the largest vote ever given for any man for any office in the State, thus showing the high appreciation of his merits by his political opponents."[58]

The years during which Walker served on the supreme court tested the man and the institution. He expressed support for the Union until Florida seceded; then he gave his loyalty to the Confederate States. Through the conflict he served on the supreme bench, and, when it had ended, he emerged as a, if not the, leading political figure among the state's white residents. They elected him on November 29, 1865, as their governor, an office that he assumed on January 18, 1866. As Florida's chief executive, Walker faced difficulties at every step. His inability to forestall violence against blacks and loyalists, coupled with economic and personal devastation in the war's wake, limited his ability to forge an agenda for state reconstruction. By March 1867, with enactment of congressional Reconstruction, his actions were subjected to military approval. The recognition on July 4, 1868, of his Republican successor Harrison Reed finally removed him from the governor's office.[59]

During the remainder of the Reconstruction era, Walker acted as a rallying point for Democrats. He feuded with Reed and often aided attempts to remove the Republican from office. Through the period he practiced law. Philoclea Walker died on May 7, 1868, and the former governor married Elizabeth Duncan in 1875. After Democrats regained political control in the state, Walker benefited through appointment in 1879 as judge of the second circuit. His health waned in the following years, but Walker presided as judge until his death at Tallahassee on July 20, 1891. "[T]he state has sustained the loss of one of her ablest and most faithful public servants," declared Governor Francis P. Fleming, "who, from early manhood to the close of a long and useful life, was honored by his fellow citizens with places of public trust, which he filled with fidelity and ability."[60]

William Augustus Forward, Supreme Court Justice, 1860–1865

Justice William Augustus Forward's family background contrasts plainly with David S. Walker's patrician southern heritage, as does Forward's Democratic philosophy with Walker's aristocratic Whig perspectives. Forward was born in New York in 1812, just as his father began serving in the state militia during the War of 1812. Although the Forwards enjoyed strong family connections—cousin Walker Forward later became secretary of the treasury under William Henry Harrison—William's father decided, about 1816, to relocate to Canada. William subsequently studied law but became embroiled in the Canadian rebellion of 1837–38. British authorities arrested him and, afterward, banished him from the country.[61]

Exiled from Canada, Forward once again made his home in New York. Former congressman Isaac H. Bronson befriended the young lawyer, and, when Bronson accepted an East Florida judgeship in 1840, he encouraged his protégé to travel to the territory with him. At St. Augustine Forward established a law practice and a political career. He quickly began participating in the kinds of Democratic party functions that he soon would be leading. In the process Forward adopted as his own most of the South's ideological assumptions. By 1850 he was a slaveowner. Forward also was building a new family. His wife, Almira, had died on November 11, 1841, and their daughter, Almira Anita, had followed within eight days. Forward then remarried on June 9, 1842, to Mary Hutchinson, daughter of a New York attorney and granddaughter of a Dartmouth College president.[62]

East Florida's resistance to statehood and support for territorial division spurred Forward's career in public office. Although a Democrat, he urged territorial division and worked with area Whigs to accomplish the goal. In 1844 he attained election to the territorial house of representatives from St. Johns County, and in January 1845 he achieved selection as speaker. He did not return to the capitol in the first elections after statehood, but the resignation of Senator George Center resulted in a decision by county voters to put him in the state senate in time for the November 1845 adjourned session. He chaired the judiciary committee and also worked with the finance and banking panels. He earned a reputation for careful attention to public expenditures, once questioning requested funds for rehabilitating the supreme court chambers. Rather than approving the funds, he arranged for appointment of a committee to "report whether any repairs are actually and *indispensably* necessary, and to report the amount required to complete said repairs."[63]

Forward's legislative career continued in the years after 1845. He served in the house in 1847 and returned to the senate the following year, but the times proved frustrating as Whigs controlled both chambers and Democratic programs seldom achieved passage. He worked principally in the areas of the judiciary, government operations, education, and federal relations. He opposed popular election of circuit judges and the lengthening of judicial terms but backed popular election of probate judges. On the other hand, the lawmaker contributed substantially toward passage of legislation granting criminal defendants rights of appeal. Forward doubtlessly felt more comfortable as a senator during the 1850 session, as his party once more organized the assembly. He chaired the corporations committee and extended his efforts for the judiciary and federal relations committees. He renewed his opposition to popular election of circuit judges and unsuccessfully proposed a plan for gubernatorial appointment subject to senate confirmation.[64]

Forward's legislative service offers an example of how complicated partisan and personal relationships could become. As a house member in 1847, he opposed the selection of Jacksonville's Joseph Bradford Lancaster as speaker but then worked well with the Whig leader. Serving on the judiciary and other committees, he helped Lancaster to sidetrack inflammatory resolutions regarding the Wilmot Proviso. Questioned about why a states' rights man would act thus, Forward later insisted—in good political style—that he acted only because the resolutions should have been referred to a standing, as opposed to a select, committee.[65]

As illustrated by his cooperation with Lancaster, Forward's party spirit fell short of that of some of his more extreme colleagues. When Lancaster won a judgeship, Forward even proposed a resolution thanking the controversial speaker "for the able, dignified and impartial manner in which he has discharged the duties of his station."[66] The legislator was well liked by many, who believed him to be "a sound lawyer and a conscientious and honest man."[67] Yet in regard to the rewards of office, Forward lost to more serious partisans. With Democrats in control in 1845, he withdrew by necessity from a contest for the southern circuit judgeship. Again, five years later, Democratic majorities in both legislative chambers failed to elect him to the bench, this time as justice and as circuit judge. Finally, in 1853 a difficult contest with incumbent Thomas Douglas, who had defeated Forward in 1850, led to victory as Forward pieced together house and senate votes to assume the East Florida circuit judgeship. Proclaimed a Jacksonville newspaper, "[Forward] will make an able, honest, and impartial judge."[68]

With the judicial election Forward reestablished residence in East Florida, having in 1851 opened a law partnership at Tallahassee with former comptroller Simon Towle. He settled at Jacksonville, and his return to the area was "hailed with much pleasure by our citizens."[69] The judge fulfilled his duties "with credit to himself and to the approbation of the public" but resigned the position after four years to pursue the law with John P. Sanderson. Many citizens regretted hearing the news.[70] "He has preserved the ermine of his office from even the breath of contamination," a newspaper noted. "His high professional attainments and obliging disposition cannot fail to command a liberal share of business."[71]

The former judge's life thereafter encountered additional changes and new directions. Forward removed his home to Palatka, and, in 1859, he secured popular election to the supreme court. With President Abraham Lincoln's election, the justice supported secession. He also volunteered for service as a private in the Second Florida Infantry but, upon reflection, remained on the supreme court. The war's conclusion found Forward at Palatka, where, in July 1865, he contracted the illness that killed him. He died at Savannah, on October 19, on his way north to seek treatment. "The death of this excellent man and citizen," eulogized a Jacksonville newspaper, "is truly a loss to this State, where his great probity of character, his eminent abilities as a jurist, his Christian virtue, and his genial traits of character, made him honored and loved."[72] Added representatives of attorneys who had worked with him, "[W]e shall ever cherish the memory of Wm. A. Forward, with love for his gentle and noble qualities as a man and with the highest respect and veneration as one of the most able and talented Lawyers that have ever adorned the Supreme Bench of Florida."[73]

Chapter 9

Antebellum Opinions

During its first fifteen years of existence, the supreme court of Florida considered a broad range of issues while attempting in difficult circumstances to establish its organization and credibility. As previously discussed, the process at times moved haltingly and occasionally broke down, but through the years the tribunal succeeded in its basic tasks. Naturally, many rulings were controversial, while the individual perspectives and political principles of the justices influenced decisions. Floridians expected such a state of affairs. Nonetheless, the following summary of court opinions well illustrates the solid foundation laid for Florida jurisprudence in those early years. Further testimony to the success of that building process will be found in part 3's discussion of court accomplishments under the stress of war and Reconstruction.

Before commencing the review, note should be made that Florida law, at first, limited the supreme court's jurisdiction to civil cases. Hence, the earliest opinions often dealt with commercial and probate matters. By the 1850s lawmakers expanded the scope of court action to include appeals in criminal cases, equity decisions, and all other orders and judgments of circuit courts. Given the nature of state development and issues of the times, questions regarding slavery, women's rights, and economic development emerged as special concerns.[1]

Procedural Issues

Procedural and jurisdictional rules lie at the heart of any court's ability to fulfill its responsibilities. Not surprisingly, then, the supreme court's first opinion concerned just such a question, specifically its jurisdiction to hear appeals from the territorial courts. The issue arose from a general assembly directive transferring all cases pending in the territorial court of appeals to the supreme court. Litigants argued in *Stewart* v. *Preston* that the legislature held no authority to pass such a law and that the matter lay within the exclusive domain of the federal courts. Justice Thomas Baltzell's opinion quickly dispensed with the arguments and asserted the court's authority, but related issues continued to surface. In *Beatty* v. *Ross*, for example, a defendant demanded that his case be transferred to a federal court with concurrent jurisdiction. Baltzell again upheld the authority of Florida courts, finding in 1847 that, in such circumstances, state courts had an obligation, as well the power, to adjudicate the cases transferred to them from the territorial courts. The court affirmed the opinion even though Baltzell acknowledged that it ran contrary to a United States Supreme Court decision.[2]

The passage of a few years and the creation of an independent supreme court raised the level of artistry involved in court reasoning as to its position relative to federal courts. The curious decision in the 1851 case of *In Re John Innerarity* v. *Curtis and Griswold, Trustees* also hints that the justices may have been more interested in influencing the outcome of a private land claim than in procedural niceties. In this particular instance, the court declined to order its clerk to transfer records to a United States district court, even though the materials were received from the territorial court of appeals and directly concerned issues under litigation in the federal court. Justice Leslie Atchinson Thompson wrote for the court that a congressional act granting authority to transfer the papers to the supreme court's clerk did not give the court jurisdiction to tell the clerk what to do with them. Legislators overturned the decision at the first opportunity, specifying the court's control of court of appeals materials.[3]

Another issue of procedural concern stemmed from appeals in which a court member previously had served as counsel of record. Once the justice recused himself, could a circuit judge then be appointed to sit and decide the case? The constitution provided that "No Governor, Justice of the Supreme Court, Chancellor, or Judge of this State, shall be eligible to election, or appointment, to any other and different station, or office, or post of honor, or emolument, under this State, or to the station of Senator, or Representative in the Congress of the United States, from this State, until one year, after he shall have ceased to be such Governor, Justice, Chancellor, or Judge."[4]

The question commanded the court's attention in 1851, when Judge Thomas Douglas asked for its opinion after he had been asked to hear a case as a temporary member of the tribunal. Justice Thompson avoided the prohibition of the constitution's language by finding that "other" applies to an office "different in its structure, character, duties and the nature of its function." The problem resolved, statutory language permitting the appointments then passed constitutional muster.[5]

A subsequent, though related, concern involved the court's authority to hold term with two justices present. In *Griffin* v. *Orman*, Thompson, who was subject to disqualification, found for the court that three judges must be present for the panel to act and that the chief justice could appoint a circuit judge to sit with the court in instances of disqualification.[6] As examined in chapter 8, continuing differences within the court over this rule contributed to the embarrassing controversies of 1859 between Chief Justice Baltzell and Justice Charles H. DuPont.

Although some of these decisions suggest an activist spirit, most justices believed they based their opinions upon a philosophy of judicial conservatism. Justice George W. Macrae, for instance, once dismissed a petition for rehearing that had been filed within the designated period but after the court's adjournment. He argued lack of jurisdiction, insisting that the petition had to be submitted during the same term of court.[7] Similarly, the court's 1851 *In Re White* opinion stressed conservative interpretation. Despite its constitutional grant of power to issue writs of injunction, mandamus, quo warranto, habeas corpus, and such other remedial and original writs "as may be necessary to give [the court] a general superintendence and control of all other courts," the tribunal held that its jurisdiction merely was appellate and that it could not grant a writ of mandamus in an original proceeding.[8]

Thomas Baltzell's approach, whether considered pragmatic or eccentric, offered an exception to the conservative philosophy. An illustration comes from his reaction to the problem of delays after disqualification of a judge who had either participated in litigation as counsel of record or presided over the matter in a lower court. In one such instance he reached an agreement with the parties at the trial level. He would render a decision, and they would appeal it for resolution in the supreme court while authorizing his participation at the appellate level. "A man may waive his objections to a juror, or select as arbitrators persons totally disqualified, and yet it is his own concern," Baltzell wrote. "The provision is for the benefit of [the] parties, and such [a] one as, in my opinion, they may very properly waive."[9] While Justice Hawkins agreed in principle, in order to avoid deadlock he joined with the court's 1849 majority in *Darden* v. *Lines*, which declared that, given the arrangement, no final decision actually had been reached at the trial level and, as such, no appeal could lie.[10]

The 1855 court evidenced a more generous attitude in the consideration of circuit court powers than it did for its own power in *Darden*. In a decision hailed at the time as "greatly beneficial to small suitors at large, and satisfactory to the legal profession," it held that decisions of justices of the peace were subject to circuit court review. The justices reasoned in *Dibble* v. *Jacksonville and Alligator Plank Road Company* that constitutional provisions granting appellate jurisdiction to the supreme court should not be construed so as to preclude circuit courts from exercising jurisdiction over inferior courts.[11] Interestingly, the supreme court utilized a detailed history of superior court jurisdiction during the territorial period upon which to base its decision.[12]

Probate

Several cases of significance concerning probate received court attention during the antebellum period. At its first term, the tribunal in 1846 determined in *Parkhill's Administrators* v. *The Union Bank* that the powerful financial institution could not sue Martha Manley as administrator of Parkhill's estate once she had been removed from that capacity. The following term the panel considered a related question. Could the creditor of a deceased person sue the administrator of an estate in his individual capacity after discharge if the former administrator allegedly had engaged in improper activity while administrator? A statute arguably absolved such persons from liability, but Justice Douglas construed the law to mean that, while a suit could not be brought against an individual after discharge in his capacity as administrator, one could be entertained against that person upon proof that "at the time when the discharge was granted, the defendant had *not* faithfully and honestly discharged the trust and confidence reposed in him."[13] Baltzell unsuccessfully opposed the majority's logic, arguing that "The Statute, in my view creates a new remedy, providing a prospective bar to operate unless suit be commenced . . . within five years after [the administrator's] discharge."[14]

The problem of an executor's liability in probate cases refused to die, and, in the 1851 case of *Gregory* v. *Harrison*, the court again addressed the issue. Once more, the newly independent court varied the precedent of the former panel of circuit judges. On this occasion the decision provided that an administrator could maintain an action against a removed estate executor. The court reasoned that the executor, notwithstanding the revocation of letters testamentary, still held an interest in estate chattels reduced to possession. The interest belonged not to the executor personally but to him as trustee for the creditors, legatees, and distributees. Further, the panel determined that in intestate cases, where creditors already had been paid, the probate judge could appoint an administrator to distribute the estate's remainder.[15]

Residency issues sparked debate, as well. In 1848's *Blewitt* v. *Nicholson*, the court considered whether a county judge could grant administration to a husband by virtue of his marital rights upon his wife's estate, even though she was a nonresident at death and died in another state. State law failed to address the situation, and, in the circumstances, the justices relied upon English common law. They held that the granting of administration did not concern the question of jurisdiction. Since the statute was silent, the county judges could grant administration in such cases under their general powers.[16]

Related questions of residency arose nine years later in *Smith* v. *Croom*. Hardy B. Croom had perished, along with his family, in a shipwreck. The case required determination of two questions: first, who predeceased whom among Croom and his children; second, whether Croom at his death held domicile in North Carolina or Florida. Relying upon the testimony, the court found that the father died before his children. By reference to his correspondence, in which Croom stated that he was not planning to settle in Florida, the tribunal declared that Croom intended North Carolina as his domicile even though the planter had purchased Florida land and participated in a territorial election. The decision established a landmark in the law of domicile and survivorship.[17]

Commercial Litigation

Florida's early statehood years were in stark economic contrast to the final half-decade of the territory's existence. From depression and stagnation, a dynamically developing state had emerged. Both good and bad times produced litigation, however, and much of the civil agenda of the courts related to disputes involving promissory notes, foreclosures, bank failures, arbitration, and contracts. Many decisions ignited controversy because personal attitudes of individual judges could significantly affect large sums, vast acreage, and scores of slaves. The same influences were felt at times on the supreme court.

Far more often than not, the supreme court's decisions in commercial cases enjoyed unanimous agreement of the justices. In the panel's first term, for example, only one such case divided the court. The defendants in *White* v. *Camp* claimed lack of consideration, proper endorsement, and fraud in a suit over a promissory note. The issue depended upon whether a law that did not require the plaintiff to present evidence other than the note itself applied to an assignee. Justice Hawkins wrote the majority opinion. The statute did not apply to a bona fide purchaser assignee, he reasoned. It "should be construed strictly, for it is laid down that a statute, which takes away a common law remedy, ought never to have an equitable construction."[18] Thomas Douglas concurred after examination of the law's purpose, which he concluded "was to increase the quantity of negotiable paper, in a new country, where there were few mercantile transactions, and the circulating medium was scarce." Accordingly, Douglas observed, "[the] provisions of this statute only apply, as between the immediate parties to the transaction, or such others as have taken these instruments after due, or have not acted in good faith, or with due circumspection in cases attended with suspicion."[19] Justice Baltzell agreed with the result but criticized his colleagues for dictum relating to the burden of proof. The opinions, he declared, "lead in my opinion to a very great embarrassment in practice, if not to serious injury and injustice to parties."[20]

The difficulties encountered in foreclosure actions focused court attention in the 1848 case of *Wilson* v. *Hayward*, which also afforded opportunity for Baltzell to stress the panel's commitment to equity as opposed to rigid application of common-law rules. "The statute for the foreclosure of mortgages by the Courts of Common Law, under which this proceeding was had," Baltzell commented, "has created no little embarrassment in the decision of cases based upon it." He then argued that, although the legislature had directed common-law courts to decide such issues, the lawmakers had not intended the statute to revive common-law rules and principles. Rather, mortgages really existed as creatures of courts of equity. As such, all claimants should be brought as parties in litigation concerning them to allow adjustment of all conflicting rights and interests.[21]

The issue of foreclosures took on practical and political importance during the antebellum period far beyond what appearance might suggest. The collapse of banking institutions during the early 1840s had raised questions not only of debtor liability but also of a stockholder's civil and criminal liability for corporate actions. Consequently bank supporters—mostly Whig planters, professionals, and businessmen—desired courts to enforce collection of debts owed to financial institutions while upholding corporate powers. Many Democrats, to the contrary, sought to relieve debtors and to hold bank backers responsible for damages caused by irresponsible corporate policies.

The principal case illustrating this clash of interest and political philosophy carried the style *Union Bank of Florida* v. *Parkhill's Administrators* and was decided in 1849 before the creation of an independent state supreme court. A key issue related to enforcement of a promissory note given in payment of bank shares. Democrat Baltzell, acting as trial court judge, offered jury instructions effectively piercing the corporate shell by asserting that bank bonds backed by the territory "were in effect and actually bonds of the stockholders." He insisted that the bank acted as agent for the shareholders and that, as soon as bonds were sold, the "shares of stock were paid in full." When the matter came before the supreme court, constitutional rules barred Baltzell's participation, and Whig leader Joseph Bradford Lancaster subsequently wrote the court opinion. Recognizing the legal and political implications of Baltzell's instructions, Lancaster pointedly rejected them by emphasizing the protections of the corporate form. This and similar cases brought home to Whig leaders the need for a sympathetic appellate tribunal and served as context for the 1850 selections of supreme court justices through legislative vote swapping.[22]

Most often decisions related not to broad political issues and legal concepts; instead, they dealt with narrow details of law and jurisprudence. Sometimes the cases prompted justices to step into the role of law professors in a state without a law school. During the term in which the *Union Bank* decision was reached, the justices also deliberated in *O'Bryan* v. *Reed* as to whether, under the "Act Concerning Arbitrations and Awards," an arbitration award not signed by both parties could be enforced. The tribunal's answer was no.[23] Assumpsit rules received consideration in *Gordon* v. *Camp*. The decision detailed when an action in assumpsit could lie and explained that nonfeasance, misfeasance, and malfeasance could give rise to such action when the plaintiff waived the tort and relied on circumstances forming a breach of promise.[24] The next year the differences between executed and executory contracts likewise produced a reasoned court explanation as well as court notice that an equity court could restrain further collection of purchase money when a vendor could not comply with covenants.[25]

Occasionally the issues at point held deeper implications or else required jurisprudential pioneering. One such case grew out of the law of partnership. The plaintiff in *Fillyau* v. *Laverty*, decided in 1850, had filed suit against a representative of a deceased partner. The estate representative defended by insisting that the creditor first had to name the surviving partner as a party and pursue the action against him. Justice George Sydney Hawkins, attempting to find equity, adopted what has become the modern viewpoint. "[C]reditors should possess every facility of enforcing their demands against the estates of those who contracted the obligations," he found, "without being obliged to await the law's delay." Hawkins added, "[N]or can we see any good reason why the death of one of the partners should place the creditor, as to the efficiency of his remedy, in a worse position than if the death had not occurred." The justice noted, as well, the existence of a nonclaim statute, which barred demands not exhibited within two years of death. Relying upon his interpretation of the law's intent, Hawkins observed, "This statute is virtually a statute of limitations, passed not only for the security of the legal representatives, but for the benefit of the heirs and distributees, to effect a speedy and final settlement of estates."[26]

Liens and Attorney Fees

Questions of foreclosure and other commercial issues could divide the justices, but unanimity came easily when the matter at controversy concerned attorney's fees. The first such case, *Randall* v. *Archer*, resulted in an 1854 decision in favor of a lawyer's authority to assert a lien over a mortgage and bond in his possession. The opinion relieved the attorney of any responsibility for filing a claim over liabilities received by his client.[27] A decision of even greater significance was aired the following year. The main issue concerned how lawyers' fees should be determined when no contract specified an amount or a method. Baltzell's recusal brought circuit judge William Augustus Forward to the supreme bench. Forward's opinion for the high court in *Carter* v. *Bennet* remanded the question to the trial court, instructing the judge to entertain evidence at the final hearing as to a reasonable fee.[28] The judge's determinations then were appealed as *Carter* v. *Davis*. Writing for the court in 1858, Judge B. A. Putnam, sitting for Baltzell, directed that the principle of *quantum meruit* would determine compensation in such cases. Lawyers were entitled, he added, to a lien on any amount rendered in judgment.[29] Reportedly, the issue "for many years occasioned much interest in the Middle and Western sections of the State."[30] *Carter* continues to be cited to this day.

Constitutionality and Separation of Powers

The United States Supreme Court's reluctance to find laws of Congress unconstitutional found no counterpart in the Florida judiciary. Within three years of its creation, the state supreme court in *Flint River Steam Boat Company* v. *Allen* had invalidated an 1847 law that permitted entry of a judgment in some circumstances simply upon submission of an affidavit of claim for services rendered on board a watercraft on the Apalachicola River. Chief Justice Douglas referred to the 1838 Constitution and its language that "the right of trial by jury shall forever remain inviolate." The words, he declared, did "not merely imply that the right of jury trial shall not be abolished or wholly denied, but that it shall not be *impaired*." By denying jury trial prior to judgment, the law in question had impaired the right to a jury trial and, therefore, was unconstitutional.[31]

Three years later the panel declared an 1832 territorial act void. The court also asserted its authority to examine the nature of a legislative act in order to determine whether its character was legislative or judicial. The case involved a law granting a divorce. According to Justice Semmes's reasoning in *Ponder* v. *Graham*, the federal law that created the legislative council constituted a grant of power, not a restriction of preexisting power. Therefore, the council's authority did not extend beyond what it was granted: that is, the power to make the laws. The lawmaking function, Semmes believed, concerned future conduct. An act granting a divorce dealt primarily with past conduct and required judicial, rather than legislative, determination. In such a situation the principle of separation of powers—"[which] the wisest and best of men have considered the only safe guarantee to public liberty and private rights"—compelled the supreme court to declare the purported law void. "The fundamental principle of every free and good government," Semmes wrote, "is that these several co-ordinate departments forever remain separate and distinct . . . for it is this which gives to our system energy, vitality and stability."[32]

When a separation-of-powers dispute affected the executive branch, the court seemed to exhibit more deference than it did when considering legislative actions. The 1850 case of *Bemis* v. *State* concerned a state suit against former comptroller of public accounts Nathaniel P. Bemis. The comptroller in 1847 had received just under $600 in funds owed to the territorial government but had retained the money because he was owed about the same amount for services rendered to the public. No state law permitted such an offset, the court noted, and, in the situation, the state could sue an officer on his bond.[33] In another comptroller-related case, the court limited judicial power to order executive officers to act through issuance of writs of mandamus. Specifically, Chief Justice Douglas held that, in a matter requiring an executive officer's judgment and discretion, "the Court could not by *mandamus*, act directly upon the officer and guide and control his judgment and discretion in the matters committed to his care in the ordinary discharge of his official duties." The proper remedy for a sheriff whose claim for services had not been paid by the comptroller, Douglas added, was a memorial to the general assembly for relief.[34]

While the court evidenced willingness to curb extensions of the legislature's power, one area of legislative action—support of internal improvement projects—earned approval. The Whig party had destructed by the early 1850s, with a number of its adherents moving into the Democratic fold. Democrats always had voiced some support for internal improvements, but by mid-decade many party members had set aside their opposition to special corporate privileges and immunities in order to encourage state development and private gain. Whether a constitutional prohibition against "perpetuities and monopolies" prevented such programs remained open to question until, in 1855, the state supreme court held in *Barbee* v. *Plank Railroad Co.* that it did not. As Justice DuPont reasoned, the term *perpetuity* applied only to estates. He determined, as well, that corporations did not constitute monopolies because anyone theoretically could become a shareholder.[35]

Other internal improvement-related issues received court review. In 1856 the justices affirmed the constitutionality of an act that offered land grants for construction and operation of specified projects and permitted local governments to subscribe to stock in the favored corporations. The specific concern arose, as Justice Baltzell's dissent mentioned, from a constitutional ban on expenditure of tax funds other than for "necessary expenses of government." Justice DuPont for the court dismissed Baltzell's assertions as unfounded.[36] A similar concern stemmed from a state law that permitted riparian owners to build wharves in streams or waters of bays and harbors. Under its provisions, the court found, Key West could grant private persons rights to construct wharves, even though the municipal charter conveyed no specific authority for such grants and the action arguably constituted a divestiture of sovereign lands.[37]

Taxation

How state and local government could raise funds for its needs, including support of internal improvements, sometimes found the justices approving of specific actions while disapproving of others. In *Levy* v. *Smith*, for instance, the supreme court declined in 1851 to assent to arguments by Moses Levy that a law establishing three categories of land for assessment purposes violated constitutional requirements for an "equal and uniform mode of taxation." The panel stressed that uniformity of application throughout the state satisfied the constitution even when some defects marred the law.[38] The court proved not so flexible when Monroe County attempted to impose a tax of 1 percent on auction sales. Chief Justice Anderson observed that statutes limited county taxes to levies upon persons and species of property. The tax in question, Anderson determined, constituted a commission or tax on sales and, as such, did not come within the county's lawful authority.[39]

Torts

Among appeals related to tort law, one case stands as the antebellum period's most significant. The question presented in 1850's *City of Tallahassee* v. *Fortune* concerned whether a municipality could be held liable for loss of a mare because of the town's failure to repair a ditch. Defense attorneys insisted that, first, trespass did not lie against a municipal corporation and, second, the action does not lie when injury resulted from the plaintiff's negligence. Justice Lancaster rejected the defenses. The act of incorporation, he found, granted the city power and authority "to prevent and remove nuisances." A large ditch, gully, or chasm that was situated on a public highway appeared to him to be such a nuisance. The city's power to prevent and remove nuisances, he continued, "carried with it the implied legal obligation to remove them." Of the question of plaintiff's negligence, he added, "It is the custom of the people generally, when in the streets, to hitch their horses to a hook, peg, post, tree or rack, and leave them while the riders attend respectively to their own business." He concluded, "The thing is daily (and frequently every day) done by the most careful as well as by the careless persons, and cannot, in our opinion, form a ground of allegation of negligence or want of ordinary care, in the plaintiff; but horses so hitched often escape, and this is accident rather than negligence."[40]

Slavery and Free Blacks

Two court opinions illustrate the panel's attitude toward the rights of slaves and free blacks in the pre-Civil War era. Both involved criminal cases in which the justices reversed convictions while expressing their support for the institution of slavery and their belief in the inferiority of blacks.

The first case, *Luke, a slave* v. *The State,* reached the court in 1852 and revolved around trial judge Thomas Douglas's refusal to charge a jury with instructions that a slave could commit no criminal offense if he was acting under the control and direction of his master. The highly controversial question presented the court with a dilemma that it preferred at that time to avoid. The panel managed to do so by deciding the matter based upon procedural grounds. Its opinion vacated Luke's sentence because he had been charged under a general law rather than under a law providing punishment for slaves. Punishment laws providing such distinctions met with the court's "approbation." The opinion declared:

> The perpetuation of the institution [of slavery], indeed the common safety of the citizens during its continuance, would seem to require that the superiority of the white or Caucasian race over the African negro, should be ever demonstrated and preserved so far as the dictates of humanity will allow—the degraded caste should be continually reminded of their inferior position, to keep them in a proper degree of subjection to the authority of the free white citizens. And thus there is an obvious propriety in visiting their offences with more degrading punishment than is inflicted on the white citizens, while the humanity of the law is demonstrated by securing to them the same forms of law in making defence—a trial by jury—compulsory process for their witnesses—the aid of counsel—and indeed, as full, fair, and impartial a trial, as can or may be claimed by a white person.[41]

The court's serious attitude about safeguarding the limited rights afforded blacks found expression in several additional decisions. Particularly, in *Simon, a slave* v. *The State* the tribunal reversed a conviction based upon a confession extracted while an excited crowd milled outside the building where the slave was confined and after the town mayor had informed the man that he surely would be hung if he did not confess.[42] On the other hand, the decision in *Clark*

v. *Gautier*, rendered in 1859, established that a writ of habeas corpus was not the proper method for trying the right of a black man to freedom. Thomas N. Gautier had filed for such relief on behalf of Dick, a mulatto. The trial court granted the writ, but putative owner William Clark appealed. Writing for the court, Justice Baltzell reasoned, in light of the United States Supreme Court's *Dred Scott* decision, that habeas corpus proceedings were intended for the protection of personal liberty of free men and were not designed or used to try any right of property.[43]

Women's Rights

Two major decisions, both issued in 1855, concerned women's rights. *Maiben* v. *Bobe* concerned Rosanna Shomo's rights to dispose of property deeded to her without restriction by her brother. Justice DuPont dissented from the majority opinion, insisting that "the enjoyment of the *use* may clearly exist without the right of disposal." For the court, however, Justice Baltzell held otherwise. He commented broadly on laws purporting to require both husband and wife to join all sales and transfers:

> [T]his restriction upon the rights of married women implies a distrust not by any means flattering to them or to the other sex. Are those of our state less to be trusted or confided in, in this respect than the women of England or New York, and other states of the Union where freedom of alienation prevails; are they more imbecile? have they less character, less self reliance and ability to assert their rights, or have those of the other sex greater disposition to impose upon, oppress and take advantage of their weakness and infirmities? We think not. If they are unfit to be trusted with powers of alienation, their right of ownership may well be doubted. Their sound judgment, good sense, and intelligence, their virtue and native energy, with the gallantry and sense of justice of the other sex are their surest and safest reliance. The world has an experience in its past history, not to be forgotten, of the effects of special guardianships of this kind. This experience has demonstrated that to hedge their property with restrictions and guards is as important and useless as to surround their persons by stone walls, to prevent injury and insult.[44]

Differences in outlook between Baltzell and DuPont carried over into *Sanderson* v. *Jones*. Robert Harrison had transferred slaves and other property in trust to himself and his wife. Later he shifted ownership of a few of the trust's slaves to another trust for the benefit of his daughter, who married John P. Sanderson. When Mrs. Sanderson died, Mrs. Harrison sought a court order directing that the slaves be returned to the original trust, arguing that the transfer to Mrs. Sanderson's trust had been improper. The supreme court disagreed, with Baltzell finding that Harrison could transfer his interest in the trust property to his daughter, that the transfer was unrestricted, and that Sanderson was entitled to claim an interest in his wife's property. In the process Baltzell dismissed certain procedural matters in order to reach the substantive issues. DuPont reacted with strenuous objection. "If I have exceeded the limits usually assigned to a dissenting opinion," he recorded, "I claim an apology in the paramount importance of the question involved, and in the firm conviction . . . that the doctrines announced in the opinion of the Court are not only unsustained by authority, but are in direct conflict with the best interests of society, and take away the only shield which an affectionate and provident parent is allowed to interpose for the protection of his confiding and often unfortunate daughter, and her innocent and helpless progeny."[45]

Part Three

Civil War and Reconstruction, 1861–1877

Chapter 10

Civil War and the Courts

During the period beginning with statehood in 1845 and ending on the Civil War's eve, Florida retained its basic character while growing substantially. In the 1850s the population almost doubled to 140,000, with many newcomers hailing from Deep South states such as Georgia and South Carolina. Still, in mid-decade, Indian war again struck the peninsula, causing disruption and settler flight until its 1858 conclusion. Even then much of the state continued to reflect a frontier atmosphere, with cattle grazing and subsistence farming as principal industries. Many hamlets and villages dotted the landscape, but only three towns—Pensacola, Key West, and Jacksonville—boasted populations greater than 2,000.[1]

Despite sparse population and frontier conditions, indications of sustained growth presented themselves in all Florida regions. No longer were amenities of advancing civilization such as schools and libraries rare. Steamboats regularly plied waterways such as the Apalachicola, St. Johns, and Oklawaha rivers, while railroads began to link key plantation areas, naval-stores centers, and lumbering regions with port towns. Four hundred miles of track had been laid by 1860. The lines spurred the economy by shortening travel times between Jacksonville and Tallahassee, Fernandina and Cedar Key, and Pensacola and the state of Alabama.[2]

Regional hubs such as Jacksonville, Key West, and Pensacola benefited from Florida's prosperity, but the state's economic heart could be found in Middle Florida. The plantation belt—which had expanded eastward to Columbia, Alachua, and Marion counties—had matured into one of the South's most sophisticated and affluent areas. Cotton culture, worked by greater numbers of slaves, predominated. More than 61,000 bondsmen and bondswomen lived in the state in 1860, the large majority in Middle Florida.[3]

Slavery, of course, had emerged as more than an economic issue while the nation headed toward civil war. This seemingly insoluble issue had aided the destruction early in the 1850s of the Whig party. In East, South, and West Florida especially, many Whigs had drifted into the short-lived American or Know Nothing party, but secession-inclined Democrats held state-level political power firmly in their grasp. A final effort to challenge their strength was launched in 1860 in the guise of the Constitutional Union party. Nationally and in Florida the movement approved a conciliatory platform that avoided any mention of slavery and championed "the Constitution of the Country, the union of States, and the enforcement of the laws."[4]

The 1860 political challenge to Florida's Democratic power structure failed to achieve its purpose. The Constitutional Unionists convened a statewide convention at Quincy on June 27, named candidates for state and national offices, and initiated a spirited campaign. The party represented the only realistic alternative to the Democrats, as the Republican party had yet to gain a foothold in the state. But the Constitutional Unionists could overcome neither their opponents' organizational powers nor the overwhelming support given to Democrats by Florida newspapers. Nevertheless, the Constitutional Unionists scored well, especially in East, West, and South Florida. Gubernatorial candidate Edward Hopkins, for instance, gained 5,248 votes to Democrat John Milton's 6,994. It was not enough, though, as Democrats triumphed that fall in state and national contests. Democratic rule seemed secure.[5]

Americans anxiously had awaited the results of the national presidential race, and Abraham Lincoln's election stoked fears of national division and conflict. Many pro-secession Floridians demanded that the state prepare for any assault upon the state's rights or upon the institution of slavery. Union supporters vocalized their loyalty, but in some areas—Calhoun and Taylor counties provide examples—they found themselves subjected to mob violence. On November 26 Governor Madison Starke Perry welcomed the new legislature to the state capitol by advocating immediate secession of the southern states. The general assembly responded by allocating $100,000 for purchases of arms and ammunition and by scheduling a secession convention.[6]

The Convention of the People of Florida met against a backdrop of emotional support for disunion, particularly in the Deep South states from which much of the state's white population had emigrated. The assembly convened at Tallahassee on January 3, 1861. South Carolina already had proclaimed its separation from the Union, and local pro-secession forces were determined to bring Florida out second. Unionists realized the likelihood of some action. They played for time by urging delay until other southern states had considered the matter. They also battled for a statewide referendum, believing that a majority of voters would not countenance division. Pro-secession men challenged the tactics. Their leaders proclaimed that the convention held power to decide for Floridians, and their words took on added urgency as conventions began to deliberate in other states. Preliminary votes finally revealed pro-secession majorities. When a final vote on the ordinance was taken on January 10, the tally revealed 62 to 7 in favor of disunion. As Mississippi had withdrawn the day previously, Florida stood as the third state in secession.[7]

The Florida supreme court's members played a minor, but symbolically important, role in the drama. The convention directed the tribunal to oversee preparation of the final manuscript of the secession ordinance. The justices, in turn, invited Thomas Jefferson's descendant Elizabeth M. Eppes to decorate the document. Their letter addressed Miss Eppes as "a lineal descendant of the immortal author of the first Declaration of American Independence" and requested her to "lend your aid in embellishing the parchment which contains the Declaration of Independence of the Sovereign State of Florida."[8] The day following the ordinance's adoption, the justices observed with other officials as sixty-four delegates signed the parchment. Tallahassee women then presented governor-elect John Milton with the new flag of the republic of Florida: a solid white field graced with three blue stars denoting the seceded states.[9]

At the conclusion of the secession ceremony, jubilant citizens celebrated in Tallahassee's streets. In other towns cannons rang out the news, and volunteers offered their services to defend their state. Amid the euphoria Unionists for the most part held their reservations quietly. One prominent man already had voiced a note of caution, however. Tallahassee celebrants had accosted former governor Richard Keith Call shortly after the signing. "Well, Governor," they told him, "we have done it!" Call responded, "And what have you done?" Andrew Jackson's old protégé then answered his own question. "You have opened the gates of Hell," he declared presciently, "from which shall flow the curses of the damned which shall sink you to perdition!"[10]

Secession in South Carolina, Mississippi, and Florida represented only the beginnings of national division. Within a month of Florida's action, Alabama, Georgia, Louisiana, and Texas had followed. Florida's United States representatives and senators had departed from Congress on January 21, and one week later Santa Rosa County's Jackson Morton, who had fought secession, traveled to Montgomery, Alabama, to represent his state in the Confederacy's constitutional convention. On February 8 Jefferson Davis of Mississippi took office as president of the Confederate States of America, with Florida's Stephen R. Mallory accepting the post of secretary of the navy. The Confederacy subsequently adopted its constitution on March 11.[11]

In many respects the Confederate Constitution paralleled its United States counterpart, although it contained some significant variations. Rather than a separate bill of rights, it incorporated the guarantees of the federal amendments into its text. The document unabashedly acknowledged the institution of slavery. To immunize the presidency from partisan politics, its authors limited that officer's tenure to one six-year term. The chief executive received power to make line-item vetoes of appropriations, and, following the British parliamentary model, his cabinet members held seats in Congress so that they could defend the president's policies directly to lawmakers. The charter limited the Congress's powers to a greater extent than did the United States Constitution. For example, the body could not tax imports, legislate for the general welfare, or propose constitutional amendments.[12]

The Confederate Constitution's judicial provisions also resembled those of the federal document, except that states could not be sued by citizens of other states or by foreigners, including citizens who held property interests in Confederate states. As also was true of the United States Constitution, it vested judicial power in a supreme court and "such inferior courts as the Congress may, from time to time, ordain and establish." This power extended to "all cases arising under this Constitution," but the drafters eliminated the federal charter's reference to "all cases, in Law and Equity." The omission raised the possibility that the Confederate Congress could limit the discretionary power of judges by restricting their equity jurisdiction.[13]

The Confederate Constitution's judicial provisions quickly found implementation in national law. On March 16, 1861, Congress passed a judiciary act that established a supreme court with jurisdiction to hear appeals from the states. It also created several district courts and a court of admiralty and maritime jurisdiction to sit at Key West. The supreme court never materialized because some ardent secessionists feared the potential tyranny of life-tenured justices exercising judicial review over the states. Confederate administrators also abandoned the admiralty court after Union troops kept William Marvin, federal judge for the Southern District of Florida, on the bench in Key West. The district courts did commence operations, but their dockets consisted mainly of sequestration proceedings and habeas corpus petitions from conscripts seeking to avoid the Confederate draft. Other private litigation on the national level declined substantially after 1861. Both as result and as cause, the primary legal business of the Confederacy was conducted in state courts.[14]

In 1861 constitutional revision occupied the attention of Floridians as well as Confederate officials. On April 22 the state secession convention ratified the national charter unanimously. Its members also realized the fundamental constitutional changes wrought by secession, and they continued to sit to revise the state's original Constitution of 1838. They soon adopted changes to reflect current concerns and circumstances. Most symbolically the delegates replaced the original preamble with the text of the secession ordinance that had declared Florida "a sovereign and independent Nation." The new document reduced the governor's term to two years, although it exempted governor-elect John Milton, who would serve his original four-year term. The legislature received authority to establish courts with jurisdiction over offenses committed by slave and free blacks. Additionally, the revisions ended the state's experiment with popular election of jurists, providing instead for gubernatorial appointment, subject to senate confirmation, of supreme court justices and circuit judges to six-year terms. The drafters likely intended the reforms to prevent the election of Unionists to the bench, since pockets of pro-Union voters dotted the state.[15]

When the convention approved its constitutional revisions, the language seemed to mandate broad changes on the supreme court, but such did not prove the case. Sitting at the time were three men who had been elected to six-year terms in 1859. As explained in chapter 8, Charles H. DuPont, the associate justice who had disagreed so vehemently with Chief Justice Thomas Baltzell over the absence of Justice Byrd Murphy Pearson, had replaced Baltzell as chief justice. Pearson did not stand for reelection because of poor health, and William Augustus Forward and David S. Walker filled the vacancies left by Pearson's and DuPont's failure to stand for their old positions. DuPont, Forward, and Walker either supported secession or else reconciled themselves to it. In the circumstances neither Governor Perry nor Governor Milton replaced any of them, even though the new constitution did not require that they be retained. The three justices served on the court through the war.[16]

In terms of the Civil War's grand strategies, at first Florida held relatively little importance to either the Confederate government or to the United States. Through most of the period the Confederacy assigned only small forces to the state. The greater part of their duties, even when supported by local troops, consisted of guarding the Middle Florida plantation belt and defending the vital ports at the mouths of the Apalachicola, St. Marks, and St. Johns rivers. In the most significant military engagement—1864's Battle of Olustee near Lake City—rebel forces prevented Union soldiers from destroying vital supply lines between Florida and Georgia. They forestalled, as well, the threatened liberation of slaves in the Middle Florida area.[17]

Despite the absence of decisive battles, Florida's security came to be of vital concern to the Confederate war effort. By late 1863 southern troops relied on the state for subsistence supplies, and Floridians contributed beef, sugar, syrup,

Robert Bruce Van Valkenburgh

Henry Laurens Mitchell

Samuel J. Douglas

Soldiers of the War between the States. In all instances military service of justices preceded their service on the court. In May 1861, former Judge Samuel J. Douglas and his family hastily departed by ship from Key West, a town in sympathy with the Union cause, for his home state of Virginia. He provided service to the Confederacy as a military judge. Robert Bruce Van Valkenburgh, a United States congressman during the war, assumed the difficult task in a North divided between copperheads and pro-war advocates as an active recruiter in New York and as a colonel in the Army of the Potomac at Antietam, site of the bloodiest battle in the nation's history, and named by the Confederacy the Battle of Sharpsburg. Lieutenant and later Captain Henry Laurens Mitchell of the Confederacy served with Preston's Brigade in the battles near Murfreesboro, Tennessee, in 1863, and was cited in war records for his gallantry. George Pettus Raney and William Adams Hocker, not pictured, also served the Confederate cause.

salt, and shoe leather. The state also supported the Confederacy by sending more than its share of soldiers to the rebel armies. In 1863 more than one-half of the white males between sixteen and sixty years of age fought for the South. By war's end 80 percent of eligible Florida men had donned a grey uniform. At the same time about 1,200 white Floridians fought for the Union, mainly in the First and Second Florida cavalries. Perhaps 1,000 blacks, most former slaves, served in United States forces. In all, Florida contributed more soldiers per capita than any other state.[18]

While Florida escaped the most brutal ravages of war, it experienced substantial loss nonetheless. Its Confederate soldiers suffered 6,000 casualties, including 1,000 deaths. Several towns and villages—notably Jacksonville, Pensacola, Fernandina, Cedar Key, Tampa, Manatee, and Fort Meade—absorbed extensive damage, as did farms and plantations in East, West, and South Florida. Except for results of the Marianna raid of September 1864, Middle Florida escaped the conflict virtually unharmed. Still, the state's real and personal property values, not including losses caused by slave emancipation, dropped by $22 million between 1860 and 1865. Given the persistence of Unionist sentiment and the state's geographic vulnerability, many areas fell early into Union hands. Key West remained under federal control throughout the war. In the struggle's early years Union forces permanently occupied Fernandina, St. Augustine, and Pensacola. After several temporary occupations, Jacksonville received a permanent Union garrison in December 1863.[19]

War's consequences usually cannot be foreseen, and many changes that affected Florida's judiciary could be numbered among them. From necessity and a zealous intention to safeguard the state's rights, lawmakers effectively rejected the federalist court system presupposed by the United States and Confederate constitutions. Instead the legislators placed issues that once had been under federal jurisdiction, such as admiralty and diversity cases, into the hands of circuit court judges. When they did so, McQueen McIntosh, United States judge for the Northern District, resigned his post, thereby relinquishing federal judicial control over most of the state. President Abraham Lincoln soon designated Jacksonville resident Philip Fraser as his replacement, but Judge Fraser did not hold regular court sessions until after the war's end. Only in Marvin's Key West court, where Thomas Boynton presided beginning in 1863, did federal judicial authority survive. As a result, state judicial officials could not prevent the prosecution of prize vessels captured while running the Union blockades of the Atlantic and Gulf coastlines.[20]

Within the state the administration of justice suffered significantly. Wartime circumstances compelled some local and circuit courts to move their sessions or to suspend operations. Judges often contended with shortages of personnel and dockets crowded with cases transferred from federal courts. The supreme court's appellate jurisdiction survived legislative reforms intact, but the war interrupted court routine. Sessions lasted a few days each, and the tribunal consequently decided only a small number of cases. Litigation slowed further as "members of the bar wholly untrained in military tactics" abandoned their law offices "to gain fame for themselves equal to that hitherto won by trained soldiers."[21] Reportedly even Chief Justice DuPont joined volunteers in March 1865 determined to defend the Quincy courthouse from anticipated federal shelling.[22]

Many significant constitutional questions failed to receive court review due to wartime political considerations. One instance arose in December 1861, when secession convention president John McGehee called for the delegates to reassemble at Tallahassee the following month. Governor Milton, a staunch secessionist himself, believed that radical supporters of the Confederate central government who opposed some of his policies stood behind the maneuver. Accordingly he challenged McGehee's action under the wording of the convention's adjournment resolution. McGehee refused to accommodate the governor's reasoning. Milton then asked Attorney General John B. Galbraith's opinion, which Galbraith declined to give. Neither side chose to pursue the matter in the supreme court.[23]

Another important constitutional controversy emerged as a result of the January 1862 convention meeting. Delegates limited Milton's powers by creating an executive council to oversee the executive branch. The plan called for election of the council's four members by the convention and provided that they would share in the "discharge of the duties imposed and in the exercise of the power conferred" upon the governor. Milton assailed the arrangement as unconstitutional and again turned to Galbraith. The attorney general, still anxious to avoid political turmoil, declined to institute legal action. In any event the council never established a sufficient base of authority. The legislature disbanded it in November 1862.[24]

Though its influence waned during the Civil War, the supreme court continued to meet and issued about one dozen decisions from 1862 to 1864. One of its most interesting cases involved determination of the extent of a woman's right to alimony in an action for divorce. The husband in *Chaires* v. *Chaires* had argued that alimony could only be awarded in cases of the husband's adultery or extreme cruelty, not abandonment. Chief Justice DuPont, to the contrary, held for the tribunal that judges appropriately could order alimony no matter the grounds upon which the divorce was granted. It could not be presumed that the legislature's intent in passing the statute, he wrote, "would designedly seek to deprive the unfortunate wife, who may have been abandoned by a dissolute husband and doomed to drag out a weary existence in *married widowhood,* of her only hope of support." The opinion further declared that judges did not have to require a husband to pay alimony pending the outcome of the suit if the wife had income from a separate estate.[25]

Most other supreme court decisions related to routine civil and criminal appellate matters, but some dealt with weightier issues. As will be seen, the most important of those matters arose from the circumstances of war. Slavery, conscription, impressment of goods for military use, price limits, wartime speculations, and railroads numbered among the subjects of controversy mediated by the court.

Despite the obvious threat that the Civil War posed to slavery, Florida's laws changed little, while the supreme court continued to interpret the statutes as it had prior to the conflict. In *Miller* v. *Gaskins,* for instance, the panel reaffirmed the state's strict legal distinctions between free whites and black slaves. The litigation arose from a challenge to a will. Thomas Gaskins had bequeathed his slave, Sarah, to Thomas Miller "in trust, that he will allow the said Sarah to go, if she wishes, to any free state . . . ; and upon further trust that he will allow Sarah . . . to enjoy such privileges and freedom as is consistent with law." Justice Walker characterized this provision as an attempt to place Sarah "in a sort of middle state between slavery and freedom." He found that position untenable. "There is no evil against which the policy of our laws is more pointedly directed," he observed, "than that of allowing slaves to have any other status than that of pure slavery." Thus, the court found "no difficulty in pronouncing this devise null and void."[26]

The institution of slavery and defense of states' rights represented focal points of the war, while the ability to gather armies large enough to contest it formed another. In the first months after secession, volunteers poured forth to enlist in Confederate service. The enthusiasm ebbed as battlefield reverses, northern intentions to prosecute the struggle, and shortages of armaments and supplies became clear. By April 1862 military needs compelled the Confederate Congress to enact a conscription law. The act assigned each state a quota for conscription if sufficient numbers did not volunteer. Conscription agents thereupon began impressing thousands of Floridians into military service. The pressure eased in the fall, when the Confederate Congress amended the law to exempt vital occupations such as government officials, clergymen, cattlemen and cow hunters, planters, overseers, and workers engaged in critical industries. In spring and summer 1863 Governor Milton delayed the draft's execution by exhorting sufficient volunteers to enlist to meet the state quota.[27]

The exemptions and Governor Milton's best efforts failed to resolve the conscription problem, and later in 1863 the issue reheated. Florida no longer furnished sufficient volunteers, and demands for able-bodied men increased. Desertions compounded Confederate shortages. Eventually 2,000 Floridians left rebel armies, in many instances to protect and offer relief to their families, who were suffering from inflation and shortages of food and supplies as a result, in part, of the Union blockade of shipping to the South. Violent resistance met some efforts at conscription enforcement, especially in Taylor and Lafayette counties and along the Apalachicola and Peace rivers. Draft evaders sometimes joined with deserters and Unionists to raid plantations, arm runaway slaves, and destroy Confederate outposts. Rebel agents attempted to hunt down the malefactors, occasionally with bloodhounds. They destroyed camps and forced their inhabitants into service or else into prison. Homes were destroyed, and families were interned in refugee camps. Apparently the agents executed some captives by hanging.[28]

The state government usually declined to interfere as Confederate agents scoured the countryside. Governor Milton opposed harsh treatment of conscripts and deserters, but he exacerbated the situation by refusing to grant many applications for exemption. Given Florida's contributions of soldiers and supplies, a number of residents—like many of their counterparts in other southern states—objected to such a policy and to conscription generally as an insult to their honor and inappropriate for a citizenry with their resolve. They considered the situation a repudiation of the principles for which the South was fighting. Not surprisingly, then, the state supreme court heard several cases challenging the draft. In only one instance did the court refuse to grant an exemption. That case involved a physician, and the decision turned on the fact that he had neglected to follow statutory guidelines for certification as a medical doctor.[29]

Two other conscription cases commanded attention. In the first Edward L. King was arrested in October 1864 for not responding to a draft notice. The defendant claimed an exemption from service because he acted as a deacon and elder in the Methodist Episcopal Church, South. King worked primarily as a planter. On the other hand, he preached once a month in his community, performed marriages, and administered the sacraments. He did lead a particular congregation. The law exempted "every minister of religion authorized to preach according to the rules of his church, and who, at the passage of the act, shall be regularly employed in the discharge of his ministerial duties." In the circumstances the supreme court's decision in *King* v. *Daniel* resolved the matter in King's favor. Chief Justice DuPont noted that the church recognized local preachers who received no monetary compensation and who were expected to hold other employment. Since King had been ordained, preached regularly, and performed the other church services expected of him, he met the criteria for exemption. The court ordered his release.[30]

The court manifested equivalent leniency in 1864's *Hunt* v. *Finegan* by exempting a county commissioner who was elected after he had been drafted. Finding that the state constitution did not bar soldiers from running for office, Justice Forward believed that the only issue concerned whether county commissioners fell under the conscription act's exemption of "officers, judicial and executive, of the Confederate and State governments." He noted that commissioners' duties included levying taxes, appointing administrative officials, and reviewing property valuations. The justice determined that a commissioner possessed legislative, executive, and judicial powers. Again placing state needs over the army's, Forward held that "instead of the State's breaking up the army by electing soldiers to fill office, the effect will be, if they are not allowed to attend to their duties, the State organization will be broken up by the military."[31]

The Confederacy's efforts to exercise power over private property resulted in controversy, as well. As the fighting progressed, the government found itself unable to furnish adequate financial support for the war. It possessed no real property, its currency's value had declined precipitously, and it could not rely upon revenue from the unstable cotton yield. By 1863 officials found it necessary to institute a direct tax on real and personal property, an 8 percent levy on food and luxuries, a graduated income tax, a 10 percent sales tax, and certain licensing fees, in addition to existing taxes such as those on slaves and large landholdings instituted to provide funds to families of poor soldiers. An even more unpopular impressment act authorized agents to procure supplies and foodstuffs at prices set by state boards. Payment came in the form of redeemable coupons, and boards often set prices below market value. With currency inflation, the system virtually guaranteed losses to farmers. The scheme left countless Southerners fretting that "the Yankees cannot do us any more harm than our own soldiers have done."[32]

Florida's major battle concerning property seizures involved one of the state's largest landowners and most prominent political figures, David Levy Yulee. The legal contretemps ensued after Confederate authorities, anxious for rail connections between Florida food supplies and the Georgia transportation network, seized Yulee's Florida Railroad and ordered troops to relocate portions of its track. The army men refused to obey a local court order issued on Yulee's behalf. After a tense face-off law enforcement officials backed away from the trouble, leaving its resolution to postwar authorities.[33]

Yulee's attempt to find relief fell short of success in the railroad controversy, but he secured a hearing before the supreme court in a similar matter. After the 1863 harvest the former United States senator had sold sugar to the city of Savannah at a specified price. Confederate authorities seized the product, offering a lesser compensation. Yulee, asserting that he no longer owned the sugar, declined the tender. Savannah officials similarly refused and cited Yulee's rights as their reason. The Floridian eventually delivered his holdings to the army but pursued legal action for "[j]ust compensation." As required by law, he first sought arbitration from the state commission that supervised impressment agents. That panel raised the amount payable, but it did not agree with the senator's higher demands. A circuit court judge then increased the commission's valuation. An adamant Yulee appealed to the supreme court, arguing that the lower court erroneously had calculated the value as of the day the sugar was impressed rather than on the day of the trial. Defense attorneys countered that state courts had no authority to rule, since Confederate law provided a remedy.[34]

The Yulee sugar controversy permitted the supreme court to declare the right of state courts to regulate property disputes even in the face of contradictory national legislation. To obtain the result, Justice Forward narrowly construed the Impressment Act to conclude that Yulee's case involved little more than a private contractual dispute. Further he declared that the Confederate impressment agent's actions in violating legal technicalities supported the court's conclusion and left it free to decide the case upon common-law or equitable grounds. As to setting a proper valuation for the sugar, Forward rejected arguments from both sides. Instead he proclaimed that value should be decided as of the date of delivery and that the rule of just compensation in private cases applied, as well, in impressment decisions. He wrote, "[Just compensation is] what the article would sell for in the market, quality and quantity considered, and not the price which the owner might demand, or which some person for especial reason might be willing to give." Effectively the court had extended its jurisdiction to include the actions of officials of the national government.[35]

The supreme court's handling of the conscription and impressment cases symbolized the contradictions of the Confederate experiment. The secession movement had rested upon a foundation of state sovereignty. Because of the exigencies of war, however, by 1863 the Confederacy had found it necessary to exercise its authority to coerce men and property from the states. This flew in the face of the rebellion's professed commitment to states' rights and liberty from the tyranny of centralized government. The supreme court, in limiting national power under the conscription and impressment acts, typified these values. In each case the court protected the liberties of individuals as citizens of Florida rather than expanded the central government's power during wartime.

One significant area of the supreme court's Civil War-era deliberations remains to be considered. As noted, the tribunal's most important cases of the period related to the sectional conflict. Nonetheless, the court resolved other litigation that would profoundly affect the state's economic development through the century's end. Particularly several cases allowed the justices to help spur railroad construction. In good part the pertinent issues grew from the 1855 Internal Improvement Act, which authorized state land grants for construction of specified types of transportation projects. The land in question had been transferred to the state by the federal government. A board of trustees—composed of the governor, attorney general, treasurer, comptroller, and registrar of public lands—oversaw the program. The state, anticipating revenues from land sales, also guaranteed bonds issued by participating private corporations. Company stock additionally received permanent tax exemptions.[36]

From application of the Internal Improvement Act came a string of cases decided during the Civil War. Their specific origins may be traced to an 1861 law intended to encourage the deepening and widening of the Apalachicola River's shipping channel. General William D. Bailey, who owned bonds backed by state guarantees from a different venture, believed that the Apalachicola project endangered his investment and sought judicially enforced relief. He founded his objections on the 1855 law's language, which had not mentioned the Apalachicola project. The internal improvement fund's board of trustees argued that the law contemplated many projects not named. The board also contended that the act was unenforceable against it, in any event, because the law violated a state constitutional admonition that "the General Assembly shall not pledge the faith and credit of the State in aid of any corporation whatever."[37]

The court's decision rebuked the trustees and enunciated a clear policy favoring railroad development. The constitution's framers, Justice Walker explained in *Bailey* v. *Trustees of the Internal Improvement Trust Fund,* distinguished between "appropriating or pledging a fund already raised by the gift of the United States to the State of Florida, and the pledging of the faith and credit of the State to raise funds not yet in existence." Indeed, he continued, the constitution encouraged a "liberal system of Internal Improvements" through the "suitable application of such funds as may be appropriated for such improvements." Walker concluded by noting the inappropriate nature of the trustees' assertion of the unconstitutionality of "the very act which gives them existence."[38]

Neither Walker's reasoning nor the court's decision ended there. Having chastised the trustees, the justices ruled in Bailey's favor by declaring the priority of railroad construction over other projects. The 1855 act, Walker wrote, required the fund to postpone other improvements until a railroad network linking the state's major ports, plus a canal between the Indian and St. Johns rivers, had "been put into successful operation." Walker felt that the program was working and that, having reaped the benefits of the investments, Floridians could not then undermine bondholder security by jeopardizing interest payments through diversion of funds to other projects. A legislative action attempting to accomplish that end failed to meet the standards of the original law and was void.[39]

The *Bailey* decision infuriated lawmakers, who resented the judicial challenge to their authority. They directed Attorney General Galbraith to obtain a rehearing on the grounds that several of the lawyers and judges involved in the case maintained intimate connections with railroads or the internal improvement fund. Walker, for example, had served on the board as registrar of public lands and owned stock in the Pensacola and Georgia Railroad. Chief Justice DuPont had purchased stock for his minor children. When the disqualification question came before the court, however, the justices rejected challenges to Walker and DuPont and declared the legislature's action in calling for their recusal unconstitutional. The justices' interests in the case, Justice Forward ruled, were speculative. The dispute between Bailey and the fund involved no legal interests of any railroad, he insisted, nor did any railroad company or its stockholders have standing in the case. Walker, as Forward also noted, had divested himself of the railroad stock.[40]

With the conflict-of-interest question resolved, the justices turned to the legislature's interference in court affairs. Could lawmakers, by passage of a law, properly request a rehearing of a case? The court held that the assembly had no standing to intervene. "For all the Court knows," Forward observed, "the parties of the suit are satisfied with the decision of the Court. . . . But the Legislature, it seems, were not satisfied." Its action in interfering, he continued, violated the principle of separation of powers because "an act of the Legislature, directing a rehearing, is the exercise of a power properly belonging to the Judicial Department." Declaring the statute unconstitutional, Forward requested that the legislature respect the court's authority. He reminded them, "This Court has always endeavored to act with the legal deference to a co-ordinate part of the government, and at all times aimed not to tread upon the province of any of its powers."[41]

The Civil War thus tested the court. Important issues had been withheld from its review, and its influence had waned. Through the years of conflict, though, the justices doggedly pursued their responsibilities, insisting when they could on defending state and individual rights against federal encroachment and resisting efforts by legislators to take advantage of the wartime situation in order to undermine the panel's independence. With the peace in April and May 1865, however, the justices would learn that the tribulations and challenges only were beginning.

Chapter 11

Presidential Reconstruction

The Civil War's conclusion surprised few Floridians. By March 1865 most residents realized that Confederate defeat was imminent, a fact punctuated on April 1 by Governor John Milton's suicide. Senate president Abraham K. Allison, who had opposed secession, succeeded him as acting governor, but within days General Robert E. Lee had surrendered his forces at Appomattox Courthouse, Virginia. After General Joseph E. Johnston followed Lee's action later in the month, Union forces began to extend control over that portion of Florida not already subject to their authority. On May 24 Major General Quincy Gillmore declared martial law. His order permitted local judges, justices of the peace, and county court clerks to continue working. On the other hand, it suspended top state officials, including supreme court justices, from office. Soon President Andrew Johnson appointed former federal judge William Marvin as provisional governor and directed him to assemble delegates "loyal to the United States" to a convention to restore the state "to its constitutional relations to the Federal government."[1]

Governor Marvin's actions aimed at bringing Florida back into the Union pleased former Confederates while they rankled loyalists. Freedmen were not allowed to vote, although former Confederates were. The governor insisted to audiences throughout North Florida that only minimal steps need be taken to restore conservative, white control. As a result, elections in early October produced a convention dominated by Confederates and their sympathizers. Former supreme court justices Benjamin D. Wright and Thomas Baltzell numbered among them.[2]

The constitutional convention's deliberations, which began October 25, reflected Marvin's minimalist requirements. Only those concessions deemed absolutely necessary obtained approval. Otherwise, the body called for legislative elections under conditions that ensured reinstatement of the state's prewar power structure. The convention declined to guarantee rights for blacks, except to ratify the Thirteenth Amendment abolishing slavery. The governor subsequently asked former chief justice Charles H. DuPont to serve with Anderson J. Peeler and Mariano D. Papy to formulate recommendations regarding the status of blacks. DuPont and Peeler thereafter urged enactment of measures designed to restrict former bondsmen as far as possible to the condition of free blacks prior to the war. The laws they designed, later known as the "black codes," placed freedmen and freedwomen in a subservient position and limited their opportunities for political and economic advancement. These codes stood among the harshest approved by any of the southern states. With respect to the courts, blacks could testify only in actions involving other blacks, and they could not serve on juries.[3]

Constitutional revision in late 1865 changed Florida's governmental structure in several significant ways. Because of legal uncertainties experienced when senate president Allison assumed the governorship, drafters decided to create an office of lieutenant governor. The positions of governor, cabinet members, and legislators remained elective, but the governor received power to appoint supreme court justices to six-year terms with senate consent. On November 29 suspended justice David S. Walker achieved unopposed election as governor. Pensacola's W. W. J. Kelly became lieutenant governor. They succeeded to office on December 20.[4]

Walker's gubernatorial tenure proved tumultuous. Until his removal from office under the terms of congressional Reconstruction in mid–1868, he attempted to balance demands of Unionists and federal authorities with those of his political allies. His supreme court appointments illustrate his conservatism. He designated Charles H. DuPont to continue as chief justice and selected Augustus Emmet Maxwell and James McNair Baker as associate justices. The news alarmed many loyalists, black leaders, and newly arrived Northerners. DuPont's rigid views were known widely, and both associate justices had represented Florida in the Senate of the Confederate States. When Maxwell resigned in 1866, Walker replaced him with former territorial judge Samuel J. Douglas, who had advocated secession and been deported from Key West to Virginia by federal authorities. Walker also furthered a conservative agenda by successfully opposing ratification of the Fourteenth Amendment and its guarantees of black rights. "Look around you," he admonished the legislature, "and see how many persons will be left in office after this amendment is adopted."[5]

Executive branch tumult found its counterpart in court operations. On May 16, 1866, Major General John G. Foster restored to Florida's civil courts "full jurisdiction over all cases whatsoever" and withdrew "all military control except in a few specified cases."[6] Courts in many areas failed to provide justice to blacks and loyalists, however, and violence flared. By June authorities reinstated martial law in Madison, Escambia, Santa Rosa, Levy, and Alachua counties. While varying with time and region, the situation improved little in the months that followed. Still, the bench and the bar struggled to reassert judicial authority amid the chaos of war and defeat. In 1866 approximately 175 attorneys either were practicing or sitting on the bench. Twenty partnerships offered their services. Except for lawyers at Key West, the state's largest town, most legal practitioners worked in North Florida. Tallahassee accommodated twenty-five attorneys, and Pensacola, Jacksonville, and Lake City each claimed fifteen to twenty. Thirteen counties, though, found themselves without resident legal talent.[7]

The state's difficulties in adjusting to Reconstruction affected, as well, the supreme court's ability to execute its responsibilities. The state's tenuous relationship with the Union, symbolized by the continued military presence, discouraged the justices from rendering important decisions. Between March 1866 and July 1868 the tribunal considered only about twenty-five cases. Mostly they involved contracts, debts, and business partnerships that had been upset by the war. The court also heard several criminal appeals and some arguments involving jurisdictional issues stemming from local-court efforts at reorganization. None of the cases raised significant constitutional issues.[8]

The most interesting judicial opinions written during this period considered the effect of emancipation on contracts involving slaves. In 1867's *Walker* v. *Gatlin*, for example, the court held that, in a slave sales contract warranting that the bondsman was a "slave for life," the seller was not liable for breach of warranty because the slave's status was altered by unforeseen changes in the federal and state constitutions. Noting that the contract had been made only a month prior to secession, Chief Justice DuPont doubted that "at that interesting period, when all hearts were aglow with buoyant hopes of national independence, it ever entered into the mind of either party that the warranty given in the bill of sale was intended to provide against the possible contingency, which has since happened—the defeat and overthrow of the Confederate Government, and the consequent abolition of the institution of negro slavery."[9]

Similar issues received consideration in *Judge* v. *Forsyth's Executors*, also decided in 1867. Before the war, William Judge had promised to pay $2,000 to Joseph Forsyth's executors and had secured payment with a mortgage deed to five slaves. In 1866 the executors sued in Santa Rosa County to foreclose the mortgage. After the circuit court ordered payment, Judge appealed on the ground that emancipation had voided the mortgage. Justice Douglas, writing for a unanimous court, held that the circuit court possessed no jurisdiction to hear the case. Specifically, mortgage foreclosures constituted proceedings in rem, not in personam, and required "the existence of property, real or personal," to give "the party the right to proceed by petition, and the court the power to hear and determine the case." Taking judicial notice that slavery had been abolished, Douglas decided that "the property named in the mortgage had ceased to be property, and was as if it had never existed as such, and without this property the suit by petition for a foreclosure could not be maintained."[10] Much like the case in *Walker*, this decision represented an effort to protect former slaveowners from further financial loss.

In many ways the era of presidential Reconstruction represented an interim in the history of supreme court evolution, but importantly the panel's decisions were accepted and upheld as Florida's law. Before considering how respect for the court's authority persisted during the years of congressional Reconstruction, an examination of the lives of newly appointed justices James McNair Baker and Augustus Emmet Maxwell provides additional insight about the court and its personnel during the immediate postwar years.

James McNair Baker, Supreme Court Justice, 1866–1868

As had been true of several of his Florida judicial predecessors, James McNair Baker was born in North Carolina. The event occurred on July 20, 1821, in Robeson County, to Archibald S. and Catherine McCollom Baker. James's father had emigrated from Scotland as a child, while his mother was a North Carolina native of Scottish descent. The family claimed distinction from the fact that James's great-grandfather Colonel Ephrain Blaine had been commissary general to George Washington during the Revolutionary War. The details of James's education are not known, but he graduated in 1844 from Davidson College. He then studied law at Lumberton under John W. Cameron.[11]

Baker's Florida residence commenced soon after his law studies. His health had waned, and in 1846 he rode on horseback to the then-new state for relief. He achieved admission to the bar at Madison and began practicing at the Suwannee River village of Columbus, located about seventy miles east of Tallahassee. Three years later Baker relocated to Alligator (Lake City), where he continued his practice while developing a plantation. By 1850 his holdings were valued at approximately $6,000, a sizable sum for the time. Baker earned a statewide reputation for legal acuity, particularly in the field of property law. He also emerged as a Whig leader, representing Florida at the party's 1852 national convention, where he opposed the nomination of Winfield Scott. One year later Baker won election as solicitor for the eastern judicial circuit. He declined to campaign for the post on partisan grounds, an understandable position in light of his party's collapse in the 1852 state elections.[12]

Through the decade of the 1850s, Baker prospered. Politically he moved into the American or Know Nothing party, as did many other East Florida Whigs. He received the party's 1856 congressional nomination. Baker resigned as solicitor to undertake the campaign but was defeated by George Sydney Hawkins. The same year the legislature named Baker County in his honor, and the former solicitor returned to a law practice at Alligator. In 1859 he married Fannie P. Gilchrist in Fayetteville, North Carolina. Reportedly Baker's new wife aided his successful efforts to rename Alligator as Lake City. Family legend held that she refused to hang lace curtains in the windows of her new home until the change received approval.[13]

Baker returned to public office in 1859, when he secured election to the judgeship of the new Suwannee judicial circuit. The next year he supported the Constitutional Union party and its attempts to preserve the Union. Once Florida had seceded, though, Baker backed the Confederate States. In 1861 he was selected, along with Augustus Emmet Maxwell, as one of the state's Confederate senators. Reelected in 1863, he was described as "[a] respected and hardworking senator."[14] Baker chaired the public lands committee and served on other panels, including commerce and naval affairs. He advocated conservative fiscal practices and interested himself in the postal service, judicial districting, sequestration procedures, and pay scales. During his first term the senator ardently supported Jefferson Davis's administration, but he subsequently grew disenchanted with the president's policies. Baker especially opposed measures—such as high taxes, impressment, and conscription of skilled workers—that imposed economic hardships on the states.[15]

Following the war, Senator Baker returned to Lake City to resume his legal and public service careers. In 1866 Governor David S. Walker acknowledged Baker's experience and talents with appointment as a supreme court associate justice. During two years' service Justice Baker authored only nine opinions, primarily in cases that involved contract and property disputes. He left the bench when the Constitution of 1868 became effective and, once again, opened a legal office, this time at Jacksonville. His bitterness at congressional Reconstruction evidenced itself in active support of the Democratic party, and he served on its state executive committee in 1876.[16]

The former justice also returned to the supreme court, beginning in 1869, as a litigator. In cases heavily laden with political overtones, he argued for clients interested in the disposition of public lands for internal improvements and the outcome of railroad bankruptcies. Particularly he and Wilkinson Call sued railroad developer George Swepson, a participant in the celebrated Reconstruction-era Swepson-Littlefield fraud, on behalf of the city of Jacksonville. They insisted that their goal was "abstract justice." The action embarrassed many community leaders in the Republican city, who believed that it would deprive the town of needed infrastructure. A local newspaper pleaded with the lawyers, "Let us have peace, and railroads, and steamships, and let such a costly article as abstract justice take care of itself."[17]

Activities beyond the political realm occupied Baker's attention, as well. Raised a Presbyterian by his Scottish parents, he worked in the church and strongly advocated its doctrines. He served as an elder, represented the church as an attorney, and acted as a member of the Pan-Presbyterian Alliance that met in Philadelphia in 1880. The year following his journey to Philadelphia, Baker returned to the bench when Democratic Governor William D. Bloxham appointed him judge of the fourth judicial circuit. Governor Edward A. Perry retained his services until health problems forced Baker's retirement in 1890. He died at Jacksonville on June 20, 1892, of paralysis, and was buried in the city's Evergreen Cemetery. "Judge Baker was a man of commanding stature," observed his obituary, "with a strong dignified personality combined with such a benignity of expression that all saw in him a friend on whom they could rely, one of nature's noblemen, *sans peur et san[s] reproche.*"[18]

Augustus Emmet Maxwell, Supreme Court Justice, 1866, 1889–1890; Supreme Court Chief Justice, 1887–1889

Justice Augustus Emmet Maxwell's early life paralleled that of Justice Baker in significant ways. The two men were born at about the same time in adjoining southeastern states and shared the traits of privileged backgrounds, university educations, similar political philosophies, and relocations to Florida near the time of statehood. Maxwell was born in Elberton, Georgia, on September 21, 1820, to Simeon and Elizabeth Fortson Maxwell. Two years afterward the family relocated to a plantation in Greene County, Alabama. After attending country schools, Augustus in 1836 commenced studies at the University of Virginia. As chairman of its student body, on one memorable occasion he presided over student assemblies after a "wild student of South Carolina shot and killed one of the prominent professors [the sole law professor] of the University."[19] Although compelled to leave school briefly due to eyesight problems, he graduated in 1841. Reportedly, Maxwell was a handsome man, with dark, curly hair. He stood approximately six feet, four inches tall. In later life he wore a beard, but as a youth he was clean-shaven. He possessed a formal demeanor and "spoke and wrote in measured and precise phrases."[20]

After graduation Maxwell's personal and professional lives blossomed. He had met Sarah Roane Brockenbrough while at the university. They married in 1843 and moved to Alabama, where he joined the bar. Maxwell practiced law in Eutaw until 1845, when the couple relocated to Florida. The move resulted from family connections, particularly encouragement from the lawyer's brother-in-law, Florida congressional delegate William Henry Brockenbrough. With such assistance Maxwell opened a Tallahassee law office and enjoyed the honor of becoming the first attorney admitted to practice before the supreme court of Florida. He soon also obtained appointment as attorney general and secretary of state in Governor William D. Moseley's cabinet. Unfortunately, Maxwell's early years in the state ended sadly when Sarah died on December 16, 1847, at age twenty-five. She left her widowed husband the care of three infant children.[21]

Maxwell's personal loss found no counterpart in his political career. In 1847 he achieved election to the state house of representatives from Leon County as a Democrat. The next year he received appointment to the party's state central committee, and in 1849 voters promoted him to the state senate. During 1849 he shared with Robert B. Hilton the ownership and editorship of the Tallahassee *Floridian*, which they merged with the *Southern Journal* to form the *Floridian and Journal*. As state senator, Maxwell involved himself in a myriad of concerns, including education and constitutional revision. He chaired key senate committees on the judiciary and federal relations. The senator also received consideration in 1851 for election as a supreme court associate justice. One year later Maxwell became the first Democrat elected to Congress from Florida. His margin of victory was sixty votes.[22]

Following his 1852 election to Congress, Maxwell, in November 1853, detoured to Pensacola on his way to Washington. There he celebrated nuptials with Julia Hawks Anderson, daughter of supreme court chief justice Walker Anderson. The couple subsequently had six children, one of whom, Evelyn Croom Maxwell, followed his father and grandfather on Florida's supreme bench. The marriage, in turn, prompted Congressman Maxwell, a lifelong Baptist, to join the Episcopal church. He served as a vestryman in Pensacola's Christ Church from 1858 to 1868 and as a lay delegate to the diocesan councils from 1878 to 1888.[23]

At first, the congressional forum proved a congenial one for Maxwell. Democratic circles received him well. One party organ called him "one of that gallant band of sterling young democrats now in Congress who have contributed so much during the present session to elevate the character of the House of Representatives, and to give confidence to the masses of our party in its continued ascendancy."[24] Florida Democrats likewise waxed enthusiastic about their representative. In 1854 all but two counties at the state party convention endorsed the congressman for reelection, and he thereafter defeated former Whig governor Thomas Brown. In Congress, Maxwell championed internal improvements and land grants for railroad development.[25]

Despite his official success, Maxwell's congressional tenure ended after his second term. Apparently he did not enjoy Washington political life. Increasingly he eschewed legislative debates that did not bear directly on Florida concerns and, in 1856, announced that a "duty too controlling to be resisted, bids me relinquish a public service in which I cannot continue with due regard to private responsibilities."[26] He moved his family to Pensacola, where he built his plantation, Oakfield, six miles north of the town. Maxwell worked part time as the federal government's navy agent, handling the financial affairs of the Pensacola Navy Yard. He also served as president of the Alabama and Florida Railroad Company until its rails and rolling stock were confiscated by Confederate authorities.[27]

Maxwell supported secession. No opponent of slavery, while in Congress he had urged passage of the Kansas-Nebraska Act. When Florida withdrew from the Union, he pledged funds to help equip two companies of Confederate volunteers. In 1862 he was elected to the Confederate Senate along with James McNair Baker. Given Pensacola's vulnerability to Union occupation, the senator moved his family to a home near Evergreen, Alabama, named Rebel Haven. Oakfield for a time thereafter served Confederate forces as a headquarters.[28]

As a Confederate legislator, Maxwell concerned himself with a broad range of subjects, although he held special concerns for the elimination of speculation on goods. After Governor John Milton called for an end to the "villainous traffick" in the "prime necessities of life," the senator unsuccessfully proposed price controls on all goods. Over time, such legislative frustrations and his wartime experiences drained Maxwell's enthusiasm for the Confederate cause. By 1864 he voiced support for a negotiated armistice, but he never actively participated in the Confederate peace movement.[29]

As did his colleague Senator Baker, Maxwell returned after the war's end to the law. He served briefly in 1866 on Florida's supreme court as Governor David S. Walker's appointee but resigned to accept the presidency of the Alabama and Florida Railroad. The justice also opened a legal practice at Pensacola with former Confederate navy secretary Stephen R. Mallory. Both indulged in Conservative and Democratic politics. In 1877 Maxwell represented the Tilden electors in quo warranto proceedings to dismiss Republican claims to presidential victory in Florida. His reward came the same year when Democratic governor George F. Drew named Maxwell to the first judicial circuit at Pensacola. He served in that capacity until 1885, when he formed a new law partnership with Stephen R. Mallory, Jr. In addition, Maxwell represented Escambia County in the 1885 constitutional convention, in which he chaired the committee on the executive department.[30]

The one-time justice returned to the supreme bench in 1887, when Governor Edward A. Perry of Pensacola designated him to replace Chief Justice George Gray McWhorter. When provisions of the state's new constitution requiring judicial elections became effective in 1888, voters retained Maxwell in office. As the charter provided for staggered terms, court members drew lots to determine their tenure. As a consequence, Maxwell served only two additional years on the bench. In a similar drawing he lost his position as chief justice to George Pettus Raney.[31]

Following his second period of service on the supreme court, Maxwell practiced law at Pensacola with his son, Evelyn, with whom the justice had lived since the death of wife Julia in 1886. He continued to promote the Democratic party and its candidates. As late as 1896, he helped lead opposition in the state to "free silver" and accepted nomination as an elector for the "Gold Democrat" ticket of John M. Palmer and Simon B. Buckner.[32] When Evelyn received a circuit court judgeship in 1896, his father retired from the law. Maxwell lived at Chipley and Marianna with the family of his daughter Elizabeth's husband, Francis C. Wilson, M.D., as Elizabeth, then his only living daughter, had died in 1889. Maxwell died in Chipley on May 5, 1903. He was buried in St. John's Cemetery, Pensacola.[33]

Chapter 12

Congressional Reconstruction

In the Civil War's aftermath, President Andrew Johnson attempted to execute a vision of national reconciliation. The program is known to history as presidential Reconstruction, and it offered relatively unsevere conditions by which the former Confederate States could resume normal ties with the Union. Johnson believed that his plan carried out policies designed originally by Abraham Lincoln. Still, by refusing to demand suffrage rights for freedmen and by permitting most Confederate veterans to vote, Johnson enabled the prewar power structures in states such as Florida once again to assume the reins of government.[1]

The president's efforts to design moderate Reconstruction policies stirred opposition from within the Republican party, from black leaders, and from southern loyalists who felt betrayed after their wartime sacrifices. The controversy intensified as the reconstructed state governments enacted "black codes" that virtually reinstituted slavery and failed to quash violence against blacks and white loyalists. Soon, concerns about presidential policies focused upon ratification of the Fourteenth Amendment to the United States Constitution, which guaranteed certain rights to freedmen and freedwomen. Southern governors such as Florida's David S. Walker led opposition to the amendment, and most southern legislatures refused to ratify it. Following the national elections of 1866, congressional Republicans (labeled as radicals) responded by enacting over Johnson's veto laws mandating harsher policies. Their program was embodied in the Reconstruction acts. The era begun by their enactment is called congressional Reconstruction.[2]

The Reconstruction acts, the first of which became law in March 1867, dramatically altered the southern political climate in the face of angered opposition from most white Southerners. They lumped the former Confederate States, except for Tennessee, into five military districts and gave district commanders powers of martial law. Their terms required states seeking readmission to the Union to rewrite their constitutions to grant voting rights to adult black males and subjected the revised charters to congressional approval. Congressional favor further was conditioned upon legislative ratification of the Fourteenth Amendment. Former Confederates, who before the war had taken an oath of allegiance, could not sit in the conventions, and otherwise-qualified blacks could vote in elections for delegates.[3]

Seemingly overnight, the assertion of congressional authority over Reconstruction gave birth to the Republican party in the South. Party adherents generally controlled the constitutional conventions, although divisions among Republicans evidenced themselves from the outset. Whites from the North known as carpetbaggers, black leaders, and southern loyalists all vied for influence. Florida's assembly, uniquely, stood about equally divided between these elements, even though almost half the state's population consisted of former slaves.[4]

Florida's convention succeeded in crafting constitutional revisions, but the process evolved through turmoil and produced bitter divisions among Republicans. Two principal factions emerged: the aggressive "Mule Team" and a more moderate regular party organization within which loyalist Ossian Bingley Hart of Jacksonville and carpetbaggers Harrison Reed, Thomas W. Osborn, and Marcellus L. Stearns provided much of the leadership. After seizing initial convention control, the Mule Team eventually lost its power struggle to the regulars. Still, the resulting document altered Florida's governmental structure profoundly. "The Constitution of 1868 satisfied no one entirely," historian Jerrell Shofner explained, "yet it made concessions to the divergent groups in the state." He continued, "Although some of these concessions detracted from the excellence of the document, it was a good Constitution. . . . It was by far the most liberal organic law up to that time in Florida."[5]

The new constitution's most striking feature embodied the grant of almost imperial powers to the governor. For one thing the chief executive officer, who served a four-year term, could succeed himself. He could veto legislation and call special legislative sessions. More significantly, the governor possessed authority to appoint all state and county officials except for United States representatives and senators, the lieutenant governor, state legislators, and constables. One Illinois congressman later complained that the scheme "erects a little oligarchy down there in Florida."[6] As factions vied for political control in subsequent years, the struggles necessarily centered upon the governor's office more than at any other time in state history. Not surprisingly, the nature and extent of the powers also became subjects of supreme court consideration.

With respect to the judiciary, the Constitution of 1868 retained a supreme court of three justices appointed by the governor and subject to senate confirmation. Still, the term of office was changed to service during good behavior, and, for the first time, justices were subjected to constitutional qualifications.

The language limited service to a person who was "twenty-five years of age and a practicing attorney in this State." The charter called for January, April, and October court sessions and prescribed annual salaries of $4,500 for the chief justice and $4,000 for associate justices. It required, as well, an annual appropriation of $2,000 for the court's library, although this supplement and the salary provisions overstated actual value since payments often were made in depreciated state scrip. The legislature soon proposed constitutional amendments, later ratified, to reduce the dollar amounts to $3,000 per year for each of the justices.[7]

The court system contemplated by the 1868 charter—exclusive of justice of the peace, municipal, and federal courts—encompassed two levels of inferior courts and a supreme court with broad jurisdiction. Circuit courts held original jurisdiction over felonies, suits regarding the title or boundaries of real estate, and matters of equity exceeding $300. They also exercised appellate jurisdiction in misdemeanor cases and civil suits of more than $100. County courts heard misdemeanors and civil suits, and their judges entertained probate matters. An innovation permitted attorneys to act as referees in civil cases if both parties and the appropriate court agreed. Another provision, aimed at easing the way for northern lawyers, permitted any attorney authorized to practice in another state or before a federal court to become a member of the bar in Florida.[8]

Constitutional drafters carefully enumerated supreme court jurisdiction. The tribunal received appellate authority over all cases in equity and all cases in law that "involved the title to, or right of, possession of real estate, or the legality of any tax, impost, assessment, toll, or municipal fine, or in which the demand or the value of the property in controversy exceeds three hundred dollars." The court also could hear appeals from all other civil cases "not included in the general subdivisions of law and equity." Regarding criminal matters, the tribunal could hear "questions of law alone" in felony cases. Court authority included power to issue writs of mandamus, prohibition, certiorari, and quo warranto, as well as other writs "necessary or proper to the complete exercise of its appellate jurisdiction." Each justice could issue writs of habeas corpus on his own authority, and all court members sat with the governor and attorney general to consider remission of fines and forfeitures, commutation of punishments, and the grant of pardons after conviction.[9]

Given the governor's appointive influence on the judiciary, conservatives feared the worse from the court system. The editor of Pensacola's *West Florida Commercial*, for example, quickly recognized the active role that judges would play in Reconstruction politics. He particularly criticized the "vast power of appointment in the Governor," which allowed him to place justices on the supreme bench for life and judges on the circuit courts for eight-year terms.

This power, he declared, existed "in derogation of the voice of the people." With a judiciary "thus organized and coming into office," he concluded, "with judges selected, probably for their known and unequivocal Radicalism, the entire judicial system and tone of the State will be permanently in the interest of the negro."[10]

Florida's first government under the new constitution achieved organization in the summer of 1868, and Republican governor Harrison Reed's initial supreme court appointments failed to assuage conservative fears that the court would become the third branch of carpetbag rule. He named Thomas J. Boynton as chief justice and, as associate justices, Ossian Bingley Hart and Edwin M. Randall. The chief justice-designee barely missed qualifying as a carpetbagger. A Missouri Republican, he had moved to Florida in 1861 to serve as United States attorney under Judge William Marvin and had replaced Marvin on the Southern District bench when the judge resigned in 1863. Hart hailed from one of the state's oldest and most prominent families, and he was respected for his legal abilities; but he had remained loyal to the Union, had helped to found the state Republican party, and was known for his radical views. Randall, whose family held close connections in national and Wisconsin Republican circles, had arrived in Florida after the war's close, and reports had linked him with Reed in the distribution of bribes during the constitutional convention.[11]

Among some conservatives, anger greeted Reed's initial supreme court appointments. Displaced chief justice Charles H. DuPont expressed the sentiments felt by many former leaders at the turn of events. In a reluctant farewell message delivered on July 28, 1868, he declared, "[T]he administration of your State Government has been forcible wrested from you and committed to the hands of a stranger." Although the state's military commander had ordered him to yield his office, DuPont refused to do so. In the circumstances, though, he was compelled to act. "[D]eprived of the aid of the Executive, to sustain the Judicial Department in the exercise of its legitimate functions, and opposed by the entire Legislative and Military authority of the United States," he continued, "I have no other alternative than to announce to you a *suspension* of the exercise of the functions of my office as Chief Justice, until such time as the same may be resumed without endangering the peace and good order of society."[12]

The intensity of such sentiments soon found a measure of relief as the summer weeks passed. Shifting and uncertain Republican coalitions reinforced Reed's inclination to achieve a working relationship with conservative whites. From early on he had appointed some conservatives to state and local office, among them Tallahassee Democrat James Diament Westcott, Jr., as attorney general. Westcott, whose father had represented Florida in the United States Senate, had served as private secretary to a Democratic governor and as a Confederate official. Though he was young, he held close ties among the state's white elite. Boynton's surprise refusal of appointment as chief justice afforded Reed further opportunity to ally with Westcott's friends. First, he pleased his old patron, United States Postmaster General Alexander Williams Randall, by redesignating his brother, Edwin M. Randall, as chief justice. Then the governor promoted Westcott to Randall's associate justiceship. The actions lent more balance to the tribunal, with a moderate northern Republican as chief justice, flanked by a native Republican loyalist and a native Democrat who had supported the Confederacy. Indeed, Hart and Westcott became the first native Floridians to sit on the court.[13]

The court lineup of Randall, Hart, and Westcott offered broader credibility to the tribunal and, as will be seen, enabled it to resolve successfully many of the Reconstruction era's controversies. One surviving description of panel members suggests, though, the continued animosity directed at carpetbaggers and Reconstruction by many whites, a fact that shortly would lead to bloodshed and political fraud on both sides of the equation. "Westcott is a solid looking juryman, with the air of a student," the court visitor recalled, "and can no doubt get away with a plate of beans in short order." He continued: "Hart is a tall white-haired old gentleman, who has the respect of nearly everybody, without regard to sex or previous condition, and is said to play a rattling game of poker. [He is the] impersonification of law, literature, and the fine arts." Of the presiding justice, he added: "Chief Justice Randall occupied the middle seat on the bench. Randall is a little, snarling, dried-up importation from Wisconsin, and having no reputation of his own, is always careful to have it known that he is the brother of a Randall who was Andy Johnson's Postmaster General."[14]

As the new supreme court set to work, Governor Reed's administration encountered repeated challenges. He endured and survived numerous attempts at impeachment, and allegations of corruption and misgovernment circulated widely. By 1870 many black leaders, centered around State Senator Charles H. Pearce and other adherents of the African Methodist Episcopal (AME) church, had begun to coalesce against carpetbag rule as represented by Reed and United States Senator Thomas W. Osborn. In that year they achieved the election of Josiah H. Walls as Florida's first and only black congressman and of white loyalist Samuel T. Day as lieutenant governor. Two years later they successfully backed Justice Hart for election as governor to succeed Reed.[15]

After Governor Hart took office in January 1873, Florida entered a period of relative peace and progress. Hart's reputation for honesty and integrity, com-

Ossian Bingley Hart

Edwin M. Randall

James Diament Westcott, Jr.

The supreme court during Reconstruction. The 1868 Florida Constitution provided for supreme court justices to "hold their offices for life or during good behavior." Governor Harrison Reed appointed Republican Edwin M. Randall as chief justice and two native Floridians, Republican Ossian Bingley Hart and Democrat James Diament Westcott, Jr., as associate justices. When Hart became governor in 1873, he appointed his replacement to the high court, Franklin D. Fraser, who served only fifteen months and was followed by Robert Bruce Van Valkenburgh. Randall was chief justice for a record of almost seventeen years, and Randall, Westcott, and Van Valkenburgh served together on the court for a record of eleven years. The concurrence of Randall and Van Valkenburgh with Justice Westcott's opinion in 1876 placed a Democrat once again in the governor's office.

bined with support from black leaders and some white conservatives, permitted him to maintain law and order while revamping state administration and finances. He led the legislature in proposing numerous amendments to the constitution, including a requirement for biennial, rather than annual, legislative sessions. One of his earliest recommendations found enactment as the state's first civil rights act. Unfortunately, Hart had contracted pneumonia while campaigning in 1872 and never fully recovered. The exertions required by his official duties complicated the health problems, and he died on March 18, 1874. Lieutenant Governor Marcellus L. Stearns, a carpetbagger, thereupon became governor.[16]

During his gubernatorial tenure Hart had not forgotten the supreme court. In order to ensure that he, rather than Reed, appointed his successor, he resigned only when he prepared to take the oath as governor. Shortly afterward he filled the vacancy by naming Pennsylvania-born Franklin D. Fraser, the brother of United States District Judge Philip Fraser, a longtime Hart friend. Within two months after Hart's death, Fraser resigned to return to Pennsylvania. Governor Stearns, in turn, appointed New Yorker Robert Bruce Van Valkenburgh to the court, where he remained until 1888.[17]

While the Stearns administration governed the state, Florida politics again witnessed divisions, intrigues, and frauds similar to those associated with the Reed years. The problems climaxed in the controversies surrounding the presidential and gubernatorial elections of 1876. In those circumstances the supreme court found itself at the center of a political storm. Although formed of a majority of Republicans, the tribunal resolved the state election by permitting installation of Democrat George F. Drew as governor, thus bringing the era of Reconstruction to an end in Florida.[18] The details of the court's deliberations in that and other key proceedings during congressional Reconstruction are discussed in chapter 13. For a closer look at the men behind them, biographical sketches of Randall, Hart, Westcott, Fraser, and Van Valkenburgh follow.

Edwin M. Randall, Supreme Court Chief Justice, 1868–1885

More than any other member of Florida's supreme court, Edwin M. Randall properly can be known as the chief interpreter of the Constitution of 1868. He was born in Canajoharie, Montgomery County, New York, on April 5, 1822, the son of Phineas and Sarah Beach Randall. Edwin received his early education in the public schools of his native city. Doubtless his father's career as an attorney and judge influenced the young man. Randall read law under his father, achieved admission to the bar in 1844, and, the following year, joined his brother, Alexander Williams Randall, in a practice at Waukesha, Wisconsin.

Marriage followed in 1847, when he wed Julia Mills in Milwaukee. Through the ensuing decade Randall devoted increasing time to his law office while his brother pursued a political career that resulted, in 1857, in his election as Wisconsin's governor. During the period, Edwin also made the acquaintance of newspaper editor Harrison Reed, then living in Madison.[19]

Alexander Randall's political advancement paved the way for Edwin's subsequent career. An effective wartime governor, Alexander Randall came to Abraham Lincoln's attention. In 1863 the president called Alexander to Washington as first assistant postmaster general and charged him with helping to prepare for the 1864 reelection campaign. The connection resulted in Edwin's 1864 appointment as a federal tax commissioner for Louisiana, an office he held for two years. By 1867 Alexander occupied the position of postmaster general in President Andrew Johnson's administration. He employed Edwin as a postal inspector and dispatched him to Florida to work on post office and political matters with Harrison Reed, the state's postal agent. Edwin arrived in the state soon after passage of the first Reconstruction acts, assessed his prospects, and announced his intention to reside in Florida permanently.[20]

The partnership between Randall and Reed assisted both men in their careers. They teamed during the 1868 constitutional convention to dispense Republican party funds in opposition to the Mule Team's aggressive leadership and in favor of proposals backed by the regular—and more conservative—Republican organization to which they belonged. Reed emerged from the convention as the party's candidate for governor, an office to which he was elected in May. As the campaign progressed, rumors surfaced in the national press that Governor Reed would secure United States Senate election for either Alexander or Edwin. Exposure canceled any such plans. Additional reports then suggested that Reed, who had reached out for an alliance with white conservatives, would place former governor David S. Walker on the supreme court along with Edwin as chief justice. Walker apparently lost interest in the appointment, but on July 9 the governor announced Randall's designation as an associate justice. When chief justice-designee Thomas J. Boynton declined his seat, Reed elevated Randall to the chief justiceship and, at the same time, carried out his desire to impress white conservatives by appointing Democrat James Diament Westcott, Jr., as an associate justice.[21]

Reed's designation of Randall as chief justice reflected political wisdom from the governor's perspective. Reed desired a mutually beneficial working relationship with white conservatives and Republican powerbrokers. Although a Republican, Randall was known for his moderate, pro-business views; connections with the conservative Johnson administration; and experience as a lawyer. Conservatives could respect him. On the other hand, the state's carpetbag element could see him as one of their own, while Republicans generally could regard him as fair.[22]

In seventeen years of service Randall guided the court through one of its most difficult periods. According to George Pettus Raney, he dealt with the divisive issues of Reconstruction "as if the most commonplace of causes had been on trial."[23] In doing so the chief justice authored opinions in the cases of greatest constitutional significance during his tenure, earning him the designation of chief interpreter of the Constitution of 1868. In a separate constitutional role, Randall presided in 1872 over an impeachment trial of Harrison Reed, a task that he undertook with probity and decorum. Further, Randall's involvement in the aftermath of the disputed presidential and gubernatorial elections of 1876 offered extremely difficult and sensitive challenges. Under his leadership the supreme court ordered state officials to recount ballots and award the governor's chair to Democrat George F. Drew, even though many of the same officials were Randall's political and personal friends. Numerous Floridians credited Randall and his court colleagues with rising above party and politics to resolve the dispute.[24]

Legal abilities and personal demeanor aided Randall's court accomplishments. Future justice James Bryan Whitfield noted in 1885 that "Judge Randall has always been a close student, and his thorough knowledge of the law, and his experience in applying it to cases, have made him master of his profession."[25] Another future justice remembered that Randall's insistence upon distance from petty political disputes stood out as an important quality. George Pettus Raney particularly recalled that, on one occasion, Randall had been invited to advise the house committee on finance and taxation on a new revenue law. He agreed; but after listening briefly as debate degenerated into partisan bickering, the chief justice "quietly disappeared from the room." Raney commented favorably on "the striking contrast [Randall] bore to the general personality of the Republican element assembled at the Capital."[26]

Though possessing a reserved and dignified bearing, Randall also approached his work with a sense of humor. One example arose in 1874, when Randall wagered Mariano D. Papy that the chief justice could introduce humor into a judicial opinion without destroying its dignity. The case involved a debtor who failed to pay for a horse and buggy and sought to enjoin his creditor from repossessing them in satisfaction of the debt. Randall commented that he felt "the same kind of embarrassment which was experienced by a French Judge when a youth, convicted of murdering his own father and mother, appealed for mercy on the ground that he was a poor orphan." While using humor to illustrate that the case did not belong in a court of equity, Randall also won his bet.[27]

Not all Floridians shared a high regard for Randall's contributions. Many black leaders chafed at his conservative approach, and Republican partisans reacted angrily to his pivotal role in placing Drew in the governor's office. A hint of scandal also touched him on occasion. In 1868, for instance, Randall's name was linked with the disappearance of key documents in a sensitive case then before the federal district court, although a panel of three lawyers headed by former justice James McNair Baker cleared him of the charges. Not long afterward the chief justice's friendship with railroad speculator and political operative Milton S. Littlefield similarly prompted talk of improper conduct. However, no charges ever were filed or sustained in the matter.[28]

Randall retired from the supreme bench on January 7, 1885, not long after the installation of Democratic governor Edward A. Perry. He returned to his Jacksonville home, where he formed a legal partnership with John T. Walker, George U. Walker, and Stephen E. Foster. That year Randall served, as well, as Duval County delegate to the state constitutional convention, within which Florida's Democrats rewrote the work of Republicans seventeen years earlier. In the assembly he introduced a resolution providing for submission of the final draft of the constitution for approval by the people.[29]

Following his constitutional convention service, Randall continued to practice law at Jacksonville, sometimes alone and occasionally in partnership. Briefly in the early 1890s he acted as Jacksonville city attorney. By 1893, though, Randall's health had begun to decline. Two years later, on July 12, 1895, he succumbed to complications of Bright's disease at his Jacksonville home. Commenting on Randall's supreme court service, a local newspaperman declared, "[H]e was considered a fair jurist in every respect, and won the respect of the entire state, not only among the republicans, but among the democrats as well."[30]

Ossian Bingley Hart, Supreme Court Justice, 1868–1873

Ossian Bingley Hart held the distinction of being the first native-born Floridian to sit on the state's supreme court and to achieve election as its governor. He was born January 17, 1821, on a farm near King's Ferry, which was located on the south bank of the St. Marys River along the Florida-Georgia border. Within four months, his family, including parents Isaiah David and Nancy Nelson Hart, had begun to move southward to the St. Johns River. Isaiah soon helped found on the site of their settlement the town of Jacksonville. Ossian grew up in the tiny port community, where his father tended store, held a series of public offices, and developed a family plantation. As a lad of not quite sixteen, Ossian volunteered as a soldier in the Second Seminole War, achieving the rank of sergeant. His early education was described as the "old field" variety, but he briefly attended Moses Waddell's prestigious academy at Willington, South Carolina, in 1838–39.[31]

Back in Florida after his stay at Willington, Hart set about establishing professional and personal ties. He read law with his father and with future justice Joseph Bradford Lancaster, after which he passed examination for the bar in October 1842. The previous year Hart had met Catharine Smith Campbell of Newark, New Jersey, who was in Jacksonville visiting relatives. After corresponding with her for two years, Hart married Catharine at her father's Newark home on October 2, 1843. They had no children, but they raised several girls, including Ossian's niece, Mary Ellen Beers Hart, and Flora Henderson, daughter of Hillsborough County state senator John A. Henderson.[32]

Hart experienced a varied and challenging professional life. Catharine's health was delicate, and Ossian, desirous of establishing a plantation in an area free from winter frosts where he might also practice law, convinced her to move to the vicinity of the frontier outpost at Fort Pierce. Ten days after their 1844 arrival, fire destroyed their possessions and supplies. After a brief sojourn in Key West, where friends advanced funds for a second start, they returned to work their claim. That year local voters elected Hart to represent the new county of St. Lucie in the territorial council. He ran as a Whig, but his victory reflected personal, more than partisan, appeal. He sat at Tallahassee during January–March 1845 in Florida's final territorial legislature, where he joined his father and other East Florida Whigs in fighting statehood. His most personally satisfying act as a legislator, he later maintained, was to secure passage of the married woman's property act. He also successfully sponsored several bills to develop St. Lucie County and open it to commerce.[33]

The legislative work bolstered Hart's standing in St. Lucie County, but his residence proved short term. Fellow settlers soon placed him on the county commission and accepted his leadership in numerous local endeavors. In November 1846, though, nature again struck a blow when a hurricane destroyed his house and citrus groves. He and Catharine left the ruins for a more civilized home in Key West, where Ossian anticipated a lucrative career practicing admiralty and salvage law in Judge William Marvin's court. "I have heard Ossian say [that] for the practice of law [this] is the best place in Florida," Catharine wrote. "The Law[y]ers here frequently made from 6 to 7 hundred dollars on one case."[34] After a slow start Hart overcame resentments of the newcomer to establish a successful practice, earning by the early 1850s a legal income second only to his rival, soon-to-be United States senator Stephen R. Mallory. He also spent four years from 1849 to 1853 as solicitor for the state's southern judicial circuit.[35]

Catharine's health, political setbacks, and poor economic conditions prompted another move in the mid–1850s. Ossian's mentor Joseph Bradford Lancaster died at Tampa in November 1856. The next year the Harts moved there, and Ossian took over Lancaster's law practice. Again he emerged as a community leader, serving one term in 1860 as a town councilman. His most notable legal case occurred in 1859 when Hart defended a slave, Adam, accused of murdering a white man. The lawyer obtained from the state supreme court a reversal of his client's conviction, but, in the wake of John Brown's raid on Harper's Ferry, a mob lynched Adam. The episode deeply affected Hart's views on race relations and the value of law and an ordered society. Tampa nonetheless remained his home through the Civil War, except for time spent after Isaiah's 1861 death in managing the family plantation and serving as estate executor.[36]

Loyalism and continued opposition to the Confederacy characterized Hart's stance during the Civil War. He ardently had opposed secession, and, afterward, he urged devotion to the Union "until, by the events of the war, the protection of the National Government could not reach him, and common prudence compelled silence."[37] Although Hart was "a large slave holder and property owner," the *Jacksonville Herald* noted in 1865, "nothing could induce him to participate in the rebellion."[38] Actually he never purchased a slave. In 1857 Isaiah Hart had given Ossian a family of four blacks, and he inherited others. He also controlled several score of slaves as estate executor. In 1864 Hart was drafted into the Confederate Army, but he avoided service through a medical exemption.[39]

Hart's loyalism translated itself with the peace into support for Reconstruction. He advocated the grant of equal rights for blacks, including the right to vote. At first he also supported autonomy for the former Confederate States and criticized federal efforts to restructure southern race relations. Events soon convinced him, though, that the state could not be reconstructed without military supervision and mandated black suffrage. In late 1865 he moved his family back to Jacksonville, where he immersed himself in politics, becoming a founder of the Union party in 1866. For two years he served as civil agent of the Freedmen's Bureau in Duval County and as bureau counsel for the state. He gained support of many blacks, loyalists, and northern Republicans, while maintaining personal and business ties with prominent conservatives such as former

United States senator David Levy Yulee, one-time Confederate congressman John P. Sanderson, and Governor David S. Walker.[40]

In the immediate postwar years Jacksonville stood out as the state's premier town of industry and commerce. Its community included hundreds of northerners who adhered to the Republican party, even though their personal philosophies ranged from conservative to moderate. As the town's largest landlord and a leading anti-Confederate, Hart emerged as a catalyst for political action. Within days of enactment of the First Reconstruction Act, he and his allies, black and white, attempted to assume control of town government with Hart as mayor, an action forestalled by military authorities. On March 27 he gathered black and white leaders in his law office to draft a declaration of principles, thereby founding the state Republican party. Hart won election as its first chairman.[41]

As a result of intraparty power struggles during 1867, carpetbaggers pushed Hart out of his Republican party leadership post. Through the influence of state military commander John T. Sprague, he became the state superintendent of voter registration, accomplishing the task of preparing for and holding the first elections under congressional Reconstruction. Sprague praised him as "a patriot grown gray in the service of his country" and for his "cordial and honest support." The colonel also noted that Hart's official duties had been performed "without hesitation, and without partisan rancor."[42] During the constitutional convention of January and February 1868 Hart provided key advice to party regulars, helped draft the constitution subsequently adopted, and eventually took a seat as delegate.[43]

Hart departed the constitutional convention believing that his reward would be selection to the United States Senate. Carpetbaggers won both senate seats, however, in legislative maneuvering. Governor Harrison Reed, whose political debt to Hart and his fellow loyalists was great, then tendered Hart appointment as an associate justice of the supreme court. On the high court Hart exerted less influence on jurisprudence than did fellow members Edwin M. Randall and James Diament Westcott, Jr. He authored only seventeen opinions and missed several sessions due to other commitments. His work stressed, though, the importance of respect for the court and the law. "Whatever some men may choose to think of others as men," he wrote, "the tribunal must be everywhere respected by at least implicit obedience to its process." He continued: "Without this, the fabric of jurisprudence, erected by the experience of ages, the best constituted safe-guard of human rights, must fall. Great, beneficial and beautiful as it is, it is a delicate structure, and cannot maintain its usefulness under frequent shocks of disrespect. It has its enemies, as is patent in this case, so also has everything that is beautiful and good."[44]

While on the court Hart yearned for a more active political role. He helped to resolve disputes among party factions, but his eyes remained set on the United States Senate. In 1870 the legislature elected him to that body, asserting that incumbent senator Abijah Gilbert had been selected improperly. Hart attempted to claim the seat, but the senate's members refused to unseat Gilbert. Two years later black and loyalist leaders, angry at carpetbag corruption and mismanagement, combined to secure Hart the Republican gubernatorial nomination. In November 1872 he defeated Democrat William D. Bloxham for the office.[45]

Hart's gubernatorial campaign had stressed the importance of "debt reduction, internal improvements, universal education, and honest government."[46] In office he revised the tax structure, revamped state finances, replaced numerous incompetent officeholders, and supported increased appropriations for education, social services, and railroad construction. The initial act passed during his administration was the state's first civil rights act. When breakdown of law and order threatened, he reacted quickly and competently. By January 1874 he could boast in his annual legislative message "that the spirit of political hatred and bitterness is well nigh extinguished, and that the people of all parties are more united and harmonized than they have been for many years."[47]

The exertions of political life took too great a toll on Hart. He developed pneumonia during the 1872 campaign and never fully recovered. After the 1874 legislative session he returned to Jacksonville, where he attempted once again to recuperate. On March 18, 1874, he died at his home. Hart is buried in the city's Evergreen Cemetery. At the supreme court's chamber on April 15, justices and lawyers gathered to pay their respects. A memorial resolution—prepared by Mariano D. Papy, R. B. Hilton, and John Friend—noted, "[I]n the death of Governor Hart the people of this State have lost an honest and faithful public officer; one whose purposes and aims were directed to the promotion of their best interests and to the supremacy of the Constitution and law." The resolution concluded, "[T]hough he had been removed from the bench and from direction association with the bar, we feel it due to his character as a lawyer and a judge to bear testimony to the uprightness, integrity, ability, and faithfulness which illustrated his professional and judicial career."[48]

James Diament Westcott, Jr., Supreme Court Justice, 1868–1885

The contributions of James Diament Westcott, Jr., a Democrat, formed a key element in the supreme court's successful efforts to build a creditable reputation during Reconstruction. He was born in Tallahassee on June 18, 1839, the son of James Diament Westcott, Jr., and Rebecca B. Westcott. Although the younger Westcott actually was the third person in the family to bear his grandfather's name, he used the suffix "Jr." throughout his life. The father had moved from New Jersey to Florida in 1830, receiving upon arrival appointment as territorial secretary. He later worked as United States attorney for the Middle District. The elder Westcott actively supported Florida's drive for statehood, served as a delegate to the 1838 constitutional convention, and helped found Florida's Democratic party. In 1845 he went to Washington with David Levy Yulee as one of the state's first senators. Westcott did not run for reelection in 1858, moving instead to New York City before retiring to Canada in 1862.[49]

Despite his father's relocation from Florida in the 1850s, the younger Westcott remained in the state and advanced his career through education and a series of political positions. First, he received instruction in Tallahassee schools, primarily West Florida Seminary. "Even in boyhood," an observer noted, "he evinced intellectual powers of a high order."[50] He subsequently read law with a local attorney while establishing himself in political circles. In 1858 Westcott achieved designation as assistant secretary of the state senate. One year later, at age twenty, he received appointment from Madison S. Perry as the governor's private secretary. During the Civil War Westcott worked as clerk of the Confederate States District Court for the District of Florida. He also served the Confederate Army as an assistant commissary officer for the state.[51]

The end of hostilities offered Westcott chances for further advancement. He won election to the state house of representatives from Leon County and served in that body during 1866. Unlike many Confederate sympathizers, though, Westcott evidenced flexibility regarding the South's new circumstances. "He was conservative in his politics," one commentator recorded, "and while he had always voted the Conservative ticket, it was known that his politics were of the most liberal kind."[52] His appearance in elective office foretold, as well, Westcott's increased standing as a lawyer. On March 1, 1867, he and Mariano D. Papy, former state attorney general, formed a partnership that prospered representing railroad companies. Perhaps at Papy's suggestion, Governor Harrison Reed named Westcott in July 1868 as attorney general in the state's first Republican administration. The action pleased conservatives but prompted opposition from Republicans aghast at the promotion of a one-time Confederate official who maintained close connections with one-time secessionists.[53]

Westcott's elevation to the supreme bench proceeded quickly after his appointment as attorney general. As discussed earlier in this chapter, Reed desired to strengthen his ties with white conservatives. When Thomas J. Boynton declined the chief justiceship and the governor thereafter named Edwin M. Randall, a vacancy existed for an associate justice. Reed grasped the opportunity to name a well-regarded Democratic attorney such as Westcott. The appointment partially succeeded in allaying fears that the governor was packing the court with Republican carpetbaggers. The Westcott appointment did not satisfy some diehard former secessionists, however, who criticized Westcott for taking office in the Republicans' "bogus government."[54]

On the bench Westcott's personal qualities eased tense situations and, thereby, furthered the court's work. Robert Wyche Davis described the justice's demeanor. "He was genial, good natured, companionable, and quickly saw the bright or the amusing side of things," the 1885 Florida house speaker recalled. On one occasion, Davis continued, the court had ruled against his client. Westcott, noting the surprise on Davis's face, asked, "You are disgusted, aren't you?" Davis apologized for allowing his emotions to show, but Westcott replied with a laugh, "Oh, don't try to suppress them; we allow disappointed lawyers great latitude, and if it will relieve you any, you may tell your client when you get home that we are a set of asses."[55] The justice's amiable personality sparked memories from others who argued before him. They recollected that Westcott often would leave his chambers before court began to chat with attorneys and warm his hands over the open-hearth fireplaces in the courtroom. He also enjoyed entertaining guests at his Tallahassee residence, where, reportedly, he "dispense[d] an elegant hospitality."[56]

Westcott's capacity for legal research and scholarship further aided accomplishment of the court's mission. Davis recorded that, in one case, he had spent weeks preparing briefs and arguments involving numerous novel points of law. A few days after oral arguments, Westcott delivered an opinion in favor of Davis's client. In doing so, the lawyer remembered, the justice "cited numberless authorities which I had never seen and never been able to find."[57] Colleagues on the bench recognized Westcott's talent and assigned him to write decisions in many of the most complex cases, especially those concerning equity. In all he penned 267 opinions, the most prolific output of any court member, save Chief Justice Randall, through 1885. George Pettus Raney later commented that Westcott "took pleasure in tracting [the law's] principles down through the intricacies and mists of decision and treatise, to the present." Westcott's thoroughness reflected more than academic interest. A conservative jurist guided by formalist principles of adjudication, Westcott held strictly to precedent and "regard[ed] new departures as dangerous."[58]

As a well-regarded Democrat on a Republican court, Westcott occupied a unique position in Florida government and politics. Circumstances surrounding the election of a United States senator in 1873 testify to that fact. Governor Ossian Bingley Hart's allies had deposed incumbent carpetbagger Thomas W. Osborn, but they had been unable to dictate the choice of his successor. In the complicated maneuvering that followed, the choice narrowed to Westcott and Republican Simon B. Conover, speaker of the house and former state treasurer. Westcott received considerable support from Republicans, but finally Conover triumphed with Democratic votes. Democratic leaders later explained that they would have supported the justice but wanted to retain his services on the supreme court.[59]

Westcott's competence and amiability brought respect and admiration, but his eccentricities provoked curiosity and may have contributed to his early death. A lifelong bachelor, he lived, according to Robert Wyche Davis, "with his books and his dog and gun." The friend continued, "He had faults—faults that were regretted and that probably cut short his career, possibly even his life."[60] From whatever cause, ill health dictated his resignation from the supreme court in January 1885. For slightly more than two years he battled health problems before succumbing at Tallahassee on April 29, 1887.[61] Fourteen years earlier a court visitor had summarized well Westcott's contributions. "His course," the man recorded, "has been such as to give him the confidence of the substantial, thoughtful men of each side."[62]

Note should be made that Westcott's generosity of spirit continued to benefit Florida long after his death. He left most of his estate to the West Florida Seminary. The gift served "[p]artly as a personal memorial," wrote the seminary's historian, "but more as a contribution to the welfare of the institution and as an aid to Leon County students who aspired to an education." Under the terms of the gift, the then substantial amount of $2,000 in interest annually subsidized the institution, half of which was earmarked for the benefit of local children. The bequest marked, asserted the historian, "a complete change in the fortunes and history of the institution."[63] In 1936 the Florida State College for Women, the seminary's successor and the forerunner of Florida State University, named the school's administration building in Westcott's honor.[64]

Franklin D. Fraser, Supreme Court Justice, 1873–1874

Franklin D. Fraser received appointment to the Florida supreme court in January 1873 as a result of newly inaugurated governor Ossian Bingley Hart's need for a reliable ally on the panel. He was born at Montrose, Susquehanna County, Pennsylvania, on April 23, 1819, the son of Dr. Charles Fraser and his wife, Mary. He attended schools at Montrose and at Oxford, New York, prior to entering Union College at Schenectady, New York. After graduation Fraser read

James Diament Westcott, Jr., Memorial Building. The Board of Control in 1936 named the administration building at Florida State College for Women, Tallahassee, in honor of Justice James Diament Westcott, Jr. A trust established by Westcott provided income from commercial and residential property and from bonds to the West Florida Seminary on his death in April 1887. The case, *Lewis v. Gaillard*, discussed in chapter 19, had as its focus Westcott's will. The supreme court of Florida in 1911 held that the terms of the will were still valid even though West Florida Seminary no longer existed.

law at Montrose with Judge William Jessup, Sr., and was admitted to the bar in 1842. A friend of the time recalled, "As a lawyer he was very careful and painstaking; and, as is very happily expressed in the resolution, 'he was careful in examining a case and slow in forming an opinion, but when once intelligently formed he held it with the utmost tenacity.'"[65]

During his first two decades of professional life, Fraser established a sturdy reputation and began a family. One attorney who practiced with him noted, "He was kind and courteous to his fellow members of the bar and he ranked among us as a man of great ability and fine legal attainments."[66] He worked in Susquehanna and Wyoming counties, more as an "office lawyer" than a trial attorney.[67] "For a number of years," Franklin's older brother Philip recalled, "he [also] held the office of Prosecuting Attorney in Pennsylvania and gave complete satisfaction."[68] On the personal side, Fraser married Jane B. Clark, and the couple had one daughter, Fannie.[69]

Philip Fraser was the future justice's connection with Florida. Philip had moved to Jacksonville in the 1840s and had prospered thereafter as a lawyer, town mayor, Whig leader, and loyalist. In the process he became a close personal and political associate of Isaiah D. Hart and his son, Ossian Bingley Hart. Apparently Franklin visited Philip in Duval County prior to the war, but the brothers next were united when Philip returned to Montrose following the 1862 Union evacuation of Jacksonville. Not long afterward, President Abraham Lincoln designated Philip as federal judge of the Northern District of Florida. When Judge Fraser returned to the state in 1863 to assume his duties, Franklin probably accompanied him. At St. Augustine the younger brother worked as the Northern District's deputy clerk.[70]

Fraser's Florida sojourn lasted only a short time. He returned to Pennsylvania before the war's conclusion and remained there for several years. With the onset of congressional Reconstruction, Philip endeavored to find his brother a position that would draw him back to the South. He attempted first to secure an appointment as federal district attorney for Florida's Northern District, but his efforts proved unavailing until mid–1869, when Franklin was designated the district's register in bankruptcy. At Jacksonville Franklin associated himself with Republican politics and, once again, gained Ossian Bingley Hart's personal notice. Likely with Hart's encouragement, acting governor Samuel T. Day, a loyalist and Hart friend, offered Fraser the judgeship of the fourth judicial circuit in February 1872, but the lawyer declined.[71]

Not long after declining the circuit judgeship, Fraser considered a second judicial position. In November 1872 Hart won the state's gubernatorial contest but refused to resign his supreme court seat until he could appoint his own successor. When that opportunity came to hand in January 1873, the governor turned to Fraser, naming him an associate justice. Given Fraser's known abilities and Hart's legislative influence, the nomination encountered no serious opposition. However, the justice's tenure lasted only sixteen months. Hart died in office in March 1874, and Fraser resigned from the court in May, "deeming the salary inadequate and finding the state of Southern society very distasteful to his feelings." He left a legacy of seven opinions, all in minor cases.[72]

Fraser resided in Pennsylvania after his departure from Florida. He resumed his legal practice and attended his brother Philip, who lay ill from the disease that would kill him in 1876. Franklin D. Fraser's sudden death on November 10, 1879, from pneumonia shocked friends and acquaintances at Montrose. "Ten days previous to Judge Fraser's death," a colleague recorded, "he was apparently in as sound and robust health as he ever was, and as the best of us." He continued, "I do not remember of any serious illness he ever had until that which resulted in his death."[73] The former justice's fellow legal practitioners convened a few days later to pay respects to his memory. They resolved, in part, "[I]n the death of Judge Fraser this Bar has lost one of its oldest and ablest members, a man of ripe experience and great legal attainments, a counsellor of strict integrity, and one who was an honor to the profession."[74]

Robert Bruce Van Valkenburgh, Supreme Court Justice, 1874–1888

Robert Bruce Van Valkenburgh, born at Prattsburg, Steuben County, New York, on September 4, 1821, replaced Franklin D. Fraser on Florida's supreme bench. Van Valkenburgh was the first of twelve children born to Jacob Van Valkenburgh and Eunice Bethia Higgins Van Valkenburgh. He attended schools in Auburn, New York, before relocating in 1837 to read law in Buffalo with the firm of Henry W. Rogers and Joseph G. Matsen. As did Justice William Augustus Forward, Van Valkenburgh participated in the Canadian rebellion of 1838. He refused an offer to serve as aide to a principal rebel leader, but during the conflict he helped to cut the steamer *Caroline* out of the ice in Buffalo harbor "and by a singular accident was prevented from being on board of her when she was destroyed by the Canadians."[75]

During 1838 Van Valkenburgh returned to Prattsburg to continue his formal education at Franklin Academy. Subsequently, he read law under David Rumsey, Jr., in the Steuben County seat of Bath. After admission to the bar in 1843, Van Valkenburgh and Rumsey formed a partnership. On September 10, 1844, the junior partner married Rumsey's sister, Catherine. Van Valkenburgh thereafter cultivated a successful practice, particularly in criminal cases. The firm eventually earned a reputation as "a training school for the judiciary."[76] Two firm members became New York trial judges, another became a Massachusetts supreme court justice, and Van Valkenburgh graced the supreme court of Florida.[77]

Van Valkenburgh actively supported New York's Whig party and otherwise involved himself in politics. From 1840 to 1841 he edited the *Constitutionalist,* a Whig newspaper. In 1851 he ran for the state assembly and became the only Whig elected in his district. Van Valkenburgh left the assembly after one term, but, in 1856, he ran again and defeated the incumbent by 1,250 votes. He held important assembly positions, including chairmanship of the committee that oversaw New York City government. In 1860 he missed election as house speaker by one vote. A description written at the time described Van Valkenburgh as "a tall handsome man, with dark full eyes, even and ruddy features." He possessed a striking countenance and was "really one of the most noticeable men in the House." The representative spoke with "a particularly melodious voice, very like that of Pierre Soule, ex-U.S. Senator and ex-minister to Spain, although [Van Valkenburgh] is native 'and to the manor born,' and has not the '*accent.*'"[78]

The young lawyer and politician boasted talents as a skilled and formidable debater and as a natural leader, qualities that earned him victories in the legislature and the courtroom. In 1854 and 1856, for example, he appeared before New York senate committees to support the construction of a Hudson River bridge. Arrayed against some of the state's top legal talent, he helped convince the lawmakers to approve the bill and then aided its final passage through the assembly. While undertaking such tasks and practicing law, Van Valkenburgh also served as a colonel in the state militia. In 1855 he contributed to state commission work aimed at designing rules and regulations for New York's armed forces.[79]

The Civil War era found Van Valkenburgh greeting other challenges for his talents. In 1861 he won election as a Republican to the United States House of Representatives, where he served two terms. During the war he commanded a recruiting bureau in Elmira, New York, where he raised the first regiment to report to Washington after President Abraham Lincoln called for volunteers. He ultimately organized sixteen additional volunteer regiments and also chaired the militia committee in the House. In 1862 Van Valkenburgh commanded the 107th Regiment of New York Volunteer Infantry at the Battle of Antietam. His commanding officer reported that, despite their lack of military experience, Colonel Van Valkenburgh and his troops "did not flinch in the discharge of their duties." He added, "They fought like veteran soldiers."[80] At the end of

1862 Van Valkenburgh resigned his military commission to attend to his ill wife. She died in April 1863, leaving no children.[81]

Following the war Van Valkenburgh held several positions in President Andrew Johnson's administration. In 1865 he served briefly as acting commissioner of Indian affairs. In late 1865 Johnson appointed him as minister to Japan, where he remained until November 1869. On November 25, 1865, shortly after arriving to take up his duties, he married his second wife, Anna Simpson Schoyer. Family lore maintains that Van Valkenburgh's ties with Anna benefited Florida's citrus industry. Reportedly, when the couple came to the state, Anna brought with her the Satsuma variety of the orange. As minister, Van Valkenburgh successfully opened the city of Osaka and the port of Hiogo for trade with the United States.[82]

One account suggests that the future justice displayed considerable courage, as well as leadership, in Japan. According to Chief Justice Edwin M. Randall, a group of rebels who opposed the Japanese government's invitation to outsiders planned to massacre foreigners in Tokyo. The plotters conspired to capture an old Confederate warship, the *Stonewall*, that recently had been purchased from the United States by the Japanese rulers. From its anchorage the ship's guns could bombard all city quarters occupied by foreign residents. One evening Van Valkenburgh received notice from the mikado, the Japanese head of government, that he had been captured and, in Randall's words, "probably before morning would be minus a head, unless assistance were sent." Within the hour minister Van Valkenburgh had "taken possession of the vessel in the name of the United States, had three hundred armed men on board, and the next morning had four thousand armed men on the streets of the city." He then "speedily organized an army, advanced upon the rebels, surprised them in their camp, slew many by the sword, and drove others into the sea." The Van Valkenburghs later decorated their Florida home with gifts presented to them in gratitude for his heroics.[83]

The diplomat's health provided the immediate reason for his eventual settlement in Florida. Van Valkenburgh had suffered from rheumatism since the Civil War, and his Japanese experiences taxed him further. He returned to the United States "with his voice entirely gone, . . . barely able to speak above a whisper."[84] In April 1871 he moved to Duval County seeking relief. There the former legislator again indulged in politics, particularly the liberal Republican movement that had emerged as a reaction to Grant administration corruption and inefficiency. In Jacksonville's large population of conservative northern-born businessmen, he found many friends. With them he campaigned in 1872 for liberal Republican presidential candidate Horace Greeley. Since the state liberal Republicans backed the Democratic gubernatorial candidate, Van Valkenburgh also likely worked for the election of William D. Bloxham and against Ossian Bingley Hart.[85]

The liberal Republican candidates for president and governor met defeat in Florida, but Van Valkenburgh's involvement in the party resulted in his appointment to the supreme court. Governor Hart died in March 1874, and his lieutenant governor, northern-born Union officer Marcellus A. Stearns, ascended to the office. As a member of the discredited "Osborn Ring" of carpetbaggers, Stearns quickly sought allies among the liberal Republicans in anticipation of the 1876 elections. When Hart's associate Franklin D. Fraser resigned from the supreme court in May 1874, the governor seized the chance to attract liberal Republicans by his appointment on May 20 of a respected member of their movement to the tribunal.[86]

Unlike Hart's earlier elevation of Fraser, Van Valkenburgh's appointment brought considerable criticism on the governor. Although a Republican newspaper insisted that Stearns's action was "a wise and judicious act," the state's Democratic press, especially editor Charles E. Dyke of the Tallahassee *Weekly Floridian,* used the incident to denounce carpetbaggers and the politics associated with them.[87] Complaining that the nomination had "taken the public by surprise," Dyke asserted that its goal was to strengthen carpetbag rule in the face of a Democratic resurgence after Hart's death. The appointment, the editor continued, "appears like an absolute prostitution of Executive power to the base end of converting the highest Judicial tribunal in the State to a mere political engine for party purposes and personal aspirations, without regard to public interests and the welfare of the people." Among other things Dyke highlighted the facts that Van Valkenburgh "had probably never brought a suit in this State, and . . . at the time of his appointment was actually not a member of the [bar of the] court upon whose bench he was placed."[88] The latter accusation carried real teeth, since the constitution forbade appointment to the court of any person who was not "a practicing attorney in this State."[89] Fortunately for Van Valkenburgh, he was admitted to practice before the supreme court on the day before he was sworn in as justice.[90]

The Van Valkenburgh appointment ushered in a period of stability for the court, as no vacancy occurred until Chief Justice Randall and Justice James Diament Westcott, Jr., resigned in 1885. The new justice also brought to the court expertise in criminal law, and he was assigned many of the criminal appeals that came before the panel. Van Valkenburgh's health prevented him, however, from fully participating in court responsibilities. He averaged only eight opinions per term, as compared to sixteen per term for Westcott and twenty per term for Randall. After Anna Van Valkenburgh died at Mayport on September 5, 1887, her husband's health deteriorated further. During the last few months of the court's 1888 term, he was "unable to occupy his seat on the bench because of continued illness."[91] Justice Van Valkenburgh died at Suwannee Springs, still a court member, on August 1, 1888. He was buried in St. Nicholas Cemetery, south of Jacksonville.[92]

Chapter 13

Business of the Court, 1868–1877

From political, constitutional, and jurisprudential necessity, the supreme court of Florida emerged during congressional Reconstruction as a more dynamic and influential body than it had been at any previous time. Its involvement spread across the full range of issues normally subject to appellate review, but for the first time justices officially embroiled themselves in determination of sensitive cases affecting control of the state's political power. That the court was able to do so while building and maintaining a reputation for independence and integrity is a high compliment to the men who served on the tribunal during that tumultuous era.

Constitutional Changes

Immediately following the adoption of the Constitution of 1868, state supreme court members began interpreting key provisions of the new document. As implementation of Reconstruction generated increasing controversy, the panel became more closely involved in resolving such questions as well as related disputes that arose from the political rancor created by Republican rule and conservative (or Democratic) opposition. Its responsibility—first and foremost—required the court, amid partisan machinations and financial chicanery on both sides of the political divide, to bring a sense of fairness and integrity to state government. Its members succeeded. Most Floridians, at least, would have agreed with the conservative who declared, in 1872, that the justices "are men not easily corrupted."[1]

In setting about its tasks, the tribunal adjusted to changes in its operations mandated by the new constitution. The change most visible concerned where the court sat. Prior to the Civil War, sessions were held at Tallahassee, Marianna, Jacksonville, and Tampa. Now the panel met only at the capitol in Tallahassee. The changed routine did not involve substantive consequences, as the court had rarely spent more than two days per year in any one location other than Tallahassee and often adjourned such sessions without conducting any business.[2]

In addition to the original provisions of the Constitution of 1868, the supreme court also contended with a series of amendments proposed during the administrations of governors Harrison Reed and Ossian Bingley Hart. Some of the amendments related specifically to the tribunal. One permitted the legislature to establish rules "for calling into the Supreme Court a judge of the circuit court to hear and determine any matter pending before the court in the place of any justice thereof who shall be disqualified or disabled in such case from interest or other cause."[3] Another clarified the panel's appellate jurisdiction.[4]

Some of the most significant supreme court decisions during congressional Reconstruction concerned the effect of Florida constitutional changes on state common law as viewed within the context of a new federal constitutional system grounded in national supremacy and symbolized by the Thirteenth, Fourteenth, and Fifteenth amendments to the United States Constitution. These changes placed substantive limits on state action. The Constitution of 1868 provided, for instance, that all judgments and decrees rendered in any Florida court since secession involving "the sale or purchase of slaves, are hereby declared set aside, and the plea of failure of consideration shall be held a good defence in all actions to said suit."[5] Within two years of the charter's effective date, the supreme court in *McNealy* v. *Gregory* had negated the language, while asserting its own authority within the new constitutional framework.

The litigation in *McNealy* had begun when Adam McNealy, the holder in due course of a promissory note from Jason Gregory, sued Gregory in an action of assumpsit. Gregory insisted that the matter was not actionable under the new constitution because the note's consideration was the price and value of a slave purchased after secession. The supreme court countered Gregory's argument. It found the state constitutional clause unconstitutional and, thereby, void as a violation of three provisions of the federal constitution. First, the clause impaired the obligation of contracts retrospectively by voiding agreements backed by consideration that was legal at the time the contracts were made. Second, assuming the clause's purpose was to punish people who had traded in slaves, it constituted an impermissible bill of attainder. Finally, it violated the Fourteenth Amendment by depriving citizens of their property without due process of law.[6]

The *McNealy* decision entailed short- and long-term consequences. It shielded former slaveowners from further economic losses resulting from emancipation. Purchasers who bought slaves on credit could not use the fact of emancipation as a pretext for avoiding their debts. Of more importance, the case affirmed the judiciary's role as the ultimate arbiter of the powers of the branches of government and the rights of its citizens. Justice James Diament Westcott, Jr.'s, opinion clearly stated the principle. Even as the constitutional convention was promulgating the questionable rule, he declared, "there was a body of magistracy . . . to which the trust of *exercising the judicial powers of government* was confided by the people of the State, by the Congress of the United States, and by the President of the United States."[7]

The necessity of interpreting a new constitution, coupled with the highly political nature of Reconstruction, forced the court to confront constitutional issues more directly than it had in the past. In fact, framers of the document ushered the court to the forefront of political discourse. They did so by voiding the jurisprudential necessity of a case or controversy. They declared, "The Governor may at any time require the opinion of the Justices of the Supreme Court as to the interpretation of any portion of this Constitution, or upon any point of law, and the Supreme Court shall render such opinion in writing."[8]

Governors often availed themselves of the opportunity for securing an opinion, and the first example arose within months after the Republican takeover. As soon as the new court convened in October 1868, Governor Harrison Reed sought an advisory opinion on the eligibility of former Confederates to hold office. Desirous of including within his administration prominent conservatives, Reed specifically inquired as to whether "a person who was a member of the Secession Convention, and signed the ordinance of secession, can hold any official position . . . or act as deputy for any officer, or act in a *clerical* capacity in any department of the government."[9] In response, the high court considered the constitutional bar on office holding by state or federal officers and legislators who had engaged in rebellion against the United States after taking an oath to support the United States Constitution. The tribunal held that the provision did not outlaw all government employment, such as working as a clerk or a laborer. Further, the justices found that secession convention delegates were neither legislators nor executive or judicial officers. Unless a delegate previously had taken an oath of office in some official capacity, he could hold public office under the new constitution even if he had fought for the Confederacy or otherwise given aid and comfort to the enemies of the United States. Thus, some of Florida's most prominent politicians were permitted to continue their involvement in state government.[10]

Pleased with the results of his initial inquiry of the court, Reed invoked the advisory opinion clause again in 1869. The controversy related to the Florida legislature's election of a new United States senator. In July 1868 the body had named carpetbagger Abijah Gilbert for a term that would not begin until the following year. Commonly accepted reports indicated that the decision resulted from Gilbert's promise to buy enough state bonds to fund the state's nearly empty treasury. Several of Gilbert's disappointed opponents challenged the action on grounds that the legislature had not abided by procedures specified in federal law. Reed avoided taking a stand; instead, he requested the justices to determine the legality of the original election. Chief Justice Edwin M. Randall delivered the panel's statement on January 29, 1869. He acknowledged Gilbert's arguments that "the questions involved in the inquiry are not matters of judicial cognizance, and that the 'opinion' of this Court is binding on no person, the matter being purely of legislative interpretation and adjudication." Nevertheless, Randall observed, the constitution required the court to answer questions "upon any point of law" at the governor's request. So, he continued, "we are constrained to comply."[11]

Turning to the facts of the case, the court through Randall concluded that Gilbert's election "was irregular, but it is out of our power to *decide* that the election was 'illegal and void,' that question being exclusively for the Senate of the United States." Despite irregularities, the Senate could determine that the election "was a fair expression of the power in whom was vested the duty of selection." Until the Senate acted the validity of the election would "remain an open question."[12] The opinion established important precedent. Thereafter, the supreme court of Florida guarded its prerogative to decline issuing advisory opinions on questions that were blatantly political. In this particular case, the senatorial election's legal ambiguity prompted the legislature in 1870 to declare a new election. None of the original complainants achieved a victory. Rather, the assembly turned to Ossian Bingley Hart. The United States Senate thereafter declined to seat the Florida justice, principally because the state's carpetbag senior senator, Thomas W. Osborn, favored his fellow carpetbagger. Hart returned to the court until he assumed the office of governor in January 1873.[13]

Impeachments of Governor Harrison Reed

Governor Reed's frequent invocation of the constitution's advisory opinion clause typified his administrative style, which eschewed political compromise in favor of executive fiat. A political maverick whose only previous experience in public office consisted of an appointment to the federal direct tax commission during the Civil War, Reed sporadically attempted, without success, to woo conservatives while forging cooperation among the disparate racial, regional, and commercial interests that made up the Republican party. As one historian observed, "[the governor] failed to win over many Democrats and fostered increased Republican opposition."[14]

With elements of virtually all camps opposing Reed at times, attempts to remove him from office loomed as inevitable. The first try occurred four months into his administration. A special legislative session in November 1868 passed an appropriation of additional legislative compensation for expenses incurred in attending the meeting. Reed vetoed the per diem allowances. The assembly overrode the veto, and, on November 3, the house of representatives passed fourteen articles of impeachment that accused Reed of lying, incompetence, embezzlement, and graft. The same day Lieutenant Governor William H. Gleason, an old friend of Reed from Wisconsin, declared himself acting governor and established an office in a hotel across the street from the capitol. Many of Reed's cabinet members joined Gleason, including Secretary of State George Alden, who carried the Florida seal to the pretender's hotel headquarters.[15]

Circumstances soon involved the state supreme court in the affair. The state constitution placed the sole power for impeachment in the house and directed that the trial be conducted in the senate with the chief justice presiding. While these guidelines seemed to place impeachment solely within the legislature's powers, the executive article authorized the governor to request advisory opinions of the court. Seeing a possible solution to his political dilemma, Reed on November 9 sought the court's backing. He argued the unconstitutionality of impeachment because a quorum had not been present in the senate when the house preferred charges against him. Four of the senators, he explained, had just been appointed by him to state offices, a fact that made them ineligible to sit in the upper house. Gleason claimed, in response, that the court possessed no jurisdiction over the matter under the wording of its constitutional grant of authority.[16]

As to the jurisdictional question, the justices declined to accept the lieutenant governor's reasoning. They concluded, instead, that Reed's points were well taken. The senate had not validly convened, and the house's action was invalid. Impeachment did not consist, Chief Justice Randall explained, merely of drafting articles of impeachment by the assembly. It included actual presentation of those articles to a duly constituted senate. Just as a criminal court could not act on an indictment until it was "presented to the court in actual, open, and legal session, and received and filed therein," the supreme court could not "recognize a declaratory resolution of the Assembly as constituting an effective impeachment, until the declaration of impeachment or accusation be made to [the senate]." Since no such declaration had been made, the court did not reach Gleason's further argument that the governor was disqualified from carrying out official duties while an impeachment trial was pending.[17]

The advisory opinion spurred Reed to a counterattack on Gleason. The governor ordered Attorney General Almon R. Meek to obtain a writ of quo warranto against the lieutenant governor, seeking his removal from office on the grounds that Gleason had not resided in Florida for three years prior to his election, as required by the constitution. Gleason, represented by former justice and governor David S. Walker, admitted that he had not satisfied the residency requirement, but he argued that he should not have to respond to the writ because the court did not have jurisdiction to issue such writs unless they were related to an appeal from a lower court.[18]

Once again the lieutenant governor's reasoning proved insufficient. On November 24 Justice Westcott ruled on the jurisdictional question. The constitution provided, he noted, that "the Court will have power to issue writs of mandamus, certiorari, prohibition, quo warranto, habeas corpus, and also all writs necessary or proper to the complete exercise of its appellate jurisdiction." Walker had argued that the provision limited the court's authority in nonappellate cases and had cited the court's 1851 opinion in *Ex parte White*, in which Justice Leslie Atchinson Thompson held that the court's original jurisdiction extended only to matters involving the supreme court's supervision of inferior tribunals. Westcott held, however, that the new constitution invalidated *White*. Under the antebellum constitution the court "was expressly restricted to appellate jurisdiction only," he wrote, whereas "here we have no analogous clause." The fact that the framers of 1868 "adopted different language shows that they intended to make a change in the power."[19]

Justice Westcott then turned to a determination of the meaning of the constitutional clause governing the issuance of writs and thereby offered an important definition of court authority. Gleason had contended that the phrase "necessary or proper to the complete exercise of its appellate jurisdiction" modified the first portion of the sentence related to the power to issue common-law writs. Westcott concluded otherwise. He explained that the words "and also all writs" indicated that only those writs not specified in the first part of the sentence were limited to appellate matters. The jurist summarized, "[T]he jurisdiction of this court is twofold: appellate jurisdiction proper, with power to issue all writs necessary to its full exercise, and original jurisdiction to issue the specified writs when they are the appropriate remedies." The decision turned, in part, on Westcott's understanding of the role of American appellate tribunals. Reviewing the powers granted to other courts of last resort, he asserted that "the Supreme Courts of the States are, as a general thing, clothed with powers in addition to those which are *appellate in their character.*"[20]

Gleason repeatedly attempted over the ensuing three weeks to save his position. His lawyers filed motion after motion challenging the quo warranto action. The lieutenant governor contended, among other things, that Reed had solicited him to run for office; that Reed had instituted the proceedings for "malicious and vindictive motives, and to gratify a spirit of revenge and recrimination"; that he could only be removed from office through impeachment; and that Attorney General Meek was not a valid officer, his appointment having been made after the governor was impeached and disqualified from his duties. The court rejected each of the arguments, although Westcott noted in dissent that government officials appointed by the governor after his impeachment "occupy no better position than if his appointment was made by some citizen."[21] Gleason also alleged that justices Randall and Hart did not meet the constitutional requirements for holding public office. Westcott dismissed the contention as a "legal proposition absurd upon its face."[22]

Failing before the supreme court, Gleason sought to remove the case to federal court under the Civil Rights Act of 1866. In a thundering affirmation of federalism, Randall refused to grant the petition, for "[t]o do so would be to destroy all necessity for and power of State courts, and destroy all harmony between the courts of the United States and the State courts." He concluded, "It would result in a revolution of the judicial system."[23] On December 15 the court declared Gleason's ineligibility for holding office. The lieutenant governor tried to appeal the ruling to the United States Supreme Court, but Randall declined to sign the writ of error because the case involved no federal question. When the legislature reconvened in January 1869, Gleason retained his post as president of the senate for one week before resigning.[24]

Reed's shrewd invocation of the constitutional process for advisory opinions saved him from this initial impeachment attempt, but growing dissatisfaction with his administration led in 1869 and 1870 to renewed efforts to remove him from office. The final, but most serious, attempt to challenge Reed's tenure began on February 2, 1872, when the house voted unanimously to impeach the governor. The articles contained allegations that Reed had fraudulently issued internal improvement bonds, received payoffs for favors, lied to a state senator, and attempted to influence a justice of the peace. The senate convened as a court of impeachment, with Chief Justice Randall presiding, but a majority of senators soon voted to adjourn. This tactic kept Reed out of office without undertaking a politically charged trial, while placing Lieutenant Governor Samuel T. Day, a Florida loyalist, in power.[25]

The legislative legerdemain failed to defeat the suspended governor, and Reed again turned for relief to the supreme court. On April 27 he learned that Day had gone to Jacksonville to attend a Republican meeting. Reed reappeared at the capitol, declared himself the true governor, and asked the justices for an advisory opinion, arguing that the senate's adjournment constituted a judgment of acquittal. The governor's opponents felt confident that Justice Hart would rule against Reed, but they remained unsure about Westcott, a Democrat, and Randall, a political ally and friend of the chief magistrate. Accordingly Day called a special legislative session so that impeachment could proceed if the court ruled in the governor's favor. The tensions heightened on April 29, when both the house and senate adjourned so that members could attend the supreme court's session. According to one senator, Reed's opponents "were in high spirits, as Hart had privately informed them that things were all right, and that the court would sustain Day."[26]

The rumors misled to some extent. First, all three justices agreed with Reed that the meaning of constitutional language regarding an "acquittal by the Senate" was not restricted to a formal judgment of acquittal but also meant any action other than conviction that dismissed or discontinued the prosecution. Beyond that, the court members could not agree with unanimity. Westcott and Hart held for the tribunal that the matter was "beyond our jurisdiction entirely," since the senate constitutionally sat as a court of impeachment with "exclusive original and final jurisdiction." Referring to the recent mandamus and quo warranto decisions, the opinion noted that "[t]his court can say to an officer, you are not elected or qualified," but only a senate court of impeachment "can say to him, we admit that you are selected by the people; that you were in all respects qualified, and notwithstanding all this, you shall . . . no longer discharge the functions of [your] office."[27]

Additional aspects of the controversy received attention. The constitutional grant of power to the governor to require advisory opinions of the supreme court suggested that, even if the court could not order the senate to reinstate Reed, the panel was bound to render a legal opinion on the propriety of the senate's actions. Nonetheless, in a curious piece of circular reasoning Westcott held that, because Reed was suspended, "his power as Governor to demand our opinion upon any question of law ceases." The justice reached the conclusion even though the question at hand concerned whether senate adjournment had ended Reed's suspension. Complicating the situation, Westcott found that, even had acting governor Day submitted the question, the court's answer would be merely advisory and not binding on the senate. His decision informed Reed that "[a] purely voluntary expression of an opinion by this court upon a subject of the greatest importance then pending before the Senate, might be calculated to embarrass its action and might perhaps be viewed as an impertinent suggestion as to its duty in the premises." Westcott added, "Whether you are entitled to a discharge[, the senate] must determine."[28]

Chief Justice Randall dissented, claiming both that the court possessed no jurisdiction over the matter and that Reed should be reinstated. On the jurisdictional issue, he invoked the doctrine of separation of powers to demonstrate that no branch should be allowed to exercise exclusive political and judicial power. "If all political and judicial supervisory power is lodged in any one body of men," he wrote, " . . . then are such several departments [of government] mere cheats and shams, baubles and playthings invented to delude and ensnare." Randall conceded that the impeachment proceedings were beyond the court's control, but he insisted that the tribunal could consider senate actions to determine "what results legally flow from such action." As to whether senate adjournment constituted an acquittal, the chief justice paid careful attention to the practical effect of the adjournment. Reed's term would have expired by the time the senate convened again, and he would have been denied the privileges of office without a hearing. Since an impeachment court's jurisdiction extended only to public officials, "the postponement to a day when it will have no jurisdiction of the officer is an absolute dismissal of the matters." He concluded, "A refusal to try is a refusal to convict."[29]

The court's impeachment decisions established significant precedents. They clarified constitutional impeachment authority. The 1868 opinion defined the requirements necessary to constitute a lawful impeachment, while the 1872 decision affirmed that the senate possessed exclusive jurisdiction to determine questions of law and fact. Because subsequent state constitutions have used language similar to that of the 1868 charter in providing for impeachment, the findings remain valid precedent. Of greater significance, the quo warranto proceedings against Gleason offered the justices opportunity for defining broad parameters for the court's original jurisdiction. The claims made in those troubled days would resist encroachment thereafter.

The Second Lieutenant Governor Controversy

During the period in 1872 when the supreme court examined the constitutional sufficiency of Governor Reed's impeachment, it considered other matters of importance to the state and its government. Particularly it rendered, within weeks after the impeachment opinion, a decision that dealt a serious blow to Republican power and Justice Hart's chances for election as governor to succeed Reed. The case, which had lingered since the elections of 1870, involved an attempt by William D. Bloxham, the conservative lieutenant governor candidate, to oust apparent winner Samuel T. Day from office. Incidents of fraud and intimidation revealed by the case embarrassed both parties and raised concerns about the legitimacy of Florida's state government.[30]

The events surrounding the 1870 elections constituted some of the bloodiest in Florida's history. By that year conservatives had organized to resist Republican power at a time when the Ku Klux Klan and other vigilante organizations spread violence among Republicans, black and white. The violence especially flared during the summer of 1870, prompting Governor Reed to request the presence of federal troops in the most affected counties on election day. As the time for polling approached, the incidents increased. Many of them carried tragic results. Some conservatives cheered the malefactors, and on election day vigilantes drove numbers of black voters from polls or otherwise kept them from voting. In Jefferson County, for example, whites prevented up to five hundred blacks from casting ballots when William Capers Bird, a conservative member of the 1865 constitutional convention, brandished a pistol at black state senator Robert Meacham on the steps of the Monticello courthouse. Reportedly Bird warned Meacham that "no damned nigger shall vote here."[31]

When the polls closed on election day 1870, conservatives (increasingly known again as Democrats) apparently had gained narrow victories in the congressional and lieutenant governor's races. They also claimed legislative majorities. Republicans hastened to reverse these results by various mechanisms, including fraud in some instances. Bloxham, determined that his win not be snatched from him, sought to enjoin the Republican-dominated state board of canvassers from announcing adjusted results. Circuit judge Pleasants W. White, a conservative and one-time Confederate official appointed to office by Governor Reed, granted the injunction. A federal grand jury then indicted White for violation of the Enforcement Act of 1870, which had expanded federal jurisdiction over voting rights.[32]

White's arrest invited Republican countermeasures. With the judge resting in a Jacksonville jail, the state board of canvassers counted the votes without interference. After rejecting ballots from nine counties and three Duval County precincts, the board declared victory in the lieutenant governor's race for Samuel T. Day and in the congressional race for Josiah T. Walls, both Republicans. The board also announced Republican majorities in the legislature. Conservatives complained that the Republicans had defrauded them of the election by refusing to count votes that they—the conservatives—had obtained in the excluded counties.[33]

After the canvassing board's announcements, the dispute moved to the supreme court. On January 10, 1871, Bloxham petitioned for a writ of mandamus requiring the board to recount all ballots. Attorney General J. C. B. Drew responded that the court did not have the power to direct a recount. He argued that, because the board had adjourned sine die after it had certified the election results, it could not be reconvened. Chief Justice Randall rebuffed the attorney general's position. He forcefully affirmed the court's power, through the writ of mandamus, to compel government agencies to perform their duties. The board, Randall held, had not completed its legal duty "to ascertain the whole number of votes cast, and who had received the highest number of such votes." Thus, the canvassers "did not conclude their duties as canvassers, nor put an end to their powers as canvassers by an adjournment *sine die.*" The court could compel them to count all the ballots.[34]

Republican leaders, anticipating Randall's opinion, had prepared another gambit. Party legislators changed the rules of the game by repealing the law that created the board of canvassers, effectively dissolving the board. As the supreme court prepared to deliver a judgment in Bloxham's favor, the legislation came to Randall's attention. Black state senator John Wallace, who associated closely with Bloxham, later observed, "It was very singular that the Chief Justice should take judicial notice of a paper when he did not know whether it was fictitious or genuine, especially when it involved the rights of all the people in the State."[35] Although the justices believed that the board had a duty to count all votes in the canvass, they informed Bloxham that the court could not compel a nonexistent governmental entity to do anything, "not even to finish what they have commenced."[36]

While Bloxham pursued his writ of mandamus, another player entered the field. Incumbent Edmund C. Weeks petitioned the court for a writ of quo warranto, claiming that he rightfully held the office of lieutenant governor. Reed had appointed Weeks in the wake of William H. Gleason's departure from office. At the time the governor also had called for an election for lieutenant governor to take place at the November 1870 general election. Reed based his actions on constitutional language providing that "when no mode is provided by this Constitution . . . for filling [a] vacancy, the Governor shall have power to fill such vacancy by granting a commission, which shall expire at the next election."[37] Weeks maintained that he should serve until the next regular election for lieutenant governor, scheduled for 1872, rather than until the 1870 general election. The court disagreed. Its members concluded that the constitution only contemplated that an appointee would fill the office until an election could be properly held, not until the expiration of the term of the replaced official. To hold otherwise would be "in opposition to the true principles of republican government."[38]

Bloxham persisted in his efforts to win the lieutenant governor's office. On February 20, 1871, he applied to the supreme court for a writ of quo warranto, challenging Day's claim. Because the case arose under the court's original jurisdiction, its commencement was delayed until November 15, when the justices appointed special masters to collect evidence and testimony in the affected voting districts. The trial began on May 28, 1872, with former justice Samuel J. Douglas representing Bloxham and future justice George Pettus Raney appearing for Day. On June 1 the court surprised Floridians by ruling, based upon the factual information gathered by special masters, that Bloxham had been duly elected. For the victor the results were bittersweet. Since the legislature did not meet again before his term expired on January 3, 1873, Bloxham enjoyed no opportunity to preside over the senate, the lieutenant governor's principal duty. When Bloxham ran for governor in 1872, he was defeated by Justice Hart. Nevertheless his 1870 victory, confirmed by the supreme court, signaled, according to one historian, "the beginning of the end of Reconstruction in Florida."[39] The Democrats had become a politically potent force once again, a fact with which the Republicans were compelled to reckon.

Economic Development and Associated Frauds

Although partisan squabbling characterized the congressional Reconstruction period, the primary concerns of most Floridians centered elsewhere than on state politics. Even most carpetbaggers had been lured to Florida by opportunity for economic gain rather than for political advancement. Reconstruction leaders, explained a leading historian of the period, "were business-oriented men who recognized that the state needed to be developed if the problems created by the Civil War were to be permanently solved."[40] Contending interests naturally clashed in such pursuits, and litigation arising from the various efforts at development soon reached the supreme court.

Contrary to some Old South myths, Florida experienced growth and some prosperity during Reconstruction. From a population of about 140,000 in 1860, the number of Floridians had grown to almost 190,000 in 1870 and reached 270,000 a decade later. This increase resulted largely from immigration, primarily by whites from North and South but also by black agricultural workers and some foreigners, especially Cubans coming to the state's largest town, Key West. Agriculture remained the primary economic activity, and the cultivation of citrus fruits and winter vegetables began to replace the production of cotton in importance. Lumber and naval stores industries took firmer hold, particularly in West Florida. Perhaps most significantly for the future, travelers increasingly wintered at resort towns such as Jacksonville, St. Augustine, Palatka, and Key West.[41]

Economic growth required internal improvements on a large scale. The building of canals and railroads would open formerly inaccessible lands to settlers. The advances also would encourage commercial interests to lend their funds and newcomers to invest labor in developing the region. Residents viewed railroads, above all other improvements, as most essential. The Civil War had halted construction of Florida's nascent rail networks, and many of the lines had been dismantled by Union and Confederate forces. Onlookers described the tracks that were supposed to link the state's towns and regions as "two streaks of rust running thru the wilderness."[42] To surmount the problems, the legislature in 1869 approved an act "to Perfect the Public Works of the State." This statute pledged state aid to complete the construction of numerous unfinished railroads, many of which were owned by unscrupulous speculators.[43]

To prevent legal challenges from stalling completion of the needed railroads, Governor Harrison Reed sought a supreme court advisory opinion on the 1869 statute's constitutionality. The law had achieved enactment pursuant to a constitutional provision that empowered the legislature to issue state bonds "for the erection of State buildings, support of State institutions, and perfecting public works."[44] Reed asked the justices if railroads constituted public works and if the legislature could aid their construction. The court, writing seriatim, upheld the law. Justice Westcott, a former railroad attorney, noted that the constitution authorized state aid to *perfect* public works. He concluded, after historical inquiry, that "these incompleted lines of railway . . . were the unperfected 'public works' which the Constitution of 1868 contemplated."[45] Justice Hart concurred. "As one who was a member of the Convention that framed the Constitution," he wrote, "I cannot unlearn or ignore the certainty that those words had special reference to our great unfinished railroad system, so necessary to the settlement, development, and prosperity of Florida, and so convenient, useful, and beneficial to the whole public."[46]

Even in the face of his myriad political troubles, Governor Reed remained a steadfast proponent of railroad expansion. He called a special legislative session in 1869 to spur completion of a railroad system "as early as possible, in order that . . . the State may receive her full share of the immigration and capital now flowing Southward." He urged that the lawmakers offer "the widest inducements . . . for the profitable investment of capital."[47] The governor used his position as chairman of the internal improvement trust fund to generate momentum. The Internal Improvement Act of 1855, previously discussed in part 2, had provided that the fund could offer no more than $10,000 per mile of track in assistance of railroad construction. In 1869 Reed convinced the legislature—one historian claimed that "[w]holesale bribery" played a crucial role—to raise this amount to $14,000 per mile, then in 1870 to $16,000.[48]

Two railroads received the greater part of this type of state assistance, the

Florida Central and the Jacksonville, Pensacola, and Mobile. Both were incorporated in 1869 by North Carolinian George W. Swepson and his associate, former Union general Milton S. Littlefield of Maine. The promoters had assembled the lines from three defunct companies subject to state control and had purchased them on extremely favorable terms. Notably the governor had accepted as payment of the $1.5 million price old state bonds at par value (they had been secured at perhaps one-third the sum) and a personal check from Swepson. In return, the internal improvement fund promised to provide $4 million in aid to the railroads, raised by the sale of state bonds. Littlefield, as Swepson's Florida agent, bribed state officials to remove requirements that the state have a first lien on the property and that they prove clear title before Florida issued new state bonds.[49]

Unfortunately Swepson and Littlefield were swindlers with little interest in building Florida's future. Swepson's check, for instance, proved worthless. The funds available to the developer had been given to him in trust by the state of North Carolina to finance railroad projects there. In the end the two men managed to bilk Florida out of a fortune. As for developing the state, not even one-third of the money raised from bonds benefited railroad construction, the rest being used to pay private debts and to fund a European tour. Although most political leaders, Democrat and Republican, initially had supported the venture, growing evidence of waste, fraud, and mismanagement convinced the legislature to revoke the sale of the remaining $1 million of state bonds. Littlefield and two state senators were convicted of bribery. The political damage weighed heavily on Reed, who faced a third attempt at impeachment when allegations arose that he had accepted a Swepson bribe. Further mismanagement by Reed landed the internal improvement fund in federal receivership, where it remained for years.[50]

The Swepson-Littlefield railroad schemes prompted a series of lawsuits that would not be resolved until after the conclusion of Republican rule in Florida. The first cases arose prior to disclosure of the full extent of the frauds. In September 1869, shortly after the railroad purchase, several stockholders filed suit against the state. Circuit judge Alva A. Knight placed the Jacksonville-to-Quincy line in receivership after he found that Swepson and Littlefield had engaged in collusion. Two weeks later the supreme court set aside the judgment and ordered receiver James W. Johnson to return the company's control to Swepson. Johnson refused to comply. The justices held him in contempt of court and ordered him jailed without bail. Justice Hart's concurring opinion expressed personal ire at the receiver's conduct. "[T]he *tribunal* must be everywhere respected by at least implicit obedience to its process," Hart declared. "Without this, the fabric of jurisprudence, erected by the experience of ages, the best constituted safe-guard of human rights, must fall. Great, beneficial and beautiful as it is, it is a delicate structure, and cannot maintain its usefulness under frequent shocks of disrespect."[51]

As news spread of the fraudulent schemes, bondholders, personal and business creditors, part owners of the railroads, and North Carolina officials sued Swepson, Littlefield, and others associated with the companies. Courts in Florida, North Carolina, Georgia, New Jersey, and New York heard the actions. Because of financial and legal difficulties, construction ceased on the roads in 1872, leaving Florida virtually without rail lines west of Apalachicola or south of Cedar Key. On existent lines poor service continued, rails and equipment fell into disrepair, and financial and labor problems plagued the companies. Events forced Swepson out of control by 1873, but the legal troubles faced by the railroads persisted.[52]

The controversies surrounding the railroad frauds simmered for decades, but beginning in 1876 the state supreme court offered hope for resolution of the legal difficulties. In that year the justices invalidated the bond issue for the benefit of the Jacksonville, Pensacola, and Mobile Railroad. Justice Westcott and two circuit judges decided the case because justices Van Valkenburgh and Randall once had served as counsel in the litigation. Westcott reaffirmed the court's earlier decision that the legislature could grant state aid to railroads. However, he continued, at the time the constitution received approval, all the planned railroad lines had terminal points within the state. Because the Jacksonville, Pensacola, and Mobile featured a track from Quincy to Mobile as one of its primary lines, it fell outside the scope of the "public works" that the legislature could "perfect." The court recognized that a connection to Mobile might "be of much greater benefit to the people" than the more limited system contemplated by the Internal Improvements Act and the state constitution, but it refused to consider "questions of policy of this character." Thus, the bond issue was unconstitutional, and the state avoided liability for the debt. The decision did not relieve the railroad of its obligations, and the state maintained a lien on behalf of the bondholders, mostly investors with no complicity in the swindle.[53]

During the next two years the justices sorted out the conflicting claims of stock owners and bondholders affected by their 1876 ruling. Meanwhile the legislature, ostensibly to prevent another such fiasco, proposed a subsequently approved constitutional amendment to prohibit the state from pledging its credit to any individual or company or becoming "a joint owner or stockholder in any company, association or corporation."[54] In 1879 they repudiated the state's debt resulting from the Swepson-Littlefield fraud. Also that year, the United States

Supreme Court upheld the supreme court of Florida's judgment regarding the bond issue's propriety.[55]

Problems associated with railroad financing also adversely affected other efforts to undertake internal improvements. Beginning in 1869, for example, the internal improvement trust fund agreed to sell huge tracts of South Florida lands to former lieutenant governor William H. Gleason if he agreed to make the area accessible through drainage projects. The plans came to a halt in December 1870, however, when worried New York investor Francis Vose obtained a federal court injunction against transferring state lands other than for cash.[56]

The Vose injunction caused reverberations throughout Florida's political and business circles. Prodded by the federal court that issued the order, the trustees of the internal improvement fund eventually attempted to rescind its agreement with the former lieutenant governor. The matter came before the supreme court in 1875 in the case of *Trustees of the Internal Improvement Trust Fund* v. *Gleason.* The trustees contended that, under the 1862 decision in *Bailey* v. *Trustees of the Internal Improvement Fund* (see chapter 10), it could pledge state lands only to pay the interest to original holders of railroad bonds. The fund's arguments suggest that this may have been a collusive suit, as counsel Horatio Bisbee pointed out that the fund was bound to follow this rule no matter how it might "arrest every effort at internal improvement, however wise and advantageous . . . , render impossible every noble enterprise to develop the resources of the State; stifle every industry, repel capital and labor from our shores, until all industries of the State shall perish." Bisbee concluded, perhaps sardonically, that the "consequences of the law can never be considered in passing a judgment of what the law of a given subject is."[57]

In the *Gleason* case, the state supreme court found for the defendant and against the trustees. It did so by limiting *Bailey* to the specific facts of that litigation. The decision declared that *Gleason,* as opposed to *Bailey,* involved an effort "to improve the trust estate, by using a portion of it to render the balance more valuable." To contend that using part of the fund to increase the total value violated the trust, Justice Westcott held, "would render these trustees powerless to drain one acre of the millions of acres of swamp lands now in their hands, thus preventing their improvement, and would prevent them from carrying out the manifest policy and spirit of the law." Because the justice sensed that the fund trustees "assume[d] an attitude hostile to" the bondholders, the court withheld final judgment until the bondholders could be made parties to the action. Nevertheless, the principles explained in *Gleason* constituted an endorsement of a broad system of internal improvements and ended the common perception left by *Bailey* that railroads were the only acceptable projects for internal improvement.[58]

Economic development and internal improvements proceeded slowly through congressional Reconstruction, but not because the supreme court of Florida thwarted economic activity. Rather, political ambition, greed, and an overzealous commitment to growth enticed Florida's leaders, including Democrats as well as Republicans, into unsound financial schemes that produced few improvements to the state's infrastructure. Yet when reviewing litigation arising from the development controversies, the court gave broad sanction to the state's power to facilitate internal improvements. These decisions would prove a boon to development in the years ahead.

The Election of 1876 and "Redemption"

By 1876 the Democratic party had regained much of the organization it had lost in the early years of congressional Reconstruction. Although Republicans still controlled the state's political machinery, their opponents felt confident that they could select viable candidates with a winning electoral appeal for staunch Democrats, northern conservatives, and old-line Whigs. At the party convention in June, Democrats selected as their gubernatorial candidate George F. Drew, a New Hampshire native who had moved to Madison County around 1840 and established a lumber-mill operation. A former Whig who had generally abstained from politics, Drew and his candidacy enjoyed popularity. He had supported the Union during the Civil War, but his opposition to radical Reconstruction appealed to former Confederates. Furthermore, Drew's lack of prior affiliation with the traditional elements of either party attracted voters, including some blacks, weary of official corruption and broken Republican promises. On their part, Republicans, after a bruising intraparty struggle, proposed Marcellus L. Stearns, who had ascended to the governorship upon the death of Ossian Bingley Hart and who was associated closely in the public mind with carpetbagger politics as usual.[59]

The elections of 1876 featured violence, fraud, and voter intimidation. Despite the presence of small detachments of federal troops assigned to a few areas to protect against voting abuse, Democratic party faithful resorted to night riding, kidnapping, and other means to prevent blacks from voting or to persuade them to vote for Democrats. Republicans, with official control of the ballot boxes, generally relied on more subtle means of ensuring victory. Their methods included the creation of spurious voting rolls, the exercise of multiple voting, and creative ballot counting.[60]

Initial election-day returns indicated a narrow Democratic sweep of statewide and national offices. Drew had beaten Stearns by about five hundred votes, while Democratic presidential candidate Samuel Tilden had edged Rutherford B. Hayes by less than one hundred. However, statutes required the state board of canvassers to ratify the tallies before the results became official. Board membership comprised Secretary of State Samuel B. McLin and Comptroller Clayton A. Cowgill, both Republicans, and Democratic Attorney General William Archer Cocke. On December 6, after discarding ballots from a number of precincts, the board announced that the Republican candidates for presidential elector had won by several hundred votes. Future justice George Pettus Raney, a member of the Democratic executive committee, obtained an injunction from the Tallahassee circuit court ordering the canvassers simply to count the votes for the state elections without passing on their validity. The board ignored the injunction and, after discounting some votes, reported that the Republican candidates for governor and lieutenant governor had triumphed.[61]

Subsequent to the certifications, Democratic lawyers approached the supreme court for relief. Particularly, Drew petitioned for a writ of mandamus directing the canvassers to recount the ballots. Although the court had recessed for the year, the justices convened in special session because an early resolution was necessary so that the elected officials could take their offices at the proper time. Drew's petition insisted that the board had overstepped its authority by considering evidence on the validity of ballots, a function that belonged to the courts. Republican board members agreed to abide by the court's decision, since Chief Justice Randall and Justice Van Valkenburgh belonged to their party and Justice Westcott had received his appointment from a Republican governor. On December 14 the panel granted the writ, ordering the board either to count all of the election returns or show cause why it could not do so.[62]

The canvassing board filed its answer on December 16. Its lawyers contended that the board had been empowered, as a quasi-judicial agency, to reject any clearly fraudulent ballots. Manatee County elections had involved so much corruption, they added, that no method of determining the actual vote existed. They also argued that the board had ceased to exist upon completing its duties and, therefore, was not under the court's jurisdiction. Drew's attorneys insisted that the board had no authority except to deliver an exact count of all votes and that its duties would not be complete until it rendered the proper decision.[63]

The justices acted with dispatch. On December 23 they unanimously ordered the board of canvassers to recount the ballots based solely on the county returns. Justice Westcott passed over the jurisdictional issue, noting that the 1871 *Bloxham* case provided authority. The state constitution, he wrote, vested the judicial power solely in the state courts. Consequently, the "general nature" of the board's power was strictly "ministerial," meaning that the state canvassers could only tally the votes submitted by the county canvassers and "declar[e] the results as *shown by the returns.*" While the justices admitted that the law permitted the board to reject ballots that were "so irregular, false, or fraudulent that the Board shall be unable to determine the true vote," the opinion distinguished a "true" vote from a "legal" one. The former referred to a determination that the votes were part of the official returns certified by the county's canvassers, while the latter involved a question of whether individual votes were fraudulent. "Whether irregularities or fraud in an election will authorize the rejection of a vote case, counted and returned in a genuine, *bona fide* return, is a question of law not within the power of this Board to determine." The view that the canvassing board "is a tribunal having power strictly judicial, such as is involved in the determination of the legality of a particular vote or election," Westcott concluded, "cannot be sustained."[64]

The unanimous decision surprised state Republicans. Chief Justice Randall's vote especially galled them, since he was seeking support for an appointment to a federal bench vacancy. Randall and Stearns shared a personal enmity, though, and some onlookers interpreted the chief justice's vote as a direct attack on the governor. "Randall was only glad of an opportunity to sacrifice Stearns," McLin informed a Republican official. "The traitor would have destroyed the electoral vote if necessary to make his spite on Stearns and one or two others."[65]

The court's opinion received national attention because, if the same reasoning were applied to the vote for presidential electors, it could affect the selection of the next president. The *New York Times*, for example, criticized it as a "JUDICIAL CRIME."[66] Drew's attorneys carefully had limited their complaints to the state races, so that federal courts could not become involved. Nevertheless, the court's holding that the canvassing board could make only a ministerial count called into question Hayes's Florida victory, since the board also had disqualified votes for Tilden. The justices, themselves, were unsure about the effect of their ruling on the presidential election. Westcott stated privately that he thought Hayes had carried the state since some East Florida voters had split their tickets. Three days afterward, when the crucial nature of Florida's vote became apparent, he recanted. Chief Justice Randall later expressed surprise that a similar mandamus proceeding was not attempted to challenge the electoral vote.[67]

As news of the Florida decision spread, national party officials tried to broaden their intervention in state affairs. Republican national secretary William E. Chandler's actions offer an example. He directed Stearns and other state party leaders to ignore the supreme court ruling, subsequent to which McLin canceled a scheduled meeting of the canvassing board. At approximately the same time Republican leaders in other areas of the country, realizing the implications of the court decision on the presidential election, planned federal court actions. Meanwhile in Florida, Attorney General Cocke insisted that the canvassing board meet. McLin and Cowgill eventually agreed, and on December 28 the board reported that Drew had beaten Stearns by 24,179 votes to 23,984. The two Republicans emphasized, though, that they did not regard that result as valid and asked that "this protest may be admitted as part of such [election] return, and become of the record of the Court." They attempted, as well, to make the presidential election an issue. Over Cocke's objections, the board majority reported that it had recanvassed the votes for president elector, based on the court-imposed standards, and found that the Republican electors had received the majority.[68]

The supreme court's rejoinder was not long in coming. On January 1, 1877, the tribunal denied the board's right to their protest. As explained by Justice Westcott, the board's members had received their hearing and now had only the "simply duty . . . to obey the writ and to make a certificate of their obedience." The justice additionally refused to consider the board's findings in any race other than that for governor. "The only relator in this case is George F. Drew," he observed, "[and] all of the other persons mentioned in these papers as receiving votes for various offices, and who are declared elected to such offices, are in no manner parties to this controversy."[69]

The ballot recount gave the governor's office to Drew. Democrats also had won a majority in the legislature, so, with Drew's inauguration on January 2, 1877, Democratic rule returned to Florida. Democratic partisans called the transition "Redemption," and they have been known to history as "Redeemers." Nonetheless, the political drama still had not run its course. The national presidency was undecided, and many state Democrats, flush with victory, refused to be contented with half a loaf. Several abortive initiatives, including petitions to the supreme court, marked their initial postelection attempts to capture Florida's electoral votes for Tilden. Then the Democratic legislature called a new canvassing board to recount the presidential votes. On January 18 that body declared Tilden the winner, even though Republican officials already had sent to Washington a certification of Hayes's win. One week following the recount, circuit judge Pleasants W. White ruled in favor of the Tilden electors in a quo warranto proceeding. The Republicans appealed, but the supreme court refused to hear the matter until its June session.[70]

Prior to the time the court convened in June, Washington political machinations had rendered the state canvassing board's recount meaningless. Southern Democrats in Congress, in return for concessions, agreed not to challenge the findings of a national joint high commission, composed of ten congressmen and five United States Supreme Court justices, that Hayes had won the election. This Compromise of 1877 marked the final stages of congressional Reconstruction in Florida and in other southern states. Although Florida's Democrats exulted in their renewed control of the state, their celebrations carried one note of regret. Had Florida's electoral votes been counted for Tilden, he—and not Hayes—would have won the presidency.[71]

The results of the elections of 1876 settled uneasily on many Floridians, and their certainty remained open to question well into 1877. Stearns continued to seek help from state leaders in securing the governorship. In February 1877 one-time United States senator Thomas W. Osborn advised him to test the supreme court once again in a quo warranto proceeding. Stearns considered the proposal but expressed skepticism. His reply to Osborn revealed bitterness at the court, especially Chief Justice Randall. "I cannot talk to Randall and I could have no faith in what he would say to me," Stearns related. "I think some of our friends whom he would trust and at the same time fear to betray . . . should do the talking with him and get his views and pledges &c." If they could "put [Randall] to the test & squarely pledge him," then Stearns would "undertake the case and can & will raise the money here to carry it through." He warned, "I don't propose to run any risk by giving Randall a chance simply to ratify their other illegal action and throw further doubt upon the electoral vote." In the end Stearns decided not to pursue a further court hearing, and the question lapsed.[72]

In contrast to Republicans who expressed sentiments similar to those of Stearns, Democrats praised the supreme court and its members. Typically George Pettus Raney lauded the tribunal for its ability to withstand the partisan scrutiny surrounding the case. "The decision of the court," he wrote after Randall's 1895 death, "resulted in maintaining the wholesome control of the courts over such bodies [as the board of canvassers], the preservation of judicial power against legislative invasion, . . . the enforcement of the will of the people as expressed at the ballot box . . . , and the deliverance of the State from the rule of strangers."[73] Raney exaggerated the court's influence, but he aptly summarized the spirit of the court's rulings during Reconstruction. In the midst of political dislocation and social turmoil, the court established itself as an independent, co-equal branch of government capable of resolving disputes that divided Floridians.

During a period characterized by civil war, political upheaval, and economic dislocation, the supreme court of Florida proved to be a remarkably stable institution. That fact can be attributed largely to low turnover and capable jurists. The same justices who were elected in 1859 served through the Civil War, and

Charles H. DuPont continued to serve as chief justice until 1868. Five different justices occupied the court between the ratification of the Constitution of 1868 and the end of congressional Reconstruction in 1877, but two of them—Randall and Westcott—sat throughout the period. Indeed, after Van Valkenburgh joined the tribunal in 1874, court composition did not change until 1885. Of the eleven men who worked on the tribunal during the Civil War and Reconstruction, only three left the bench for reasons other than death or constitutional change.

The supreme court also maintained its stability and reputation through the prudent exercise of a departmental concept of judicial review, enhancing its powers generously in areas of judicial competence but usually refraining from interference in purely political disputes. Thus, the justices could expand their original jurisdiction or strike a constitutional provision that impaired the court's power to enforce contracts, while leaving control of impeachment proceedings in legislative hands and allowing the legislature and governor to define the state's economic needs. Even the court's most politicized decision, that declaring a Democratic majority in the 1876 election, turned on a finding that the board of canvassers had usurped judicial authority by determining the legality of election returns. While many decisions held political ramifications, the court was able, in the words of one lawyer who practiced before it, to "rise above partisan and sectional considerations."[74] During a period when legislators of both parties engaged in chicanery and short-sighted schemes and a governor kept his job in the face of repeated impeachment attempts, Florida's supreme court retained respect for judicial institutions and played an important role in stabilizing the state's economic and political structure.

Part Four

Redemption and the Bourbons, 1877–1896

Chapter 14

Post-Reconstruction Florida

When Republican rule ended early in 1877, Florida entered a new political era. Critics called the white conservatives who seized control the Bourbons, insisting that they resembled the French and Spanish royal families, as historian C. Vann Woodward put it, because of their "obstinate adherence to the old loyalties and abhorrence of the new."[1] The new rulers in this and other southern states viewed their accomplishments as having almost divine significance, believing that they had "redeemed" the state from the evils of Republican domination.[2] Thus, the two decades following Reconstruction's end are known as either the Bourbon period or the Redemption.

Florida's political upheaval of 1877 carried enormous changes in its wake, but the state already was undergoing transformations that would revolutionize it in social and economic terms and lay the foundation for the modern era. Population was growing, demographics were changing, national and world publicity was attracting attention, and the economy was recovering from the negative effects of the Panic of 1873. What Florida lacked as a catalyst for major improvement was a reliable and inexpensive transportation network. During the next two decades these trends would accelerate, and that transportation network would become a reality with dramatic results.[3]

The manner in which the population grew and its composition otherwise altered held important implications. After the Civil War blacks and whites represented almost equal proportions of the state totals, but during the 1870s the size of the slight white majority began to increase. By 1880, the percentage stood at 53.5. Five years later it had risen to 56.8, then in 1890 to 57.5, and finally in 1895 to 58.5 percent. In total numbers, Florida grew from 187,748 inhabitants in 1870 to 464,639 twenty-five years afterward. Some portion of the increase reflected emigration from northern and western states. The largest numbers, though, came from Confederate states such as Georgia and Alabama, with the immigrants bringing demands for conservative white government.

Movement also occurred within the state that affected the political and social equations. Increasingly, African Americans left what had been heavily black Middle Florida counties. During 1880 to 1885, for example, Gadsden, Jefferson, Leon, Liberty, and Madison counties all lost population. Some of these individuals moved out of state to find employment. More relocated to the developing peninsula or to Florida's growing cities.[4]

As suggested, during the Bourbon period some of Florida's towns developed into cities. At the era's commencement, Key West, with 5,000 or 6,000 residents, claimed honors as the largest town. By 1895 that figure essentially had tripled to 16,500. Still, other locations registered greater increases. Tampa's 800 inhabitants in 1870 had mushroomed to more than 15,000. Pensacola's 14,000 signified more than a quadrupling. The state's most populous urban center five years before the century's end was Jacksonville with 25,000. Beyond these increasingly urban areas, new communities prospered, so that 1895 census takers also concerned themselves with places such as Titusville, Melbourne, Orange Park, Palm Beach, Punta Gorda, Clearwater, Leesburg, Tavares, Orlando, and Kissimmee.[5]

The roots of Florida's growth could be traced to the initiatives of Republicans and northern-born residents during Reconstruction. Ministers of the northern Methodist church in the immediate postwar period had seen northern immigration as central to the future of Florida and its freedmen and had urged the state's attractiveness upon northern newspaper readers. Under the Constitution of 1868, the Republicans created the office of commissioner of lands and immigration, and that official worked to broaden public awareness and interest. Popular writers carried on the work. Harriet Beecher Stowe, of *Uncle Tom's Cabin* fame, settled at Mandarin on the St. Johns River and extolled Florida living in her publications. Similarly, Georgia poet Sidney Lanier's guidebook, published in 1875, portrayed an exotic and pleasing clime filled with opportunities for the newly arrived.[6]

As a result of the publicity, some wealthy northerners perceived possibilities for Florida and launched investments during the 1870s, especially in the easily accessible St. Johns River valley. For example, William Astor planned communities, rehabilitated the moribund rail link between St. Augustine and the St. Johns, and helped to sponsor Jacksonville's commercial expansion. Connecticut-born general and diplomat Henry S. Sanford's activities drew even more attention. With a fortune derived from the Civil War-related industrial boom, he engaged in large-scale citrus and agricultural developments centered upon his town of Sanford. These and similar initiatives vitalized the river valley's economy, encouraging the growth of tourism, spurring the building of resort hotels, and ushering in a golden era of steamboating on the St. Johns and Oklawaha rivers.[7]

Many Floridians looked longingly at the boom times in the St. Johns River area, for the whims of nature and a political deal had deprived them of the one element crucial to their prosperity: easy transportation. Much of the state—particularly the western Panhandle and the peninsula—remained rural and isolated, if inhabited at all. Few navigable waters passed through the sparsely populated regions, and roads consisted mainly of sand tracks that often were muddy bogs when they were not entirely flooded. Railroads answered the need, but in 1870 Republican governor Harrison Reed and former United States senator David Levy Yulee, a Democratic leader, had connived to block the building of lines that would compete with Yulee's Florida Railroad, which was the state's only link between the Atlantic Ocean and the Gulf of Mexico. Their understanding resulted in the granting of a federal court injunction prohibiting the state from using its public lands to support construction of internal improvements. Because a creditor of Yulee's road, Francis Vose, had filed the original suit, the action became known as the Vose injunction.[8]

The Vose injunction's restrictions lasted through the 1870s, until Governor William D. Bloxham arranged to pay Vose's claims in 1881 by selling 4 million acres of state lands to Philadelphia industrialist Hamilton Disston at twenty-five cents an acre. Disston, who needed ready cash to make a down payment, in turn disposed of half his purchase to Sir Edward J. Reed, a British investor and parliamentarian, for $600,000. The two men thereupon embarked upon huge land sales and development campaigns that brought Florida worldwide notice. Disston's Florida Land and Improvement Company, for instance, concentrated upon opening the Kissimmee and Caloosahatchee river valleys for navigation, commerce, and settlement. In the process the tiny cattle outposts of Orlando, Kissimmee, and Fort Myers found themselves expanding into substantial towns, and thousands of immigrants streamed into the remote locations.[9]

The schemes of Disston and Reed depended for their ultimate success upon railroad construction, and, with the Vose injunction no longer standing in the way, state government offered generous bounties in land and other benefits to entrepreneurs who were willing to supply the iron rails and locomotives. Hundreds of individuals and groups stepped forward with proposals, but three men moved into the forefront and dominated Florida's rail network.

In West Florida, the railroad was the Louisville and Nashville and its manager William D. Chipley. In return for what eventually amounted to well over 2 million acres of public lands, Chipley engineered construction eastward from

Pensacola across the Apalachicola River to a junction with existing lines in Middle Florida. A timber industry boom followed the extension of the rails, and Pensacola expanded into a thriving port city.[10]

Despite Chipley's accomplishments, much of West Florida continued to be heavily underpopulated, but a different story unfolded in the peninsula. There, Henry B. Plant and Henry M. Flagler scripted a tale of remarkable achievement. Plant came first. A Connecticut native who had made millions through his Southern Express Company, he began collecting small southern railroads after the Civil War's end. By 1881 he possessed interests in several Florida lines and had linked Jacksonville directly with Savannah. The businessman then pondered further expansions.[11]

Plant's empire blossomed within only a few years. Particularly, in 1883 he gained control of the South Florida Railroad. The line held a state charter to build from the St. Johns to the Gulf, but its money had run out in 1882, with construction completed only from Sanford through Orlando to Kissimmee. Plant also gained rights from, and possibly control of, a second line, the Jacksonville, Tampa, and Key West Railroad, which possessed a similar charter. If he could complete a railroad from Kissimmee to Tampa by January 25, 1884, he would gain 13,840 acres of land from the state for every mile of track he laid. For months crews of thousands of workers, predominantly black, toiled under sometimes inhuman conditions to meet the deadline. Orlando, Kissimmee, and Tampa boomed, while new communities such as Lakeland, Auburndale, Lake Alfred, Winter Haven, and Plant City sprang up from flat land. Finally, on January 23 officials drove the last spike in the line. The St. Johns River to Tampa Bay corridor opened wide for settlement, with Tampa remolded as a resort city destined to become Florida's largest.[12]

Floridians also realized Henry B. Plant's hand in the building of a second major line, the Florida Southern Railroad, chartered to construct a road from Lake City to Charlotte Harbor, with a branch to Palatka. Backers commenced work in 1881. Within five years the tracks passed south through Gainesville, Ocala, Brooksville, and other locales to reach the old Polk County cattlemen's center of Fort Meade. That year, 1886, the work proceeded down the east side of Peace River to Charlotte Harbor, where developer Isaac Trabue had planned a resort community, Punta Gorda. For almost two decades the end of the line in southwestern Florida rested there. Not until 1904 would the tracks be extended to Fort Myers.[13]

Henry B. Plant's great triumphs remain little known, mostly because those of his friend and competitor Henry M. Flagler resulted in much greater accomplishments. Like Plant, Flagler hailed from Connecticut. He had shared a partnership in the Standard Oil Company with John D. Rockefeller. Although he had visited Florida as early as 1878, he began wintering there in 1883–84. Taken with the charm and possibilities of St. Augustine, he determined to make it a world-class resort, beginning with construction of his grand hotel, the Ponce de Leon (now Flagler College). He soon accumulated and improved several short rail lines to link Jacksonville, St. Augustine, and the Daytona area. By 1888 the Ponce de Leon had opened, and two years later his railroad bridges crossed the waters of the St. Johns at Jacksonville and Palatka.[14]

Having accomplished his initial goals, Flagler then gazed upon further horizons. "With the vastness of the Florida east coast south of St. Augustine still undeveloped," a biographer explained, "Flagler next set out to rid himself of his railroad partners and then to control the development of the Florida east coast."[15] In 1892 he ordered construction of rails south from Daytona to New Smyrna. The Florida legislature then offered a new subsidy program, by which the entrepreneur could gain 8,000 acres of public lands for each mile of track laid from Daytona down the coast. Flagler in 1893 reorganized as the Jacksonville, St. Augustine, and Indian River Railway Company and sped crews to work sites. By the next year his rail tracks had reached and passed his new or enhanced towns of West Palm Beach and Palm Beach. In April 1896 they extended to the remote village of Miami.[16]

The legacies left to Florida by Chipley, Plant, and Flagler involved much more than the simple construction of rail lines. The latter two, especially, introduced into the state innovations and a level of sophistication previously unknown or, at least, rarely seen in Florida. Plant's luxurious resorts at Tampa and Punta Gorda vied with Flagler's in locations such as St. Augustine, Ormond, Palm Beach, and Miami. The men either brought to such communities (or influenced others to develop) services as basic as running water and fire-fighting programs or as up-to-date as electrical power, telephone connections, adequate medical facilities, street railway systems, and golf courses. They constructed public buildings, paved town ways, and laid sewers. Modernity touched the state, sparking desires by other locales to emulate the achievements. Beyond that, the financing necessary for such accomplishments compelled the emergence of more efficient banking and insurance systems. Public perception of local bonding for services and facilities changed substantially for the better, with old tales of carpetbagger corruption left behind in drives for the municipal amenities of the late nineteenth century.[17]

Transportation advances and related innovations, in turn, permitted and sparked greater diversity of Florida's economy. Tourism surged, although the visitors primarily represented individuals of substantial means. The cigar industry found homes at Key West, Tampa, and Jacksonville. Agriculture remained an important component of the economy, but new crops including strawberries, celery, watermelons, eggplant, cantaloupes, and grapefruit competed with the antebellum staples of cotton, sugar, and tobacco. Citrus production, which thrived in the central peninsula and around the Peace and Indian river areas, ballooned from 400,000 boxes shipped in 1880 to 5 million in 1894. Southwestern Florida's cattle industry, out of which commercial empires such as the Lykes Corporation grew, also prospered.[18]

Floridians looked increasingly to the state's abundant natural resources as a source of development. In the late 1880s phosphate mining began in the Peace River region and soon expanded to additional locations. New sawmills appeared in the virgin pine forests of the Panhandle and the rich cypress stands of the Gulf coast, producing more than 14 billion board feet of lumber by the century's end. The pine operations also provided northern ship owners with a much needed source of turpentine and other naval stores, while cypress pencils from Florida trees graced offices, schools, and homes throughout the nation. Floridians made greater use, as well, of the resources of the sea. Sponge fishing developed in Key West and Tarpon Springs; seafood became a large industry on both coasts. By 1889, for example, Cedar Key shipped 1 million pounds of mullet annually.[19]

Florida's rosy economy of the 1880s and early 1890s did not extend itself without interruption or impediment. Disease appeared repeatedly, scaring residents and tourists alike. The yellow fever outbreaks of 1887–88 alone took hundreds of lives, and thousands fled the scourge. Fire remained a constant threat, and during this era towns and cities such as Key West, DeLand, and St. Augustine suffered substantial damage. Nationally and regionally, agricultural prices declined, with farmers caught in an ever-tightening credit vise. The state's new industries proved vulnerable to world pricing and demand, just as had agriculture. Phosphate companies additionally suffered from overexpansion and capital shortages, leaving some areas by the mid–1890s struggling for stability. Then, in late 1894 and early 1895 killer freezes ravaged the peninsula. The chilly invasions destroyed farm crops, froze citrus trees to the roots, struck down countless animals in the fields, and left many Floridians in poverty and misery. Still, the state emerged from the Redemption era with great hopes, praying that it now possessed a solid foundation for future prosperity and phenomenal growth.[20]

Great changes in politics and social affairs mirrored Florida's economic transformation. The Redeemers grasped control of the government in 1877, and, for the most part, they resembled the Bourbon Democrats of other southern states. Their ranks encompassed secessionists, planters, industrial entrepreneurs, small businessmen and professionals, some small farmers, and more than a few former Unionists and Republicans. They articulated no unified political philosophy. Nevertheless, they tended to be linked by four tenets: white supremacy, limited government, fiscal austerity, and support for economic investment. The new regime's fiscal policy clarified itself early, when Governor George F. Drew announced in his first address to the legislature: "Spend nothing unless absolutely necessary and pay all bills when made, or at the earliest possible moment thereafter." Warning that "the pruning knife must be used with a fearless and impartial hand," he slashed more than 40 percent of the state's budget, while cutting taxes and reducing state debt.[21]

Drew's pay-as-you-go economic policy meshed well with the Bourbons' belief in less government, and to some extent the times merited it. The Republicans had left the state with a $90,000 deficit and a large bonded indebtedness, with the effects of the national depression brought on by the Panic of 1873 still in evidence. On the other hand, some cuts undermined legitimate advances under the Republicans and harmed the state in the long run. Florida's public school system, for instance, suffered from underfunding; nonetheless, Bourbons eventually reduced the already inadequate support by half. When the trustees of the Florida Agricultural College voted in 1877 to move the school from Eau Gallie to a central location, Drew immediately closed the college, leaving the state without a comprehensive institution of higher learning. Redeemer efforts to make the prison system self-supporting led to the establishment of one of the harshest institutions in state history, the convict lease system.[22]

For Bourbon rule's first eight years, circumstances compelled Redeemers to proceed with their reforms at a slower pace than extreme Democrats preferred. For one thing, Drew, a former Republican, held moderate views on some questions. His successor William D. Bloxham articulated more conservative ideas, but he sometimes showed a paternalistic interest in problems of the state's racial minority. Additionally, the Constitution of 1868 and state law afforded protections to black political participation, and black representatives continued to serve in the legislature in numbers similar to those evidenced during Reconstruction. The potential for a political alliance of blacks and disaffected Democrats remained high. Also, the possibility of federal interference muted some initiatives.[23]

Given the limitations, once in power Democrats acted quickly to solidify their hold on the state's political machinery. Using the sweeping powers of appointment bestowed on him by the Constitution of 1868, Drew packed state and local offices with the party faithful, reserving only an occasional minor office for a conservative black. In 1877 the general assembly passed legislation proposed by Drew that required a complete purging of county voter rolls to eliminate the false registrations that, it was argued, characterized many precincts. Democratic county commissioners would then conduct a new registration process. This measure perhaps helped to remedy the electoral fraud that had plagued some elections in the 1870s, but it also permitted Democrats to weaken further the Republican party and raised the possibility of the eventual disfranchisement of black voters.[24]

As the transition to Democratic control proceeded, Republicans gamely attempted to hold on to their offices. Most white loyalists had withdrawn from the party, though, and growing numbers of African Americans over time were choosing to refrain from voting rather than support white carpetbaggers. Regardless, as late as 1880 black Republican George Washington Witherspoon was probably denied West Florida's congressional seat through electoral shenanigans, while white Republican Horatio Bisbee represented East Florida until 1885. Bloxham's gubernatorial victory of 1880 came with widespread complaints of fraud and irregularities, and one historian concluded that the Bourbons were compelled to use "extreme measures to keep the state from going Republican."[25] Given black immigration into towns and cities, Republican power in many urban areas surged in the 1880s, with Fernandina, Pensacola, Key West, St. Augustine, and numerous other places often dominated by the party.[26]

Many more extreme Democrats were unwilling to acquiesce in a Republican renaissance. In 1884, they coalesced around the gubernatorial candidacy of Pensacola's Edward A. Perry. Behind the one-time Confederate general stood a coterie of influential conservatives, including West Florida's William D. Chipley, General William Miller, Confederate senator Augustus Emmet Maxwell, Milton attorney George Gray McWhorter, and future United States senator Charles W. Jones. They wrested the nomination from Governor Bloxham and backed a platform that called for a constitutional convention. In order to appeal to voters in the developing peninsula, Perry accepted a young Leesburg lawyer, Mississippi-born Milton Harvey Mabry, as his ticketmate for lieutenant governor.[27]

The Perry slate faced strong opposition. Two years earlier some disenchanted Democrats had combined with a part of the Republican leadership in the Independent movement. In 1884 the Independents rebounded mightily with the gubernatorial candidacy of Madison County's Frank W. Pope. The anti-Bourbon coalition—which expressed full support for more and better schools, fairer election laws, and full voting rights regardless of race—attracted many black Republicans. In the end, the Democrats triumphed amid cries of ballot-box stealing and other electoral frauds. The winning margin came from South

Florida's newly swelled voter rolls, where former Confederates from other states turned out for Perry and Mabry.[28]

The new administration moved quickly following the January 1885 inaugural. On the one hand, Governor Perry rewarded his supporters by securing approval of a state pension for Confederate veterans. With the other hand, he sent a strong signal to his political opponents. Using his Republican-controlled hometown of Pensacola as an example, the governor arranged for passage of legislation abolishing Pensacola's charter and vesting control of its government in Perry's designees. The action succeeded in placing Pensacola under conservative control, but it failed to stem black and Republican power in other municipalities. Accordingly, before the decade's end Democrats utilized the same strategy to divest Republicans of authority in Key West and Jacksonville.[29]

Next came the summer's constitutional convention. Ever since the Democrats had regained state control, calls had arisen for revision of the 1868 charter. Still, for the most part the response before 1884 had been lukewarm. Unlike some other southern constitutions drafted by Reconstruction conventions, Florida's had resulted from a coalition between Democrats (then called conservatives) and moderate Republicans. It had preserved the franchise for ex-Confederates, apportioned the legislature to favor Democratic counties, and ensured white control of predominantly black counties by giving the governor power to appoint county officials. When serious need for revision had presented itself, the amending process had afforded opportunity for reasonable satisfaction. Voters had specifically rejected a convention in 1880, with many white Democrats in black counties supporting the existing system of gubernatorial appointment of local officers. Thousands of Democrats in other areas simply believed that they could control the opposition by other means.[30]

The call for the 1885 convention ultimately emerged from the factionalization of the Democratic party. Its members divided themselves on the basis of personal philosophies, sectionalism, and patronage. Antipathy between George F. Drew and William D. Bloxham framed politics as a matter of personality as much as party loyalty, to the chagrin of moderates. The Disston purchase drew criticism from Drew supporters who accused Bloxham of corruption, from taxpayers who questioned the favorable terms that Disston had received, and from land squatters who would be compelled to relocate. Moreover, isolated South Florida residents objected to the Bloxham administration's apparent commitment to the development of the Panhandle at their expense. Finally, younger party members resented the preference in county appointments that older Democrats received. Many of the discontented Democrats supported the Independents and then cast a favorable vote in November 1884 for a convention.

Numerous old-line Democrats joined them, as did a substantial faction of Republicans who believed that the authorization of local elections would return control of many counties to their party. The tally reflected overwhelming approval for revision.[31]

Democrats controlled the convention, which met in June 1885, by a large majority. The resulting document represented compromise between party factions, as determined in party caucuses. It borrowed liberally from the 1868 charter but contained significant alterations. The Declaration of Rights that opened the new constitution reiterated virtually every guarantee of its predecessor, but, with symbolic importance, drafters changed the assertion that "all men are by nature free and equal" to a guarantee that "all men are equal before the law." As discussed in chapter 15, delegates voted for an elective supreme court. They decentralized state government. In the process they stripped the governor of much of his power by making the cabinet and many other state and local offices elective, but they left control of county commissions in the governor's hands so as to ensure Democratic oversight of elections. Public schools received continued authorization, except that the law would require them to be racially segregated. As to the right to the ballot, the Democrats approved ominous changes. They authorized the legislature to "enact such laws as will preserve the purity of the ballot given under this Constitution." More important, they submitted for ratification a provision permitting enactment of laws requiring payment of a poll tax as a prerequisite for voting.[32]

Almost one and a half years elapsed after the convention's adjournment and the ratification election of November 1886, and political developments of significance occurred during the period. First, the plight of farmers throughout the South increased as crop prices sagged and the power of corporations grew. Increasingly rural residents looked upon railroads as an enemy, with calls issuing forth for state regulation of their rates and operations. Simultaneously, a national labor union, the Knights of Labor, initiated widespread organizational efforts in the region, including within their ambit thousands of black workers. In Florida the union combined with some black Republican leaders to seize control of Key West city government and to field some legislative candidates and one congressional aspirant. In the situation, voters approved the constitution and the poll tax authorization, while electing a legislature determined to regulate railroads and resist the potential threat of the Knights and their black allies. Three months later the Knights coalition took control of Jacksonville.[33]

With these events well in mind, the legislature, when it met in April 1887, took several steps. First, it opted not to impose the poll tax immediately, but it did further tighten voter registration procedures and permitted municipal reorganizations based upon a system that isolated black voters into one or two wards. With respect to Fernandina and Palatka, it required wards. Then, the legislators added the state's first law mandating racial segregation on railroads. Further, with regard to the transportation companies, it responded to farmer discontent by creating a state railroad commission for regulatory purposes and placing certain legal restrictions on the carriers' activities.[34]

During the remainder of 1887 and through 1888, political tensions boiled. The Knights organization spread deep into the Panhandle and the peninsula, scoring electoral victories in a number of locales. At general elections held in November 1888 came achievements that the Bourbons could not overlook. With Knights' support, black candidates won election as sheriff and county judge of Monroe County and as clerk of the circuit court and criminal court judge in Duval County. In the next few months, St. Augustine and Palatka residents followed the trend by voting themselves under Republican control.[35]

Retribution came when legislators convened for their 1889 session. They imposed a poll tax and other restrictions on registration and voting, including a complicated "eight ballot-box" system. The solons rechartered St. Augustine under the ward system and placed government at Key West and Jacksonville in the governor's hands. The actions broke the power of the Knights organization and sundered all hopes for a Republican resurgence. Effectively, many poor people, black and white, were deprived of the franchise and direct participation in state politics. The doors that had opened with passage of the Reconstruction acts in 1867 and 1868 had been slammed shut with finality.[36]

By taxing the privilege of voting, the 1889 elections law revisions also broke the back of the farmers' revolt in Florida before it had effectively begun. The national Farmers' Alliance held its annual meeting in the state in 1890 and issued its famous "Ocala Demands" for reform, but the local organization failed to muster sufficient support even for a bill to enhance the powers of the state railroad commission. As a result, pro-railroad legislators joined with disillusioned reformers in 1891 to abolish the commission entirely. The next year the Populists, a third party that germinated from Alliance activities, could not defeat the gubernatorial candidacy of Bourbon leader and one-time supreme court justice Henry Laurens Mitchell nor take control of the legislature. Accordingly, the initiatives for reform and regulation awaited a new political day that would have to dawn after 1896.[37]

The voting law restrictions of 1889 symbolized, as well, a new era of race relations patterns in Florida. During the Reconstruction period some limited advances were achieved toward a racially integrated society, at least in the sense of public accommodations, transportation, and institutions. Redeemers did not immediately repeal the laws that served as a foundation for equal access, and neither did they quickly pass laws mandating racial segregation. By the early 1880s some facilities and transportation companies, reacting to or anticipating white demands, began to insist upon racial segregation in seating and service. In 1882 the determination of African Methodist Episcopal bishop Daniel A. Payne in resisting forced segregation on a train delayed for several years the full implementation of what would soon be called Jim Crow seating. Even after the 1887 legislature passed the state's first Jim Crow law, which required racial segregation in seating on railroad cars, some lines resisted its enforcement. Not until 1891 did Florida legislators craft an act that effectively brought racial segregation to the railroads and ushered in an era when the iron rule of Jim Crow split society firmly—and seemingly irrevocably—upon racial grounds.[38]

Chapter 15

The Post-Reconstruction Court

During the twenty years that followed Reconstruction's end in 1877, the supreme court experienced profound alterations in personnel, perspective, method of its selection, constitutional authority, and other important matters. Yet for most of the period's first decade the tribunal remained as it had existed beginning in 1874. Two conservative Republicans, Chief Justice Edwin M. Randall and Associate Justice Robert Bruce Van Valkenburgh, sat with moderate Democrat James Diament Westcott, Jr. As will be considered in chapter 16, the jurists maintained the court's reputation for bipartisan collegiality, integrity, and sober—if not innovative—decision making.

The court reached a fundamentally important turning point in January 1885, when former Confederate general Edward A. Perry assumed office as governor. Within hours, two of the three justices had resigned. Randall, almost sixty-three years of age, desired to spend more time at his Jacksonville home and to buttress his personal finances with income from a private law partnership. An ailing Westcott required all his energies to battle the health problems to which he would succumb two years later. The vacancies permitted Perry to remold the tribunal dramatically. He turned to two fellow West Floridians who had associated closely with him in Democratic politics. To replace Randall, he chose Milton lawyer George Gray McWhorter, a former Democratic speaker of the Florida house of representatives, Democratic presidential elector, and Perry campaign aide. George Pettus Raney, who followed Westcott, possessed similar credentials. He had served as a Democrat in the house of representatives, designed party legal initiatives that resulted in the supreme court's decision in favor of Democratic gubernatorial candidate George F. Drew, acted as state attorney general for Drew and his successor William D. Bloxham, and urged Perry's election in 1884.[1]

Democratic organs and party advocates exulted in Perry's choices. The Tallahassee *Weekly Floridian* typically praised the "high legal standing" of the new justices.[2] Jacksonville attorney L. I. Fleming lauded Raney as "one of the most honorable, capable, upright and in every way fitting men that could possibly have been found in the state."[3] In the same vein, McWhorter, who was not well known outside the Panhandle area, received acknowledgment of his reputation as "a gentleman of sterling integrity, possessing a well stored and highly cultivated mind."[4]

The January 1885 designations reoriented the court's perspective on key issues with substantial repercussions for Floridians; but the year still was young, and further changes were in the offing. At the Democrat-dominated constitutional convention that met in June, delegates reconsidered the judicial branch's structure, the supreme court's role, and the method of judicial selection. Without too much rancor, debates resulted in a series of amendments that provided more flexibility and authority in the county and circuit courts and permitted creation of criminal courts of record in the relatively urban counties of Escambia and Duval. One new provision pleased black leaders. "The Justice-of-the-Peace Court system has been a wholesale disfranchising machine to disqualify blacks," explained Duval delegate Thomas V. Gibbs. "About 3,000 voters for trivial offences or on trumped up charges have been disfranchised." He continued, "This, under the proposed constitution, if ratified, will be stopped, as only courts of record can impose penalties which carry with them disfranchisement."[5]

The changes also conferred on the supreme court a somewhat expanded jurisdiction. The language finally approved specified for the panel "appellate jurisdiction in all cases at law and in equity originating in Circuit Courts, and of appeal from the Circuit Courts in cases arising before Judges of the County Courts in matters pertaining to their probate jurisdiction and in the management of the estates of infants, and in cases of conviction of felony in the criminal courts, and in all criminal cases originating in the Circuit Courts." Drafters carried over from the Constitution of 1868 powers regarding the issuance of writs. Also, the new state charter subjected justices to the same constitutional qualifications as did the 1868 document, requiring them to be attorneys of at least twenty-five years of age.[6]

Controversy ensued when delegates turned to consideration of methods of judicial selection. Each of the four previous state constitutional conventions had witnessed major debates on the subject, and Florida had experimented with various permutations of judicial election, gubernatorial appointment, life tenure, and fixed judicial terms ranging from six to eight years. In 1885, with state government securely in Democratic control, many party members demanded popular election. "All important offices should be filled by the sovereign power, that power, here, being the people," insisted one influential official.[7] Some leaders in black-majority counties dissented, though, wary of ushering an era of black county judges and justices of the peace. "I can conceive of no greater local misfortune happening to our people," typically declared a conservative lawyer.[8] Similarly the influential Jacksonville *Florida Times-Union* argued, "Under the elective system . . . the honors will always be carried off by the Oily Gammons of the profession."[9] Hopeful that the worried Democrats were correct about the local elections, some Republicans also supported popular selection.[10]

With the convention's judicial article committee almost evenly split on the issue, a Democratic caucus resolved the dilemma through compromise. Circuit judgeships would remain subject to gubernatorial appointment, while justices and other local judicial officers would stand for election. In the case of justices, the decision came only after assurances to pro-appointment delegates that the court's members would be given terms long enough to insulate them from direct popular pressures. "The Bourbons got the circuit Judges and County Commissioners appointive, thus saving their election machinery," noted Delegate Gibbs, "and the Liberals succeeded in having the Supreme Bench, county Judges, and Justices of the Peace made elective."[11]

As finally agreed, the first election for court members would be held at the general election in 1888, to take office in January 1889. Each candidate would run for one of three supreme court justice positions, with the victors casting lots for selection of a chief justice. Except for members chosen at the first election, each justice would serve a six-year term. Lots would be utilized to determine length of initial terms beginning in 1889, with one justice retaining office for two years, one for four years, and one for the full term.[12]

As it became clear that the state's new constitution would entrench Bourbon rule in Florida, Republican delegates led by former Chief Justice Randall, who represented Duval County, successfully demanded that the charter be subjected to popular ratification. The effort paid off in forcing Bourbons to moderate some of their more extreme positions. A key issue arose as to when to hold the ratification election. Republicans favored an immediate vote, whereas Democrats feared that, if ratification were the only issue on the ballot, the Republicans could mobilize their constituents to defeat the document. The Democratic majority prevailed, and voters approved the constitution at the general election held late in 1886.[13]

With judicial elections not scheduled until 1888, Governor Perry enjoyed an additional opportunity to work his impact upon the court. In mid–1887 Justice McWhorter resigned his seat to accept appointment to the state's railroad commission. The governor replaced him with a Pensacola friend, Augustus Emmet Maxwell, who had represented Florida in the Confederate Senate, sat on the supreme bench in 1866, and presided as judge of the first circuit under governors Drew and Bloxham. Also a delegate to the 1885 constitutional convention, Maxwell had chaired the committee on the executive department. In August 1888 Justice Van Valkenburgh died, and, by then, power had begun to flow away from Perry's office. One historian remarked that, under the Constitution of 1885, "the Democratic state convention . . . replace[d] the governorship as the most important political institution in Florida."[14] As if to pay homage to that fact, Perry appointed Tampa lawyer and circuit judge Henry Laurens Mitchell, the party's previously selected court nominee. With the designation, the tribunal's bipartisan composition ended.[15]

The elections of 1888 returned to the court the Democratic activists who already sat upon it. By a large majority justices Raney, Maxwell, and Mitchell overwhelmed their Republican opponents, former Chief Justice Edwin M. Randall, Jesse H. Goss, and Charles Swayne. The victory represented, as earlier forecast by the *Florida Times-Union*, "an unqualified indorsement of the appointments originally made by Governor Perry."[16] When the winners took their oath of office in January 1889, they acted to determine their tenure. As a method of casting lots, each man opened a book and looked at the first letter of the page's first word. The jurist who chanced upon the letter nearest to the first letter of his last name won. Raney drew the six-year term, and Mitchell gained one of four years. In a separate lottery, Raney also attained the chief justiceship.[17]

When the first elected court under the new constitution met on January 9, the tribunal continued to hold its sessions in the south wing of the capitol, constructed in 1845. Located on the first floor, the room lay directly beneath the senate chamber. Befitting its pioneer origins, the courtroom's atmosphere remained informal. Inexpensive bookshelves lined the walls, and upon them sat the court's inadequate library. During the winter months lawyers and justices would congregate around two plain wood fireplaces at opposite ends of the room. An 1882 visitor commented that the space resembled neither "a severely official appearing apartment" nor a room "of the awe-inspiring style so usual with court rooms." Rather, he found "a decidedly cosey, domestic appearance, quite pleasant and reassuring."[18] Most of the furnishings derived from the original 1845 purchase, although the court received new carpeting and some additional furniture in 1887. The justices typically shared an office until 1891, when workers partitioned a small area of the capitol lobby so that each court member could enjoy private space.[19]

Most lawyers who appeared before the court through the Redemption era were white. An account of its organization in 1889, for instance, mentioned fifteen white lawyers in attendance, as well as Attorney General William B. Lamar and Judge E. K. Foster. The jurists and the advocates socialized easily, attending together that evening an elegant ball at Tallahassee's Leon Hotel.

Often, though, African-American attorneys practiced before the court's bar. The case of Isaac Lawrence Purcell offers an example. After leaving law studies at the University of South Carolina in 1877, Purcell relocated to Palatka, where he studied law privately. In 1889 he qualified for admission to the local bar, followed two years later by an appearance before the state's highest tribunal. "Our ambitious young men, and our hopeful old men, were cheered by the appearance of I. L. Purcell, Esq., in the supreme court this week," boasted the black-owned *Florida Sentinel*. "Palatka is justly proud of this rising young attorney, and the entire state can unite in the boast."[20] Purcell believed that he received fair treatment before the supreme court, noting that it "meted out to the Negro even against the white man a lenient form of justice."[21]

The evolution in court personnel experienced new movement in 1891. In January, Leesburg attorney Milton Harvey Mabry took a seat. Governor Perry's one-time lieutenant governor had secured the 1890 Democratic nomination for Justice Maxwell's place on the bench and had won easily in November. Also in January 1891, Justice Mitchell resigned to accept a circuit judgeship, preparatory to entering the governor's race in 1892. Governor Francis P. Fleming, a one-time Jacksonville attorney, turned for his replacement to Gainesville lawyer Robert Fenwick Taylor. As had become traditional, Taylor enjoyed a reputation as "one of the most faithful workers in the Democratic ranks."[22] He had represented Alachua County in the 1885 constitutional convention, where his law partner, Edward C. F. Sanchez, had chaired the judicial article committee. The appointment met with popular approval, as voters elected Taylor to his own term in 1892.[23]

The new court evidenced a generational shift. For the first time men born after statehood composed the panel. Two of the three—Raney and Mabry—had received legal training at law schools rather than by reading law, and only Raney had served in the Civil War. The trend extended itself in 1894. Chief Justice Raney resigned to resume private practice and now-governor Henry Laurens Mitchell named forty-year-old Benjamin Sullivan Liddon of Marianna, a well-regarded West Florida lawyer who had served as counsel to the state railroad commission. Voters ratified the choice that November.[24]

Thus, the Redemption era brought six new justices to the supreme court. As discussed in chapter 16, they facilitated significant changes in Florida politics, law, and society. Before examining those changes, a closer look at each of the individuals is merited.

George Gray McWhorter, Supreme Court Chief Justice, 1885–1887

The Redemption era's first new supreme court appointee was George Gray McWhorter. The fifth of eight children born to Alwyn Amzi and Sarah Hamlin

McWhorter, he came into the world on February 27, 1833, at Coosada, Autauga County, Alabama. His father, a lawyer and cotton grower, prospered from the gains of his Coosa River plantation and, by 1840, already owned fifty-four slaves. The senior McWhorter, according to one source, "gave his children good opportunities for education," but George preferred "the freedom and sports of country life more than he did the confinement of institutions of learning."[25]

Although he ultimately attended the universities of Alabama and Georgia, young McWhorter "did not settle down early to any definite line of life."[26] Then, in 1856, he married Mary Louise Roche of Columbia, South Carolina, and the following year set out to discover opportunities in remote Santa Rosa County, Florida. Family legend indicates that Mary Louise, who enjoyed the delights of antebellum society in Montgomery, resisted the move. As their stagecoach plodded through piney woods north of Milton, the couple heard the cries of a panther. "Grandmother was terrified lest one should leap from a limb onto the back of one of the horses," remembered a descendant, "and then proceed to devour us all!" Perhaps as a result of her reservations, the two young people remained only a few months at Milton before relocating to Birmingham. There George read the law. They returned to Milton in 1859, where he honored a promise to erect them a fine home.[27]

McWhorter achieved admission to the bar the year of his Milton homecoming and over time earned a reputation as a skillful and eloquent attorney, particularly in representing local timber and, eventually, railroad interests. "His power of concentrating analytical thought enabled him to cut directly through irrelevant matter to the heart of the subject," recalled a fellow practitioner, "[and] he had strength before a jury that was almost irresistible."[28] A senior Jacksonville attorney once watched McWhorter argue before the supreme court. "[I] was forcibly struck with his easy and able conduct of his case," the man related. "He impressed me as a learned lawyer, one familiar with the law as a science and well versed with the common and statute laws of the land."[29]

The Civil War and Reconstruction years launched McWhorter into politics. He was already disposed by background to support the antebellum southern way of life, and the war seemed to harden his sentiments. Perhaps some of the underlying causes can be traced to two Union raids on Milton during 1862. During the first Mary Louise was compelled to flee to the city jail for refuge when gunfire erupted near their home. On the second occasion, with no warning, Minie balls from Union guns shattered her front windows, again sending her fleeing. After the unpleasantness the family refuged at Montgomery until the conflict's end. When they returned in 1865 their home still stood, but its interior had been stripped by Union soldiers down to and including the doorknobs and mantelpieces.[30]

The future justice's services to the Confederacy are uncertain, but upon his return to Florida McWhorter quickly joined with a coterie of fervent West Florida Confederate supporters that included his old friend and fellow lawyer General Edward A. Perry, General William Miller, Confederate senator Augustus Emmet Maxwell, future United States senator Charles W. Jones, and Colonel William D. Chipley. The group formed the backbone of the Democratic party in West Florida for the remainder of the century. Their politics stressed the hard edge of white resistance to Reconstruction.[31]

Political involvement led McWhorter into high government office in 1877. His Democratic associates had aligned themselves with area lawyers, merchants, and small farmers to demand state support for construction of a railroad in the Panhandle. West Florida had played a crucial role in the redemption of Florida, they argued. If the state would not reward them by sponsoring a rail line and developing Pensacola's port, they threatened to seek annexation into Alabama. McWhorter had won election in 1876 to the house of representatives, and the bloc's members demonstrated their strength immediately upon arrival in Tallahassee the following January by securing McWhorter elevation to the speakership.[32]

McWhorter left the legislature following his two-year term, but he continued his active involvement in Democratic politics. In 1880 he canvassed the state for the party's candidates, and two years afterward friends promoted him for Congress as "a highly accomplished gentleman, a powerful and eloquent speaker, and a steadfast and consistent democrat."[33] During the 1884 general election his oratorical skills served the party well. The Independent movement was attempting to fuse a coalition of moderate Democrats and Republicans against Bourbon rule, and leaders such as the future justice went on the attack. At Lake City, for example, McWhorter, in the words of an approving newspaper account, "blended facts, fun, argument and sledge-hammer blows at Independentism, and prophesied a glorious victory for the nominees of the Pensacola and Chicago [Democratic] Conventions."[34] That year he cast one of Florida's electoral college ballots for Democrat Grover Cleveland, the first party president since the Civil War.[35]

One aspect of McWhorter's 1884 political activities resulted in his placement on the supreme court. Edward A. Perry secured the Democratic gubernatorial nomination after a bitter struggle with more moderate former governors George F. Drew and William D. Bloxham. McWhorter stood shoulder to shoulder with his friend, enjoying the honor of nominating Perry. When Chief Justice Randall resigned in January 1885, Governor Perry quickly chose McWhorter to fill the vacancy. Relatively unknown outside West Florida, his elevation nonetheless pleased Bourbon leaders. "I have no acquaintance with Chief Justice McWhorter," one such individual declared, "but understand he is a good lawyer, which is the first requisite of a good and able judge."[36]

The chief justice's brief tenure on the court proved serviceable but not spectacular. On July 1, 1887, having occupied his seat for only a little more than two years, he resigned from the bench in order to accommodate Governor Perry's request that he chair the newly established Florida Railroad Commission. One cynical editor, who clearly believed that McWhorter was unwilling to apply himself, predicted his early resignation as commissioner "if the position required him to write out opinions and be kept busy as a school-master solving difficult problems."[37] The Democratic press generally praised the appointment, suggesting that the partisan editors did not consider him indispensable on the court. Fellow justices remembered him more favorably. "While he sat upon this bench he performed well and ably his share of its labors," their memorial declared. "The especial characteristics of the opinions delivered by him are clearness, sound reasoning and brevity without obscurity."[38]

Unlike colleagues such as George Pettus Raney, who enjoyed Tallahassee social life, McWhorter's "literary tastes and domestic habits incline[d] him to private rather than public life."[39] Nevertheless, he commanded respect for his intellect and good humor. "Probably there is not a more profound thinker in the State," asserted one newspaper, "and he is distinguished for the lucid, clear-cut ideas which he entertains on all important subjects." The account added: "He remembers everything he reads, he never forgets anything, not even a joke, and he is hard to beat telling one. He is a giant, physically and intellectually."[40]

Health problems, especially rheumatism, beset an aging McWhorter. He unsuccessfully sought treatment at New Orleans, but the malady forced him on April 30, 1891, to resign from the railroad commission. He returned to his country home in Santa Rosa County, where he died on May 21, 1891. Explained a Pensacola friend, "For several months just preceding his death the disease became complicated with some affection which caused occasional spasmodic difficulty in his breathing, so that it was necessary to keep constant watch over him, especially when asleep."[41] An obituary recalled, "As a judge, in the short time he was on the supreme court bench, he made a good reputation, and was greatly respected and admired by the members of the bar." The notice concluded, "His memory will long be cherished and honored by the people of Florida."[42]

George Pettus Raney, Supreme Court Justice, 1885–1889; Supreme Court Chief Justice, 1889–1894

Florida's second new justice in 1885, George Pettus Raney, was born at Apalachicola on October 11, 1845. His parents, David Greenway Raney, a merchant, and Harriet Frances (Jordan) Raney, were native Virginians who had met after David moved to Florida in 1826. George's early education came primarily from a tutor, W. W. Fay. In 1862 he entered the University of Virginia but withdrew a year later to enlist in the Confederate Army. Raney served as a private in Georgia and Florida before attaining the rank of sergeant major. At the war's end he returned to Charlottesville, where he studied law. In 1867 Raney achieved admission to the bar in Florida and established a practice at Apalachicola.[43]

Political involvements arrived hand in hand with Raney's law practice. In 1868 he won election as a conservative (Democrat) to represent Franklin County in the first state legislature under the Reconstruction constitution. He assumed an active role in that body, standing as his party's candidate for house speaker and serving as chairman of the judiciary committee. As a legislative leader, Raney played a prominent role in the various attempts to impeach Republican governor Harrison Reed. His appearance was described a few years afterward by an acquaintance. "Raney is of fair height, with rather slender physique," the man commented. "His feature[s] are acquiline, more so from the fact that he discards beard or mustache." He added, "He is a fluent and forcible speaker, and bears the reputation of being a sound, well-read lawyer."[44]

Legislator Raney enjoyed Tallahassee life and in 1869 opted to make the town his home. He first practiced law there with Anderson J. Peeler, then for two years beginning in 1873 partnered with Mariano D. Papy, Florida's antebellum attorney general. During this time Raney also served as a Leon County commissioner. On November 4, 1873, he married Mary Elizabeth Lamar in Athens, Georgia. Elizabeth, the daughter of Thompson B. and Sarah Bailey Lamar, was the niece of United States Supreme Court Justice Lucius Q. C. Lamar.[45]

During Reconstruction and Redemption, Raney worked prominently on behalf of the Democratic party and the state. In the crucial election year of 1876, he served on the party's executive committee and as a candidate for presidential elector. He also formulated the plan to use mandamus and injunctive relief to secure George F. Drew's gubernatorial victory. He then helped to represent Drew in his related suit before the supreme court. The litigation's outcome ended Republican rule in Florida. As a reward, Drew appointed Raney as his attorney general, a position that Raney retained upon the election of Drew's successor, William D. Bloxham. In the position his most important work revolved around his role as counsel for the state's internal improvement fund. He represented it in the numerous lawsuits that emanated from legislative land grants to railroads and canal builders, bond issues to finance railroads, and the default and sale of failed railroad ventures supported by the state. In 1881 he assisted in negotiations with Philadelphia industrialist Hamilton Disston for the purchase of 4 million acres of publicly owned lands, a transaction that permitted the state to free itself from federal receivership and spurred an explosion of railroad building.[46]

During this time the future justice substantially influenced the practice and administration of the law. Particularly, he wrote a manual of evidence and procedure for justices of the peace and county judges. He also joined with John A. Henderson and Pleasant W. White in revising James F. McClellan's *Digest of the Laws of Florida*, which revision was published in 1881. Raney's manual and *McClellan's Digest* were the only compilation of Florida statutes and rules of procedure available to state practitioners, and they became required reading for lawyers throughout Florida.[47]

Raney's supreme court tenure began on January 13, 1885, when Governor Edward A. Perry named him to succeed Justice James Diament Westcott, Jr. The two justices were close personally and professionally, and Westcott's influence may have prompted Perry's action. Three years after Raney's initial appointment, in the first judicial elections under the Constitution of 1885, voters continued his incumbency as one of three justices. He drew a six-year term by lot. Selected also by chance as chief justice, Raney became the first native Floridian to hold that post.[48]

As might be expected from someone with his extensive knowledge of Florida law, Raney left a significant mark upon the supreme court, authoring more than three hundred opinions. His jurisprudential philosophy might best be described as conservative. He refused to countenance the view that judges must consider changing social circumstances when interpreting the constitution. Chief Justice Jefferson B. Browne remembered that Raney opposed the "monstrous doctrine" that popular will, "rather than the constitution, should be the guide for the courts." Raney rebuked the "disciples of the new creed" who believed that "whatever fad or fancy might temporarily gain ascendancy . . . must be given full sway," even if it "trespasses upon the rights of property and of personal liberty."[49] Yet the justice could not be considered simply a doctrinaire adherent of laissez-faire philosophy. In his most significant opinions—those regarding the constitutionality of legislative efforts to regulate railroads—he balanced the rights of corporations to earn a profit against the state's power to regulate in the public interest. Raney proved himself a quintessential common-law judge, as well, filling his opinions with pages of encyclopedic references to the decisions of other states' courts. Francis Beauregard Carter remarked that "his opinions are models of completeness, replete with citations sustaining his conclusions, clear and satisfactory in criticism of opposing authorities." The justice added, "While many of his opinions seem lengthy, they are not unduly so, but are merely thorough."[50]

Raney's service on the court ended on May 31, 1894, when he resigned to return to private practice and, soon, active political life. For the first three years he associated with John A. Henderson, then finished his career in partnership with a nephew, Judge William J. Oven. The one-time justice specialized in representing railroads, earning a reputation as a fierce advocate. One Jacksonville attorney recalled his first meeting with Raney at a strategy session of railroad lawyers. "It occurred to me that in what was called a conference, we, who were visitors, talked, Judge Raney decided, and about all that was left was a petition for rehearing, with the usual results," he noted. "I reported to my people that I felt co-operation with Judge Raney was impossible."[51]

After the turn of the century Raney spent much of his time representing client interests before the state railroad commission. Beginning in 1903 he did so as division counsel of the Seaboard Air Line Railway, an appointment that caused controversy. The former justice then served as state senator from Leon County, and some persons speculated upon the potential for conflict of interest. Raney apparently considered resigning from the legislature but soon announced that he would "serve out his term in that office the same as if the [railroad] appointment had not been made at this time."[52] As one of his first actions as division counsel, Raney negotiated a settlement between the railroad and the railroad commission, which had complained of the line's poor passenger accommodations in Tallahassee. The commissioners thereupon suspended their investigation, and the railroad agreed to make certain improvements.[53]

As suggested by the 1903 controversy, Raney early returned to the political arena. In 1896 he appeared on Florida ballots as a candidate for presidential elector, and, by the next year, supporters had pressed his candidacy before the legislature for election to the United States Senate. In that instance the lawyer's ties to railroad interests sparked sufficient opposition to forestall a Raney victory. He represented the state on the national Democratic executive committee from 1900 to 1904. Already, Leon County voters had sent him to the state house in 1899, followed by four years in the senate beginning in 1903. He also held numerous offices in the state and local party organizations.[54]

During these postcourt years, Raney gained a reputation for offering a helping hand to aspiring young attorneys and also for the strength of his personality as a lawyer. He assisted several men in preparation for the bar, examining their knowledge in nightly meetings at his home. On the other hand, while he treated young county judges with "the same gracious deference which he would have shown to the Supreme Court of the United States," he sometimes gave them unsolicited advice. Reportedly, on one occasion a probate judge abandoned Raney in the middle of a legal argument to answer a fire alarm as a volunteer fireman. When the jurist returned, "he discovered that Judge Raney had waited patiently, and the latter quietly but firmly suggested that since he, the county judge, had now assumed an official county position, he should resign his connection with the fire department." Concluded the report, "Naturally, the advice was promptly heeded."[55]

As one of Tallahassee's well-respected citizens, Raney led an active social life. In doing so, though, he was a creature of habit, and his familiar dress and mannerisms evoked strong images. A friend described him in later years as a "tall, spare man." He continued, "The broad white shirt front, the black tie, long coat and lighter trousers, the soft felt hat, all picturing a countenance whose [complexion] was more sallow than pale, a clean-shaven face, a nose more Roman than acquiline, thin hair, piercing eyes, but more than anything else, I was impressed by the convergence of the lips, indicating a man of much force."[56] Similarly, a biographer commented: "He always wore, according to the custom of his early years, a long frock coat, in the rear pocket of which he almost always carried pecan nuts, which he would take out and crack and eat during his progress down the street. He varied this practice by sometimes blowing a tuneless whistle through his teeth, an indication of great concentration."[57]

Raney took great pride in his state and his city and strongly backed them both. He once applauded students at Tallahassee's Florida State College for attending school in the state, telling them that they were "forming attachments that will in after life make you feel that there is something to be proud of in proclaiming wherever you are: I am a Floridian."[58] In 1905 he helped to found the Florida Historical Society. On the local level, he bitterly fought attempts to move the state capital from Tallahassee. In 1900 he campaigned throughout the state on the issue, exclaiming to audiences that "I love the red clay hills of dear old Leon."[59]

While Justice Raney's last decade held wonderful moments, the years encompassed tragedy, as well. His first wife died as the nineteenth century neared its end. Then, on November 13, 1901, he remarried to Evelyn Bird Cameron, sister of Virginia governor William Evelyn Cameron. Within one year, while Raney visited Apalachicola, she burned to death in a tragic accident. Raney's health suffered thereafter. During the summer of 1910 he fell ill and was persuaded by doctors to vacation in the mountains of New England. He returned to his law practice that fall, apparently fully restored, but early in the new year he contracted pneumonia. On January 8, 1911, he died at his Tallahassee home, aged sixty-five years.[60]

Henry Laurens Mitchell, Supreme Court Justice, 1888–1891

South Floridians found representation on the supreme court in 1888, with the appointment of Henry Laurens Mitchell. The new justice was born on September 3, 1831, in Jefferson County, Alabama, the child of Thomas and Elizabeth (Starns) Mitchell. Fifteen years afterward the family relocated to Florida, driving a team of oxen more than eight hundred miles to settle on the frontier in eastern Hillsborough County. Young Mitchell, known in adult life as Laurens, received his education first in the common schools of Alabama, then at the hands of a Methodist parson tutor in Florida. By 1852 he had tired of tending crops and livestock on the frontier and moved to the tiny village of Tampa to read law under James A. Gettis. To support himself in the endeavor, he taught in the local public schools. After four years he gained admission to the bar, joining Gettis as a partner.[61]

A governmental career quickly followed upon the opening of Mitchell's legal office. In 1857 area voters elected him solicitor of the southern judicial circuit as a Democrat. In that capacity he represented the state in numerous cases before the supreme court during its Tampa sessions, which meetings were required by prewar statutory rules. The position also thrust young Mitchell into his most controversial legal role. In 1859 he prosecuted a slave, Adam, for murder, while future justice Ossian Bingley Hart led the defense. During the "long and acrimonious" trial, Mitchell pressed his case with forceful determination and appeal to emotion, so much so that Hart successfully sought a supreme court order for a retrial. After news arrived of the order, a mob pulled the prisoner from his cell and lynched him.[62]

Mitchell served as solicitor until 1861, finding time also to sit as a member of the Tampa town council in 1860. With the Civil War's outbreak, though, he soon enlisted in the Sunny South Guards, a Confederate unit that became Company K, Fourth Florida Infantry. Its members elected him first lieutenant. In October 1862 Mitchell achieved promotion to captain, and superiors commended him for bravery at the first Battle of Murfreesboro, Tennessee. The following August authorities dispatched him to Florida on recruiting duty. While there, Hillsborough County voters elected the captain to the Florida house of representatives. Mitchell resigned his commission in November 1864.[63]

The Confederate surrender in 1865 found Mitchell attempting to restart a law practice in the devastated Tampa area. His responsibilities increased the next year when he married Mary Eugenia Spencer, the daughter of land investor William Samuel Spencer. Needing a more secure income than the law assured, he accepted the editorship of the Spencer family's newspaper, the Tampa *Florida Peninsular.* That circumstances compelled Mitchell to turn away from the law would not have been unusual at all for Florida practitioners of the era. As historian William T. Cash observed, "As late as 1880 no more than two-thirds of the Florida attorneys practiced law as an exclusive vocation."[64] In the role of editor, Mitchell emerged as a passionate advocate of conservative resistance to Reconstruction. In doing so he reserved special ire for his former legal colleague Ossian Bingley Hart, who had become a leader among loyalists and Republicans. "This poor tool of Radicalism," Mitchell observed in 1868, "has stooped to everything low and mean to negroize Florida."[65]

Beyond newspaper advocacy, Mitchell involved himself in party building and contests for office. By 1870 he chaired Hillsborough County's Democratic executive committee, and two years afterward county electors rewarded him with a seat in the Florida house. The election coincided with Hart's elevation to the governor's office, and Mitchell used his legislative position in a bid to thwart Hart's programs. As chairman of the judiciary committee, he sought to curtail the governor's constitutional powers of appointment. More immediately, he attempted unsuccessfully to block passage of Hart's Civil Rights Act. Despite the failures, conservatives recognized a talented partisan fighter. They returned him to the house for an additional term and, upon Redemption in 1877, conferred upon him the judgeship of the sixth judicial circuit.[66]

Judge Mitchell sat on the circuit bench for more than a decade, dispensing justice but sometimes encountering controversy. In 1879, for example, some South Floridians alleged his involvement in attempts to persecute former Republican officials by bringing false charges and tampering with the jury selection process. Mitchell heatedly denied the charges and joined with other officials to force the court clerk's resignation. Politics also played a role in the most famous trials at which the judge sat. Members of a vigilante group known as the Sarasota Assassination Society had marked some men, mostly Republicans, for death and had acted on the threats in several cases. Mitchell presided over their trials at Manatee County's isolated seat of Pine Level, the journey to which required him to "swim horses and drive through water for miles and miles."[67]

National attention centered on the rustic courthouse, with its floor of "one part sawdust, two parts fleas."[68] Given scorching summer heat, high humidity, and harsh conditions, Mitchell's health suffered. The weakened judge lasted through the trial of the first three defendants before being forced to request a replacement to preside over the remaining trials.[69]

The judge's appearance and temperament provoked numerous comments from acquaintances and other observers. One historian insisted that Mitchell was "undoubtedly the homeliest man" to hold public office in Florida.[70] Others noted his quick temper. On one occasion a Tampa newspaper published a poem that satirized the future justice's habit of always wearing a sword at his side. When the poet later happened to appear in Mitchell's courtroom, the judge reportedly chased him outdoors, waving his weapon over his head and shouting, "I'll teach you to make fun of my sword."[71] Yet many Tampans warmed to his good nature and appreciated his sense of humor. Chief Justice Robert Fenwick Taylor remembered that "it was beautiful to see him, impelled by the bigness of his heart, speedily making amends for a harsh word used in hastiness of temper."[72] Another man recalled the night when Mitchell was awakened by a shivaree outside a room on the same floor where he had an apartment. Rather than complaining, the judge joined the crowd, barefoot and clad in red flannel underwear, and cheered on its members.[73]

Besides his labors as circuit judge, Mitchell worked for Tampa area development, particularly railroad construction to the port town. When Henry B. Plant's South Florida Railroad appeared about to become a reality in the early 1880s, Mitchell, who enjoyed friendly relations with railroad executives, "found out" the line's intended route. Thereupon, he launched himself upon a career as entrepreneur and town father by laying out near his family's old eastern Hillsborough County homestead the site of Plant City. His foresight and initiative paid off handsomely for the judge.[74]

Mitchell's initiative found expression in other areas of his professional life, a fact that led him to the supreme bench. Pursuant to the 1885 constitution, supreme court offices became elective in 1888. Sensing opportunity, Mitchell successfully vied for a Democratic nomination at the party's convention that year. Several months later, but before the general election, Justice Robert Bruce Van Valkenburgh died. Governor Edward A. Perry then turned to his party's nominee to fill the vacancy, perhaps with the encouragement of the judge's brother Dr. Charles L. Mitchell, who served Perry as state commissioner of lands and immigration. Justice Henry Laurens Mitchell took the oath of office on August 7. That November, voters ratified the appointment. In January 1889 Mitchell drew, by lot, a four-year term. His court tenure proved brief, though.

Anticipating his race for governor in 1892, he resigned from the supreme court on January 1, 1891, to return to the judgeship of the sixth judicial circuit.[75]

Mitchell's star continued to rise after his departure from the supreme court. In the face of 1892's populist revolt, he grasped the Democratic gubernatorial nomination, representing the party's conservative wing. An experienced politician, Mitchell ran on a platform that appealed broadly to Floridians and won election with a large majority. Adherence to the status quo characterized his administration, a product both of his limited view of the scope of state responsibility and the fiscal difficulties connected with instituting reforms during economic depression following the Panic of 1893. He rejected proposals to increase school funding and enhance teacher training, and he sided with the railroads against the reestablishment of a state railroad commission. Florida's financial woes were exacerbated by two hard freezes in the winter of 1894–95 that crippled the citrus industry and further reduced state revenues. Mitchell also faced the disaster that followed the hurricane of 1896, when 135-mile-per-hour winds destroyed Cedar Key and lashed much of northeastern Florida. The governor briefly received national attention when he took a stand against prize fighting, seeking unsuccessfully to prevent a bout between "Gentleman" Jim Corbett and Charlie Mitchell.[76]

Mitchell's life after leaving the governor's office in 1897 proceeded quietly but lasted only a short while. Just before leaving the capitol, he signed his own commission for the office of clerk of the Hillsborough County circuit court, to which he had been elected in November 1896. The selection came as a reward from Mitchell's influential constituents for his many years of service to Tampa and the state. The lucrative fee system by which clerks were paid kept him comfortable in his old age. In January 1901 he moved to his last elected position, county treasurer for Hillsborough County. On October 14, 1903, Mitchell died at Tampa, aged seventy-two.[77]

Milton Harvey Mabry, Supreme Court Justice, 1891–1894, 1897–1903; Supreme Court Chief Justice, 1895–1897

Peninsular Florida's growing population and political clout found recognition in the career of Milton Harvey Mabry. The future justice was born on June 17, 1851, in Pickens County, Alabama, to Jesse H. Mabry and Sarah Caroline Prude. His merchant father relocated the family on several occasions during Milton's youth. In 1856 they moved from Bridgeville, Alabama, to DeSoto Parish, Louisiana, where they remained for four years. Then the Mabrys transferred to Lee County, Mississippi. Too young to participate in the Civil War, Milton received his education in common schools, particularly at Verona, Mississippi. About

1868 he entered the literary department of the University of Mississippi at Oxford. After two years' study, he transferred to the law department at Cumberland University, Lebanon, Tennessee. He graduated from that institution in 1872.[78]

Mabry's return to Mississippi initiated his practice of the law and of politics. At Tupelo, he soon was elected the town's mayor, in which capacity he served for two years. His involvements reached into the heart of state Democratic politics. The young lawyer witnessed firsthand the bloody election battle of 1875 and subsequent events that led to the end of Mississippi's Reconstruction and the beginning of white Democratic rule. There, also, he forged long-term relationships. First, between 1872 and 1874 he entered into a friendship with another young lawyer, William Adams Hocker, who was teaching Latin and Greek at the Franklin Institute in Columbus. Then, in 1876, he married Ella D. Bramlett, the daughter of a farmer with extensive holdings in Verona. The couple eventually would have five sons and one daughter.[79]

Apparently the friendship with Hocker brought about Mabry's move to Florida. Hocker had made the journey in 1874, settling not far from Leesburg in what then was Sumter County. He had prospered. Local Democrats sent him to the legislature in 1877, and party leaders had recognized his merit with appointment that year to be state's attorney for the fifth judicial circuit. Within a few years he virtually controlled Sumter County Democratic politics. Probably at Hocker's urging, an ailing Mabry joined him at Leesburg in 1879, where the two men formed a law partnership.[80]

The combination of Mabry's and Hocker's talents and drive benefited both men and, by 1882, had resulted in Mabry's election as Sumter County's state representative. First, though, it had caused controversy that made them both a powerful enemy, Florida's Confederate hero John J. Dickison. The situation developed beginning in July 1881 when local men pulled J. J. Dickison, Jr., from a Leesburg jail and lynched him for the murder of a popular resident. As it turned out, the original victim survived, but the younger Dickison did not. Hocker, sensitive to local voter displeasure, pursued a low-key investigation as state prosecutor. Dickison, until the previous January Florida's adjutant general, reacted in fury. Mabry defended his law partner by publishing a letter that seemed to justify the lynching. Dickison insisted upon bringing his own attorney to present evidence and witnesses to the grand jury, but that panel in Hocker's presence declined to indict anyone. Dickison vowed to continue his fight for punishment of the lynchers, and unresolved questions followed Mabry and Hocker as they pursued successful political careers.[81]

Dickison's displeasure created embarrassment for Mabry but did not block his rise. In 1884 state Democrats nominated former Confederate general Edward A. Perry for governor. Aware of the growing electoral strength of Democrats in the peninsula and needing a lieutenant governor candidate to balance his West Florida background, Perry backed Mabry for the position. Since the thirty-three-year-old had resided in the state for only five years, the nomination came as a surprise. Still, Mabry brought assets to the ticket. As a new Floridian, he had not been embroiled in the internecine squabbles that had threatened to fracture the party. He could, therefore, appeal to a broad spectrum of voters. Moreover, Mabry attracted several constituencies whose support would be vital to defeat the powerful alliance represented by the Independent movement of that year. South Floridians who felt no loyalty to Pensacolan Perry certainly numbered among them. The youthful Mabry also appealed to a new generation of voters who barely remembered life under the Confederacy and might not be impressed by Perry's record as a Civil War hero.[82]

The Democratic ticket triumphed in November 1884 elections, and Mabry entered the lieutenant governor's office in January 1885. The position's responsibilities related mostly to ceremony, a fact recognized by the constitutional convention of 1885, which abolished the office as of the end of Mabry's term. The principal duty consisted of presiding over the Florida senate. Mabry gained a reputation as a conciliator in that role, although dynamic leadership qualities did not evidence themselves in his work. "Not possessing the mannerism so common to public men," a friendly correspondent explained, "Governor Mabry is not fully appreciated by those who judge the man by his superficial qualities." He continued: "But to know him is to appreciate him for what he is, a clear-headed, large-hearted gentleman with punctilious ideas of the proprieties and amenities of life. His knowledge of State affairs is full, and his judgment is clear and correct."[83]

After stepping down from the lieutenant governor's office in January 1889, Mabry remained out of elective office only briefly. Temporarily he practiced law at Leesburg, but in 1890 he secured the Democratic nomination for Justice Augustus Emmet Maxwell's seat on the supreme court. Winning an easy victory that November, he joined the tribunal in January 1891. Francis Beauregard Carter, who sat alongside Mabry for the last half of his court tenure, remembered his colleague as a conscientious and original legal mind whose opinions were models of clarity. According to Carter, Mabry concerned himself more than most of his peers with preserving constitutional liberties, particularly the writ of habeas corpus. This writ, he believed, should be "free from cost, from formalities in obtaining it, and from technicalities in the procedure."[84]

Justice Mabry contributed to the court and its decisions for well over a decade before personal considerations compelled him to seek other opportunities. In January 1903 he announced that he would not seek a third term but

Hall of Science, Stetson College of Law

Milton Harvey Mabry

Thomas M. Shackleford

Mary Stewart Howarth

Justices assist Florida's first law school. Justice (and later clerk of the court) Milton Harvey Mabry and Justice Thomas M. Shackleford provided support with Justice Wiliam Adams Hocker (not pictured) to Dean Albert J. Farrah when his budget permitted the employment of only one full-time teacher at Florida's first law school. The College of Law of John B. Stetson University opened its doors in DeLand in October 1900. Future justice Roy H. Chapman graduated in 1908, as did Mary Stewart Howarth, the first woman to graduate from a Florida law school. The Hall of Science was the home of the Stetson College of Law in DeLand from 1902 to 1946.

would instead "take up private practice at Tampa in order that he may lay up something for himself and family before old age creeps upon him."[85] At least one prominent state newspaper, appalled that a jurist of Mabry's stature would be forced to make such a choice, called on the legislature to increase the justices' salaries from $2,500, about one-fourth of what skilled private practitioners in the large cities earned. This measure, the newspaper argued, would allow the state to "retain men on the bench who have become familiar enough with the work to keep up with it" rather than merely provide talented attorneys with a prestigious post that they could parlay into financial gain after one or two terms.[86]

After departing from the bench, Mabry split the remainder of his life between the Tampa area and Tallahassee. In 1904 he joined his son Giddings Eldon Mabry in a law partnership at Tampa that lasted for one year. Then, in 1905 the justices, who were seeking a new supreme court clerk, unanimously turned to their former colleague. According to Justice Thomas M. Shackleford, each of the jurists wrote Mabry a personal letter to convince him to accept the appointment. He agreed and remained in the position until failing health forced him to resign in 1915. While serving as clerk, he remarried. His first wife had died in 1903, and in 1906 he wed Irene Washburn, formerly of Louisville, Kentucky. The couple moved from Tallahassee to Clearwater in 1915, before they settled at Tampa. Mabry died in his home there on March 3, 1919, after a lingering illness. "In his death," declared the *Tampa Morning Tribune,* "the state has lost one of its old time, old school, gentlemen and lawyers, a man whose code of honor was the code of noblesse oblige." The journal added, "He gave a long and useful life in the service of his state."[87]

Robert Fenwick Taylor, Supreme Court Justice, 1891–1897, 1905–1915, 1917–1923; Supreme Court Chief Justice, 1897–1905, 1915–1917, 1923–1925

South Florida produced, in addition to Justice Milton Harvey Mabry, yet another supreme court member in 1891, who would become the longest-serving justice of his era. Robert Fenwick Taylor was born on March 10, 1849, on his family's plantation in Beaufort District, South Carolina. His father, cotton and rice planter John Morgandollar Taylor, boasted a long and venerable lineage. Similarly, Robert's mother Maria (Baker) Taylor traced her ancestry to distinguished individuals, including Revolutionary War hero and minister Richard Furman, who founded the Furman Theological Seminary (now Furman University).[88]

Before the child's third birthday, the family relocated to Florida. They settled on an estate that became known as Osceola plantation in Marion County. There young Taylor received his early education from tutors before enrolling at Ocala's East Florida Seminary. He developed an interest in pursuing the profession of law, but the Civil War's onset limited his opportunities and diverted him from studies. As one account put it, "Instead of settling down to Blackstone at the age of fifteen years, the military fever of the time seized him."[89] Too young to enlist in the regular Confederate Army, Taylor nonetheless fought as a volunteer in the 1864 engagement at Gainesville, where area men, defending their homes from Union attack, entered the fray crying "Victory or Death."[90]

The 1865 Confederate surrender afforded Taylor the chance to further his professional training. He attended the Maryland Military Institute in Baltimore but left the school six months before graduation. Returning to Florida, the future justice read law with his brother-in-law James B. Dawkins, a Gainesville attorney who had served in the Florida secession convention and the Confederate Congress. He achieved admission to the bar at Ocala in 1870. For seven years, until Dawkins accepted appointment as circuit judge, the two lawyers practiced together as the Gainesville firm of Dawkins and Taylor. During that period Taylor served by court request with two other local attorneys as examiners for Florida's black United States congressman Josiah T. Walls, enthusiastically recommending his admission to the bar. After Dawkins assumed his judicial duties, Taylor for a time worked as a sole practitioner but soon affiliated with another prominent Democratic leader, Edward C. F. Sanchez. According to one state legal historian, their partnership represented "the largest practice in that section of the state."[91]

Through the 1870s Taylor's interests expanded beyond the legal profession. On February 1, 1872, he married Amelia Evans Haile, the daughter of a prominent Alachua County planter family that also had immigrated to Florida from South Carolina. Their only child to survive adolescence, Serena Haile Taylor, would marry future Florida attorney general and supreme court justice William Hull Ellis. Taylor involved himself in Democratic politics and resistance to Reconstruction. He labored on county and state party committees, becoming, as one observer described, "One of the most faithful workers in the Democratic ranks."[92] Until 1885, though, he declined to seek office for himself, disdaining that kind of personal involvement in the rough-and-tumble of political campaigning. Then, Democrats in Alachua County rewarded him, along with his partner Edward C. F. Sanchez, for their support of party interests by naming them to represent the county in the 1885 constitutional convention. He chaired the assembly's committee on style and arrangement.[93]

The respect that Taylor earned within the legal profession and the Democratic party finally brought him appointment to the supreme court in January 1891, upon the resignation of Justice Henry Laurens Mitchell. The next year's elections ensured him retention of his seat. He would win five more successive electoral contests, despite occasionally taking unpopular stances in his decisions. Conservative by nature, he resisted some legal and political trends that arrived with the Progressive era. "When the politicians were crying out against the corporations, and were attempting to destroy property rights," recalled Justice Jefferson B. Browne, "he stood firm against public clamor, and frequently took upon himself the brunt of popular displeasure."[94] Further, Taylor defended personal rights against public pressures for faster criminal punishments in an era of increasing racial injustice. Browne continued, "He has not heeded the popular demand for more convictions, but has stood firm for constitutional rights of life and liberty, it mattered not what the result." He added, "Where hate and fanaticism have run riot, and the public careers of men threatened unless they would bow to its behests, he has stood unmoved and unshaken."[95]

Taylor's personal philosophy recalled the conservatism of an earlier age. He believed that "greater attention [should be given] to the proper training of the youth of the country, and the inculcation in them of rigid principles of old-fashioned honesty and integrity, whether dealing with individuals or corporations, and a proper respect for age, law and order, and the rooting out from their minds the idea that the acquisition of money is the only thing worth a life's striving." He once offered advice to those interested in a successful legal career. "To the young man who selects the law as his profession," he declared, "I would say that no matter what may be his natural gifts, he is doomed to utter failure unless he unreservedly and unremittently submits himself to the eternal work demanded by the most jealous of all mistresses—the law."[96]

Justice Taylor's contributions to the court came in many forms. His opinions in equity cases and his decisions on the power of mandamus proved especially influential, being cited frequently in treatises and other state court opinions. In a more immediate sense and on a more personal scale, he aided the enhancement of the court's working environment. In 1902 he sat on a committee with Governor William Sherman Jennings and his cabinet to select new furnishings for the capitol. After spending hours examining fixtures and furniture on display at Tallahassee's Leon Hotel, Taylor was significantly impressed with the quality and appearance of H. D. Hartt's rugs and carpets. As a result and before regular bids were opened, the court ordered that "beautiful brussels carpet [be] put on the floor at once."[97]

Eventually Taylor sat upon the supreme bench for thirty-four years, twice as long as any justice before him. His tenure on the tribunal included three terms as chief justice. Before his February 28, 1925, resignation, he authored 564 opinions and participated in nearly 8,000 decisions. Given those statistics, Taylor had involved himself in about 76 percent of the cases decided by the court since its inception. Recognizing his remarkable record, the 1926 state legislature voted him retirement at full pay.[98]

Away from the court Taylor enjoyed a varied personal life. Active in numerous fraternal organizations, he also was an enthusiastic and insatiable reader. In 1923 he employed his extensive knowledge of Florida legal history in revising the "bench and bar" chapter in Henry Gardner Cutler's *History of Florida*. Taylor enjoyed outdoor recreation, as well, particularly hunting, fishing, and riding. He pursued such physical activities throughout his life, but at least once his pleasure almost produced his death. In 1919, at the age of seventy, the justice, while riding "a spirited horse," was "thrown over the head of the animal to the hard ground." The accident victim was taken "in an insen[s]ible condition" to his daughter's nearby home, but fortunately Taylor quickly recovered.[99]

Taylor survived his 1919 accident, but the one-time justice remained in frail health and would not live through the following decade. In mid-February 1927 an aging Taylor contracted bronchial pneumonia. Doctors pronounced his condition grave, although he showed some signs of recovery after the passage of a week. Then, on February 26 he suffered a relapse and died of kidney failure at his Tallahassee home, having survived his wife by twenty-five years. The event came two weeks short of Taylor's seventy-ninth birthday. Kinsmen buried him in the family cemetery at Kanapaha, near Gainesville. Five years previously Justice Browne, upon receiving on behalf of the court an official portrait of Taylor, had spoken of the man. "The artist in this instance has caught two of his most admirable qualities, his gentleness and his tolerance," Browne remarked. "Another artist might show his wonderful strength of character; still another his fearlessness; another his massive intellect, but I am content that his gentleness and tolerance and charity shall beam from that portrait on the generations of men of his profession who will visit this chamber in the years to come."[100]

Benjamin Sullivan Liddon, Supreme Court Chief Justice, 1894; Supreme Court Justice, 1895–1897

The Redemption era's early preference for justices from West Florida reasserted itself in 1894 with the appointment of Benjamin Sullivan Liddon to the supreme court. Born on September 7, 1853, in Marianna, he was the son of Benjamin G. Liddon and Susan (Sullivan) Liddon. Both sides of the family claimed distinguished ancestors and had pioneered the settlement of the Jackson County area. The future justice's father early involved himself in public affairs. He helped to lead the Whig party in the Panhandle, publishing at Marianna beginning in 1847 the influential *Florida Whig.* He also fought the evils of abuse of alcohol through active participation in the Sons of Temperance. Unfortunately for his son, the elder Liddon died in 1864 while serving as a sergeant in the Confederate Third Georgia Infantry. His demise came at Petersburg, Virginia, during the celebrated Battle of the Crater.[101]

Following his father's death, young Liddon confronted difficult obstacles. "His mother was left with a family of children," one account noted, "and, like everyone else in the South at that time, was not in affluent circumstances." It added, "Judge Liddon had to fight his own battles."[102] He attended available schools at Marianna and at Madison, Georgia, then briefly studied at Southern University in Greensboro, Alabama. For the most part, though, he taught himself. One popular story asserted that "he studied his Latin on his wagon, loaded with wood, as he drove it to town."[103] Upon reaching adulthood, Liddon chose to teach others. For lawyers of the period, teaching proved a popular alternative. William T. Cash determined, for example, that more than one-fourth of the small-town attorneys at the century's end initially had assumed teaching positions. From 1877 to 1879 Liddon also served as Jackson County's superintendent of schools.[104]

Income from teaching permitted Liddon the time to read the law. He did so in the chambers of Allen H. Bush, a leading attorney in Marianna and author of *Bush's Digest of the Laws of Florida.* He achieved admission to the local bar in 1875. Working at first as a sole practitioner, he soon formed a partnership with William D. Barnes, a power in state Democratic circles. By 1879 Barnes had reached the presidency of the state senate and then served from 1881 to 1890 as state comptroller. After Barnes's rise to the comptroller's office, Liddon invited the first student to study law with him, Francis Beauregard Carter, to join in a second partnership. It lasted until 1889. As illustrated by his assistance to Carter, Liddon gained a reputation as a superb instructor of the law, and he ultimately trained numerous Panhandle attorneys. Reportedly, he set high standards for his clerks, primarily in taking dictation and transcribing correspondence and legal documents. "There were no typewriters in this section in those days," recalled John Carter, "and stenographers were considered a species of crank that would soon become extinct."[105] Many Liddon charges ended up on the bench, including Carter, who succeeded his mentor on the supreme court.[106]

Perhaps from his association with Barnes, Liddon embraced active involvement in Democratic party affairs. For four years during the 1880s he held office as Marianna mayor, and his 1884 support for Edward A. Perry's gubernatorial campaign earned his appointment to the board of education of the West

Florida Seminary (now Florida State University). His voice carried louder than those of many other partisans for two reasons. First, as an advocate in the courtroom or on the campaign trail, he benefited from a magnificent voice. One attorney friend remembered it as "irresistible," noting that "it charmed and swayed juries and won their verdicts."[107] Second, from 1881 he published the Marianna *Courier* as a party organ. Its editorials received attention throughout the state.[108]

Legal skills and political contacts advanced Liddon's professional career during the 1880s and early 1890s. He gained heightened stature by accepting responsibilities as counsel for the state railroad commission, particularly with respect to the Louisville and Nashville Railroad's unsuccessful challenge of the commission's rate-making powers. As a criminal lawyer, he excelled, as well, sometimes defying local passions. An observer praised him in one instance, for example, for "acquitting his client in the face of the most pronounced popular opinion."[109] In 1886 Liddon appeared in the supreme court as a litigant, winning his appeal in a case that clarified the requirements for proving adverse possession in a property dispute.[110]

It was thus as an attorney with high standing in the profession and solid Democratic contacts that Liddon appeared to Governor Henry Laurens Mitchell in May 1894 as a prime candidate for appointment to the supreme court to replace resigning Chief Justice George Pettus Raney. "He is a lawyer of solid judgment and of wide learning," commented the Jacksonville *Florida Times-Union*. "But while it is the business of a judge to administer the law as he finds it, fairly and impartially, he needs something more than legal attainments," the newspaper continued. "He needs a broad sympathy with his fellow men, and an insight into the conditions which surround them. We believe Judge Liddon possesses those qualifications for his position."[111] The Democratic party concurred by nominating Justice Liddon for a full term, which he won in the general election of November 1894. He did not serve out his six years. Instead, in 1897 Liddon resigned from the bench to resume private practice. "He was restless under the restraint which hems in a judge," explained former student and judge Cephas L. Wilson, "and he longed to return to the scenes of forensic battles."[112]

The former justice's postcourt life included political activism but revolved around legal practice in West Florida. Settling at first in Pensacola, he opened an office with Republican leader John Eagan. After Eagan received appointment in 1901 as United States attorney for the Northern District of Florida, Liddon returned to Marianna. He invested in and served as counsel for banks, railroads, and insurance companies, including the Louisville and Nashville

Railroad. Politically, he identified himself with the progressive wing of the Democratic party, especially through his support of Jacksonville's Duncan Upshaw Fletcher. In 1900 he chaired the Florida delegation to the Democratic national convention. During the administrations of progressive governors William Sherman Jennings and Napoleon B. Broward, he headed a statutory revision commission that produced, in 1906, a sorely needed update of state laws. He aided the party, as well, through his careful efforts in leading the prosecution in the politically sensitive 1897 impeachment of state treasurer Clarence B. Collins, who had been accused of misusing state funds. Negotiations led to Collins's resignation after impeachment but before a senate trial.[113]

Likely the most well-known instances of Liddon's postcourt involvement in the admixture of law and Democratic politics occurred early in the 1900s and involved his friend, Congressman William B. Lamar of Jefferson County. First, in 1902 an irate constituent, Walter Taylor, assaulted Lamar with fatal intent. Given the circumstances surrounding the assault, the local state's attorney refused to prosecute. Liddon, over the objections of the state's attorney, appeared upon the judge's invitation, presented a case to the grand jury, and influenced the panel to act.[114] That body then indicted the defendant for assault with intent to commit murder, and a jury subsequently convicted him of assault with intent to commit manslaughter. Taylor appealed to the supreme court, which, in a divided 1904 opinion, upheld the indictment and conviction. Thereafter, Lid-don's personal actions became the subject of disbarment proceedings. In them the former justice triumphed, although only after prolonged distress.[115]

Meanwhile, Liddon and Lamar had combined in an attempt to remove United States District Judge Charles Swayne. The lawyer, who arrived in Florida from Pennsylvania in 1885, unsuccessfully vied for the supreme court three years later as a Republican. President Benjamin Harrison the next year appointed him to the federal bench for the Northern District of Florida. In that capacity Swayne insisted on the prosecution of Democratic officials whom he believed guilty of elections law violations. He also joined with Republican leaders wishing to reform Florida's newly enacted restrictions on registration and voting.[116]

Naturally, Swayne's actions angered Democratic officials, especially Lamar's close ally Samuel Pasco of Jefferson County, who had become a key figure of the party's conservative wing. In 1903 Pasco arranged for a legislative demand for Swayne's impeachment for alleged "corruption, absenteeism, ignorance and incompetence, and the wasting of the assets of bankrupts."[117] Lamar followed with a congressional impeachment resolution. On behalf of Florida's legislature, Liddon assembled evidence and offered his findings to the house judiciary committee. One source described his presentation as a "masterly argument," and the committee's report charged that a "disgraceful perversion of justice was made possible by the complacency, stupidity, or worse of Judge Swayne."[118] The house then impeached the jurist. Even some Democratic lawyers opposed removal, though, and demanded acquittal. "It seems . . . ," one wrote, "that this is a matter upon which the judgement of the bar is more trustworthy than the opinions of editors and politicians."[119] A split senate agreed and on February 27, 1905, exonerated Swayne of all charges.[120]

Liddon's personal life, through the tumultuous years of his political involvements, had proceeded quietly but ended suddenly. In 1880 he married Virginia M. Harvey of Jackson County. Together they had nine children. The lawyer spent much of his leisure time studying the volumes in his extensive library, and he maintained his knowledge of current events through attending lectures and reading periodicals. He wrote poetry as well as obituaries and marriage notices for the Marianna newspaper. By late in the new century's first decade he was described as flourishing "in the full vigor of sound middle age."[121] Yet soon his health began to suffer. In December 1909 he traveled to New Orleans for his son's wedding, and there he died on the twenty-first, at age fifty-six.[122]

Chapter 16

Case Decisions and the Redemption

The twenty-year period that commenced in 1877 saw Florida, as discussed in chapter 14, advance into the modern era. The state, its economy, and its residents diversified and grew in complexity; so, too, did the supreme court's work. The inventions, innovations, and economic changes that marked the United States in the century's final quarter prompted a plethora of litigation that raised difficult questions regarding the range and limits of governmental regulatory power as well as new implications for contract, property, tort, and criminal law. Since poor and isolated Florida had experienced the coming of progress relatively late, the state's high tribunal often could benefit from the pioneering decisions of federal and other state courts. Still, local circumstances presented the justices with an immediate context that sometimes flavored their decisions. In many areas, heated passions, partisan sympathies, and parochial interests demanded attention and assumed influence. The fragility of Redemption served as the backdrop to one particularly important group of decisions, while a second one concerned balancing the public interest against that of the railroads.

Electoral Contests

Political tensions lay heavily upon the age. Through the first two decades of the Redemption era, Bourbon state leaders found their control of government subject to constant challenge. Republicans clung to power in some areas for years. By the early 1880s, elements within the Democratic party also had erupted in an anti-Bourbon revolt known as the Independent movement. The period 1886–89 witnessed black Republicans uniting with the Knights of Labor. After passage of the poll tax and other elections-related legislation in 1889 undercut labor and Republicans, farmers demanding reform under the banner of the People's party soon challenged pro-business Democrats. Naturally, the repeated contests entailed court review of elections results, the processes of law, and governmental attempts to suppress dissent.

Among the electoral disputes addressed by Florida's courts, two conspicuously frame the era's Bourbon dilemma. The first resulted from an 1878 race for the state's eastern congressional district. The incumbent, northern-born Union Army veteran Horatio Bisbee, Jr., enjoyed substantial popularity among African Americans and with many of the whites who lived at Jacksonville and other northeastern Florida port cities of pronounced Republican strength. His challenger, Sanford merchant and Democratic lieutenant governor Noble Hull, seemed to Bisbee's supporters likely to favor the interests of central Florida residents over their own, a fact that spurred efforts in the congressman's behalf.[1]

In the situation, second district Democrats, who controlled county election boards, shamelessly manipulated voting and counting processes on election day. The town of Madison provides an example. Both parties there agreed to alternate their voters through the day to avoid confrontation. Yet Democrats deliberately stalled their balloting. Almost two hundred black voters, finding themselves unable to reach the polls, cast informal ballots at a general store. Democrats in an outlying precinct invited a cooperative courier to join them for a drink of whiskey, then stole the ballot box that he was carrying. Similarly, in the Republican stronghold of Marion County, Democrats stuffed the ballot box during an inspector's recess.[2]

Despite the Democratic frauds, the final polling results stood close to equal between the candidates. The returns showed Bisbee leading Hull by about two hundred votes, with the tallies from sparsely populated Dade and Brevard counties unreceived. Hull then directed Orlando businessman Nathaniel Poyntz to travel to Brevard to determine what might be done to secure a margin of victory. "I would give anything if this could be accomplished," the candidate reportedly declared.[3] Poyntz, in turn, dispatched Orlando attorney J. H. Allen to the scene, where the emissary bribed the court clerk to add 190 votes to Hull's total.[4]

The irregularities quickly became public and set the controversy on a path to judicial review. First, the Democrat-run state canvassing board rejected all returns from Madison and Brevard counties, giving Hull a forty-vote victory. Bisbee appealed to the supreme court. Acting as his own counsel, the congressman demanded an order compelling the board to count all bona fide returns. In the matter of *The State of Florida ex rel. H. Bisbee, Jr.* v. *The Board of State Canvassers*, the tribunal's two Republican justices comprised the majority. Chief Justice Edwin M. Randall's opinion granted relief, finding that state law compelled the counting of "unimpeached returns."[5] Democrat James Diament Westcott, Jr., dissented, insisting that no statute "obliged [the board] to accept the face of the returns."[6]

The initial decision presaged further controversy. The recount indicated a Bisbee victory, but Democratic governor George F. Drew contrarily certified Hull as the winner. Bisbee returned to the supreme court, seeking a writ of mandamus against the governor. The court's Republican majority refused the writ, declaring in *The State of Florida ex rel. H. Bisbee, Jr.* v. *Geo. F. Drew, Governor* that "the Governor of the State of Florida cannot be commanded by the courts to perform any act which may be required of him by a law of the State relating to the executive office, or any duty which he may be required to perform of a political nature, even though private rights may be involved."[7] Interestingly, Democrat Westcott backed Bisbee's petition. "This court," he opined, "has held that officers of the executive department of the government are subject to control by the courts in the exercise of ministerial powers pertaining to elections."[8]

Rebuffed by the court, Bisbee finally gained satisfaction in Washington. In January 1880, after a lengthy investigation, the United States House of Representatives expelled Hull. By that time he had served in office for nearly one year. The Florida legislature also investigated the now deposed congressman but determined that he had no knowledge of the fraud. A federal grand jury at Jacksonville disagreed and indicted him. Apparently, though, prosecution did not ensue. Eventually, local officials in Madison, Brevard, and Marion counties were convicted of election-law fraud. As for Bisbee, he achieved reelection in 1880 and 1882 and the distinction of being the last major Republican leader to retain power.[9]

Thirteen years after the Bisbee-Hull contretemps, Florida politics had changed significantly. Republicans no longer constituted a factor except in some local elections, but deep divisions within the Democratic party threatened Bourbon rule. One major fight brewed over the legislative election of a United States senator in 1891. Incumbent Wilkinson Call represented the party's more progressive wing, especially in his opposition to land grants to railroads and to the arrogant exercise of power by the lines. Pensacola's William D. Chipley, a force in the Democratic party, particularly resented Call's actions and their potential effect on his railroad's interests. Accordingly the Bourbons, with Governor Francis P. Fleming's cooperation, opted to purge Call by denying him reelection. The ensuing legislative session erupted into wild excitement, with charges of bribery sounding amid confusion. Recalcitrant members, frustrated at Call's strength, finally tried to deny a quorum by leaving town, earning themselves the sobriquet "Babes in the Woods." Nonetheless, Call persevered and won a majority vote the next day. The absent solons thereafter complicated matters upon their return. Specifically, they altered the senate journal to throw doubt on the victory.[10]

Governor Fleming seized the opportunity to deny Call his seat despite the vote. He denounced the election as illegal and designated a Bourbon former congressman, Robert H. M. Davidson of Quincy, to fill the vacancy. Secretary of State John L. Crawford, a Call ally, countered by refusing to attach the state's great seal to Davidson's commission. Attorney General William B. Lamar backed Crawford and declined to represent Fleming in the governor's attempt to secure a supreme court order directing the secretary of state to act. Thus, in the case of *The State of Florida ex rel. Francis P. Fleming, Governor,* v. *John L. Crawford, Secretary of State,* state senator and Tallahassee lawyer Frederick T. Myers spoke for the governor. He found the going easy. "It is in our judgment clearly the official duty of the Secretary to affix the seal of the State to the appointment, and to countersign or attest the same as evidencing the official act of the executive authority of the State in appointing a Senator in the Congress of the United States," wrote Chief Justice George Pettus Raney for a unanimous tribunal composed of Bourbon activists, "and this duty is one involving no official discretion or judgment on his part."[11]

Like Bisbee, Call attained redress in the nation's capital. In December 1891 the Senate seated him pending review by its committee on privileges and elections. The next February its unanimous and favorable report led to final action securing the seat for Call. "The conservative Bourbons," concluded one Florida historian, "had suffered their first serious defeat since Reconstruction."[12]

Political Violence

Just as the restoration of Democratic rule did not eliminate electoral shenanigans, criminal appeals to the supreme court indicated that political violence continued to plague the state. One noteworthy example again concerned Madison County and a congressional candidacy of Horatio Bisbee. After the congressman's 1882 reelection victory, Republican charges of Democratic frauds prompted another investigation. This time, the inquiry was conducted by Florida's federal collector of internal revenue, Dennis Eagan, who also exercised political power as the Republican boss of Madison County. Eagan provided a forum at Madison in which one of his local lieutenants, Charles H. Savage, proffered accusations of voter intimidation against attorney Frank Patterson, the partner of Democratic leader Frank W. Pope, then Madison's mayor. Racial tensions in the community were profound, with several violent encounters reported. When the hearings resumed the day after Savage's testimony,

Patterson accosted the witness, declaring, "You are, I suppose, the black son of a bitch that reported me."[13] Patterson then attempted to shoot Savage, but his pistol misfired, after which the black leader killed his assailant. In the confusion another black Republican, Howard E. James, had come to his friend Savage's assistance.[14]

Some local whites determined to punish Eagan, Savage, and James. A mob seized Savage, crying "kill him" and "shoot him," to which, according to one account, Mayor Pope responded, "No, chop his * * * head off."[15] Fortunately for Savage and James, the local militia hustled them to the protection of the local jail. Meanwhile, Eagan fled during the night into Georgia. A justice of the peace issued warrants for their arrest—Savage for murder and James and Eagan for being "feloniously present, assisting, aiding and abetting said Savage in the said murder."[16] Authorities soon traced Eagan to Albany, Georgia. He was arrested under the Madison County warrant and delivered to the custody of Leon County's sheriff, who placed him in the Tallahassee jail. Savage and James also had been removed to the protection of the same facility.[17]

Eagan immediately sought relief from the supreme court. He petitioned for a writ of habeas corpus, while denying his guilt and insisting upon an investigation. Justice James Diament Westcott, Jr., writing for a unanimous, bipartisan court, declined to accept Eagan's assertion that he could not obtain justice in Madison County and remanded the case to the local magistrate for further inquiry. The attorney general and the state attorney apparently foresaw problems and intervened, requesting that the high tribunal conduct the investigation, "seeing that great expense would be saved to the State by having the examination before the Supreme Court."[18] The court acceded and held extensive hearings. Fifteen days after Eagan's original petition, the justices ordered in the matter of *Ex-parte Dennis Eagan* that the Republican leader be freed, having concluded that the evidence did not warrant further proceedings against him.[19]

Savage and James did not find such swift justice. In April 1881 a Madison County grand jury indicted them, respectively, for murder in the first and second degree. At a trial held at Jasper, in Hamilton County, they were convicted, but not before they had questioned the organization and composition of the grand and petit juries and asserted insufficiency of counsel. They appealed the guilty verdict to the supreme court, based upon these grounds as well as trial and procedural errors. Chief Justice Randall penned the court's opinion in *Charles H. Savage and Howard E. James* v. *The State of Florida.* Regarding critical allegations of racial discrimination in jury selection, he dismissed the complaints for failure of the accused to prove their allegations. On numerous procedural questions Randall relied on the "sound discretion" of the local judge.[20]

The court found, nonetheless, grounds for reversal of the convictions. Particularly, the justices criticized limits placed on the ability of the defense "to inquire on cross-examination as to *all* the witness saw after he had testified to part of it."[21] The decision also faulted jury instructions that required James to be found guilty of murder in the second degree if Savage was found guilty of murder in the first degree and jurors believed that his friend "was present aiding and abetting." Randall commented, "The reason is that one who is guilty of murder in the first degree must be charged and proved to the satisfaction of the jury to have done the act charged with a formed design to effect the death, and this is the law as to the principal in the second degree as well as in the first degree."[22]

The good news of the order for a new trial turned tragic for Savage and James. In August 1882 officials transported them from Tallahassee by train, bound for a retrial at Jasper. When the cars stopped at Madison's depot, twenty armed men attacked the prisoners. A local man reported the results. "Savage was riddled with bullets, and fell dead in the car," he detailed, "but James, though shackled, ran out of the back door and up towards town. He was pursued by a number from the party in the train, volley after volley being fired after him." After James's death on the Madison street, the attackers turned their attention again to the first victim. They placed his body by the railroad tracks and then fired anew into the corpse. Many, perhaps most, local residents condemned the killings. "Such blood-thirstiness is at all times reprehensible," they declared in a public gathering, "but more especially so when the unfortunate victims were on their way to appear before a judicial tribunal and to be tried according to law and the evidence."[23]

As the supreme court attempted to safeguard legal rights and procedures for Republican criminal defendants, it also sought to ensure the penalty of the law for legitimately convicted criminals, even when their crimes were based in Democratic partisanship. One such case involved a vigilance committee in southwestern Florida popularly known as the Sarasota Assassination Society. The secret cabal, comprised primarily of young, unreconstructed, southern-born Democrats, committed itself to using violence and terror against its political enemies. In June 1885, for example, three members were convicted of killing Charles Abbe, the Sarasota postmaster and a federal court commissioner who had testified against society members in various legal proceedings.[24]

A related case tried about the same time concerned the murder of another local man, Harrison "Tip" Riley, by society members. When circuit judge Henry

Laurens Mitchell requested a replacement to sit on the trial, the supreme court designated sixth circuit judge E. K. Foster. Future Florida senate president Joseph B. Wall of Hillsborough County led the defense, which called only one witness. The jury subsequently found Edmond P. Bacon guilty of murder in the first degree, with two other men convicted of accessory before the fact of murder in the first degree. Sentenced to hang, the defendants appealed to the supreme court. The panel undertook a careful review of the testimony to determine the correctness of the judge's refusal to grant a new trial. Finding that a jury could pass upon the credibility of an accomplice's testimony, the court in *Edmond P. Bacon, Leonard F. Andrews and Alfred B. Bidwell* v. *The State of Florida* upheld the judge's ruling and the verdict. "The charge of the court was full and explicit upon this subject," declared Associate Justice Robert Bruce Van Valkenburgh, "and the jury had the whole case fairly submitted to them."[25] Eventually two of the men escaped from custody, and one secured a commutation of sentence to life imprisonment.[26]

Bourbon Political Power versus Home Rule

During Redemption's first decade, Republicans found a sanctuary of sorts in many Florida towns and cities. Often they controlled municipal government, to the anger of white Democrats. In rural areas personal and economic intimidation, combined with growing disenchantment with white Republican leaders, caused many blacks to refrain from voting. On the other hand, protection for Republican voters came somewhat more easily in towns, where blacks increasingly resided during the late 1870s and early 1880s. Ports and resorts such as Fernandina, Pensacola, Jacksonville, Palatka, Green Cove Springs, and St. Augustine especially witnessed persistent Republican influence.[27]

Bourbon leaders chafed at the continued existence of these Republican power centers, sentiments fueled by charges of corruption and mismanagement. As early as 1879, some legislators unsuccessfully acted to promulgate a statute usurping Pensacola's governmental powers. When Governor William D. Bloxham took office in January 1881, he initiated a more substantial attempt to rectify the situation. He achieved passage of laws purporting to affect certain classes of municipalities but effectively dissolving only the charters of Pensacola and Fernandina. The measures placed power in the hands of gubernatorial appointees.[28]

Republicans refused to accept the political assault and presented the question to the supreme court which, at that point, still consisted of two Republicans and one Democrat. The key decision related to a request for a writ of quo warranto in the matter of Fernandina and was decided unanimously. Speaking for the tribunal in *The State of Florida, ex rel. Christian A. Haley* v. *Gustave Stark*, Justice Westcott rejected the Bourbon initiative as improper under the 1868 constitution. "In view of the plainest deductions and conclusions which follow the application of a simple, honest judgment to these facts, can it be said that that is a uniform system of municipal government in which such plain differences may exist in cities in the same situation and the same class?" he questioned. Westcott concluded for the court, "The Constitution, which is a limitation upon the powers of the Legislature, not a grant of powers to it, provides that 'the Legislature shall establish a uniform system of county, township and municipal government,' and any action of that department of the government which destroys the uniformity of a pre-existing system, and permits and authorizes, in cities similarly situated, systems of government differing essentially in the manner of the selection of offices, their terms of office, and the manner of the assessment and collection of revenue, cannot be sustained."[29]

Four years later the high court's composition had changed, as one-time Confederate general Edward A. Perry grasped control of state government. At the time of Perry's inauguration as governor in January 1885, Chief Justice Randall and Associate Justice Westcott resigned, permitting Perry to place upon the supreme tribunal two distinguished lawyers, George Gray McWhorter and George Pettus Raney, who were also his reliable Bourbon allies. The same month Perry moved to wrest political control of his Pensacola hometown from the Republicans. His legislative allies pressed for passage of a bill permitting the governor, under certain limited circumstances, to take control of a municipality through his designees.[30]

Once more, the Republicans resisted by demanding supreme court review. Superficially at least, the case seemed to fit the facts in the 1881 Fernandina dispute. Yet the new tribunal did not settle on that precedent. "This court will not perpetrate an insincerity by denying that the reputed condition of [Pensacola] led to its enactment," Associate Justice Raney conceded.[31] Nonetheless, he concluded on the court's behalf that the constitution permitted the legislature to classify municipalities based upon reasonable criteria. As to the decision in *Haley* v. *Stark*, Raney distinguished the facts. In the Fernandina case private individuals could ascertain when conditions warranted dissolution of the municipal corporation, while the new law placed that responsibility in a public official, the governor. That distinction ascertained, Raney's opinion proceeded logically. "The law is general as to the whole class, and not special as to any one of the class, and it is not local to one city or town, as contradistinguished from another in the situation or condition making the class."[32] The precedent established, the legislature within four years seized Key West and Jacksonville and remade other towns to minimize black voting strength and Republican power.[33]

Railroad Litigation

While Bourbon attempts to retain the reins of state government dominated politics in the two decades after Reconstruction, the construction and operation of railroads surpassed in dynamism all other sectors of Florida's economy and business life. As the years passed, though, emphasis changed from dealing with problems created before or during Reconstruction, to providing state support for construction, to regulating corporate behavior. Earlier courts had interpreted the state's constitutional ability to assist the lines, but the Redemption-era courts nonetheless found themselves enmeshed in controversies that placed the justices center stage in the economic struggles of the times.

A series of cases decided in the late 1870s and early 1880s concerned taxation of railroads and the complexities of the state's rights in lines built with state assistance. As to taxation, the supreme court of Florida in the 1876 matter of *Atlantic and Gulf Railroad* v. *Allen* and 1878's *Gonzales* v. *Sullivan* held that the tax exemptions granted to railroads under the Internal Improvement Act devolved to any successor companies. Writing for the court, Justice Westcott labeled this finding to be bad public policy but felt constrained by United States Supreme Court precedents in the premises.[34] Then, in 1882, an intervening United States Supreme Court decision compelled the high court to reverse the earlier decisions.[35] Accordingly, Westcott in *Palmes* v. *Louisville and Nashville Railroad* declared such exemptions a "personal privilege" that could not be transferred.[36] The fact that the legislature was attempting to levy taxes in spite of earlier exemptions, and the court's approval of the action, represented the beginning of the shift from subsidy to regulation of railroads by the state.

A related instance of litigation concerned the state's rights versus those of foreign bondholders with respect to bonds issued to assist railroad development during Reconstruction. The conflict issued from one of the period's great scandals, the dealings of developers George W. Swepson and Milton S. Littlefield with Republican governor Harrison Reed. Democrats eagerly desired to separate the state from responsibility for the bonds and any financial obligations entailed thereby. Bondholders resisted the inclination strenuously.[37]

Many of the issues arising from the Swepson-Littlefield machinations came to a head in the 1878 case of *The State of Florida and The Trustees of the Internal Improvement Fund* v. *The Jacksonville, Pensacola and Mobile Railroad Company and Milton S. Littlefield.*[38] A court composed of Justice Westcott and circuit judges Augustus Emmet Maxwell and Pleasant W. White (Chief Justice Randall and Associate Justice Van Valkenburgh earlier had been involved in the railroad's affairs) reexamined Florida's authority to subsidize lines. The tribunal confirmed the constitutionality of the general principle of grant subsidies, but it held that the wording of the Internal Improvement Act that authorized the assistance did not encompass lines laid within certain geographical areas, thereby rendering void any bonds issued in support of the unapproved portions of the railroads. In regard to the priority of the state's liens, the jurists determined that, pursuant to statute and with one exception, the lien of the internal improvement fund took precedence over that of the state as trustee for foreign bondholders. "The bonds were not valid as a primary obligation against the state," explained Justice Westcott, "but they were effective when held by *bona fide* purchasers, as showing who were the *cestuis que trust* under the statute."[39] The decision emboldened Democratic lawmakers in 1879 to repudiate the obligations of that portion of the state's railroad debt deemed "unconstitutional."[40]

The burst of railroad construction that began in the early 1880s brought with it for the court's resolution a wide range of novel issues or, at least, issues relating to newly complicated circumstances. The number of cases appealed to the tribunal mushroomed, and it became clear that significant social costs, including damage to property and injuries to passengers and employees, accompanied the economic benefits of steam locomotion. Many state courts had confronted these problems when railroading was in its infancy, and they had adopted common-law doctrines such as assumption of risk, contributory negligence, and the fellow-servant rule to protect the nascent industry from crippling lawsuits. The later emergence of the industry in Florida enabled the court to distribute more evenly the costs of development, both because the industry was on a more sound economic footing and because statutory law existed to guide the court in its policy judgments.[41]

The era's disputes extended well beyond torts, with major cases decided regarding property law and taxation. Several examples will permit a closer look at the types of issues considered. The court's 1887 decision in *Florida Southern Railway Co.* v. *J. B. Brown* concerned the rights of adjacent property owners when a rail line was constructed along a street. Finding no unlawful taking when the adjacent owner does not own the soil under the street, the justices permitted special damages arising when his right to use of the way is denied. On the other hand, when the adjacent owner does own the soil under all or part of the street, that person "has such property in his portion of the street as will prevent the taking thereof or any part of his side of said street by the imposition thereon of an additional burden on the soil to the usual requirements of travel, to wit: by the laying of a railroad track thereon and the operation thereof by steam without first making just compensation therefor."[42]

Similarly, in two cases styled *Jacksonville, Tampa & Key West Railway* v. *Charles S. Adams*, decided in 1891 and 1894, the supreme court addressed the powers of eminent domain. The tribunal upheld the rights of railroads to exercise the power and broadly articulated the extent of permissible conduct, affirming to the railroads, based upon statutory authority, the power even after a determination that a line acted "without complying with the law regulating the exercise of such power" and "whether or not it has or has not been ousted from its former or illegal possession."[43] Further, the justices insisted that the Constitution of 1885 mandated a jury determination of compensation for appropriated property and that the jury's action must be unanimous.[44]

On the subject of taxation, the court in the matter of *F. R. Osborne* v. *State of Florida*, heard in 1894, examined how the state might levy license taxes on lines engaged in interstate commerce. Chief Justice George Pettus Raney authored the opinion, which partially backed state power. "The Southern Express Company may carry on any and all business that constitutes interstate or foreign commerce, free from regulation by or under our laws," he wrote, "but business strictly of a state or local character cannot be exempted from our laws, or put beyond our authority, by its engaging at the same time in interstate or foreign commerce."[45]

The Railroad Commission

Although the Disston purchase of 1881 spurred much needed development of a key industry, the rapid growth of railroads created new issues. Excessive competition and minimal profits forced many smaller companies into bankruptcy and compelled the others to adopt questionable business practices. Passengers and shippers in underserved areas paid exorbitant rates to subsidize the lower rates that common carriers charged in highly competitive regions. The railroads offered rebates, free passes, and other incentives to large shippers, thus discriminating against less affluent customers. Perhaps most unfairly, local shippers paid higher rates than interstate shippers. "As strange as it may seem," one journalist proclaimed in 1878, "it costs more to ship a bushel of corn from Quincy to Jacksonville, some two hundred miles, than it does to bring the same quantity from St. Louis or Louisville, a distance of over a thousand miles."[46] A decade later the problem persisted. The discriminatory practices, along with general complaints about poor service and public opposition to railroad efforts to avoid taxation, convinced legislators that the public interest would no longer be served by subsidizing the lines but, rather, by regulating them.[47]

Other states confronted with these problems had adopted one of two solutions. Some had passed general regulatory legislation and left it to the courts to enforce the provisions. At least twenty-five other states by 1886 had created regulatory commissions to oversee the industry. Since 1866, Florida had attempted to regulate through legislation, passing statutes that prohibited rate discrimination and established maximum passenger rates. Railroad critics believed that this piecemeal approach was ineffective, whereas industry supporters partially blamed legislative micromanagement for the industry's earlier failures. Thus, a consensus developed, amid pressures for further legislative action, for the establishment of a railroad commission with authority to oversee the industry but with flexibility to adapt to the industry's changing needs.[48]

By the mid–1880s the issue of a railroad commission already had received statewide attention. During the 1884 election, Independent gubernatorial candidate Frank W. Pope campaigned against the power of the railroads and promised to establish a regulatory body. Delegates at the constitutional convention of 1885 considered requiring a similar agency. The attempt failed, but the final document did authorize the legislature to "pass laws for the correction of abuses and to prevent unjust discrimination and excessive charges by persons and corporations engaged as common carriers."[49]

When Florida's legislature convened in 1887, the question of a commission stood near the top of the public agenda. Perhaps the most striking aspect of the debate that year was the lack of any serious opposition from the railroads. One road president, Sherman Conant, expressed the sentiments of many railroad men when he spoke in favor of "a fair, just and conservative law." The primary benefit of a commission, in Conant's view, would be to mediate the inevitable disputes that would arise between the common carriers and their customers in such a rapidly growing enterprise. An impartial board of arbitration, "composed of sensible, level-headed men, free from the control of railroads on the one hand and from demagoguery on the other," would benefit the public and the railroad companies. "There is no real antagonism between the railroad companies and the people," he insisted. "The best interest of the one is the best interest of the other." Conant recognized that public desire for regulation was so high that the establishment of a commission was probably inevitable. Still, he reminded his interviewer that "the people derive vast benefits from the roads and therefore ought to be willing to deal fairly with them."[50]

The themes sounded by Conant found ready ears among many Bourbon leaders worried about increasing farmer dissatisfaction. Governor Perry reiterated the message in his address to the 1887 legislature. While supporting the principle of a regulatory commission, he reminded lawmakers that the railroads were "the greatest factors in Florida's progress" and that a punitive law would "turn back the wheels of progress." The interests of the people and of the railroads were "to a greater extent than is generally imagined identical," he asserted. Perry insisted that the goal of any regulation should be to balance the people's interests, the railroads' rights, and the state's needs.[51] On June 2 he signed into law a Florida railroad commission bill. It had passed unanimously in the senate and with only three dissenting votes in the house of representatives.[52]

The new commission closely resembled the one already established in Georgia. It consisted of three members appointed by the governor with the senate's approval. The commissioners served staggered terms of four years and could not own stock in, be employed by, or have any interest in a railroad company. The commission could set rates and review agreements among competing companies. A significant revision of the Georgia model, added during senate debate, permitted railroad companies to appeal rates to a board of revisers composed of the attorney general, the comptroller, the secretary of agriculture, the secretary of state, and the state treasurer. The commission could initiate suits against violators through the state's attorney in the county where the violation occurred. A judge could levy fines of between $100 and $5,000, which would be used to benefit county schools.[53]

Commission organization quickly followed the law's approval. In August Perry designated Chief Justice George Gray McWhorter, former circuit judge Enoch Vann, and Sumter County farmer and one-time Democratic legislator William Himes as the initial commissioners. The men hurriedly addressed the tedious task of making the fledgling agency operational. They consulted with other state railroad commissions and the interstate commerce commission, established rules and forms for compliance with and protest of the panel's decisions, and conducted public hearings. On October 1 they announced a schedule fixing passenger and freight rates. The tariffs satisfied neither the public, who desired even lower rates, nor the railroad companies, which maintained that the commission had a responsibility to guarantee a "reasonable profit."[54] The commissioners spent the rest of the year hearing petitions for individual exceptions to the published rates, which they granted in some cases. Some dissatisfied companies appealed to the board of revisers, which generally upheld the commission's rulings.[55]

The regulatory board met increasing resistance to its orders as it endeavored to hold the line on rate increases in the face of significant economic disruptions affecting the industry, such as the yellow fever epidemic of 1888. In the circumstances some railroads began to challenge the board's authority with actions that ranged from refusal to cooperate to outright defiance. Numerous companies objected to filing an annual report as required by law, and all but one submitted the compilations late. Finally, the commission agreed not to question the reports' accuracy if the railroads would merely file them. Since the commissioners did not possess jurisdiction over interstate rates, some companies inflated those tariffs to compensate for what they considered inadequate local rates. Other lines raised intrastate rates and used the threat of retaliation to discourage shippers from protesting to the commission.[56]

None of the twenty-seven railroads subject to the commission's authority gave it more annoyance than the Pensacola and Atlantic. Its founder, Bourbon loyalist William D. Chipley, had opposed the panel's creation from the beginning. Since the rates on other lines of the railroad's parent company, the Louisville and Nashville, were higher than those permitted by the commission, Chipley felt compelled to challenge the agency's powers. Particularly, he ignored many of its rules and rates. Thereafter, the commissioners requested Attorney General Charles M. Cooper to sue Chipley's line in several counties. By January 1889 the state had won six cases with combined judgments of $14,000.[57]

Chipley vigorously opposed the commission's enforcement actions. Initially he challenged the body's rulings through its own established procedures for petition, protest, and appeal to the board of revisers. As suits against his company mounted, though, he directly attacked the commission's legitimacy. Insisting that, by not fixing rates that were "reasonable and just," the commissioners had exceeded their authority in what amounted to an unconstitutional taking of private property without just compensation, he obtained injunctive relief from first circuit judge James F. McClelland to stop prosecution.[58] After a series of legal maneuvers, Attorney General Cooper appealed the decision to the supreme court. On its behalf, Chief Justice Augustus Emmet Maxwell in 1888's *Railroad Commissioners* v. *The Pensacola and Atlantic Railroad Company* dissolved the injunction and dismissed Chipley's complaint. The action, he reasoned, was a prohibited suit against the state. "The law refuses authority to enjoin the discretionary action of executive officers," Maxwell wrote. "It does not matter that the exercise of the discretion works an injustice or wrong."[59] Instead of injunctive relief, Chipley could raise objections as part of his defense to any commission enforcement effort. Noting that, if the commission law were unconstitutional, the commissioners would not be clothed with protection, Maxwell then examined the act and pronounced it constitutional as a proper exercise of state police powers.[60]

Although the case affirmed the commission's legality, it left unanswered questions about the scope of its powers. Since Chipley had other litigation pending in the supreme court, the attorney general recommended that the commission postpone further action until the high tribunal had ruled on the commission's substantive authority, particularly its rate-setting power. The court heard

The Pensacola and Atlantic Railroad Company v. *The State* at January term 1889. Its opinion, scripted by Chief Justice George Pettus Raney, circumscribed the commission's flexibility to some extent. It found that rates must be set at a level sufficient to meet a road's operating expenses but declared that, when reasonable disagreement exists about the remunerative value of the tariff schedule, the courts should not substitute their judgment for that of the commissioners. According to one credible source, this decision was the first instance in which a state supreme court held that a railroad commission's prescription of freight and passenger rates that would not support railroad expenses constituted a taking of property in violation of due process.[61]

Although the second *Pensacola and Atlantic* case represented a slight infringement on the powers of the railroad commission, since it now had to justify its rates when challenged in court, the rulings generally solidified the body's authority and settled authoritatively that the legislature could create regulatory agencies to carry out its constitutional power to oversee the railroads. As the lines adjusted to the new rules, compliance increased, and, by 1891, only one railroad was charging rates higher than allowed by the commission. In 1889 the legislature also amended the law to increase some of the commission's powers and streamline its operations, such as by eliminating the board of revisers and authorizing the commission to present cases to the interstate commerce commission. Shippers began to realize genuine savings. Then, in 1891, disgruntled pro-railroad legislators combined with anti-railroad lawmakers, who feared railroad domination of the panel through new appointments, to repeal the commission's charter. Nonetheless, the supreme court's rulings would endure to permit future legislatures to regulate economic enterprise through governmental agencies, an opportunity that Progressive-era lawmakers would embrace with enthusiasm.[62]

Regulation of Other Industries

Once involved in regulation of the railroad business, the state slowly reached its regulatory arms toward other industries. Phosphate mining, especially, drew interest after individuals and companies began extracting that resource in the late 1880s. Two statutes, passed in 1887 and 1891, purported to subject the industry to state authority, created a board of phosphate commissioners, and claimed rights in mineral deposits under navigable waters. In 1893 the court backed the legislative initiative, rejecting in *State* v. *Black River Phosphate Co.* an attempt by one industry arm to assert mining rights as a riparian owner.[63]

The court upheld, as well, regulatory measures undertaken by the state's emerging towns and cities in the interest of public health and safety. As it did generally during the period regarding exercise of police powers, the tribunal adopted a "reasonableness" test and established itself as the ultimate arbiter of reasonableness. The 1890 decision of *City of Jacksonville* v. *William M. Ledwith* offers a case in point. Chief Justice Raney asserted for the court that Jacksonville, by ordinance, could "prescribe the time and places for the sale of the articles [that the ordinance] covers; and such restrictions as to times and places being reasonable with reference to the welfare of the community, and not being in general restraint of trade, they may likewise prohibit the sale of such articles elsewhere."[64]

Criminal Law

The increasingly sophisticated economic and social side of Florida life, taken with broader jurisprudential developments, introduced new perspectives on criminal law and procedure. Nationally, the late nineteenth century witnessed a trend toward what has been described as "modernization" of the law, changes that afforded greater attention to formal due process, bureaucratization, and streamlining of court administration coupled with less tolerance for self-help.[65] In Florida, the court's dockets listed a wide variety of cases that explored various aspects of emerging issues. The mention of a few decisions demonstrates the range of supreme court consideration. *Finch* v. *State* (1876) examined defendants' rights in capital cases, while the next year's *Gibson* v. *State* upheld the use of six-person juries in criminal and civil cases.[66] *Bond* v. *State*, heard in 1886, determined that prior threats of a homicide victim were not admissible when the defendant instigated the attack.[67] *Garner* v. *State* explored, in 1891, the subjects of self-defense and the defense of intoxication, and 1892's *Lovett* v. *State* defined reasonable doubt.[68]

Voting Rights

The preservation of Bourbon control of Florida government depended upon the withdrawal of many blacks from the voting booth. Already in 1877 some black voters had evidenced disenchantment with white carpetbagger leadership by declining to exercise the franchise, and in numerous rural counties economic and physical intimidation by Democrats enhanced the decline in electoral participation. The Constitution of 1868 also contributed to the diminution of the black vote. Article 14 specified that no person convicted of "felony [shall] be qualified to vote at any election unless restored to civil rights" and provided further, "The legislature shall have power and shall enact the necessary laws to exclude from . . . the right of suffrage, all persons convicted of bribery, perjury, larceny, or of infamous crime."[69] The 1868 assembly thereafter banned from the polls "persons hereafter convicted of felony, bribery, perjury, larceny, or other infamous crime."[70]

Once in power in 1877, the Bourbons utilized justice of the peace courts, headed by gubernatorial appointees, to process thousands of cases for petty offenses, with the result of a conviction that prohibited the defendant from voting. One man who had been convicted of the misdemeanor of petty larceny challenged the practice in the 1881 case of *State of Florida ex rel. Richard Jordan* v. *T. E. Buckman*. The supreme court's Republican majority combined with Justice Westcott, a Democrat, to dismiss the appeal in a brief opinion. "The Legislature may, or may not, under this Constitution, so legislate as to annex to petty larceny the punishment of a misdemeanor," Westcott wrote, "but neither such a statute, nor any other which the Legislature might pass, can disconnect from it that punishment which the Constitution makes it the duty of the Legislature to annex to it, which is disqualification to vote."[71]

The *Jordan* decision illustrated the court's tendency to decide cases involving race relations in a formalistic manner without regard to social or political realities, and the same approach was evidenced in a second important voting rights case, 1880's *State of Florida ex rel. Charles Scott* v. *The Board of County Commissioners of Jefferson County*. The litigation centered on an 1877 law pressed by the Bourbons that commanded a new voter registration process that granted boards of county commissioners, again gubernatorial appointees, extensive powers to eliminate individuals from the rolls. In Jefferson County in 1878 the board acted so aggressively that it impeded reregistrations by qualified blacks. Particularly, the commissioners "assumed and pretended power under the statute by holding short sessions of their board, by refusing to remain in session from day to day till their duty was performed, by formalities in conducting business, by failure of a quorum of said board to attend, and in various other ways, that it was impossible, prior to [the 1878] general election, for but comparatively few persons, whose names had been so erased from said book, to have their names restored thereto."[72] Even in those circumstances the court declined to order the board to fulfill its lawful responsibility. "Mandamus is never granted in anticipation of a sup[po]sed omission of duty," Chief Justice Randall declared, "however strong the presumption may be that the persons whom it is sought to coerce by the writ will refuse to perform their duty when the proper times arrives."[73]

Regulation of the Legal Profession

As the courts grappled with more and more complex legal issues, legal educators and professionals began reconsidering the appropriate standards for training and admission to the bar. In 1870, Christopher Columbus Langdell, the new dean of Harvard Law School, introduced the "case method" of legal education, emphasizing the "legal science" of inductively deriving generally applicable legal principles from a careful reading of common-law cases. As colleges and universities across the country added law schools that adhered to Langdell's conception of law as a formal academic discipline, other methods of legal training, such as "reading law" as an apprentice in a law office, fell into disrepute. The American Bar Association, established in 1878, sought to solidify the status of law as a profession—rather than as a mere trade—by encouraging states to require a degree from a university-affiliated law school and the successful completion of a standardized examination for admission to the bar.[74]

Changes came slowly to the legal profession in Florida. The legislature did not respond immediately to the national pressures for reform, leaving authority over bar admission and discipline in the hands of circuit judges. As the jurists applied more rigorous standards on an ad hoc basis, though, attorneys challenged the legality of those judicial actions in the supreme court, presenting the justices with the opportunity to shape the character of the state's legal profession. In general the jurists acted conservatively, stressing individual fitness for the practice of law, as opposed to standardized qualifications, and creating a presumption against disbarment as a means of disciplining attorneys.[75]

Some problems required particular attention. From the territorial days, for example, applicants for the bar had been required to be twenty-one years old, demonstrate "good moral character," and pass an examination before a circuit judge. In practice, the age requirement had often been waived through special legislation. Then, the Constitution of 1885 prohibited the legislature from passing special acts "relieving minors from legal disabilities."[76] This provision was adopted partly to end the practice of admitting minors to the bar and probably constituted a reaction to the call for stricter standards. Still, the constitution did not prohibit general legislation to emancipate minors, and in 1889 the legislature authorized circuit judges to remove the disabilities of minors to manage their estates, which authorized them to do all "things that he or she could do if twenty-one years of age."[77]

The new statute prompted an early challenge regarding the right to practice law. In 1889 Herbert Lamson, an emancipated minor, sought bar admission from a circuit court. The judge refused an examination, arguing that the act of that year only permitted courts to allow some minors to conduct their personal affairs. It did not, he reasoned, affect the age requirement for the bar, which the constitution's framers had wished to preserve. Lamson petitioned the supreme court for a writ of mandamus compelling administration of an examination. Chief Justice Raney, for a unanimous court, complied. He noted in *State of Florida ex rel. Herbert Lamson* v. *James M. Baker* that circuit judges had been authorized since 1875 to grant minors the power to manage their estates and argued that the new legislation contemplated broader powers. Under the new act, Raney observed, judges were to consider the applicant's "character, habits, and mental capacity for business," not simply his ability to manage his own affairs. A minor whose disabilities had been removed under the act was "in the same position as to applying for admission to the bar that he would be had a special act been passed authorizing him to be examined, and if found qualified to be admitted." Thus, the court refused to allow examining judges to impose bar qualifications that were more strict than those specifically provided by the constitution or statute.[78]

Similarly, the high court refused to sanction the use of disbarment to remove attorneys who violated professional expectations unrelated to moral fitness. Two 1892 cases involved lawyers who faced disbarment for careless errors that did not affect the outcome of litigation or benefit the attorneys financially. *State of Florida ex rel. Geo. P. Fowler* v. *Jesse J. Finley* concerned an attorney who faced removal for correcting a clerical error in a legal decree after it had been signed and approved by the circuit court. The correction noted the county in which the decree had been executed and had no effect on the document's meaning. The justices disapproved of tampering with court decrees, but "when such an interference . . . is made unauthorizedly or incautiously, but without any bad motive or fraudulent design, it partakes more of the character of a contempt of the court, than of that moral turpitude that stamps the perpetrator as being an unfit person to exercise the office of an attorney." Disbarment's purpose, the court specified, was "protection, not punishment." In this instance, the proper remedy was to punish Fowler for his "unauthorized and highly reprehensible act" through a reprimand, fine, or suspension, "as there were no elements in it that marked him as a corrupt practitioner against whom the public should be protected by destroying his official life as an attorney."[79]

State of Florida ex rel. Benton C. Rude v. *William B. Young* presented more striking circumstances. An attorney had been disbarred for his handling of a criminal case, having arranged for the defendant to pay small sums to a burglary victim and to the presiding judge for court costs in exchange for case dismissal. The lawyer maintained that he did not know that the defendant had been charged with a crime and thought that he had been mediating a settlement in a replevin action. Overturning the disbarment, the supreme court prohibited such action unless a "clear preponderance" of evidence proved the commission of an unprofessional act *and* "bad motive," emphasizing that disbarment was intended only to remove those who were morally unfit to practice law. "Illegal acts," the court insisted, "are not necessarily corrupt." By interpreting the facts in a manner highly favorable to the defendant, the tribunal demonstrated the high burden of proof required for disbarment. The fact that a deputy sheriff showed an arrest warrant to the lawyer, for instance, did not prove that he "ever read the warrant or was aware of its contents." Finding nothing that suggested to the justices "a hope of benefit" to the lawyer, the justices concluded that his conduct must be "attributed . . . to a misapprehension or inattention to his duty, than to a criminal intent." The court again had viewed professional responsibility more as an issue of personal character than technical expertise.[80]

Not until the closing years of the nineteenth century did the national movement for more formalized bar admission procedures successfully reach the Florida legislature. The result and the supreme court's reaction to it are discussed in chapter 19.

Part Five

Before the Great War, 1897–1916

Chapter 17

Progressive Florida

The January 5, 1897, inauguration of William D. Bloxham as governor, beginning the Democrat's second term after a lapse of twelve years, offered Floridians a misleading sign of the future. The event directed them, not ahead, but back to earlier days. Narrowly chosen lieutenant governor in the contested election of 1870, defeated for elevation to the office of chief executive in 1872, and finally seated in the governor's chair in 1881, the Leon County planter's continued presence in politics reminded his fellow residents of the tumultuous years of Reconstruction and Redemption. In that earlier time, the state had existed in an isolated and undeveloped condition, depending primarily upon agriculture for its inhabitants' livelihoods. Long-sought prosperity had eluded most, while experiments in race relations had ended amid violence and struggles for political supremacy.[1]

Already in 1897, though, Florida had begun to change in a dramatic fashion that its political character had yet to reflect. The 1880s and early 1890s had ushered an era of development that, in turn, had spurred tremendous population growth. When Bloxham had achieved election as governor in 1880, the state still contained only about 270,000 residents. Fifteen years later, just before his second term, the figure had increased by almost 200,000. During the two decades after 1895, further development fueled remarkable gains as the population bolted upward by 98 percent. The total in 1915 approached close to 1 million.[2]

As the population grew, whites predominated to an ever greater extent. In the Civil War's aftermath, black Floridians and their white counterparts each comprised about one-half of the population. By the mid–1880s the number of blacks had dipped to approximately 44 percent, with a further drop of 2 percent in the following decade. After a slight resurgence during 1895–1905, the share plummeted seven points to 39 percent in 1915. This decrease of blacks as a percentage of the overall population accompanied an enhanced urban presence. Where 36 percent of black Floridians resided in cities and towns in 1905, 43 percent did so in 1915. Florida's largest city that year was Jacksonville, in which 36,000 blacks lived, comprising 54 percent of the town's citizens. Other communities with black majorities included Tallahassee, Apalachicola, Daytona, Fernandina, Palatka, Quincy, and Sanford.[3]

Just as more blacks lived in the state's urban areas, so, too, did more Floridians generally. The state's largest town, Key West, had boasted fewer than 10,000 residents in 1880, with Jacksonville and Pensacola each possessing several thousand fewer still. Tallahassee, with 2,500, still claimed prominence among the larger communities. By the mid–1890s Jacksonville's 25,000 dwarfed Key West's 16,000 and Pensacola's 14,000. The trend accelerated over the next twenty years. In 1915, 67,000 lived at Jacksonville and 23,000 at Pensacola. Key West lagged in growth with a total of only 18,495, but two much newer communities had assumed positions of significant population concentration. Tampa for a time in the 1870s virtually had been depopulated, and 1880 census takers had discovered only 720 who claimed the town as their home. Fifteen years afterward, however, 5,532 were counted, and, in 1915, 48,160. Similarly, in 1895 the tiny village of Miami found no entry on census takers' lists. Given an almost 200 percent increase between 1910 and 1915, the latter year's final tally rested at about 15,600 for the Dade County community.[4]

The movement of Floridians from countryside to town found a parallel in regional population shifts. Political and economic power had concentrated before the Civil War in Middle Florida, the plantation-oriented area between the Suwannee and Apalachicola rivers. During the decade and a half after 1880 its counties had stagnated. Madison, Jefferson, and Leon actually lost population, with growth thereafter for all Middle Florida counties attaining relatively modest levels, at best. On the other hand, Escambia and Duval anchored northwestern and northeastern Florida's surges with substantial increases. The most telling revisions came in the upper and central peninsula. Baker, Orange, Osceola, Alachua, Marion, Hillsborough, and Polk posted large gains. After 1895 the momentum for growth shifted further east and south. Between 1905 and 1915 the thirteen counties of South Florida averaged 75 percent increases in population, with Dade achieving 102 percent, Polk 110 percent, Lee 119 percent, St. Lucie 184 percent, and Osceola 202 percent. To the state's thirty-nine counties in 1880 had been added six in 1895. After legislators created Broward County in 1915, the total reached fifty-one. The largest of them were Duval (94,834), Hillsborough (83,682), Escambia (41,117), Polk (37,423), and Alachua (35,366).

Multiple factors prompted these demographic changes. As discussed in part

4, railroad construction and related immigration and tourism programs provided a solid foundation. Encouraged by generous programs of land grants and other public assistance, West Florida's William D. Chipley and East Florida's Henry B. Plant and Henry M. Flagler remade the state. In the 1880s Plant's South Florida and Florida Southern railroads provided access to the central and southwestern portions of the peninsula, creating or benefiting towns such as Orlando, Kissimmee, Winter Haven, Lakeland, Plant City, Tampa, and Punta Gorda. Meanwhile, Flagler built a rail and commercial empire along the Atlantic coast. He began at St. Augustine and, by 1896, had extended his line, known later as the Florida East Coast Railway, to remote Miami. His grand tourist hotels drew winter guests by the thousands, and his touch proved magical for Ormond Beach, Daytona, Fort Pierce, Palm Beach, and other locales.[5]

While construction on these lines essentially had been completed before 1897, much of the benefit obtained from them occurred in the two decades that followed. The rails offered the transportation to the state and the developers provided accommodations. Yet despite widespread advertising, most vacationing Americans still did not consider Florida as a likely destination. In the circumstances, a war finally provided the necessary stimulus.

The Spanish-American War of 1898, though brief, induced substantial changes in the United States and, particularly, in Florida. As Theodore Roosevelt, one of its most renowned participants, noted, "It wasn't much of a war, but it was the best war we had."[6] With patriotic passions stirred by mass-circulation newspapers and politicians anxious to divert public attention from other problems, the conflict particularly gave Americans a chance to put aside bitter memories of the Civil War as northerners and southerners joined in a popular cause. It began in February 1898 when the United States battleship *Maine* exploded and sank in the harbor at Havana, Cuba. Rumors circulated wildly that the island's overlords, the Spanish, had destroyed the vessel and killed many members of its crew. "THE MAINE BLOWN UP WITH TORPEDO" cried a *Tampa Morning Tribune* headline.[7] Few heeded words of caution such as those expressed by the *Micanopy Hustler*'s editor:

> The Maine is lost when Freedom's cause
> Did very badly need her;
> Let's find out [for] certain if she was
> Blowed up by a torpeder.[8]

The incident led to a declaration of war by the United States Congress, and soon Florida had become a center for war mobilization and coordination. Most particularly, Tampans called the War Department's attention to the city's advantages as a supply base and point of embarkation. The newly built railroads seemed ideally suited for troop and supply transportation, and the owners facilitated their use. By May 25, 23,000 officers and men crowded Tampa, while auxiliary camps dotted the landscape at Lakeland, Jacksonville, Fernandina, and Miami. Each of the locales suffered to some degree from disease and crime as a result, but benefits substantially outweighed the costs. Beyond the ring of local cash registers, for instance, Tampa and Pensacola emerged with improved harbors and defenses. Key West benefited by the construction of a deeper channel, a modern navy yard, improved coaling facilities, and added defenses. Moreover, the state gained an incalculable advantage in favorable publicity, largely the result of press attention. War Department expenditures aided the railroads, as well, permitting significant additions and improvements to roadbeds and equipment.[9]

One of the war's most unpleasant sides illustrated another factor—beyond rail construction, tourism, immigration, and war mobilization and coordination—that fostered Florida's demographic changes in the late nineteenth and early twentieth centuries. In the 1890s enhanced efforts were undertaken aimed at erecting a color line in southern society. This line was marked by the passage of statutes and ordinances known to us as "Jim Crow laws." When black troops from the North and West passed through the South on their way to Florida in 1898, they bristled at the racial segregation codes and demeaning treatment. At Tampa the tensions exploded into rioting after white Ohio volunteers, on a drunken spree, used a black child for target practice. Black soldiers tore into sections of the city, destroying bars, restaurants, and brothels.[10]

The racial tensions and violence were not limited to soldiers at Tampa. Florida had known vigilante action since the beginning of the territorial era, but, during the 1890s, racial violence and lynchings reached their most intense points in the state's history. From 1890 to 1900 at least seventy-four blacks died from lynch law, with an additional fifty-one falling victim in the succeeding decade. Forty-nine more individuals perished between 1910 and 1917. The problem especially beset rural areas and small towns. When that fact was coupled with poor economic conditions for farmers, it encouraged many blacks to remove their families to Florida cities. Increasingly in the early 1900s the refugees moved, as well, to northern cities where industrial jobs beckoned. By 1915 railroads and other businesses were recruiting workers in Florida for employment elsewhere, and thousands of black Floridians thereafter joined the great migration.[11]

For those blacks who remained in the state, Florida's urban centers for a time furnished some chances for improvement and security. In the first decade of the 1900s, cities such as Pensacola, Fernandina, St. Augustine, Gainesville,

Ocala, Tampa, and Key West boasted small, but well-established, black middle classes. With blacks dominating construction trades in many locales, state growth permitted rewarding employment under reasonable conditions. In such circumstances, black professionals, merchants, and tradesmen could flourish. Not surprisingly, then, in 1911 Pensacola possessed within its black community thriving churches, a normal school and high school, literary and social clubs, and other amenities of urban life.[12]

Jacksonville, in regard to active discrimination, was Florida's least onerous environment for blacks. Prior to 1907 its black residents participated in city governance, and some thereafter continued to control substantial property interests and commercial enterprises. At the turn of the century, for instance, Stansbury Boyce possessed assets worth $75,000, gained through operation of "two or three very large dry goods establishments." At the same time Abrams Lincoln Lewis joined with others to found the mutual benefit association that became the Afro-American Life Insurance Company. Until fired by the Woodrow Wilson administration in 1913, lawyer Joseph E. Lee ran the United States government's revenue collection operations for the state from offices there. Generations of Florida's most promising black children received their educations at its Stanton High School, Cookman Institute, and Edward Waters College. Individuals of importance who attended included T. Thomas Fortune, James Weldon Johnson, A. Philip Randolph, and Zora Neale Hurston.[13]

As suggested by Joseph E. Lee's professional affiliation, black lawyers continued to serve their communities in the early twentieth century, and their ability to practice extended to the supreme court of Florida. While Key West's James Dean, Tampa's Peter W. Bryant, and others received degrees at institutions such as Howard University, typically an attorney-to-be read law in the state. James Weldon Johnson did so in the offices of white attorney Thomas A. Ledwith at Jacksonville. Johnson described the experience:

> His office was in the Law Exchange Building, and there I spent a part of each day. . . . After I had been studying about six months Mr. Ledwith turned over to me the duty of drawing most of the necessary papers. This lightened his work and was very advantageous for me. He had a good practice in divorce matters, and I gained proficiency in drawing bills in these cases. He gave me a good deal of his time in discussing knotty questions and in quizzing me in various legal subjects. At the end of eighteen months my friend—we had become friends—said he thought I ought to try the examination for admission to the bar. I didn't feel so sure about it as he [and the] nearer the day approached, the more anxious I grew.[14]

Johnson took his bar examination about 1899. "This was the first time in Duval County . . . ," he recorded, "that a Negro had sought admission to the bar through open examination in a state court." He explained, "There were two or three Negro lawyers in Jacksonville, but each of these, I believe, had been admitted in the Federal Courts during or shortly after the Reconstruction period, and were admitted to practice in the state courts through comity." The event proved less forbidding than Johnson had feared. Future United States senator Duncan Upshaw Fletcher and local attorney E. J. L'Engle eased his way over the objections of lawyer W. B. Young to the admission of a black man. After Young stalked from the courthouse, Fletcher moved Johnson's admission, upon which the attorneys present offered their congratulations. As Johnson related further, his journey into the profession had not yet ended:

> In the following spring the state teacher's association met at Tallahassee. I was bound by duty to go, and [a friend] thought that it would be a good thing for both of us to be there and look for the opportunity to be admitted to the State Supreme Court. In quest of that opportunity, we climbed the central red hill of the town, up to the capitol. In one of the corridors we met a man who shouted, "Hey, what are you two fellows doing here?" The man was Frank T. Clark, a Jacksonville lawyer. We told him that our main reason for visiting the capitol was to find someone, if we could, who would help us in being admitted to the Supreme Court. Mr. Clark said at once, "Why, come along with me; I'll do it myself." We followed him into the Supreme Courtroom, and in less time than it takes to tell about it he had made the motion and we had been admitted. A short while afterwards Mr. Clark was elected to Congress.[15]

Economic and social conditions worsened for blacks as the twentieth century moved toward its third decade. Innovative leaders endeavored to offer assistance. After Jacksonville's Great Fire of 1901, Eartha Mary Magdalene White launched a career as social worker, helping to create the Union Benevolent Association and founding a home for the elderly. In 1904 Mary McLeod Bethune opened the Daytona Normal and Industrial Institute for Negro Girls, the predecessor of Bethune-Cookman College, and in 1913 Spelman College graduate Blanche Armwood established schools of household arts at Tampa. Similar efforts can be identified in most state cities, but they suffered to an extent from Florida's loss of talent to the North. It was, after all, Floridians Fortune, Johnson, Randolph, Hurston, and their fellow émigrés who contributed so much to black cultural and political life in America during the twentieth century.[16]

The sweeping changes that were marshaling Florida's trend toward urban-

James Weldon Johnson. Johnson began studying law in Jacksonville a few years before the turn of the century and passed the bar examination in a state court. While visiting Tallahassee, Johnson was admitted to practice before the supreme court upon motion of a Jacksonville attorney. He was one of several black lawyers practicing in Jacksonville.

ization lessened its dependence upon agriculture, although farm products remained the single largest source of income within the state. Agricultural pursuits broadened, though. The cotton economy waned, while expanded commerce in timber, cattle, citrus, and winter vegetables fostered growth. Phosphate and fertilizer industries utilized advanced production techniques. Electric lights and telephones began to diminish the stern isolation of rural areas, an eventuality further encouraged when the seeds of a "good roads" movement were planted at Jacksonville in 1910 by the opening of Atlantic Boulevard, the state's first improved highway. Four years previously owners operated fewer than three hundred automobiles in Florida, one-fourth of which were located at Daytona, with Miami having thirty-eight. The number more than doubled within two years, and, by 1915, 15,000 horseless carriages speedily transported Floridians along added miles of improved roads.[17]

As residents adjusted to the momentous changes occurring in the state, so, too, did Florida's politicians and politics, though not so quickly and completely. Nationally, the movement known as progressivism acted to transform concepts of government away from laissez-faire restraint to increased governmental activism in favor of reform. Southern advocates proved more cautious than backers in the North and West, stressing the need for patience, deliberateness, and unhurried change. The reforms southern progressives advanced were relatively mild and grounded within the context of continued white control. Their most visible demands regarded the regulation of business, particularly control of corporations, by state governments.[18]

Florida progressivism arose as a faction of the Democratic party. Although its philosophy tended to be liberal by southern standards, the term easily could mislead. No typical progressive could be found because no single person supported all of the causes associated with the movement. Instead, adherents found guidance in broad principles of business regulation, "good government," and social reform. Rather than evidencing hostility toward industry as such, the progressives favored careful supervision of railroads and related concerns so as to maximize Florida's appeal to investors and potential settlers. They launched campaigns, as well, to provide for the helpless, increase agricultural productivity, teach the unlearned, and reorganize government to cut expenses by eliminating waste rather than services. No governor who served during 1897 to 1916 did so as an avowed progressive, but the movement influenced the administrations of each to greater and lesser extents.[19]

The era opened, as noted at the beginning of this chapter, with the second administration of William D. Bloxham. Floridians had expected him to continue the Bourbon traditions of the preceding two decades. Although Bloxham represented conservative strength in the state, increasing demands for reform moved the governor and legislators to take constrained actions. In 1897 and 1899, for instance, the legislature reinstated the railroad commission and increased its enforcement powers. The solons also enacted measures to prevent monopolies of beef sales and to institute pure-food regulations. Bloxham expanded state regulatory authority through creation of what became the office of auditor, an investigative unit to root out fraud and waste in government. By the time he left office, Bloxham had overseen the beginnings of fire insurance company regulation, adoption of a uniform textbook law, and the first service of women as notaries public.[20]

Illinois-born William Sherman Jennings, who came to Florida in 1885, followed Bloxham in the executive office in 1901. The advent of this recently arrived northerner, who resided in the fast-growing central-peninsular region, symbolized in politics the movement from old-line Middle Florida planter influence toward the enhanced power of the state's "new men." By inclination a conservative, Jennings nonetheless backed numerous progressive programs. He fought to reclaim for the state 3 million acres of public lands previously granted to corporations, and he initiated plans for draining the Everglades. He urged improvement of educational programs, saw to an enlargement of the capitol, and arranged better terms for the leasing of state convicts. Perhaps most significantly, he helped write into law the Primary Election Law, by which all Democratic candidates after 1901 would be selected by vote in a white-only primary. Viewed as a progressive reform, this effort proved, as one Florida historian explained, "The gifts of Jeffersonian democracy were to be accorded only to the white population."[21]

Florida progressivism probably achieved its crest in the administration of Napoleon Bonaparte Broward, which began in 1905. The Jacksonville native implemented programs for state assistance to public schools, compulsory school attendance, regulation of child labor, fish and game conservation laws, food and drug inspection, prison reform, and equitable legislative apportionment. He successfully urged the legislature to reorganize higher education, from which came the institutions now known as the University of Florida, Florida State University, and Florida Agricultural and Mechanical University. Broward also oversaw construction of the state's first governor's mansion, but not all of his ideas succeeded so well. He urged, for example, a national program to buy up all property owned by Negroes and to colonize them in a nation of their own. Likely his most notable achievement was implementation of state-funded plans for Everglades drainage, which encouraged increased settlement in the southern peninsula.[22]

The ensuing terms of governors Albert W. Gilchrist and Park Trammell, respectively from DeSoto and Polk counties, revealed a continuing legacy of mild progressive influence. Among their activities from 1909 to 1917, Gilchrist worked for laws to safeguard the health of humans and of livestock, and Trammell brought about election campaign finance reform and property assessment equalization. Through the four administrations of the progressive era, judicial organization and the administration of justice also found themselves as subjects of reform demands. The results and the individuals who served on the supreme court during the period are examined more closely in the chapter that follows.[23]

Chapter 18

Court Expansion and Other Reforms

The waves of change that swept through Florida in the late nineteenth and early twentieth centuries significantly affected Florida's judiciary just as they did other facets of government and society. In the process, the supreme court of Florida underwent alterations that resulted in the expansion of its membership and, to some extent, the subjects of its responsibilities. Demands were placed upon its members to decide issues critical to the new society that they served, although, typically, the men who sat on the tribunal represented through their origins an earlier era when planters exercised power and state government responded to their needs. The challenges they faced proved greater in light of that fact, but the justices nonetheless exercised their responsibilities forthrightly and, sometimes, courageously.

In 1897, which roughly dates the beginning of the Progressive era in Florida, the supreme court operated pursuant to the provisions of article 5 of the Constitution of 1885. As the document specified, three justices held office for staggered terms of six years. Each was elected by popular vote unless a vacancy occurred, in which event the governor appointed a successor to serve out the term. A chief justice was to be chosen by lot of the justices. Strictly speaking, no "associate justices" sat on the court; rather, they appropriately were addressed as "chief justice" and "justice." The members serving on January 1 included Chief Justice Milton Harvey Mabry, Justice Robert Fenwick Taylor, and Justice Benjamin Sullivan Liddon. Early in the month Liddon resigned, and Governor William D. Bloxham designated Francis Beauregard Carter to serve in his stead. The court thereupon selected Taylor to preside as chief justice.[1]

Florida's population growth and the resulting increased litigation soon placed unmanageable demands upon the three-man court. For years already, attorneys and their clients had complained of congested dockets that sometimes resulted in backlogs of up to four years. In many cases, as one report noted, the problem "deprived [litigants] of a verdict until they were dead or the issues involved had become too old to be of interest." Accordingly, in 1901 the legislature acted to rectify the situation. It proposed a constitutional amendment that, in addition to increasing the number of judicial circuits, doubled the number of justices.[2]

Pending ratification of the amendment by voters in 1902, the legislators provided temporary relief for the case overload problem. It permitted the justices "to select and call to its assistance three persons, residents and citizens of Florida, and learned in the law, of good moral and professional character," to act as commissioners of the court. Commissioners' duties encompassed assisting in the disposition of the caseload and rendering other services as directed by the justices. The court exercised this authority by naming as commissioners William Adams Hocker, chief judge of the fifth circuit; Evelyn Croom Maxwell, chief judge of the first circuit; and Tampa lawyer James F. Glenn. "The justices are entitled to hearty congratulations upon securing the services of three such talented and capable lawyers and jurists to assist them," proclaimed the capital's principal newspaper. The editor added: "They are also entitled to the thanks of the people of Florida for the wise and worthy selections they have made. Since the appointments have been announced there need be no doubt whatever that the Supreme Court Commission will render valuable service to the State."[3]

The next year voters endorsed court expansion by a vote of 5,515 to 3,147. The amendment specified that for the year 1905, and for subsequent years, the legislature was to provide for the election of the justices as it might determine and to prescribe terms of office not to exceed six years, except that the number of justices holding office at any one time could not be less than three nor more than six. In the meantime the amendment permitted the governor immediately to appoint three additional justices. Governor William Sherman Jennings, after the November 1902 ratification, named as interim justices Thomas M. Shackleford, Commissioner Maxwell, and Robert Spratt Cockrell. At the time of the November election, Commissioner Hocker had been elected to replace Justice Mabry, who had retired.[4]

As the justices settled into their new offices and courtroom in the new capitol, they organized for work. The tribunal's members divided themselves into two divisions. Chief Justice Taylor presided over the first, which included justices Mabry and Shackleford. Justice Carter headed the second, with justices Cockrell and Maxwell. Plans called for the two divisions to work separately unless a disagreement required their members to sit *en banc* to resolve the dispute. Since the commissioners no longer were needed, their positions were vacated, and Commissioner Glenn returned to Tampa to enter private practice.[5]

Housing the court, 1902–13. The 1845 capitol was enlarged and improved at the turn of the century following another attempt to move the seat of government. Spacious north and south wings, an impressive dome, and other embellishments were designed by architect Frank Milburn to enhance the exterior. Justices had individual offices, and steam heat replaced wood-burning fireplaces. The supreme court in 1902 had been expanded, and a new bench was purchased to accommodate the six justices.

Further statutory and personnel alterations affected the court. On February 15, 1904, Governor Jennings selected James Bryan Whitfield to replace Justice Maxwell, who had resigned. Later in the year, pursuant to a legislative plan approved in 1903, four justices stood for reelection: the chief justice and the three appointed members. The man selected to succeed the chief justice was to serve a term of six years, while the law subjected the others to staggered terms decided by lot. The plan provided further for the election of successors to the two remaining justices at the general election immediately preceding the expiration of their terms so that, after 1904, two justices would be elected at each general election. As a result of the November 1904 contest, Justice Taylor achieved reelection over W. B. Sheppard. Justices Whitfield, Shackleford, and Cockrell likewise enjoyed approval for a return to the court. When the latter three court members drew their lots, Whitfield received the two-year term, Shackleford the four-year term, and Cockrell the six-year term.[6]

Housing the court, 1913–49. In 1913 the supreme court of Florida moved into a new building on Jackson Square shared with the Florida Railroad Commission. The $100,000 structure, designed by Atlanta architect P. Thornton Marya, had a marble-floored lobby, a courtroom, a grand staircase, and an elevator. Local residents believed that this second state building would firmly anchor the seat of government in Tallahassee. The photograph was taken from the cupola of the capitol.

The reorganizations of 1901–4 presaged additional court changes. In January 1905 panel members selected Justice Whitfield as chief justice to serve through June, after which Justice Shackleford presided for four years. Justice Whitfield again fulfilled the responsibilities of chief justice from 1909 to 1913. In May 1905, Justice Carter resigned, arranging in the process to exchange positions with Charles Breckenridge Parkhill, then a judge of the first circuit. Thereafter, Cockrell, Hocker, Parkhill, Shackleford, Taylor, and Whitfield formed the supreme court until Justice Parkhill resigned in January 1912. By that time the court's backlog problem had been remedied, and the 1911 legislature had decided to eliminate one seat on the tribunal, reducing its membership to five. Ironically, the legislation's sponsor was Representative Glenn Terrell, who would be appointed to the court after the sixth seat again was authorized in 1923.[7]

In 1911 progress also was made in providing a new home for the supreme court. Governor Albert W. Gilchrist appointed a commission to select an appropriate site for a building to house the court, the railroad commission, and a library. The structure's location was to be "not more than 1500 feet from the center of the Capitol Building." On October 5 Tallahassee's city council voted to deed Jackson Square—which lay between Duval and Adams streets on the west and east and two opposing portions of Madison Street on the north and south—to the state for the purpose. Contractors completed the $100,000 building in time for its occupancy in 1913. Thirty-nine years later state officials designated the structure as the Whitfield Building, in honor of Justice James Bryan Whitfield. It would be known as such until its destruction in 1978.[8]

The tribunal that first occupied the new supreme court building soon faced additional alterations. In 1913 members once more turned to Justice Shackleford to preside, which he did until 1915, when Justice Taylor commenced two additional years of service in that capacity. In 1914 Justice Hocker chose not to seek reelection; as a result William Hull Ellis joined the court after the year's general election. Two years later, after a hotly contested Democratic primary election, former state senate president Jefferson B. Browne of Key West ousted Justice Cockrell. In 1917 Justice Shackleford left the panel, to be replaced with the appointment of Thomas M. West by new governor Sidney J. Catts. Thus ended the period's changes in court makeup.[9]

While this brief outline of changes on the court during 1897–1916 necessarily omits much of the color and texture of court personalities and operations during the Progressive era, the following look at the justices who served in those years will offer further insight into those subjects.

Francis Beauregard Carter, Supreme Court Justice, 1897–1905

Francis Beauregard Carter's career at the bar came courtesy of a future member of the Florida supreme court. Carter was born near Neal's Landing on the Chattahoochee River in Jackson County on August 12, 1861. Educated in Marianna public schools, he later trained as a printer. Attorney Benjamin Sullivan Liddon, who would join the state's highest tribunal in 1894, needed a bright young man to help with his Marianna practice and recognized Carter's potential. Accordingly, the younger man read law in Liddon's office. After Carter achieved admission to the bar in 1882, the two men formed the partnership of Liddon and Carter, which soon enjoyed a reputation as one of the state's leading firms. When Liddon's justiceship ended the partnership, Carter formed a new Marianna firm with his brother, John H. Carter.[10]

In Jackson County, Carter's professional and personal lives flourished. He achieved election as Marianna mayor and actively participated in Democratic party politics. He attended the 1896 state party convention as a Jackson County representative, where he supported national convention delegates pledged to the candidacy of William Jennings Bryan. In turn, he received designation as a party elector and cast a presidential electoral vote in Bryan's favor. Carter also pursued his religious commitments through work within the Episcopal church. In 1885 he had married Margaret Henrietta Dickson, the daughter of a Jackson County planter, and over the next dozen years the couple celebrated the births of seven children. An eighth child was born much later in Pensacola in 1908.[11]

In 1897 Benjamin Sullivan Liddon again figured importantly in Carter's professional development. The justice had resigned from the supreme court to enter private practice at Pensacola. Carter thereupon sought the seat through appeals to Governor William D. Bloxham. At first his chances seemed remote. The governor had offered the position to former governor Francis P. Fleming. A Marianna delegation, led by Mayor C. L. Wilson, urged Carter's candidacy upon Bloxham, but the effort initially resulted only in an attempt "to persuade Mr. Carter to strive for the circuit court judgeship of Pensacola district." Carter "declined to come out of the race for the supreme bench, being sanguine that with his influential backing he could secure it." His persistence was rewarded. Mrs. Fleming's reluctance to move to Tallahassee prompted her husband's withdrawal from consideration, and Bloxham turned to Carter in January 1897.[12]

The new justice's appointment received popular ratification, but his tenure on the bench ended after eight years of service. Well liked for his affability, his "obvious love of good food," and his reputation as the most studious man on the high court, his success could have been forecast. As required by law, Carter faced the voters in 1900, and he defeated Republican Henry C. Goodell by 26,255 votes to 5,179. Although he was securely seated on the bench, party activists kept Carter's name and influence alive, and in 1904 he considered, but declined, running for governor. Rather, he preferred a change of scene. His wife did not enjoy life at Tallahassee, and he looked forward to joining his old friend Liddon in Pensacola. Accordingly, on May 25, 1905, Justice Carter resigned his position to accept the judgeship of the first judicial circuit, which encompassed the area between the Perdido and Apalachicola rivers. In doing so, he exchanged places with Charles Breckenridge Parkhill, who left the circuit judgeship to accept Carter's place on the supreme court.[13]

Stepping down from the high court proved only the first transitional step for Carter. Within two years he left the bench to reenter private practice as a partner with the Pensacola firm of Blount, Blount, and Carter, where his labors yielded success and he earned an excellent legal reputation. The firm specialized in corporate law, and Carter served particularly as counsel for the Louisville and Nashville Railroad. As an attorney in private practice, he argued numerous cases before the state supreme court. During the period one editor, greeting his arrival at the capitol to appear before the tribunal, called him "one

Mr. and Mrs. Francis Beauregard Carter. This photograph of Francis Beauregard Carter and his wife, Margaret Henrietta, "Etta," Dickson Carter, was taken a few years prior to his service on the high court. Justice Carter was thirty-five years old when he was appointed to the supreme court of Florida in January 1897.

The seven children of Justice and Mrs. Francis Beauregard Carter, circa 1900. From left standing: Francis Beauregard, Jr., Pattie Williams, and Philips John. From left seated: Helen May, Dickson Herndon, John Harden, and Eugenia Woods. Not pictured is the Carter's eighth child, Margaret Henrietta, who was born in Pensacola in 1908.

of the State's best and most useful citizens." Millard F. Caldwell, who came to know Carter well through "some tedious litigation," described the former justice as a pleasant and courteous man, somewhat reserved, having gray hair, standing about five feet, nine inches tall, and "rotund." Carter presented the image of a man personally and professionally conservative, best known as a "splendid lawyer of unquestioned integrity" who was "possibly the most studious member of the Pensacola Bar."[14]

In the 1910s and 1920s Carter pursued his legal career, his family relations, and other personal interests. During 1919–20 he unsuccessfully attempted to secure appointment to the United State Fifth Circuit Court of Appeals, in which endeavor several sitting Florida justices supported him. In 1921, upon the death of his firm's senior partner, William A. Blount, Carter formed Carter and Yonge, consisting of himself; his sons Francis Beauregard Carter, Jr., and Dickson Herndon Carter; and J. E. D. Yonge. As the firm established itself, a longtime political relationship endured and grew. Carter's old favorite William Jennings Bryan had moved to Florida, and they came to know each other well. Their friendship lasted until Bryan's death in 1925. The next year the former justice vied for a state supreme court seat against Justice Louie W. Strum, an appointee of Governor John W. Martin. In the June primary, Strum defeated his opponent by a substantial majority.

Carter lived for more than another decade, dying on January 9, 1937, at the age of seventy-five. As a supreme court resolution declared, "His influence upon the judicial history of Florida was wholesome and constructive." Francis Beauregard and Margaret Henrietta Carter are buried in Riverside Cemetery, Marianna.[15]

William Adams Hocker, Supreme Court Justice, 1903–1915

Justice Francis Beauregard Carter's experience in replacing a friend and legal partner on the supreme court found its parallel in the career of William Adams Hocker. Unlike Carter, Hocker could not boast of Florida roots, having entered the world in Virginia. He was born on December 5, 1844, at his father's plantation, Oak Grove, located in Buckingham County between the James River and the north fork of the Slate River. The estate was a grand one, including about 2,300 acres worked by the labor of one hundred or more slaves. The family residence was "typical of the home of the well-to-do planter of Virginia before the war."[16]

The future justice's education pursued a course typical for the son of an affluent planter. Until 1858 Hocker received tutoring at home, after which hc attended a neighborhood school at a nearby plantation home. He mastered

Latin and Greek and was recognized as "an enthusiastic student, accomplished in the classics and well instructed in piano." In 1862 Hocker matriculated at Hampden-Sidney College, but on January 26, 1864, he joined the Virginia cavalry under General Fitzhugh Lee. Reportedly, he left for war with "two horses, a dappled gray and a roan, and a negro body servant." Hocker saw action in the campaigns around Petersburg; at the April 1, 1865, Battle of Five Forks; and in subsequent skirmishes at Amelia Springs, High Bridge, and Farmville.[17]

Hocker's education and personal development, interrupted by the war, were pursued in its aftermath. In October 1865 he entered the University of Virginia to study law, at his father's instigation. Believing that his life as the son of a wealthy planter would continue despite the Confederate defeat, the younger Hocker only reluctantly acquiesced. His accomplishments gained him admission to the Virginia bar in 1868, and he became a member of the firm of Mosely and Hocker, at Buckingham County Court House. On November 11 of that year he married Gertrude Venable of Prince Edward County. He brought her to the family plantation, Oak Grove, where they remained for several years. In 1871 they were compelled to relocate when Oak Grove was sold to satisfy debts of his now deceased father's estate. As of that time, one biographer asserted with some creative license, Hocker "had never earned a dollar, his father's ample fortune being at his command."[18]

Out of the turmoil produced by postwar economic chaos and his father's death, the future justice's life took several unexpected turns, leading eventually to a new Florida home. Through the influence of a relation of his wife, Hocker was offered a position as professor of Latin and Greek at the Franklin Institute in Columbus, Mississippi. Arriving in time for the fall 1872 term, the new professor discovered dim prospects in Mississippi and soon opted to move. In June 1874 he and a friend, Thomas Spicer, settled in the Florida peninsula at Yalaha on Lake Harris, about fifteen miles from Leesburg. There the two men erected log houses, Hocker naming his Bendemeer. After journeys involving transportation by rail, river, and mule, their wives and families joined them in the autumn. Already on July 16, 1874, Hocker had achieved admission to the bar at Leesburg. While waiting for his practice to build, he taught school there, commuting each day from his rural homestead.[19]

Contacts made through teaching and legal practice led Hocker into politics. A conservative Democrat, he won election to the Florida legislature in 1876 at the same time that Governor George F. Drew redeemed the state for Hocker's party. As the 1877 session unfolded, the lawmaker endeared himself to party regulars by blocking land grants to Republican-controlled railroad projects. At session's end Drew rewarded his ally with appointment as state attorney for the fifth judicial circuit, a post that Hocker then held until August 1886.[20]

After 1877 Hocker emerged as a power in state Democratic politics. By the early 1880s he virtually controlled party affairs in old Sumter County, and his influence expanded significantly when his junior law partner, Milton Harvey Mabry, entered the office of lieutenant governor in 1885. Not long thereafter Hocker accepted a seat as delegate in the state constitutional convention. In that body, which produced the Constitution of 1885, he distinguished himself as a champion of Democratic railroad interests and as an opponent of railroad regulation and chain-gang reforms.[21]

Hocker's high profile as a corporate lawyer and political powerbroker necessitated that he live closer to Leesburg. In the circumstances he moved his family to an orange grove, Kenderton, situated about two miles from town and farmed it until the great freeze of 1895. There for a time he lived the life of a well-born and well-bred Southerner, enjoying boating, shooting, fishing, hunting, and frequent visits from his Virginia relatives. By 1887 the lawyer opened a home in Leesburg from which, in 1890, voters sent him to represent recently created Lake County in the state senate. Two years afterward he joined Mabry at Ocala, where the attorneys resumed their partnership. Continued influence in Democratic party affairs led to Hocker's June 1893 designation by Governor Henry Laurens Mitchell as fifth judicial circuit judge and to an unsuccessful campaign for selection as United States senator four years later. Governor William D. Bloxham recommissioned him as judge in 1899, and he exercised the judicial responsibilities until his 1901 resignation following appointment as a supreme court commissioner.[22]

Events of the twentieth century's opening years affected Hocker in important ways. With the 1901 appointment, he and his family transferred their home to Tallahassee. There on November 17, 1901, Gertrude Hocker died, having borne five children. Eight years later, on December 1, 1909, Hocker married his cousin Mattie Novell Glover of Roanoke, Virginia. By then Hocker had held a seat on the state supreme court for more than half a decade. He first won election to the tribunal in November 1902, replacing Milton Harvey Mabry. Upon Hocker's Democratic primary victory the previous summer, the *Ocala Star* had noted, "[W]e are confident that his well-trained and thoroughly developed judicial mind, as well as his large experience in grappling with knotty questions eminently qualify him to occupy a position on the supreme bench of the state." Its editor followed by lauding Hocker as "a man whose private character and life are above reproach and whose public career has always borne the stamp of honesty, ability, and faithfulness in the performance of his every duty."[23]

Hocker served on the supreme bench until January 5, 1915, easily winning reelection in 1908. As his second term neared conclusion, however, ill health forced him to retire from active duty, and voters named William Hull Ellis as his successor at the 1914 general election. Justice Hocker lived until 1918, dying at Jacksonville on July 17, aged seventy-three years. At a February 1919 memorial service, Gainesville's W. W. Hampton recalled his friend. "He was a charming man," Hampton declared, "wonderfully cultured, a great reader, most attractive and a fluent conversationalist . . . a man of scientific research and wonderful learning." Hampton concluded, "I have yet to hear any criticism of Judge Hocker's judicial administration, either on Circuit or Supreme Bench, or as State Attorney of our Circuit, and our people loved him."[24]

Thomas M. Shackleford, Supreme Court Justice, 1902–1905, 1909–1913, 1915–1917; Supreme Court Chief Justice, 1905–1909, 1913–1915

As illustrated by Justice William Adams Hocker's career, Florida became home in the late 1800s to numerous immigrants seeking their fortunes from the growth sparked by railroad and land development. Not too dissimilar from Justice Hocker's experience was that of his colleague Thomas M. Shackleford. Born in Fayetteville, Tennessee, on November 14, 1859, he was the child of Daniel Park and Alethea (Young) Shackleford. Tall, thin, and gregarious later in life, Shackleford would be described as the epitome of a southern gentleman. He received his formal education at Burritt College, Spencer, Tennessee, and, later, at Harvard University. Beyond these studies, he prepared for the practice of law by reading in law offices in his native state. He gained admission to the local bar in 1882.[25]

The years immediately following his licensing as an attorney brought profound changes for Shackleford. First, in 1882 he married Nannie Clopton Rhea, with whom he would have a son. Then the couple left their familiar Tennessee environs for a new home in Florida. They initially settled in the peninsula at Lake Weir, where Shackleford added citrus farming to his occupations. In 1883, however, they moved on to Brooksville, remaining there for a decade. In Hernando County the young lawyer prospered. At the town he edited two newspapers, indulged himself as local correspondent for the *Louisville Courier-Journal* and the *Nashville American*, and wrote a novel, *Amaskohegan, a Story of Lake Weir*. His good fortune apparently was interrupted only by the early death of his wife in 1887. Shackleford remarried on December 13 of the next year to Lena A. (Jane) Wooten of Russelville, Kentucky, with whom he would have three children.[26]

During the period of his residence at Brooksville, Shackleford established strong connections within the Democratic party. By 1888 he had achieved selection as a delegate to the national Democratic convention, and four years afterward he voted as a Florida presidential elector in favor of Grover Cleveland. With the law and politics came important friendships. Especially, Shackleford and fellow lawyer William Sherman Jennings grew close. In later years the former Tennessean would remind Governor Jennings of their days together. "Being with you called to my mind so many happy memories of dear old Brooksville days," he wrote on one occasion, "when we were all younger than we are now and were just fairly beginning our life work." Their friendship would work strongly in Shackleford's favor.[27]

The future justice's connections and established reputation soon offered him lucrative opportunities. In 1893 he formed a legal partnership with Hugh C. Macfarlane at Tampa, a town then mushrooming from tourism and phosphate development. As the two men came to exercise enhanced influence in local and state affairs, Shackleford and his wife involved themselves, as well, in many civic endeavors. Together, for example, they helped to organize the town's First Christian Church. The lawyer also found time to write another novel, *By Sunlit Waters: A Tampa Story*. From 1900 to 1902 Shackleford's legal responsibilities included those of Tampa's city attorney.[28]

The lawyer's path toward the supreme bench began in 1900, when his friend Jennings launched a successful campaign for governor. Shackleford worked on Jennings's behalf in the Tampa Bay area, although some of his efforts met with frustration. "I am very sorry to inform you that I am left off the state [Democratic convention] delegation," he informed the candidate in May. "I was kept off by cold blooded treachery of my so called friends, kept off solely as I find because of my loyalty to you." The disappointment notwithstanding, Jennings secured nomination and election. Thereafter the two friends stayed in touch. Shackleford felt little hesitation about lobbying the governor on matters of interest, including a proposed law "creating a greater Tampa," which he opposed because "[i]t would mean a heavy financial blow to Mr. Macfarlane."[29]

Beyond influencing the governor's stance on legislation, Shackleford hoped for personal recognition of his professional and political aptitudes. "Referring to our conversation concerning the position of Justice of the Supreme Court I wish to be perfectly frank with you," he intimated to Jennings in June 1902. He continued, "This office has been for many years and still is the goal of my ambition." The possibility of Jennings's satisfying that ambition had arisen when, in 1901, the legislature had proposed a constitutional amendment adding three justices to the court, the first incumbents being subject to the governor's appointment. Until a statewide vote of approval was taken in November 1902, though, Jennings could make no appointment. In the meanwhile, Shackleford labored on behalf of candidacies important to Jennings, including that of William Adams Hocker to replace Milton Harvey Mabry on the high court. When Hocker secured the all-important Democratic nomination over Judge Joseph Baisden Wall of Tampa, Shackleford congratulated the governor, declaring that "[t]he administration achieved a great victory."[30]

The November election returns carried Shackleford closer to his reward, as voters approved court expansion. The prospective jurist had reassured Jennings days before the polling of his availability and capability, even to insisting that treatment had rectified a slight hearing problem. "I have been very much improved in every way, both physically and mentally," he told his friend, "so much so that it is a subject of comment with many who come in contact with me." Ten days later he touched upon the appointment again. "After the amendment has been officially declared adopted I want you to carefully examine my endorsements and weigh well my fitness and qualifications for the high position to which I am aspiring." Shackleford added, "Divest yourself for the time being of any feeling of personal friendship for me, and determine whether or not my endorsements are of such a character and my character, qualifications, habits and ability are such as to warrant and justify you as Governor in appointing me." After the candidate furnished further endorsements and testimonials from influential Democrats and Tampa area citizens, Jennings acceded to his request and, by December 1, 1902, had appointed Shackleford a justice.[31]

Once upon the supreme tribunal, Justice Shackleford remained there until 1917. From 1905 to 1909 and again from 1913 to 1915 he acted as chief justice. He discovered, as had many of his judicial colleagues, that personal financial demands often outstripped his public compensation. "Tom's expenses at the university together with my expenses here demand about all my salary," he commented in a friendly letter to ex-governor Jennings in 1906, "but I am economizing all I can." Still, the financial strain compelled him to consider using Jennings's influence "in having [a] loan placed with Mr. Barnett's bank." He easily achieved a final reelection in 1914, but the possibility of greater earnings prompted him on August 27, 1917, to resign, permitting Governor Sidney J. Catts to name Attorney General Thomas M. West to replace the jurist. Shackleford then returned to Tampa. He joined the firm of Shackleford and Shackleford, created by his sons, and practiced law until his death on September 21, 1927.[32]

The deceased justice's work on the supreme bench had brought him credit and public honors. The University of Florida, for instance, awarded Shackleford an honorary LL.D. degree in 1910. At the time of his retirement the *Tampa Tribune,* after describing his homecoming there as "full of honors," proudly noted that the jurist's opinions were quoted "over the land." His peers on the supreme court shared the high regard. "Judge Shackleford," their resolution read after his death, "was an able and upright judge. His painstaking and very excellent work is preserved in many volumes of the supreme court reports." They concluded, "He was a man of great strength of character and a most valuable citizen of Florida."[33]

Evelyn Croom Maxwell, Supreme Court Justice, 1902–1904

When in late 1902 Governor William Sherman Jennings placed his friend Thomas M. Shackleford on the supreme court of Florida, he faced a complicated dilemma. Although three appointments were at his disposal, the reality of state politics required that he recognize factors in addition to professional competence and personal regard. Particularly, circumstances necessitated that the governor's designations reflect Florida's continued regionalism, Democratic party factionalism, and the influence of prominent families. With this situation in focus, Jennings, through his remaining high court appointments, illustrated the exercise of an adroit political hand.

Evelyn Croom Maxwell descended from one of Florida's most powerful and well-regarded political families. His grandfather, Walker Anderson, helped to draft the Constitution of 1838, served in both houses of the legislature, and ranked as a leader of the Democratic party. From 1851 to 1853 Anderson sat on the state supreme court as chief justice. Late in Anderson's final year on the court, his daughter Julia Hawks Anderson married United States Representative Augustus Emmet Maxwell. The Democratic congressman, who would also serve, in 1866, on Florida's highest court, gained election in 1862 to the Confederate States Senate. To protect his family from Union forces operating in the vicinity of family properties near Pensacola, he moved them to an estate not far from Evergreen, Alabama. There on July 27, 1863, a son, Evelyn Croom Maxwell, was born.[34]

As a scion of the Anderson and Maxwell families, Evelyn Croom Maxwell's life and career evolved in a steady and secure fashion. He attended public schools at Pensacola, after which he graduated from the University of Nashville, Tennessee, in 1882 with the degree of licentiate of instruction. For a time he taught in Pensacola public schools while studying law in the offices of J. C. Avery. Maxwell secured admission to the bar in 1885 and, in 1892, was appointed judge of the criminal court of record of Escambia County. From 1896 to September 1901 he sat as a judge of the first judicial circuit. His resignation from the circuit bench followed his selection by Governor Jennings as a commissioner of the supreme court. Maxwell's elevation to the supreme bench followed in December 1902.[35]

Maxwell's legal and judicial abilities enjoyed widespread regard, but his tenure on the supreme court lasted only fifteen months before he resigned on February 15, 1904, to return to private practice at Pensacola. A robust man, more than six feet in height, "who appeared to be in splendid condition," he was considered by colleagues such as Millard Caldwell to be "a thorough going gentleman and a capable lawyer." Caldwell noted that Maxwell, a conservative man professionally and politically, possessed a "good and logical mind" but worked best amid clutter. According to Caldwell: "He had large, roomy, well furnished and equipped offices. His original desk was very large, and instead of having a secretary and filing clerk, he just stacked his correspondence on top of the desk until it got to be about two feet high. He moved to his little conference table which was large enough to seat eight and continued to stack the mail and pleadings on top of the table as he had his desk. After he moved his chair all around the table and finally got his filings so high they began to topple, he moved to his secretary's desk—she had been gone for some years."

Despite the absence of organization, Maxwell's system worked. Caldwell remembered that "when I was a young lawyer and had business with him . . . we needed a particular document which had been sent to him many years before." Added the future governor, "[Maxwell] walked back to his original desk and straight to the pile of documents and pulled our paper from the mess."[36]

Following his supreme court service, Maxwell remained in Pensacola, where he enjoyed the fruits of a prosperous legal practice. Widely respected in the community, he contributed substantially to the city's civic, religious, and cultural sectors. He died at the Warrington home of his daughter, Mrs. Albert D. Gray, on November 17, 1954. Justice Maxwell's wife, Wilhelmina Thornton Maxwell, whom he had married at Pensacola on February 1, 1894, predeceased him.[37]

Robert Spratt Cockrell, Supreme Court Justice, 1902–1917

Where West Florida family and political connections had stood Evelyn Croom Maxwell in good stead with Governor William Sherman Jennings, East Florida served as Robert Spratt Cockrell's base of support. The lawyer was born at Livingston, Alabama, on January 22, 1866. When Robert still was a child, his father, A. W. Cockrell, relocated the family to Florida, settling at the state's emerging financial and business center of Jacksonville. The younger Cockrell attended local schools before entering the University of Virginia, where he received the degrees of bachelor of arts, master of arts, and bachelor of laws. Subsequently he completed postgraduate work at the University of Berlin.[38]

A legal career awaited Cockrell upon his return from Germany. He successfully stood for admission to the bar at Jacksonville in 1891 and joined A. W. Cockrell and Son, a firm that included his father and two brothers. By that time the senior Cockrell had emerged as one of Jacksonville's premier attorneys, and the firm's members, accordingly, enjoyed social prominence as well as professional standing. The father especially represented Duval County's powerful Democratic politician Napoleon Bonaparte Broward, who, in turn, maintained close relations with Governor Jennings and who, with Jennings's endorsement, himself would achieve election as governor in 1904.[39]

When the possibility of a supreme court appointment became evident in 1902, the Cockrell family commenced a broad-based campaign to secure a seat on the bench for Robert. In ten years of practice, he had established a reputation as a good, very technical lawyer. Building upon that basis, family members sought out endorsements from prominent Democrats. Particularly, one brother approached William James Bryan, Broward's close friend and ally, whom Governor Broward would appoint to the United States Senate. Although Bryan did not know Robert, he nonetheless urged Jennings to make the appointment, noting that A. W. Cockrell, Jr., was "a good friend of mine politically." He continued, "I am told by those who know him that Mr. [Robert] Cockrell . . . is a safe, conservative, conscientious and thorough student of law, possessed of a well trained legal mind."[40]

The family efforts extended well afield from Jacksonville and Duval County. Since Robert potentially was competing for the appointment with South Florida's Thomas M. Shackleford of Tampa, petitions were circulated on Cockrell's behalf in legal and political circles in Hillsborough, Polk, Manatee, and Monroe counties to demonstrate support in those influential areas. Even Shackleford was approached to endorse Cockrell as "well qualified." The prospective justice's backers then publicized the support gained thereby in the Jacksonville *Evening Metropolis,* one of the state's leading newspapers. Its editor proclaimed the candidate as "learned in the law, a . . . student and a gentleman of high character."[41]

The successful campaign culminated with Cockrell's December 1902 appointment to the supreme court. He served on the bench for the next fifteen years, after securing a six-year term by popular vote in the 1904 general election. During that period he authored numerous opinions, marked by brevity, with a laconic style and tone. Some of the opinions challenged powerful railroad interests, and they drew him opposition in the 1916 Democratic primary from one-time senate president Jefferson B. Browne. Cockrell's academic and gentlemanly style did not serve him well as campaign assets, and, when the votes were tallied, he became one of the few Florida justices denied reelection.[42]

One personal legacy of Cockrell's tenure on the supreme court was his marriage at Tallahassee on October 30, 1903, to Courtney Walker, daughter of former governor and justice David S. Walker. The couple enjoyed an active and diverse social life in the state capital, while they raised four children. Unfortunately, Courtney Cockrell suffered an untimely death in October 1914 at Black Mountain, North Carolina, where she had been convalescing from a lengthy illness. She had survived only to her thirty-eighth year.[43]

Following his failure to secure reelection, Justice Cockrell engaged in private practice at Jacksonville before pursuing a teaching career. Previously he had served on Duval County's board of public instruction. In 1919 he became professor of law at the University of Florida in Gainesville. One student, Justice Richard W. Ervin, described him in those days as "a thin emaciated type of about six feet," with dark curly hair and a dark brown, "wizened" type of face. Cockrell's charges recalled him chewing tobacco while teaching. Ervin remembered his penchant for ribald jokes and stories "quite shocking to middle class morality Baptist students in the class" and suggested that "some of his stories still must glimmer dimly around the [University of Florida's] Holland Center." Ervin added: "[H]e seemed to cater to the more affluent students, especially those from Jacksonville, his hometown. He liked athletics, attended football practices and the games. He was a tough professor, usually giving only a 75% grade to his freshmen in his criminal law class. He was cantankerous and cynical openly, but underneath he had a kind heart."[44]

Justice Cockrell taught more than a generation of law students at the University of Florida Law School before retiring in 1940. He lived until June 23, 1957, when he died in Miami at the age of ninety-one. He was buried at Tallahassee beside the resting place of his long-deceased wife, Courtney Walker Cockrell.[45]

James Bryan Whitfield, Supreme Court Justice, 1904–1909, 1913–1935, 1937–1943; Supreme Court Chief Justice, 1905, 1909–1913, 1935–1937

The importance of quality education, legal ability, and political sensitivity—coupled with family connections and fortuitous timing—to obtaining a seat on the Florida supreme court early in the twentieth century finds an additional illustration in the career of James Bryan Whitfield. His beginnings were auspicious. The son of Judge Richard Allen Whitfield and Mary Whitfield Croom, he was born on the family plantation near Goldsboro, Wayne County, North Carolina, on November 8, 1860. When the boy had attained the age of one year, his parents transferred the family by wagon train to a Leon County, Florida, plantation. The younger Whitfield remained there through the Civil War. He received a basic education at Tallahassee's West Florida Seminary, after which he attended the University of Virginia. He earned a degree as bachelor of laws in 1886, though not before he had reported news from the 1885 state constitutional convention and authored the informative *Florida State Government* the same year.[46]

Back at Tallahassee the young lawyer struggled to commence a practice before turning to public service. In February 1888 he began the transition by accepting a position as cashier of the Florida Sub-Tropical Exposition at Jacksonville, a festival featuring state agricultural products. He admired "the busy field of rigid competition and flattering possibilities . . . calculated to animate the spirits and aspirations of young men" that he found in that city. On the other hand, he yearned to return to the state's sleepy capital. "You well know I prefer living in Tallahassee to any place in the world," he informed his father, "and it is because of that feeling that I have persistently determined not to leave the state or get too far away from home." He added, "If there is any possible hope for improvement in the conditions that control the future of Tallahassee I will be only too glad to return there to stay."[47]

Likely through Richard Allen Whitfield's agency, opportunities for his son soon emerged at Tallahassee. Temporarily the young lawyer labored as secretary to Governor Edward A. Perry, while preparing a campaign for election as Leon County judge. He secured the position at the general election held in November 1888, although his tenure proved brief. Early in 1889 a vacancy occurred in the office of clerk of the supreme court of Florida. Whitfield accepted the appointment in March and held the clerkship until 1897, when he resigned to resume a private legal practice. "He has performed the duties of the office during his incumbency with ability and integrity," declared the court's members. They concluded by praising his "kind, truthful and courteous character that mark the man a gentleman."[48]

The months after Whitfield's departure from supreme court duties presented him with a prestigious new position and with personal tragedy. In late spring 1897 newly inaugurated Governor William D. Bloxham, a Leon County planter and old friend of the Whitfield family, called upon the former clerk to serve as state treasurer in the aftermath of the incumbent treasurer's decision to resign rather than face impeachment. "He will be safe," the Jacksonville *Daily Florida Citizen* informed state residents. "He will be a conservative guardian of the public funds. He has no special banker friends [and] has no one to reward." Former governor Henry Laurens Mitchell concurred by observing that "Whitfield is a native Floridian, a fine lawyer, a perfect gentleman, and entirely reliable." The appointment came in June, and within four months joy turned to pain. Whitfield had married on November 25, 1896, to Leila Rebecca Nash. The following September she gave birth to a son but died as a result on October 4, 1897. Heartbroken, the treasurer did not remarry until June 12, 1901. He and his second wife, Margaret Hayward Randolph Whitfield, would share four children.[49]

The Tallahassee attorney established himself securely in the office of state treasurer, although he seems to have yearned before long for greater challenges. He won election to the treasurer's post in 1898 and reelection in 1900. At the time a local newspaper noted, "Judge Whitfield is the right man in the right place, and his administration of this responsible trust merits universal approval." While successfully contending for reelection, though, the treasurer threw his political support to the candidacy of William Sherman Jennings for governor. "I always stand ready to serve you and the party in any way I can," he informed Jennings in July after the Democratic primary election. That month Whitfield offered Jennings the use of a luxurious home that he had constructed in Tallahassee across the street from the capitol but had not occupied after this wife's death. When the November general election confirmed Jennings's victory, the treasurer organized the new governor's inaugural ceremony and ball. "You will I trust be assured," Whitfield had informed Jennings in November 1900, "that it shall be my highest purpose to aid you in making a success of your administration."[50]

Recognition of Whitfield's abilities, political influence, and loyalty to Jennings came in February 1903 when the governor appointed the treasurer as attorney general. Context for the designation derived from Jennings's desire for higher office. While praising the appointment of a "lawyer of note" such as Whitfield, one newspaper explained: "The Governor wants to go to the United States Senate, and as most ambitious men do, is making a strong effort to form political alliances that will land him the coveted seat." The friendship between the two men grew closer during the year, and, when Jennings absented himself from the capitol, Whitfield virtually ran state government on his behalf. When the 1904 election year began, Jennings offered an additional mark of preferment. Justice Evelyn Croom Maxwell resigned from the supreme court in February, and the governor presented the seat to Whitfield. Required to stand for election almost immediately, Whitfield easily withstood the challenge while Jennings's senate candidacy faltered.[51]

The Whitfield family. This 1909 photograph was taken at the family's home on Monroe Street across from the capitol. From left: Chief Justice James Bryan Whitfield, Mary Croom, James Bryan, Jr., Margaret Randolph Whitfield holding Randolph, Julia Croom, and John Nash.

Justice Whitfield's popularity with voters displayed itself throughout his tenure on the high bench. "[H]e has given entire satisfaction and has added many new friends and supporters to his host of admirers," proclaimed one editor in December 1904. Following his selection by lot as chief justice the next month, the newspaperman added, "The selection of Hon. Jas. B. Whitfield as chief justice . . . is but a continuation of a series of success enjoyed by few men of his age in this country." The justice would serve on the supreme court for thirty-nine years. In 1905, 1909–13, and 1935–37 he would act as chief justice. During the period he was required by political considerations to prepare for a campaign only once, in 1918. In that year he went so far as to draft an advertisement, but, when no opposition surfaced, he dispensed with further campaigning.[52]

As a supreme court member, the magnitude and quality of Whitfield's labors placed him above many of his colleagues in the esteem of the bar. From 1904 to 1943 he authored 1,958 opinions, a fact that made him the most prolific writer in the court's history. He also drafted numerous significant statutes. As early as 1895, he had scripted the general election law, and in 1913 he designed the text necessary to authorize direct election of United States senators.

His writing talents produced, as well, *Whitfield's Notes*, a study of Florida political and legal history. The *Florida Historical Quarterly*, the *Yale Law Journal*, and the *American Law Review* benefited from his essays on the culture and history of his era.[53]

The justice's accomplishments, as well as his willingness to be helpful to others, found recognition and drew praise. When in September 1945 the University of Florida conferred on Whitfield the honorary degree of doctor of laws, Justice Glenn Terrell commented: "He is in every sense a great craftsman of the law. His faith in democracy, his devotion to our constitutional theory and his fidelity to Florida are his compelling traits." Judge Lamar Warren remembered him as "perhaps the most revered member of the court," while Justice B. K. Roberts called him "a very kindhearted person, particularly to beginner lawyers." Roberts recounted a personal experience. Just after the lawyer had lost an appeal before the high tribunal, Whitfield took him aside. "Well, you may have lost the judgment," the justice observed, as apparently was his habit, "but remember you have made a contribution to the jurisprudence of the state with your brief and your argument, and you have assisted in the development of a principle of case law which, though not serving your client in this case, may serve many of your clients in the future."[54]

One area in which the justice departed from the strict interpretations of many of his brethren involved the principle of separation of powers. Whitfield maintained close, personal relations with many incumbent state officeholders. One justice referred to him as the "private counselor to governors of the state." While recognizing the existence of constitutional limitations on legislative actions, he also strove to find constitutional foundations for new laws. Justice Richard W. Ervin noted Whitfield's critical nickname, "Slippery Jim," for his "spidery type opinions" that justified the constitutional legitimacy of legislative initiatives. Still, Whitfield took very seriously his responsibilities as a jurist. "The bench offers no great glamour," he once observed. "For the most part it compels hard, exacting work. Yet, at times, when the lamp burns low and the first rays of dawn filter dimly through the chamber windows onto the finished draft of an opinion expanding the borders of charted legal territory, a judge for the moment captures the feeling that the result is worth all the effort."[55]

Justice Whitfield retired from the court in 1943. He died in his sleep at home in Tallahassee on August 21, 1948, aged eighty-seven, and was buried in the city's Episcopal cemetery. A memorial statement in the *Biennial Report of the Attorney General* noted "[h]is culture, his profound learning, and his simple urbanity." It noted further that "he had more to do with directing the current of the law than any single person in the history of this state." The report concluded: "He was in every sense a great craftsman of the law whose social response was not dulled by use. . . . [N]o judge in Florida has ever been more generally beloved and respected for his integrity, modesty and personal charm. His learning, culture and temperament made him a great cornerstone to, and bulwark for, the present legal structure of our state."[56]

Charles Breckenridge Parkhill, Supreme Court Justice, 1905–1912

The life story of Justice Charles Breckenridge Parkhill echoes many of the themes that sounded in Justice James Bryan Whitfield's biography. Like Whitfield, Breckenridge hailed from a distinguished planter family and grew to manhood in Leon County. He was born on June 22, 1859, at Tuscawilla, the family plantation near Tallahassee. His parents boasted distinguished lineages. Elizabeth Brooks Bellamy Parkhill traced her family involvement in Florida affairs to pre-territorial days, while Dr. George Washington Parkhill could point to Middle Florida family prominence for almost as long. The couple named the future justice after his uncle, United States Vice President John Charles Breckenridge, who, when the child was one year old, lost the 1860 presidential election to Abraham Lincoln.[57]

Parkhill's family fortunes suffered from the Civil War. His father, a Unionist, joined with former governor Richard Keith Call and others to delay secession; but when it came, he joined the Second Florida Regiment, CSA, and was killed in action. As Charles matured, his mother coped with maintaining family properties in the midst of postwar economic turmoil. Nonetheless, she enabled her son to attend Randolph-Macon College from 1876 to 1878. He earned an appointment to the United States Military Academy at West Point but hearkened to his mother's fears of losing another family member to war and returned to manage a Parkhill plantation in Jefferson County until he could save sufficient funds to attend law school. After two years of work he pursued legal education at the University of Virginia, where Woodrow Wilson studied as his classmate. Parkhill edited the campus magazine, joined the Beta Theta Pi fraternity, and played varsity baseball. He earned his degree in law in 1882.[58]

Parkhill's search for a legal position in Florida led him into good fortune, personally and professionally. He joined the Pensacola law offices of his father's wartime colleague, former Confederate general Edward A. Perry. At the time Perry possessed substantial influence within state legal circles and the Democratic party. A young James Bryan Whitfield, for example, described Perry in early 1885 as a lawyer who "stands at the head of the bar." In November 1884 Perry won election as governor. By then the ties between the partners had grown ever closer. In May 1884 the young lawyer had married Perry's daughter,

Genevieve. One year afterward she delivered a daughter, Genevieve. Three days later, on June 2, 1885, the mother died of "child bed fever." As a grieving widower, Parkhill dedicated himself to his work and to the care of his daughter, who was said to be "the image of her mother."[59]

The changes in Parkhill's life encompassed career decisions. He left the Perry offices to build his own practice. Utilizing the political connections and experience gained through his association with Perry, he also vied for elective office. In 1888 Escambia County voters sent him to Tallahassee as their senator. During the 1889 session, which convened in the aftermath of a yellow fever epidemic that struck cities around the state, he particularly addressed health concerns, introducing legislation to create the state board of health. Also during that legislative session, Parkhill came to know well Judge Joseph Baisden Wall of Tampa, the senate president, and his daughter, Helen. Helen captivated Charles, and, following a brief courtship, they married at Tampa on November 30, 1891. They were to have eight children.[60]

Parkhill did not remain in the senate after 1889, preferring to tend to his growing family and expanding legal practice at Pensacola. He returned part time to public office in 1897 when Governor William D. Bloxham designated him as solicitor for the Escambia County criminal court of record. He participated, as well, as an officer in the local militia organization. The former senator maintained a high profile in Democratic party affairs, earning a reputation for public speaking. "Everybody in Florida has known 'Charlie' Parkhill for years," one newspaperman later commented, "and thousands have enjoyed his eloquence." In 1900 he backed Jefferson County's Dannitte H. Mays, the house speaker, for governor and then switched his support to William Sherman Jennings. Congratulating Jennings that November, Parkhill exulted to the governor-elect, "I hope to have the pleasure of taking my [militia] company in the [inaugural] parade." In January 1901 Parkhill fulfilled the aspiration.[61]

Jennings's governorship permitted Parkhill enhanced access to state corridors of power. He began to recommend friends for appointments and, by summer 1901, was inquiring on his own behalf about the position of adjutant general. An appointment was not forthcoming until January 1904, however, when Jennings named Parkhill as judge of the first judicial circuit. "[H]e has become one of the leading lawyers of West Florida," commented Tallahassee's *Daily Capital* in approving the action. Then, in May 1905, Justice Francis Beauregard Carter suggested that he and Parkhill exchange jobs. When asked about the arrangement, Jennings reportedly responded that "anything they worked out between themselves was all right with him." The two jurists agreed to the swap, which included occupancy of Carter's Tallahassee home by the Parkhills.[62]

The Pensacola prosecutor and corporate lawyer discovered quickly the limitations inherent in living on a state justice's salary. Family responsibilities, some left in the wake of his father's death, placed demands upon his finances, just as thoughts of his own mortality pressed ever more intently. Within five years after his appointment to the supreme court he initiated ultimately unsuccessful efforts to obtain a federal judicial position. He wrote at the time, "I have been just taking matters and life as they come, drifting without trying to force the current of my life, but I am growing old—time is passing—and maybe I should decide on a definite course for the future." Anxious for relief, he resigned from the court in January 1912 and announced his intention to seek election to the United States House of Representatives. Family considerations soon compelled him to withdraw from the campaign.[63]

The problem's solution appeared as a result of the December 1912 death of his father-in-law, Joseph Baisden Wall. The decedent's law practice beckoned, and Helen fervently desired to live again in Tampa. Accordingly, the Parkhills relocated to that city. Charles accepted appointment there as city attorney, in which capacity he worked until 1917. During World War I, he entered the army as a major in the judge advocate general's corps and assisted in the settlement of war claims on General John J. Pershing's staff in France. After his return to Tampa in 1920, the former justice achieved election as state attorney. He launched a campaign for governor in 1924, during which the state's principal newspaper, the Jacksonville *Florida Times-Union*, endorsed him as "clean, brainy and capable." As with his 1912 congressional race, though, Parkhill decided to not finish the primary contest. "If I had continued in the race for Governor," he wrote his daughter, "I would have had to be on the go all the time, day and night, in cold and heat and rain and spend so much money." He concluded, "It is not worth the price."[64]

After the 1924 gubernatorial race, Parkhill executed the responsibilities of his office as Hillsborough County's state attorney. His fervor in prosecuting wrongdoing at times jeopardized the former justice's safety. On one occasion, remembered his son John, defense attorney Pat Whitaker intimated that Parkhill had acted unethically in his tactics. The charge infuriated the prosecutor, who charged at Whitaker, hitting him in the jaw. "Whitaker in turn hit Poppa," John explained, "and when he did, I went and jumped on Whitaker's back and hit him as hard as I could with my little fists." Thereafter, "We all three got tangled up, we fell against a table, it broke, law books fell to the floor, [and it] sounded like cannons." Bailiffs intervened and ended the pandemonium by separating the three. The judge held both adults in contempt of court, fining each $100.[65]

Parkhill achieved a final reelection as state attorney in 1932, announcing that he would retire upon expiration of the term. On election day he received news of the death of his son Joe. Coupled with the realization that his son had lost the Tuscawilla plantation to creditors, the death sparked the father's nervous breakdown. While convalescing with his daughter Genevieve at Houston, Texas, he died on May 13, 1933. Of his last days of public service, the supreme court noted in a memorial: "Judge Parkhill was faithful to the last to his arduous duties as a state attorney. His last appearance before the supreme court was representative of the State in the Lewis Leavine appeal case. He was so overwrought in urging the court to sustain Leavine's death sentence that we permitted him to make his final argument from his chair." The memorial closed by declaring, "It was evident that the strain of years of public service had taken its toll."[66]

William Hull Ellis, Supreme Court Justice, 1915–1937; Supreme Court Chief Justice, 1927–1929, 1937–38

During the twentieth century's first decades, most Florida justices shared similar backgrounds and temperaments. A genteel, Old South spirit pervaded the supreme court chambers, with overtones of academic disengagement. One glaring exception can be found, however, in the person of William Hull Ellis. The justice, a "short, stocky, bald-headed, red faced" man who was "very eloquent in his speech," earned respect for his "Churchillian" judicial opinions. Still, Ellis represented a dissenting tradition that reached back to the antebellum experiences of Justice Thomas Baltzell. As one court member recalled, Ellis often "clearly and emphatically expressed his displeasure with what the majority of the Court was doing." Beyond that, in his later years the justice possessed a fiery, occasionally ungovernable temperament. An avid golfer, he displayed this side of his personality particularly on the links. Friends recalled that "at times he would break his golf clubs and in some instances throw them at his caddie." Added another, "In his later years it became difficult to get anyone to caddie for him because of his temper."[67]

As distinguished from the plantation roots of many of his colleagues, Ellis's family sought its fortune in building contracting. His father, North Carolina-born Charles H. Ellis, had moved to Pensacola to pursue that occupation before William was born on September 17, 1867. Charles died in 1871, and his widow, Julia F. Wilson Ellis, returned with her son to her native Gadsden County. William spent his youth and adolescence at Quincy, where he received a public school education, with a brief attendance at an Atlanta business college. At age twenty-one, the future justice enjoyed his first election to public office when Quincy voters placed him on the town council. He served the body as its president and would continue to sit on the panel, more often than not, through the 1890s. During the period Gadsden County electors granted him a position on the board of county commissioners, which he served as chairman. Ellis read law in Quincy and, in 1889, gained admission to the bar.[68]

The 1890s witnessed Ellis's personal and professional maturity. In June 1894, for instance, he married Ramelle Nicholson of Attapulgus, Georgia. The couple would have three children before she died on December 25, 1902. After years of individual practice, Ellis in 1897 joined prominent attorney E. C. Love in legal partnership at Quincy. The young lawyer busied himself, as well, with politics. A gift for public speaking resulted in appearances in many parts of the state on behalf of Democratic candidates and causes. By the twentieth century one pundit could refer to him as "the silver-tongued orator of the State of Florida." In 1900 the party chose him as a presidential elector, and he received more general election votes than any other member of the slate. When the completion of capitol remodeling was celebrated at Tallahassee in December 1902, Ellis delighted the crowd with his remarks. One onlooker characterized his presentation as "something few in the hall will ever forget."[69]

Ellis's longtime services on behalf of the Democratic party led to a series of important state government appointments. In 1903 he helped to draft legislation reorganizing the state's auditing process, and Governor William Sherman Jennings designated him to fill the newly created auditor's office. Reportedly, the "brethren of the press" showed "considerable surprise" when Ellis agreed to take the job, for they believed him to be "slated for the Attorney Generalship." The state auditor did not have to wait long for the promotion. When Attorney General James Bryan Whitfield resigned in February 1904 to accept Jennings's offer of a seat on the supreme court, the governor elevated Ellis to the vacancy. With administration backing, he handily defeated the well-regarded Alfred St. Clair-Abrams in the May party primary. By 1904 the general election presented no obstacle to the Democratic candidate.[70]

The 1904 general election ushered in a new era in Florida politics with the election of Napoleon Bonaparte Broward as governor. The activist Democrat spurred numerous initiatives with which Attorney General Ellis assisted, especially projects involving internal improvements and drainage. Ellis contributed additionally to the legal profession by backing the creation of the Florida State Bar Association in February 1907. He served on its committee on constitution and bylaws and was elected its vice president for the second circuit. During the Broward years Ellis remarried, a fact that promised political advantage. His bride, Serena Haile Taylor, was the daughter of Justice Robert Fenwick Taylor,

Justice William Hull Ellis. The "silver-tongued orator of the State of Florida" may have used this photograph in one of his campaigns for attorney general in 1904 or 1908. Ellis was one of nine justices of the supreme court of Florida to have served as attorney general prior to sitting on the high court.

and the ceremony occurred in Taylor's Tallahassee residence in April 1906. As the town's *Weekly True Democrat* noted, "The bride belongs to one of our first families." Two daughters subsequently were born to the Ellises.[71]

After one term as attorney general, Ellis's political career temporarily came to a halt. He stood for reelection in 1908, boasting that "the record I have made is clean, and shows that my services have been efficient." His plans did not take proper account, however, of the political ascendance of soon-to-be governor and United States senator Park Trammell of Polk County. The Trammell juggernaut overwhelmed Ellis in the Democratic primary and compelled the incumbent to retire to private practice in Quincy. Three years later Ellis toyed with the idea of running for Congress but, in the end, declined to make the race. Instead, he accepted appointment under Governor Albert W. Gilchrist, an old Gadsden County acquaintance, as general counsel for the trustees of the internal improvement trust fund. His work for the fund brought him recognition as an effective proponent of Everglades drainage, a then-popular program. In 1914 he utilized the popularity gained thereby to offer his candidacy for the supreme court upon the retirement of Justice William Adams Hocker. Following election, he took the oath of office to join the court in January 1915.[72]

Ellis remained a member of the high court for more than two decades following his swearing in. He won reelection without opposition in 1920, 1926, and 1932 and served as chief justice during 1927–29 and 1937–38. Additionally, in 1919 he acted as president of the state bar association. Ill health and failing eyesight beset the justice in the 1930s. When those factors were combined with Judge Elwyn A. Thomas's announcement that he would oppose the justice, Ellis acknowledged in late 1937 that he would not seek another term. That year Stetson University honored his judicial contributions by awarding him an honorary degree of doctor of laws.[73]

Retirement facilitated Ellis's movement into a private legal practice at Quincy. Within a few weeks after leaving the supreme court, he returned to its bar to argue on behalf of a client. The action stirred criticism, and the court responded by barring retired justices from practicing before it. In the 1940s Justice and Mrs. Ellis relocated to Gainesville. He died in a Jacksonville rest home on April 14, 1948, and was interred at the Quincy Episcopal Church.[74]

Chapter 19

Progressive Era Court Perspectives

The period lasting from 1897 to 1916 brought to the supreme court of Florida hundreds of cases affecting most aspects of contemporary jurisprudence. While most of the litigation reflected issues of long-standing interest, some concerned new facets of the state's commercial and social lives. For example, in 1900 the supreme tribunal considered the question of competition between municipalities and private enterprise in the generation and sale of electrical power. The court held, in *Capital City Light & Fuel Co.* v. *City of Tallahassee*, that a utility company had waived its franchise rights by failing to construct electric power plants or a distribution system. In such circumstances, the justices recognized legislative power to grant a second franchise to a city without unconstitutionally impairing the utility's contract.[1]

Another innovation similarly commanded court attention. The increasing presence of automobiles in the state had led the legislature in 1905 to impose on owners certain duties and obligations, mandate licenses and numbering to identify the vehicle and driver, and require that automobiles, when driven on a public highway, be operated so as not "to endanger the life or limb of any person" and "in [the] case of horses or other draft animals, to prevent frightening the same." In *Atlantic Coast Line R. Co.* v. *Weir*, decided in 1912, the high court determined that the licensing requirement did not abrogate the right of an owner of an unregistered vehicle to recover from a railroad for operation of its trains in violation of statutory duty.[2] Five years later the justices, in *Anderson* v. *Southern Cotton Oil Co.*, cited the legislation as evidence that the state had enacted special regulations pertaining to automobiles "in recognition of the many and great dangers incident to their use." Pursuant to the finding, the court held that an employer was vicariously liable for the negligent operation of a motor vehicle by his employee.[3]

Regulation of an expanded legal profession also required scrutiny. Coincident with innovations such as electric power and automobiles had come population growth with attendant business and commercial expansion. The situation required significantly greater numbers of attorneys to handle legal affairs. In turn, the conditions attracted to Florida many out-of-state lawyers whose competence to practice was questioned by local professionals. To resolve the potential problem, legislators in 1897 created a five-member state board of legal examiners to be appointed by the supreme court. Subsequently the court considered a challenge to the law and declared it unconstitutional. The decision in *State ex. rel. Clyatt* v. *Hocker* hinged upon a finding that the statute gave the supreme court power to appoint state officers when the constitution directed such officers either to be elected or appointed by the governor. Afterward, an amendment approved in 1899 required that an applicant be examined for fitness by two members of the bar in open court.[4]

Besides these types of cases, the Progressive era offered new political and governmental initiatives in areas ranging from race relations to social and educational reform to regulation of corporations and beyond. In almost every area the court found itself confronted with sensitive issues and difficult decisions. The following discussion provides a sampling of that work and of the court's reasonings.

Race Relations

By 1897 legal segregation had begun to find a firm footing in southern soil, spurred partly by the United States Supreme Court's decision of the previous year in *Plessy* v. *Ferguson,* which accepted the doctrine of "separate but equal." Already, laws enacted in Florida in the late 1880s and through the 1890s effectively had deprived most blacks and many poor whites of the ballot. White supremacy stood as a cornerstone of the state Democratic party. As the *Orlando Sentinel-Reporter* noted in 1901 of Governor William Sherman Jennings, "He was the choice of an undivided party, and he assumes office with the question of the right of the white man to rule, which has distracted the South [for] so many years, forever settled."[5]

Within this environment several important issues reached a state supreme court whose members, for the most part, shared conservative legal perspectives as well as backgrounds steeped in the traditions of the Old South's planter world. In the cases the court displayed sensitivity to rights guaranteed in the state and federal constitutions, as interpreted in light of the United States Supreme Court's guidelines. To some extent the justices's opinions reflected a spirit of paternalism, what Justice Robert Spratt Cockrell referred to in 1910 as an "atmosphere of that tender consideration so generally shown to the illiterate negroes by the descendants of the slave owner class."[6]

Some matters that the court reviewed represented unresolved questions left as vestiges of slavery. In 1899's *Adams* v. *Sneed*, for instance, the court examined the inheritance rights of lineal descendants of slaves. Since slaves were considered property and were not allowed to marry legally, their issue were not considered to be legitimate. When couples married after the Civil War, their living children became legitimate in the eyes of the law, but *Adams* concerned property ownership when no post-emancipation marriage ceremony had taken place. The court held that the issue of such marriages had no heritable blood for purposes of the laws of descent. Children of the unratified marriages "simply have no status one way or the other."[7] Responding to the decision, the legislature quickly legitimated all such offspring. In 1904 the high court confirmed the constitutionality of the new law.[8]

The justices reached one decision of fundamental importance in 1908. The issue in *Montgomery* v. *State* concerned the systematic exclusion of blacks from panels of prospective jurors and whether such exclusion resulted in deprivation of a fair trial for a black defendant. Evidence demonstrated that Duval County courts consistently had chosen white jurors for trials of all defendants, even though more blacks than whites resided in the county. Montgomery alleged that the county commissioners "in selecting names for the jury box . . . discriminated against all men of color, on account of their race, color and previous condition of servitude; and failed and refused to select any for jury duty."[9]

The court decided the question based upon the equal protection clause of the Fourteenth Amendment of the United States Constitution. It found that a black defendant, while not possessing a constitutional right to have a black juror on the jury that was to decide his fate, was entitled to have blacks on the panel from which the jury was selected. Exclusion of blacks offended the equal protection doctrine. In Justice James Bryan Whitfield's words: "The constitutional guarantee of equal protection of the laws does not give to any person a right to a jury composed in whole or in part of his own or of any particular race; but every person being tried in a court of justice is entitled to have a jury selected and summoned without illegal discrimination of any character."[10]

The application of the *Montgomery* rule was tested in 1913's *Bonaparte* v. *State*. Again, the issue involved an all-white Duval County jury. The trial judge had not allowed the defense to cross-examine the deputy sheriff, who had gone into the community to round up the jury panel, as to whether in his years of performing this duty he had ever brought a black prospective juror into court. With Justice Robert Fenwick Taylor writing for the majority, the supreme court stated that the defense could cross-examine as to composition of previous jury panels because that procedure represented the sole method of determining whether the *Montgomery* rule was being followed.[11]

In the era's atmosphere of racial animosity, these rulings signify a court concern for justice and fairness for black defendants. One national commentator observed: "In this Florida court then, the civil right of every negro to trial by juries open to negroes has been vigorously upheld. It is such occurrences as this, unheralded because undramatic, that indicate, more accurately than the doings of the ruffian or the mob, in what direction the American people are moving." Perhaps the rulings' importance was best expressed by United States Supreme Court Justice Hugo Black, who in 1948 informed Florida's Senator Claude Pepper, "I have read the decision of Justice Whitfield in the case of *Montgomery v. State*, 55th Fla. 97." He continued, "The opinion is splendidly written. That Judge Whitfield should have written it in 1908 is a tribute to his courage and character."[12]

Prohibition

Along with racial matters, the question of the prohibition of the sale and consumption of alcoholic beverages remained a passionately contested issue in the last decade of the nineteenth century and the first two decades of the twentieth. The court heard a number of cases related to various aspects of the controversy. By way of example, it had frequent occasion to consider appeals involving the powers of counties and municipalities to tax or ban the sale of alcohol. A related concern involved the "local option" provisions of the state constitution, which permitted counties and municipalities to vote themselves "dry." Interestingly, at least one editor considered such dry votes as a bane to the legal profession. Commenting on the departure of one Monticello attorney to accept a bank job in Alabama, he wrote, "Handling the funds of a hundred thousand dollar bank, is better than practicing law in a 'dry town,' and we congratulate Mr. Clarke upon his good fortune."[13]

Several appeals stemmed from a 1901 law and its subsequent amendments. The first act provided that "Whoever sells, or causes to be sold, any spirituous, vinous, malt or other intoxicating liquors in any county or precinct which has voted against the sale of such liquors" shall be guilty of a crime. The court upheld its constitutionality in 1903 and 1905 in *Brass* v. *State* and *Caesar* v. *State*, respectively.[14] Subsequent legislation increased the penalties to "imprisonment not exceeding one year or by fine of not more than one thousand dollars." Court ratification of the propriety of the change came in 1908's *Ladson* v. *State* and 1909's *Hallbeck* v. *State*.[15]

Often application of the laws involved novel questions, such as in *McGriff* v. *State*, where the alleged unlawful sale was made in Seminole County, which, in 1913, had been created out of portions of Orange County. Orange had voted dry, but newly organized Seminole had yet to hold an election. Justice Thomas M. Shackleford, writing for the court, determined that the formation of a new county from an old one that had voted dry "cannot have the effect of nullifying such election and authorizing the sale of liquors" in the new county.[16]

Many of these issues at least temporarily were mooted within a few years. In 1918 Florida voters approved a constitutional amendment, effective January 1, 1919, prohibiting the sale of alcoholic beverages throughout the state. In *Correlis* v. *State* the supreme court upheld the conviction of a defendant accused of selling the beverages in a dry county after the date of ratification but before January 1, 1919. It reasoned that the old enforcement laws remained in effect until the effective date of the amendment.[17] Then, the Eighteenth Amendment to the United States Constitution, ratified in Florida on November 27, 1918, achieved final approval on January 29, 1919. Prohibition thereafter became a matter of national concern.[18]

Higher Education Reform

Reorganization and reform of Florida's higher education system stood as a centerpiece of Governor Napoleon Bonaparte Broward's 1905 legislative agenda. The ensuing Buckman Act created a board of control to manage all state institutions of higher learning. The legislation has been described as a "great step forward" for higher education in Florida, which meant that "Florida would no longer lag behind most of the states in the promotion of advanced learning." Specifically, it abolished the University of Florida at Lake City, Florida State College at Tallahassee (earlier, West Florida Seminary), the white Normal School at Defuniak Springs, Gainesville's East Florida Seminary, South Florida College at Bartow, and the Florida Agricultural Institute in Osceola County. To succeed them, the law established the University of Florida, which soon was located at Gainesville, and the Florida State College for Women at Tallahassee. The Colored Normal School, also known as the Florida State Normal and Industrial School, was continued, also at Tallahassee.[19]

The Buckman Act engendered much opposition and criticism from those who believed that the "schools of the common people" had been abolished and that the new entrance standards limited higher education to the wealthy. Critics took their cases to court and challenged the law's constitutionality in *State ex rel. Moodie* v. *Bryan*. The 1905 decision, written for a unanimous court by Justice Charles Breckenridge Parkhill, upheld the Buckman Act. It concluded with the observation, "[W]e again wish to call attention to the fact that with the wisdom or folly of the act, justice or injustice thereof, we have nothing to do." Parkhill added, "The sole question we are called upon to decide is does the act conflict with the constitution? If not, we are bound to uphold it."[20] In a later case, *Lewis* v. *Gaillard*, the court in 1911 held that a testamentary devise to the West Florida Seminary did not lapse when the Buckman Act changed the institution's name to Florida State College for Women and substantially changed the curriculum by abolishing coeducation at the school. Justice Cockrell wrote for the court majority, while justices Whitfield and Shackleford dissented.[21]

Primary Election Law

The turn of the century introduced into Florida the statewide primary system for elections. At the time the concept represented a liberal attempt to eliminate the stranglehold that Bourbon Democrat powerbrokers held on the party through the convention system. A secondary consideration involved defining political parties as private organizations in control of their own membership, thereby skirting the suffrage guarantees for blacks contained in the Fourteenth and Fifteenth amendments to the United States Constitution. Local, informal, primary elections dated in the state to the 1870s, but the initial attempt to provide guidelines on a statewide basis arose in 1897. Legislators refined the law in 1901, 1906, 1909, and 1913, and their efforts succeeded. Voting decreased in the state from more than 60 percent of eligible voters in the 1880s to 30 percent by 1910. Portions of the laws also required candidates to publish statements of campaign expenses and lists of workers and placed limits on the amount a candidate could spend in most elections.[22]

The primary system's impact began to be felt in 1900, when William Sherman Jennings became the first governor chosen under its provisions. By 1902 the legislature had subjected the selection of nominees for all statewide elected offices to the law. Challengers soon brought the scheme into court. Particularly, the election code, as amended in 1906, provided that the standing committee of any political party, as part of its authority to oversee the contests, could "decide who have been chosen by the majority vote cast in the primary election." In 1908 the supreme court established limits on the legislature's jurisdiction by ruling, in *D'Alemberte* v. *State ex rel. Mays*, that the committee's power did not supplant that of the judiciary to determine protests and contests of election results.[23]

Because the statutes mandated that a primary election had to be won by a majority of all votes cast, results frequently required a runoff election to decide between the two top vote getters. Fiscally conservative legislators reasoned that the expense could be avoided through a scheme subsequently known as the Bryan Primary Law. Enacted in 1913, the statute extensively revised the primary election process. Its main feature was a requirement that the ballot contain, after the name of each candidate, a place for "first choice" and "second choice." The law directed the canvassing board to tally the results in each column. If one candidate received a majority of first choice votes, he was the winner; if no candidate achieved a majority, the board added the total number of second place votes to totals of the leading contenders. The candidate then enjoying the highest revised total was to be declared the winner.[24]

This innovative, yet questionable, plan resulted in a spectacular first trial, the 1916 Democratic gubernatorial primary. Described by one historian as "probably the most confused [election] in Florida's political history," the race saw Sidney J. Catts and William V. Knott emerge from a field of five. State Comptroller Knott represented a moderate to conservative philosophy. Political outsider Catts engaged in a freewheeling, demagogic campaign, resorting especially to stirring anti-Catholic sentiments. In the primary Catts and Knott gained 30,092 and 24,720 votes, respectively. Knott's 8,449 second-place votes outdistanced Catts's 3,337, but the frontrunner still possessed a total margin of 260 votes. Knott protested the count and demanded another tally, alleging fraud and confusion. A trial court agreed, after which the supreme court upheld the recount order in *State ex rel. Knott* v. *Haskell.*[25]

The 1916 election fireworks intensified. Officials concluded from the court-ordered recount that eighteen counties' returns were inaccurate and posted a revised tally that gave Knott the primary victory by twenty-one votes. The party embraced the comptroller as its gubernatorial nominee, despite legal skirmishes that prompted three additional supreme court opinions.[26] Meanwhile, much of Florida's press decried the process, which appeared to deny the rightful winner his nomination. Catts, who had insisted throughout the legal skirmishing that he would run in the general election, accepted in October the Prohibition party's nomination. The candidate lambasted the Democratic party and the supreme court at every opportunity, referring to the tribunal as "the Court of Supreme Contempt" and arguing that its members had stolen the Democratic nomination from him. The voters agreed, and in November Catts easily bested Knott by 39,000 votes to 30,000.[27]

Public versus Private Rights

During the Progressive era the state launched several attempts to assert public rights against private claims. Many of these actions will be discussed in the following sections, but a key court decision regarding the doctrine of sovereign immunity also deserves attention. The matter's origins can be traced to 1879, when, pursuant to several laws, Governor George F. Drew appointed Sidney Wailes as the state's agent to resolve, with the federal government, certain state claims arising out of the century's Indian wars. The contract granted Wailes 15 percent of all sums collected. As the agent endeavored to fulfill his end of the bargain, the matter dragged on year after year. Finally, in 1902 Congress authorized a settlement. The state received $1,089,158.66, of which Wailes demanded $163,373.80 as his commission, to be shared with the estate of his associate William K. Beard.[28]

State officials, sensitive to public perceptions as to the enormity of Wailes's claim, balked at the payment. Since Wailes was barred from suing in state court through the doctrine of sovereign immunity and in federal court through the provisions of the Eleventh Amendment to the United States Constitution, which prohibits a suit against a state for money damages, he pressed for support in the court of public opinion. The matter evolved into a cause célèbre, with accusations made that the state was reneging on its contractual obligations. In 1903 the legislature acted to rid itself of the concerns by appropriating $25,000 for the claimants.[29]

Wailes refused the legislative compromise and eventually sought redress in the courts. In 1910 he asked the Leon County circuit court to direct the state comptroller to pay his claim in full. The judge denied the requested writ of mandamus, and Wailes appealed to the supreme court. Two years afterward the justices sided with the state. Their opinion, in *Wailes* v. *Croom,* declared that the legislature possessed sole power to settle claims against the state. Facts in evidence disclosed that the assembly had fully considered Wailes's demands, referred the matter to a committee that had taken testimony and otherwise investigated the claim, and issued appropriate reports. Thereafter, the legislators had acted within the limits of their authority to offer a compromise by appropriating the $25,000. "The result, whether equitable and just," the decision observed, "is not for us to judge."[30]

Public Lands and Private Rights

By 1900 close ties between old-line Bourbon Democratic officials and railroad company executives had resulted in grants of millions of acres of state lands to railroad companies and private interests. Often the cessions had been justified by the benefits that internal improvements, such as railroads, could bring to the state, but the generosity had been exercised at times under questionable circumstances. The result by century's end was that little land remained in the once extensive public domain. This fact posed a problem for Governor William Sherman Jennings, who wished to implement a program of land reclamation and drainage of swamp and overflowed lands, primarily in South Florida's Everglades. To finance such a program without proposing unpopular new taxes, Jennings believed it was necessary to sell public lands. His dilemma revolved around the question of how to obtain title to them.[31]

One potential answer for Jennings's dilemma concerned the manner in which lands had been granted. At times officials had deeded property outright, but on other occasions they merely had issued certificates that established claims to lands once the United States government had properly patented them to the state, as provided in federal law. In the situation Jennings, as chairman of the board of trustees of the internal improvement trust fund, caused the board to refuse to execute deeds under prior railroad grant certificates, asserting that the grants had not been ones of absolute title but "only residuary grants" subject to the trustee's superior title. The board's official argument insisted that its predecessor boards could not bind their successors by creation of encumbrances on lands that were not patented to the trustees when certificates were issued.[32]

Federal court litigation followed the board's action, and the struggle broadened when Jennings in 1903 secured title for the state from the federal government for almost 3 million acres of South Florida lands. Napoleon Bonaparte Broward, who followed Jennings as governor, designated Jennings as counsel for the board and added the argument that these newly patented lands could not be claimed under certificates because, as a condition of the patents, the proceeds from their sale must be used for drainage and reclamation. A dozen or more suits swirled through various courts, but a federal district judge in 1906 permitted the state to proceed with sales of 100,000 acres.[33]

The federal decision sparked passage of legislation and the filing of additional contests. In 1905 the legislature enacted a series of laws, one of which created a state board of drainage commissioners to oversee Everglades reclamation. Amendments in 1913, 1915, 1917, and 1919 strengthened the laws. The activities of the Everglades Drainage District, which possessed authority over 4 million acres, brought on a land sales boom, with investors streaming to South Florida from across the nation. Supreme court decisions along the way added the security of legal propriety to the initiatives. In 1917, for example, the justices in *Lainhart* v. *Catts* found the 1913 act to be constitutional, finding that drainage and reclamation of swamp and overflowed lands were proper exercises of legislative authority. In utilizing that authority, the solons could choose to create taxing and regulatory districts and place them in charge of administrative officers and commissions. Accordingly, the court would not enjoin the assessment and collection of acreage taxes levied by drainage districts.[34]

Lainhart v. *Catts* foreshadowed other opinions concerning drainage and reclamation activities. In *Bryan* v. *Dade Muck Land Co.*, the court in 1918 upheld the issuance of a writ of mandamus directing the Broward County clerk to accept funds in redemption of tax certificates issued when landowners had not paid assessments levied by the Everglades Drainage District. Under statutory limitations, the court stated, title to the properties had yet to vest in the district. Two years afterward, in *Bannerman* v. *Catts*, the 1913 act again was pronounced constitutional. Legislative determination of the amount of the benefits to be derived from and the assessments to be levied by the district was held to be conclusive and would not be overturned unless arbitrary and abusive.[35]

As illustrated by the *Dade Muck Land* case, the court discovered some limits on the exercise of authority by drainage districts. For instance, in 1919 *Forbes Pioneer Boat Line* v. *Board of Commissioners of Everglades Drainage District* explained that the law did not authorize the commissioners to levy and collect a toll for the use of locks in the district's North New River Canal. The enabling legislation had omitted reference to any such power. The day the decision was announced, the legislature attempted to validate prior toll collections. The boat company attacked the new law as ex post facto, impairing the obligation of a contract, and depriving the company of property without due process of law. In 1920 the state supreme court rejected the arguments and upheld the new law.[36]

The toll collection question moved into federal court, and there it found resolution. In 1922 the United States Supreme Court overturned the state decision. Justice Oliver Wendell Holmes posed the dispute in simple terms. "Stripped of conciliatory phrases," he wrote, "the question is whether a state legislature can take away from a private party a right to recover money due when the act is passed." Writing for the majority, Holmes held that it could not. If the drainage district commissioners did not possess the right to collect the tolls in the first instance, then the boat company enjoyed the right to receive reimbursement of the improperly collected funds. Any law passed by the legislature after the litigation's conclusion could not deprive one of the parties of the right to collect the amount owed.[37]

Public Ownership of Land Touched by Navigable Waters

Developers, state officials, and concerned citizens confronted issues related to the ownership of lands periodically overflowed by navigable waters. In *State ex rel. Ellis* v. *Gerbing*, for instance, the court in 1908 considered the question of title to lands lying between the ordinary high and low water marks of a navigable stream. The respondent, Gerbing, had marked and staked Amelia River oyster bars for his personal benefit. He claimed title to the property from an individual who had received a deed from the state through the trustees of the internal improvement fund. Justice James Bryan Whitfield's opinion in the *Gerbing* case enunciated an important doctrine as to the public's rights in such lands. The state, he wrote, possessed title to lands under navigable waters within its borders, including the shore or space between high and low water marks. That title was held in trust for the use of Florida's inhabitants, it being essential to the sovereignty of the state and to the welfare of the people. While the state may make limited disposition of such lands or may permit their use, it may not convey title to a private person.[38]

The year following the *Gerbing* decision, the high court considered several related matters, including how to determine what is a navigable water. The case concerned Lake Jackson in Leon County. The lake periodically dried up, and, during one dry spell, certain owners of shore lands had claimed title to portions of lake's bottom. In *Broward* v. *Mabry* the justices held that the owner of uplands bordering a navigable body of water has title only down to the ordinary high water line. Capacity for navigation, not usage for that purpose, would determine the navigable character of the water body for purposes of ownership of land covered by such waters. In this case, "[the] conditions of the lake" were "such that in its ordinary state" it was navigable. Consequently, title to the bed of the lake was vested in the people.[39]

The supreme court decided another significant definitional case in 1912. An 1883 state law had permitted homesteaders to purchase up to eighty acres of swamp or overflowed lands for twenty-five cents an acre upon meeting certain conditions. By virtue of their opinion in *Trustees of the Internal Improvement Fund* v. *Root,* the justices decided what constituted such lands. Swamplands, they held, are those that require drainage of excess water or moisture to make them fit for cultivation. Overflowed lands are those that are covered by non-navigable waters or that are subject to periodic overflows of non-navigable waters; additionally, they require drainage, levies, or embankments to remove or keep out the water so as to make the lands suitable for cultivation.[40]

Corporate Regulation and the Railroads

Restraint of corporate powers and activities in the interest of the public good constituted a principal focus of Progressive era legislative efforts. Since railroads nationally and in Florida occupied the forefront of corporate enterprise, they naturally became the target of reform-minded legislators. Florida's Constitution of 1885 had opened the door to regulation by investing in the legislature "full power to pass laws for the correction of abuses and to prevent unjust discrimination and excessive charges by persons and corporations engaged as common carriers in transporting persons and property."[41]

Initial attempts at implementation of railroad supervision by the public had suffered setbacks, but in 1897 the legislature revisited the subject by adopting a more comprehensive regulatory act. It called for the appointment of three commissioners by the governor, subject to state senate confirmation. Their duties included making "reasonable and just rates of freight and passenger tariff to be observed by all railroad companies." They could investigate company financial records to ascertain compliance as well as all contracts, agreements, bills of lading, and other such documents to determine if they were reasonable and just. The law specified penalties and created a private cause of action against railroad companies by private individuals injured as a result of rules violations. The commissioners could direct the attorney general to institute court proceedings to compel rules compliance by common carriers.[42]

The solons took a further step in 1899 when they substantially revised the 1897 law. As a result, the commission received additional authority, including power to regulate schedules; passenger terminals and union depot companies; and charges for storage, wharfage, and demurrage. Beyond that, the commissioners' powers of investigation were strengthened, and they were permitted to compel examinations under oath. Language in the law required a person to testify even when that testimony might tend to incriminate him, but it specified that the testimony could not be used against that person in any criminal proceeding. The statute required companies to submit annual reports, answer additional demands for information, and submit contracts between railroads doing business within the state to the commissioners for approval. The amendment added additional and more severe penalties and established rights on behalf of private individuals to recover damages from any common carrier found in violation of commission rules. Finally, the act expanded powers of the railroad commission to cause state and local law enforcement officials to seek court relief.[43]

Railroads and other corporations qualifying as common carriers tested the new laws soon after their passage. In 1899's *State* v. *Jacksonville Terminal Co.*, the supreme court upheld commission attempts to require a terminal company to admit a railroad company to the privileges and benefits of its common passenger station or terminal. The opinion noted that, for purposes of the decision, it was immaterial whether the terminal company was operating wholly within the state or that the railroad company desiring to use the terminal operated on an interstate basis. Commission orders effecting this purpose did not constitute an unconstitutional interference with interstate commerce and did not deprive the terminal company of property without due process of law. Concluding, the court held that the law of 1899 permitted railroad commissioners to ascertain facts necessary in order to fix and adjust reasonable rates for passenger terminal use.[44]

The commission's rate-setting authority endured numerous challenges. In *State* v. *Seaboard Airline Railway*, for instance, the court held in 1904 that, in determining whether the rates of freight and passenger tariffs established by the commissioners were reasonable, the costs of construction properly could be excluded from estimated earnings under proposed rates. The justices decided, as well, a series of cases concerning whether the commission exceeded its authority in fixing the amounts that railroads could charge for hauling commodities, generally upholding the commission's authority.[45]

Commission rules imposing charges upon railroads for detaining properly loaded cars received attention in *State* v. *Atlantic Coastline R. Co.* The railroad insisted that authority to mandate such charges lay outside the commission's statutory base and that they constituted a burden on interstate commerce and an unlawful penalty that deprived the company of its property without due process of law. Once again, the tribunal upheld commission action. Writing for the court, Justice James Bryan Whitfield outlined its test:

> The statute and the rule have a just relation to the regulation of intrastate transportation by common carriers, a proper subject of legislative classification and action, they are authorized by the laws of the State, they are applicable alike to all under similar circumstances, they do not appear to be unreasonable in their terms or operation, they do not impose unusual or undue or excessive burdens or restrictions upon rights secured by the organic law, they do not directly or materially burden interstate commerce, and, consequently when properly constructed and applied, they do not appear to deprive the carrier of property without due process of law, nor to deny to it the equal protection of the laws nor to interfere with the authority of Congress as to interstate commerce, in violation of the constitution or laws of the United States.[46]

Similarly, in 1910 the court considered the validity of a commission rule limiting the amount a railroad could charge for switching cars. In supporting the commission's position in *State* v. *Atlantic Coastline R. Co.*, the justices once more set forth a test. "[T]he service in question is cognate to and so intimately connected with the public service involved in the carriage and delivery of freight by the railroad company," wrote Justice Charles Breckenridge Parkhill, "as to constitute a part of such service and consequently subject to governmental control."[47]

The supreme court was not always so amenable to the reach of the railroad commissioners in the exercise of their rule-making powers. *State* v. *Louisville and Nashville R. Co.* (1906) involved a defendant railroad company that had refused to accept a commission order that it act as a common carrier to transport certain goods. The company did not own or operate a line traveling the complete distance required by the order. While it could connect with other lines, it did not possess a right to use the other lines. On the court's behalf Justice William Adams Hocker found that the commission had exceeded its authority. The 1899 act, he declared, did not "confer upon the Railroad Commissioners any power to compel one railroad to transport freight over the line of another railroad which the former does not own, control or operate."[48]

One case in which the court prescribed limits on commission authority concerned a rule that required every railroad company immediately to report by telegram any wreck occurring on its line within the state, specifying as nearly as possible the cause of the wreck, the extent of the damage, and the number of persons killed and injured. A unanimous decision in *State* v. *Louisville and Nashville R. Co.* held in 1909 that commission powers were special and limited. The commissioners could exercise only such authority as was legally conferred by the express provisions of the law or such as might "by fair implication and intendment" be determined to be included in the authority expressly conferred. The court concluded that the act of 1899 did not offer any such express or implied authority.[49] Likewise, the 1909 decision in *State* v. *Florida Eastcoast Ry. Co.* reined in the commission's reach. The railroad had refused to comply with commission orders concerning its schedules, asserting that the company had changed the schedule from the one ordered by the state so as to avoid delay and inconvenience to its passengers. In the circumstances the justices, while acknowledging the commission's general right to have its orders obeyed, permitted the company to disregard an unreasonable order.[50]

Earlier the same year the court had laid the foundation for the pro-railroad decision in an opinion that upheld the railroad commission's basic right to regulate schedules. In a case also captioned *State* v. *Florida Eastcoast Ry. Co.*, the tribunal recognized commission power to make just and reasonable regulations of schedules with reference to connections so as to afford convenience and comfort to the public affected by the service. "Even where a particular regulation causes a pecuniary loss to the carrier," Justice Whitfield wrote, "if it is reasonable with reference to the just demands of the public to be affected by it and it does not arbitrarily impose an unreasonable burden upon the carrier, the regulation will not be a taking of property in violation of the constitution."[51]

Despite setbacks, the commission over time and with the assistance of legislators delved more deeply into regulatory schemes, and often the court validated the efforts. For example, the 1899 act had permitted adoption of rules to ban discrimination in rate charges and the provision of services. In *State* v. *Atlantic Coastline R. Co.*, decided in 1906, the court held that, where a railroad company that qualified as a common carrier voluntarily transported and delivered employees and freight for one corporation engaging in providing telegraph services and refused to offer similar services to others without sufficient excuse, the railroad was guilty of unjust discrimination and could be compelled to perform like services for reasonable compensation for other telegraph companies.[52] In 1912 a related theme commanded court consideration in the case of *State* v. *Louisville & Nashville R. Co.* On that occasion the justices condoned regulations that required rail companies, under some circumstances, to transport passengers and freight in separate trains where necessary for passenger safety. That the railroad's profits might suffer did not reduce the regulation to an unreasonable burden.[53]

In 1907 the legislature moved to enhance consumer protection from railroad defaults, and a subsequent challenge resulted in court backing for stricter regulation. The new law required common carriers to pay a claim for any freight losses or damages and for any overcharge within sixty days of presentation of the claim. Further, it specified that, if the claimant succeeded in obtaining a judgment in excess of the amount offered by the carrier in settlement, the trial court should add a 50 percent annual interest charge to the principal sum of the claim, together with reasonable attorney's fees "which shall be fixed by the court not to exceed fifteen dollars, if the amount recovered does not exceed one hundred dollars, and not to exceed fifteen per cent on any amount recovered greater than the sum of one hundred dollars."[54] The 1910 decision in *Atlantic Coastline R. Co.* v. *Coachman* found no constitutional deficiency. "[W]e are not prepared to say, beyond a reasonable doubt," noted Justice Parkhill, "that the penalty is so exorbitant and unreasonable as to render the statute unconstitutional; on the contrary, the regulations herein appear to be reasonably necessary and conducive to the public welfare."[55]

Beyond claims for defaults, problems also surfaced when companies discontinued passenger service in order to place corporate emphasis on more lucrative freight business. The railroad commission in 1908 attempted to slow, if not stop, the practice by requiring companies to obtain the commissioners' consent before canceling any regular passenger service routes. The court in two

1911 decisions, both titled *State* v. *Atlantic Coastline R. Co.*, rejected railroad complaints. Justice Whitfield observed that, while the initial discretion as to operation of a passenger train belonged to the railroad, discretion to continue such service was subject to lawful governmental regulation.[56]

In addition to guaranteeing passenger service, commissioners looked toward ensuring adequate terminal facilities. A commission order directed one line to improve its depot facilities by reconstructing toilet rooms, substituting electric lights for kerosene lamps, and enlarging waiting rooms, baggage rooms, and sheds. The railroad, deeming its facilities adequate, sought court relief. In 1912 Justice Whitfield's majority opinion rejected the company's arguments. He specified, "It is the duty of the carrier to anticipate the needs of the public and to provide appropriate and reasonably adequate facilities and accommodations to meet the present and prospective demands for the safety, comfort and convenience of the public who have a right to use the facilities and accommodations." Whitfield concluded, "The reasonable requirements of a growing community or of an increasing business should be anticipated by a carrier in the performance of its public duty."[57]

Two years afterward a similar question came before the tribunal. Offering its ruling in *State* v. *Florida Eastcoast Railway Co.*, the court determined that a 1906 statute provided railroad commissioners with authority to require railroads to establish freight and passenger depots so as to ensure the safety and convenience of passengers and prompt delivery of freight. Again Justice Whitfield penned the court's decision. "To afford reasonably adequate facilities at its own stations is an absolute duty of the carrier," he opined. "A proper test is not whether the facilities required by the order are in fact *necessary*, but whether they are reasonable for the convenience and safety of the public to be served, and the expense to the carrier is not so unreasonably out of proportion to the convenience afforded to the public as to impose an unlawful burden upon the carrier."[58]

The legislature slowly extended the commission's powers beyond common carriers. In 1911, for instance, the body received responsibility to regulate telephone companies and service. Commission powers otherwise specified by law were made applicable to the new duties. In *State* v. *Southern Telephone and Construction Co.*, the justices in 1913 held that the 1911 act did not confer upon the commissioners judicial powers to determine complaints filed by individuals against a telephone company, at least where the complaints involved something other than a violation of commission rules and regulations.[59]

Lastly, one of the era's most cited decisions concerned an initiative by Attorney General William Hull Ellis, a future justice, to require the Atlantic Coastline Railroad to place its equipment, roadbed, and track in a condition sufficient to permit the line to discharge its responsibilities and duties to the people of Florida. Ellis alleged that the company had received various charters and enjoyed other benefits from the state. Nonetheless, the railroad had allowed its roadbeds to fall into disrepair and otherwise failed to provide "adequate and sufficient terminals for forwarding and delivering such freights to connecting lines." It also had "failed and is failing to supply and furnish flat and box cars in sufficient numbers to load the freights actually offered and being offered to it for transportation." Additionally, the road had "failed and is failing to provide sufficient motive power for the proper handling of its cars and freights and passenger traffic over said lines of railroad." Insisting that the people of Florida had been subjected to "great confusion, inconveniences, hindrances, delays and injury" by the company's inattention, Ellis requested from the supreme court a writ of mandamus directing the railroad to put its affairs in order through specified actions.[60]

Writing for a unanimous court in 1907, Justice Whitfield reasoned in *Ellis v. Atlantic Coast Line Railroad Company* that the issuance of a writ of mandamus constituted a proper remedy to "enforce the performance of a duty to the public imposed by law upon a common carrier railroad corporation," whether the duty was created by statute or was "raised by implication of law from the nature of the public duty authorized by law to be performed and which is being performed by such corporation." He found that the service rendered by the carrier "directly and vitally affects the public" and is a "beneficial right which the public are entitled to enjoy." Failure to perform adequately would result in loss and inconvenience and possibly endanger life and property. "[T]herefore," Whitfield asserted, "it is a fundamental duty of the state to rigidly require a proper rendering of this useful public service." The decision represented one of the first attempts by a state court to formulate a doctrine that a public service corporation owes a duty to the public which has priority over its duty to its stockholders.[61]

With these and similar decisions, the supreme court of Florida helped to move state jurisprudence into the twentieth century. Though sometimes haltingly, the justices recognized the tremendous social and political changes affecting the state in the Progressive era. Within limits established by the state and national constitutions and decisions of the United States Supreme Court, they encouraged a public correction of public ills and set the stage for commitment to greater public responsibility in future years.

Notes

Abbreviations

F&J	*Tallahassee Floridian and Journal*
FSA	Florida State Archives, Tallahassee
FSCHS	Florida Supreme Court Historical Society, Tallahassee
FT-U	*Jacksonville Florida Times-Union*
FT-U&C	*Jacksonville Florida Times-Union and Citizen*
FU	*Jacksonville Florida Union*
LC	Library of Congress
MSCF	Minutes of the Supreme Court of Florida, Supreme Court, Tallahassee
NA	National Archives
PG	*Pensacola Gazette*
PKY	P. K. Yonge Library of Florida History, University of Florida, Gainesville
RG	Record group
SAHSRL	St. Augustine Historical Society Research Library, St. Augustine
TP	*Territorial Papers of the United States, Florida*
TS	*Tallahassee Sentinel*
WF	*Tallahassee Weekly Floridian*
WPA	Work Projects Administration

Chapter 1: Andrew Jackson and the Beginnings of the Florida Judiciary

1. Boyd and Reder, "A History of the Supreme Court of Florida," *University of Miami Law Review* 35 (September 1981): 1019–21.
2. Tebeau, *History of Florida*, 89–115; Martin, *Florida during the Territorial Days*, 1–3.
3. See Patrick, *Florida Fiasco*; Peters, *Florida Wars*, 17–59; Mahon, *Second Seminole War*, 18–28.
4. Martin, *Florida during the Territorial Days*, 3–14.
5. *United States Statutes at Large*, 3:523.
6. Remini, *Andrew Jackson*, 1:365–98.
7. Ibid., 399; James, *Andrew Jackson*, 19.
8. Remini, *Andrew Jackson*, 1:399; James Monroe to Andrew Jackson, January 24, 1821, Andrew Jackson papers. Among other sources, Monroe's letter also may be found in Bassett, *Correspondence of Andrew Jackson*, 3:38.
9. Among the outstanding biographies available on Jackson, see James, *Andrew Jackson*, and Remini, *Andrew Jackson*.

10. Bassett, *Correspondence of Andrew Jackson,* 3:39.
11. Ibid.
12. Remini, *Andrew Jackson,* 1:400–401; Doherty, *Richard Keith Call,* 1–15; Bassett, *Correspondence of Andrew Jackson,* 3:39.
13. Bassett, *Correspondence of Andrew Jackson,* 3:42–46.
14. Carter, *TP,* 22:8–9; *Acts of the Legislative Council of the Territory of Florida Passed at Their First Session* (1822), iv, x–xxi.
15. Carter, *TP,* 22:10, 13–16; Bassett, *Correspondence of Andrew Jackson,* 3:42–44.
16. Carter, *TP,* 22:13–16.
17. Ibid., 22:28–29, 57; Brown, "'Sarrazota, or Runaway Negro Plantations,'" 5–17.
18. Transfer of possession of East Florida occurred on July 10, 1821, at St. Augustine. Colonel Robert Butler, adjutant general for the southern district, accepted the territory on behalf of Governor Jackson and the United States. Tebeau, *History of Florida,* 118–19.
19. The judicial offices held by DuVal and Fromentin should not be confused with the superior court judgeships later authorized for the territory. Among others, President Monroe appointed Alexander Anderson of Tennessee and Georgian John G. Bird as United States attorneys, New Yorker James G. Forbes as United States marshal, George Walton of Georgia as secretary for West Florida, and William G. D. Worthington of Maryland as secretary for East Florida. Tebeau, *History of Florida,* 119; Doherty, *Richard Keith Call,* 17–18.
20. Remini, *Andrew Jackson,* 1:321; Doherty, *Richard Keith Call,* 16–17; Bassett, *Correspondence of Andrew Jackson,* 3:56.
21. Bassett, *Correspondence of Andrew Jackson,* 3:56.
22. *Acts of Territorial Florida* (1822), i–viii.
23. Ibid., xv.
24. Martin, *Florida during the Territorial Days,* 23–25.
25. Jackson's ordinances for West Florida were issued as broadsides by the Pensacola office of the *Floridian,* which published its first issue on August 18, 1821. Richard W. Edes and Company at St. Augustine, which began publishing the *Florida Gazette* on July 14, 1821, issued the ordinances for East Florida in pamphlet form. Given slight differences in spelling and punctuation, the texts of the ordinances for East and West Florida are virtually identical, but some provisions apply only to one town or province. The *Florida Gazette* published the first four East Florida ordinances in Spanish in its editions of September 8 (ordinances 1, 2, and 3) and September 15 (ordinance 4), 1821. Ordinance 5, relating to proceedings in county courts, appears in the St. Augustine pamphlet but is not preserved among the West Florida broadsides. See McMurtrie, *Ordinances.*
26. Ibid. The quotations from Jackson's ordinances that follow in the main text also are from McMurtrie, *Ordinances.*
27. Hoffman, "Talleyrand," 56; Carter, *TP,* 22:36.
28. Bassett, *Correspondence of Andrew Jackson,* 3:49.
29. Carter, *TP,* 22:161.
30. For excellent discussions of issues and events related to *The Heirs of Vidal* v. *John Innerarity,* see Coker and Watson, *Indian Traders,* 330–49, and Doherty, *Richard Keith Call,* 21.

31. Doherty, *Richard Keith Call,* 21.
32. Carter, *TP,* 22:184–89; Pensacola *Floridian,* April 20, 1822.
33. Carter, *TP,* 22:250–58, 262–63.
34. Ibid., 22:317–18, 347; Snyder, "Nancy Hynes DuVal," 24.
35. Bassett, *Correspondence,* 3:122.
36. Ibid., 3:129.
37. Martin, *Florida during the Territorial Days,* 31.
38. Hoffman, "Talleyrand," 56.
39. Carter, *TP,* 22:36, 160–61; Hoffman, "Talleyrand," 56.
40. Fromentin's actual title was "Judge of the United States for West Florida and for that part of the Floridas which lies westward of the cape." Typically for territorial Florida's initial presidential appointees, his term was "during good behavior, and until the end of the next session of the Senate of the United States, and no longer." Bassett, *Correspondence of Andrew Jackson,* 3:49; Carter, *TP,* 22:36; Hoffman, "Talleyrand," 56.
41. Hoffman, "Talleyrand," 56.
42. Carter, *TP,* 22:263.
43. Ibid.
44. Ibid., 22:299.
45. Ibid., 22:317–18.
46. Hoffman, "Talleyrand."
47. Much of the information for William Pope DuVal's biographical sketch came from Snyder, "William Pope DuVal"; Snyder, "Nancy Hynes DuVal"; Knauss, "William Pope DuVal"; and *National Cyclopaedia of American Biography,* 11:376.
48. William Pope DuVal to Richard Keith Call, September 5, 1842, Call papers. Also quoted in Snyder, "Nancy Hynes DuVal," 34. Nancy Hynes DuVal died of yellow fever at St. Joseph, Florida, July 14, 1841. Snyder, "Nancy Hynes Duval," 33.
49. Carter, *TP,* 22:3–4, 42, 51, 55.
50. Ibid., 22:3–4.
51. Ibid., 22:42–43.
52. Ibid., 22:160; Martin, *Florida during the Territorial Days,* 26.
53. Carter, *TP,* 22:284–85, 299.
54. Ibid., 22:371–72.
55. Ibid., 22:469–70; *United States Statutes at Large,* 3:654.
56. William Pope DuVal to Andrew Hynes, September 18, 1828, St. Augustine Historical Society Collection, St. Augustine.
57. Snyder, "Nancy Hynes DuVal," 32–33; Carter, *TP,* 24:992.
58. Carter, *TP,* 24:3; Knauss, "William Pope Duval."
59. St. Augustine *Florida Herald and Southern Democrat,* May 12, 1848; Knauss, "William Pope DuVal," 130–39.
60. Myers, "Some Early History," January 16, 1903, 4.

Chapter 2: Superior Courts and a Territorial Court of Appeals

1. United States Congress, *Debates and Proceedings,* 17th Congress, 1st sess., 38:226.
2. Ibid., 2578–84. The act also is found in *United States Statutes at Large,* 3:654.
3. Myers, "Some Early History," January 9, 1903.
4. Farris, "Courts of Territorial Florida," 346; *United States Statutes at Large,* 3:654.

5. For an overview of early territorial Florida, see Martin, *Florida during the Territorial Days*.
6. Tebeau, *History of Florida*, 122; Martin, *Florida during the Territorial Days*, 35–36.
7. *Acts of Territorial Florida* (1822), 3–5, 9–11, 91–94, 190–92; Farris, "Courts of Territorial Florida," 346–49.
8. Tebeau, *History of Florida*, 122; Carter, *TP*, 24:613.
9. See *Acts of Territorial Florida* (1822).
10. Ibid., 53–54; Carter, *TP*, 24:610.
11. Carter, *TP*, 24:613.
12. Ibid., 22:416.
13. Ibid., 22:318, 451.
14. Pensacola *Floridian*, July 20, 1822; Carter, *TP*, 22:554–55.
15. Carter, *TP*, 22:677.
16. Farris, "Courts of Territorial Florida," 347–48.
17. Doherty, *Richard Keith Call*, 27–30; Farris, "Courts of Territorial Florida," 347–48.
18. *United States Statutes at Large*, 4:45.
19. Carter, *TP*, 22:53, 656; St. Augustine *East Florida Herald*, July 29, 1824.
20. Sources on Joseph Lee Smith's life and career include "Life of Judge Joseph Lee Smith" in Joseph Lee Smith family materials, SAHSRL; Fredriksen, "Lawyer, Soldier, Judge"; and Kilbourn, *Bench and Bar*, 147, 290.
21. Kilbourn, *Bench and Bar*, 147.
22. Noll, *General Kirby Smith*; Fredriksen, "Lawyer, Soldier, Judge," 118.
23. *American State Papers: Naval Affairs*, 3:922; Noll, *General Kirby Smith*.
24. Carter, *TP*, 24:409.
25. Ibid., 22:416.
26. Noll, *General Kirby Smith*, 7, 10.
27. "Life of Judge Joseph Lee Smith," 11, 13–17.
28. Douglas, *Autobiography*, 73–74.
29. Carter, *TP*, 23:39–40.
30. Ibid., 23:58–60.
31. Ibid., 59.
32. Ibid., 23:169–70, 194–95.
33. Ibid., 23:373–74.
34. Ibid., 23:392–93.
35. Doherty, *Richard Keith Call*, 36–37; Carter, *TP*, 23:411–12, 437–38, 506–14, 556.
36. On the Nucleus, see Doherty, "Political Factions," and Doherty, "Andrew Jackson's Cronies."
37. Doherty, *Richard Keith Call*, 36; Fredriksen, "Lawyer, Soldier, Judge," 104.
38. Carter, *TP*, 24:4–5, 520.
39. Fredriksen, "Lawyer, Soldier, Judge," 104.
40. Hall, *Politics of Justice*, 16, 23; Hall and Rise, *From Local Courts to National Tribunals*, 12–13; Doherty, *Whigs of Florida*, 1–7.
41. St. Augustine *Florida Herald*, November 28, 1833; Hall and Rise, *From Local Courts to National Tribunals*, 13, appendix B, 171; Fredriksen, "Lawyer, Soldier, Judge," 118; "Life of Joseph Lee Smith," 17–18.

42. On Brackenridge's life, see Keller, *Nation's Advocate.* Much of the material for this biographical sketch is from its pages.
43. Ibid., 16–17.
44. Ibid., 36; Brackenridge, *Recollections,* 14–16.
45. Brackenridge, *Law Miscellanies,* 571.
46. Among the legal treatises studied by Brackenridge were Burlemaqui's works on general law, Martens's and Vattel's on international law, and standard texts on shipping, promissory notes, bills of exchange, and insurance. Brackenridge, *Recollections,* 110–15; Brackenridge, *Views of Louisiana.*
47. Thomas Jefferson to Henry Marie Brackenridge, March 16, 1814, Jefferson papers, LC.
48. Keller, *Nation's Advocate,* 166; Parton, *Life of Andrew Jackson,* 1:xvi.
49. Keller, *Nation's Advocate,* 184.
50. Bornholdt, *Baltimore and Early Pan-Americanism,* 85.
51. Ibid., 103–4.
52. *St. Louis Enquirer,* October 7, 1820; Parton, *Life of Andrew Jackson,* 2:615; Thomas, *A History of Military Government,* 69.
53. Barfield, "First Civil Governor."
54. Pensacola *Florida Gazette,* September 1, 1821.
55. Evidencing his faith in Florida's potential, Brackenridge, in 1822, purchased several hundred acres of land on Pensacola Bay. He improved the tract, which contained a live oak grove, with peach, lemon, orange, and additional live oak trees. He studied live oak growth and the preservation of live oak for construction of naval vessels. The plantation failed to prosper, and, in 1827, congressional delegate Joseph M. White arranged for its purchase by the United States Navy. Brackenridge aided the naval live oak program with his "Letter on the Culture of Live Oak" to Secretary of the Navy Samuel Southard. The secretary and President John Quincy Adams soon accepted the judge's offer to superintend the new naval live oak preserve. In this paid position, Brackenridge became the first forester for the United States and superintendent of its first experimental forestry station. Carter, *TP,* 23:1064–65. On live oak culture and use, see also Wood, *Live Oaking.*
56. Paisley, *Red Hills of Florida,* 84; Keller, *Nation's Advocate,* 290.
57. Carter, *TP,* 22:318.
58. Ibid., 22:451.
59. Pensacola *Floridian,* July 20, 1822.
60. Henry M. Brackenridge to secretary of state, June 1, 1823, misc. letters, General Records, Department of State. This was Brackenridge's report on the *Carmen* case.
61. Ibid.; Carter *TP,* 22:447–48.
62. *Pensacola Gazette and West Florida Advertiser,* August 21, 1824.
63. Ibid., March 4, 1826.
64. Ibid., May 18–June 22, 1827.
65. Carter, *TP,* 24:610.
66. Ibid., 611–15.
67. *Pensacola Gazette and Chronicle,* October 22, 1831.
68. Ibid., October 22, 1831.

69. Carter, *TP*, 22:860–62.
70. Ibid., 22:864.
71. *Pensacola Gazette and West Florida Advertiser*, September 11, 1824; Carter, *TP*, 22:967.
72. Carter, *TP*, 23:213–14.
73. Ibid., 23:935–37, 959–64; Keller, *Nation's Advocate*, 322.
74. Ibid., 23:936; Keller, *Nation's Advocate*, 327.
75. Carter, *TP*, 24:704.
76. Brackenridge, *Judge Brackenridge's Letters*, 2; *Niles' Weekly Register*, October 10, December 19, 1840; Brackenridge, *Sixty Years*.
77. *Pittsburgh Daily Gazette*, January 18, 1871.
78. Carter, *TP*, 22:656; St. Augustine *East Florida Herald*, July 31, 1824.
79. Whatley and Cook, "East Florida Land Commission," 41; Carter, *TP*, 22:413, 580.
80. Carter, *TP*, 22:945–46.
81. Ibid., 22:941, 953–54.
82. St. Augustine *East Florida Herald*, July 31, 1824.
83. Woodford, *Mr. Jefferson's Disciple*, 18. This work provided the basic information for the biographical sketch of Augustus Brevoort Woodward.
84. Ibid., 21.
85. Ibid., appendix 10.
86. A. B. Woodward to Thomas Jefferson, August 16, 1802, Jefferson papers, Alderman Library; Woodford, *Mr. Jefferson's Disciple*, 31; Hall and Rise, *From Local Courts to National Tribunals*, 174.
87. Hall and Rise, *From Local Courts to National Tribunals*, 174.
88. Woodford, *Mr. Jefferson's Disciple*, 86; Hall and Rise, *From Local Courts to National Tribunals*, 174.
89. Woodford, *Mr. Jefferson's Disciple*, 90.
90. Ibid., 74.
91. Ibid., 173–81; Carter, *TP*, 23:53.
92. Groene, *Ante-Bellum Tallahassee*, 19; Myers, "Some Early History," March 13, 1903.
93. Johnson, *Red, White and Bluebloods in Frontier Florida*, 64.
94. Carter, *TP*, 23:151.
95. Ibid., 153.
96. Johnson, *Red, White and Bluebloods*, 64–66; Carter, *TP*, 23:724–26, 798, 813, 875.
97. Hall and Rise, *From Local Courts to National Tribunals*, 8–9.
98. Carter, *TP*, 23:960; Hall and Rise, *From Local Courts to National Tribunals*, 174.

Chapter 3: A Maturing Judicial System

1. Martin, *Florida during the Territorial Days*, 97–123; Schafer, "A Class of People"; Brown, "Race Relations."
2. See Smith, *Slavery and Plantation Growth*.
3. Groene, *Ante-Bellum Tallahassee*, 13–23; Ellis and Rogers, *Tallahassee and Leon County*, 6–7; *United States Statutes at Large*, 4:45.
4. Mahon, *Second Seminole War*, 29–55.
5. Smith, *Slavery and Plantation Growth*, 22.
6. Ibid., 22–23; Harper, "Ante-Bellum Census Enumerations," 42–45; Martin, *Florida during the Territorial Days*, 109.

7. Martin, *Florida during the Territorial Days*, 37–38; Doherty, *Richard Keith Call*, 48–49.
8. Doherty, *Richard Keith Call*, 48–50.
9. Dodd, "Wrecking Business," 173–80.
10. Diddle, "Adjudication," 44.
11. Dodd, "Wrecking," 180–81; *American Insurance Company* v. *356 Bales of Cotton*, 26 *US* 511 (1828).
12. Carter, *TP*, 24:968; Dodd, "Wrecking," 181–84; *United States Statutes at Large*, 4:291
13. For a discussion of crime and criminal law in territorial Florida, see Hall and Rise, *From Local Courts to National Tribunals*, 8–20. This quotation is found on p. 9. Also see Denham, "Rogue's Paradise."
14. Hall and Rise, *From Local Courts to National Tribunals*, 9; *Territory of Florida* v. *Charles Hershile*, May 10, 1837, United States District and Superior Court of Florida records, Pensacola, 3:10.
15. Martin, *Florida during the Territorial Days*, 71–78; *Richard Meade* v. *The United States*, 2 *Court of Claims Reports*, 243; *Richard Meade* v. *The United States*, 9 *Wallace*, 723.
16. Doherty, *Richard Keith Call*, 39–40; Call, *Journal*, 51–52.
17. Doherty, *Richard Keith Call*, 36; *United States Statutes at Large*, 4:284–86.
18. *Maryland Biographical Cyclopedia*, 531.
19. Doherty, *Richard Keith Call*, 57–59. Regarding the Arredondo and Forbes claims, see also Martin, *Florida during the Territorial Days*, 77–82; Coker and Watson, *Indian Traders*, 350–62; Rogers, *Outposts on the Gulf*, 5–47.
20. Call, *Journal*, 58; Doherty, *Richard Keith Call*, 58–60.
21. *American State Papers: Public Lands*, 3:718–19; Doherty, *Richard Keith Call*, 60–63.
22. Call, *Journal*, 62–64; Doherty, *Richard Keith Call*, 63–64.
23. Call, *Journal*, 66–67; Doherty, *Richard Keith Call*, 64–67.
24. Doherty, *Richard Keith Call*, 64–67; Carter, *TP*, 24:158.
25. Carter, *TP*, 23:1057.
26. Ibid., 24:830, 856.
27. Ibid., 24:983.
28. Hall and Rise, *From Local Courts to National Tribunals*, 167, 173.
29. Doherty, *Richard Keith Call*, 80–82.
30. Hall and Rise, *From Local Courts to National Tribunals*, 155–56, 167, 171, 173.
31. *Maryland Biographical Cyclopedia*, 531; Hall and Rise, *From Local Courts to National Tribunals*, 167.
32. Ibid.
33. *Maryland Biographical Cyclopedia*, 531; Shofner, *History of Jefferson County*, 21–27.
34. Quincy, *Memoirs*, 7:247; Carter, *TP*, 23:882.
35. Carter, *TP*, 23:882.
36. Ibid., 882–83, 965–66.
37. Myers, "Some Early History," March 13, 1903.
38. Carter, *TP*, 25:537.
39. Thomas Randall to William Wirt, April 7, 1833, Wirt papers.
40. Laura Randall to mother, December 19, 1827, ibid.
41. Henry Marie Brackenridge to Caroline Brackenridge, October 2, 1827, Brackenridge letters.
42. Laura Randall to mother, January 8, 1828, Wirt papers.

43. Tallahassee *Floridian*, January 11, 1834.
44. Myers, "Some Early History," March 13, 1903.
45. Shofner, *History of Jefferson County*, 26–27, 94–95; Laura Randall to mother, December 19, 1827, Wirt papers.
46. Long, *Florida Breezes*, 146–48.
47. *Maryland Biographical Cyclopedia*, 531; Carter, *TP*, 24:591, 25:236, 26:124.
48. Thomas Randall to Elizabeth Wirt, July 15, 1837, Wirt papers.
49. Ellen Wirt Vass to Catherine G. Wirt, June 23, 1839, Wirt papers.
50. Dovell, *History of Banking*, 29.
51. Manuscript returns, Seventh and Eighth United States Decennial Censuses, 1850 and 1860, Leon and Jefferson counties, Florida (population and agricultural schedules).
52. Carter, *TP*, 25:268.
53. *F&J*, March 30, July 27, 1850; "Quincy Conservative Convention," 268.
54. *Maryland Biographical Cyclopedia*, 531; petition regarding the estate of Thomas Randall, August 11, 1877, file 788, Leon County probate records.
55. *United States Statutes at Large*, 4:291; Carter, *TP*, 24:10–11; Hall and Rise, *From Local Courts to National Tribunals*, 173; Shofner, *Jackson County*, 28–29.
56. Carter, *TP*, 23:214, 731, 24:10–11.
57. Ibid., 24:51.
58. Ibid., 24:112.
59. Ibid., 24:231.
60. Henry Marie Brackenridge to Caroline Brackenridge, September 1, 1828, Brackenridge letters.
61. Ibid., August 23, 1830.
62. Carter, *TP*, 24:685–86.
63. Quoted in Hammond, "Wreckers," 247.
64. Rerick, *Memoirs of Florida*, 2:72–73.
65. Dodd, "Wrecking Business," 185.
66. Hammond, "Wreckers," 248.
67. Diddle, "Adjudication," 45.
68. Browne, *Key West*, 165.
69. Diddle, "Adjudication," 46–47; Dodd, "Wrecking Business," 184; Hall and Rise, *From Local Courts to National Tribunals*, 11–12.
70. Carter, *TP*, 25:273–74.
71. Hall and Rise, *From Local Courts to National Tribunals*, 11, 172.
72. Boyles, "Governor Reid"; Hall and Rise, *From Local Courts to National Tribunals*, 168; Miller, *Bench and Bar*, 2:182–83. For more on Reid, see Fouraker, "Administration of Robert Raymond Reid," and *National Cyclopaedia of American Biography*, 11:377.
73. Miller, *Bench and Bar*, 2:183.
74. Hall and Rise, *From Local Courts to National Tribunals*, 168.
75. Miller, *Bench and Bar*, 2:182–237.
76. Carter, *TP*, 24:705; Boyles, "Governor Reid"; Miller, *Bench and Bar*, 2:204–5.
77. Carter, *TP*, 24:862–63, 874–75.
78. Reid, "Diary," 47.
79. Carter, *TP*, 25:80–82.

80. Reid, "Diary," 25.
81. Ibid., 64.
82. Ibid., 4.
83. Mrs. C. F. Andrews memoirs. At the beginning of the Civil War, Martha Reid followed her son Raymond Jenckes to Richmond, Virginia, where he served in the Second Florida Regiment (Perry's Brigade), CSA. For the war's duration Martha served as matron of the Hospital for Florida Soldiers at Richmond, which she helped to organize and maintain with Dr. Thomas Palmer of Perry. Her devotion to the patients, whose wounds she dressed with linens donated by her Florida friends, was so appreciated that she came to be called "Mother Reid." Even on the day she learned that Jenckes Reid had been killed at the Battle of the Wilderness, she continued nursing the sick and dying. In commemoration of the sacrifices endured by Martha and her family during the conflict, the Jacksonville chapter of the United Daughters of the Confederacy (the first such unit in Florida) in 1894 took the name "Martha Reid Chapter."
84. The principal work on the Second Seminole War is Mahon, *Second Seminole War.*
85. Doherty, *Whigs of Florida,* 1–4; Brown, "Race Relations," 306–7; Dodd, *Florida Becomes a State,* 29–46.
86. Reid, "Diary," 1–2.
87. Dodd, *Florida Becomes a State,* 47–48.
88. Doherty, *Richard Keith Call,* 81.
89. Boyles, "Governor Reid."
90. Doherty, *Whigs of Florida,* 7–17; St. Augustine *News,* December 27, 1839.
91. Tallahassee *Floridian,* December 28, 1840.
92. Martin, *Florida during the Territorial Days,* 254–55; Mahon, *Second Seminole War,* 265–66; Meltzer, *Hunted Like a Wolf,* 174–76. Also see Covington, "Cuban Bloodhounds."
93. Martin, *Florida during the Territorial Days,* 254–55.
94. Cash, *Story of Florida,* 2:624.
95. Judicial Conference, *Judges of the United States,* 76; Powell, *Dictionary,* 311–12.
96. Carter, *TP,* 24:704.
97. Ibid., 24:880–81.
98. Ibid., 24:852.
99. Ibid., 25:229–30.
100. Ibid., 24:922–23.
101. Powell, *Dictionary,* 311–12.

Chapter 4: Momentum toward Statehood and a Supreme Court

1. See Martin, *Florida during the Territorial Days,* 53–164; Smith, *Slavery and Plantation Growth,* 122–70.
2. Mahon, *Second Seminole War,* 29–113; Brown, "Race Relations," 287–307.
3. Brown, "Race Relations," 287–307; Brown, "Ossian Bingley Hart," 42–77.
4. Dovell, *History of Banking,* 9–40.
5. Doherty, *Whigs of Florida,* 1–17; Martin, *Florida during the Territorial Days,* 262–66; Brown, "Race Relations," 306–7.
6. Dodd, *Florida Becomes a State,* 34–35.

7. Ibid., 37.
8. Doherty, *Whigs of Florida*, 5–15; Dodd, *Florida Becomes a State*, 47–70; Brown, "Ossian Bingley Hart," 76–78.
9. Doherty, *Whigs of Florida*, 7–17.
10. Dodd, *Florida Becomes a State*, 146, 162–65, 169, 198–202, 206–8.
11. Ibid., 314.
12. Ibid., 312–15.
13. Carter, *TP*, 24:657–58, 1000–1001. On Apalachicola, see also Rogers, *Outposts on the Gulf*, and Willoughby, *Fair to Middlin.'*
14. Carter, *TP*, 25:234–35.
15. *United States Statutes at Large*, 5:5; Carter, *TP*, 25:234, 270–72, 435–44, 516.
16. Carter, *TP*, 25:467–69.
17. Cash, *Story of Florida*, 1:629–30.
18. Manuscript returns, Sixth U.S. Decennial Census, 1840, Escambia County, Florida; Carter, *TP*, 24:198–99, 25:516.
19. Carter, *TP*, 24:138–39.
20. Ibid., 24:138–40, 198–99, 25:516; Richard C. Allen biographical materials at Constitutional Convention State Museum; Groene, *Ante-Bellum Tallahassee*, 48–49.
21. Carter, *TP*, 25:135, 195.
22. Ibid., 25:438, 452–54; Rogers, *Outposts on the Gulf*, 12–13.
23. Carter, *TP*, 25:516.
24. Dodd, *Florida Becomes a State*, 201.
25. Carter, *TP*, 25:570; Tallahassee *Floridian*, July 28, 1838; *St. Joseph Times*, quoted in Tallahassee *Floridian*, August 14, 1841.
26. *Pensacola Mail*, January 30, 1872.
27. Carter, *TP*, 25:515, 26:132; Hall and Rise, *From Local Courts to National Tribunals*, 162–63.
28. Carter, *TP*, 25:513; Hall and Rise, *From Local Courts to National Tribunals*, 14.
29. *New Yorker*, quoted in *PG*, undated clipping, c. 1841.
30. Carter, *TP*, 26:132, 161–62.
31. Walker, *Trial and Imprisonment*, lxiv–lxviii, 10–14, 33–43, 54–55.
32. Carter, *TP*, 26:513, 1084; Florida *Senate Journal* (1845), 85–99; *Pensacola Mail*, January 30, 1872.
33. Bruington, *St. Michael's Cemetery*, 62; Hall and Rise, *From Local Courts to National Tribunals*, 162; *Pensacola Mail*, January 30, 1872.
34. *Pensacola Mail*, January 30, 1872.
35. The principal source of information on Marvin's life is his autobiographical essay contained in Kearney, "Autobiography." The quoted material is found on p. 181. See also *National Cyclopaedia of American Biography*, 11:379, and William Marvin to Charles B. Pendleton, December 5, 1889, Marvin biographical file.
36. Kearney, "Autobiography," 182–87.
37. Ibid., 188–89.
38. Ibid., 188–94.
39. Carter, *TP*, 25:143–44, 596–97; Kearney, "Autobiography," 194–98.

40. Carter, *TP,* 25:143–44, 596–97; Marvin to Pendleton, December 5, 1889, Marvin biographical file.
41. Marvin to Pendleton, December 5, 1889, Marvin biographical file.
42. Kearney, "Autobiography," 200–201; Durkin, *Confederate Navy Chief,* 9, 19–20, 23, 31–32, 70.
43. Kearney, "Autobiography," 200.
44. Brown, "Ossian Bingley Hart," 151–52; Clerk of the House of Representatives, *People of Lawmaking,* 61; Dodd, *Florida Becomes a State,* 169.
45. Kearney, *Autobiography,* 203–4.
46. Ibid., 203–6.
47. Ibid.
48. Carter, *TP,* 26:132, 25:143–44, 596–97; Hall and Rise, *From Local Courts to National Tribunals,* 14.
49. Marvin, *Rules;* Marvin, *Law of Wreck and Salvage.*
50. Quoted in Hall and Rise, *From Local Courts to National Tribunals,* 11.
51. Kearney, "Autobiography," 207.
52. Ibid., 214; Maloney, *Sketch,* 63.
53. Kearney, "Autobiography," 215–19; Shofner, *Nor Is It Over Yet,* 34–57.
54. Kearney, "Autobiography," 219–20.
55. Ibid., 219–22; Morris, *Florida Handbook,* 325; Marvin, *Authorship.*
56. Hall and Rise, *From Local Courts to National Tribunals,* 154.
57. James, *Andrew Jackson,* 263–64.
58. Carter, *TP,* 26:124–25.
59. Ibid., 26:128–29.
60. Groene, *Ante-Bellum Tallahassee,* 108.
61. Martin, *Florida during the Territorial Days,* 106–7; Carter, *TP,* 26:337.
62. Carter, *TP,* 26:129.
63. Hall and Rise, *From Local Courts to National Tribunals,* 16–17.
64. Carter, *TP,* 26:365.
65. Hall and Rise, *From Local Courts to National Tribunals,* 154.
66. Isaac H. Bronson biographical materials, SAHSRL. Some accounts argue that Bronson was born at Rutland, Jefferson County, New York. His tomb inscription concurs. See *Biographical Directory of the American Congress,* 675; St. Augustine *Record,* January 5, 1944.
67. Isaac H. Bronson biographical materials; *United States Statutes at Large,* 5:263–64; *Biographical Directory of the American Congress,* 675, 1870; Martin, *Florida during the Territorial Days,* 38–39.
68. Isaac H. Bronson biographical materials; Carter, *TP,* 26:123–24, 871.
69. Tallahassee *Floridian,* July 28, 1838.
70. St. Augustine *News,* June 5, 1840; Carter, *TP,* 26:165.
71. Carter, *TP,* 26:609.
72. Mahon, *Second Seminole War,* 276; Carter, *TP,* 26:267.
73. Carter, *TP,* 26:971; Ott and Chazal, *Ocali Country,* 41–42.
74. *Biographical Directory of the American Congress,* 675; *F&J,* August 25, 1855; Hall and Rise, *Local Courts to National Tribunals,* 156; Florida *Senate Journal* (1845), 85–99.

75. Michaels, *River Flows North,* 82–85, 317; *F&J,* August 25, 1855.
76. Hall and Rise, *From Local Courts to National Tribunals,* 16.
77. *F&J,* January 19, 1850.
78. Ibid.; James, *Andrew Jackson,* 25; Tindall, *America,* 1:532.
79. *F&J,* January 19, 1850.
80. Tallahassee *Florida Sentinel,* January 1, 1850.
81. *F&J,* January 19, 1850.
82. Ibid.; Hall and Rise, *From Local Courts to National Tribunals,* 157; Carter, *TP,* 26:372.
83. Carter, *TP,* 26:618–19.
84. Tallahassee *Florida Sentinel,* January 1, 1850; *F&J,* January 19, 1850.
85. Florida *Senate Journal* (1845), 85–99; *PG,* December 20, 1845.
86. *F&J,* January 19, 1850.
87. Tallahassee *Florida Sentinel,* January 1, 1850.
88. Carter, *TP,* 26:377–79; Hall and Rise, *From Local Courts to National Tribunals,* 16; Clerk of the House of Representatives, *People of Lawmaking,* 12; Doherty, *Whigs of Florida,* 18.
89. *WF,* November 18, 1873; Hall and Rise, *From Local Courts to National Tribunals,* 159; Myers, "Some Early History," March 13, 1903.
90. Groene, "Justice Samuel Douglas," 272.
91. Carter, *TP,* 26:377–79.
92. Ibid., 26:377–79, 444.
93. Ibid., 26:434–35.
94. Ibid.
95. Tallahassee *Florida Sentinel,* February 4, 1842; Groene, *Ante-Bellum Tallahassee,* 100–101.
96. *Army and Navy Chronicle,* March 9, 1843, 275–77.
97. *WF,* November 18, 1873; Hall and Rise, *From Local Courts to National Tribunals,* 159; William Marvin to "Brown," February 21, 1896, Marvin biographical file.
98. *WF,* November 18, 1873; Browne, *Key West,* 90–93, 219; Kearney, "Autobiography," 215–16.
99. Marvin to Brown, February 21, 1896, Marvin biographical file.
100. Boyd and Reder, *History,* 1032–33; *WF,* November 18, 1873.
101. Marvin to Brown, February 21, 1896, Marvin biographical file.
102. *WF,* November 18, 1873.

Chapter 5: Florida in the Antebellum Era

1. James, *Andrew Jackson,* 499–500; Florida *Senate Journal* (1845), 4.
2. Regarding Jonathan Walker, see Walker, *Trial and Imprisonment.*
3. Mahon, *Second Seminole War,* 314–20; Covington, *Billy Bowlegs War;* Brown, *Florida's Peace River Frontier,* 34–74, 106–20.
4. See generally Mahon, *Second Seminole War,* and Covington, *Billy Bowlegs War;* Brown, *Florida's Peace River Frontier,* 75–90, 123–26; VanLandingham, *Pictorial History of Saint Lucie County,* 8; Covington, "Armed Occupation Act."
5. Tindall, *America,* 1:470–74, 568–71; Willoughby, *Fair to Middlin,'* 54.
6. Harper, "Ante-Bellum Census Enumerations," 42–51.

7. Ibid., 47–49; manuscript returns, Seventh U.S. Decennial Census, 1850, Florida (population schedules).
8. Generally, see Smith, *Slavery and Plantation Growth.*
9. Womack, *Gadsden,* 58.
10. Smith, *Slavery and Plantation Growth,* 56–57, 122–52; manuscript returns, Seventh and Eighth U.S. Decennial Censuses, 1850 and 1860, Florida (population and slave schedules).
11. Harper, "Ante-Bellum Census Enumerations," 51–52.
12. Stirling, *Letters,* 224–25.
13. Manuscript returns, Eighth U.S. Decennial Census, 1860, Florida (population, manufacturing, and agricultural schedules); Richard, "Notes," 15.
14. See Kennedy, *Population of the United States in 1860;* Fernald, *Atlas,* 132; Brown, *Florida's Peace River Frontier,* 63–105.
15. Manuscript returns, Seventh U.S. Decennial Census, 1850, Florida; Rogers, "Way They Went," 91.
16. Rogers, "Way They Went," 91.
17. Manuscript returns, Seventh U.S. Decennial Census, 1850, Florida (mortality schedules).
18. Tebeau, *History of Florida,* 196–98; Brown, *Florida's Peace River Frontier,* 227–31.
19. Smith, *Slavery and Plantation Growth,* 189–91; Tebeau, *History of Florida,* 195–96.
20. Pyburn, *History,* 54–56; Florida *Senate Journal* (1854, appendix), 6–8.
21. Ibid.
22. Regarding Florida in 1860, see manuscript returns, Eighth U.S. Decennial Census, Florida; Hentz, *Planter's Northern Bride.*
23. Dovell, *History of Banking,* 44–47.
24. Florida, *Territorial Laws* (1845), 24–25; Florida, *Territorial House Journal* (1845), 81–87; Hall, *Magic Mirror,* 159.
25. See Garvin, "Free Negro"; Bates, "Legal Status"; and Brown, "Race Relations."
26. Ibid. On the Proctor family, see Warner, *Free Men in an Age of Servitude.*
27. Bates, "Legal Status," 161–63; *Laws of Florida* (1848), 69–70.
28. Bates, "Legal Status," 162.
29. Quoted in Brown, "Ossian Bingley Hart," 200.
30. See, for example, Genovese, *Roll, Jordan, Roll.*

Chapter 6: Creation and Organization of the Supreme Court

1. Doherty, *Whigs of Florida,* 12–15; Brown, "Ossian Bingley Hart," 121–23; Florida *Territorial Senate Journal* (1845), 1–5.
2. Doherty, *Whigs of Florida,* 15.
3. Ibid., 14–15.
4. Rerick, *Memoirs of Florida,* 1:212–13; Florida *Senate Journal* (1845), 23.
5. Florida *Senate Journal* (1845), 20.
6. Ibid., 23; Florida *House Journal* (1847), 40; Rerick, *Memoirs of Florida,* 1:215.
7. Tebeau, *History of Florida,* 172–73; Doherty, *Whigs of Florida,* 16–17.
8. Dodd, *Florida Becomes a State,* 314.
9. Ibid., 313.

10. Florida *House Journal* (1845), 103; Florida *Senate Journal* (1845), 69.
11. *Laws of Florida* (1845), 83.
12. Ibid.
13. Dodd, *Florida Becomes a State*, 94.
14. Florida *Senate Journal* (1845), 85–106.
15. Ibid., 85–99.
16. Ibid., (1845, adjourned session), 11; Florida *House Journal* (1845, adjourned session), 91; St. Augustine *Florida Herald*, December 2, 1845; Tallahassee *Florida Sentinel*, December 9, 1845.
17. Florida *Senate Journal* (1845, adjourned session), 4, 77, 82–84, 95; Tallahassee *Florida Sentinel*, December 9, 16, 1845.
18. St. Augustine *Florida Herald and Southern Democrat*, December 23, 1845.
19. *PG*, December 20, 1845.
20. Ibid., December 27, 1845.
21. Doherty, *Whigs of Florida*, 20–21; Florida *Senate Journal* (1846); Tallahassee *Florida Sentinel*, January 12, 1847; Tallahassee *Floridian*, January 2, 1847.
22. Dodd, *Florida Becomes a State*, 312–13.
23. Ibid., 315.
24. MSCF, January 6–February 4, 1846; 1 *Florida Reports* (1846), 1–8.
25. MSCF, January 5–February 4, 1846.
26. *Laws of Florida* (1846), 23–24.
27. 1 *Florida Reports* (1846), ix.
28. Ibid.
29. *Biographical Directory of the United States Congress*, 1156–57; Carter, *TP*, 26:329–30, 514–15; Stanley, *History of Jackson County*, 235.
30. Doherty, *Whigs of Florida*, 10–11; Carter, *TP*, 26:329–30; *Biographical Directory of the United States Congress*, 1156–57.
31. Carter, *TP*, 26:514–15.
32. Shofner, *Jackson County*, 105–6; Florida *Senate Journal* (1845), 3–4, 20, 86, 103.
33. *Newport Gazette*, December 15, 1846.
34. Tallahassee *Floridian*, November 21, 1846.
35. *WF*, March 26, 1878.
36. Florida *House Journal* (1848), 170–71; Tallahassee *Florida Sentinel*, March 23, 1853; *F&J*, April 23, 1853.
37. Florida *Territorial House Journal* (1840), appendix, 77–79; Franklin County, tax rolls, 1845–50; Manuscript returns, Seventh U.S. Decennial Census, 1850, Franklin County, Florida (population schedule); *F&J*, January 9, 1858.
38. *F&J*, May 18, 1850, July 15, 1854, May 17, 1856; Shofner, *Jackson County*, 207–8.
39. *Congressional Globe*, December 4, 1860, 7; Brevard, *History of Florida*, 2:52; *Biographical Directory of the United States Congress*, 1155–56.
40. Davis, *Civil War and Reconstruction*, 434; *Biographical Directory of the United States Congress*, 1155–56; *Marianna Courier*, March 21, 1878, quoted in *WF*, March 26, 1878.
41. *Marianna Courier*, January 25, 1867; Tallahassee *Semi-Weekly Floridian*, January 30, 1866; Stanley, *History of Jackson County*, 88; Pyburn, "Thomas Baltzell," 1–9.
42. Groene, *Ante-Bellum Tallahassee*, 105.

43. Florida *Territorial Council Journal* (1832), 1–10, 30–57, 97.
44. *Apalachicola Gazette,* March 23, 1839; Dodd, *Florida Becomes a State,* 146; Knauss, *Territorial Florida Journalism,* 222–23.
45. Rerick, *Memoirs of Florida,* 1:172.
46. *Apalachicola Gazette,* April 6, 1839.
47. Doherty, *Whigs of Florida,* 7; Dodd, *Florida Becomes a State,* 69.
48. Tallahassee *Florida Sentinel,* September 23, 1842; Carter, *TP,* 26:28, 39; Cutler, *History of Florida,* 1:14–15; Tallahassee *Floridian,* June 15, 1839, March 21, 1840; Morris, *Florida Handbook,* 254–55.
49. Florida *Territorial House Journal* (1840), appendix, 77; Tallahassee *Florida Sentinel,* June 6, 1843; Carter, *TP,* 26:877, 885–87, 892, 902–3; Doherty, *Whigs of Florida,* 7.
50. Clerk of the House of Representatives, *People of Lawmaking,* 5; Florida *Senate Journal* (1845), 99; Cutler, *History of Florida,* 1:119; Florida *Territorial House Journal* (1840), 87.
51. Paisley, *Red Hills of Florida,* 113; *F&J,* October 31, 1846.
52. Tallahassee *Floridian,* October 31, 1846; Tallahassee *Southern Journal,* April 3, 1848.
53. *F&J,* March 31, 1849.
54. Florida *House Journal* (1850), 313.
55. Manuscript returns, Seventh U.S. Decennial Census, 1850, Leon County, Florida (population and slave schedules); Leon County tax rolls, 1846–51.
56. *F&J,* April 24, 1852; Tallahassee *Florida Sentinel,* March 22, 1853; St. Augustine *Ancient City,* August 13, 1853.
57. St. Augustine *Ancient City,* August 13, 1853.
58. Ibid., October 15, 1853.
59. *F&J,* September 20, 27, 1856.
60. Ibid.
61. Boyd and Reder, *History of the Supreme Court,* 1027–28.
62. Wallace, *Carpetbag Rule,* 11–12; Tallahassee *Semi-Weekly Floridian,* January 16, 1866.
63. Florida *House Journal* (1865), 282–85; Tallahassee *Semi-Weekly Floridian,* January 16, 23, 1866.
64. Tallahassee *Semi-Weekly Floridian,* January 16, 1866.
65. Douglas, *Autobiography,* 14–15.
66. Ibid., 17–37.
67. Ibid., 51.
68. Ibid., 52–53.
69. Ibid., 53–54.
70. Boyd and Reder, *History of the Supreme Court,* 1022; Douglas, *Autobiography,* 53–54.
71. Carter, *TP,* 23:554; Douglas, *Autobiography,* 60–61, 68–69.
72. Douglas, *Autobiography,* 72–74.
73. *Jacksonville Courier,* August 27, 1835; Carter, *TP,* 24:607, 25:8; 159 *Florida Reports,* xxx; St. Augustine *Florida Herald,* June 24, August 27, 1835.
74. Douglas, *Autobiography,* 73.
75. *Jacksonville Courier,* August 6, 1835; Graham, *Awakening of St. Augustine,* 36; Douglas, *Autobiography,* 114–15.
76. Isaac H. Bronson to William D. Moseley, August 28, 1845, Florida governors' correspondence, series 679, box 2, folder 8.

77. Manuscript returns, Sixth U.S. Decennial Census, 1840, St. Johns County, Florida; St. Johns County tax rolls, 1845–57.78. Carter, *TP*, 24:167–68, 178–82, 354–55, 455–57, 475–76, 563–64, 712, 715–16, 868–69; Douglas, *Autobiography*, 87–88.
79. Isaac H. Bronson to William D. Moseley, August 28, 1845. Florida governors' correspondence, series 679, box 2, folder 8.
80. Douglas, *Autobiography*, 88; Florida *Senate Journal* (1845, adjourned session), 11.
81. Boyd and Reder, *History of the Supreme Court*, 1024–27; *Pensacola Gazette*, July 30, 1853.
82. Boyd and Reder, *History of the Supreme Court*, 1027.
83. Quoted in Tallahassee *Florida Sentinel*, January 2, 1849. 84.
84. Jacksonville *Florida News*, September 15, 1855. See also *F&J*, September 15, 1855.
85. Tallahassee *Florida Sentinel*, March 10, 1846.
86. Returns of election of November 4, 1844, Monroe and Dade counties, Florida Election Returns, series 21, boxes 8 and 31; *FH&SD*, December 3, 1844.
87. Florida *Territorial Senate Journal* (1845), 3–6; Tallahassee *Floridian*, quoted in *FH&SD*, May 6, 1845.
88. Tallahassee *Star of Florida*, March 28, 1845.
89. Ibid.
90. *FH&SD*, June 3, 1845; Florida *Senate Journal* (1845), 23.91. Tallahassee *Florida Sentinel*, March 10, 1846.
92. *Pensacola Gazette*, January 23, 1847.
93. William R. Hackley diary, entry of April 28, 1848, PKY; Tallahassee *Florida Sentinel*, January 16, 1847.
94. Gordon, *Biographical Census*, 328.
95. Carter, *TP*, 22:946–47, 23:226; St. Augustine *East Florida Herald*, August 9, 1823, March 26, 1825; Brown, "Ossian Bingley Hart," 55.
96. Doherty, *Richard Keith Call*, 41–42, 46–51; Brown, "Ossian Bingley Hart," 55–56.
97. Gordon, *Biographical Census*, 328; Brown, "Ossian Bingley Hart," 55–57, 76–78; *Jacksonville Courier*, August 6, 20, 1835.
98. Carter, *TP*, 23:847; Florida *Legislative Council Journal* (1832), 4; Clerk of the House of Representatives, *People of Lawmaking*, 55; *Jacksonville Courier*, January 7, 1836; Tallahassee *Florida Sentinel*, January 9, 1849.
99. Doherty, *Whigs of Florida*, 9–17; Brown, "Ossian Bingley Hart," 76–78; Tallahassee *Star of Florida*, February 9, 1843.
100. Laura Lancaster to Thomas M. Vincent, May 7, 1857, Vincent family papers.
101. St. Augustine *News*, January 31, 1845; *FH&SD*, February 25, 1845; Florida *House Journal* (1845, adjourned session), 91; Florida *Senate Journal* (1846), 88, appendix, 61–64.
102. Davis, *History of Jacksonville*, 293; Tallahassee *Floridian*, October 16, December 25, 1847; *FH&SD*, November 11, 1847; Clerk of the House of Representatives, *People of Lawmaking*, 55; Florida *House Journal* (1847), 5.
103. Florida *House Journal* (1847), 144–46; Tallahassee *Floridian*, December 25, 1847; Tallahassee *Florida Sentinel*, January 9, 1849.
104. "Key West and Salvage in 1850," 59.

105. Brown, "Ossian Bingley Hart," 162–67; Brown, "Tampa and the Coming of the Railroad," 13; Stone, "Know Nothings," 3–8; *F&J*, October 25, 1856.
106. Tampa *Florida Peninsular*, December 27, 1856.

Chapter 7: An Independent Supreme Court

1. Tindall, *America*, 1:600.
2. Ibid., 1:600–11.
3. Doherty, *Whigs of Florida*, 23–29.
4. Ibid., 28.
5. MSCF, 1847; Tallahassee *Florida Sentinel*, January 13, 1846; Tallahassee *Floridian*, May 1, 1847.
6. *Laws of Florida* (1847), 15–16; Tallahassee *Floridian*, July 31, 1847.
7. Tallahassee *Florida Sentinel*, October 12, November 2, 1847; Tallahassee *Floridian*, October 16, 1847; Apalachicola *Commercial Advertiser*, October 28, 1847; Florida *House Journal* (1848), 165.
8. Florida *House Journal* (1848), 165–66.
9. Ibid.
10. Ibid. (1847), 53.
11. Tallahassee *Florida Sentinel*, November 14, 1847; Florida *House Journal* (1847), 133–45.
12. Doherty, *Whigs of Florida*, 28–32; Davis, *Civil War and Reconstruction*, 32.
13. Florida *House Journal* (1848), 9.
14. *Laws of Florida* (1848), 18.
15. Ibid.; Florida *House Journal* (1847), 165–66.
16. *Laws of Florida* (1848), 18–19.
17. Florida *House Journal* (1848), 34–42; Florida *Senate Journal* (1848), 187–89; *PG*, January 20, 1849; Doherty, *Richard Keith Call*, 126.
18. Davis, *Civil War and Reconstruction*, 35.
19. Jacksonville *Florida Republican*, February 1, 1849.
20. Doherty, *Whigs of Florida*, 42–45; *PG*, October 12, December 14, 1850.
21. MSCF, 1849–50.
22. Doherty, *Whigs of Florida*, 45–46.
23. Florida *Senate Journal* (1850), 10–13.
24. Ibid.
25. Florida *House Journal* (1851), 278.
26. Ibid. (1850), 122.
27. *PG*, January 18, 1850.
28. Doherty, *Richard Keith Call*, 142–43; Thompson, "Railroad Background"; *New York Daily Tribune*, April 15, 1853; Florida *House Journal* (1851), 311–13.
29. Florida *House Journal* (1850), 300 et seq.
30. Ibid., 311–13.
31. Thompson, "Railroad Background," 181, 189–93; Florida *House Journal* (1851), 312–402; *F&J*, January 18, 1851.
32. *National Cyclopaedia of American Biography*, 12:59;Wentworth, "Walker Anderson."

33. Anderson, "Tales," 4–5; *National Cyclopaedia of American Biography*, 12:59.
34. *PG*, December 1, 1838.
35. Anderson, "Tales," 4–5.
36. Yonge, "Walker Anderson," 173–74; 160 *Florida Reports*, xliii.
37. Clerk of the House of Representatives, *People of Lawmaking*, 3; St. Augustine *News*, October 8, 1842.
38. Dodd, *Florida Becomes a State*, 394.
39. Tallahassee *Floridian*, June 15, 1839; Carter, *TP*, 26:373–74; Wentworth, "Walker Anderson."
40. Clerk of the House of Representatives, *People of Lawmaking*, 3.
41. Florida *Territorial Senate Journal* (1845), 3, 17, 23, 36–39, 174–77; *PG*, June 14, 1845.
42. St. Augustine *News*, July 19, 1845.
43. Yonge, "Walker Anderson," 178.
44. Carter, *TP*, 26:877, 885–87, 892, 902–3; *PG*, September 19, 1846; Wentworth, "Walker Anderson."
45. Wentworth, "Walker Anderson"; *PG*, May 20, 1848, October 27, 1849, March 2, 30, August 24, September 7, 1850; *F&J*, June 23, 1849.
46. Tallahassee *Floridian*, June 20, 1846; Florida *Territorial Senate Journal* (1845), 175.
47. *PG*, May 20, 1848; *F&J*, June 23, 1849, October 19, 1850; Florida *House Journal* (1848), 48, 127.
48. *F&J*, January 4, 1861; Florida *House Journal* (1850), 166–73; Yonge, "Walker Anderson," 179–80.
49. Florida *House Journal* (1850), 313, 400–401; *Pensacola Gazette*, quoted in *F&J*, February 8, 1851.
50. *National Cyclopaedia of American Biography*, 12:59; *F&J*, February 28, 1857; Pensacola *West Florida Times*, January 20, 1857.
51. Pensacola *West Florida Times*, January 20, 1857.
52. Bureau of Historic Sites and Properties, *Delegates to the Saint Joseph Constitutional Convention*, 283. On Albert Gallatin Semmes generally, see Semmes, *Semmes and Allied Families*.
53. Tallahassee *Floridian*, February 8, 1851.
54. *Apalachicola Gazette*, March 1, 1838; Franklin County tax rolls, 1850–51.
55. *Apalachicola Gazette*, July 12, 1838.
56. Bureau of Historic Sites and Properties, *Delegates to the Saint Joseph Constitutional Convention*, 284.
57. Dodd, *Florida Becomes a State*, 230, 329; *Apalachicola Gazette*, December 26, 1840; *St. Joseph Times*, March 23, 1839; *PG*, May 6, 1848; Tallahassee *Southern Journal*, May 1, 1848; Tallahassee *Floridian*, February 8, 1851.
58. Bureau of Historic Sites and Properties, *Delegates to the Saint Joseph Constitutional Convention*, 284.
59. Ibid., 285.
60. 159 *Florida Reports*, xxxii.
61. Groene, *Ante-Bellum Tallahassee*, 121; Knauss, *Territorial Florida Journalism*, 79; Tallahassee *Florida Sentinel*, June 6, 1843; Ley, "Tallahassee Fire," 165.
62. Thomas H. Hagner to Peter Hagner, November 3, 1838, Maryland Historical Society; Leon County tax rolls, 1850–53; Tallahassee *Floridian*, July 31, 1847; Tallahassee

Florida Sentinel, April 25, 1848; Florida *Territorial Council Journal* (1832), 8, 15, 107; Carter, *TP*, 25:479, 26:28–29, 72, 221; Groene, *Ante-Bellum Tallahassee*, 50.

63. Dodd, *Florida Becomes a State*, 48–56; Doherty, "Political Factions," 138–39; *F&J*, August 25, September 1, 1849.
64. Doherty, "Political Factions," 138–39; Tallahassee *Star of Florida*, August 30, 1844; Tallahassee *Florida Sentinel*, September 9, 1845, August 13, 1850; Tallahassee *Floridian*, July 31, 1847; Boyd and Reder, *History of the Supreme Court*, 1025; Florida *House Journal* (1852), 59–61, 72, 164, 330; Florida *Senate Journal* (1852), 237; Rerick, *Memoirs of Florida*, 2:87–88; Act of December 27, 1845, chap. 45, chap. 46, 117, 118, *Acts and Resolutions of the First General Assembly of the State of Florida*; Thompson, *A Manual or Digest of the Statute Law of the State of Florida*, 1847, v, viii–ix.
65. *F&J*, August 25, September 1, 1849, January 25, 1851.
66. Ibid., February 8, 1851.
67. 159 *Florida Reports*, xxxii; Tallahassee *Florida Sentinel*, June 13, 1854.
68. 159 *Florida Reports*, xxxii.
69. Carter, *TP*, 22:66, 913, 956, 23:350–51, 400; Doherty, *Richard Keith Call*, 26, 76–77; Family records from William B. Wright III, Orange Park, Florida, 1991.
70. Tallahassee *Florida Intelligencer*, March 11, 1826; Carter, *TP*, 24:935–37, 959–64.
71. Carter, *TP*, 22:549–50, 585, 24:334.
72. Ibid., 24:239, 226–27, 305.
73. Brackenridge, *Judge Brackenridge's Letters*, 11–12.
74. Ibid., 12.
75. Doherty, *Richard Keith Call*, 72, 76–77, 119.
76. Clerk of the House of Representatives, *People of Lawmaking*, 107; Florida *Territorial Council Journal* (1832), 20, 57–58, (1833), 11.
77. Dodd, *Florida Becomes a State*, 48.
78. Ibid., 146–47, 169, 255; Doherty, *Richard Keith Call*, 112.
79. Dodd, *Florida Becomes a State*, 434, 449; Knauss, *Territorial Florida Journalism*, 64; *PG*, April 12, 1845; Florida *Senate Journal* (1845, adjourned session), 4.
80. Knauss, *Territorial Florida Journalism*, 21–22; *PG*, July 11, 1846.
81. *PG*, July 11, 1846.
82. Ibid., August 1, 1846; Knauss, *Territorial Florida Journalism*, 65.
83. MSCF, January 20, 1848; *PG*, June 8, August 24, 1850; Knauss, *Territorial Florida Journalism*, 64.
84. Manuscript returns, Fifth and Seventh U.S. Decennial Censuses, 1830 and 1850, Escambia County, Florida; Escambia County tax rolls, 1850–53; Boyd and Reder, *History of the Supreme Court*, 1025.
85. Cutler, *History of Florida*, 1:377; Wallace, *Carpetbag Rule*, 12; Shofner, *Nor Is It Over Yet*, 57; Davis, *Civil War and Reconstruction*, 434; 160 *Florida Reports*, xli.

Chapter 8: Popular Elections and Internal Divisions

1. Boyd and Reder, *History of the Supreme Court*, 1026.
2. *F&J*, March 6, 1852, April 8, 1853.
3. Doherty, *Whigs of Florida*, 52–58.
4. Florida *House Journal* (1852), 154–55.
5. *Laws of Florida* (1852), 98–99.

6. 4 *Florida Reports*, 175; *Law of Florida* (1852), 100–102.
7. Tallahassee *Floridian*, November 28, 1846.
8. *FH&SD*, March 7, 1848; Tallahassee *Florida Sentinel*, December 3, 1850; St. Augustine *Ancient City*, August 31, October 5, 1850.
9. Dodd, *Florida Becomes a State*, 201; Tallahassee *Florida Sentinel*, December 3, 1850.
10. Florida *Senate Journal* (1852), appendix, 120; Florida *House Journal* (1852), 266; *Laws of Florida* (1852), 189–91.
11. Boyd and Reder, *History of the Supreme Court*, 1025–26; Dodd, *Florida Becomes a State*, 201; Clerk of the House of Representatives, *People of Lawmaking*, 107.
12. 5 *Florida Reports*, 332; *PG*, July 30, 1853, *F&J*, August 20, 1853.
13. *F&J*, July 9, 16, 30, 1853; St. Augustine *Ancient City*, July 9, August 27, 1853; *PG*, August 13, 1853; Jacksonville *Florida News*, July 2, 1853.
14. *PG*, July 30, September 3, 24, October 1, 1853; *F&J*, September 17, 1853; Jacksonville *Florida News*, September 17, 1853.
15. Jacksonville *Florida News*, July 2, 9, November 12, 1853; St. Augustine *Ancient City*, July 16, October 29, 1853; *F&J*, October 24, 29, 1853.
16. MSCF, 1854–55; *F&J*, April 8, 1854, December 15, 1855.
17. *F&J*, January 26, 1856.
18. Ibid., February 7, 1857.
19. Ibid., January 9, 1858.
20. MSCF, January 18, 1859.
21. Ibid.
22. Ibid., January 25, 1859.
23. Ibid.
24. *F&J*, February 12, August 20, 1859.
25. *F&J*, February 26, March 19, 1859; Tampa *Florida Peninsular*, March 12, 1859; Fernandina *East Floridian*, October 6, 1859.
26. 8 *Florida Reports*, 459, 465, 467, 494.
27. MSCF, April 14, 1859; 8 *Florida Reports*, 495.
28. *F&J*, May 21, 28, 1859; 8 *Florida Reports*, 495–516.
29. *Laws of Florida* (1858), 165; *F&J*, October 22, 1859; St. Augustine *Examiner*, October 29, 1859.
30. *F&J*, March 12, April 30, May 7, June 4, August 20, September 24, October 1, 22, 1859; Fernandina *East Floridian*, July 14, 28, 1859; St. Augustine *Examiner*, October 29, 1859.
31. Rerick, *Memoirs of Florida*, 2:89; 16 *Florida Reports*, v–x.
32. Rerick, *Memoirs of Florida*, 2:86.
33. Ibid.; 2:16 *Florida Reports*, v–x; Womack, *Gadsden*, 39; Florida *Territorial House Journal* (1840), appendix, 79; manuscript returns, Fifth U.S. Decennial Census, 1830, Gadsden County, Florida.
34. Florida *Territorial Council Journal* (1834), 11–12, (1835), 25, 30, 59; Clerk of the House of Representatives, *People of Lawmaking*, 29; Doherty, *Whigs of Florida*, 25; Doherty, *Richard Keith Call*, 125–26.
35. Carter, *TP*, 24:453, 815, 967, 25:47, 284–85; Womack, *Gadsden*, 25; Rerick, *Memoirs of Florida*, 2:89.

36. Carter, *TP*, 26:329; Tallahassee *Floridian*, April 11, 1846.
37. 16 *Florida Reports*, vii; MSCF, January 26, 1846; Tallahassee *Florida Sentinel*, March 22, 1853; Gadsden County tax roll, 1853.
38. Tallahassee *Florida Sentinel*, March 5, May 7, 1850; Womack, *Gadsden*, 63.
39. Florida *House Journal* (1850), 400–401, (1852), 59–60, 381, 386; *F&J*, May 21, 1853; Boyd and Reder, *History of the Supreme Court*, 1027–33.
40. Boyd and Reder, *History of the Supreme Court*, 1032; Shofner, *Nor Is It Over Yet*, 44, 51–52.
41. Davis, *Civil War and Reconstruction*, 232, 460; 16 *Florida Reports*, v–x; Shofner, *Nor Is It Over Yet*, 131–32, 259–60; *WF*, March 14, 1871.
42. Avant, *Illustrated Index*, 215; *WF*, July 17, 1877; 16 *Florida Reports*, ix–x; Jacksonville *Weekly Florida Union*, October 20, 1877.
43. 16 *Florida Reports*, xii–xiii.
44. 160 *Florida Reports*, xlii; Rerick, *Memoirs of Florida*, 2:88; manuscript returns, Seventh U.S. Decennial Census, 1850, Benton County, Florida.
45. Tallahassee *Florida Sentinel*, May 7, 1850; *F&J*, May 4, 1850.
46. Jacksonville *Florida Republican*, November 4, 1852; MSCF, February 18, 1852; Rerick, *Memoirs of Florida*, 2:89.
47. *F&J*, September 3, 1853.
48. Boyd and Reder, *History of the Supreme Court*, 1027.
49. *F&J*, April 16, 1859.
50. Edwards, *Grave Markers*, 111.
51. *TS*, June 18, 1868; *WF*, July 25, 1891; Doherty, *Richard Keith Call*, 4.
52. Florida *Senate Journal* (1845), 3–4, 20, 28, 111, (1846), appendix, 64–69; MSCF, January 15, 1846; *F&J*, July 11, 1846.
53. Florida *House of Journal* (1848), 3, 18, 34, 42, 46, 49, 127, 133, 162, 170–71.
54. Tallahassee *Florida Sentinel*, July 20, August 17, November 19, 1850; *PG*, July 20, 1850.
55. Florida *Senate Journal* (1850), 115–17; *F&J*, July 29, 1854.
56. *F&J*, November 4, 1854; *TS*, June 18, 1868.
57. Rerick, *Memoirs of Florida*, 1:230.
58. *F&J*, January 9, 1858, January 8, 1859; Rerick, *Memoirs of Florida*, 1:230; *TS*, June 18, 1868.
59. Davis, *Civil War and Reconstruction*, 218–19, 355–56, 366–68, 409, 430, 435; Shofner, *Nor Is It Over Yet*, 88–93, 101–103, 199; Florida *House Journal* (1866), 9.
60. Shofner, *Nor Is It Over Yet*, 199, 220; *WF*, July 25, 1891; Savannah *Daily News and Herald*, May 18, 1868.
61. *F&J*, October 1, 1859; *FU*, December 2, 1865; Rerick, *Memoirs of Florida*, 2:89.
62. William Augustus Forward biographical materials, SAHSRL; William A. Forward biographical materials, Putnam County Division of Archives and History, Palatka; *FT-U*, July 16, 1896; manuscript returns, Seventh U.S. Decennial Census, 1850, St. Johns County, Florida.
63. Dodd, *Florida Becomes a State*, 407–8; Florida *Senate Journal* (1845, adjourned session), 4, 20–21, 26, 77, 91; Tallahassee *Florida Sentinel*, December 9, 16, 1845.
64. Florida *House Journal* (1847), 160, 179, 185; Florida *Senate Journal* (1848), 3, 23, 25, 52, 78, 95–97, 144–45, 152, 195, 252–53, 272, (1850), 3, 25, 73, 270, 273, 310.

65. Florida *House Journal* (1847), 4–5, 24–25, 38, 51, 60, 155–56, 166.
66. Ibid., 145.
67. *FU*, November 4, 1865.
68. Tallahassee *Florida Sentinel*, December 9, 16, 1845; Florida *House Journal* (1850), 310–17, 323–29, 340–43, 360–65, 399–402; Tallahassee *Florida Sentinel*, January 4, 1853; *F&J*, January 8, 1853; Jacksonville *Florida News*, February 19, 1853.
69. *F&J*, October 4, 1851; Jacksonville *Florida News*, February 19, 1853; St. Augustine *Ancient City*, June 18, 1853.
70. *FU*, November 4, 1865.
71. *F&J*, June 20, 1857.
72. Rerick, *Memoirs of Florida*, 1:246; *FU*, November 4, 1865; Michaels, *River Flows North*, 74–77, 91.
73. Tallahassee *Semi-Weekly Floridian*, November 17, 1865.

Chapter 9: Antebellum Opinions

1. See chapters 7 and 8.
2. 1 *Florida Reports*, 198.
3. 4 *Florida Reports*, 175; *Laws of Florida* (1852), 98–99.
4. Dodd, *Florida Becomes a State*, 317.
5. 4 *Florida Reports*, 4, 7.
6. 8 *Florida Reports*, 459.
7. 1 *Florida Reports*, 197.
8. 4 *Florida Reports*, 165, 170.
9. 2 *Florida Reports*, 585.
10. Ibid., 569–83.
11. Jacksonville *Florida News*, March 3, 1855.
12. 6 *Florida Reports*, 279.
13. 1 *Florida Reports*, 343.
14. Ibid., 354.
15. 4 *Florida Reports*, 56.
16. 2 *Florida Reports*, 200.
17. 7 *Florida Reports*, 81.
18. 1 *Florida Reports*, 94, 99.
19. Ibid., 102–4.
20. Ibid.
21. 2 *Florida Reports*, 29.
22. Ibid., 660, 692.
23. Ibid., 448
24. Ibid., 422
25. 3 *Florida Reports*, 269
26. Ibid., 72, 103, 105
27. 5 *Florida Reports*, 438
28. 6 *Florida Reports*, 214
29. 8 *Florida Reports*, 183

30. *F&J*, January 9, February 27, 1858
31. 2 *Florida Reports*, 102, 114
32. 4 *Florida Reports*, 23, 42
33. 3 *Florida Reports*, 12
34. Ibid., 202, 213
35. 6 *Florida Reports*, 262, 267–68
36. Ibid., 610, 640
37. 8 *Florida Reports*, 325
38. 4 *Florida Reports*, 154–55
39. Ibid., 402
40. 3 *Florida Reports*, 19, 26
41. 5 *Florida Reports*, 185, 195
42. Ibid., 285
43. 8 *Florida Reports*, 360
44. 6 *Florida Reports*, 381, 399–400, 411–12.
45. Ibid., 430, 482.

Chapter 10: Civil War and the Courts

1. Covington, *Billy Bowlegs War*; Johns, *Florida during the Civil War*, 2; Davis, *Civil War and Reconstruction*, 33–34.
2. Doherty, "Florida in 1856," 60–64; Johns, *Florida during the Civil War*, 134; Dovell, *Florida*, 1:400, 2:613–14.
3. See, particularly, Smith, *Slavery and Plantation Growth.*
4. Doherty, *Whigs of Florida*, 57–62; Johns, *Florida during the Civil War*, 8–9.
5. Johns, *Florida during the Civil War*, 9–10.
6. Ibid., 11–12; Reiger, "Secession of Florida," 358–64; Florida *House Journal* (1860), 8–12, 30–34.
7. Reiger, "Secession of Florida," 358–68.
8. *Journal of the Proceedings of the Convention of the People of Florida* (1861), 44.
9. Dovell, *Florida*, 2:476; Johns, *Florida during the Civil War*, 20–21; Gammon, "Gover nor John Milton," 79.
10. Doherty, *Richard Keith Call*, 158.
11. Johns, *Florida during the Civil War*, 43–44; Tindall, *America*, 1:640–42; Doherty, *Richard Keith Call*, 158; Durkin, *Confederate Navy Chief*, 131.
12. See DeRosa, *Confederate Constitution.*
13. Ibid., 101, 147.
14. Ibid.; Robinson, *Justice in Grey*, 197, 209, 304–6; Hall and Rise, *From Local Courts to National Tribunals*, 32–33.
15. Dovell, *Florida*, 1:475–77.
16. Boyd and Reder, *History of the Supreme Court*, 1030–31.
17. On the Civil War in Florida generally, see Johns, *Florida during the Civil War*, and Davis, *Civil War and Reconstruction*. As to the Battle of Olustee, see Coles, "A Fight, a Licking, and a Footrace," and Nulty, *Confederate Florida*.
18. Davis, *Civil War and Reconstruction*, 224; McPherson, *Battle Cry of Freedom*, 615; Nulty, *Confederate Florida*, 61–68, 222–23; Klingman, *Neither Dies nor Surrenders*, 5.

19. Davis, *Civil War and Reconstruction*, 322; Gammon, "Governor John Milton," 193–94; Shofner, *Nor Is It Over Yet*, 3; Brown, *Florida's Peace River Frontier*, 146–75.
20. Hall and Rise, *From Local Courts to National Tribunals*, 31–36.
21. Boyd and Reder, *History of the Supreme Court*, 1032; Davis, *Civil War and Reconstruction*, 247; Hall and Rise, *From Local Courts to National Tribunals*, 31–36; Johns, *Florida during the Civil War*, 78–79; Paisley, *Red Hills of Florida*, 208.
22. Cash, *Story of Florida*, 2:646.
23. Johns, *Florida during the Civil War*, 87.
24. Ibid., 89–95.
25. 10 *Florida Reports*, 308, 314.
26. 11 *Florida Reports*, 73–74, 78.
27. Coulter, *Confederate States*, 314–15; Brown, *Florida's Peace River Frontier*, 152–53; Gammon, "Governor John Milton," 173–97.
28. Davis, *Civil War and Reconstruction*, 359–64; McPherson, *Battle Cry of Freedom*, 506–7, 600–611.
29. Ibid., 213; 11 *Florida Reports*, 100.
30. 11 *Florida Reports*, 91–99.
31. 11 *Florida Reports*, 105, 109.
32. Davis, *Civil War and Reconstruction*, 185–87; McPherson, *Battle Cry of Freedom*, 615–17.
33. Gammon, "Governor John Milton," 150–55; Davis, *Civil War and Reconstruction*, 193–95; Cash, *Story of Florida*, 2:649–50.
34. 11 *Florida Reports*, 9–10.
35. Ibid., 53, 58–60.
36. *Laws of Florida* (1854), 9–19; Johnson, "Railroads of Florida," 20–21; Brown, "Florida, Atlantic and Gulf Central Railroad," 416–18.
37. 10 *Florida Reports*, 112, 119–20; Lewis, "Railroad Cases," 4.
38. 10 *Florida Reports*, 126–28.
39. Ibid., 122, 127, 129–31; Lewis, "Railroad Cases," 4–5.
40. 12 *Florida Reports*, 213.
41. Ibid., 249, 253, 255.

Chapter 11: Presidential Reconstruction

1. Coles, "Terrible and Sad Result," 150–58; Davis, *Civil War and Reconstruction*, 327–34; 3 *Florida Statutes* (1941), 159–60.
2. Shofner, *Nor Is It Over Yet*, 37–39; Brown, "Ossian Bingley Hart," 248–50; Davis, *Civil War and Reconstruction*, 359–61.
3. Shofner, *Nor Is It Over Yet*, 39–44, 50–56; Davis, *Civil War and Reconstruction*, 361–64.
4. Shofner, *Nor Is It Over Yet*, 46.
5. Tallahassee *Florida Sentinel*, January 6, 1866; Boyd and Reder, *History of the Supreme Court of Florida*, 1032–33; Browne, *Key West*, 91–93; Dovell, *Florida*, 2:540; Davis, *Civil War and Reconstruction*, 435–37.
6. *Fernandina Courier*, May 16, 1866.
7. Shofner, *Nor Is It Over Yet*, 83–90; Cash, *Story of Florida*, 2:652–53.
8. See, generally, *Florida Reports*, vols. 11–12.

9. 12 *Florida Reports,* 9, 13.
10. 11 *Florida Reports,* 257–60, 263, 266.
11. *FT-U,* June 21, 1892; Margaret Baker Berg to Brian S. Polley, March 12, 1984, Baker files.
12. *Biographical Souvenir,* 38; Cutler, *History of Florida,* 2:34; Warner and Yearns, *Biographical Register,* 11; Columbia County tax rolls, 1847–50; *F&J,* October 22, 1853; Jacksonville *Florida News,* October 15, 1853.
13. Cutler, *History of Florida,* 2:34; Gold, *History of Duval County,* 355; *FT-U,* December 20, 1856; Utley, "Origin of the County Names in Florida," 30; *Biographical Souvenir,* 38; Berg to Polley, March 12, 1984, Baker files.
14. *F&J,* February 12, 1859; Fernandina *East Floridian,* June 2, 1859; Cutler, *History of Florida,* 2:34; Wakelyn, *Biographical Dictionary,* 84–85; Warner and Yearns, *Biographical Register,* 11.
15. Wakelyn, *Biographical Dictionary,* 84–85; Warner and Yearns, *Biographical Register,* 11.
16. Cutler, *History of Florida,* 2:34; Gold, *History of Duval County,* 355–56.
17. *FU,* October 14, 1869.
18. *FT-U,* June 21, 1892.
19. Adelaide Bell, "Augustus Emmet Maxwell," Maxwell file.
20. Ibid.; Maxwell, *Maxwell Family,* 39.
21. Augustus Emmet Maxwell genealogical data, Maxwell file; Bell, "Augustus Emmet Maxwell," Maxwell file; Tallahassee *Floridian,* December 25, 1847; Rerick, *Memoirs of Florida,* 2:86.
22. Minutes of the Florida supreme court, January 6, 1846; Rerick, *Memoirs of Florida,* 2:86; Florida *Senate Journal* (1850), 24–25; Florida *House Journal* (1850), 324–29, 341, 360; *F&J,* October 27, 1849, October 30, 1852; Tallahassee *Southern Journal,* March 27, 1848.
23. Augustus Emmet Maxwell genealogical data, Maxwell file; Norman Simons to Mr. and Mrs. Frank P. Maxwell, November 22, 1978, Reder files, box 1; Pensacola *Public Record,* July 6, 1940; Armstrong, *History of Escambia County,* 228; Maxwell, *Maxwell Family,* 39–40.
24. *F&J,* February 11, July 8, 1854.
25. Ibid., July 8, November 4, 1854.
26. Ibid., February 9, 1856, February 7, 28, 1857.
27. *Dictionary of American Biography,* 6:439; Maxwell, *Maxwell Family,* 40; Pensacola *Public Record,* July 6, 1940.
28. 45 *Florida Reports,* xvi–xvii; *F&J,* June 3, 1854; Yonge, "Secession in Florida," 283–85; Wakelyn, *Biographical Dictionary,* 317.
29. Yearns, *Confederate Congress,* 133, 178.
30. Durkin, *Confederate Navy Chief,* 397–409; Shofner, *Nor Is It Over Yet,* 190, 336; Williamson, *Florida Politics,* 134.
31. Cutler, *History of Florida,* 1:214.
32. Quincy *Florida Herald,* August 20, 1892; Bell, "Augustus Emmet Maxwell," Maxwell file.
33. Simons to Maxwell, November 22, 1978, Maxwell file; *New York Herald,* May 7, 1903.

Chapter 12: Congressional Reconstruction

1. Foner, *Reconstruction,* 176–227.
2. Ibid., 228–60; Shofner, *Nor Is It Over Yet,* 81–107; Brown, "Ossian Bingley Hart," 271–75.
3. Foner, *Reconstruction,* 276–77.
4. Hume, "Membership of the Florida Constitutional Convention," 3–4, 9, 16–17; Klingman, *Neither Dies nor Surrenders,* 18–22; Shofner, "Constitution of 1868," 358–59.
5. Shofner, "Constitution of 1868," 369; Shofner, *Nor Is It Over Yet,* 177–86; Brown, "Ossian Bingley Hart," 327–50.
6. Shofner, *Nor Is It Over Yet,* 187; *Pensacola Observer,* October 3, 1868; Pensacola *West Florida Commercial,* January 16, 1869.
7. Wallace, *Carpetbag Rule,* 416–19, 429–30; Article 6 and article 16, section 30, Florida Constitution of 1868; Davis, *Civil War and Reconstruction,* 649–50.
8. Wallace, *Carpetbag Rule,* 416–19.
9. Ibid., 414, 416–17.
10. Clipping, Pensacola *West Florida Commercial,* c. 1868, FSCHS.
11. *TS,* July 9, 1868; Boyd and Reder, *History of the Supreme Court,* 1034–35; Hall and Rise, *From Local Courts to National Tribunals,* 33–37, 155; Brown, "Ossian Bingley Hart," 336–37, 341–42.
12. *WF,* July 28, 1868.
13. Shofner, *Nor Is It Over Yet,* 196–97; Brown, "Ossian Bingley Hart," 371–73.
14. *Savannah Daily Advertiser,* May 4, 1872, quoted in Brown, "Ossian Bingley Hart," 374–75.
15. Brown, "Carpetbagger Intrigues." See also Shofner, *Nor Is It Over Yet,* and Davis, *Civil War and Reconstruction.*
16. Brown, "Ossian Bingley Hart," 449–92.
17. Ibid., 455; Dobson, "Robert Bruce Van Valkenburgh."
18. Shofner, *Nor Is It Over Yet,* 300–339.
19. *National Cyclopaedia of American Biography,* 2:458, 12:215; *FT-U,* July 13, 1895.
20. *Dictionary of American Biography,* 8:344–45; *FT-U,* July 13, 1895; *TS,* July 15, 1867; Tallahassee *Semi-Weekly Floridian,* August 9, 1867.
21. Brown, "Ossian Bingley Hart," 361–62, 371–72.
22. Shofner, *Nor Is It Over Yet,* 196; Brown, "Ossian Bingley Hart," 362–63; *New York Tribune,* February 5, 1868.
23. 36 *Florida Reports,* xvii, xix–xx.
24. Ibid.; Rerick, *Memoirs of Florida,* 2:98.
25. Whitfield, *Florida State Government,* 32.
26. *National Cyclopaedia of American Biography,* 13:215; 36 *Florida Reports,* xi, xv.
27. 14 *Florida Reports,* 366, 368; 36 *Florida Reports,* xvii.
28. *FU,* December 12, 1868, February 4, 1869; *Savannah Morning News,* November 4, 1869.
29. *FT-U,* June 18, 1885, July 13, 1895.
30. Ibid., July 13, 1895.

31. Brown, "Ossian Bingley Hart," 34–67; *TS*, August 24, 1872. On Ossian Bingley Hart generally, see also Campbell, *Biographical Sketch*, and Brown, "Justice Ossian Bingley Hart."
32. Brown, "Ossian Bingley Hart," 81–83, 92–94; Campbell, *Biographical Sketch*, 5–6.
33. Brown, "Ossian Bingley Hart," 100–124.
34. Catharine S. Hart to "My dear Sister," April 16, 1848, Snodgrass collection; Brown, "Ossian Bingley Hart," 131–38.
35. Brown, "Ossian Bingley Hart," 138–63.
36. *TS*, August 24, 1872; Brown, "Ossian Bingley Hart," 175–203.
37. *TS*, August 24, 1872.
38. *Jacksonville Herald*, September 15, 1865.
39. Campbell, *Biographical Sketch*, 7; Brown, "Ossian Bingley Hart," 182–83, 226–27, 243.
40. Shofner, *Nor Is It Over Yet*, 165, 277; Brown, "Ossian Bingley Hart," 251–86.
41. Brown, "Ossian Bingley Hart," 301–5.
42. *TS*, July 9, 1868; Brown, "Ossian Bingley Hart," 310–67.
43. Brown, "Ossian Bingley Hart," 342–50.
44. 13 *Florida Reports*, 55; Brown, "Ossian Bingley Hart," 374–76.
45. See Brown, "Carpetbagger Intrigues."
46. *TS*, August 24, 1872.
47. Florida *Senate Journal* (1874), 12–21; Brown, "Ossian Bingley Hart," 449–88.
48. 14 *Florida Reports*, xiv; Brown, "Ossian Bingley Hart," 488–92.
49. Marks, *Who Was Who in Florida*, 260; Juneanne Westcott Glick to Larry S. Paarlberg,, December 26, 1989, Westcott materials in Dobson files; St. Augustine *Florida Herald*, March 18, 1845.
50. *WF*, May 5, 1887; Dodd, *History of the West Florida Seminary*, 70; Whitfield, "Judge James Diament Westcott," 17.
51. *F&J*, November 27, 1858; Whitfield, "Judge James Diament Westcott," 17; Robinson, *Justice in Grey*, 615.
52. Whitfield, "Judge James Diament Westcott," 17–18; *Savannah Morning News*, February 24, 1873.
53. Unidentified clipping announcing Papy and Westcott partnership, Westcott materials in Dobson files; Lewis, "Railroad Cases," 10; Shofner, *Nor Is It Over Yet*, 44, 160; Whitfield, "Judge James Diament Westcott," 17–18.
54. Pensacola *West Florida Commercial*, September 3, 1868; Brown, "Ossian Bingley Hart," 372–73.
55. Tallahassee *Weekly True Democrat*, September 14, 1906.
56. Ibid.; Barbour, *Florida for Tourists*, 82.
57. Tallahassee *Weekly True Democrat*, September 14, 1906.
58. 24 *Florida Reports*, vi; Rerick, *Memoirs of Florida*, 2:101.
59. Shofner, *Nor Is It Over Yet*, 290; Brown, "Ossian Bingley Hart," 458–60.
60. *FT-U*, September 23, 1906.
61. *WF*, May 5, 1887.
62. *Savannah Morning News*, February 24, 1873.
63. Dodd, *History of the West Florida Seminary*, 70.

64. *Tallahassee Daily Democrat,* December 11, 1936.
65. *Montrose* [Pa.] *Democrat,* November 19, 1879; Brown, "Ossian Bingley Hart," 455; Stocker, *Centennial History,* 86.
66. *Montrose* [Pa.] *Democrat,* November 19, 1879.
67. Stocker, *Centennial History,* 86.
68. Philip Fraser to S. P. Chase, October 29, 1868, general records of the Department of Justice, RG 60, box 211, folder "Fraser, P."
69. Stocker, *Centennial History,* 87.
70. Brown, "Ossian Bingley Hart," 79–80; *Montrose* [Pa.] *Democrat,* November 19, 1879; Stocker, *Centennial History,* 86–87; Case record, *Dunham* v. *Fraser,* file F41, box 104, St. Johns County court records.
71. Fraser to Chase, November 7, 1868, general records of the Department of Justice, RG 60, box 211, folder "Fraser, P."; Stocker, *Centennial History,* 87; Davis, *History of Jacksonville,* 120; *Montrose* [Pa.] *Democrat,* November 19, 1879; *WF,* February 27, 1872; *FU,* June 24, July 1, 1869.
72. Brown, "Ossian Bingley Hart," 455; Boyd and Reder, *History of the Supreme Court,* 1038; Supreme court opinion statistics, Dobson files.
73. *Montrose* [Pa.] *Democrat,* November 19, 1879.
74. Ibid.
75. Bungay, *Pen and Ink Portraits,* 72; Dobson, "Robert Bruce Van Valkenburgh," 10.
76. Dobson, "Robert Bruce Van Valkenburgh," 12.
77. Ibid.; *FT-U,* August 3, 1888.
78. Bungay, *Pen and Ink Portraits,* 73.
79. Ibid., 72–73.
80. 160 *Florida Reports,* xlv; *National Cyclopaedia of American Biography,* 7:529–30; Whitfield, *Florida State Government,* 85; Dobson, "Robert Bruce Van Valkenburgh," 11.
81. Dobson, "Robert Bruce Van Valkenburgh," 11.
82. Robert Bruce Van Valkenburgh materials, Dobson files; Van Valkenburg, *Genealogy,* 1:174; *Hiogo and Osaka* [Japan] *Herald,* supplement, January 4, 1868.
83. *FT-U,* August 3, 1888.
84. Ibid., August 2, 1888.
85. Ibid.; Brown, "Ossian Bingley Hart," 440–42.
86. MSCF, May 19, 20, 1874; *WF,* May 26, 1874.
87. Jacksonville *Tri-Weekly Florida Union,* May 21, 1874.
88. *WF,* May 19, 26, June 9, 1874.
89. Wallace, *Carpetbag Rule,* 434.
90. MSCF, May 19, 20, 1874.
91. Supreme court opinion statistics, Dobson files; *FT-U,* August 10, 1888.
92. *FT-U,* August 10, 1888.

Chapter 13: Business of the Court, 1868–1877

1. *Savannah Daily Advertiser,* May 4, 1872; *Savannah Daily Republican,* April 24, 1872, quoted in Brown, "Ossian Bingley Hart," 375–76.
2. Generally, see MSCF, 1852–68.
3. *Laws of Florida* (1871), 52–53.

4. Ibid. (1874), 117, (1875), 49.
5. Wallace, *Carpetbag Rule,* 432.
6. 13 *Florida Reports,* 417–45.
7. Ibid., 445.
8. Wallace, *Carpetbag Rule in Florida,* 415.
9. 12 *Florida Reports,* 651.
10. Ibid.; Boyd and Reder, *History of the Supreme Court,* 1035–36.
11. Shofner, *Nor Is It Over Yet,* 193, 206–7; 12 *Florida Reports,* 688.
12. 12 *Florida Reports,* 688–89.
13. Brown, "Ossian Bingley Hart," 395–406.
14. Klingman, *Neither Dies nor Surrenders,* 28.
15. Davis, *Civil War and Reconstruction,* 547–48; Shofner, *Nor Is It Over Yet,* 200–201, 204–5.
16. Shofner, *Nor Is It Over Yet,* 204–5.
17. 12 *Florida Reports,* 653, 678.
18. Ibid., 191, 199.
19. 4 *Florida Reports,* 165; 12 *Florida Reports,* 205–6.
20. 12 *Florida Reports,* 200, 207–8.
21. Ibid., 210, 236.
22. Ibid., 257, 261.
23. Ibid., 243–44.
24. Ibid., 267–71; Florida *Senate Journal* (1869), 18–21.
25. Boyd and Reder, "History of the Supreme Court," 1036–37; Ewing, "Florida Reconstruction Impeachments," 305; Brown, "Carpetbagger Intrigues," 281; Davis, *Civil War and Reconstruction,* 632–33.
26. Shofner, *Nor Is It Over Yet,* 221–22; Brown, "Ossian Bingley Hart," 423–29; Wallace, *Carpetbag Rule,* 188.
27. 14 *Florida Reports,* 289, 295–96, 300; Wallace, *Carpetbag Rule,* 188.
28. 14 *Florida Reports,* 307, 309.
29. Ibid., 310–12, 317.
30. Brown, "Ossian Bingley Hart," 430–31.
31. Peek, "Election of 1870," 357–59; Brown, "'Where are now the hopes I cherished?'" 17–18.
32. Peek, "Election of 1870," 360–61.
33. Ibid., 361; *WF,* November 22, 1870.
34. 13 *Florida Reports,* 72–73.
35. Wallace, *Carpetbag Rule,* 138–39; Peek, "Election of 1870," 363; 13 *Florida Reports,* 77.
36. 13 *Florida Reports,* 77.
37. Ibid., 9, 17; Wallace, *Carpetbag Rule,* 413.
38. 13 *Florida Reports,* 9, 17; 14 *Florida Reports,* 9.
39. Peek, "Election of 1870," 364–65, 368.
40. Shofner, "Political Reconstruction," 146.
41. Shofner, *Nor Is It Over Yet,* 258–74.
42. Pettengill, *Florida Railroads,* 21.
43. *Laws of Florida* (1869), 29–38; Lewis, "Railroad Cases," 5, 10.

44. Wallace, *Carpetbag Rule*, 424.
45. 13 *Florida Reports*, 699, 714–15.
46. Ibid., 717.
47. *FU*, June 17, 1869.
48. Davis, *Civil War and Reconstruction*, 660–61.
49. On the Swepson-Littlefield frauds generally, see Fenlon, "Notorious Swepson-Littlefield Fraud."
50. Shofner, "Political Reconstruction," 156–57; Rerick, *Memoirs of Florida*, 1:316–17; Fenlon, "Notorious Swepson-Littlefield Fraud," 240–46.
51. Shofner, *Nor Is It Over Yet*, 246; 13 *Florida Reports*, 33, 55.
52. Shofner, *Nor Is It Over Yet*, 248–49; Fenlon, "Notorious Swepson-Littlefield Fraud," 258.
53. 15 *Florida Reports*, 455, 533.
54. *Laws of Florida* (1874), 116.
55. Wallace, *Carpetbag Rule*, 327; Lewis, "Railroad Cases," 11; 103 *United States Supreme Court Reports*, 188, 144.
56. Shofner, *Nor Is It Over Yet*, 251–53; Brown, "Ossian Bingley Hart," 410–12; 28 *Federal Case Reports*, 1298.
57. 15 *Florida Reports*, 385–86.
58. Ibid., 398–99; *TS*, July 17, 1875.
59. Shofner, *Nor Is It Over Yet*, 288–304.
60. Ibid., 304–13.
61. Shofner, "Florida Courts," 28–31.
62. 16 *Florida Reports*, 17, 24; Shofner, "Florida Courts," 29–31.
63. Shofner, "Florida Courts," 31–32; 16 *Florida Reports*, 25–43; Brown, *Florida's Peace River Frontier*, 210–13.
64. 16 *Florida Reports*, 43–45, 49, 52.
65. Samuel B. McLin to William E. Chandler, December 24, 1876, William E. Chandler papers; Shofner, "Florida Courts," 32.
66. *New York Times*, December 29, 1876.
67. *WF*, November 14, 1876; Shofner, *Nor Is It Over Yet*, 313; Shofner, "Florida Courts," 32–33; 36 *Florida Reports*, xvii.
68. Shofner, "Florida Courts," 34; 16 *Florida Reports*, 57–60.
69. 16 *Florida Reports*, 57–60.
70. Shofner, "Florida Courts," 41.
71. See Woodward, *Reunion and Reaction*.
72. Williamson, "The Election," 90–91.
73. 36 *Florida Reports*, xvii.
74. Tallahassee *Weekly True Democrat*, September 14, 1906. On the departmental concept of judicial review, see Hall, *Supreme Court and Judicial Review*.

Chapter 14: Post-Reconstruction Florida

1. Woodward, *Origins of the New South*, 14.
2. Ayers, *Promise of the New South*, 8.

3. For the Bourbon period generally, see Williamson, *Florida Politics,* and Tebeau, *History of Florida,* 257–308.
4. McRae, *Fourth Census,* 16–19; *FT-U,* September 20, 1885.
5. Walker, *Ninth Census,* 98; McRae, *Fourth Census,* 16–17; *FT-U,* September 3, 1895.
6. Foster and Foster, "John Sanford Swaim"; Foster and Foster, "The Last Shall Be First"; Nolan, *Fifty Feet in Paradise,* 58–59; Lanier, *Florida.* On the efforts of Florida's lands and immigration commissioner, see, for example, Eagan, *Sixth Annual Report.*
7. *Savannah Morning News,* March 12, 1874; Jacksonville *Florida Daily Times,* February 3, 1882; *FT-U,* April 27, 1892; Nolan, *Fifty Feet in Paradise,* 65–72.
8. Brown, "Ossian Bingley Hart," 410–12, 462–67, 497–99.
9. Tebeau, *History of Florida,* 278–80; Hanna and Hanna, *Lake Okeechobee,* 97–99; Davis, "Disston Land Purchase"; Grismer, *Fort Myers,* 105.
10. Tebeau, *History of Florida,* 282–83.
11. Pettengill, *Story of Florida Railroads,* 63–64.
12. Ibid., 64–68, 76; Johnson, "Henry Bradley Plant," 118–23; Brown, *Florida's Peace River Frontier,* 274–75; Grismer, *Tampa,* 171–75.
13. Peeples, "Charlotte Harbor Division"; Brown, *Florida's Peace River Frontier,* 268–71.
14. Akin, *Flagler,* 113–36; Tebeau, *History of Florida,* 284.
15. Akin, *Flagler,* 136.
16. Ibid., 136–45, 161–63.
17. See, for example, Flagler's contributions to West Palm Beach and Palm Beach in Akin, *Flagler,* 143–59, and Plant's to Tampa in Grismer, *Tampa,* 190–95.
18. Dovell, *Florida,* 2:607–40; Rerick, *Memoirs of Florida,* 1:335, 344–45; Covington, *Story of Southwestern Florida,* 1:190; Akerman, *Florida Cowman,* 117–19.
19. Brown, *Florida's Peace River Frontier,* 312–18; Dovell, *Florida,* II, 607–40; Rerick, *Memoirs of Florida,* 1:344–45; Covington, *Story of Southwestern Florida,* 1:191.
20. Tebeau, *History of Florida,* 290–91; Covington, *Story of Southwestern Florida,* 1:194–96; Brown, *Florida's Peace River Frontier,* 316–17, 321–23; Ayers, *Promise of the New South,* 187–213.
21. Florida *Senate Journal* (1877), 37–39; Rerick, *Memoirs of Florida,* 1:334–42; Williamson, *Florida Politics,* 22–23.
22. Rerick, *Memoirs of Florida,* 1:334–43; Williamson, *Florida Politics,* 23, 36.
23. On the Drew and Bloxham administrations generally, see Williamson, *Florida Politics,* 1–95.
24. Rerick, *Memoirs of Florida,* 1:340, 346; Shofner, *Nor Is It Over Yet,* 343; Williamson, *Florida Politics,* 28.
25. Klingman, *Neither Dies nor Surrenders,* 76–87; Williamson, *Florida Politics,* 52–69; Brown, *Florida's Black Public Officials,* in press.
26. Brown, *Florida's Black Public Officials,* in press.
27. Williamson, *Florida Politics,* 106–8; Woolsey files.
28. Williamson, *Florida Politics,* 83–85, 91–93, 97, 104–5, 114–17, 120–27; Klingman, *Neither Dies nor Surrenders,* 88–93.
29. Williamson, *Florida Politics,* 129–30; Brown, *Florida's Black Public Officials,* in press.
30. Bell, "Constitutions and Politics," 313–15; Cash, *Democratic Party,* 79; Klingman, *Neither Dies nor Surrenders,* 95.

31. Bell, "Constitutions and Politics," 315–24; Cash, *Democratic Party*, 74–78; Williamson, *Florida Politics*, 96–128; Klingman, *Neither Dies nor Surrenders*, 95.
32. Wallace, *Carpetbag Rule*, 406; Declaration of rights, section 1, Florida Constitution of 1885, in *Journal of the Proceeding of the Constitutional Convention of the State of Florida*, 589; Williamson, *Florida Politics*, 133–40; Klingman, *Neither Dies nor Surrenders*, 95–98. See also Williamson, "Constitutional Convention of 1885."
33. Williamson, *Florida Politics*, 141–49; Brown, *Florida's Black Public Officials*, in press; Akin, "When a Minority," 127–28.
34. *Laws of Florida* (1887), 52–66, 116, 181–91, 195–203; Long, "Florida's First Railroad Commission, 1887–1891 (Part I)," 108–10.
35. Philadelphia *Journal of United Labor*, December 3, 1887, January 21, February 18, May 12, August 2, 1888; Brown, *Florida's Black Public Officials*, in press; *New York Age*, December 1, 1888; *FT-U*, November 15, 1888, April 13, 1889; *DeLand Weekly News*, February 2, 1889; St. Augustine Council minute book E (August 1887–June 1892), 238, SAHSRL.
36. *Laws of Florida* (1889), 13–14, (1889, 2d sess.), 88–108; Brown, *Florida's Black Public Officials*, in press; Akin, "When a Minority," 137–39; Browne, *Key West*, 55; Jackson, "The Negro and the Law," 94.
37. Tebeau, *History of Florida*, 298–302; Williamson, *Florida Politics*, 163–89.
38. Brown, "Bishop Payne," 23–39. On the rise of Jim Crow racial discrimination generally, see Woodward, *Strange Career of Jim Crow*.

Chapter 15: The Post-Reconstruction Court

1. Boyd and Reder, *History of the Florida Supreme Court*, 1040. On the political backgrounds of justices McWhorter and Raney, see their biographical sketches in this chapter.
2. *WF*, January 13, 1885.
3. *FT-U*, January 14, 1885.
4. Ibid.
5. *Journal of the Proceedings of the Constitutional Convention of the State of Florida, Which Convened at the Capitol, at Tallahassee, on Tuesday, June 9, 1885*, 455–66 (hereafter, *Proceedings*); *FT-U*, October 4, 1885; *New York Freeman*, September 12, 1885.
6. *Proceedings*, 466; Boyd and Reder, *History of the Florida Supreme Court*, 1041.
7. *FT-U*, June 28, 1885.
8. Ibid., October 4, 1885.
9. Ibid., June 28, 1885.
10. *Proceedings*, 458–63.
11. *FT-U*, July 22, 1885; Williamson, "Constitutional Convention of 1885," 121–22; *New York Freeman*, September 12, 1885.
12. *Proceedings*, 465.
13. *FT-U*, June 18, 1885; Williamson, *Florida Politics*, 142–43.
14. Regarding justices Augustus Emmet Maxwell and Robert Bruce Van Valkenburgh, see their biographical sketches in chapters 11 and 12, respectively. Boyd and Reder, *History of the Florida Supreme Court*, 1041; Williamson, *Florida Politics*, 141.
15. *WF*, June 7, 21, 1888; *FT-U*, August 7, 10, 1888.

16. *FT-U*, August 10, 1888; *WF*, January 1, 1889.
17. *FT-U*, January 10, 1889; Tallahassee *Daily Democrat*, January 23, 1923.
18. Jacksonville *Florida Daily Times*, January 28, 1882; *FT-U*, August 9, 1888.
19. Tallahassee *Weekly True Democrat*, September 14, 1906; Galbraith and Miller, *Historical Documentary Research Project*, 24, 35, 37–39, 196.
20. *FT-U*, January 10, 1889; Smith, *Emancipation*, 278; Gainesville *Florida Sentinel*, quoted in Tallahassee *Florida Bureau of Immigration Monthly*, February 1891.
21. Smith, *Emancipation*, 278.
22. See Milton Harvey Mabry biographical sketch in this chapter. Boyd and Reder, *History of the Florida Supreme Court*, 1042; Whitfield, *Florida State Government*, 55.
23. See Robert Fenwick Taylor biographical sketch in this chapter. Boyd and Reder, *History of the Florida Supreme Court*, 1042.
24. See Benjamin Sullivan Liddon biographical sketch in this chapter. Boyd and Reder, *History of the Florida Supreme Court*, 1042–43.
25. The editor appreciates the generosity of Nathan Woolsey, Milton, Florida, for sharing his historical notes and files on the life of Justice George Gray McWhorter (hereafter, Woolsey files). Pensacola *Daily News*, May 23, 1891.
26. Pensacola *Daily News*, May 23, 1891; 32 *Florida Reports*, xii–xiv.
27. Woolsey files.
28. Whitfield, *Florida State Government*, 84.
29. *FT-U*, January 14, 1885.
30. Woolsey files.
31. See, for example, McWhorter's comments in the *Pensacola Observer*, September 5, 1868; Woolsey files.
32. Williamson, *Florida Politics*, 21–22.
33. 27 *Florida Reports*, xii, xiv; Pensacola *Advance Gazette*, March 13, 1882.
34. *WF*, August 19, 1884.
35. *FT-U*, January 15, 1885.
36. Williamson, *Florida Politics*, 106–8; Prince, "Edward Alysworth Perry," 75; Woolsey files; *FT-U*, January 14, 1885.
37. *Ocala Star Banner* paraphrased in Long, "Florida's First Railroad Commission, 1887–1891 (Part I)," 110–11.
38. 27 *Florida Reports*, xiv.
39. Whitfield, *Florida State Government*, 84.
40. *FT-U*, January 15, 1885.
41. Pensacola *Daily News*, May 23, 1891; Woolsey files.
42. Pensacola *Daily News*, May 23, 1891.
43. Tallahassee *Weekly True Democrat*, January 13, 1911; Meginnis, "George Pettus Raney," 81–82; Rerick, *Memoirs of Florida*, 2:103; *Savannah Morning News*, January 25, 1881; *Makers of America*, 3:38.
44. Tallahassee *Weekly True Democrat*, January 13, 1911; Davis, *Civil War and Reconstruction*, 613, 616, 635–36; *Savannah Morning News*, January 25, 1881.
45. 77 *Florida Reports*, 4; Williamson, *Florida Politics*, 19; Meginnis, "George Pettus Raney," 82–83, 86; *WF*, May 20, 1873, May 26, 1874; Whitfield, *Florida State Government*, 85; Tallahassee *Weekly True Democrat*, January 13, 1911.

46. Meginnis, "George Pettus Raney," 83–84; Rerick, *Memoirs of Florida*, 1:336–39; Shofner, *Nor Is It Over Yet*, 329–30; *Makers of America*, 3:39–41; Williamson, *Florida Politics*, 74.
47. Raney, *Manual*; *Weekly Tallahassean*, January 17, 1901; Tallahassee *Weekly True Democrat*, January 13, 1911; Meginnis, "George Pettus Raney," 86–87; Cash, *Story of Florida*, 2:667.
48. Meginnis, "George Pettus Raney," 81, 84; Buford, "Something about the Supreme Court of Florida"; 24 *Florida Reports*, vi–vii.
49. 77 *Florida Reports*, 2.
50. Ibid., 2, 10.
51. *FT-U*, March 26, 1897; *Tallahassee Democrat*, August 21, 1908; Meginnis, "George Pettus Raney," 83; 77 *Florida Reports*, 35.
52. 77 *Florida Reports*, 1, 22, 36; Meginnis, "George Pettus Raney," 85; Tallahassee *Weekly True Democrat*, January 13, 1911; *Weekly Tallahassean*, December 13, 1900, April 24, 1903, December 2, 1904.
53. *Weekly Tallahassean*, July 24, 1903.
54. Meginnis, "George Pettus Raney," 85; *Weekly Tallahassean*, August 30, November 22, 1900, February 14, 1901, April 24, 1903; Raney biographical materials.
55. *Makers of America*, 3:43; Meginnis, "George Pettus Raney," 87–89.
56. 77 *Florida Reports*, 35.
57. Meginnis, "George Pettus Raney," 88.
58. *Weekly Tallahassean*, March 20, 1903.
59. 77 *Florida Reports*, 1, 49.
60. Tallahassee *Weekly True Democrat*, January 13, 1911; Meginnis, "George Pettus Raney," 82, 86; *Weekly Tallahassean*, October 24, 1902.
61. Whitfield, *Florida State Government*, 89; McKay, *Pioneer Florida*, 2:402; Grismer, *Tampa*, 121–22, 317; *Tampa Tribune*, November 7, 1954; 160 *Florida Reports*, xliv. On Henry Laurens Mitchell's life generally, see Church, *Life of Henry Laurens Mitchell*.
62. 160 *Florida Reports*, xliv; Tampa *Florida Peninsular*, March 19, 1859, March 10, 1860; Brown, "Ossian Bingley Hart," 194–97; Brown, "Politics, Greed, Regulator Violence, and Race in Tampa," 27.
63. Tampa *Florida Peninsular*, February 4, 1860; Hartman and Coles, *Biographical Register*, 1:450.
64. Church, *Henry Laurens Mitchell*, 20–21; Grismer, *Tampa*, 317–18; Cash, *Story of Florida*, 2:659.
65. Church, *Henry Laurens Mitchell*, 20–28; Tampa *Florida Peninsular*, July 4, 1868.
66. Church, *Henry Laurens Mitchell*, 28–29; Brown, "Ossian Bingley Hart," 460–61; Whitfield, *Florida State Government*, 89.
67. Tampa *Sunland Tribune*, June 12, 1879; *Tampa Guardian*, December 6, 1879; Brown, *Florida's Peace River Frontier*, 242–43, 292–94; Matthews, *Edge of Wilderness*, 315–358.
68. Matthews, *Edge of Wilderness*, 358.
69. Ibid., 359–61.
70. Cash, *History of the Democratic Party*, 88.
71. McKay, *Pioneer Florida*, 2:405.
72. 46 *Florida Reports*, xiv–xv.

73. McKay, *Pioneer Florida,* 1:49.
74. Hawes, "On the Track in Plant City."
75. *FT-U,* August 10, 1888; Whitfield, *Political and Legal History,* lxxiv; 160 *Florida Reports,* xliv; Dobson, "Supreme Court of Florida."
76. 160 *Florida Reports,* xliv; Tebeau, *History of Florida,* 302; Klingman, *Neither Dies nor Surrenders,* 107; Quincy *Florida Herald,* August 20, 1892; Ayers, *Promise of the New South,* 313; Proctor, *Napoleon Bonaparte Broward,* 74–76.
77. 160 *Florida Reports,* xliv; Grismer, *Tampa,* 318; Cash, *Story of Florida,* 2:663.
78. Rerick, *Memoirs of Florida,* 2:105; Whitfield, *Florida State Government,* 78; Cash, *Story of Florida,* 2:667; *National Cyclopaedia of American Biography,* 5:397.
79. Whitfield, *Florida State Government,* 78; *National Cyclopaedia of American Biography,* 5:397; 81 *Florida Reports,* 6; *Tampa Morning Tribune,* March 4, 1919; Foner, *Reconstruction,* 560–63. On William Adams Hocker, see his biographical sketch in chapter 18.
80. *Tampa Morning Tribune,* March 4, 1919; William Adams Hocker biographical sketch, chapter 18.
81. *WF,* July 19, 1881; Thomas C. Lanier to Hugh A. Corley, October 11, 1881, RG 593, series 914, box 25, FSA; Madison *New Era,* August 7, 1884; Tampa *Sunland Tribune,* October 22, 1881.
82. Williamson, *Florida Politics,* 108; *WF,* February 19, 1885.
83. Morris, *Florida Handbook,* 35; *FT-U,* May 1, 1887.
84. 81 *Florida Reports,* 20–21.
85. *Weekly Tallahassean,* January 23, 1903.
86. Ibid.
87. Whitfield, *Political and Legal History,* lxxxviii; 81 *Florida Reports,* 1, 5–6; Grismer, *Tampa,* 368; *Tampa Morning Tribune,* March 4, 1919.
88. *Makers of America,* 2:104; Rerick, *Memoirs of Florida,* 1:696–97.
89. Rerick, *Memoirs of Florida,* 1:697; Cutler, *History of Florida,* 1:214, 3:184.
90. Rerick, *Memoirs of Florida,* 1:697; Dickison, "Florida," 110.
91. Whitfield, *Florida State Government,* 51; Rerick, *Memoirs of Florida,* 1:697; Klingman, *Josiah Walls,* 53.
92. *Makers of America,* 2:105; Rerick, *Memoirs of Florida,* 1:697; Whitfield, *Florida State Government,* 55.
93. *Makers of America,* 2:105; Cutler, *History of Florida,* 1:214; *FT-U,* February 27, 1928; 85 *Florida Reports,* 5–6.
94. *Weekly Tallahassean,* October 9, 1903, May 13, 1904; *FT-U,* February 27, 1928; Cutler, *History of Florida,* 3:185; 85 *Florida Reports,* 5–6.
95. 85 *Florida Reports,* 6.
96. *Makers of America,* 2:106.
97. 85 *Florida Reports,* 2–3; *Weekly Tallahassean,* October 31, 1902.
98. Tallahassee *Weekly True Democrat,* January 8, 1915; *Tallahassee Daily Democrat,* January 3, 1923; *FT-U,* February 27, 1928; 85 *Florida Reports,* 1–2.
99. Cutler, *History of Florida,* 1:iv, 3:185; *Tallahassee Daily Democrat,* March 29, 1919, February 27, 1928.
100. *FT-U,* February 27, 1928; *Tallahassee Daily Democrat,* February 27, 1928; 85 *Florida Reports,* 5.

101. Rerick, *Memoirs of Florida,* 1:601; *Makers of America,* 4:493; Shofner, *Jackson County,* 110, 167.
102. *FT-U,* May 27, 1894.
103. 81 *Florida Reports,* 9.
104. Rerick, *Memoirs of Florida,* 1:601; *Makers of America,* 4:493; Cash, *Story of Florida,* 2:669.
105. *Makers of America,* 4:494; Rerick, *Memoirs of Florida,* 1:601–2; *FT-U,* April 26, 1890; 81 *Florida Reports,* 9, 17–18, 21.
106. See Francis Beauregard Carter biographical sketch in chapter 18.
107. Rerick, *Memoirs of Florida,* 1:602; *Makers of America,* 4:494–95; Shofner, *Jackson County,* 327; 81 *Florida Reports,* 10.
108. Shofner, *Jackson County,* 374.
109. *Makers of America,* 4:495; Rerick, *Memoirs of Florida,* 1:602; Long, "Florida's Railroad Commission, 1887–1891 (Part II)," 250–51.
110. *Liddon* v. *Hodnett,* 22 *Florida Reports,* 442.
111. *FT-U,* May 27, 1894.
112. *Makers of America,* 4:494; 81 *Florida Reports,* 15.
113. *Makers of America,* 4:494–95; Cash, *Story of Florida,* 2:667; Flynt, *Duncan Upshaw Fletcher,* 42; Morris, *Florida Handbook,* 126.
114. 49 *Florida Reports,* 69–123; *Weekly Tallahassean,* December 2, 1904.
115. 49 *Florida Reports,* 69–123; Shofner, *Jefferson County,* 404.
116. Klingman, *Neither Dies nor Surrenders,* 106–7; Hall and Rise, *From Local Courts to National Tribunals,* 54, 172.
117. Hall and Rise, *From Local Courts to National Tribunals,* 54.
118. Ibid.; *Makers of America,* 4:494.
119. Klingman, *Neither Dies nor Surrenders,* 107.
120. Hall and Rise, *From Local Courts to National Tribunals,* 56.
121. *Makers of America,* 4:495.
122. *Tampa Morning Tribune,* December 23, 1909; New Orleans *Daily Picayune,* December 23, 1909.

Chapter 16: Case Decisions and the Redemption

1. Williamson, *Florida Politics,* 40–42.
2. Ibid., 43–44.
3. *WF,* March 4, 1879.
4. Ibid.; Williamson, *Florida Politics,* 44.
5. 17 *Florida Reports,* 32–39.
6. Ibid., 47.
7. Ibid., 83–84.
8. Ibid., 85.
9. Williamson, *Florida Politics,* 44–45; Rerick, *Memoirs of Florida,* 1:346.
10. Roberts, "Wilkinson Call, Soldier and Senator, Part II," 185–87; Williamson, *Florida Politics,* 166–77.
11. Roberts, "Wilkinson Call, Soldier and Senator, Part II," 189–90; 28 *Florida Reports,* 503.

12. Roberts, "Wilkinson Call, Soldier and Senator, Part II," 190; Williamson, *Florida Politics*, 178.
13. Williamson, *Florida Politics*, 81; 18 *Florida Reports*, 915–19; Philadelphia *Christian Recorder*, March 3, 1881.
14. Philadelphia *Christian Recorder*, March 3, 1881; Williamson, *Florida Politics*, 81.
15. Philadelphia *Christian Recorder*, March 3, 1881.
16. Ibid.; 18 *Florida Reports*, 195.
17. Williamson, *Florida Politics*, 82; 18 *Florida Reports*, 194.
18. 18 *Florida Reports*, 200–201.
19. Ibid., 254.
20. Ibid., 952.
21. Ibid., 958.
22. Ibid., 962–63.
23. Fernandina *Florida Mirror*, September 2, 1882.
24. Matthews, *Edge of Wilderness*, 356–59.
25. Ibid., 361–62; 22 *Florida Reports*, 82.
26. Matthews, *Edge of Wilderness*, 362–64.
27. Brown, *Florida's Black Public Officials*, in press.
28. *Laws of Florida* (1881), 110–16; *Savannah Morning News*, April 19, 1881; Fernandina *Florida Mirror*, July 9, 1881.
29. 18 *Florida Reports*, 264.
30. Brown, *Florida Black Public Officials*, in press; *Laws of Florida* (1885), 46–49.
31. 21 *Florida Reports*, 309.
32. Ibid., 326.
33. Brown, *Florida's Black Public Officials*, in press.
34. 15 *Florida Reports*, 637; 16 *Florida Reports*, 791.
35. The intervening decision was *Wilson* v. *Gaines*, 103 *United States Reports*, 417.
36. 19 *Florida Reports*, 231.
37. See Fenlon, "Notorious Swepson-Littlefield Fraud."
38. 16 *Florida Reports*, 708.
39. Ibid., 718–22.
40. Lewis, "Railroad Cases," 10–11.
41. Ibid.
42. 23 *Florida Reports*, 104, 121.
43. 28 *Florida Reports*, 631.
44. 33 *Florida Reports*, 608.
45. 33 *Florida Reports*, 162, 203.
46. Long, "Florida's First Railroad Commission, 1887–1891 (Part I)," 103–4, 117; *WF*, March 26, 1878.
47. Long, "Florida's First Railroad Commission, 1887–1891 (Part I)," 103–4, 117; Lewis, "Railroad Cases," 12.
48. Long, "Florida's First Railroad Commission, 1887–1891 (Part I)," 103–4.
49. Ibid., 104–5; Article 16, section 30, Florida Constitution of 1885.
50. *FT-U*, March 31, 1887; Long, "Florida's First Railroad Commission, 1887–1891 (Part I)," 104–5.

51. *WF*, April 7, 1887.
52. Long, "Florida's First Railroad Commission, 1887–1891 (Part I)," 105–6, 108; Williamson, *Florida Politics*, 150–51.
53. *Laws of Florida* (1887), 118–26.
54. Long, "Florida's First Railroad Commission, 1887–1891 (Part I)," 110–16.
55. Ibid., 116–24.
56. Ibid., 248–50.
57. *FT-U*, January 10, 1889; Long, "Florida's First Railroad Commission, 1887–1891 (Part II)," 250–52.
58. 24 *Florida Reports*, 466; Long, "Florida's First Railroad Commission, 1887–1891 (Part II)," 250.
59. Long, "Florida's First Railroad Commission, 1887–1891 (Part II)," 250; 24 *Florida Reports*, 466–70.
60. 24 *Florida Reports*, 470–75.
61. 25 *Florida Reports*, 310–42; *Makers of America*, 3:41–42.
62. Long, "Florida First Railroad Commission, 1887–1891 (Part II)," 251–57; Williamson, *Florida Politics*, 174.
63. 32 *Florida Reports*, 82.
64. 26 *Florida Reports*, 163, 192.
65. See, for example, Bodenhamer, *Fair Trial*, and Friedman, *Crime and Punishment.*
66. 15 *Florida Reports*, 633; 16 *Florida Reports*, 291.
67. 21 *Florida Reports*, 738.
68. 28 *Florida Reports*, 113; 30 *Florida Reports*, 142.
69. Article 14, sections 2 and 4, Florida Constitution of 1868.
70. *Laws of Florida* (1868), 1, 3.
71. 18 *Florida Reports*, 267, 270.
72. 17 *Florida Reports*, 712–13.
73. Ibid., 713.
74. Hall, *Magic Mirror*, 211–25.
75. Cash, *Story of Florida*, 2:669–70.
76. Article 3, section 20, Florida Constitution of 1885; 25 *Florida Reports*, 598–604.
77. *Laws of Florida* (1889), 126–27; 25 *Florida Reports*, 598–604.
78. 25 *Florida Reports*, 604–7.
79. 30 *Florida Reports*, 325, 345–46.
80. Ibid., 85, 105–7, 110, 113, 116.

Chapter 17: Progressive Florida

1. Morris, *Florida Handbook*, 330–31.
2. McRae, *Fourth Census*, 15.
3. Ibid., 15, 70, 73.
4. Department of the Interior, *Statistics of the . . . Tenth Census*, 117–19; Grismer, *Tampa*, 152–53, 178; Department of Commerce, *Thirteenth Census of the United States . . . : Population*, 2:311; McRae, *Fourth Census*, 70, 73–77.
5. Tebeau, *History of Florida*, 282–85.
6. Hicks, *Short History*, 560.

7. *Tampa Morning Tribune,* February 18, 1898.
8. *Micanopy Hustler,* quote in *FT-U&C,* March 2, 1898.
9. Tebeau, *History of Florida,* 309–26.
10. Woodward, *Strange Career of Jim Crow;* Ayers, *Promise of the New South,* 330–31.
11. Howard, "Vigilante Justice," 32–33; Grossman, *Land of Hope,* 16–17, 69.
12. Washington, D.C., *Colored American,* June 25, 1898; *New York Age,* October 19, 26, November 2, 30, 1911.
13. Akin, "When a Minority"; Washington, D.C., *Colored American,* June 25, 1898; *FT-U,* April 12, 1913, March 26, 1920; Jones and McCarthy, *African Americans in Florida,* 46–49, 60–65, 75–80.
14. Gordon, *Afro-Americans of Hillsborough County,* 22; Key West *Daily Equator & Democrat,* March 1889 (trade edition); Johnson, *Along This Way,* 141–42.
15. Johnson, *Along This Way,* 142–46.
16. Jones and McCarthy, *African Americans in Florida,* 60–63, 72–74, 87–89. For Florida's contribution to the Harlem Renaissance and black cultural and political life in the twentieth century, see, for example, Johnson, *Along This Way.*
17. Davis, *History of Jacksonville,* 237–38; Cash, *Story of Florida,* 2:538–39, 559.
18. Ayers, *Promise of the New South,* 413–17.
19. Waddell, "William V. Knott," chapter 5. See also Proctor, *Napoleon Bonaparte Broward,* and Flynt, *Duncan Upshaw Fletcher.*
20. Ibid.
21. Morris, *Florida Handbook,* 333; Proctor, *Napoleon Bonaparte Broward,* 173–74.
22. Proctor, *Napoleon Bonaparte Broward,* 216–91; Tebeau, *History of Florida,* 331–32.
23. Morris, *Florida Handbook,* 334–35.

Chapter 18: Court Expansion and Other Reforms

1. Boyd and Reder, *History of the Supreme Court,* 1040–43.
2. *Weekly Tallahassean,* September 12, 1901; *Laws of Florida* (1901), 19.
3. *Laws of Florida* (1901), 42; *Weekly Tallahassean,* August 1, 1901.
4. Boyd and Reder, *History of the Supreme Court,* 1043–44.
5. *Weekly Tallahassean,* October 10, December 5, 1902.
6. *Laws of Florida* (1903), 64–65; *Weekly Tallahassean,* December 16, 1904.
7. Buford and Roberts, *Judicial System,* 22.
8. Tallahassee *Weekly True Democrat,* June 30, October 6, 13, 1911; "Whitfield Building" in supreme court vertical file, Florida Collection.
9. Boyd and Reder, *History of the Supreme Court,* 1046–47.
10. Waddell, "William V. Knott," 19.
11. Ibid.
12. *FT-U,* January 6, 1897.
13. Waddell, "William V. Knott," 14, 19; Tallahassee *Weekly True Democrat,* May 26, 1905, May 15, 1914; John R. Parkhill to Brian S. Polley, January 27, 1984, Miscellaneous Manuscript Collection, FSCHS.
14. Waddell, "William V. Knott," 20; Tallahassee *Weekly True Democrat,* May 15, 1914; Caldwell questionnaire.
15. *FT-U,* January 10, 1937; Carter file.

16. Venable, *William Adam Hocker,* 3.
17. Ibid., 7.
18. *FT-U,* April 7, 1891; Venable, *William Adams Hocker,* 21.
19. Ibid.
20. *FT-U,* April 7, 1891; Williamson, *Florida Politics in the Gilded Age,* 31.
21. Williamson, *Florida Politics in the Gilded Age,* 88, 108, 134, 136, 151.
22. Venable, *William Adam Hocker,* 24; Proctor, *Napoleon Bonaparte Broward,* 157.
23. Venable, *William Adam Hocker,* 30–31; *Ocala Star,* July 5, 1902.
24. Tallahassee *Daily Democrat,* July 18, 1918; 77 *Florida Reports,* 23.
25. Foster questionnaire; 100 *Southern Reporter, Second Series,* 47; Grismer, *Tampa,* 354.
26. 100–101 *Southern Reporter, Second Series,* 47.
27. Ibid.; Thomas M. Shackleford to William Sherman Jennings, June 9, 1902, Jennings papers.
28. 100–101 *Southern Reporter, Second Series,* 47.
29. Shackleford to Jennings, April 28, May 5, 1900, January 21, May 3, 1901, Jennings papers.
30. Ibid., June 9, 11, 24, 30, July 19, 1902.
31. Boyd and Reder, *History of the Supreme Court,* 1043–45; Shackleford to Jennings, October 15, 18, 28, November 15, 1902, Jennings papers; 100–101 *Southern Reporter, Second Series,* 47.
32. 100–101 *Southern Reporter, Second Series,* 47; Shackleford to Jennings, March 1, 1906, Jennings papers; Tallahassee *Weekly True Democrat,* October 16, 1914; Tallahassee *Daily Democrat,* August 30, 1917, September 22, 1927.
33. Grismer, *Tampa,* 354; *Tampa Tribune,* quoted in Tallahassee *Daily Democrat,* August 30, 1917; Tallahassee *Daily Democrat,* September 22, 1927.
34. See biographical sketches of Walker Anderson (chapter 7) and Augustus Emmet Maxwell (chapter 11).
35. Buford, "Something about the Supreme Court of Florida," 30–31; Cutler, *History of Florida,* 3:58–59.
36. Caldwell questionnaire.
37. *FT-U,* November 19, 1954.
38. Jacksonville *Evening Metropolis,* November 12, 1902.
39. Ervin questionnaire; Proctor, *Napoleon Bonaparte Broward,* 128, 133–34, 191, 197.
40. William James Bryan to William Sherman Jennings, n.d., Jennings papers; Proctor, *Napoleon Bonaparte Broward,* 203, 269–75.
41. Shackleford to Jennings, November 11, 1902, F. M. Simonton to William Sherman Jennings, November 5, 1902, Jennings papers; Jacksonville *Evening Metropolis,* November 12, 1902.
42. Ervin questionnaire; Boyd and Reder, *History of the Supreme Court,* 1045.
43. Tallahassee *Daily Democrat,* October 23, 1914.
44. Ervin questionnaire; *Tallahassee Democrat,* June 25, 1957.
45. *Tallahassee Democrat,* June 25, 1957.
46. Cash, *Story of Florida,* 3:319; Whitfield alumni questionnaire; Neeley and Whitfield, "Our Father," 1–3.

47. Neeley and Whitfield, "Our Father," 10–11; James Bryan Whitfield to Richard A. Whitfield, May 10, 1888, Miscellaneous Manuscript Collection, FSCHS.
48. Whitfield questionnaire; *FT-U*, February 23, 1897.
49. Jacksonville *Daily Florida Citizen*, June 4, 1897; *WF*, June 12, 1897; Whitfield questionnaire.
50. *Weekly Tallahassean*, October 18, 1900; James Bryan Whitfield to William Sherman Jennings, July 9, 20, November 12, December 20, 27, 1900, Jennings papers.
51. *Weekly Tallahassean*, February 13, March 13, 1903; Whitfield to Jennings, June 20, 29, 1903, Jennings papers; Boyd and Reder, *History of the Supreme Court*, 1046; Proctor, *Napoleon Bonaparte Broward*, 187–97.
52. *Weekly Tallahassean*, December 16, 1904, January 6, 1905; Whitfield biographical materials.
53. Neeley and Whitfield, "Our Father," 10; Tallahassee *Daily Democrat*, September 10, 1945.
54. Neeley and Whitfield, "Our Father," 12; Warren, "Yesterday," 11–12; Justice B. K. Roberts interview, April 21, 1980, Whitfield biographical notes, Reder file, box 2.
55. Roberts interview, April 21, 1980, Reder file, box 2; Ervin questionnaire; *University of Florida Law Review* 1 (Fall 1948): dedication and 11–12.
56. *Biennial Report of the Attorney General, State of Florida, From January 1, 1947, to December 31, 1948*, 3–5.
57. Cutler, *History of Florida*, 2:95–96; *FT-U*, February 6, 1889.
58. Doherty, *Richard Keith Call*, 157–58; Cutler, *History of Florida*, 95–96; Parkhill biographical materials.
59. Lykes, *Gift of Heritage*, 23–26; Whitfield, *Florida State Government*, 77.
60. Grismer, *Tampa*, 391; Davis, *History of Jacksonville*, 180–86; Parkhill biographical materials.
61. Tallahassee *Daily Capital*, January 31, 1904; Lykes, *Gift of Heritage*, 36–42; Charles Breckenridge Parkhill to William Sherman Jennings, December 13, 1900, Jennings papers; *Weekly Tallahassean*, January 10, 1901; Proctor, *Napoleon Bonaparte Broward*, 157, 162.
62. Parkhill to Jennings, June 3, 1901, March 4, 1902, Jennings papers; Tallahassee *Daily Capital*, January 31, 1904; *FT-U*, May 25, 1905; Parkhill to Polley, January 27, 1984, Miscellaneous Manuscript Collection, FSCHS.
63. Charles Breckenridge Parkhill to William A. Blount, n.d., March 2, 5, 16, 1910; *FT-U*, January 6, 1912, Miscellaneous Manuscript Collection, FSCHS.
64. Lykes, *Gift of Heritage*, 114–15, 121–22; *Tampa Morning Tribune*, November 2, 1923; Grismer, *Tampa*, 391.
65. John R. Parkhill interview, February 17, 1984.
66. *Tampa Tribune*, May 14, 1933; *FT-U*, May 14, 1933; Tallahassee *Daily Democrat*, May 14, 1933.
67. Roberts interview, Reder file, box 2.
68. Cutler, *History of Florida*, 3:160; Quincy *Gadsden Democrat*, April 29, 1892; *Quincy Florida Herald*, March 25, 1893, April 28, 1894, February 23, 1895; *FT-U*, February 14, 1895.

69. Cutler, *History of Florida,* 3:160–61; *Weekly Tallahassean,* August 16, December 13, December 20, 1900, January 10, June 6, 1901, November 14, December 12, 1902.
70. *Weekly Tallahassean,* February 27, August 28, 1903, May 13, 1904.
71. Proctor, *Napoleon Bonaparte Broward,* 208, 211, 230; Cutler, *History of Florida,* 3:160; Tallahassee *Weekly True Democrat,* April 20, 1906; William Hull Ellis biographical materials.
72. Cutler, *History of Florida,* 3:160–61; Tallahassee *Weekly True Democrat,* April 17, 1908, January 5, 1912.
73. Tallahassee *Daily Democrat,* April 15, 1948; *FT-U,* April 15, 1948; *Miami Herald,* December 10, 1937; *Miami Daily News,* November 21, 1937.
74. Roberts interview, Reder files, box 2; *FT-U,* April 15, 1948; Tallahassee *Daily Democrat,* April 15, 1948.

Chapter 19: Progressive Era Court Perspectives

1. 42 *Florida Reports,* 462.
2. 63 *Florida Reports,* 74; *Laws of Florida* (1905), 120.
3. 73 *Florida Reports,* 432, 440.
4. Dovell, *Florida,* 685; 39 *Florida Reports,* 477; *Laws of Florida* (1897), 73, (1899), 131.
5. Ayers, *Promise of the New South,* 326–27; Tebeau, *History of Florida,* 289–90; *Orlando Sentinel-Reporter,* quoted in *Weekly Tallahassean,* January 17, 1901.
6. 59 *Florida Reports,* 459.
7. 41 *Florida Reports,* 151.
8. *Laws of Florida* (1899), 135; 48 *Florida Reports,* 76.
9. Brief of plaintiff in error, *Montgomery* v. *State,* June Term 1907, Florida Supreme Case Files, FSA.
10. 55 *Florida Reports,* 97, 98.
11. 65 *Florida Reports,* 287.
12. New York *Outlook,* April 4, 1908, 768–69; Hugo Black to Claude Pepper, January 29, 1948, Whitfield biographical notes, Reder file, box 2.
13. *Weekly Tallahassean,* October 9, 1903.
14. 45 *Florida Reports,* 1; 50 *Florida Reports,* 1; *Laws of Florida* (1901), 58.
15. 57 *Florida Reports,* 15; *Laws of Florida* (1907), 203.
16. 66 *Florida Reports,* 332.
17. 78 *Florida Reports,* 44.
18. Tindall, *America,* 2:1036–37; Tebeau, *History of Florida,* 367.
19. Cash, *Story of Florida,* 2:539–40; Proctor, *Napoleon Bonaparte Broward,* 225–28, 236, 278; Neyland and Riley, *History of Florida Agricultural and Mechanical University,* 54.
20. 50 *Florida Reports,* 293, 406.
21. 61 *Florida Reports,* 819.
22. Kousser, *Shaping of Southern Politics,* 226; Cash, *History of the Democratic Party,* 105–6; Proctor, *Napoleon Bonaparte Broward,* 155–58.
23. Proctor, *Napoleon Bonaparte Broward,* 173–75; *Laws of Florida* (1906), 244; 56 *Florida Reports,* 162.
24. *Laws of Florida* (1913), 242–68.

25. Flynt, "Sidney Catts," 114; 72 *Florida Reports*, 176.
26. 72 *Florida Reports*, 232, 251, 253.
27. Flynt, "Sidney Catts," 115–16.
28. Cash, *Story of Florida*, 2:532.
29. Ibid.
30. Ibid.; 62 *Florida Reports*, 284, 302.
31. Cash, *Story of Florida*, 2:540–41.
32. *Minutes of the Board of Trustees, Internal Improvement Fund of the State of Florida*, 7:534.
33. Ibid., 537–38.
34. *Laws of Florida* (1905), 22–23, (1913), 129–77, (1915), 362–403, (1917), 117–26, (1919), 197–98; Tebeau, *History of Florida*, 348–51; 73 *Florida Reports*, 735.
35. 80 *Florida Reports*, 170.
36. 77 *Florida Reports*, 742; *Laws of Florida* (1919), 197–98; 80 *Florida Reports*, 252.
37. 258 *United States Reports*, 338, 339.
38. 56 *Florida Reports*, 603.
39. 58 *Florida Reports*, 398, 412.
40. 63 *Florida Reports*, 666.
41. Article 16, section 30, Florida Constitution of 1885.
42. *Laws of Florida* (1897), 82–94.
43. *Laws of Florida* (1899), 76–93.
44. 41 *Florida Reports*, 377.
45. 40 *Florida Reports*, 114; 48 *Florida Reports*, 129, 146, 150.
46. 56 *Florida Reports*, 617, 668.
47. 59 *Florida Reports*, 612, 628; 60 *Florida Reports*, 218.
48. 51 *Florida Reports*, 311, 320.
49. 57 *Florida Reports*, 526, 528.
50. 58 *Florida Reports*, 524.
51. 57 *Florida Reports*, 522, 526.
52. 51 *Florida Reports*, 578.
53. 63 *Florida Reports*, 274.
54. *Laws of Florida* (1907), 101, 102.
55. 59 *Florida Reports*, 130, 151.
56. 60 *Florida Reports*, 465; 61 *Florida Reports*, 799.
57. 63 *Florida Reports*, 491, 506.
58. 67 *Florida Reports*, 83, 100.
59. *Laws of Florida* (1911), 127, 128; 65 *Florida Reports*, 270.
60. 53 *Florida Reports*, 650, 679–82.
61. Ibid., 673–74.

Bibliography

Manuscripts

Allen, Richard C. Biographical materials. Constitutional Convention State Museum, Port St. Joe, Florida.

Anderson, William E. "Tales of a Grandfather." Collection of Walter W. Manley II, Tallahassee.

Andrews, Mrs. C. F. Memoirs. SAHSRL.

Baker, James M. Files. FSCHS.

Brackenridge, Henry Marie. Letters. University of Pittsburgh Library.

Bronson, Isaac H. Biographical materials. SAHSRL.

Caldwell, Millard F. Questionnaire. FSCHS.

Call, Richard Keith. Papers. Florida Historical Society Collection, University of South Florida Library, Tampa.

Carter, Francis B. File. FSCHS.

Chandler, William E. Papers. LC.

Dobson, Nancy. Files. FSCHS.

Ellis, William Hull. Biographical materials. FSCHS.

Ervin, Richard W. Questionnaire. FSCHS.

Florida Supreme Court Historical Society. Interview files.

Forward, William Augustus. Biographical materials. SAHSRL.

Hackley, William R. Diary, 1831–57. Unpublished manuscript, PKY.

Hagner, Thomas H., to Peter Hagner. Letter dated November 3, 1838. Maryland Historical Society, Baltimore.

Jackson, Andrew. Papers. LC.

Jefferson, Thomas. Papers. Alderman Library, University of Virginia.

Jefferson, Thomas. Papers. LC.

Jennings, William Sherman. Papers. FSCHS.

Marvin, William. Biographical file. Florida Historical Society Collection.

Maxwell Family. Biographical file. Pensacola Historical Society.

Miscellaneous Manuscript Collection. FSCHS.

Parkhill, Charles Breckenridge. Biographical materials. FSCHS.

Parkhill, John R. Interview. February 17, 1984. FSCHS.

Raney, George Pettus. Biographical materials. FSCHS.

Reder, Randall. Files. FSCHS.

Richard, John Charles. "Notes and Observations Upon the Present Condition of Florida [c. 1848]." Collection of Walter W. Manley II, Tallahassee.

Smith, Joseph Lee. Family materials and history. SAHSRL.

Snodgrass, Dena E. Collection. PKY.

Supreme Court. Vertical file. Florida Collection, State Library of Florida, Tallahassee.

Vincent, Thomas McCurdy. Family papers. Special Collections, Louisiana State University, Baton Rouge.

Wentworth, T. T. "Walker Anderson: Biographical Sketches of Early Citizens of Pensacola." Clipping dated August 17, 1940. Biographical file, Florida Collection, State Library of Florida, Tallahassee.

Whitfield, James B. Alumni questionnaire, University of Virginia Alumni Association, Charlottesville. Copy at FSCHS.

———. Biographical materials. FSCHS.

Wirt, William. Papers. Microfilm at Maryland Historical Society, Baltimore. Copies available at Tallahassee Historic Preservation Board.

Woolsey, Nathan. Historical notes and files. Milton, Florida.

Wright, Benjamin D. Family records. William B. Wright III, Orange Park, Florida.

Public Documents, Public Records, and Maps

Acts and Resolutions Passed by the Legislative Council of the Territory of Florida at Its Twenty-First Session. Tallahassee: Office of the Star of Florida, 1845.

Acts of the Legislative Council of the Territory of Florida Passed at Their First Session, 1822. Pensacola: Floridian Press, 1823.

American State Papers: Naval Affairs. 4 vols. Washington, D.C.: Gales and Seaton, 1832–61.

American State Papers: Public Lands. 8 vols. Washington, D.C.: Gales and Seaton, 1832–61.

Biographical Directory of the United States Congress, 1774–1989. Washington, D.C.: Government Printing Office, 1989.

Bureau of Historic Sites and Properties, Division of Archives, History, and Records Management, Florida Department of State. *The Delegates to the Saint Joseph Constitutional Convention, 1838–1839.* Tallahassee: Florida Department of State, 1980.

Carter, Clarence E., ed. *Territorial Papers of the United States,* vols. 22–26, *Florida Territory.* Washington, D.C.: Government Printing Office, 1956–62.

Clerk of the House of Representatives. *People of Lawmaking in Florida, 1822–1991.* Tallahassee: Florida House of Representatives, 1991.

Congressional Globe, 36th Congress, 2d sess., *Court of Claims Reports.*

Columbia County. Tax rolls, 1845–1878. Available on microfilm at FSA.

Department of Commerce, Bureau of the Census. *Thirteenth Census of the United States Taken in the Year 1910: Population.* 3 vols. Washington, D.C.: Government Printing Office, 1913.

Department of Justice. General records. RG 60, NA.

Department of State. General records. RG 94, NA.

Department of the Interior, Census Office. *Statistics of the Population of the United States at the Tenth Census (June 1, 1880).* Washington, D.C.: Government Printing Office, 1883.

Eagan, Dennis. *Sixth Annual Report of the Commissioner of Lands and Immigration of the*

State of Florida, for the Year Ending December 31, 1874. Tallahassee: State of Florida, 1874.

Escambia County. Tax rolls, 1845–60. Available on microfilm at FSA.

Federal Case Reports.

Florida. Constitutions, 1839, 1868, 1885.

———. *House Journal.* 1845–1917.

———. *Journal of the Proceedings of the Constitutional Convention of the State of Florida, Which Convened at the Capitol, at Tallahassee, on Tuesday, June 9, 1885*. Tallahassee: N. M. Bowen, State Printer, 1885.

———. *Journal of the Proceedings of the Convention of the People of Florida*. Tallahassee: N.p., 1861.

———. *Laws of Florida*, 1845–1917.

———. *Minutes of the Board of Trustees, Internal Improvement Fund of the State of Florida*. 39 vols. Tallahassee, 1902–74.

———. *Senate Journal.* 1845–1917.

———. *Statutes*, 1941.

———. *Territorial Council Journal.* 1822–38.

———. *Territorial House Journal.* 1839–45.

———. *Territorial Senate Journal.* 1839–1845.

Florida, Office of the Attorney General. *Biennial Report of the Attorney General, State of Florida, from January 1, 1947, to December 31, 1948*. Tallahassee: State of Florida, 1948.

Florida, Office of Elections. Division of election returns, 1824–1916. RG 156, series 21, FSA.

Florida, Office of the Governor. Governors' correspondence. RG 101, series 679, FSA.

Florida Reports. Florida Superior Court, Eastern and Southern District. Record book, 1830–19, PKY.

Florida Supreme Court. Case Files, 1825–1997. RG 1100, series 49, FSA.

———. Minutes. 1846–1916.

Franklin County. Tax rolls, 1845–60. Available on microfilm at FSA.

Gadsden County. Tax rolls, 1845–60. Available on microfilm at FSA.

Judicial Conference of the United States. *Judges of the United States.* 2d ed. Washington, D.C.: Government Printing Office, 1983.

Kennedy, Joseph C. G. *Population of the United States in 1860: Compiled from the Original Returns of the Eighth Census.* Washington, D.C.: Government Printing Office, 1860.

Leon County. Probate records. Available on microfilm at FSA.

———. Tax rolls, 1845–60. Available on microfilm at FSA.

McRae, W. A. *The Fourth Census of the State of Florida Taken in the Year 1915*. Tallahassee: T. J. Appleyard, State Printer, 1915.

Putnam County. Last will and testament of William A. Forward.

Putnam County Department of History and Archives.

St. Augustine Council. Minute Book E, August 1887–June 1892. St. Augustine Historical Society Research Library.

St. Johns County. County court records. SAHSRL.

———. Tax rolls, 1845–60. Available on microfilm at FSA.

Southern Reporter. Second series.

The Third Census of the State of Florida Taken in the Year 1905. Tallahassee: Capital Publishing Company, State Printer, 1906.

Thompson, Leslie A. *A Manual or Digest of the Statute Law of the State of Florida*. Boston: Little, Brown, 1947.

United States Congress. *The Debates and Proceedings of the Congress of the United States.* Washington, D.C.: Gales and Seaton, 1855.

United States Congress Serial Set. Washington, D.C.

United States Decennial Censuses, 1820–1920. Manuscript returns. Available at FSA.

United States District and Superior Court of Florida, Pensacola. Court records, vols. 3–4, PKY.

United States Reports.

United States Statutes at Large.

Walker, Francis A. *Ninth Census.* Volume 1: *The Statistics of the Population of the United States.* Washington, D.C.: Government Printing Office, 1872.

Whitfield, J. B. *Florida State Government, 1885: An Official Directory of the State Government.* Tallahassee: Floridian Steam Book and Job Office, 1885.

Newspapers and Periodicals

Apalachicola *Commercial Advertiser,* 1847.

Apalachicola Gazette, 1838–40.

Army and Navy Chronicle, 1843.

DeLand Weekly News, 1889.

Fernandina Courier, 1866.

Fernandina *East Floridian,* 1859.

Fernandina *Florida Mirror,* 1879.

Hiogo and Osaka [Japan] *Herald,* 1868.

Jacksonville Courier, 1835–36.

Jacksonville *Daily Florida Citizen,* 1897.

Jacksonville *East Florida Advocate,* 1839–40.

Jacksonville *Evening Metropolis,* 1902.

Jacksonville *Florida Daily Times,* 1882.

Jacksonville *Florida News,* 1853–55.

Jacksonville *Florida Republican,* 1849.

Jacksonville *Florida Times-Union,* 1882–97, 1903–54.

Jacksonville *Florida Times-Union and Citizen,* 1897–1903.

Jacksonville *Florida Union,* 1865–81.

Jacksonville Herald, 1865.

Jacksonville *Tri-Weekly Florida Union,* 1874.

Key West *Daily Equator & Democrat,* 1889.

Marianna Courier, 1866–67.

Miami Daily News, 1937.

Miami Herald, 1937.

Montrose [Pa.] *Democrat,* 1879.

The Nation, 1868.

New Orleans *Daily Picayune,* 1909.

New York Age, 1888, 1911.
New York Daily Tribune, 1853.
New York Herald, 1903.
New York *Outlook*, 1908.
New York Times, 1876.
Newport Gazette, 1846.
Niles' Weekly Register [Baltimore], 1840.
Palatka Daily News, 1887.
Pensacola *Daily News*, 1891.
Pensacola *Floridian*, 1821–22.
Pensacola *Advance Gazette*, 1882.
Pensacola Gazette, 1838–53.
Pensacola Gazette and Chronicle, 1831.
Pensacola Gazette and West Florida Advertiser, 1824–28.
Pensacola Mail, 1872.
Pensacola News-Journal, 1971.
Pensacola Observer, 1868.
Pensacola *Public Record*, 1940.
Pensacola *West Florida Commercial*, 1869.
Pensacola *West Florida Times*, 1857.
Philadelphia *Christian Recorder*, 1866–85.
Philadelphia *Journal of United Labor*, 1887–88.
Pittsburgh Daily Gazette, 1871.
Quincy Florida Herald, 1892–95.
Quincy *Gadsden Democrat*, 1892.
St. Augustine *Ancient City*, 1850–53.
St. Augustine *East Florida Herald*, 1824–25.
St. Augustine Examiner, 1859.
St. Augustine *Florida Herald*, 1833–35.
St. Augustine *Florida Herald and Southern Democrat*, 1844–48.
St. Augustine *News*, 1839–42.
St. Augustine Record, 1944.
St. Joseph Times, 1839.
St. Louis [Mo.] *Enquirer*, 1820.
Savannah Daily Advertiser, 1872.
Savannah *Daily News and Herald*, 1868.
Savannah Daily Republican, 1872.
Savannah Morning News, 1869–74.
Tallahassee *Florida Bureau of Immigration Monthly*, 1891.
Tallahassee *Daily Capital*, 1904.
Tallahassee Daily Democrat, 1914–48.
Tallahassee Democrat, 1957–65.
Tallahassee *Florida Intelligencer*, 1826.
Tallahassee *Florida Sentinel*, 1842–66.
Tallahassee *Floridian*, 1830–47.

Tallahassee *Floridian and Advocate*, 1829.
Tallahassee *Floridian and Journal*, 1850–59.
Tallahassee *Semi-Weekly Floridian*, 1865–66.
Tallahassee Sentinel, 1868–75.
Tallahassee *Southern Journal*, 1848.
Tallahassee *Star of Florida*, 1843–45.
Tallahassee *Weekly Floridian*, 1868–98.
Tallahassee *Weekly True Democrat*, 1905–14.
Tampa *Florida Peninsular*, 1856–60, 1868.
Tampa Guardian, 1879.
Tampa *Sunland Tribune*, 1879.
Tampa Tribune, 1898–1994.
Washington, D.C., *Colored American*, 1898.
Weekly Tallahassean, 1900–1903.

Secondary Sources

Abbey, Kathryn T. "The Union Bank of Tallahassee: An Experiment in Territorial Finance." *Florida Historical Quarterly* 15 (April 1937): 207–31.

Akerman, Joe A., Jr. *Florida Cowman, A History of Florida Cattle Raising*. Kissimmee: Florida Cattlemen's Association, 1976.

Akin, Edward N. *Flagler: Rockefeller Partner and Florida Baron*. Kent, Ohio: Kent State University Press, 1988.

———. "When a Minority Becomes the Majority: Blacks in Jacksonville Politics, 1887–1907." *Florida Historical Quarterly* 53 (October 1974): 123–45.

Armstrong, H. Clay. *History of Escambia County, Florida*. St. Augustine: Record Company, 1930.

Avant, David A. *Illustrated Index of J. Randall Stanley's History of Gadsden County, 1948*. Tallahassee: Avant Studios, 1985.

Ayers, Edward L. *The Promise of the New South: Life after Reconstruction*. New York: Oxford University Press, 1992.

Barbour, George M. *Florida for Tourists, Invalids, and Settlers*. New York: D. Appleton, 1882. Reprint ed., Gainesville: University of Florida Press, 1964.

Barfield, William D. "The First Civil Governor and the Capital of Florida." *Papers of the Jacksonville Historical Society* (1949): 75–89.

Bassett, John Spencer. *Correspondence of Andrew Jackson*. 6 vols. Washington, D.C.: Carnegie Institution of Washington, 1926–35.

Bates, Thelma. "The Legal Status of the Negro in Florida." *Florida Historical Quarterly* 6 (January 1928): 159–81.

Bell, John Luther, Jr. "Constitutions and Politics: Constitutional Revision in the South Atlantic States, 1864–1902." Ph.D. diss., University of North Carolina, 1969.

Biographical Souvenir of the States of Georgia and Florida. Chicago: F. A. Battey and Company, 1889.

Bodenhamer, David J. *Fair Trial: Rights of the Accused in American History*. New York: Oxford University Press, 1992.

Bornholdt, Laura. *Baltimore and Early Pan-Americanism: A Study in the Background of the Monroe Doctrine*. Northampton, Mass.: Smith College Studies in History, 1949.

Boyd, Joseph A., and Randall O. Reder. *A History of the Supreme Court of Florida.* Tallahassee: Florida Bar, 1983. The greater part of this work originally appeared in *University of Miami Law Review* 35 (September 1981): 1019–66.

Boyles, Hallie. "Governor Reid . . . Forgotten Man?" *Tallahassee Democrat,* June 20, 1965.

Brackenridge, Henry Marie. *History of the Late War, between the United States and Great Britain, Containing a Minute Account of the Various Military and Naval Operations.* Baltimore: Joseph Cushing, 1816.

———. *Judge Brackenridge's Letters.* Washington, D.C.: N.p., 1832.

———. *Law Miscellanies: Containing an Introduction to the Study of Law.* Philadelphia: P. Byrne, 1814.

———. *Recollections of Persons and Places in the West.* Philadelphia: James Kay, Jr., and Brother, 1829.

———. *Sixty Years in the North and Twenty Years in the South.* Pittsburgh: Barr and Myers, 1865.

———. *Views of Louisiana; Together with a Journal of a Voyage up the Missouri River in 1811.* Pittsburgh: Cramer, Spear, and Eichbaum, 1814.

Brevard, Caroline Mays. *A History of Florida from the Treaty of 1763 to Our Own Times.* 2 vols. DeLand: Florida Historical Society, 1924–25.

Brown, Canter, Jr. "Bishop Payne and Resistance to Jim Crow in Florida during the 1880s." *Northeast Florida History* 2 (1994): 23–40.

———. "Carpetbagger Intrigues, Black Leadership, and a Southern Loyalist Triumph: Florida's Gubernatorial Election of 1872." *Florida Historical Quarterly* 72 (January 1994): 275–301.

———. "The Florida, Atlantic and Gulf Central Railroad, 1851–1868." *Florida Historical Quarterly* 69 (April 1991): 411–29.

———. *Florida's Black Public Officials, 1867–1924.* Tuscaloosa: University of Alabama Press, in press.

———. *Florida's Peace River Frontier.* Orlando: University of Central Florida Press, 1991.

———. "Justice Ossian Bingley Hart." *Florida Supreme Court Historical Society Review* 4 (1991–94): 1–3, 16–17.

———. "Ossian Bingley Hart: Florida's Loyalist Reconstruction Governor." Ph.D. diss., Florida State University, 1994.

———. "Politics, Greed, Regulator Violence, and Race in Tampa, 1858–1859." *Sunland Tribune* 20 (November 1994): 25–30.

———. "Race Relations in Territorial Florida, 1821–1845." *Florida Historical Quarterly* 73 (January 1995): 287–307.

———. "The 'Sarrazota, or Runaway Negro Plantations': Tampa Bay's First Black Community. *Tampa Bay History* 12 (Fall/Winter 1990): 5–19.

———. "Tampa and the Coming of the Railroad, 1853–1884." *Sunland Tribune* 17 (November 1991): 13–18.

———. "'Where are now the hopes I cherished?' The Life and Times of Robert Meacham." *Florida Historical Quarterly* 69 (July 1990): 1–36.

Browne, Jefferson B. *Key West, the Old and the New.* St. Augustine: Record Company, 1912. Reprint ed., Gainesville: University of Florida Press, 1973.

Bruington, Lola Lee Daniell. *St. Michael's Cemetery, 1807–?* Pensacola: Lola Lee Daniell Bruington, 1986.

Buford, Rivers. “Something about the Supreme Court of Florida.” *Florida State Bar Association Law Journal* 6 (May–June 1932): 29–35.

Buford, Rivers, and B. K. Roberts. *Judicial System of Florida. 2 Florida Decisions*, ix.

Bungay, G. W. *Pen and Ink Portraits of the Senators, Assemblymen, and State Officers of the State of New York*. Albany: J. Munsell, 1857.

Call, Richard Keith. *Journal of Richard Keith Call*. Unpublished manuscript, Federal Writer's Project.

[Campbell, Emma F. R.] *Biographical Sketch of Honorable Ossian B. Hart*. New York: James T. White and Company, 1901.

Cash, William T. *The History of the Democratic Party in Florida*. Tallahassee: Democratic Historical Foundation, 1936.

———. *The Story of Florida*. 4 vols. New York: American Historical Society, 1938.

Church, George B., Jr. *The Life of Henry Laurens Mitchell, Florida's 16th Governor*. New York: Vantage Press, 1978.

Coker, William S., and Thomas D. Watson. *Indian Traders of the Southeastern Spanish Borderlands: Panton, Leslie & Company and John Forbes & Company, 1783–1847*. Pensacola: University of West Florida Press, 1986.

Coles, David James. “‘A Fight, a Licking, and a Footrace’: The 1864 Florida Campaign and the Battle of Olustee.” Master's thesis, Florida State University, 1985.

———. “‘A Terrible and Sad Result’: The End of the Civil War in Florida, March–June 1865.” In *The Proceedings of the 90th Annual Meeting of the Florida Historical Society at St. Augustine May 1992*. Tampa: Florida Historical Society, 1992.

Commemorative Biographical Record of Northeastern Pennsylvania. Chicago: J. H. Beers and Company, 1900.

Coulter, E. Merton. *The Confederate States of America, 1861–1865*. Baton Rouge: Louisiana State University Press, 1950.

Covington, James W. “The Armed Occupation Act of 1842.” *Florida Historical Quarterly* 40 (July 1961): 41–52.

———. *The Billy Bowlegs War, 1855–1858: The Final Stand of the Seminoles against the Whites*. Chuluota, Fla.: Mickler Publishers, 1982.

———. “Cuban Bloodhounds and the Seminoles.” *Florida Historical Quarterly* 33 (October 1954): 111–19.

———. *The Story of Southwestern Florida*. 2 vols. New York: Lewis Historical Publishing Company, 1957.

Cutler, Henry Gardner. *History of Florida Past and Present*. 3 vols. Chicago: Lewis Publishing Company, 1923.

Davis, T. Frederick. “The Disston Land Purchase.” *Florida Historical* Quarterly 17 (January 1939): 200–10.

———. *History of Jacksonville Florida and Vicinity 1513 to 1924*. Jacksonville: Florida Historical Society, 1925. Reprint ed., Jacksonville: San Marco Bookstore, 1990.

Davis, William Watson. *The Civil War and Reconstruction in Florida*. New York: Columbia University Press, 1913. Reprinted., Gainesville: University of Florida Press, 1964.

Denham, James M. “From a Territorial to a State Judiciary: Florida's Antebellum Courts and Judges.” *Florida Historical Quarterly* 73 (April 1995): 443–55.

———. "A Rogue's Paradise: Violent Crime in Ante-Bellum Florida." Ph.D. diss., Florida State University, 1988.

DeRosa, Marshall L. *The Confederate Constitution of 1861: An Inquiry into American Constitutionalism.* Columbia: University of Missouri Press, 1991.

Dickison, John J. "Florida." In *Confederate Military History.* Edited by Clement A. Evans. 13 vols. Atlanta: Blue and Grey Press, 1899.

Diddle, Albert W. "The Adjudication of Shipwrecking in Florida in 1831." *Tequesta* 7 (1947): 44–49.

Dobson, Nancy. "Robert Bruce Van Valkenburgh: 'Soldier, Statesman, Jurist.'" *Florida Supreme Court Historical Society Review* 4 (1989–90): 10–13.

———. "The Supreme Court of Florida—A Century Ago." *Florida Supreme Court Historical Society Review* 3 (1987): 5, 8–9.

Dodd, Dorothy. *Florida Becomes a State.* Tallahassee: Florida Centennial Commission, 1945.

———. "The Wrecking Business on the Florida Reef, 1822–1860." *Florida Historical Quarterly* 22 (April 1944): 171–99.

Dodd, William G. *History of the West Florida Seminary.* Tallahassee: Florida State University Press, 1952.

Doherty, Herbert J. "Andrew Jackson's Cronies in Florida Territorial Politics." *Florida Historical Quarterly* 28 (October 1949): 131–42.

———. "Ante-Bellum Pensacola." *Florida Historical Quarterly* 37 (January–April 1959): 337–56.

———. "Florida in 1856." *Florida Historical Quarterly* 35 (July 1956): 60–70.

———. "Political Factions in Territorial Florida." *Florida Historical Quarterly* 34 (July 1955): 3–29.

———. *Richard Keith Call, Southern Unionist.* Gainesville: University of Florida Press, 1961.

———. *The Whigs of Florida, 1845–1854.* Gainesville: University of Florida Press, 1959.

Douglas, Thomas. *The Autobiography of Thomas Douglas.* New York: Calkins and Stiles, 1856.

Dovell, J. E. *Florida: Historic, Dramatic, Contemporary.* 4 vols. New York: Lewis Historical Publishing Company, 1952.

———. *History of Banking in Florida, 1828–1954.* Orlando: Florida Bankers Association, 1955.

Durkin, Joseph T. *Confederate Navy Chief: Stephen R. Mallory.* Chapel Hill: University of North Carolina Press, 1854. Reprint ed., Columbia: University of South Carolina Press, 1987.

Edwards, Lucy Ames. *Grave Markers of Duval County, 1808–1916.* Jacksonville: Lucy Ames Edwards, 1955.

Ellis, Mary Louise, and William Warren Rogers. *Tallahassee & Leon County: A History and Bibliography.* Tallahassee: Florida Department of State, 1986.

Ewing, Cortez A. M. "Florida Reconstruction Impeachments." *Florida Historical Quarterly* 36 (April 1958): 299–318.

Ezell, John Samuel. *The South Since 1865.* 2d ed. Norman: University of Oklahoma Press, 1978.

Farris, Charles F. "The Courts of Territorial Florida." *Florida Historical Quarterly* 19 (April 1941): 346–67.

Fenlon, Paul E. "The Notorious Swepson-Littlefield Fraud: Railroad Financing in Florida, 1868–1871." *Florida Historical Quarterly* 32 (April 1954): 231–61.

Fernald, Edward A., ed. *Atlas of Florida*. Tallahassee: Florida State University Foundation, 1981.

Flynt, Wayne. *Cracker Messiah: Governor Sidney J. Catts of Florida*. Baton Rouge: Louisiana State University Press, 1977.

———. *Duncan Upshaw Fletcher: Dixie's Reluctant Progressive*. Tallahassee: Florida State University Press, 1971.

———. "Sidney Catts: The Road to Power." *Florida Historical Quarterly* 49 (October 1970): 107–28.

Foner, Eric. *Reconstruction: America's Unfinished Revolution, 1863–1877*. New York: Harper and Row, 1988.

Foster, John T., Jr., and Sarah Whitmer Foster. "John Sanford Swaim: A Life at the Beginning of Modern Florida." *Methodist History* 26 (July 1988): 229–40.

———. "The Last Shall Be First: Northern Methodists in Reconstruction Jacksonville." *Florida Historical Quarterly* 70 (January 1992): 265–80.

Fouraker, Warren G. "The Administration of Robert Raymond Reid." Master's thesis, Florida State University, 1949.

Fredriksen, John C. "Lawyer, Soldier, Judge: Incidents in the Life of Joseph Lee Smith of New Britain, Connecticut." *Connecticut Historical Society Bulletin* 51 (Spring 1986): 103–21.

Friedman, Lawrence Meir. *Crime and Punishment in American History*. New York: Basic Books, 1993.

Galbraith, Christine, and Barbara Miller. *Historical Documentary Research Project: 1902 Florida Capitol Restoration Reports*. Tallahassee: Historic Tallahassee Preservation Board, 1979.

Gammon, William Lamar, II. "Governor John Milton of Florida, Confederate States of America." Master's thesis, University of Florida, 1948.

Garvin, Russell. "The Free Negro in Florida before the Civil War." *Florida Historical Quarterly* 46 (July 1967): 1–18.

Genovese, Eugene D. *Roll, Jordan, Roll: The World the Slaves Made*. New York: Pantheon, 1974.

Gold, Pleasant Daniel. *History of Duval County, Florida*. St. Augustine: Record Company, 1928.

Gordon, Julius J. *Afro-Americans of Hillsborough County, Florida, 1870–1890*. Tampa: Julius J. Gordon, 1993.

———. *Biographical Census of Hillsborough County, Florida, 1850*. Tampa: Julius J. Gordon, 1989.

Graham, Thomas. *The Awakening of St. Augustine*. St. Augustine: St. Augustine Historical Society, 1978.

Grismer, Karl H. *The Story of Fort Myers: The History of the Land of the Caloosahatchee and Southwest Florida*. St. Petersburg: St. Petersburg Printing Company, 1949. Reprint ed., Fort Myers Beach: Island Press Publishers, 1982.

———. *Tampa: A History of the City of Tampa and the Tampa Bay Region of Florida*. St. Petersburg: St. Petersburg Printing Company, 1950.

Groene, Bertram H. *Ante-Bellum Tallahassee*. Tallahassee: Florida Heritage Foundation, 1981.

———. "Justice Samuel Douglas As Governor Marvin Remembered Him." *Florida Historical Quarterly* 49 (January 1971): 268–77.

Hall, Kermit L. *The Magic Mirror: Law in American History*. New York: Oxford University Press, 1989.

———. *The Politics of Justice: Lower Federal Judicial Selection and the Second Party System, 1829–1861*. Lincoln: University of Nebraska Press, 1979.

———. *The Supreme Court and Judicial Review in American History*. Washington, D.C.: American Historical Association, 1985.

Hall, Kermit L., and Eric W. Rise. *From Local Courts to National Tribunals: The Federal District Courts of Florida, 1821–1990*. Brooklyn: Carlson Publishing, 1991.

Hammond, E. A. "Wreckers and Wrecking on the Florida Reef, 1829–1832." *Florida Historical Quarterly* 41 (January 1963): 239–73.

Hanna, A. J., and Kathryn Hanna. *Lake Okeechobee: Wellspring of the Everglades*. New York: Bobbs-Merrill, 1948.

Harper, Roland M. "Ante-Bellum Census Enumerations in Florida." *Florida Historical Quarterly* 6 (July 1927): 42–52.

Hartman, David W., and David Coles, comps. *Biographical Register of Florida's Confederate and Union Soldiers, 1861–1865*. 6 vols. Wilmington, N.C.: Broadfoot Publishing Company, 1995.

Hawes, Leland. "On the Track in Plant City." *Tampa Tribune*, April 21, 1984.

Hentz, Catherine Lee Whiting. *The Planter's Northern Bride*. Philadelphia: T. B. Peterson, 1854.

Hicks, John D., and George E. Mowry. *A Short History of American Democracy*. 2d ed. Boston: Houghton Mifflin and Company, 1956.

Hoffman, M. M. "Talleyrand: An American Copy." *Catholic World* (April 1943): 54–60.

Howard, Walter T. "Vigilante Justice and National Reaction: The 1937 Tallahassee Double Lynching." *Florida Historical Quarterly* 67 (July 1988): 32–51.

Hume, Richard L. "Membership of the Florida Constitutional Convention of 1868: A Case Study of Republican Factionalism in the Reconstruction South." *Florida Historical Quarterly* 51 (July 1952): 1–21.

Jackson, Jesse Jefferson. "The Negro and the Law in Florida, 1821–1921." Master's thesis, Florida State University, 1960.

James, Marquis. *Andrew Jackson: Portrait of a President*. New York: Bobbs-Merrill, 1937. Universal Library ed., New York: Grosset and Dunlap, 1937.

Johns, John E. *Florida during the Civil War*. Gainesville: University of Florida Press, 1963. Reprint ed., Macclenny, Fla.: Richard J. Ferry, 1989.

Johnson, Dudley Sady. "Henry Bradley Plant and Florida." *Florida Historical Quarterly* 45 (October 1966): 118–31.

———. "The Railroads of Florida, 1865–1900." Ph.D. diss., Florida State University, 1965.

Johnson, James Weldon. *Along This Way: The Autobiography of James Weldon Johnson*. New York: Penguin Books, 1990.

Johnson, Malcolm B. *Red, White and Bluebloods in Frontier Florida.* Tallahassee: Rotary Club, 1976.

Jones, Maxine D., and Kevin M. McCarthy. *African Americans in Florida.* Sarasota: Pineapple Press, 1993.

Kearney, Kevin E., ed. "Autobiography of William Marvin." *Florida Historical Quarterly* 36 (January 1958): 179–222.

Keller, William F. *The Nation's Advocate: Henry Marie Brackenridge and Young America.* Pittsburgh: University of Pittsburgh Press, 1956.

"Key West and Salvage in 1850." *Florida Historical Quarterly* 8 (July 1929): 47–63.

Kilbourn, Dwight C. *The Bench and Bar of Litchfield County, Connecticut, 1709–1909.* Litchfield, Conn.: Dwight C. Kilbourn, 1909.

Klingman, Peter D. *Josiah Walls, Florida's Black Congressman of Reconstruction.* Gainesville: University of Florida Press, 1976.

———. *Neither Dies nor Surrenders: A History of the Republican Party in Florida, 1867–1970.* Gainesville: University of Florida Press, 1984.

Knauss, James Owen. *Territorial Florida Journalism.* DeLand: Florida State Historical Society, 1926.

———. "William Pope DuVal, Pioneer and State Builder." *Florida Historical Quarterly* 11 (January 1933): 95–139.

Kousser, J. Morgan. *The Shaping of Southern Politics: Suffrage Restriction and the Establishment of the One-Party South, 1880–1910.* New Haven: Yale University Press, 1974.

Lanier, Sidney. *Florida: Its Scenery, Climate, and History.* Philadelphia: J. B. Lippincott and Company, 1875. Reprint ed., Gainesville: University of Florida Press, 1973.

Lewis, Robert B. "Railroad Cases in the Florida Supreme Court, 1845–1887." *Florida Supreme Court Historical Society Review* 1 (Winter 1985): 3–5, 10–12.

Ley, Fred P. "The Tallahassee Fire of 1843." *Florida Historical Quarterly* 7 (October 1928): 164–67.

Long, Durward. "Florida's First Railroad Commission, 1887–1891 (Part I)." *Florida Historical Quarterly* 42 (October 1963): 103–24.

———. "Florida's First Railroad Commission, 1887–1891 (Part II)." *Florida Historical Quarterly* 42 (January 1964): 248–57.

Long, Ellen Call. *Florida Breezes; or Florida, New and Old.* Facsimile reproduction of the 1883 ed., Gainesville: University of Florida Press, 1962.

Lykes, Genevieve Parkhill. *Gift of Heritage.* N.p., 1969.

Makers of America, Florida Edition. 4 vols. Atlanta: A. B. Caldwell, 1909.

Meginnis, Benjamin A. "George Pettus Raney, 1845–1911." *Apalachee* (1944): 81–89.

Mahon, John K. *History of the Second Seminole War, 1835–1842.* Gainesville: University of Florida Press, 1967.

Maloney, Walter C. A *Sketch of the History of Key West, Florida.* Newark, N.J.: Advertiser Printing House, 1876. Reprinted., Gainesville: University of Florida Press, 1968.

Marks, Henry S. *Who Was Who in Florida.* Huntsville, Ala.: Strode Publishers, 1973.

Martin, Sidney Walter. *Florida during the Territorial Days.* Athens: University of Georgia Press, 1944.

Marvin, William. *The Authorship of the Four Gospels.* Albany, N.Y.: Weed, Parsons, and Company, 1885.

———. *Rules of the Superior Court for the Southern Judicial District of Florida: In Admiralty.* New York: N.p., 1840.

———. *A Treatise on the Law of Wreck and Salvage.* Boston: Little, Brown, and Company, 1858.

Maryland Biographical Cyclopedia of Representative Men of Maryland and the District of Columbia. Baltimore: National Biographical Publishing Company, 1879.

Matthews, Janet Snyder. *Edge of Wilderness: A Settlement History of Manatee River and Sarasota Bay, 1528–1885.* Tulsa, Okla.: Caprine Press, 1983.

Maxwell, Henry D. *The Maxwell Family: Descendants of John and Ann Maxwell, 1701–1894.* Easton, Pa.: Easton Express Print, 1895.

McKay, Donald B. *Pioneer Florida.* 2 vols. Tampa Southern Publishing Company, 1959.

McMurtrie, Douglas C. *Ordinances of the Provinces of the Floridas.* Chicago: John Calhoun Club, 1941.

McPherson, James M. *Battle Cry of Freedom: The Civil War Era.* New York: Oxford University Press, 1988.

Meltzer, Milton. *Hunted Like a Wolf: The Story of the Seminole War.* New York: Farrar, Straus, and Giroux, 1972.

Michaels, Brian E. *The River Flows North: A History of Putnam County, Florida.* Palatka: Putnam County Archives and History Commission, 1986.

Miller, Stephen F. *The Bench and Bar of Georgia: Memoirs and Sketches.* 2 vols. Philadelphia: J. B. Lippincott and Company, 1858.

Morris, Allen. *The Florida Handbook, 1991–1992.* Tallahassee: Peninsular Printing Company, 1991.

Myers, Oscar A. "Some Early History." *Weekly Tallahassean,* January 9–May 1, 1903.

National Cyclopaedia of American Biography. 75 vols. New York: James T. White and Company, 1888–1984.

Neeley, Julia Whitfield, and Randolph Whitfield. "Our Father, James Bryan Whitfield." *Florida Supreme Court Historical Society Review* 3 (1987–88): 1–3, 10–12.

Neyland, Leedell W., and John W. Riley. *The History of Florida Agricultural and Mechanical University.* Gainesville: University of Florida Press, 1963.

Nolan, David. *Fifty Feet in Paradise: The Booming of Florida.* San Diego: Harcourt Brace Jovanovich, 1984.

Noll, Arthur H. *General Kirby Smith.* Sewanee, Tenn.: University Press at the United of the South, 1907.

Nulty, William H. *Confederate Florida: The Road to Olustee.* Tuscaloosa: University of Alabama Press, 1990.

Ott, Eloise Robinson, and Louis Hickman Chazal. *Ocali Country, Kingdom of the Sun: A History of Marion County, Florida.* Ocala: Marion Publishers, 1966.

Paisley, Clifton. *The Red Hills of Florida, 1528–1865.* Tuscaloosa: University of Alabama Press, 1989.

Parton, James. *Life of Andrew Jackson.* 3 vols. New York: Mason Brothers, 1859–1861.

Patrick, Rembert W. *Florida Fiasco: Rampant Rebels on the Georgia-Florida Border, 1810–1815.* Athens: University of Georgia Press, 1954.

Peek, Ralph L. "The Election of 1870 and the End of Reconstruction in Florida." *Florida Historical Quarterly* 45 (April 1967): 352–68.

Peeples, Vernon E. "Charlotte Harbor Division of the Florida Southern Railroad." *Florida Historical Quarterly* 58 (January 1980): 291–302.

Peters, Virginia Bergman. *The Florida Wars.* Hamden, Conn.: Archon Books, 1979.

Pettengill, George W., Jr. *The Story of the Florida Railroads, 1834–1903.* Boston: Railway and Locomotive Historical Society, 1952.

Powell, William S., ed. *Dictionary of North Carolina Biography.* Volume 1: A–C. Chapel Hill: University of North Carolina Press, 1979.

Prince, Sigsbee C. "Edward Alysworth Perry, Florida's Thirteenth Governor." Master's thesis, University of Florida, 1949.

Proctor, Samuel. *Napoleon Bonaparte Broward: Florida's Fighting Democrat.* Gainesville: University of Florida Press, 1950. Paper ed., Gainesville: University Press of Florida, 1993.

Pyburn, Nita Katharine. *The History of the Development of a Single System of Education in Florida, 1822–1903.* Tallahassee: Florida State University, 1954.

———. "Thomas Baltzell and Universal Education." In *Florida Educators,* by the Florida State University Research Council. Tallahassee: Florida State University, 1959.

Quincy, Josiah. *Memoir of the Life of John Quincy Adams.* Boston: Phillips, Samson, and Company, 1859.

"Quincy Conservative Convention." *Florida Historical Quarterly* 18 (January 1940): 267–69.

Raney, George P., comp. *Manual of the Statutes of Florida Applicable to Justices of the Peace and County Judges.* Tallahassee: Tallahassee Book and Job Office, 1900.

Raymond, Mrs. Henry L. "Ralph Waldo Emerson in Florida & Emerson's Largely Unpublished Little Journal and St. Augustine, January, February, March, 1827." *Florida Historical Quarterly* 27 (October 1939): 75–83.

Reid, Robert Raymond. "Diary of Robert Raymond Reid, 1833, 1835." Unpublished manuscript, Jacksonville: WPA Historical Records Survey, 1939–40.

Reiger, John F. "Secession of Florida from the Union—A Minority Decision?" *Florida Historical Quarterly* 46 (April 1968): 358–68.

Remini, Robert V. *Andrew Jackson and the Course of American Empire, 1767–1821.* New York: Harper and Row, 1977.

Rerick, Rowland W. *Memoirs of Florida.* 2 vols. Atlanta: Southern Historical Association, 1902.

Roberts, Albert Hubbard. "Wilkinson Call, Soldier and Senator." *Florida Historical Quarterly* 12 (April 1934): 179–97.

Robinson, William M., Jr. *Justice in Grey: A History of the Judicial System of the Confederate States of America.* Cambridge: Harvard University Press, 1941.

Rogers, William Warren. *Outposts on the Gulf: Saint George Island & Apalachicola from Early Exploration to World War II.* Pensacola: University of West Florida Press, 1986.

———. "The Way They Went: Death in Leon County in 1860." *Apalachee* (1980–83): 89–95.

Schafer, Daniel L. "'A Class of People Neither Freedmen nor Slaves': From Spanish to American Race Relations in Florida, 1821–1861." *Journal of Social History* 26 (Spring 1993): 587–609.

Semmes, Raphael Thomas, comp. *The Semmes and Allied Families.* Baltimore: Sun Book and Job Printing Office, 1918.

Shofner, Jerrell H. "The Constitution of 1868." *Florida Historical Quarterly* 41 (April 1963): 356–74.

———. "Florida Courts and the Disputed Election of 1876." *Florida Historical Quarterly* 48 (July 1969): 26–46.

———. *History of Jefferson County*. Tallahassee: Sentry Press, 1976.

———. *Jackson County, Florida—A History*. Marianna: Jackson County Heritage Association, 1985.

———. *Nor Is It Over Yet: Florida in the Era of Reconstruction, 1863–1877*. Gainesville: University of Florida Press, 1974.

———. "Political Reconstruction in Florida." *Florida Historical Quarterly* 45 (October 1966): 145–70.

Smith, J. Clay, Jr. *Emancipation: The Making of the Black Lawyer, 1844–1944*. Philadelphia: University of Pennsylvania Press, 1993.

Smith, Julia Floyd. *Slavery and Plantation Growth in Antebellum Florida, 1821–1860*. Gainesville: University of Florida Press, 1973.

Snyder, Frank L. "Nancy Hynes DuVal: Florida's First Lady, 1822–1834." *Florida Historical Quarterly* 72 (July 1993): 19–34.

———. "William Pope DuVal: An Extraordinary Folklorist." *Florida Historical Quarterly* 69 (October 1990): 195–212.

Stanley, J. Randall. *History of Jackson County*. Marianna: Jackson County Historical Society, 1950.

Stirling, James. *Letters from the Slave States*. London: John Parker and Son, 1857.

Stocker, Rhamanthus M. *Centennial History of Susquehanna County, Pennsylvania*. Philadelphia: R. T. Peck, 1887. Reprint ed., Baltimore: Regional Publishing Company, 1974.

Stone, Spessard. "The Know Nothings of Hillsborough County." *Sunland Tribune* 19 (November 1993): 3–8.

Tebeau, Charlton W. *A History of Florida*. Coral Gables: University of Miami Press, 1971.

Thomas, David Yancey. *A History of Military Government in the Newly Acquired Territory of the United States*. New York: Columbia University Press, 1904.

Thompson, Arthur W. "Confederate Finance: A Documentary Study of a Proposal of David L. Yulee." *Florida Historical Quarterly* 30 (October 1951): 193–207.

———. "The Railroad Background of the Florida Senatorial Election of 1851." *Florida Historical Quarterly* 31 (January 1953): 181–95.

Tindall, George Brown. *America: A Narrative History*. 2 vols., 2d ed. New York: W. W. Norton and Company, 1988.

Utley, George B. "Origin of the County Names in Florida." *Florida Historical Quarterly* 1 (October 1908): 29–35.

Van Valkenburg, Paul I. *Genealogy of the Van Valkenburg Family in America*. National Association of the Van Valkenburg Family, 1976.

VanLandingham, Kyle S. *Pictorial History of Saint Lucie County, 1565–1910*. Fort Pierce: Sun Bank of Saint Lucie County, 1976. Revised ed., Fort Pierce: Sun Bank/Treasure Coast, N.A., and Saint Lucie County Historical Society, 1988.

Venable, Elizabeth Marshall. *William Adam Hocker: Justice of the Florida Supreme Court*. Jacksonville: Miller Press, 1941.

Waddell, Cynthia Roberson. "William V. Knott: A Plain, Old Fashioned Democrat." Ph.D. diss., Florida State University, 1994.

Wakelyn, John L. *Biographical Dictionary of the Confederacy.* Westport, Conn.: Greenwood Press, 1976.

Walker, Jonathan. *The Trial and Imprisonment of Jonathan Walker, at Pensacola, Florida.* Boston: Anti-Slavery Office, 1845. Reprint ed., Gainesville: University of Florida Press, 1974.

Wallace, John. *Carpetbag Rule in Florida: The Inside Workings of the Reconstruction of Civil Government in Florida after the Close of the Civil War.* Jacksonville: Da Costa Printing and Publishing House, 1888. Reprint ed., Kennesaw, Ga.: Continental Book Company, 1959.

Warner, Ezra J., and W. Buck Yearns. *Biographical Register of the Confederate Congress.* Baton Rouge: Louisiana State University Press, 1975.

Warner, Lee H. *Free Men in an Age of Servitude: Three Generations of a Black Family.* Lexington: University of Kentucky Press, 1992.

Warren, Lamar. "Yesterday." *Florida Supreme Court Historical Society Review* 2 (1985–86): 11–13.

Whatley, George C., and Sylvia Cook. "The East Florida Land Commission." *Florida Historical Quarterly* 50 (July 1971): 39–52.

White, Joseph M. *A New Collection of Laws, Charter and Local Ordinances of the Governments of Great Britain, France and Spain.* 2 vols. Philadelphia: T. and J. W. Johnson, 1839.

Whitfield, James B. *Florida State Government: An Official Directory of the State Government.* Tallahassee: Floridian Steam Book and Job Office, 1885.

———. "Judge James Diament Westcott." *Florida State Bar Association Law Journal* 1 (November 1927): 17–19.

———. *Political and Legal History of Florida.* Atlanta: Harrison Company, 1943.

Williamson, Edward C. "The Constitutional Convention of 1885." *Florida Historical Quarterly* 41 (October 1962): 116–26.

———. *Florida Politics in the Gilded Age, 1877–1893.* Gainesville: University of Florida Press, 1976.

———, ed. "The Election of 1876 in Florida." *Florida Historical Quarterly* 32 (October 1953): 81–91.

Willoughby, Lynn. *Fair to Middlin': The Antebellum Cotton Trade of the Apalachicola/Chattahoochee River Valley.* Tuscaloosa: University of Alabama Press, 1993.

Womack, Miles Kenan. *Gadsden: A Florida County in Word and Pictures.* Quincy: Gadsden County Bicentennial Committee, 1976.

Wood, Virginia S. *Live Oaking: Southern Timber for Tall Ships.* Boston: Northeastern University Press, 1981.

Woodford, Frank B. *Mr. Jefferson's Disciple: A Life of Justice Woodward.* East Lansing: Michigan State College Press, 1953.

Woodward, C. Vann. *Origins of the New South.* Baton Rouge: Louisiana State University Press, 1951.

———. *Reunion and Reaction: The Compromise of 1877 and the End of Reconstruction.* 2d revised ed. Garden City, N.Y.: Doubleday and Company, 1956.

———. *The Strange Career of Jim Crow.* 3d revised ed. New York: Oxford University Press, 1974.

Yearns, William Buck. *The Confederate Congress.* Athens: University of Georgia Press, 1960.

Yonge, Julia J. "Walker Anderson, 1801–1857." *Florida Historical Quarterly* 11 (April 1933): 173–83.

Yonge, Julian Chandler. "Secession in Florida: Pensacola on Its Own." *Florida Historical Quarterly* 26 (April 1948): 283–99.

Index

Under names for individuals, the subheadings "legal career of" and "political career of" refer in general to activities leading up to Supreme Court appointment and other positions. Page references followed by "n." refer to material found in notes, while page references in *italics* refer to illustrative material.

Walter W. Manley, II, professor of business administration at Florida State University, has been a visiting professor at Oxford and Cambridge universities. He is the author of five books, including *Critical Issues in Business Conduct: Legal, Ethical and Social Challenges for the 1990s*.

E. Canter Brown, Jr., historian in residence at the Tampa Bay History Center, is the author of numerous books, including *Ossian Bingley Hart, Florida's Loyalist Reconstruction Governor* and *Florida's Peace River Frontier* (UPF, 1991).

Eric W. Rise, assistant professor of criminal justice at the University of Delaware, is the author of several books, including *The Martinsville Seven: Race, Rape, and Capital Punishment*.